**2**ND
EDITION

# A Primer
# for Management

Michael P. Dumler | Steven J. Skinner

Illinois State University | University of Kentucky

THOMSON
\*
SOUTH-WESTERN

Australia · Brazil · Canada · Mexico · Singapore · Spain · United Kingdom · United States

**THOMSON**

**SOUTH-WESTERN**

**A Primer for Management, Second Edition**
Michael P. Dumler and Steven J. Skinner

**VP/Editorial Director:**
Jack W. Calhoun

**VP/Editor-in-Chief:**
Dave Shaut

**Sr. Acquisitions Editor:**
Joe Sabatino

**Associate Developmental Editor:**
John Abner

**Marketing Manager:**
Kimberly Kanakes

**Content Project Manager:**
Starratt E. Alexander

**Manager of Technology, Editorial:**
John Barans

**Technology Project Manager:**
Kristen Meere

**Manufacturing Coordinator:**
Doug Wilke

**Editorial Assistant:**
Ruth Belanger

**Production House:**
ICC Macmillan Inc.

**Printer:**
Edwards Brothers, Inc.
Ann Arbor, Michigan

**Art Director:**
Tippy McIntosh

**Internal Designer:**
Patti Hudepohl

**Cover Design:**
Diane Cartheuser

**Cover Image:**
© Getty Images

Library of Congress Control Number:
2006940879

For more information about our
products, contact us at:

Thomson Learning Academic Resource
Center

1-800-423-0563

**Thomson Higher Education**
5191 Natorp Boulevard
Mason, OH 45040
USA

# BRIEF CONTENTS

# 2

## PLANNING | 85

# ORGANIZING | 163

A s we introduce the second edition of *A Primer for Management,* we first want to thank the many adopters who have not only used our book but provided feedback and encouragement. Several years ago when we began developing the first edition we asked ourselves the question: Is there a need for a college textbook the presents a succinct statement of current theory and practice of contemporary management, while at the same time allowing the instructor the flexibility to use supplementary material? You have answered that question in the affirmative and that is exactly what we tried to do in this edition.

Our objectives in writing the second edition of the *Primer* remained the same: first, to give the instructor and student a text that provides the basic theories and concepts necessary for gaining an understanding of the process of management; second, to empower the instructor through choice—the *Primer* provides the content and a select set of pedagogical tools, yet allows the instructor the flexibility to include additional material that adds richness, detail, and flair to the learning environment; and third, to present material in a format that would offer the market a significantly lower-priced alternative to existing textbooks.

## What's New About the Second Edition?

Based on extensive feedback from adopters, students, and reviewers, and our own insights, we have made a number of significant changes and enhancements to this edition:

- *New Chapter 2: History of Management.* This chapter provides a complete history of management beginning with its origin through contemporary influences. Formerly an appendix, this chapter has been updated, expanded, and moved into the body of the text at the request of adopters.

- *New Chapter 4: The Global Management Environment.* This chapter examines the nature and importance of the global economy. Different types of organizations in the global economy, the environment for global business, regulation of international business and multinational market groups are discussed.

- *New Chapter 11: Individual Behavior.* The addition of this exciting new chapter adds greater depth to the coverage of individual behavior at work. Personality, perception, and attitude formation are a few of the topics discussed in the context of work situations.

- *Revised and Expanded Chapter 3: The Organizational, Social, and Ethical Environment.* This chapter has undergone a major revision and includes new sections on social responsibility and ethics. The responsibility of managers to consumers, employees, the environment, and investors, as well as factors influencing ethical behavior, are presented.

- *New Content and Updates throughout.* Each chapter has been updated and there are discussions of emerging topics such as online pre-employment testing, team building, collaborative technologies, and more.

- *New and Updated Management Highlights throughout.* Each Management Highlight box serves one of three purposes: to inform, to provide personal assessment, or offer a decision making context.

The **Informational Management Highlight** boxes help students appreciate management issues in contemporary situations. Several examples include:

| Understanding Dell™as a system.
| Social responsibility in the aftermath of hurricane Katrina.
| Ford Explorer/Firestone tire debacle.
| Planning for success at Jet Blue, Air Tran, and Southwest.
| Pre-employment testing online.
| Leadership in stressful situations.
| Improving non-verbal communication skills.
| When a team is a bad idea.
| Managing organizational change.

**Personal Assessment Management Highlights** include a short assessment exercise that helps students develop insights about their own behavior. The personal assessment Management Highlights can be used individually or as an integrative assignment that helps students know more about themselves and their potential for a career in management. Some examples of self-assessment exercises include:

| How strong is your motivation to manage?
| Evaluating your ethical behavior.
| Determining your willingness to delegate.
| Assessing your personality (Myers-Briggs Type Indicator).
| Does work meet your needs?
| Self-leadership assessment.
| Listening skills.
| Determining team readiness.
| Analyzing forces for and against change.

And lastly, the **Analytical Management Highlight** offers the opportunity to make a decision, or solve a problem that has business implications. For instance,

| McDonald's™: bureaucracy or system?
| The new car purchase decision.
| Are GM and Ford planning for the future or reacting to it?
| Implementing an ECO-Friendly strategy in the small car market.
| Unwelcome advances at work.
| Understanding the pressures for and against change.

| *New Margin Notes.* Key terms and succinct definitions are presented in the margin next to where the terms are introduced in the text to facilitate learning.

| *New Discussion Questions.* Included at the end of each chapter, discussion questions are meant to be used for in-class discussion but can also be used as a quick written assignment in class. Whether for credit or not, students can use these questions to evaluate their understanding of the material in each chapter.

> *New Video Cases.* Each chapter contains a contemporary case with an accompanying video and discussion questions focused on the inner workings of well-known companies such as Pepsi, P.F. Chang's, and Lonely Planet. Case material is closely tied to the content of the chapter provides a rich context in which to examine the efficacy of management theories.

> *New BizFlix Exercises.* Each chapter also contains an exercise related to short film clips from popular Hollywood movies—such as *The Bourne Identity, Patch Adams, Seabiscuit,* and *The Breakfast Club*—which visually reinforce and connect abstract management concepts to experiences familiar to students. These high impact video clips are great vehicles to begin a chapter discussion!

# How Will the *Primer* Benefit You and Your Students?

Students benefit immediately with a low-cost/high-content alternative to the traditional text. Our easy to access website offers student several features that they report help improve test scores—self-test key terms and definitions and our handy online quizzes. Both resources help students increase their content comprehension. Instructor will find that our philosophy of—more for less—delivers the rich detailed content you expect. *Primer* uses a functional approach covering the traditional terrain of planning, organizing, leading, and controlling. Yet, a strong behavioral emphasis is evident throughout the book. For instance, the role of the manager, decision making, individual behavior, groups and teams, leadership, motivation, communication, and organizational change are all covered in separate chapters. All of these topics emphasize the role of the individual at work. The bottom line is that *Primer* offers functional coverage you expect with behavioral content emphasized by AACSB.

## Enrichment Materials

Adopting faculty and their students have a full spectrum of coordinated resources from which to choose as it relates to their unique teaching and learning needs.

### Instructor's Manual with Test Bank | (ISBN: 0-324-38006-2). An Instructor's Manual with Test Bank, geared toward making teaching with the Primer more effective, is available to faculty who adopt. Learning outcomes; lecture outlines; lecture enhancement material (activities and extra examples); questions for discussion and review (with suggested answers); complete Video Case notes, teaching notes for utilizing the BizFlix exercises, and suggested answers to end of chapter Discussion Questions.

The original Test Bank, written by text authors Mike Dumler and Steve Skinner, has been revised and updated to fill out the manual, providing instructors with a full complement of questions in true/false, multiple-choice, and essay formats.

### PowerPoint™ Presentation Slides | (ISBN: 0-324-38008-9). A set of PowerPoint presentation slides accompanies every chapter, providing instructors with a complete set of basic notes for lectures and students with a helpful set of review materials. These slides, which highlight and synthesize key concepts for greater recall, are available for download at http://www.thomsonedu .com/management/dumler. A duplicate set can also be found on the Instructor's Resource CD-ROM.

### Video Chapter Cases and BizFlix DVD | (ISBN: 0-324-54522-3). This DVD contains all of the videos related the end of chapter Video Cases and BizFlix Exercises. The Video Cases provide students with an insider's view of management concepts in practice at familiar companies such

as P.F. Chang's, Pepsi, Loney Planet, NEADS, and Organic Valley. The BizFlix short film clips from popular Hollywood movies—such as *The Bourne Identity, Patch Adams, Seabiscuit,* and *The Breakfast Club*—visually reinforce and connect abstract management concepts to experiences familiar to students

**ExamView® Testing Software** (ISBN: 0-324-38008-9). ExamView, South-Western's computerized testing program available on the Instructor's CD-ROM, contains all the questions in the printed Test Bank. This easy-to-use test-creation program is compatible with both Microsoft® Windows and Macintosh systems and enables instructors to create printed tests, Internet tests, and LAN-based tests quickly. Blackboard- and WebCT-ready versions of the Primer's Test Bank are also available to qualified instructors. Contact your South-Western/Thomson sales representative for more information.

**Instructor Resource CD-ROM** (ISBN: 0-324-38008-9). This CD-ROM contains the Microsoft Office application files of various teaching resources (the Instructor's Manual with Test Bank and the PowerPoint slides), along with our ExamView testing program and test files.

**Product Support Site** (http://www.thomsonedu.com/management/dumler). An enriching Web site complements the text, providing many extras for students and instructors. The informative resources include: (1) interactive quizzes, (2) downloadable support materials, and (3) key terms and definitions.

# Acknowledgments

Revising *Primer for Management* required the insight of many reviewers who reacted to our ideas and helped us shape the final product. We gratefully acknowledge those who helped us with the first edition of *Primer for Management* and those who played a part in the second edition. Their comments were a helpful sounding board for our ideas.

- Christen S. Adels, Geneva College
- Tope Adeyemi-Bello, East Carolina University
- Gene Marie Black, Arkansas Technological University
- Paula Brown, Northern Illinois University
- Murray Brunton, Central Ohio Technical College
- Ray Coye, DePaul University
- Joe Dodson, Western Illinois University
- Robert A. Donnelly, Jr., Goldey-Beacom College
- Lon Doty, San Jose State University
- Jerry E. Estenson, California State University at Sacramento
- Jud Faurer, Metropolitan State College of Denver
- Francis Green, Penn State University
- Francis E. Hamilton, University of South Florida
- Linda Hefferin, Elgin Community College
- Gordon F. Holbein, University of Kentucky
- James Keebler, St. Cloud State University

- S. Beth Kost, Nicolet Area Technical College
- Thomas Lloyd, Westmoreland Community College
- Michael Mahler, Montana State University
- Art Meiners, Marymount University
- Dan Moshavi, Montana State University
- Donald C. Mosley, Jr., University of South Alabama
- Christopher P. Neck, Virginia Tech
- Carolyn Kelly Ottman, University of Wisconsin at Milwaukee
- Lisa Ritzler-Crawford, Wright State University
- Linda B. Shonesy, Athens State University
- Gary L. Taylor, South Dakota State University
- Joseph Tomkiewicz, East Carolina University
- Barry L. Van Hook, Arizona State University
- Patricia Kramer Voli, University of North Carolina, Wilmington
- Michael W. Wakefield, Colorado State University at Pueblo

The second edition of *Primer* benefited from the support of our colleagues at Illinois State University and the University of Kentucky. The advice and opinions of Gail Russ, John Lust, Peter Foreman, Mathew Sheep, Iris Varner, and Ardyth Allen were all appreciated. Our special thanks go to Ross Mechan (Virginia Tech), who oversaw the revision of the *Primer's* complete ancillary package. Finally, the authors would like to acknowledge that this book was supported in part by sabbatical leave programs at their respective institutions.

*M. P. Dumler* | *S. J. Skinner* | *January 2007*

## Dedication

The authors would also like to dedicate this book to the following:

To my family, Kathleen, Irena, and Danny for their love and understanding.
—MPD

To Moira, Aaron, and Carrie Skinner.
—SJS

# About the Authors

**MICHAEL P. DUMLER** is a Professor of Management in the Department of Management and Quantitative Methods in College of Business at Illinois State University. Over the years, he has taught undergraduate, graduate, and on-site professional MBA courses. Previously, he taught at the University of Wisconsin—Eau Claire and worked for the University of Chicago at Argonne National Laboratory. Professor Dumler has been an active consultant to several health care organizations, facilitating organization change, compensation planning, and employee assessment.

Dr. Dumler has been the recipient of the College of Business Research Award and the University Research Initiative Award; and he is a member of Beta Gamma Sigma. He has made many presentations to professional organizations, including the Academy of Management and the Decision Sciences Institute. Dr. Dumler has authored research articles that have appeared in the *Journal of Occupational and Organizational Psychology, Group and Organization Management, Journal of Managerial Issues, Psychological Reports, Administration and Society, Journal of Educational Leadership, Journal of Business Communications, Journal of Management Systems,* and *Journal of Social Behavior and Personality,* among others.

**STEVEN J. SKINNER** is the Rosenthal Professor in the Gatton College of Business and Economics at the University of Kentucky, where he has taught undergraduate and graduate courses in the School of Management for over twenty years. He was previously on the faculty at Illinois State University and was formerly a research administrator for State Farm Insurance Companies. He has also consulted with a variety of large and small organizations.

Dr. Skinner has authored or co-authored seven books, including the recently published *High Performers: Recruiting and Retaining Top Employees* (South-Western, 2004), part of South-Western's Professional Portfolio. Dr. Skinner's research has been published in a number of journals, including the *Academy of Management Journal, Journal of Marketing Research, Journal of Retailing, Journal of Business Research, Public Opinion Quarterly, Journal of the Academy of Marketing Science, Journal of Advertising Research, Journal of Risk and Insurance,* and *Journal of Personal Selling and Sales Management.* He has received the Mu Kappa Tau Award for the best article in *Journal of Personal Selling and Sales Management.*

# Managing and the Environment

# 1

# MANAGEMENT AND MANAGERS

Have you ever overheard someone say this? "I work for a poorly run company; management is totally incompetent." Or have you heard the converse? "My boss stays on top of the details; really, this is a great place to work." Perhaps you have voiced similar sentiments yourself. If so, what precisely did you mean? These statements, both the complaints and the compliments, underscore some important principles about management: (1) management is a type of work; and (2) management can be performed quite well sometimes, and at other times, quite miserably. When we charge that an organization is inadequately managed, how obvious are the mistakes that have been made? How easy would it have been to avoid them?

Don't let anyone fool you. Managing well is neither easy nor obvious. If it were, there would be a lot less acrimony in the world and a lot more certainty associated with every business decision ever made. But learning to be a better manager involves much more than just reading a few good books on the subject. It requires dedication of purpose, an advanced understanding of how organizations really work, and knowledge of human behavior. As a field of study, management draws on a vast array of accumulated research about organized activities and task-based human behavior, complemented with the applied experience and skills of people who actively strive to attain organizational goals. Managers are people who plan, organize, lead, and control organizations. A good manager, then, is someone with knowledge, skills, and experience who attains goals in an effective manner. Remember also, as you begin your formal study of management, that it is not a new concept. As long as humans have roamed the planet, some among us have made plans, organized activities, motivated others, and led those individuals toward goal attainment. History is filled with stunning examples of human accomplishment achieved through management. The pyramids at Giza, the Parthenon in Greece, and the Great Wall of China would not have been possible without managers—people who understood the principles of management and applied them, sometimes relentlessly, for better or worse.

## Organizations versus Markets

Managers perform their work in organizations. Organizations are structural arrangements of people brought together to accomplish a goal or goals. A local church, a large corporation, a police department, a prison, and a professional baseball team are all organizations. Each of them has a different membership and purpose. Some organizations are voluntary, such as a church; others, such as a prison, are coercive (forced membership); still others attract membership based on economic exchange, such as a business.[1]

It almost goes without saying that organizations are important to society. Without them, how would we accomplish commerce, maintain social order, or gather together to worship? Well, the answer might surprise you. The alternative to an organization is a market, a place where buyers and sellers congregate to bid on products or services. Without organizations we would have to go to a market, like the farmer's market or eBay. Although markets are useful, they might not be efficient for repetitive transactions. Imagine engaging in a bidding war every time you want to grab a sandwich for lunch. To solve this problem, organizations evolved. A distinct advantage of organizations over markets relates to hierarchy.[2] Through hierarchy, an organization classifies work into its component parts, assigning people with specialized skills to complete tasks necessary to the purpose of the organization. Organizations—by performing similar tasks faster, more accurately, or at lower cost than a market—provide an efficient means of exchange. Also, they are handy because they represent one-stop shopping. When we want lunch in a hurry, we go to McDonald's or a similar business whose goal is to quickly provide food to the public. In summary, *hierarchies* are adept at performing repetitive tasks where value and price are clear; they are thus useful facilitators of exchange. *Markets* also facilitate exchange, but they do so most advantageously in situations where a product is unique and its value and price are unclear.

Not all organizations are created equal. What makes some organizations better than others are the people who inhabit them. In the context of this book, we are particularly interested in managers. Their organizational success can be understood by evaluating how they work and what they accomplish. Similarly, we can gauge the quality of an organization in two basic ways: efficiency and effectiveness. Efficiency (i.e., productivity) is using the minimum resources necessary to produce a product or service. In other words, an efficient organization is not wasteful. Waste is a cost of production that should be minimized. Effectiveness is the ability of the organization to achieve a goal or goals. One goal might be to make a 5 percent profit after taxes; another might be to achieve a balance in hiring underrepresented groups; still another might be to expand business operations into a wider geographic area. Usually, organizations have multiple goals that they attempt to achieve simultaneously. The degree to which they are successful at goal attainment is a measure of their overall effectiveness. Organizational performance is an outcome that assesses the degree to which an organization is both efficient in using resources and effective in attaining stated goals. Normally, the determination of organizational performance is a comparative process. Organizational performance is often compared to an expected standard (i.e., market share, return on investment), specific competitors (e.g., a strategic group), or performance average for a specific industry.

## Organizations as Systems

A metaphor is a figure of speech that describes one thing in terms of another. Thus, metaphorically speaking, an organization is a system. You can imagine how useful a metaphor might be in portraying a complex organization like Vivendi Universal. "An organization is a personal computer" is a metaphor commonly used to convey the idea that an organization is a network of specialized component parts (or processes) that creates, markets, and distributes products or services.

Envisioning the organization as a system creates opportunities for finding and solving organizational problems. In other words, a problem that might occur in just one part of the organization is seen as affecting the entire organization when that organization is viewed as a system. A poor-quality TV, for example, might be the result of purchasing inferior parts. Solve the problem of inferior input, and the whole system surges forward. With that in mind, a system can be defined as a collection of interrelated entities (subsystems) that operate interdependently to achieve common goals. The concept of synergy means that a system is greater than the sum of its parts. Thus, subsystems are more effective working interdependently as an integrated system than is each subsystem working independently as a separate part. As shown in Exhibit 1.1, a system consists of three subsystems: input, processing, and output (IPO). An input subsystem, such as purchasing, ensures that resources are available to produce the product or service. A processing subsystem creates the good or service. Manufacturing facilities build or construct the physical product for later sale. An output subsystem makes the product or service available to distributors or customers. Organization problems are normally associated with one of the three subsystems.

EXHIBIT

**1.1**

**Organizations as Systems (IPO Model)**

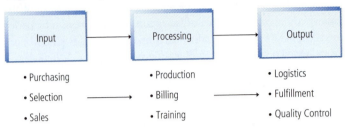

So as you can see, understanding systems theory greatly helps the manager in visualizing situations and diagnosing problems.

As mentioned earlier, it is useful to think of an organization as a system. Management scholars agree that organizations are open systems in which the organization receives inputs from the external environment, utilizes the inputs in the internal organization, and transmits organizational output back to the external environment. Systems theory helps us envision the organization as a series of specialized components. If one component is bad, the whole system is degraded. Think about the systems theory metaphor in the following situation.

A small organization consists of a sales force, a production facility, and a logistics department, all controlled by an accountant who happens to own the company. Salespeople generate business, production makes the good or service, and logistics delivers the product to the consumer while accounting ensures that costs are contained on the road to profitability. However, the production workers are sitting idle, and the logistics department has a truck at the loading dock, but there is nothing to load. What is the problem? Not enough information, you say. Well, more information might help, but systems theory leads us to examine the input side of the IPO model for answers. One explanation might be that the sales force needs to generate more business. Whether the demand for the product or service exists is another issue entirely. Either way, the systems theory metaphor helps diagnose, evaluate, and offer an explanation for the situation.

## Organizations and the Economy

Business organizations are embedded in a larger economic context. Evolutionary activity occurs over long periods of time. This gradual evolutionary activity allows the economy to expand or contract and organizations to become more efficient by weeding out the inefficient producers. We see market forces in action when a producer who charges more than his competitors for a comparable product is forced (i.e., by lack of demand) to lower price or lose sales and ultimately go out of business. Revolutionary activity occurs periodically to forever alter the nature of business transactions. Economic revolution occurs when a new innovation, such as new methods of production, are introduced into the economy. For example, desktop computing put the power of the computer at our fingertips and transformed many aspects of daily life. Desktop computers allowed small companies the same computing advantages as much larger companies.

All organizations require resources in the form of land, labor, and capital to support economic activity. However, the basis of worldwide economic activity has changed over time. Early agrarian economies (before 1830), characteristic of the post-revolutionary era, were based on small family-owned farms and small shop production. Craftsmen and trade workers created products to meet the needs of individual farms and shops. The agrarian form fit the demand of the time with the means of production. The industrial economy (1830–1950) was ushered in by technological revolutions, beginning with the invention of steam power. Steam power created the energy necessary for mass production. Coupled with the revolution in production, the influx of immigrants created the demand for more products and services than the craft system could provide. The economies of the industrial age built the world as we now know it. Post–World War II economies scurried to rebuild the world, supplying products and services to a growing population. The development of computer technology during World War II set the stage for the knowledge economies that we see in their infancy today. Knowledge economies are based on information and intangibles such as computer software and financial services. Compared to the industrial economies of the post–World War II era, knowledge economies represent new challenges and opportunities that require special management skills. A more detailed treatment of management history is reviewed in Chapter 2, "History of Management."

## Organizations Worldwide

Business management today is often global. Components are outsourced from around the world, assembled off shore, and then transferred to the home country for sale in the domestic market. This means today's managers require a broader understanding of business. The three dominant world economies—the United States, Japan, and Germany—are driven by the economic engines of business organizations. Additionally, France, India, China, and Korea have all made dramatic progress in recent years as global sources for manufacturing or services. All these successful organizations have one thing in common: a steady supply of trained managers who understand the principles of modern management in a global economy. Further, each country has nurtured economic growth as the basis for a stable society. Economic stability requires a growing gross domestic product, or GDP, which is a measure of the purely domestic output of a country; stable currency; and low unemployment. Each of these countries has seen the growth of major corporations that dominate trade in their respective industries: Microsoft and Exxon-Mobil in the United States, Sony in Japan, Siemens in Germany, Alcatel in France, Hindustan Motors in India, Geely Group in China, and Hyundai in Korea. Managers of these companies around the world have one thing in common—the goal of generating above-average economic returns for investors. According to Lester Thurow, world economies have formed three major trading alliances to help them compete worldwide.[3] To remain competitive, other countries have followed suit and have developed trading partnerships that assure economic stability in their region of the world. The North American Free Trade Agreement (NAFTA), Central America Free Trade Agreement (CAFTA), EU (European Union), OPEC in the Middle East, and in the Pacific Rim the Asian Pacific Economic Cooperation (APEC) group are several such partnerships. Russia and the former eastern block countries represent still another potential partnership that may formally coalesce in the future. However, they also demonstrate that economic stability is not possible without political stability. Politicians create the environment in which organizations can succeed or fail. Managers strategically respond to environmental conditions by aligning the organization's resources and capabilities with the environmental opportunities. Over the long run, organizations that survive fulfill consumer needs efficiently.

Whereas organizations have been part of human existence from the beginning of time, organizations that emerged in the United States during the twentieth century relied on extensive investments in both machine and human capital. Managers helped to plan, organize, lead, and control these organizations that led to the urban industrial economy. Today, managers worldwide direct or oversee the work and performance of other individuals toward the attainment of organizational objectives.

**KEY** TERMS

**industrial economy** An industry-based economy, prevalent between 1830 and 1950, that was ushered in by technological revolutions, beginning with the invention of steam power, which created the energy necessary for mass production.

**knowledge economies** Economies that are based on information and intangibles, such as computer software and financial services, and that resulted from the development of computer technology during World War II.

**gross domestic product (GDP)** The total value of goods and services produced by a nation.

# Management and Managers Defined

## Management as a Process

Management is a process of achieving organizational goals and objectives through the efforts and contributions of other people. The management process uses the functions of planning, organizing, leading, and controlling to accomplish organizational goals. For example, the planning function is used to identify goals and develop plans to attain the goals. The organizing function might include implementing human resource plans by developing a selection process to hire employees for a new plant opening. Managers are individuals who use principles of management to guide, direct, or oversee the work and performance of others.

## Management as a Discipline, or Field of Study

Designating management as a discipline implies that it is an accumulated body of knowledge that can be learned by study. Thus management is a subject with principles, concepts, and theories. We study management to understand these principles, concepts, and theories and to learn how to apply them in the process of managing.

## Management as People

Whether you say, "that company has an entirely new management team," or "she's the best manager I've ever worked for," you're referring to the people who guide, direct, and thus manage organizations. The word *management* used in this way refers to the people (managers) who engage in the process of management. Managers are primarily responsible for guiding people toward the attainment of organizational goals and objectives. People are an organization's lifeblood. Without people, there is no such thing as a profitable firm or a successful new product launch.

## Management as a Career

"Jose Cardenas is on the fast track in the marketing department. He has held three management positions and is now, after ten years, being promoted to the vice president level." Jose has moved through a sequence of jobs on a career path. He has a management career.

The different meanings and interpretations of the term *management* can be related as follows: *People* who wish to have a *career* as a manager must study the *discipline* of management as a means of practicing the *process* of management. Thus, we define management as the process undertaken by one or more persons to coordinate the work activities of other persons and to allocate resources such as capital, materials, and technologies in order to achieve high-quality results not attainable by any one person acting alone. Are you cut out to be a manager? What is your motivation to manage? Completing the Management Highlight on page 7 will help you assess your predisposition to engage in common managerial behaviors.

Completing the Management Highlight on page 7

# The Process of Management

As mentioned earlier, the process of management is the execution of the management functions in pursuit of organizational goals. The traditional management process identifies the functions as planning, organizing, and controlling, linked together by leading. Planning determines *what* results the organization will achieve; organizing specifies *how* it will achieve the results; and controlling determines *whether* the results are achieved.

**KEY TERMS**

**management** A process of achieving organizational goals and objectives through the efforts and contributions of other people.

**managers** Individuals who use the principles of management to guide, direct, or oversee the work and performance of others.

MANAGEMENTHIGHLIGHT

## HOW STRONG IS YOUR MOTIVATION TO MANAGE?

Instructions: Answer each question below, using the scale provided, in reference to the degree to which the statement accurately describes you.

| Extremely Weak Desire | Very Weak Desire | Weak Desire | Average Desire | Strong Desire | Very Strong Desire | Extremely Strong Desire |
|---|---|---|---|---|---|---|
| 1 | 2 | 3 | 4 | 5 | 6 | 7 |

1. *I have a desire to meet managerial role requirements* by developing positive relationships with superiors.
2. *I have a desire to meet managerial role requirements* by engaging in competition with my peers by competing in games or sports.
3. *I have a desire to meet managerial role requirements* by engaging in competition with peers involving occupational or work-related activities.
4. *I have a desire to meet managerial role requirements* by behaving in an active and assertive manner involving activities that in this society are often viewed as masculine.
5. *I have a desire to meet managerial role requirements* by appropriate work relationships with subordinates; by using organizational resources to influence others toward goal attainment; and by applying appropriate organizational sanctions for inappropriate behavior or lack of performance.
6. *I have a desire to meet managerial role requirements* by assuming a highly visible management presence.
7. *I have a desire to meet managerial role requirements* by engaging in activities that are often seen as mundane and associated with day-to-day administrative work.

Record your responses from the survey and total the column to determine the strength of desire to manage: the higher the cumulative score, the greater the motivation to manage.

| Question Number | Factor | Maximum Score | Your Score |
|---|---|---|---|
| 1 | Authority figures | 7 | |
| 2 | Competitive games | 7 | |
| 3 | Competitive situations | 7 | |
| 4 | Assertive role | 7 | |
| 5 | Imposing wishes | 7 | |
| 6 | Standing out from the group | 7 | |
| 7 | Routine administrative functions | 7 | |
| | Total Score | 49 | |

Adapted from: J.B. Miner and N. Smith, "Decline and Stabilization of Managerial Motivation Over a 20-Year Period," *Journal of Applied Psychology* (June 1982): 298; and R. Kreitner and A. Kinicki. *Organizational Behavior* ( Chicago: Irwin, 1995): 12.

## | Planning

The planning function is the capstone activity of management. Planning activities determine an organization's objectives and establish appropriate strategies for achieving them. The organizing, controlling, and leading functions all derive from planning in that these functions carry out the planning decisions.

Managers at every level of the organization plan. Through their plans, managers communicate expectations and specific actions necessary for success. Although plans may differ in focus, they are all concerned with achieving short- and long-term organizational goals. Taken as a whole, an organization's plans are the primary tools for managing changes in the business environment.

Strategic planning is a multidimensional concept that provides a firm with vision, direction, a sense of unity, and purpose. It's the integrative blueprint for the organization. Strategic planning assures that the right products are produced to meet or exceed customer expectations. An important aspect of strategic planning is creating a sustainable competitive advantage over competitors. Strategy serves to obtain a match between the firm's external environment and internal capabilities. If a competing firm lowers price, then the firm's strategy must address that environmental force.[4]

## Organizing

After developing a strategy, objectives, and plans to achieve the objectives, managers must design and develop an organization that can accomplish the objectives. Thus, the organizing function is used to create a structure of task and authority relationships that supports the attainment of organizational goals.

The organizing function takes the tasks identified during planning and assigns them to individuals and groups within the organization so that objectives set by planning can be achieved. Organizing, then, involves turning plans into action. The organizing function also provides an organizational structure, enabling the organization not only to function effectively as a whole but also to achieve objectives.

## Leading

Sometimes called directing or motivating, leading involves influencing organization members to perform in ways that accomplish the organization's objectives and goals. Leaders are responsible for the design, manufacture, and distribution of products and services. Successful leaders satisfy consumer needs while making a profit for the owners or stockholders.

The leading function focuses directly on the employees in the organization. Its major purpose is to channel human behavior toward organizational goals such as improved quality. Effective leadership is important in organizations. As we have seen in the Enron debacle,[5] not all leaders operate in the best interests of organizational stakeholders. In fact, questions of insider trading, personal arrogance, and downright greed often are the prime motivation of some leaders. But over the long run, these leaders are exposed and driven out of the organization.

## Controlling

Finally, a manager must make sure that the organization's actual performance conforms to planned performance. This controlling function of management requires three elements: (1) established *standards* of performance, (2) *information* that indicates deviations between actual performance and the established standards, and (3) *action* to correct performance that fails to meet the standards. Simply speaking, the purpose of management control is to make sure the organization efficiently produces a product or service that meets or exceeds standards.

Over the long run, the four functions of management must be learned in the context of quality improvement and maintenance. Management functions and quality are related; they should not be separated. Performance of one function depends on the performance of the other functions. A plan requires leaders, an organization, and control to be properly carried out. If a plan fails to incorporate quality considerations, it will be only a matter of time until failure becomes the reality.

The Ford Edsel's failure, a classic case in mismanagement, highlights this point.[6] Plans for entering the Edsel into the medium-priced auto field were elaborate. The 1950s saw a growing trend toward medium-priced cars: Pontiac, Oldsmobile, Buick, and Dodge all targeted the middle-income car buyer. Marketing research led Ford to introduce the Edsel, with great fanfare, in 1958. But Ford's high expectations resulted in a $350 million loss. It was the biggest new-car failure in automotive history. Contributing to the loss were such factors as a recession, poor promotion, and changing consumer preferences for even smaller cars. However, lack of quality was the Edsel's true Achilles heel. In getting the Edsel to market on schedule, production was rushed; numerous defects were not cleared up. Brakes failed, oil leaked, there were rattles, and the car didn't start properly. Edsel owners were driving an inferior product. Before these defects could be corrected, the car became known as a lemon. The Edsel's poor quality became the butt of many jokes and the standard of poor quality for a generation of Americans.

Planning, organizing, controlling, and leading were all carried out at Ford. Its managers followed these functions to the letter—the Edsel was a textbook example of how to manage a product from an idea to the market. Unfortunately, quality was neither the primary objective nor the driving focal point in the management process. The Edsel case clearly illustrates the need to integrate the functions of management with an overriding quality umbrella. Failure to build in quality will result in an opportunity for the competition to gain advantage.

Today we see Ford facing lost market share and struggling to control operating costs.[7] Toyota took over Ford's long-standing position as number 2 in market share behind GM in the United States domestic market. To survive, Ford has taken dramatic steps to cut costs, including workforce layoffs estimated at 40,000 as of September 2006.[8] All the efforts at Ford represent issues of control. Faced with declining demand, they must scale down the entire company to match the expected demand for their products. In the long run, Ford must design, build, and sell new products that meet the needs of consumers worldwide. Rumor has it that Ford and GM have even discussed merger or a strategic alliance to stem the tide competition from Toyota and Honda.[9] Like their 2006 advertising campaign heralded, Ford needs to make some "Bold Moves"; otherwise, Ford will join the ranks of such dearly departed automobile manufacturers as Hudson, Nash, Studebaker.

## Types of Managers

For a good example of management evolution, consider Dell Computer Corporation in Austin, Texas. Since 1984, when Michael Dell started the company, its leadership has changed from a single entrepreneur to a team of many managers with many subordinates. The development of different types of managers is a further result of such evolution.

Now let's look at a more general case. Assume that a successful firm, led by CEO Rose Fernandez, decides to add some new products and sell them to new markets. As she becomes more overworked due to the increased complexity of her job, Fernandez may decide to specialize *vertically* (i.e., creating more levels from top to bottom in the organization) by assigning the task of supervising subordinates to other people (Exhibit 1.2). She may also choose to specialize *horizontally* by creating new areas within the organization—such as production, marketing, finance, and purchasing—and by hiring a manager to supervise each new area (Exhibit 1.3). Whichever method Fernandez chooses, the management process in her organization is now shared, specialized, and thus more complex. The various management levels are described in the following subsections.

## First-Line Management

First-line managers coordinate the work of others, that is, workers who aren't themselves managers. People at the first-line management level are often called supervisors, office managers, or foremen. The first-line manager might oversee the work of blue-collar workers, salespeople, accounting clerks, or scientists, depending on the particular tasks carried out by that subunit of the business (for example, production, marketing, accounting, or research). First-line managers are responsible for the organization's basic work; they are in daily or near-daily contact with workers. They must work with their own workers and with other first-line supervisors whose tasks are related to their own.

## Middle Management

The middle manager is known in many organizations as the department manager, plant manager, or director of operations. Unlike first-line managers, those in middle management plan, organize, control, and lead the activities of other managers. Yet, like first-line managers, they are subject to the

EXHIBIT **1.2**    **Vertical Specialization**

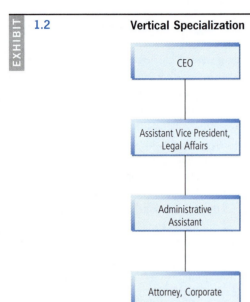

EXHIBIT **1.3**    **Horizontal Specialization**

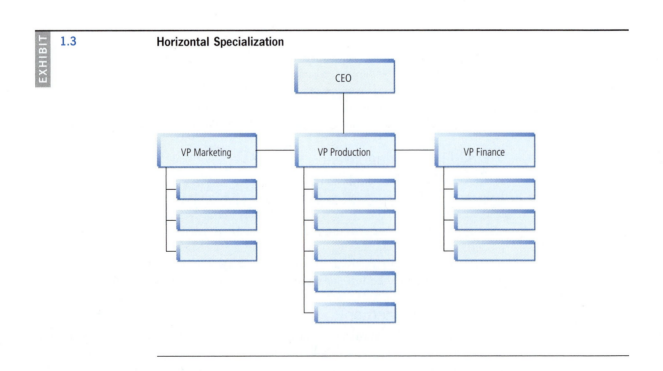

managerial efforts of a superior. The middle manager coordinates the work activity (for example, marketing) of a subunit.

Over the past ten years, firms such as Sears, General Motors, Ford, GE, Xerox, IBM, and General Dynamics have laid off many middle managers. Organizations like these have downsized the management cadre, especially middle-level management. Changes in the environment, competitive pressures, cost overruns, lost market share, and operations inefficiencies have stimulated the move to downsize. Management reductions in large companies are expected to continue into the twenty-first century.

## Top Management

A small group of senior executives (usually including a chief executive officer, president, or vice president) constitutes top management. Top management is responsible for the performance of the entire organization. These executives rely on middle management to carry their plans for action to each of their respective departments. Unlike other managers, the top manager is accountable to the board of directors and owners of the company or stockholders.[10] Of course, top-level managers depend on the work of all their subordinates to accomplish the organization's goals and mission.

The designations *top, middle,* and *first-line* classify managers based on their vertical rank in the organization. Completing a task usually requires completing several interrelated activities. As these activities are identified, and as the responsibility for completing each task is assigned, that manager becomes a functional manager.

As the management process becomes horizontally specialized, a functional manager is responsible for a particular activity. The management functions in a manufacturing firm could include quality and production, marketing, and accounting. Thus, one manager may be a first-line manager in quality and production, while another may be a middle manager in marketing. The function refers to what *activities* the manager oversees as a result of horizontal specialization of the management process. A manager's management level refers to the *right to act and use resources* within specified limits as a result of vertical specialization of the management process.

## Managerial Skills

Regardless of the level at which managers perform, they must learn and develop many skills.[11] A skill is an ability or proficiency in performing a particular task. Various skills classifications are important in performing managerial roles. Managerial skills are described in the following subsections; Exhibit 1.4 illustrates the management skills required at each level of management.

## Technical Skills

Technical skills are the *specific* knowledge, techniques, and resources used in performing work. Accounting supervisors, engineering directors, and nursing supervisors need technical skills to perform their management jobs. Effective managers know the work they manage. Without task-specific knowledge, a manager will have neither the respect of workers nor the ability to solve technical problems. Technical skills are especially important at the first-line management level,

**EXHIBIT 1.4**

### Management Skill by Level

| Level | Primary Skills | Secondary Skills |
| --- | --- | --- |
| First-Line Management | Technical Decision-Making People | Communication Computer |
| Middle Management | Analytical Decision-Making People | Communication Computer |
| Top Management | Analytical Conceptual Decision-Making People | Communication Computer |

because daily work-related problems must be solved quickly. The technical skill of measuring performance is especially important. As we will see in Chapter 13, "Leadership," managers have many control techniques at their disposal to ensure that plans come to fruition.

## Analytical Skills

Analytical skills involve the ability to analyze or logically diagnose problems and develop solutions. Analytical reasoning powers help managers to gain a broad understanding of a complex situation or problem. Analytical techniques—in the form of computer software—are powerful tools that assist managers in logically assessing and solving specific problems. For example, techniques such as materials requirement planning, inventory control, activity-based cost accounting, forecasting, and human resource information systems help managers develop solutions to complex business problems. In short, analytical tools help the manager to identify key factors, understand how they interrelate, and develop alternative solutions for decision making. Analytical skills of diagnosis, evaluation, and solution are important management problem-solving tools. They help managers not only understand problems better but also develop action plans for overcoming the problems.

## Decision-Making Skills

All managers must make decisions by choosing between several equally viable alternatives. The quality of these decisions determines that manager's effectiveness. A manager's decision-making skill in selecting a course of action is greatly influenced by her analytical skill. Poor analytical proficiency inevitably results in poor decision making. Some decisions are best made by an individual manager; others might best be made by a group. A wise manager knows when to allow a wider range of participation in the decision-making process. However, time pressures and preference for a course of action often drive him to an independent decision. If the manager hopes to gain support in the long term, he must then sell his decision to other members of the organization.

## Computer Skills

Computer know-how is an important management skill. In many cases, computers can substantially increase a manager's productivity. In minutes, computers can perform tasks in financial analysis, human resource planning, and other areas; it can take hours, even days, to complete such tasks without a computer. The computer—which instantly places at a manager's fingertips a vast array of information in a flexible, usable form—is invaluable in decision making. Software enables managers to manipulate the data and perform "what-if" scenarios, looking at the projected impact of different decision alternatives.

Today, basic management literacy includes computer skills and knowledge of business software. But managers need more than the basics for success. Today, that means using essential desktop software in daily business transactions such as e-mail, forecasting, and budgeting. Additionally, knowledge of the Internet and Web-based business solutions can mean the differences between profit and loss. For example, L.L. Bean traditionally employed catalog sales as its medium for generating sales. Now L.L. Bean sales are predominantly made through the company's website.[12] As a rule of thumb today, Internet sales increase at a rate of 25 percent per year while catalogue sales remain constant or decline. Thus, the L.L. Bean experience is not unique. In coming years, digital sales will continue to account for an increasingly larger percentage of all business sales. Additionally, business-to-business marketing, or B-to-B as it is commonly called, assures that supply chain management is fast and efficient.

As customer shopping patterns switch to Web-based transactions, managers must likewise develop the skills to manage this new technology. As part of the planning process, managers are often responsible for directing the development of websites and managing the website in support of strategic objectives. Because the technology is rapidly changing, managers need to understand how to use outsourcing versus in-house development to maximize their organizational objectives. Managers need the technical knowledge and a willingness to venture beyond their current technical abilities. Though embracing e-commerce can be a daunting and formidable obstacle for managers, the reward for the technically competent manager can be a competitive edge over the competition.

## People Skills

Because managers must accomplish much of their work through other people, managers' ability to work with, communicate with, and understand others is vital. People skills are essential at every organizational level of management; they reflect a manager's leadership abilities.

## Communication Skills

Effective communication—the written and oral transmission of common understanding—is important to success in every field. It is crucial to managers, who must achieve results through others' efforts. Communication skills involve the ability to communicate in ways that other people understand and to seek and use feedback from employees to ensure that the manager understood.

Lewis Lehr, former chairman and CEO of 3M, emphasized open communication among managers and employees. Lehr spent six months of every year away from 3M headquarters in St. Paul, Minnesota, visiting the company's numerous plants. During the visits, he participated in question-and-answer sessions with employees. Lehr believed that frequent communication was the only way to build employee trust and cooperation, which are essential to 3M's success. He also required that executives who ran 3M operations frequently visit with media, government, and education officials in their regions to talk about 3M.[13]

## Conceptual Skills

Conceptual skills consist of the ability to see the big picture—the complexities and connections of the overall organization. To keep an organization's efforts focused, it is vital to conceptualize how each part of the organization fits and interacts with other parts in order to accomplish goals and operate in an ever-changing environment.

Warren Buffett, former CEO of the investment firm Berkshire Hathaway, was concerned with making decisions about creating wealth in the future for employees and stockholders. He looks at mergers, acquisitions, and investments that may occur several decades ahead. Buffett used logic and a conceptual approach to predict future winners.[14]

Although the management skills just described are all important, the relative importance of each skill varies according to the level of the manager in the organization. Note in Exhibit 1.4 that technical and people skills are more important at lower management levels. First-line and middle managers have greater contact with the work being done and the people doing the work. In contrast, communication and computer skills are equally important at all levels of management. Analytical skills are slightly more important at higher levels of management, where the environment is less stable and problems are less predictable. Finally, decision-making and conceptual skills are critical to the performance of top-level managers. Top management's primary responsibility is to make decisions that are implemented at lower levels.

Certain characteristics, competencies, and skills are important to managerial success. Characteristics are a person's personality, or a psychological predisposition to act in a certain way, being outgoing and introducing yourself to a new customer is an example. A competency is a learned

## MANAGERIAL CHARACTERISTICS, COMPETENCIES, AND SKILLS

| Personal | Organizational | Managerial | Decision-Making |
|---|---|---|---|
| **Conscientious** Meets deadlines, arrives on time. | **Leads** Understands the vision and direction of the CEO. | **Shows Willingness** Is willing to lead and is prepared to assume responsibility. | **Accesses Information** Is able to use the Internet and other sources of information needed for decision making. |
| **Outgoing** Is willing to meet and work with other people. Takes the initiative and doesn't wait for an introduction. | **Supports Teamwork** Is willing to work on a self-directed team. Knows how to be a good team member. | **Is Trusted** Develops a sense of trust. Lets people know that he or she can be trusted. | **Finds Problems** Seeks to identify problems. What decisions need to be made? |
| **Courteous** Is polite and respectful of the rights of others. | **Understands Structure** Knows how the company is organized. | **Learns** Is open to learning new skills. | **Finds Options** Looks for alternatives that reflect the varying interests of organization members. |
| **Helpful** Is ready to help others find solutions to organizational problems. | **Understands the Politics** Understands the political aspects of the organization and how they can influence decisions. | **Adapts** Shows a willingness to change. | **Acts Strategically** Looks for opportunities and avoids threats. |
| **Open** Is open to new ideas. Is willing to change. | **Performs** Knows the job; knows what is expected and then does it. | **Networks** Develops relationships across the organization. | **Decides** Makes decisions and then stays the course. |
| | **Energy Focus** Concentrates effort and prioritizes workload. | **Advocates** Champions a cause, selling it to inform others when necessary. | |

behavior or an acquired proficiency, for example typing at a keyboard while talking to a customer on the phone. A skill is a natural ability to perform with a certain degree of consistency or success, negotiating with a supplier for a better price or making a presentation to a large group extemporaneously are examples. The Management Highlight above lists and categorizes a number of important characteristics, competencies and skills that managers need for success in today's complex organizations. At one time or another in the workplace, a manager will experience situations that require content knowledge described in the Management Highlight. Yet the importance of one skill or competency over another depends on the situation as well as the level of management (top, middle, or first-line). Demands of the situation may dictate that a manager use compassion or understanding—people skills—when dealing with an employee problem. Conversely, staying on task and meeting a deadline means balancing people skills and leadership skills to reach a timely outcome. At each level of management, different, skills, or competencies may come into play. Top management requires leadership often by creating a vision for the organization. Middle-level managers may need to develop skills in managing teams or develop an understanding of how organizational politics shape decision making.[15] First-line managers may need to access information in order to make a timely operational decision. Not to mention the fact that the first-line manager needs to be fair to all employees, knowing that fairness leads to trust. The trustworthy manager can more easily mobilize subordinate support for organizational goals.

In the end, many managerial skills can be learned or acquired with practice. Not all successful managers were successful from the beginning of their career—they had to work at it! Perhaps it is a sincere willingness and desire to work as a manager that often allows a person to overcome their deficiencies and focus their energy to overcome obstacles that leads to a successful managerial career in the long-term.

# Managerial Roles

A role is a behavior pattern expected of an individual within a unit or position. One of the most frequently cited studies of managerial roles was conducted by Henry Mintzberg. For two weeks, Mintzberg observed and interviewed five chief executives from different industries. He determined that managers serve in ten different but closely related roles.[16] The ten roles can be placed into three more general categories: interpersonal roles, informational roles, and decisional roles.[17]

## Interpersonal Roles

The three interpersonal roles of figurehead, leader, and liaison grow out of the manager's formal authority and focus on interpersonal relationships. By assuming these roles, the manager can also perform informational roles that, in turn, lead directly to performing decisional roles.

All managerial jobs require some duties that are symbolic or ceremonial in nature. The college dean who hands out diplomas at graduation, a manager who attends the wedding of a worker's daughter, and the mayor of Chicago formally meeting with the CEO of Boeing, in Boeing's new Chicago corporate offices, are all performing the *figurehead role.*

The manager's *leadership role* involves directing and coordinating subordinates' activities. This might require staffing (hiring, training, promoting, dismissing) and motivating workers. The leadership role also involves controlling, or making sure that things are going according to plan.

The *liaison role* involves managers in interpersonal relationships outside their area of command. This role might involve contacts both inside and outside the organization. Within the organization, managers must interact with many other managers and individuals. They must maintain good relations not only with the managers who send work to the unit, but also with those who receive work from the unit.

## Informational Roles

The informational role establishes the manager as the central point for receiving and sending information. As a result of the three interpersonal roles just discussed, managers build a network of interpersonal contacts. These contacts aid them in gathering and receiving information as a monitor and transmitting that information as the disseminator and spokesperson.

The *monitor role* involves examining the environment to discover information, changes, opportunities, and problems that may affect the unit. Formal and informal contacts developed in the liaison role are often useful here. The information gathered may concern competitive moves that could influence the entire organization, such as observing young people at a mall wearing a new fashion that suggests a change in a product line.

The *disseminator role* involves providing important or privileged information to subordinates. During a lunch conversation, a firm's president learns that a major customer is upset because of quality defects in the firm's products. Returning to the office, the president asks the vice president of operations and quality about the quality problem. He also instructs the vice president to personally assure him of the quality of the orders sent to the customer.

In the *spokesperson role,* the manager represents the unit to other people. This representation may be internal, when a manager makes the case for salary increases to top management; it may also be external, when an executive represents the organization's views on a particular issue of public interest to a local civic organization.

## Decisional Roles

Though developing interpersonal relationships and gathering information are important, they aren't ends in themselves. They serve as the basic inputs to the process of decision making. Some

---

**KEY**TERMS

**role** A pattern of expected behavior often associated with a job or profession.

**interpersonal role** The figurehead, leader, and liaison roles.

**informational role** The role that establishes the manager as the central point for receiving and sending information.

people believe that decisional roles—entrepreneur, disturbance handler, resource allocator, and negotiator—are a manager's most important roles.

The purpose of the *entrepreneurial role* is to improve the unit. Effective first-line supervisors continually seek new quality improvement methods to boost their unit's performance. A bank president is continually planning changes that will improve banking services. The effective marketing manager continually seeks new customer tastes.

In the *disturbance handler role,* managers make decisions or take corrective action in response to pressures beyond their control. Because decisions often must be made quickly, this role takes priority over other roles. The immediate goal is to bring about stability. When an emergency room supervisor responds quickly to a local disaster, when a plant manager reacts to a strike, or when a first-line manager responds to a breakdown in a key piece of equipment, they're dealing with disturbances in their environments. Their response must be fast, and it must return the environment to stability.

In the *resource allocator role,* a manager decides who gets which resources (money, people, time, equipment). Invariably, there aren't enough resources to go around, so the manager must allocate scarce goods in many directions. Resource allocation, therefore, is one of the manager's most critical decisional roles. A first-line supervisor must decide whether to set up overtime schedules or hire part-time workers. A worker with three projects must decide how much time to spend on each project daily. The president of the United States must decide whether to allocate more to defense and less to social programs.

In the *negotiator role,* managers must bargain with other units and individuals to obtain advantages for their unit. Negotiations may concern work, performance, objectives, resources, or anything else influencing the unit. A sales manager may negotiate with the production department over a special order for a large customer. A first-line supervisor may negotiate for new work schedules for workers. A top-level manager may negotiate with a labor union representative.

Henry Mintzberg suggests that recognizing these ten roles serves three important functions.[18] First, the roles help explain the job of managing, at the same time emphasizing that all the roles are interrelated. Neglecting one or more of the roles hinders the manager's total progress. Further, says Mintzberg, a team of employees can't function effectively if any one of the roles is neglected. Teamwork in an organizational setting requires that each role be performed consistently. Finally, the magnitude of the ten roles underscores the importance of managing time effectively so that managers can successfully perform each role.

## Contemporary Perspectives on Managing

Many of the skills described are words of wisdom and reflect a somewhat static view of organizational life. Organizational downsizing in the 1990s resulted in fewer middle managers and far fewer employees. What we are left with is a well-educated workforce in which the line between the worker and the manager is often less clear. The manager's role has changed from that of a direct supervisor to more of an employee advocate, or simply a provider of resources for employees. Even Henry Mintzberg recognizes that his roles are more useful as guideposts that mark the manager's way.[19]

Mintzberg's current view is that all managers work both inside and outside the organization. *Managers influence by managing information, by managing people, and by managing action.* Internally, managers use information to communicate and control the behavior of people inside the organization. They manage people by leading their employees. They manage action by making decisions that create internal change. Externally, managers communicate information about the organization to people outside the organization. They manage people by linking with others outside the organization. Managers complete their work by making deals and negotiations outside the organization.

**decisional role** The role of the manager, acting as entrepreneur, disturbance handler, resource allocator, and negotiator.

Successful managers learn to handle ambiguity. Most situations and problems in organizations have many possible alternatives. The right choice is never easy or clear. Today, more than ever before, managers are accomplishing their goals through groups rather than individuals. In that process, building team skills is essential to managerial success. Finally, Peter Senge suggests that managers would do well to use systems theory for problem diagnosis. He believes that managers who use a systems approach to problem diagnosis and resolution are more likely to find and develop solutions for business problems.[20]

**CONCLUSION**

## Management and Managers

Management is both a process and a discipline characterized by a constant state of change. As Mintzberg noted, managers at all levels perform three key roles—interpersonal, informational, and decisional. The dynamic nature of management means that managers must understand and apply the principles of management in daily activities. We believe that students of management should understand how management principles and managers shape the success of their organizations. Management principles are tools and techniques that can make this linkage between process and discipline successful as well as productive.

However, we believe that knowledge and appreciation of management fundamentals is the important point. As you read, analyze, and discuss the chapter content, think about how change occurs in organizations. Remember that change seldom occurs because a manager tells employees to do something. Rather, managers set the direction and then stand back and let employees use their discretion, education, experience, and common sense to effectuate change.

## Discussion Questions

1. What is the distinction between a market and a hierarchy?
2. Define each of the functions of management and provide an example of a daily managerial activity that comes under that heading.
3. Identify and define each of Mintzberg's managerial roles.

## Video Case

### Original Penguin Rides Out Turbulence

Penguins have always been cool. But golf shirts with a little flapping bird printed on them experienced a lull in coolness. In fact, their popularity remained frozen for two decades largely because they were worn by aging golfers. Now the penguins are back, flapping furiously—and, many would argue, coolly—not just on golf shirts but also on a wide array of men's and women's clothing and accessories, including shirts, shoes, hats, belts, neckties, handbags, and even bathing suits. These items represent the extreme makeover of a 50-year-old brand of clothing called Original Penguin. Now owned by Perry Ellis International, the Original Penguin brand of clothing is experiencing rejuvenation—thanks largely to Penguin's vice president, Chris Kolbe.

Chris Kolbe knows that thawing out an old brand is a daunting task under the best of circumstances. But the fashion industry is particularly difficult—the pace is dizzying, and the turbulence sometimes terrifying. Kolbe's activities as a manager are clearly characterized by variety, fragmentation, and brevity. For example, in a single day, Kolbe may be expecting several hundred samples from sources around the globe to arrive in time for a fashion show. He may have to decide whether to extend credit to a retailer or whether to drop one retailer in favor of another. He may have to review ad copy, return calls from fashion magazines, thumb through swatches of fabric, welcome sales reps arriving for a meeting, and fix his own computer. "We are always way behind and scrambling," he says with a chuckle. But Kolbe thrives on these activities because he is convinced that the time is right for his penguins to regain their place in the market among other legendary figures such as alligators and polo ponies—and he intends to make it happen.

Because the Penguin division is a tiny component of the much larger Perry Ellis, Kolbe serves all the management functions of planning, organizing, leading, and controlling—often during the course of one work day. "I take personal responsibility and accountability for everything that has the Penguin brand on it," Kolbe notes.

Kolbe also fulfills all the roles of a top manager. He considers himself a hands-on manager, communicating constantly with his staff and keeping himself "involved in every detail so I don't lose sight" of things. He develops relationships with employees so that they can work well together. "My job is really the A to Z in assembling a team of people who can focus on certain pieces of that business and deliver on the strategic goals for the company," he explains. "I feel very fortunate to have such a good team." He makes decisions about where to take the brand. Right now, he has his sights set on a more upscale market. He envisions his customers as comfortable suburbanites who want high-quality, fashionable casual clothing. But he doesn't worry too much about direct competitors in the clothing industry. Instead, he focuses on how Original Penguin can compete for consumer dollars. "My role as vice president of Penguin really is . . . I'm acting president of a very small division—a start-up company attached to a larger company," Kolbe observes. "So I really took on the A to Z of running a brand or running a company, from the . . . creative vision of the brand, to marketing the brand, to the business operations and sales of the brand."

As for that turbulence? Kolbe shrugs it off. "In every business there are roadblocks. So your ability to focus on the roadblock or work around the roadblock sometimes comes down to your ability to be successful." This is true even when the roadblock happens to be a shipment of women's flip-flops that hasn't arrived in time for the fashion show.

## Questions

1. In the context of this video example, what does it mean to say that Chris Kolbe needs conceptual skills for his job as vice president of Penguin?

2. Suppose those flip-flops—or other components of the upcoming fashion show—don't arrive in time. Describe which managerial skills will be most essential for Chris Kolbe to manage the situation through to a successful outcome.

3. From a management perspective, what do you think is the most difficult part of Kolbe's job? Why?

Sources: Company web site, http://www.originalpenguin.com, accessed July 30, 2004; "Pick up an Original Penguin," *Fashion UK* (July 8, 2004): http://www.widemedia.com/fashionuk/news/2004; Carl Swanson, "A Senior Moment," *The New York Times* (Spring 2004): 44; Stephanie Thomson, "Perry Ellis Banks on Brand Resurrections," *Advertising Age* (March 15, 2004): 14; Rima Sugi, "The Bird Is the Word," *New York Metro.com* (December 8, 2003): http://www.newyorkmetro.com.

## BizFlix

### 8 Mile

Jimmy "B-Rabbit" Smith, Jr. (Eminem) wants to be a successful rapper and to prove that a white man can create moving sounds. He works days at a plant run by the North Detroit Stamping Company and pursues his music at night, sometimes on the plant's grounds. The film's title refers to Detroit's northern city boundary which divides Detroit's white and African American populations. This film gives a gritty look at Detroit's hip-hop culture in 1995 and Jimmy's desire to be accepted by it. Eminem's original songs "Lose Yourself" and "8 Mile" received Golden Globe and Academy Award nominations.

This scene is an edited composite of two brief sequences involving the stamping plant. The first half of the scene appears early in the film as part of "The Franchise" sequence. The second half appears in the last twenty-five minutes of the film as part of the "Papa Doc Payback" sequence. In the first part of the scene, Jimmy's car won't start, so he rides the city bus to work and arrives late. The second part occurs after he is beaten by Papa Doc (Anthony Mackie) and Papa Doc's gang. Jimmy's mother (Kim Basinger) returns to their trailer and tells him she won $3,200 at bingo. The film continues to its end with Jimmy's last battle (a rapper competition).

### Questions

1. What is your perception of the quality of Jimmy's job and his work environment?

2. What is the quality of Jimmy's relationship with Manny, his foreman (Paul Bates)? Does it change? If it does, why?

3. How would you react to this type of work experience?

## *Suggested Reading*

Bossidy, Larry, Ram Charan, and Charles Burck. *Execution: The Discipline of Getting Things Done* (New York: Crown Group 2001).

Bunker, Kerry A., Kathy E. Kram, and Sharon Ting, "The Young and the Clueless" *Harvard Business Review* (December 2002): 80–87.

Walker, Carol A. "Saving Your Rookie Managers from Themselves," *Harvard Business Review* (April 2002): 97–102.

## *Endnotes*

1. Amitai Etzioni, *A Comparative Analysis of Organizations,* Revised Edition (New York: Free Press, 1975): 23–60.

2. Oliver Williamson, *Markets and Hierarchies* (New York: Free Press, 1975).

3. Lester Thurow, *Head to Head* (New York: Morrow, 1992): 56–57.

4. Charles Hill and Gareth Jones, *Strategic Management Theory,* 5th ed. (Boston: Houghton-Mifflin, 2000).

5. *Washington Post,* "Timeline of Enron's Collapse" (November 14, 2002).

6. Robert F. Hartley, *Marketing Mistakes* (Columbus, OH: Grid, 1976): 59–70.

7. Feature writer, "Toyota passes Ford to be the no. 2 U.S. Auto Retailer," *The Cincinnati Post,* Cincinnati, OH  (August 2, 2006): A6; and "Ford job cuts likely to exceed 40,000" *The Times,* London, England (Sept 14, 2006): 62.

8. Business section, "Ford job cuts likely to exceed 40,000" *The Times,* London, England (Sept 14, 2006): 62.

9. CNN wire, Ford, GM toy with merger talks, report says sources familiar say talks are not currently ongoing and may not be fruitful, paper reports, Accessed at: http://money.cnn.com/2006/09/18, September 18, 2006: 11:39 AM EDT.

10. Charles M. Farkas and Phillippe De Backer, "There Are Only Five Ways to Lead," *Fortune* ( January 15, 1996): 109–12.

11. Robert L. Katz, "Skills of an Effective Administrator," *Harvard Business Review,* (September–October 1974): 90–102.

12. "L.L. Bean Leverages Net.Commerce to Launch the Great Outdoors in Cyberspace," *E-business Solutions,* IBM Corporation, 1997.

13. Del Marth, "Keeping All the Lines Open," *Nation's Business* (October 1984): 85–86.

14. Bill Gates, "What I Learned from Warren Buffett," *Harvard Business Review* (January–February 1996): 148–152.

15. Jeffrey Pfeffer, and Gerald R. Salancik, "Organizational Decision Making as a Political Process: The Case of the University Budget." *Administrative Science Quarterly,* 19 (1974) 135–151.

16. Henry Mintzberg, *The Nature of Managerial Work* (Englewood Cliffs, NJ: Prentice-Hall, 1980).

17. Henry Mintzberg, "The Manager's Job: Folklore and Fact," *Harvard Business Review* (July–August 1975): 49–61; Jay W. Lorsch, James P. Baughman, James Reece, and Henry Mintzberg, *Understanding Management* (New York: Harper & Row, 1978): 220; Neil Synder and William F. Glueck, "How Managers Plan—The Analysis of Managers' Activities," *Long-Range Planning* (February 1980): 70–76.

18. Mintzberg, *The Nature of Managerial Work.*

19. Henry Mintzberg, "Covert Leadership: Notes on Managing Professionals," *Harvard Business Review* (November–December 1998): 140–147.

20. "Three Skills for Today's Leaders," *Harvard Management Update* (November 1999): 1–4. Peter Senge, *The Fifth Discipline: The Art and Practice of the Learning Organization* (New York: Currency Doubleday, 1990).

# 2

# HISTORY OF MANAGEMENT

M odern management traces its roots back to the era of Frederick W. Taylor, the father of scientific management. His perspective on management emphasized efficiency and the "one best way"—his way—to perform the task. Even today, we can see Taylor's ideas in practice at McDonald's or Wal-Mart. Yet, the concept of management is much older than the work of Taylor and others of his time. Managing the efforts of others is a concept that has been with us from virtually the beginning of time. In fact, the act of managing can be traced back to the ancient Romans, the Egyptians, and the Greeks. We could go even farther back in time to identify the application of management to religion and the governance of human affairs, but in this book we are primarily interested in the application of management concepts to socio-political structures and commerce. Perhaps we need think only of the miraculous inventions and abilities of ancient people to begin our journey through the development of management thought.

## Origin of Modern Management

The ancient world is full of wonders that are hard to fathom today. Knowledge of astronomy, architecture, and practical building techniques were commonplace in Rome and Greece. It is fair to say that many people who lived several thousand years ago were precise, rational, scientific, able to communicate, across cultures and stored knowledge for future generations. For example, the Greek physician Galen performed surgery on the brain and eye in 203 B.C. Grounded in science and mathematics, ancient scientists and inventors created a world that was in many ways as sophisticated as our own. For example, Ctesibius invented the water clock, and the great mathematician Archimedes invented the Archimedes screw used to pump water. Because of the great library at Alexandria, Egypt was the ancient world's repository of knowledge. At Alexandria, ancient scholars studied the writings of Socrates, Plato, and Ctesibius. The knowledge and inventions of ancient scholars allowed others who followed to provide healthcare and surgery, deliver running water to Rome (e.g., the arch structure of the aqueduct), and build a precise road system with distance markers (the Appian Way) throughout the Roman Empire. In addition, the ancient world created the pyramids, the Parthenon, the Pantheon, and other structures with phenomenal precision. Arguably, no greater example of their precision can be found than the great pyramid at the Giza plateau. Each side of the great pyramid varies by no more than 4 inches in length at the base compared to the other two sides, and the great pyramid is in precise alignment with the constellation Orion. The wonders of the ancient world represent the nexus of religion, science, and culture thousands of years before the invention of electricity, the airplane, the automobile, and space travel.

Think about it for a moment. Ancient managers, or viziers as they were known, had the ability to tell the time of day; created an infrastructure including roads; delivered running water and heated water to homes and businesses for bathing; and built structures that lasted thousands of years. Quite simply this meant ancient people engaged in the management functions of planning, organizing, leading, and controlling. In the ancient world, the principles of management as we know them today were used to accomplish goals set by powerful leaders (pharaohs, emperors, and despots). And in their day, failure was not an option!

Although the trials and tribulations of management today might not seem as dramatic as those the Egyptians might have faced thousands of years ago, management still offers plenty of excitement and challenges. The modern era of management begins with the industrial revolution, particularly as exhibited in the United Kingdom in the mid-1700s. In brief, the industrial revolution shifted manufacturing from a household setting to a factory setting. One of the first to recognize the significance of human resources was Robert Owen (1771–1858), a Scottish factory owner who refused to use child labor—a common practice of his era. Owen emphasized good working conditions, cooperation, and tolerance for differences in worker capabilities. Andrew Ure (1778–1857), another early manager who recognized the importance of human resources, provided workers with tea at breaks, medical treatment, and sickness payments. Owen and Ure, who considered workers to be more than mindless cogs, were definitely on to something. Slowly, what was meant by *management* began to change. Workers, if treated well, could perform excellently.[1]

# Modern Management

The origin of modern management is closely associated with the industrial revolution and the immigration from the old world to the new world. The industrial revolution was driven by the technology of steam power. Steam power made practical new machinery to drive mass production of goods to meet the needs of a growing and diverse population. This was a period of transition from the owner manager to the professional manager. Professional managers of that day understood scientific management principles and were willing to apply them in the pursuit of organizational goals. Modern societies depend on professional managers to oversee the production of goods and services demanded by customers. Managers are decision makers who allocate society's resources to various (often competing) ends. Managers have the authority and responsibility to build safe or unsafe products, seek war or peace, build or destroy cities, and clean up or pollute the environment. Managers establish the conditions under which we're provided jobs, incomes, lifestyles, products, services, protection, health care, and knowledge. It would be difficult to find anyone in a developed or developing nation who is neither a manager nor affected by a manager's decisions.

Understanding the development of modern management helps everyone appreciate the origin and purpose of management theories. The development of modern management can be grouped into several distinct categories, which represent different periods in the development of management thought: classical management, behavioral management, decision theory, systems theory, contingency theory, and modern influences on the evolution of management.

Each of these schools of thought is either an enhancement to our understanding of management theory or an entirely new approach (e.g., system's theory) to management theory. Collectively, these theories form modern management theory, which includes the best ideas from all these approaches and applies them with the goal of solving modern organizational problems.

# Classical Management

The hallmark of classical management was an emphasis on greater workforce productivity. A shortage of skilled labor at the turn of the twentieth century made efficient operations a priority. Classical management can be understood best by examining scientific management and classical organization theory. Scientific management concentrated on increasing the productivity of the workforce by separating the functions of management from the daily work of the organization. Managers were to do their jobs and workers their jobs. Greater efficiency was achieved through the division of labor, new work rules and methods, new standardized tools, and greater cooperation between workers and managers. Classical Organization Theory concentrated on top-level

**KEY** TERMS

**classical management** A management theory that emphasized greater workforce productivity.

**scientific management** A management theory that concentrates on increasing workforce productivity.

**classical organization theory** A theory that concentrates on top-level managers and problems of managing the entire organization.

managers and how they dealt with the everyday problems of managing the entire organization. For management students, the contributions of the classical approach are critical. These insights, in fact, constitute the core of the discipline and process of management and are the major focus of this book. Let's briefly examine each perspective.

## Scientific Management

As mentioned earlier, at the dawn of the twentieth century, business was expanding and creating new products and new markets, but labor was in short supply. Two solutions were available: (1) substitute capital for labor or (2) use labor more efficiently. Scientific management concentrated on the second solution.

**Frederick Winslow Taylor (1856–1915)** Frederick W. Taylor, called the father of scientific management, was an engineer by training. He joined Midvale Steel Works in Pennsylvania as a laborer and rose through the ranks to become a chief engineer.[2] Taylor believed that management's primary objective should be to secure the maximum prosperity for the employer and each employee. The mutual interdependence of management and workers was a common message he expressed. Taylor believed that organizations wasted human potential and physical resources. Neither skilled workers nor raw materials are unlimited, and both represent a production cost. His criticism was that managers of the day were either coercive or lazy and thereby inefficient in their approach to managing large organizations. In essence, they were unscientific. Taylor wanted to make the management of organizations more scientific and less an artistic expression of the individual practitioner. He proposed that the job of the manager be distinct and separate from the tasks of the workers. The role of management was to plan the flow of work and develop standard procedures for completing work. In Taylor's mind, this meant developing tools and equipment to better complete a task. At the heart of scientific management were two ideas: *efficiency* and *standardization.* Work should be designed and performed in the most efficient manner possible. Standardization eliminated variation in the product and decreased production uncertainty for management.[3] Taylor and his followers were driven by the notion of applying science to answer questions about efficiency, cooperation, and motivation. Taylor believed that inefficient rules of thumb used by management inevitably led to inefficiency, low productivity, and low-quality work. He recommended developing a science of management, the scientific selection and development of human resources,

**MANAGEMENT HIGHLIGHT**

**THE CONTRIBUTIONS OF FREDERICK W. TAYLOR TO SCIENTIFIC MANAGEMENT.**

| Contribution | Description | Improvement |
|---|---|---|
| Created the science of management | Through job analysis, rules and procedures were developed for all jobs. | Replaced common practices and outdated "rules of thumb" |
| Scientific selection, training, and evaluation | Developed the concept of the "first class man," and the commitment to paying well for good performance. | Increased efficiency and overall work performance |
| Cooperation between manager and worker | Cooperation ensured commonality of purpose. The role of the manager was to foster cooperation, not demand it. | Replaced the traditional adversarial relationship with a new understanding of the responsibility inherent in each job. |
| Division of work | Planning and design tasks were performed by managers. Workers were tasked with production work. | Workers were no longer expected to do their manager's work as well as their own. |

and personal cooperation between management and workers. Taylor believed that conflict among employees would obstruct productivity and so should be eliminated. The Management Highlight on the previous page provides additional insights into the importance of Taylor's contributions to the field of management.

Specialization    Taylor advocated maximum specialization of labor as one means to achieve greater efficiency. He believed each person should become a specialist and master of specific tasks. Also, he assumed that increased efficiency would result from specialization. Taylor was unhappy with anything short of the one best way. He searched, through the use of scientific methods, for the one best way to manage. This often included the design of custom tools to increase worker productivity. For example, his use of time and motion studies with stopwatches and task behavior, and his experimentation with different work methods and procedures made a scientific case for using one method or procedure over another and often encouraged others to undertake similar studies.[4] Thus began the tradition of empirical research in business.

Cooperation    Taylor tried to find a way to combine the interests of both management and labor to avoid the necessity for sweatshop management. As mentioned earlier, he believed that the key to harmony was discovering the one best way to do a job, determining the optimum work pace, training people to do the job properly, and rewarding successful performance by using an incentive pay system. Taylor believed that cooperation would replace conflict if workers and managers knew what was expected and saw the positive benefits of achieving mutual expectations.[5]

Motivation    Motivation was largely achieved through external rewards. The principle of equitable compensation meant that those who produced more would receive greater compensation. Thus, Taylor's "first class man" would receive higher wages than other employees. To the modern student of management, Taylor's ideas may not appear to be insightful. Given the times in which he developed them, however, his ideas were lasting contributions to how work is done at the shop-floor level. He urged managers to take a more systematic approach in performing their job of coordination.

Interestingly, if we evaluated scientific management on the basis of its impact on management practice at the time of its development, it would receive a low grade. Although some firms adopted scientific management, the methods of Taylor and his followers were largely ignored. In fact, many believed that Taylor's ideas would put people out of work. In 1912, the United States House of Representatives held hearings on scientific management at which Taylor testified.[6] However, Taylor's ideas garnered international interest. In fact, Lenin embraced Taylor's ideas as a solution to Russia's problems. In sum, this was quite a mixed message. Unions in the United States were worried that scientific management could put people out of work, and Lenin believed that scientific management held promise for the collective society.

The main criticism of scientific management is that Taylor and other scientific management supporters did not fully understand the psychological and sociological aspects of work. For example, scientific management made the implicit assumption that people are motivated primarily by money to work. In the late nineteenth century, this was undoubtedly a valid assumption. To assume this today, however, is far too simplistic.

| **Frank Gilbreth (1868–1924) and Lillian Gilbreth (1878–1972)** | Frank Gilbreth and Lillian Gilbreth enjoyed the title of "efficiency experts." Their main contribution was time and motion studies of work processes. They were the first to use motion picture movies to

show human movement at work. They analyzed each step in a repetitive work task and developed methods and procedures for performing the task more efficiently. The Gilbreths conducted research to demonstrate the superiority of their ideas over common practices of the day. Their famous study of bricklaying demonstrated how wasted motion could be reduced, increasing the number of bricks laid per hour from 175 to 350.[7] In their paper published in the Annals of the American Academy of Political and Social Science, they suggested that effective organizations had to consider both the welfare of the overall organization *and* the welfare of the individual worker. Lillian earned a Ph.D. from Brown University in 1915 and was a capable industrial psychologist in her own right. After Frank's untimely death of a heart attack in 1924, Lillian was left to raise their 12 children alone. As an equal partner in her husband's work, Lillian was recognized as one of the few practicing industrial psychologists of her day. Lillian was not only a pioneer in industrial psychology but also one of the few women who traveled the world, lecturing on scientific management and industrial psychology ideas. The life and times of the Gilbreths was chronicled by two of their twelve children Frank Gilbreth Jr. and Earnestine Gilbreth Carey, in the books *Cheaper by the Dozen* and *Belles on Their Toes*.

| **Henry Gantt (1861–1919)** | Henry Gantt was a close friend of Taylor and an early advocate of the scientific management movement. He was primarily concerned with the analysis of processes and the steps used to complete a task. His early work focused on *incentive systems* and **compensation plans** that included wages plus a bonus. Gantt was concerned with improving the plight of the working man and helping him gain more control over his work. Like Taylor, Gantt believed that if a man worked more than another man, he should receive a greater reward for his efforts. Additionally, Gantt emphasized the time required to complete a task rather than the quantity of the work or the units produced. His greatest contribution was the Gantt chart, an early tool of scientific management. The Gantt chart is a visual depiction of the number of steps in a process, the time required for each task, and the sequence of steps required to complete the entire project or task. Henry Gantt's chart is a basic and universal tool that is widely used today, particularly in project management applications. Gantt's contributions to scientific management enhanced and refined many of Taylor's ideas. It is fair to say that Henry Gantt is an original contributor to the field of scientific management.[8]

## Classical Organization Theory

Another body of ideas was developed at the same time as scientific management. These ideas focused on the problems faced by top managers of large organizations. Because this branch of the classical approach focused on the management of organizations (whereas scientific management focused on the management of work), it was labeled *classical organization theory*. Its two major purposes were (1) to develop basic principles that could guide the design, creation, and maintenance of large organizations; and (2) to identify the basic functions of managing organizations.

Although engineers represent many of the prime contributors to scientific management; practicing executives were the major contributors to classical organization theory. One famous engineer who spent most of his working life as an executive in a large French mining company was Henri Fayol.

| **Henri Fayol (1841–1925)** | A French mining engineer by training, Henri Fayol eventually became a managing director of a French mining and metallurgical combine, Commentary-Fourchamboult-Decazeville. Besides many articles on administration, his most famous writing was the book *General and Industrial Management,* translated by

**Gantt chart** A tool developed by Henry Gantt, that visually depicts the steps in a process, the time and the sequence of steps required to complete the entire project.

Constance Storrs and first issued in 1949.[9] Fayol divided an organization's activities into six categories:

| Technical (production, manufacturing)
| Commercial (buying, selling)
| Financial
| Security (protecting property and persons)
| Accounting
| Managerial (planning, organizing, commanding, coordinating, and controlling)

Many of Fayol's ideas are as accurate now are they were in the early twentieth century. These six categories (often under contemporary names or titles) are essential organizational activities and are present in all contemporary organizations. These ideas might appear obvious to us today, but it was Fayol who first had the vision to see the obvious.

**Fayol's Principles of Management**    Fayol proposed fourteen principles to guide the thinking of managers in resolving problems (see Exhibit 2.1). He never recommended total obedience to the principles, but he did suggest that a manager's experience and sense of proportion should guide the degree of application of any principle in a particular situation. As with scientific management, the reader should keep in mind the time in which Fayol developed his principles and his intent. He was probably the first major thinker to address problems of managing large-scale business organizations, which were a relatively new phenomenon in his time.

**Functions of Management**    Fayol was perhaps the first to discuss management as a process with specific functions that all managers must perform. He proposed four management functions:

| *Planning.* Fayol believed that managers should (a) make the best possible forecast of events that could affect the organization and (b) draw up an operating plan to guide future decisions.

**EXHIBIT 2.1**    **Fayol's Fourteen Principles of Management**

| Fayol's Principle | Description |
| --- | --- |
| 1. Division of work | Specialization of task |
| 2. Authority | Right to give orders |
| 3. Discipline | Obedience to supervisor |
| 4. Unity of command | Employee reporting to one supervisor |
| 5. Unity of direction | Individual effort focused on organizational goals |
| 6. Subordination of individual interest | Personal interests set aside for the good of the organization |
| 7. Remuneration | Fair pay |
| 8. Centralization with management | Decision making rests with management |
| 9. Scalar chain | Formal chain of command |
| 10. Order | Work conducted in a clean, orderly environment |
| 11. Equity to performance | Reward in contribution |
| 12. Stability and tenure | Stable employment |
| 13. Initiative | Self-starting responsibility |
| 14. Esprit de corps | Harmonious culture |

*Organizing*. Fayol believed that managers must determine the appropriate combination of machines, material, and humans necessary to accomplish the task.

*Commanding*. In Fayol's scheme, commanding involved directing the subordinates' activities. He believed that managers should set a good example and have direct, two-way communication with subordinates. Finally, managers must continually evaluate both the organizational structure and their subordinates; they should not hesitate to change the structure if they consider it faulty, nor to fire incompetent subordinates.

*Controlling*. Controlling ensures that actual activities are consistent with planned activities. Fayol did not expand on this idea except to state that everything should be "subject to control."

**Max Weber (1864–1920)** | Max Weber, who was born in Germany, studied law and then entered an academic career at Berlin University. He studied and reported on the theory of authority structures in organizations. He created a theory of organization to help Germany develop a social and economic form of governance necessary for social progress. His theory of organization included what we refer to today as the bureaucratic form. Weber believed that the "bureaucratic" organization is the dominant institution in society because it is the most efficient. As used by Weber, bureaucracy refers to a management approach based on formal organizational structure with set rules and regulations that rely on specialization of labor, an authority hierarchy, and rigid promotion and selection criteria.

Weber identified several benefits of the bureaucratic form:

1. *Efficiency*. The optimal use of resources to accomplish an objective.
2. *Predictability*. The use of rules, regulations, methods and procedures to ensure consistency across time and transactions.
3. *Calculability*. The ability to quantify and calculate results with great precision.
4. *Control*. Replacing the frailties of human effort with the invariability and greater consistency of technology.[10]

Another aspect of *bureaucracy* was the concept of authority. Weber made a distinction between *power* as forced compliance and *authority* as the voluntary compliance expected of a subordinate. In an authority system, those in the subordinate role (workers) see the issuing of directives by those in the authority role (managers) as legitimate. The first mode of exercising authority is based on the qualities of the leader. Weber used the Greek term *charisma* to mean any quality of an individual's personality that sets him or her apart from ordinary people. A second mode of exercising authority is through precedent and usage. In such an interpretation, managers have authority by virtue of the status and the position they have achieved or inherited.

However, most of us think of bureaucracy as rigid rules, red tape, and long lines. Bureaucracy was Weber's view of the "one best way" classical approach to solving the problems of modern life.

**Contributions and Limitations of Classical Management** | The greatest contribution of classical management was that it identified management as an important element of organized society. Management has, if anything, increased in importance in today's more global and competitive world. Advocates of the classical management believe that management—like law, medicine, and other occupations—should be practiced according to principles that managers can learn. Global managers must learn these principles to compete.

Classical management theorists believed that the identification of management functions such as planning, organizing, commanding, and controlling provided the basis for training new managers in classical management. The management functions are often presented differently, depending upon who is presenting them. But any listing of management functions acknowledges that managers are concerned with *what* the organization is doing, *how* it is to be done, and *whether* it was done.

Contributions of classical management, however, go beyond the important work of identifying the field of management and its process and functions. Many management techniques used today (for example, time and motion analysis, work simplification, incentive wage systems, production scheduling, personnel testing, and budgeting) are derived from the classical approach.

One major criticism of classical management is that most of its insights are too simplistic for today's complex organizations, which exist in a constantly changing world. Critics argue that scientific management and classical organization theory are more appropriate for the past, when most organizations operated in stable, predictable environments. The changing environment, shifting expectations of workers, increasing competition, greater workforce diversity, increasing government regulations, and a growing public concern for social responsibility and ethical behavior are all characteristics of contemporary organizations that were never contemplated by classical management theorists.

## Behavioral Management

Behavioral management developed partly because practicing managers found that the ideas of the classical approach did not lead to total efficiency and workplace harmony. Managers still encountered problems because subordinates did not always behave as they were supposed to. Thus, interest grew in helping managers become more efficient.

The behavioral management has two branches. The *human relations approach* became popular in the 1940s and 1950s. The *behavioral science approach* became popular in the 1950s and still receives a great deal of attention today.

### The Human Relations Approach

The human relations approach focuses on individuals working in group settings. Managers and workers are studied in relation to what occurs within the group. Elton Mayo is considered the father of the human relations movement.

| Elton Mayo (1880–1949) | An Australian, Elton Mayo has been called the founder of both the human relations and the industrial sociology movements. The research work that he directed at Harvard University showed the importance of the group in affecting individual behavior at work.

Mayo's initial research in textile mills was on reorganizing the work schedule to include more rest pauses for workers. Mayo expected that adding rest pauses would reduce turnover. Mayo and his team applied their knowledge and experience with rest breaks and turnover reduction from the textile mills to the Hawthorne Works of the Western Electric Company (more fully explained later in this section).

Mayo's writings and thinking led to a more complete realization and understanding of the human factor in work situations. Central to this was the discovery of the informal group as an outlet and source of motivation for workers. His work also led to an emphasis on the importance of an adequate upward-flowing communication system.

Human relations experts believed that management should consider employees' needs for recognition and social acceptance, and that they should try to fulfill these needs at work. They suggested that because groups provide members with feelings of acceptance and dignity, management must reexamine the role of the work group as a positive force on increased productivity. Therefore, effective managers will require training in people skills as well as technical skills.

| **Hawthorne Experiments** | The human relations approach traces its genesis to a series of controversial studies that were conducted beginning in the late 1920s. The Hawthorne Studies (1927–1932) at Hawthorne Works of Western Electric in Cicero, Illinois, are among the most famous in management literature.[11] The Hawthorne Works of Western Electric (which manufactured equipment for Bell Telephone System) was known for its concern for its employees' welfare. It had maintained high standards in wages and hours. The study's original aim was to determine the relationship between intensity of illumination and two groups of workers' efficiency, measured in output. The intensity of light under which one group worked was varied, but was held constant for the other group.

Before Mayo and his Harvard research team arrived, another research group had completed the initial illumination studies. Mayo and his team were presented with the findings that when illumination increased, productivity increased. However, when illumination decreased, productivity also increased. It appeared that workers reacted more to the presence and expectations of the researchers rather than to the actual increase or decrease in illumination. Scholars refer to this phenomenon as the Hawthorne effect.[12]

The Harvard researchers also set up an experiment involving the relay assembly test room at the Hawthorne plant. Six women were selected to work on assembling telephone relays in the test room. The women were studied over a long period of time, during which the researchers altered their working conditions (e.g., method of payment and length of rest periods). The researchers introduced twelve different changes and determined that in each experimental period, output was higher than in the preceding one.

The researchers concluded that changes and improvement in output were less affected by any of the twelve changes in work conditions than by the attitudes of the six work-team individuals. The cohesiveness and friendships among the team members were found to be significant. The group developed leadership and a common purpose—to increase the output rate.

The Hawthorne Studies pointed out that workers are motivated by more than economic factors. Workers' attitudes are affected by their feelings about each other and by having a common purpose. Today this theory is well accepted, but it was not generally believed when the research was being done (from 1927–1932).[13] The Hawthorne Studies were conducted before the era of collective bargaining and safety regulations, when workdays averaged ten to twelve hours and twelve-year-olds worked alongside adults.

## The Integration of Behavioral Science

Other individuals who were university trained in the social sciences such as psychology, sociology, and cultural anthropology began to study people at work. They had advanced training in applying the scientific approach to the study of human behavior. These individuals have become known as *behavioral* scientists, and their approach is considered to be distinct from the human relations approach.

Followers of this approach believe that to develop good human relations, managers must know not only why their workers behave as they do, but also what psychological and social factors influence them. Students of human relations bring to management's attention the important role individuals play in determining an organization's success or failure. They try to show how the process and functions of management are affected by differences in individual behavior and by groups in the workplace. Thus, whereas scientific management concentrates on the job's *physical* environment, the human relations approach concentrates on the *social* environment.

**KEY**TERMS

**Hawthorne Studies**
Famous studies conducted by Elton Mayo at Hawthorne Works of Western Electric in Cicero, Illinois; initially aimed to determine the relationship between the intensity of illumination and the efficiency of two groups of workers. *See also* Hawthorne effect.

**Hawthorne effect** The unexpected results of the Hawthorne Studies indicated that productivity increased in relation to the presence and attention of the researchers. *See also* Hawthorne Studies.

| Hugo Munsterberg (1863–1916) | Psychologist and philosopher at Harvard University, Hugo Munsterberg was a social scientist interested in the application of psychology to industrial settings. He is considered an early contributor to both the fields of industrial psychology and human relations. His text *Psychology and Industrial Efficiency* published in 1913 integrated scientific management with human behavior. Munsterberg believed that Taylor's quest for efficiency could be achieved only by considering the needs of the worker. As an experimental psychologist, he focused his writings on monotony and boredom at work, and the influence of the social environment and advertising on individuals. Today, many of his ideas have become integral aspects in the field of industrial psychology.[14]

| Mary Parker Follett (1868–1933) | Often considered the first female industrial psychologist, Mary Parker Follett was an accepted scholar in a field dominated by men. She made her mark in the areas of conflict management and the giving of consent (i.e., the consent to be managed) by the worker. Mary Parker Follett understood that conflict is part of a democratic culture. Resolving conflict was necessary to avoid counterproductive behavior. In society, not resolving conflict could result in revolution, whereas at work it would likely result only in lower efficiency and productivity. Yet both were outcomes to be avoided. However, Follett also recognized that not all conflict was dysfunctional. Conflict, if managed properly, was a natural consequence of human interaction. With proper integration of viewpoints, conflict leads to change. Her understanding of social and political behavior at work and the idea that workers give their consent (to be managed) was a significant advance from scientific management practices of the day. A true pioneer, her writings laid the foundation for studies in group dynamics, conflict management, and political processes in organizations that we study today.[15]

Behavioral science advocates believe that workers are much more complex than the "economic man" described in the classical approach or the "social man" described in the human relations approach. The behavioral science approach concentrates more on the nature of work itself and the degree to which it can fulfill the human need to use skills and abilities. Behavioral scientists believe that an individual is motivated to work for many reasons in addition to making money and forming social relationships.

## | Contributions and Limitations of Behavioral Management

For scholars, behavioral management contributed a wealth of important ideas and research results to the aspect of management that deals with managing people. Because managers must get work done through others, management is really applied behavioral science; that is, a manager must motivate, lead, and understand interpersonal relations.

The emphasis on efficiency characterizing the classical management approach was supplemented with a focus on people and their needs, emotions, and thoughts. The work of the behavioral management movement resulted in organizations being considered as social systems with both formal and informal patterns of authority and communications. A consideration of workers, their skills, their group involvement, and their motivation was considered to be at the core of any success achieved by management.

The basic assumption that managers must know how to deal with people appears valid, but management is more than applied behavioral science. For behavioral management to be useful to managers, it must make them better practitioners of the process of management. It must help them in problem situations. In many cases, this objective has not been achieved, because the tendency of some behavioral scientists is to use technical terms when introducing their research findings to practicing managers. is that managers either never read the report or fail to understand what action they should take. Also, in some situations, one behavioral scientist (a psychologist) might have a different suggestion from another (a sociologist) for the same management problem. Human behavior is complex, and it is studied from differing viewpoints. This complicates the job of a manager who is trying to use insights from the behavioral sciences.

# Decision Sciences

Decision sciences are a modern version of the early emphasis on the "management of work" by those interested in scientific management. Its key features are the use of decision making, information systems, mathematics, and statistics to aid in making choices when faced with production and operations problems. Thus, decision sciences focus on solving technical rather than human behavior problems.

## Origins of the Decision Sciences

The decision sciences approach has formally existed since the early part of World War II, when England was confronted with some complex military problems that had never been faced before, such as logistical support algorithms and code breaking. In an effort to solve these problems, the English formed teams of scientists, mathematicians, and physicists. The units, named *operations research teams*, proved to be extremely valuable in winning the war. When the war was over, American firms began to use these mathematical decision tools to solve business problems.

### Herbert Simon (1916–2001)
Herbert Simon, a distinguished American political and social scientist, influenced the thinking and practice of management based on decision making and information science.[16] He viewed management as equivalent to decision making, and his major interest was how decisions are made and how they might be made more effectively.

Simon describes three stages of decision making:

1. Finding occasions requiring a decision (intelligence)
2. Inventing, developing, and analyzing possible courses of action (design)
3. Selecting a course of action (choice)

In Simon's thinking, all managerial action is decision making. Economists' traditional theory is that decisions are made on the basis of rationality. However, in the real world, there are limits to rationality—such as the emotions of the decision maker. In place of the "economically rational" decision maker, Simon proposes a "bounded rationality" decision maker. He argues that decision maker "satisfice" rather than optimize. That is, decisions are made that are satisfactory or "good enough." Instead of searching for a decision to maximize profits, managers can seek an adequate profit.

Simon viewed decisions as falling on a continuum ranging from programmed, or routinely occurring, to nonprogrammed, or nonroutine and unstructured. He suggested that programmed decisions could be modeled so that a similar outcome occurred every time. Simon believed that nonprogrammed decision required a unique decision for each situation. However with computation advances, techniques that were initially used to assist in programmed decision making are now commonly used to solve far more complex non-programmed decisions. Such techniques as neural networks, transportation models, mathematical analysis, operations research, and computer simulation have gained prominence. Collectively these mathematical techniques are commonly called decision support systems. Computers and mathematics have enabled more and more elements of judgment to be incorporated into the entire decision-making process. As computer technology becomes more advanced, more complex decisions will become programmed.

KEY TERMS

**decision sciences** Modern management theories decision making, information systems, mathematics, and statistics to aid in making choices.

**| James March (1923– ) |** James March and Herbert Simon wrote the classic book *Organizations* in which they considered the motivational forces that influence people when they are confronted with choice.[17] Of course their aim was to focus on decisions made in the context of work organizations. However, their ideas about decision making have had much broader appeal over the years. March later developed another concept called the "Garbage Can" model of decision making in which he cast decisions as existing problems waiting to be solved. He saw decision makers, problems, and leadership as intertwined. To be successful, leaders needed to identify a problem and then search for a solution to the problem. By engaging member participation, influencing participants, and resolving conflict, the leader manages the decision making process to a successful climax. In other words, problems are always with us, leaders identify problems, and then those leaders make decisions that satisfy individuals or groups who have a stake in the decision resolution.

## | Contributions and Limitations of the Decision Sciences

Today, the most important contributions of the decision and information sciences management approach are to the areas of production management, operations management, and information systems. Production management focuses on manufacturing technology and the flow of material in a manufacturing plant. Management science has contributed techniques that help solve production scheduling problems, product and service quality improvement problems, budgeting problems, and maintenance of optimal inventory levels.

Operations management is similar to production management except that it focuses on a wide array of problems and includes organizations such as hospitals, banks, government, and the military, which have operations problems but don't manufacture tangible products. For such organizations, management science has contributed techniques to solve such problems as budgeting, planning for workforce development programs, and aircraft scheduling. Operations management also includes the areas of purchasing, materials management, production, inventory and quality control, maintenance, and plant management.

Information systems involve the use of computers in helping managers make better decisions and to increase an organization's efficiency. The computer now permits managers to gather and accurately process large volumes of data, produce reports in a timely manner, make projections about the future, communicate with geographically separate parts of the organization, and apply quantitative techniques to improve the enterprise's efficiency and performance.

Information is a chief ingredient used by managers. It is data evaluated or processed for a particular use. Information is disseminated up, down, and across an enterprise's units. Large volumes of information are now commonly stored in databases (centralized collections of data and/or information for a particular subject). Organizations of all sizes now depend on the flow of information and the availability of databases to make more informed and timely decisions. Planning, organizing, commanding, and controlling decisions have been enhanced through the availability of information systems.

We noted in our discussion of the behavioral approach that management is more than applied behavioral science. At this point, we should stress that decision and information sciences are no substitute for management. Decision science techniques are especially useful to the manager performing the management process. If decision science has a flaw, it is that too little emphasis has been placed on people and how they can use the tools and techniques available. What good is information provided by a computer if that information is not interpretable, relevant, or specific? What good is a new statistical quality control chart if the worker cannot interpret its meaning or even produce the chart? What good is the mathematically oriented inventory model if the data entered are inaccurate? Workers, customers, and managers using decision science techniques and approaches

**KEY** TERMS

**production management** A sphere of management science that focuses on manufacturing technology and the flow of material in manufacturing.

**operations management** A sphere of management science that includes the areas of purchasing, materials management, production, inventory and quality control, maintenance, and plant management.

**information system** A computerized system that helps managers make better decisions by permitting them to gather and accurately process large volumes of data.

EXHIBIT 2.2

**Open Systems Model**

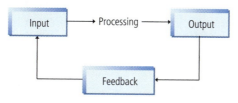

need to be viewed as users, interpreters, and benefactors. Their needs, reactions, and understanding must be weighed when deciding on an appropriate decision science technique to use.

# Systems Theory

A system consists of four components: input, processing, output, and feedback. Systems can be closed to environmental influence, such as a clock, or open to influences from the environment, as in the case of an organization with an online Internet ordering system. Exhibit 2.2 illustrates the components of a system that is open to the environment.

Systems theory is essentially a way of thinking about organizations and management problems. A system is a collection of parts that operate interdependently to achieve common goals. Minnesota Mining and Manufacturing Co. (3M) is more than a research and development, marketing, and production unit. The success of 3M is a result of a system of interrelated units that work in concert to produce new and better products.

From the systems perspective, management involves managing and solving problems in each part of the organization, but doing so with the understanding that actions taken in one part of the organization affect other parts of the organization. For example, implementing a solution to a problem in a firm's production department will likely affect other aspects of the company such as marketing, finance, and personnel. Each part of an organization is tightly linked to other parts; no single part of an organization exists and operates in isolation from the others. Thus, in solving problems, managers must view the organization as a dynamic whole and try to anticipate their decision's unintended as well as intended impact (See Management Highlight on page 34.).

# Open Systems

According to the systems approach, the elements of an organization are interconnected. The approach also views the organization as linked to its environment. The context for the systems view is the environment. The general environment contains elements that affect all organizations. The task environment contains elements that can have a more immediate impact on organizational success. Though each part of the organization performs a specific function, the sum total effect of all systems components is called the synergistic effect.[18] Some have argued that the role of management is important because the nature of the environment is quite different from one organization to the next.[19] Organizational effectiveness, even survival, depends on the organization's interaction with its environment. A battery-powered digital watch would be considered a relatively closed system. The installation of the battery is the only outside intervention. Once in place, the watch operates with no input from the external environment.[20]

**Chester Barnard (1886–1961)** | Chester Barnard bridged the behavioral school and the decision-making school. However, his contributions also included the description of the organization as a behavioral system. Barnard's ideas reflect a new understanding of leadership,

**KEY**TERMS

**systems theory** A way of thinking about organizations and management problems from a systems point of view. *See also* system.

**general environment** The overall environment containing the elements that affect all organizations.

**task environment** The environment containing elements that can have an immediate impact on organizational success.

**synergistic effect** The sum total effect of all systems components, as in an organization in which each of its parts performs a specific function.

## UNDERSTANDING DELL™ AS A SYSTEM

To further your understanding of systems theory in practice, consider Dell as an example. Dell is a computer manufacturer operating in an open system, actively interacting with its environment. Active interaction means that Dell both obtains resources from and provides resources to its environment. For example, Dell has 50 customer contact centers around the globe. In India alone, Dell employs over 10,000 employees. Dell builds computers, develops software, and runs call centers around the world. Dell obtains resources from the environment, produces its products with help from the environment, and then distributes its product to the environment. Dell also recognizes that it must protect the business environment to preserve future demand for its products.

Dell did not always exist. In fact, Dell's largest growth began in the early 1990s. Today it is an embedded member of the environment. It might be more accurate to describe Dell as a leading member of the PC and business server industry. As such it must attract the financial resources needed to build manufacturing facilities, to fund research and development (R&D) efforts, and to meet any number of other expenses. Dell obtains the funds from the environment—from banks, other lending institutions, and people who buy shares of Dell's stock. Raw materials (e.g., computer parts) are obtained from outside suppliers in the environment. Information about the latest computer product technology and about the latest products developed by Dell competitors is also needed. This information substantially influences the design and manufacture of Dell's computers. Information is obtained from the environment—from research journals, computer conferences, and other external contacts.

These inputs are acquired, coordinated, and managed in a *transformation* process that produces *output* in the form of personal and business file servers. Next, Dell almost exclusively relies on the Internet as a direct distribution channel to customers rather than on retail outlets or mass merchandisers. Is Dell successful? Only if Dell's advertising attracts customers and its products meet or exceed customer expectations over time. The customer's decision to buy from Dell or its competition provides Dell with *feedback*.

If the feedback is positive (high sales), the environment reciprocates by providing a critical input to Dell—cash that the company uses to obtain other inputs from the environment such as top-quality employees, materials, and knowledge. Negative feedback (low sales) presents Dell with a serious problem. Regardless, Dell must closely monitor feedback and act upon it. New products are developed and slow selling products are eliminated. During rapid change (the move to wireless computing), Dell needed to respond quickly to the environmental demand. Failure to respond quickly or ignore the environment signals leads to lost market share. Both General Motors (GM) and Sears have learned this lesson the hard way. Neglecting the environment will, over time, render the company noncompetitive.

Describing Dell as a system enables us to see Dell in a particular way. Thinking about Dell as an integrated system helps the analyst identify how well specialized subsystems at Dell are able to respond to the demands of the environment. In tough economic times, a systems perspective allows the analyst to pinpoint problem areas and take corrective action.

Sources: R Subramanyam, "Dell Counts on Indian Managers for New Ops," *The Economic Times of India* (Dec 6, 2005). Also see Peter Senge, *The Fifth Disipline* ( New York: Double Day: 1991).

motivation, and communication. In fact, Herbert Simon's classic text *Administrative Behavior* developed many groundbreaking ideas from Barnard's earlier work in the *Functions of the Executive*. At the time of his contributions to the management literature, Barnard was president of New Jersey Bell Telephone and a systems advocate. He viewed an organization as an aggregation of units that interact. He introduced the concept of the "system of coordination." Barnard was the first major theorist after the Hawthorne Studies to emphasize the importance and variability of individuals in the work setting.

Barnard believed that an essential element of organizations is people's willingness to contribute their individual efforts to the cooperative system. The need for cooperation and interdependence is clearly presented in Barnard's classic management book, *The Functions of the Executive*:

> A cooperative system is a complex of physical, biological, personal, and social components which are in a specific systematic relationship by reason of the cooperation of two or more persons for at least one definite end.[21]

Barnard's inducement/contribution balance is an example of how he used systems theory in a very practical manner. The inducement/contribution balance was a ratio described with a numerator that included the monetary and other inducements offered to an employee by the organization. The denominator represented the contributions made by the employee in the form

## MCDONALD'S™: BUREAUCRACY OR SYSTEM?

McDonald's corporation is familiar to us all. Realistically, the "Golden Arches" are a symbol to consumers around the world of American business, values, and culture. For better or worse, McDonald's is seen as an icon of American business. But what do we know about McDonald's operation? Probably very little. Most of have a basic familiarity with how McDonald's conducts business. But for this assignment you need to know a little bit more. To prepare, you should review your understanding of the business aspects of McDonald's; that is, what they do to produce or create an individual meal. You might think of a visit to McDonald's as a transaction. Perhaps visit a McDonald's and pay attention to how a transaction is completed. How do employees process these transactions? Remember, most people going through the drive-thru lane will spend less than five minutes at McDonald's. Next, reread the sections in this chapter on Weber and systems theory; these are different approaches to understanding work organizations.

**Assignment:** Compare McDonald's using two different approaches: Weber's theory of bureaucracy and systems theory. Following is a list of a few basic ideas from these two theories. Use each set of ideas to evaluate McDonald's. Based on your comparison, which theory helps you better understand the operational problems and successes at McDonald's?

- Weber discusses four principle benefits of bureaucracy: efficiency, predictability, calculability, and control.

- Systems theory states that organization can be viewed as systems that contain specialized subsystems for input, processing, output, and feedback.

of direct work and other helpful acts and behaviors. Barnard cast the inducement contribution balance as a state of equilibrium. Barnard predicted that when imbalance or disequilibrium occurred, action was needed to regain the state of equilibrium. For example, a disequilibrium caused by insufficient inducements (pay) for a given level of contributions (work) meant that the workers would decrease their contributions to regain equilibrium. Barnard's insights were the basis for many modern theories including the expectancy theory of motivation, equity theory, and compensation theory. It is safe to say the Barnard observed work behavior and developed several important theories that generalized far beyond New Jersey Bell Telephone Company.

## | Contributions and Limitations of the Systems Management Approach

To survive, most organizations today operate as open systems and utilize a systems perspective of management. Managers must think broadly about a problem and avoid concentrating only on desired results, because those results will affect other problems and parts of the organization as well as the environment beyond the organization. The age-old tension between the production objective of low manufacturing costs (achieved by making one product in one color and style) and the marketing objective of a broad product line (requiring high production costs) is a good example of why managers must avoid a narrow vision. Achieving both objectives at the same time is not possible, so a compromise is necessary for the overall system to achieve its objective. And in seeking a compromise, the organization must always be mindful of the environment (e.g., will customers accept the product's price or design?). The objectives of a firm's individual parts must be compromised for the objective of the entire firm. The Management Highlight above might help you understand these ideas by contrasting systems theory with bureaucracy.

Using the systems approach forces individual managers to consider a broader perspective. With a systems perspective, managers can more easily achieve coordination between the objectives of the organization's various parts and the objectives of the organization as a whole.

Critics consider the systems approach to be abstract and not very practical. According to them, discussing inputs, transformations, and outputs does not reflect the way everyday managers understand problems, make decisions, and face reality. Managers must observe, think, and respond. Awareness of resources requirements, the transformation process, sales, and the responses of the competition and customers are essential elements of managerial use of systems theory.[22] The systems concept is a great technique for thoughtful analysis, but being in the middle of daily decision-making precludes the luxury of deep systems-like analysis and thinking. Yet, it is hard to argue that maintaining an integrated view of daily events ultimately yields better decisions.

# Contingency Theory

The systems approach to management recommends that managers view organizations as systems comprising interdependent parts and understand that a change in any part affects other parts. This insight is important and certainly an improvement over the "one best way" approach advocated by Taylor, Weber, and Fayol. Managers must also see how those parts fit together, and systems theory offers a way to do that. Beyond systems theory, we enter the realm of contingency theory, which advises managers about the potential effect that the larger environment can have on the organization. Contingency theory can help management better understand the complex relationship between the internal and external environment.[23]

## The Need for Contingency Theory

In the early years of management theory, some individuals, like Frederick W. Taylor, advocated the "universal" view of management effectiveness. *Universal theorists* argued that there indeed exists "one best way" to perform different management functions. In their view, the task of management theorists is to identify these superior management prescriptions by developing and then testing theory via research.

However, other management theorists, called *situational theorists,* disagreed. They asserted that no one best approach to management exists, because each situation is too different. No one principle or prescription is supremely applicable across unique situations. In fact, situational theorists claimed that very few principles and concepts are useful across situations. Because each managerial situation is unique, a manager must approach each situation with few if any guidelines to follow. Management effectiveness first requires that a manager evaluate each situation from scratch before deciding which action to take.

A situational approach offered an explanation for those unusual organizational events that defied the rules of the "one best approach" advocates. But some situational theorists argued that all organizations are unique. Well, that nostrum left little direction for the practicing manager to follow. Built on sound theoretical principles and tested in the world of real organizations, contingency theory was born.

The contingency approach attempts to bridge the extreme points on this continuum of views. What are these contingencies that affect organizational life? Like the situational theorists, contingency theorists don't subscribe to any one best approach to management. In their view, the situations that managers face do differ and thus prohibit any one best prescription. The technology, structure, and the environment present worthy contingencies that can have an impact on organizational performance. Understanding the effect of these contingencies eliminates considerable decision-making uncertainty for managers. Ray Kroc, founder of the fast-food giant McDonald's, used contingency thinking by always searching for innovations to stay ahead of competition.

## The Impact of Technology, Structure, and Environment: A Contingency Approach

In a historical context and in the tradition of organization theory, technology, structure, and environment are important contingency variables.

Technology is best defined as the conversion process used in organizations to transform all raw materials into a complete product. Examples of three different conversion processes might be small-batch production, mass production, and continuous production such as in a refinery. Early contingency theorists speculated that both structure and technology influenced the long-term success of an organization.

**| Joan Woodward (1916–1971) |** Research exploring the relationship between organizational structure and production technology was popularized through the work of industrial sociologist Joan Woodward. Her work encouraged managers to avoid seriously considering the "one best way" claims being made by consultants and other managers. Woodward's research and writing challenged such views.[24]

While working as a professor of industrial sociology in London, Woodward—from 1953 to 1957—led the South-East Essex research team studying manufacturing firms. She investigated characteristics such as span of control (the number of workers reporting to a manager), number of levels of authority, amount of written communications, and clarity of job definitions. She found significant differences across firms. Her research brought to the forefront the role of technology as an influence on organization structure. For example, a low level of technological complexity required a small batch structure (a bakery), moderate technological complexity required a mass production structure (a toy factory), and a high level of technological complexity required a continuous production structure (a refinery). The match was referred to as the technological imperative, implying that as technological complexity increased, different structures were needed for optimal results. Her idea that technology determines the choice of structure was, at the time, seen as a breakthrough in our understanding of organizational design.

Woodward's research and case studies showed that a firm's technology plays a significant role in its structure. She, unlike Frederick W. Taylor, found that there is no best way to manage or structure an organization. She warned against accepting principles of management as universally applicable.

Woodward's work pioneered an improved understanding of how empirical research can be used to change an organization's structure. She elevated empirical work to a level where managers could derive value from the results. Woodward also illustrated how comparisons of a large number of firms could be designed so that generalizations could be made to other organizations.

**| Environment |** Two Harvard scholars, Paul Lawrence and Jay Lorsch, suggested that the nature of the environment was yet another important contingency that influenced organizational success.[25] Their rationale for its inclusion is that a high-demand environment presents an entirely different competitive situation for an organization than does a low-demand environment. Their finding suggests that successful organizations match their structure to the conditions present in the environment. In a complex and changing environment, a flexible structure with many different departments is needed to handle the complexity present in the environment. In a simple and stable environment, a machine-like structure (similar to a factory) needing fewer departments matches environmental requirements quite well.[26] Thus, the environment presents a unique contingency factor that can contribute to organizational success or failure.

**| Identifying and Evaluating Contingency Variables |** Contingency theorists stop short of asserting that all managerial situations are unique. Rather, they argue that situations are often similar to the extent that some principles of management can be effectively applied. However, the appropriate principles must be identified. This is done by first identifying the relevant *contingency variables* in the situation and then by evaluating those variables.[27] For a summary of theories, contributors, and their contributions, see Exhibit 2.3.

KEY TERMS

**technology** The conversion process used in organizations to transform raw materials into a complete product.

**technological imperative** An organization theory asserting that, as technological complexity increases, different organizational structures are needed for optimal results.

EXHIBIT 2.3

**Theories, Contributors, and Contributions**

| Theory | Proponent | Contributions of the Theory |
|---|---|---|
| Classical Theory | Frederick W. Taylor, Max Weber, and Henri Fayol | • Rules and prescriptions that apply equally in all situations.<br>• Management concepts could be learned. |
| Behavioral Theory | Elton Mayo, Fritz Roethlisberger, and William Dickson | • Role of attitudes on performance.<br>• Impact of the group on performance. |
| Decision Theory | Herbert Simon, Herbert Simon, and James March | • Selective perception.<br>• Bounded rationality as a limit in decision making. |
| Systems Theory | Chester Barnard and Peter Senge | • Organization as a cooperative system<br>• Synergistic effect gained through the integration of subsystems. |
| Contingency Theory | Joan Woodward, Paul Lawrence, and Jay Lorsch | • Defined limits to universal theories.<br>• Environment influences structure and technology. |

# Contemporary Influences on the Evolution of Management

Frederick W. Taylor, Herbert Simon, Henri Fayol, and other pioneers of twentieth-century management thinking and practice are historical sources of inspiration that management students read about. These pioneers set the course for reporting about, understanding, and studying management and workers. In addition to these historical giants are a number of contemporary philosophers and advocates of management practices. For their contributions to the shaping of management practices, the contemporary thinkers discussed in the following sections might eventually stand beside the early pioneers.

## Peter Drucker (1909–2005)

Born in Austria, Peter Drucker was educated as a lawyer and worked as a journalist in Germany. He worked as an educator, a consultant, and a philosopher whose work emphasized the importance of managers in organizational societies. Drucker believed that managers must always make economic performance the top priority. His central issue was how best to manage a business so that it is successful over time.

While many previous theorists believed otherwise, Drucker argued that profits were not the major objective of business:

> There is only one valid definition of business purpose: to create a customer. What the business thinks it produces is not of first importance—especially not to the future of the business and to its success. What the customer thinks he is buying, what he considers "value" is decisive—it determines what a business is, what it produces, and whether it will prosper.[28]

Drucker considered the present era of management to be a period of transformation; and thus the modern organization must be organized in such a way as to be flexible to accommodate constant changes. He proposed that to stay abreast of changes, management must engage in three practices. The first is continuing improvement of everything the organization does (the process the Japanese refer to as kaizen). Continuous improvement in services, product design, and product use has to become part of daily organizational life. Second, every organization must learn to exploit its knowledge. Taking the knowledge and developing one product after another from the same invention is one of the most successful practices of Japanese business. Finally, every firm must innovate. Every organization can accomplish these practices only by acquiring the most essential resource—qualified, knowledgeable people.[29]

In contemporary organizations, individuals who are not trained as managers often find themselves in managerial positions. Many people presently training to be teachers, engineers, accountants, musicians, salespersons, artists, physicians, or lawyers will one day earn their livings as managers. They will manage schools, accounting firms, symphonies, sales organizations, museums, hospitals, and government agencies. The United States and other countries are organizational societies that rely on managers to manage work, operations, and people to efficiently accomplish goals. Because the growth in the number and size of organizations is relatively new in history, the study of management is also relatively new.

## W. Edwards Deming (1900–1993)

W. Edwards Deming was born in Sioux City, Iowa. He received a Ph.D. in mathematical physics and worked for the United States Census Bureau during and after World War II.[30] In 1950, Deming went to Japan to help conduct a population census and lectured to Japanese business managers about statistical quality control. The Japanese were impressed with Deming and listened carefully to his views about quality. Deming stressed that quality is whatever the customer needs and wants. Deming was extremely critical of American management and its failure to properly address quality. He claimed that managers were responsible for 94 percent of quality problems.

Deming proposed fourteen points of total quality management that reveal an emphasis on learning, worker involvement, leadership, and continuous improvement. Deming stated: "People are born with intrinsic motivation.... People are born with a need for relationships with other people and with a need to be loved and esteemed by others.... One is born with a natural inclination to learn and to be innovative. One inherits a right to enjoy his work."[31] The three key ingredients of these fourteen points, according to Deming, are continual improvement, constancy of purpose, and profound knowledge.

## Tom Peters: Sources of Excellence

Management consultant Tom Peters (1942– ) was a principal in the consulting firm of McKinsey & Company when his first book, *In Search of Excellence,* co-authored with Robert Waterman, became a runaway best-seller.[32] Peters has since written several best-selling texts advocating a customer-oriented systems approach to organizational effectiveness. Today he travels around the world giving advice and inspirational talks about managing. His advice focuses on some basic ideas from *In Search of Excellence,* including the nine aspects of excellently run companies:

1. *Managing ambiguity and paradox*—Chaos is the rule of businesses, not the exception. The business climate is always uncertain and always ambiguous. The rational, numerical approach doesn't always work because we live in irrational times.

2. *A bias for action*—Do it, try it, fix it. The point is to try something, without fear of failure. Sochiro Honda, founder of Honda, said that only one out of a hundred of his ideas worked. Fortunately for him, he kept trying after his ninety-ninth failure.

3. *Close to the customer*—Excellent companies have an almost uncanny feel for what their customers want. This is because they are a customer of their own product and they closely listen to their customers.

4. *Autonomy and entrepreneurship*—Decision-making autonomy and the entrepreneurial spirit are essential ingredients for excellence. Great companies allow and encourage autonomy and within-company entrepreneurship.

5. *Productivity through people*—Not surprisingly, people act in accordance with their treatment. Treat them as being untrustworthy, and they will be. Treat them as business partners, and they will be. Excellent companies have taken the leap of faith required to trust their employees to do the right thing right.

6. *Hands-on, value-driven*—Practice management by walking around. Constantly ask the value added by every process and procedure.

7. *Stick to the knitting*—Stay close to your organization's basic industry. The skills or culture involved in a different industry might be a shock that is fatal to the organization.

8. *Simple form, lean staff*—Organizations with few layers of management who are unencumbered by a bloated headquarters characterize the excellent companies.

9. *Loose-tight properties*—Tight control is maintained while at the same time allowing staff far more flexibility than is the norm.

Peters believed that he designed a modest, close-to-the-customer plan in *In Search of Excellence.* In another of his books, *Liberation Management,*[33] Peters states that being close to the customer isn't really enough. Management must remove structural impediments to being close to the customer. Liberating the organization from rigid rules, hierarchies, stilted policies, and stifling demands are steps in the direction of developing what Peters calls a "symbiosis" with both domestic and foreign customers.

Peters's contribution is not found in his methods of study, the ability to replicate his conclusions, or attempts to conform to the practices he recommends. In fact, researchers have since determined that the excellent firms identified by Peters and Waterman might not have applied the principles called for by the authors. Peters's contribution is that he has stimulated managers, researchers, and theorists to think more seriously about organizations, the tasks of managers and workers, and ways to improve management practices. He and his coauthors literally put management on the front burner. Prior to the publication of *In Search of Excellence,* the popular press to considered management as a job. Peters and Waterman pointed out that excellent managers engage in many of the same activities. Peters and Waterman brought management theory to the coffee table.

## William Ouchi: Theory Z

Because many Japanese organizations were successful in the 1980s and early 1990s, many researchers and management practitioners have been motivated to analyze the factors behind these successes. One set of recommendations for American managers was introduced by UCLA management professor William Ouchi in 1981.[34] He introduced what was called Theory Z, or the combining of American and Japanese management practices, which he based on studies conducted in United States and Japanese organizations. Exhibit 2.4 compares American and Japanese organizations to a modified version, Theory Z.

Ouchi visualized a Theory Z organization as having a distinct American flavor (e.g., individual responsibility) and a unique Japanese emphasis (e.g., collective decision making). The Theory Z approach doesn't work in every situation, but it encourages managers to consider combining philosophy, methods, and tools to create a more effective organization.

## Michael Porter: Competitive Advantage

Michael Porter, a Harvard Business School professor of industrial organization and a consultant, was one of the first contemporary scholars to apply traditional economic thinking to management problems.[35] Porter explains corporate strategy in relation to a competitive marketplace. He identifies four generic strategies: (1) cost leadership, (2) differentiation, (3) cost focus, and (4) focused

**EXHIBIT 2.4**

**Comparison of Ouchi's Theory Z Typology to U.S. and Japanese Organizations**

| Type A: American Organization | Type J: Japanese Organization | Type Z: Modified American Organization |
|---|---|---|
| Short-term employment | Lifetime employment | Long-term employment |
| Individual decision making | Collective decision making | Collective decision making |
| Individual responsibility | Collective responsibility | Individual responsibility |
| Rapid promotion | Slow promotion | Slow promotion |
| Explicit control | Implicit control mechanism | Implicit informal control, with explicit, formalized measurement |
| Specialized career paths | Non-specialized career paths | Moderately specialized career paths |
| Segmented concern for the employees | Holistic concern for the employee | Holistic concern, including the family |

differentiation. Competitive advantage can be gained through lower cost or differentiation—the ability to provide unique and superior value to customers in terms of product quality, special features, or after-sale service.

Competitive scope refers to the breadth of a firm's target within its industry. A firm must choose the range of product variables it will produce, the way to distribute its products, the geographic area it will serve, and the array of industries in which it will compete.

The cost leadership strategy involves keeping costs and prices lower than those of competitors. Korean shipyards produce ships at lower costs and lower prices than their main competitors, Japanese firms. Differentiation is a strategy that attempts to improve a firm's competitive position by developing unique products. Nike's Air Jordan™ shoes are unique because of their high-technology "air" construction; Coca-Cola has a unique taste and can be bought anyplace in the world; and Benneton sweaters have unique color and patterns.

A cost focus emphasizes gaining competitive advantage through cost control in a narrow market area. Atlantic Richfield (ARCO) adopted this strategy in the early 1980s when it decided to service customers west of the Rocky Mountains. The fast-growing western states were close to the company's resource base, Alaska; ARCO was thus able to cut distribution and transportation costs. The result was a lower price of gas and paying attention to a narrower western states market area.

A focused differentiation strategy involves providing a competitive and unique product and/ or service to a narrow market area. Fiesta Food Mart has adopted a focused differentiation strategy in the border state of Texas. The store provides a unique array of foods for different ethnic groups. The food products aren't found in the natural food chains, nor are they found in the stores of other competitors. Fiesta's customers find the normal array of goods; but immigrants from Vietnam, El Salvador, Mexico, Peru, and Brazil also find familiar ethnic foods.

Porter's approach is insightful and provocative. He is unique in concluding that the best analytical focus for explaining economic performance is neither the individual firm nor macroeconomic forces. Porter proposes that the explanation about performance is found in studying why nations succeed in particular industries. A handful of nations dominate any one industry. Also, competitors tend to be tightly bunched in a geographic area within a nation (e.g., Silicon Valley in California).

## Peter Senge: Learning Organization

The leading champion of the learning organization is Peter Senge.[36] Senge argues that for organizations to be successful, they need to learn and adapt. According to Senge, learning occurs through adapting to changes in the environment. For example, children exploring their world adapt their attitudes and behaviors to what works. In the same way, organizations learn by adapting to their successes. Senge calls this adaptive learning. The next stage in becoming a learning organization

**KEY TERMS**

**competitive advantage** The advantage that can be gained through lower cost or differentiation.

**competitive scope** The breadth of a firm's target within its industry.

**cost leadership** A strategy that involves keeping costs and prices lower than those of competitors.

**differentiation** A strategy that attempts to improve a firm's competitive position by developing unique products.

**cost focus** A competitive strategy that emphasizes gaining advantage through cost control in a narrow market area.

**focused differentiation** A competitive strategy that involves providing a competitive and unique product and/or service to a narrow market area.

**adaptive learning** According to Peter Senge, an early stage that a firm goes through in becoming a learning organization; characterized by learning through adapting to its successes.

is generative learning. Generative learning involves developing a new understanding of the organization. Senge says: "Generative learning requires seeing the systems that control events."[37]

Senge believes that an organization's problems are largely built into complex systems that need to change before events will change. For example, an Internet order entry system that allows customers to order out-of-stock products without informing them of a delivery delay is a problem. The firm's customer service department will eventually receive complaints, and ultimately customers will buy from competitors, resulting in lost sales and market share. When viewed as a system, a problem in one part of the organization has the potential to affect other parts of the organization.

Senge suggests that we build a learning organization by teaching discrete new skills. These skills include developing personal mastery or competence, developing mental models, creating a shared vision, participating in team learning, and finally engaging in systems thinking. The leader's role in the learning organization is to be a teacher, designer, and visionary who encourages the development of these skills in employees.

KEY TERMS

**generative learning** According to Peter Senge, a stage that a firm goes through in becoming a learning organization and that requires "seeing the systems that control events."

## CONCLUSION

## History of Management

Our journey through the history of management began with the contributions that managers and management made to the development of the ancient world. We traced the roots of modern management to the requirements of the industrial revolution and the development of a new technology—steam power. Modern management learned that it had to deal with two often conflicting dilemmas: the need for efficiency and the needs of workers. The challenge was to balance these conflicting needs. But the payoff is substantial when the need for efficiency and the needs of workers are balanced; the relationship between managers and workers is more harmonious, and organization is more effective. Further, new management theories were reviewed that help managers better understand how to control the increasingly complex business environment. These theories included systems theory and contingency theory. Finally, the contributions of contemporary theorists offered insights into the importance of strategy and quality to competitiveness.

Management history has shown us how management theories evolved over time in reaction to changing technology, worker needs, and external forces. History also informs us that individual managers were adaptive and capable of designing efficient organizations that responded to economic competition and attracted a talented workforce. Management history teaches us that throughout time managers have met the need to increase task efficiency, motivate workers, and manage the requirements of the environment—all for the betterment of mankind.

## Discussion Questions

1. Visit a local Home Depot or Menard's and watch their operations. Notice how customers needs are met. Recall from your own personal experience what you do as a customer, what you get for your money, and how you get it.

   Then answer the following questions:

   - How does a large box store like Home Depot or Menard's employ the basic principles of scientific management in the management of their organization? Consider each of these aspects:

     - Efficient operations
     - Selection and training
     - Division of labor
     - Cooperation between management and workers

2. List and describe three characteristics of the human relations school and three characteristics of the scientific management school.

3. Discuss the contributions and limitations of classical management theory.

4. Define how contingency theory was different from other approaches to management.

5. Choose two contemporary management scholars discussed in this chapter and summarize and compare their contributions to the field of management.

## Video Case

### Original Penguin Becomes a Learning Organization

Taking charge of a company is both a challenge and a dream for any young manager. Chris Kolbe, vice president of Original Penguin, a division of Perry Ellis International, is no exception. Original Penguin is experiencing a total makeover, courtesy of Chris Kolbe and a small staff of designers, marketers, and finance managers. Once the domain of middle-aged golfers, the penguin logo now graces hats, neckties, shoes, and an entire line of fashionable women's clothing and accessories ranging from T-shirts and skirts to belts, shoes, handbags, and bathing suits. Original Penguin clothing now appears in such upscale department stores as Barney's and Saks—as well as its own retail store in midtown Manhattan. This hip new brand of clothing has come a long way from the golf courses of half a century ago.

Remaking a brand involves remaking an organization. In 1955, marketers for Munsingwear Penguin approached celebrities such as Bing Crosby and Bob Hope with the request to provide shirts for their golf tournaments. Then they contacted the Golf Association, asking for a list of its members—all men—to whom they sent sample golf shirts. The penguin logo quickly became associated with the men's pro golf tour. The company was run as a traditional organization, manufacturing a traditional product. But not anymore.

Perry Ellis has made a strategy of acquiring languishing brands, such as Jantzen bathing suits and Penguin golf wear, and breathing new life into them. When Chris Kolbe was hired by the company to turn Original Penguin around, he was given a small New York office and two staffers. There was no way he could run the company as a traditional large corporation, nor did he want to. Original Penguin was about to become a learning organization, complete with teams, empowered employees, and a free flow of information.

Kolbe relies on collaboration and communication across departments—usually just across cubicles—among team members. He helps them set goals, makes sure they have the information they need, then allows them to take responsibility for their own performance. "If you have a team, you have to give them ownership of what they do," Kolbe explains. He communicates regularly with the design team and marketing team but says that he prefers to limit the time everyone spends in meetings. "I'm a one-on-one guy. I try not to schedule a lot of meetings because meetings can be stifling."

Kolbe believes firmly in empowering employees with the freedom and resources to initiate their own ideas, make their own decisions, and perform their best. "Chris is easy to work with," says marketing manager Laura Bellafronto. "He makes you feel comfortable and secure . . . he makes you want to be here and be working with him." Kolbe is happy that he inspires that kind of loyalty. "I try to respect and treat everybody as I wish to be treated, but also I'm very comfortable with pushing people and asking a lot of them," he remarks.

The free flow of information between Kolbe and his staff is key to the rejuvenation of Original Penguin. Kolbe makes sure he communicates with every employee the goals and needs of the company. "He has a vision that he makes clear to everyone," says Laura Bellafronto.

Today, Original Penguin products sport an updated, more youthful look. "[They are] fashionably new, but not avant-garde," says Kolbe. Penguin's new customers are too young to remember leisure suits or wall-to-wall shag carpeting. Kolbe's management style is as deceptively casual as the clothing itself—comfortable but made to last. "My authority [really derives] from what I do and how I communicate with people, my directness. I know when to have fun and I know when to be serious. I try to strike that balance."

## Questions

1. As the organization has grown from just three employees, Chris Kolbe has had to delegate more decisions to others. How important is this transition to Original Penguin's success as a learning organization? Explain.

2. Do you think that Kolbe views knowledge among his employees as an important resource? Why or why not?

3. What steps might Original Penguin as a company take to ensure the satisfaction of its employees?

Sources: Company web site, http://www.originalpenguin.com, accessed July 30, 2004; Carl Swanson, "A Senior Moment," in "Men's Fashions of the Times," *The New York Times* (Spring 2004): 44; Mary Lisa Gavenas, "Brands on the Run," *DNR* (April 28, 2004): 17; Stephanie Thompson, "Perry Ellis Banks on Brand Resurrections," *Advertising Age* (March 15, 2004): 14.

## BizFlix

### In Good Company

*In Good Company* is a 2004 film featuring Dennis Quaid in the role of Dan Foreman, an advertising sales executive at a top publication. After a corporate takeover, Dan is placed under a supervisor half his age named Carter Duryea (played by Topher Grace). Matters are made worse when Carter becomes romantically involved with Dan's daughter, Alex, a beautiful college student (Scarlett Johansson). The film was originally titled *Synergy*. You can still hear references to that title that were kept in the final cut of the film.

### Questions

1. Does Carter Duryea's explanation of synergy reflect the discussion of synergy in the chapter?

2. What potential downside with Carter's plan does Dan identify during the meeting? Do you agree with Dan or Carter?

3. What kind of system is Carter Duryea describing in the clip? Explain?

## Suggested Reading

J. Michael Gotcher, "Assisting the Handicapped: The Pioneering Efforts of Frank and Lillian Gilbreth," *Journal of Management*, 18 (March, 1992): 1, 5–13.

Harold J. Levitt, "Why Hierarchies Thrive," *Harvard Business Review* (March 2003): 3–8.

Steve Lohr. "Microsoft and Google Grapple for Supremacy as Stakes Escalate," *New York Times* (May 10, 2006). (Compare today's competitors to those of the past.)

Jill R. Hough and Margaret White, "Using Stories to Create Change: The Object Lesson of Frederick W. Taylor's "Pig-tale," *Journal of Management*, 27 (2001): 585–601.

## Endnotes

1. Daniel Wren, *The Evolution of Management Thought* (New York: The Ronald Press, 1972). Also see C. S. George, *The History of Management Thought* (Englewood Cliffs, NJ: Prentice-Hall, 1972).

2. A comprehensive analysis of Taylor is found in Charles D. Wrege and Ronald G. Greenwood, *Frederick W. Taylor: The Father of Scientific Management* (Burr Ridge, IL: Business One Irwin, 1991): 131.

3. David H. Freedman, "Is Management a Science," Harvard Business Review (November–December, 1992): 1–11.

4. Frederick Taylor, The Principles of Scientific Management (New York: Norton) 1911.

5. Lyndall Urwick, *The Golden Book of Management* (London: Newman Neame, 1956): 72–79, 95–97.

6. Hearings before the special committee of the U. S. House of Representatives to investigate Taylor and other systems of shop management, United States House of Representatives Resolution 90 (1912).

7. Frank Gilbreth, *Bricklaying System* (New York and Chicago: The Myron C. Clark Publishing Company, 1909).

8. Henry Gantt, *Organizing for Work* (San Diego, CA: Harcourt, Brace, and Jovanovich), 1919.

9. Henri Fayol, *General and Industrial Management* (London: Pitman and Sons, 1949).

10. Talcot Parsons, *The Theory of Social and Economic Organization* (New York: Free Press, 1947).

11. Fritz J. Roethisberger and William J. Dickson, *Management and the Worker* (Cambridge, MA: Harvard University Press, 1931): 24.

12. Mayo, E. *The Human Problems of an Industrial Civilization* (New York: MacMillan, 1933), Ch. 3.

13. Stephen R. G. Jones, "Worker Interdependence and Output: The Hawthorne Studies Reevaluated," *American Sociological Review* (April 1990): 176–190.

14. Lyndall Urwick, *The Golden Book of Management* (London: Newman Neame, 1956): 102–105.

15. Derek Pugh (ed.), *Organization Theory* (Middlesex: Penguin Education): 147–165. Also see Lyndall Urwick, *The Golden Book of Management* (London: Newman Neame, 1956): 131–135.

16. Herbert Simon, *Administrative Behavior* (New York: Free Press, 1945); and James March and Herbert Simon, *Organizations* (New York: Wiley, 1958).

17. James March and Herbert Simon, *Organizations* (New York: John Wiley, 1958). Also see (1972) Michael D. Cohen, James G. March, Johan P. Olsen, "A Garbage Can Model of Organizational Choice," *Administrative Science Quarterly,* Vol. 17, No. 1. (March, 1972): 1–25; and Richard Cyert and James March, *A Behavioral Theory of the Firm* (Englewood Cliffs, NJ: Prentice-Hall, 1963).

18. William Dill, "Environment as an Influence on Managerial Autonomy," *Administrative Science Quarterly,* 2, (1958): 409–443.

19. Shirley Terreberry, "The Evolutionary of Organizational Environment," *Administrative Science Quarterly,* 12 (1968): 590–613. Also see Ludwig von Bertalanffy, "The History and Status of General Systems Theory," *Academy of Management Journal* (December 1972): 411.

20. Daniel Katz and Robert L. Kahn, *The Social Psychology of Organizations* (New York: Wiley, 1966): 47.

21. Chester Barnard, *The Functions of the Executive* (Cambridge, MA: Harvard University Press, 1938): 65.

22. Peter Senge. *The Fifth Discipline,* (New York: DoubleDay): 1991.

23. Fred Luthans, "The Contingency Theory of Management: A Path Out of the Jungle," *Business Horizons* (June 1973): 63–72; and Harold Koontz, "The Management Theory Jungle Revisited," *Academy of Management Review* (April 1980): 175–188.

24. Joan Woodward, *Industrial Organization: Theory and Practice* (London: Oxford University Press, 1965).

25. Paul R. Lawrence and Jay Lorsch, *Organizations and Environment* (Homewood, II: Richard D. Irwin, 1967).

26. Robert Miles. *Macro Organizational Behavior.* (Santa Monica, CA: Goodyear Publishing, 1980): 248–277.

27. Fred Luthans, "The Contingency Theory of Management: A Path Out of the Jungle," *Business Horizons* (June 1973): 63–72; and Harold Koontz, "The Management Theory Jungle Revisited," *Academy of Management Review* (April 1980): 175–188.

28. Peter F. Drucker, *The Practice of Management* (New York: Harper & Row, 1954): 37.

29. Peter F. Drucker, *Post-Capitalist Society* (New York: HarperCollins, 1993), 72.

30. Bruce Brocka and M. Suzanne Brocka, *Quality Management* (Burr Ridge, IL: Business One Irwin, 1992): 64–71.

31. W. Edwards Deming, *Out of the Crisis,* 2nd ed. (Cambridge, MA: MIT Center for Advanced Engineering Study, 1986).

32. Thomas J. Peters and RobertH. Waterman Jr., *In Search of Excellence: Lessons from America's Best Run Companies* (New York: Harper & Row), 1982.

33. Thomas Peters, *Liberation Management* (New York: Knopf, 1992).

34. William G. Ouchi, *Theory Z: How American Business Can Meet the Japanese Challenge* (Reading, MA: Addison-Wesley, 1981).

35. Michael E. Porter, *The Competitive Advantage of Nations* (New York: Free Press, 1990): 101.

36. Peter M. Senge, *The Fifth Discipline: The Art and Practice of the Learning Organization* (New York: Doubleday, 1991).

37. Peter Senge, "The Leader's New Work: Building the Learning Organization," *Sloan Management Review* (Fall 1990): 7.

# 3

# THE MANAGEMENT ENVIRONMENT, SOCIAL RESPONSIBILITY, AND ETHICS

An organization is affected by a host of environmental factors, ranging from the choices its employees make to the new, technologically sophisticated products its competitors bring to market. We begin this chapter with a discussion of some of the most significant environmental forces, both internal and external to an organization, that a manager faces when making decisions. Next, we examine different ways that a manager monitors the environment, because a manager must analyze many environmental forces to ensure the success of an organization. Then, we present a strategy for environmental analysis and subsequent action, focusing on what the organization can do to deal with uncertainty and change. We conclude the chapter with a discussion of social responsibility and ethics.

## The Internal Environment

An organization's internal environment refers to the factors within an enterprise that influence how work is done and how goals are accomplished. Employees, work flow, office or plant layout, managers' styles, and reward systems are some of the factors affecting an organization's internal environment. Taken together, these factors create a culture within an organization. Culture refers to the system of behavior, rituals, and shared meanings that distinguish a group or an organization from other similar units.[1] Managers act to define and energize an organization's culture by training employees, setting goals, and rewarding good performance in specific ways. It is one thing to say that every member of an organization, from the chief executive officer to the newly hired office clerk, shares responsibility for the firm's products and services. It is an altogether different reality to live and breathe that conviction. A unique culture that drives employee actions and attitudes and that distinguishes successful employees from also-rans can contribute to sales growth, return on assets, profits, product quality, and employee satisfaction. To perpetuate culture, each employee is expected to pass valued knowledge along to new employees. Behavioral expectations such as this underpin a company's cultural mind-set and serve as guidelines for what is appropriate and acceptable. Culture gives employees an organizational identity and establishes the rules that they follow.

> Culture by definition is elusive, intangible, implicit, and taken for granted. But every organization develops a core set of assumptions, understandings, and implicit rules that govern day-to-day behavior in the workplace.... Until newcomers learn the rules, they are not accepted as full-fledged members of the organization.[2]

Quality improvement efforts and activities have become an integral way of life for many organizations around the globe. The attempt to achieve system-wide quality changes and maintain them is generally considered to depend on cultural transformation.[3] According to some studies, however, there is no clear causal chain from organizational culture to overall performance.[4] Other research has linked elements of organizational culture to innovation. For example, researchers Francis Gouillert and James Kelly found that the following seven characteristics of organizational culture are related to innovation:

1. A stated and working strategy of innovation
2. The use of workplace teams
3. Rewards and recognition for employee creativity and innovation
4. An environment in which managers allow people to make mistakes and take risks
5. A setting in which training in creativity is provided to employees
6. A carefully managed organizational culture
7. An atmosphere in which new opportunities are actively created[5]

When a strong organizational culture emerges, the organization reaps the benefits of organizational commitment, loyalty, and cooperation. But culture can be a liability when employee behaviors and work patterns do not match the values and actions that enhance performance. Changes in the external environment might require rapid responses and adaptation, and a culture that obstructs change can inhibit or block organizational growth. IBM developed a strong culture that simply would not budge when new competitors created the need for rapid changes in product design and development. IBM's resistance to change slowed its ability to respond to strong competitors like Apple and Compaq, which were able to capture market share. In an attempt to become more responsive and regain some of the market share it lost to competitors, IBM revised its culture.

## Multiple Cultures

Research suggests that most organizations have a dominant culture and a set of subcultures.[6] Dominant culture refers to the core values shared by most of the employees in an organization. Think of the distinct characteristics of a firm such as Disney, which emphasizes quality goods and services. In a dominant culture, subcultures are most likely to develop in a unit, group, or section where employees routinely face common situations or problems. The finance department, for example, might create a subculture shared by its members.

Dominant cultures can be weak or strong.[7] In a strong culture, core values are intensely held and widely shared. Employees and role models can dramatically affect the behavior of other employees or members. In the early days at Apple Computer, Inc., employees routinely worked long after their shifts were over to complete a job. The clock at Apple meant very little, especially when a group was attempting to solve a problem.

Cultures vary from organization to organization. Southwest Airlines has a strong dominant culture, reflecting the personality of its legendary founder, Herbert Kelleher. Frequent flyers on Southwest get birthday cards, and passengers who write letters get personal responses, sometimes several pages long. Both services are part of the culture that Kelleher established and that Chief Executive James Parker and President Colleen Barrett are continuing. With a culture characterized by "keen intelligence, a deep devotion to Southwest and its employees, and a taste for a good party,"[8] the airline remains the most profitable of the major carriers.

In contrast, newly appointed General Motors CEO Rick Wagoner's major challenge is to energize the firm's dormant culture.[9] Wagoner broke with tradition by hiring two outsiders for top-level positions—head of product development and chief financial officer—and giving them more than the usual authority to solve the company's problems. Wagoner's low-key style seems to be working in tearing down the warring factions inside GM and fostering a culture of cooperation among diverse units such as design, marketing, engineering, and manufacturing.

### NINE VALUES IMPORTANT TO EMPLOYEES

1. *Recognition*—Employees want to be recognized for their accomplishments.
2. *Respect and dignity*—Employees want to be treated with respect.
3. *Autonomy*—Employees want the freedom to do the job in the way they think is best.
4. *Involvement*—Employees want to be kept informed, included, and involved in important decisions at work.
5. *Pride in one's work*—Employees want to do a good job and exercise good-quality workmanship.
6. *Lifestyle quality*—Employees want time for family and leisure.
7. *Financial security*—Employees want some security in their retirement years from inflation, economic cycles, or catastrophic financial events.
8. *Self-development*—Employees want to personally improve in order to further themselves.
9. *Feedback*—Employees want to be well informed about how they are performing.

Sources: David Jamieson and Julie O'Mara, *Managing Workforce 2000* (San Francisco: Jossey-Bass, 1991): 28–29; Daniel Yankelovich and Associates, *Work and Human Values* (New York: Public Agenda Foundation, 1983): 23; and Edward E. Lawler III, *High-Involvement Management* ( San Francisco: Jossey-Bass, 1991): 88.

## Building Culture

Many of the firms on *Fortune* magazine's list of "100 Best Companies to Work For" exhibit common values—camaraderie, loyalty, low turnover, and no secrets, to name but a few.[10] Management success in building an effective culture involves selecting, motivating, rewarding, and retaining high-performing employees. Managers must continually work at instilling commitment to a common philosophy and service, developing and rewarding competence, and finding and retaining the right people. Through the organizational socialization process, managers and coworkers offer consistent help to newcomers in developing skills and evolving into accepted team members who understand and are committed to the firm's culture.

Values represent convictions that a specific mode of conduct is personally or socially preferable to another mode of conduct. Knowing the values held by individuals is important in helping managers to interpret workers' attitudes and motivations.

The values employees bring to the workplace were largely established in their early years by parents, teachers, relatives, and friends. The discussions a young person hears at home, in the street, or at school provide a basis for values later in life. Values are relatively stable and enduring. A workforce that includes recent immigrants, Hispanics, African Americans, Asian Americans, Caucasians, and other ethnic groups will possess a variety of values spanning economic, social, religious, and political issues.

Managers today deal with a workforce that holds an array of values. Some employees value economic recognition for performance; others value time off to be with their families. Some value making a career commitment to their organizations; others value making a commitment to their profession. Often, what people lack—respect, autonomy, power, or the opportunity for promotion—by its absence becomes the thing most highly valued. Values can also shift with age, significant life experiences, increased education, and achievement of success. Because values differ, managers should not assume automatically that they know what employees value. As the Management Highlight above shows, research has a role in shaping managerial knowledge regarding what employees value in the workplace.

## The External Environment

Managers must deal not only with internal culture and subcultures but also with factors outside the organization. The external environment includes those forces outside the organization that have a direct or indirect impact on the firm's activities. Any one of these forces can dramatically

**organizational socialization** The process by which managers and coworkers offer consistent help to newcomers in developing skills and evolving into accepted team members who understand and are committed to the firm's culture.

**values** The set of convictions that specific modes of conduct are personally or socially preferable to other modes of conduct.

**external environment** The set of forces outside the organization that have a direct or indirect impact on the firm's activities, some of which are controllable and others not.

**3.1**     **Forces in the External Environment**

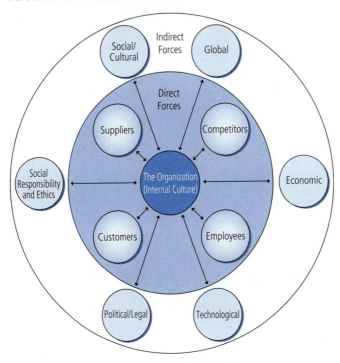

influence the course taken by an organization. Some of these forces are under the organization's control; some are uncontrollable, and their impact is difficult to predict. Exhibit 3.1, depicts the various forces constituting the external environment. In the following subsections, we examine each of these forces.

## Direct Forces

Direct forces exert an immediate and daily impact on the organization. These forces include competitors, employees, customers, and suppliers.

**Competitors** In the business world, organizations that produce similar goods or services are generally referred to as competitors. They are usually rival firms competing for the same group of customers. Failing to recognize its competition can spell disaster for an organization. At Nissan, high prices that led to the demise of the original Z line of cars: when the price of a fully loaded 300ZX reached nearly $50,000 in the late 1990s, the car was thrust into direct competition with models from Mercedes-Benz and Jaguar.[11] When introducing the new 350Z in 2002, Nissan managers recognized that competition was intense among sports cars in the medium-priced range. Although demand had fallen during the previous decade, Nissan believed competitive pricing would determine the success or failure of the new Z.

Organizations must constantly assess their competition and differentiate themselves in the marketplace. One consumer might buy her car from Volvo, which touts its reputation for safety. Another consumer may buy from Toyota because it advertises high-quality cars at reasonable prices. The critical issue for any organization is to maintain dominance in its selected market by staying a step ahead of competitors.

**KEY**TERMS

**competitors** In the business world, organizations that produce similar goods or services; usually rival firms competing for the same group of customers.

Managers must also monitor the changes their competitors are making and determine what adjustments to make in maintaining their firm's position in the market. For instance, a manager should determine if—and why—major competitors are changing product designs, distribution methods, customer service policies, or promotional methods such as advertising. Managers can obtain information about competitors' activities through direct observation as well as by surveying customers, reading trade publications, talking with employees such as salespeople, and studying market research.

| **Employees** | Employees are an organization's most important resource; they do the work of the organization. By offering a pleasant, effective work environment and attractive compensation and incentive packages, successful firms recruit, train, and retain energetic, talented employees.

Organizations compete externally not only for customers, but also for human resources. The organizations that attract and retain the most talented employees are likely in the best position to attract and retain customers. Thus, management is faced with the dual challenge of designing programs—recruiting, compensation, training, career advancement, education—that bring the best people into the organization and keep them there.

Several trends in the United States workforce are influencing the managers' job. The workforce is more diverse, and managing these differences is a significant challenge. The diversity spans age, race, and gender. The median age of the workforce, now over 40, was 28 in 1970. By 2010, one quarter of the United States population will be at least 55.[12] A workforce that was once dominated by white males now includes increasing numbers of African Americans, Hispanics, Asians, and individuals from an array of other ethnic groups. And today women comprise nearly 50 percent of the workforce. These changes require managers to develop new approaches to recruiting, training, promoting, and motivating a more diverse workforce.

| **Customers** | Customers are the lifeblood of an organization. They might include consumers who purchase an organization's goods and services, or organizational customers who purchase products for their own operations. Customers are perhaps the most critical of the direct environmental forces, because they ultimately determine whether the organization will succeed.

Most organizations make great efforts to stay close to their customers. They accomplish this goal by conducting research to identify the needs and wants of present and potential customers. Surveys typically address how satisfied the customers are with products and quality of service, and inquire about customer needs that are not being met.

| **Suppliers** | Organizations depend upon other firms to supply them with resources, including capital, raw materials, office supplies, and parts. Suppliers are important to an organization because they can directly affect the quality of goods and services produced. The quality of a car, for example, is affected by the quality of the automobile parts that a manufacturer purchases from a supplier.

Because suppliers affect product quality, it is important for organizations to have cooperative relationships with them. Many organizations use several suppliers to reduce their dependence on a single supplier. Other firms are partnering with supplier firms, in some cases investing directly in—and relying solely on—those firms for supplies. Some organizations even purchase the supplier organization to have greater control over the cost and availability of supplies.

# Indirect Forces

Although they are not directly involved in daily operations, indirect forces in the external environment also influence an organization. Indirect forces are categorized as social-cultural, economic, global, technological, and political-legal, all of which fall into the realm of social responsibility and ethics (see Exhibit 3.1).

**KEY** TERMS

**indirect forces** Forces in the external environment that influence an organization, but not directly in its daily operations; categorized as social-cultural, economic, global, technological, and political-legal.

| **Social-Cultural** | Families share certain beliefs and values that make up their social and cultural systems. So do small and large organizations—even nations. The social-cultural environment is shaped and influenced by the learned and shared values of all the individuals and organizations within that system. Because social structures and cultures are in constant flux, managers must be aware of change and incorporate that knowledge into their decisions. Organizations and managers that consider the effects of their decision making on the social-cultural environment are among the most socially responsible.

Many businesses have created policies and programs to help employees manage their home and work roles. The heightened interest in an employer work-family agenda is fueled by changing workforce demographics as well as by a growing understanding of the bottom-line benefits to employers for acknowledging and supporting people's personal lives. In determining the organizational costs of failing to have family-friendly policies, studies have found that problems with dependent care arrangements affect productivity and job effectiveness for both men and women. The benefits are measurable. Dependent care assistance has been proven to increase staff availability; work-family programs affect employee retention and reduce related stress.

Employee health is another area of growing concern to managers. The United States has become an increasingly sedentary society. Our shift to postindustrial society means an increase in indoor working and living. Americans spend about 90 percent of their time indoors, usually sleeping, eating, dressing, or watching television. Bad habits associated with a sedentary lifestyle include smoking, snacking, and drinking soda and coffee. It is generally accepted that healthy workers lose less time and have fewer accidents than unhealthy ones.

The United States spends over $800 billion a year in health care—more than 13 percent of the gross national product. In the workplace, employees are responsible for their own personal health and safety as well as that of fellow workers. Every year, 2.2 million people in the United States suffer ill health either caused or aggravated by workplace activities.[13] More and more firms are trying to improve workers' knowledge about health, lifestyles, and disease prevention. Issues such as mental stress, substance abuse, eyestrain from computer use, and improper use of equipment are covered in training programs, employee assistance programs, and new employee orientation sessions.

These examples of social-cultural factors emphasize the uncontrollable nature of the external environment. To be prepared for changes in the mix of employees, preferences of consumers, and availability of skilled employees, managers need to be aware of social-cultural trends, values, and forecasts.

| **Economic** | The economic environment influences management decisions and plans in many areas. An expanding economy directly affects demand for a firm's goods or services. If demand increases, the workforce will probably need to be expanded, or new shifts added to the workday. In a recessionary economy, decisions might have to be made about layoffs, downsizing, cutting back on the size of the firm, or even plant and office closings.

Managers must monitor changes in economic indicators—inflation rates, interest rates, unemployment rates, productivity—and make appropriate adjustments. When the economy is on the upswing, managers might decide to expand operations. Conversely, during economic downturns, demand for products can fall, along with profits, as unemployment rises; managers must be prepared to adjust to these environmental issues as well. During the economic slump at the turn of this century, most companies faced weak and falling revenues, and many firms responded by cutting jobs.

| **Global** | Throughout the world, managers are facing the same challenge—intense global competition. Large companies like IBM and AT&T as well as smaller ones like Bicknell

Manufacturing and Lucerne Farms are fighting for customers by venturing beyond domestic borders, spurred on by deregulation, privatization, and rapid technological change. A study on the internationalization of firms with 500 or fewer employees reported that 50 percent of the firms were involved in international business.[14] Global fever has now reached the ranks of United States entrepreneurs as well as the huge firms of corporate America.

As a result of this intense scramble to enter foreign markets, companies around the world are at war. Any one company has no idea where its next challenge might originate. Car companies compete with banks in credit card wars, while software firms fight with cable companies over rights on the information highway. And the target in these wars, the competitor, is always moving. Giants like Coca-Cola and Pepsi have to fight off private-label brands sold in copycat cans, and Six Flags taunts Disney in television ads, claiming that "Disney is a great vacation destination. So is Australia."

Today, size and experience count for much less than they once did. Speed and execution are critical, and battles between firms are fierce. In the United States, perhaps nothing illustrates this point better than the war among the three major long-distance carriers—AT&T, MCI, and Sprint. In Thailand, the Japanese firms Sony and Matsushita are fighting for the electronics market. Whether trying to escape flat domestic markets or building on their successes, more and more companies are looking to foreign markets for growth opportunities.

| **Technology** | **Technology** can be broadly defined as the knowledge, tools, and actions used to convert inputs into outputs. It can be as simple as a waitress taking an order, or as complex as the use of a Palm Pilot by a hospital dietician to order patients' daily meals. Technology is a part of the human condition; we give it meaning, substance, and function. So it is hardly valid to think of technology itself as being the problem, or even the reason for other problems. The expression, "We have met the enemy and he is us," can apply to people misusing technology as much as to people electing a bad government. We can either help or hurt ourselves with technology. And, because technology enables organizations to meet consumer needs, we will almost certainly continue to expand it.

Technological innovation involves all those activities that people carry out to translate technical knowledge into a physical reality, into a product that can be used. The process of technological innovation progresses from the most basic research to wide-scale marketing. The automobile is a technological innovation that has had long-term effects on the mobility of society and the purchasing patterns of consumers. Other innovations such as the telephone, airplane, radio, television, computers, and various medical technologies have also significantly influenced society.

It takes time and money to carry out technological innovation and marketing. Years might pass before an innovation in biomedicine, energy, or any other sector reaches the marketing stage. A significant environmental force, technology drives change in industries, forges relationships between firms and customers, and creates new competitors. To continue in business, managers must use technology properly. Astute managers employ technology to improve their services to customers, find new customers, lower cost, and speed the introduction of new products.

| **Political-Legal** | The political-legal environment consists of government rules and regulations that apply to organizations. The very words *rules and regulations* often make managers uneasy and resentful. No one likes being regulated. For years, the American manager has been a staunch theoretical supporter of a hands-off government policy (a policy of not interfering with business activity). Yet most managers know that the business system cannot work without some government rules and regulations to organize and monitor the external environment.

The number and variety of government regulations affecting business are huge. Some are directed toward goals as disparate as economic growth, job security, and environmental pollution

**KEY**TERMS

**technological innovation** The process consisting of all the activities that people carry out to translate technical knowledge into a physical reality, that is, into a usable or useful product or service; progresses from the most basic research to wide-scale marketing.

**3.2**          **Indirect Environmental Forces**

| Social-Cultural | Economic | Global | Technological | Political-Legal |
|---|---|---|---|---|
| Lifestyle changes | Interest rates | Trade agreements | New products | Antitrust laws |
| Life expectancies | Deficit | Exports | Patent laws | Product liability laws |
| Birth rate | Gross domestic product | Trade deficits | Productivity measurement and growth | Tax laws |
| Population growth rate (immigration included) | Unemployment levels | Cultural environment | Industry R&D | Import-export trade |
| Family arrangements | Energy sources and costs | Exchange rates | Federal support of R&D | Trade regulations |
| Consumer activism | Inflation rates | Infrastructure | Robotics | Investment tax credits |
| Shifts in population | Money supply | Competition | Computer technology | Corporate responsibility |
| Changing women's roles | | | | |

control. These regulations and government programs can be divided into those designed specifically to support business and those intended to influence various business activities. For instance, the government supports business by providing subsidies in the form of guaranteed and insured loans, support to keep the airlines flying, and money to build highways to move people and products. Numerous laws and regulatory agencies influence virtually all aspects of business, including hiring practices, workplace safety, the environmental impact of production, processes and products, and product safety, to name a few. The Securities and Exchange Commission (SEC) recently ruled that mutual fund companies, which had avoided the financial scandals that plagued many firms, must disclose how they vote in corporate proxy contests. The SEC is also looking into establishing tougher internal controls for the mutual fund industry.[15]

The political-legal environment can have an adverse effect on the organization. Firms can be fined severely for polluting the environment or engaging in other illegal practices. In some instances, the resulting negative publicity might damage the organization further. Although many organizations think they are overregulated, most observers believe government regulation will grow, especially as emerging technologies like the Internet present new avenues for abuses. Exhibit 3.2 is a useful summary of the types of indirect forces that affect organizations.

## Monitoring the Management Environment

The forces in the management environment can change; the rate of change varies depending on the specific environment. In *stable environments,* the rate of change is relatively slow, whereas *dynamic environments* are characterized by more rapid change. Additionally, some environments are more complex than others. Environmental complexity refers to the number of forces in the environment that influence the organization. Some environments are relatively simple, composed of a few factors, whereas others are more complex and include many factors.

Whether the forces in the environment change slowly or rapidly, and whether the forces are few or many, they create uncertainty for managers. Environmental uncertainty is the degree to which managers can predict how environmental factors will change and the impact these changes will have on the organization. If managers have a great deal of information about environmental forces and they are in a position to predict changes, they can reduce environmental uncertainty. Managers must constantly monitor the environment to capitalize on opportunities and minimize adverse effects that result from changes. Each element should be monitored, with special emphasis on those forces likely to have an impact on the organization. To effectively monitor changes in the environment, managers engage in environmental scanning and analysis.

Environmental scanning is the process of collecting information concerning forces in the management environment. Scanning involves gathering information through observation; reviewing business, trade, and government publications; and engaging in research efforts. Although this information is important to managers, they must be careful not to acquire so much information that the sheer volume makes analysis impossible.

Environmental analysis is the process of assessing and interpreting the information gathered through environmental scanning. A manager reviews the information for accuracy, tries to reconcile inconsistencies in the data, and interprets the findings. Analysis allows a manager to discern changes in the environment and, if possible, to predict trends and changes. By evaluating these changes, a manager should be able to determine possible threats and opportunities associated with environmental fluctuations.

Organizations should have a plan in place for responding to environmental forces. Managers use one of two general approaches. In the traditional approach, managers view the forces of the environment as uncontrollable. Thus they assume that organizations can do little to alter the influence of the various forces in the management environment. A well-managed organization taking this *reactive* approach tries to prepare itself to respond quickly to changes in the environment. For example, an organization has little power over external forces such as economic conditions and the actions of its competitors. But it can monitor the environment closely, adjusting its strategy to counter the effects of inflation and staying abreast of product improvements by competitors.

A second response to the management environment is to take a *proactive* or aggressive stance toward environmental forces. A growing number of professionals argue that the management environment can be controlled, at least to some extent. Organizations can choose to strategically manage elements of the environment to the benefit of the organization. Through lobbying, legal action, advertising of key issues, and public relations, organizations can alter some environmental forces. For instance, a firm can control its competitive environment by using aggressive pricing or competitive advertising strategies to influence the decisions of rival firms. It can lobby political officials to repeal legislation that it believes will restrict its business. Likewise, a firm can use its political skills and public relations activities to create opportunities by opening foreign markets to American businesses. Let's examine a strategic approach to environmental management.

## Strategic Management of the Environment

Strategic management of the environment is the process of identifying environmental uncertainties and developing strategies to manage or reduce those uncertainties. Successful organizations pay particular attention to critical unknowns, such as market demand and intermediate product cost. To ensure profitability, they take necessary actions both to control uncertainties and to better estimate demand and control cost. James D. Thompson, the distinguished organizational sociologist, noted that "uncertainty is the fundamental administrative problem." He suggests several environmental management strategies for reducing uncertainty in his landmark book, *Organizations in Action*.[16]

## Internal Strategies

Organizations can use internal strategies to benefit from environmental opportunities and avoid threats. Internal strategies are tactical actions that organizations can choose in adapting the organization to, reducing, or at least managing environmental uncertainty.

| **Changing Domain** | Organizations can decide where they will do business and what they will produce and market. When the competition heats up or profitability evaporates, an organization can change its domain and compete in a different market. In response to the passage of more restrictive laws regulating automobile insurers by some states, several automobile insurers stopped writing new policies in those states. (New Jersey is a notable example.) Likewise, in areas of the country where natural disasters such as flooding, fires, and hurricanes occur most often, insurers have substantially limited their risk by ceasing to write new policies. After the devastation caused by Hurricane Andrew, many home insurers simply stopped writing homeowner insurance in Florida.

| **Recruiting** | One way to manage uncertainty is by hiring top employees from a major competitor. It is not unusual to see an executive leave General Motors for a major promotion at Volkswagen. In other situations, recruitment can mean hiring a former government official who had responsibility for regulating your industry.

| **Buffering** | The strategy of buffering is a common way to maintain steady production. Organizations can buffer on either the input side or the output side of the production process. *Input buffering* manages the fluctuations caused by the interruption of supplies of materials needed to manufacture the product. This strategy often takes the form of stockpiling materials or the outright purchase of suppliers. In *output buffering,* finished goods are warehoused until they can be absorbed by the environment. Automobile manufacturers usually have big, fenced parking lots for storing vehicles until shipment. Yet even when shipped, the vehicles might be stored at a railhead facility until final delivery to the dealer. The buffering process can move fast or slow, depending on the demands of the environment.

| **Smoothing** | Smoothing is a method of maintaining continuous demand for a product or service. Pricing is a mechanism that is often used to smooth customer demand. Price increases soften demand; price reductions increase demand. In the communications industry, providers often charge more during peak hours and discount prices at off hours to attempt to influence usage patterns. Smoothing results in efficient use of assets, reducing costs by eliminating the need to buy more equipment.

| **Rationing** | We know what is likely to happen when we show up at our favorite restaurant without a reservation—no table. Restaurants and many other service providers often use rationing as a way of ensuring that all their time is productive. Without rationing, too many people to process might arrive at once, resulting in disgruntled customers who will seek service elsewhere.

## External Strategies

External strategies are organizational attempts to change environmental circumstances, thereby reducing environmental uncertainty.

| **Advertising** | We are all familiar with the effects of advertising on human behavior. Indeed, we often catch ourselves repeating familiar slogans or whistling jingles that are designed to stimulate demand for a product or service. Most organizations use advertising to signal price changes, new product features, or new locations. Organizations use advertising to provide information, create brand recognition, and encourage consumer demand: "Buy our new and improved product now—prices may never be this low again!"

**KEY**TERMS

**external strategies**
Organizational attempts to change environmental circumstances, thereby reducing environmental uncertainty.

**| Contracting |** Seasonal products such as natural gas are often sold to consumers on contract. Contracting is a mutually beneficial arrangement. The purpose of the contract is to reduce the uncertainty on both sides of the buyer-seller relationship. The buyer is assured a set price for the contract, and the seller has a guaranteed buyer. In rural communities, propane is often sold on contract in the spring and delivered the following fall. Although prices are guaranteed to the buyer, actual commodity prices might increase or decrease between the spring and fall, thus defining who benefits most from the contract deal—the propane company or its customers.

**| Co-opting |** *Co-optation* represents an attempt to influence an external party. Concerned consumers or consumer groups who complain about product design features or functions might be asked to join a customer design team. They are thereby effectively co-opted into the organization. Once an external group becomes part of the organization, their resistance to organizational actions dissipates rapidly.

**| Coalescing |** A *coalition* is an alliance of several organizations, bound by common purpose, taking a united action. Coalition building is based on the idea that there is power in numbers. When selling commodity items, vendors often grant substantial discounts for volume purchases. In healthcare, it's common for several hospitals to form an alliance to purchase common hospital supplies or share a laundry facility.

**| Lobbying |** *Lobbying* is an attempt to influence a decision maker. In business-government relations, lobbying is the act of influencing a public official to understand and appreciate an organization's or industry's perspective on an issue of mutual concern. Businesses often attempt to influence the direction of legislation in their favor. Interested business community members often write first drafts of the law, hoping that their vision of the pending legislation will be enacted into law. This form of uncertainty reduction is a way to affect or change the environment. Obviously, only the largest companies can hope to use this powerful external management strategy.

## Social Responsibility

Organizations conduct activities to produce goods and services and to generate profits. These activities greatly affect our society. Social responsibility is the awareness that business activities have an impact on society and the consideration of that impact in decision making. Society expects businesses to make a profit but also to obey laws, be ethical, and be good corporate citizens.[17] In addition to emphasizing profits, firms concerned with social responsibility voluntarily engage in activities that benefit society. Many, for instance, take an active role in supporting public education. A socially responsible firm makes deliberate, regular efforts to increase its positive impact on society while reducing its negative impact.

Practicing social responsibility costs money. But failing to emphasize social responsibility also has its costs, whether in fines, increased regulation, negative publicity, public disfavor, or loss of customers. Consumers, special interest groups, and the general public are aware of the impact of business on society and expect firms to do more than try to make profits. Most managers today regard the costs incurred in practicing social responsibility as a necessary part of doing business.[18] Business activities have an impact on consumers, employees, the environment, and those investing in the firm. The Management Highlight on page 58 examines social responsibility and disaster response.

## Responsibility to Consumers

Firms trying to succeed provide products that satisfy the needs of their customers, because dissatisfied customers eventually take their business elsewhere. But a company also needs to

**KEY**TERMS

**social responsibility**
The awareness that business activities have an impact on society and the consideration of the impact in decision making.

## SOCIAL RESPONSIBILITY AND DISASTER RESPONSE IN THE AFTERMATH OF HURRICANE KATRINA

History has seen natural disasters of epic proportions. Hurricanes have rocked the Gulf Coast. Earthquakes, forest fires, and mudslides have left the West Coast reeling. Late in 2004, a tsunami ravaged coastlines around the Indian Ocean, wiping out towns and killing thousands. Each of these disasters left many people homeless, without food or shelter, and required leaders at all levels of government to make instantaneous decisions that affected many lives. In the aftermath of Hurricane Katrina, which hit Louisiana in 2005 and is perhaps one of the worst disasters in American history, many raised questions and allegations regarding these decisions: Was the response politically or racially motivated? Are some areas of the country—west coast versus deep south—quicker to receive disaster response? Was the media coverage fair and balanced?

The answers to these questions are complex and controversial. Response to Katrina was not only slow but it shocked the world. The finger pointing began immediately with the federal government blaming the local government and the local government blaming the feds. Conservative activist Grover Norquist blamed the chaotic response on "looting in a Democratic city run by a Democratic mayor and a Democratic governor." Race was inevitably a factor, as most of the people in New Orleans seeking public shelter were poor and black. Media coverage was accused of bias, referring to victims of Katrina as "refugees" and showing pictures of blacks taking merchandise from stores; stories of young blacks helping elderly whites went unnoticed.

Though it might take years to have all the answers, some of the major problems certainly appear to be a result of breakdowns is the Federal Emergency Management Agency (FEMA) response system. FEMA experienced problems in mobilizing resources, and also was coping with personnel problems and lack of expertise in dealing with natural disasters. One thing is for certain: Hurricane Katrina put a face on poverty, and brought to light the financial plight of the poor and impoverished. Many poor people lost their savings, which they kept in cash because they are skeptical of banks. Others were unable to evacuate as ordered because they didn't own transportation or have the money for public transportation. Katrina, perhaps more than any previous natural disaster, changed many of American's thinking about poverty and disaster response.

These issues have significant consequences for those who are affected by the disaster. Natural disasters result in huge expenses and burdens, particularly for those who can afford them the least. One needs only to recall the television coverage of Katrina to picture the homeless, the losses, the crisis in leadership at all levels, the outrage, the looting, and the disenfranchised left to die. The critical question many are asking is, when faced with a natural disaster, is this: "What is the socially responsible thing to do?" Perhaps some of the lessons from Katrina will help answer this question. The lives lost cannot be brought back, but the disaster could encourage leaders to address the poverty along the Gulf Coast, empower communities to plan for a more sustainable future, and tackle the environmental problems in the region brought on by decades of abuse to land and water.

Source: Adapted from Saundra K. Schneider, "Administrative Breakdowns in the Governmental Response to Hurricane Katrina," *Public Administration Review* (September/October, 2005): 515–516; "Exploiting Disaster," *Multinational Monitor* (September/October, 2005): 5; "Special Report: When Government Fails—Katrina's Aftermath," *The Economist* (September 10, 2005): 25; Richard Wolffe, "Yet Another Gulf War," *Newsweek* (September 12, 2005): 47; "The Shaming of America," *The Economist* (September 10, 2005): 11.

consider how customers view the firm itself. Increasingly, customers are looking beyond a firm's goods and services to evaluate its policies and actions, and these customers are taking action in the marketplace.

Pressure from consumers and special interest groups has prompted many business firms to adopt socially responsible policies. Consumerism includes the activities of individuals, groups, and organizations aimed at protecting consumer rights. Consumer groups perform many activities, including testing and reporting on the safety and performance of products and service firms, informing the public and government officials of consumer issues, and advocating legislation. During his short time in office, President John F. Kennedy established the consumer "bill of rights," which includes the right to safety, the right to be informed, the right to choose, and the right to be heard. These four rights underlie many of the goals espoused by people and organizations active in consumerism today.

| The Right to Safety | The most basic consumer right is the right to products that are safe to possess and use. To ensure safety of goods, manufacturers should test them and provide buyers with explicit directions for use. In 1972, the federal government created the Consumer Product Safety Commission (CPSC) to monitor the safety of thousands of products sold to consumers. Many state and local agencies also regulate product safety.

**consumerism** The activities of individuals, groups, and organizations aimed at protecting consumer rights.

Industries in the United States have made great strides in product safety, but more progress is needed. Automobiles, appliances, children's toys, and many other products are safer today than they once were. Product packages have also been made more tamper resistant. But instances of chemicals found in foods, such as apples treated with alar (a chemical linked to cancer) or bottled water with traces of benzene (a dangerous chemical used in cleaning fluids), illustrate that safety problems continue.

| **The Right to be Informed** | Consumers have the right to receive information available about a product before they purchase it. Customers seeking a loan from a bank or other financial institution, for example, should be told of all costs and repayment terms associated with the loan. Necessary information for foods includes ingredients and detailed instructions for use. To aid shoppers making decisions in the supermarket, new FDA package labeling rules that went into effect in 1994 require food makers to adopt uniform labels for their products. The labels give consumers more information about nutrition content and limit health claims that can be made.

| **The Right to Choose** | Consumers have the right to choose and make purchases from a variety of products at competitive prices. They also have the right to expect quality service at a fair price. Consumer demand for pesticide-free foods, for example, has resulted in a movement to grow vegetables and fruits without chemicals. Thousands of farmers are experimenting with different methods of crop rotation and greater use of natural materials to control insects and increase productivity. If the experiments are successful, consumers will have the choice they desire.

| **The Right to Be Heard** | Consumers also have the right to have their opinions considered in the formation of government policies and in business firms' decisions that affect them. A number of large firms have established consumer affairs departments to address consumer concerns. Many, including Little Tykes (toys), General Electric (appliances), Nabisco (foods), and Beecham (toothpaste and other personal care products), provide toll-free telephone numbers as an easy way for consumers to ask questions, make comments, and register complaints. Small businesses might not have reason or resources to establish hot lines or hire personnel specifically for consumer relations. But small-business owners and managers can set up procedures and train employees to invite consumer comments, answer questions, and handle complaints.

## | Responsibility to Employees

Like consumers, employees hold certain expectations of business firms. They expect safe working conditions, fair compensation, equal opportunities, and adequate benefits (e.g., health insurance, vacation, and time off to care for sick children). Employees also want to know what is going on in the company and want managers to be responsive to problems or complaints. Firms aware of their responsibility to the people who work for them make every effort to meet these expectations.

In 1970, Congress passed the Occupational Safety and Health Act, which created the Occupational Safety and Health Administration (OSHA). Charged with the primary purpose of ensuring safe working conditions, OSHA has established many standards with which employers must comply. OSHA covers all employees except those working for government bodies and those covered by specific employment acts such as the Coal Mine Health and Safety Act. Under OSHA regulations, firms failing to protect the health of their employees can be held criminally liable.

Individuals also expect to be treated equally in the workplace. The Civil Rights Act of 1964 guarantees equal employment opportunities for all people regardless of age, race, sex, religion, or national origin. In addition, employers have a responsibility to ensure a working atmosphere free

**KEY** TERMS

**Occupational Safety and Health Administration (OSHA).** Passed in 1970, federal legislation whose primary purpose is to ensure safe working conditions by establishing standards with which employers must comply.

of sexual harassment. Equal employment opportunity and sexual harassment are discussed in detail in Chapter 10, "Human Resource Management."

Another major challenge facing leaders today is managing a diverse workforce. Cultural diversity refers to differences between and within cultures. Any leader who sincerely values cultural diversity must make everyone in the organization feel safe about discussing these differences. This means a change for those organizations that have been denying that differences exist while meeting equal employment opportunity or affirmative action guidelines. Valuing diversity looks at the multicultural workforce from a positive perspective rather than from a defensive position. Valuing diversity views people as having equal rights while being different and encourages the open discussion of gender, age, ethnicity, physical ability, and so on.[19] Diversity-awareness training programs can help bring these differences out into the open and identify the unique characteristics and talents of diverse individuals who are resources for the organization. Valuing diversity also requires that organizations be responsible for providing products to various races and cultures. Toy companies, for instance, are manufacturing multicultural products such as ethnic doll varieties.[20]

Although cultural diversity brings stimulation, challenge, and energy, it does not always lead to harmony.[21] A mix of genders, cultures, and alternative lifestyles can lead to conflict and misunderstanding. The job of the manager is to create an environment where differences are appreciated and a group of diverse individuals can work productively together. This is a formidable challenge, but organizations who meet this challenge face a brighter future. Diversity awareness will not work without the commitment of top executives, and it must be a business objective.[22]

## Responsibility to the Environment

The public is concerned with the impact of business on the environment in the United States and around the world. Socially responsible managers join consumers in this concern and take active measures to protect our environment. One vital environmental concern is pollution, the contamination of water, air, and land. Concern for the environment also involves conserving scarce natural resources and curbing the use of those that damage the environment. As with other social concerns, laws and regulations play a critical part in environmental issues. The Environmental Protection Agency (EPA), created by the national Environmental Policy Act of 1970, is the federal agency charged with enforcing laws designed to protect the environment.

Water pollution is caused by dumping toxic chemicals, sewage, and garbage into rivers and streams. Toxins and pollutants from buried industrial waste can also find their way into underground water supplies. A recent concern is the liberal use of agricultural fertilizers and pesticides, which drain into water supplies. Environmental laws such as the Water Quality Improvement Act of 1970 and the Water Pollution Control Act Amendment of 1972 regulate pesticides. Many other areas of the world including Japan, the former Soviet Union, Brazil, and India, are experiencing water pollution.

Air pollution is caused by carbon monoxide and hydrocarbons that come from motor vehicles as well as by smoke and other pollutants from manufacturing plants. The Clean Air Act of 1970 and the 1977 Clean Air Act Amendment provide stringent emission standards for automobiles, airplanes, and factories. The Clean Air Act Amendment of 1990 requires that motor vehicles be equipped with Onboard Systems to control about 90 percent of refueling vapors. Devices such as catalytic converters have been developed to help control air pollution.

Land pollution results from the strip mining of coal and minerals, forest fires, garbage disposal, and the dumping of industrial wastes, including chemicals and medical supplies such as used hypodermic needles. Land pollution often results in water pollution because toxic wastes drain into water supplies. The Resource Conservation and Recovery Act of 1984 requires federal regulation of potentially dangerous solid-waste disposal. Solid waste—the term for trash and garbage discarded by homes, businesses, and factories—includes paper and cardboard, grass clippings and leaves, food wastes, metals, glass, plastics, textiles, leather, wood, and rubber.

Businesses and government organizations face the problems of where to dispose of solid waste and how to do so safely. Many used products and containers do not have to go to the dump; they could be recycled. *Recycling* involves reusing materials to make other products. Newspapers, office paper, cardboard boxes, aluminum, tin cans, glass, plastic containers, and even motor oil can be recycled to reduce the drain on resources and to minimize the costs of producing new products and containers, and to slow the need for more and bigger landfills.

## Responsibility to Investors

Managers also have a responsibility to the people who invest money in their firms. Many investment-related abuses have come to light in recent years. The public, government regulatory agencies, and many business leaders are concerned with problems such as mishandling of investors' funds, insider trading of stocks, and excessive compensation of executives.

Firms have responsibility to manage funds properly and return a fair profit to investors. Investment scams have probably existed since people started using money. The United States saw many during the California Gold Rush in the 1800s, when scores of hapless investors bought worthless mines. In recent years, some investors have been equally unfortunate, discovering that their money went for gold mines or oil wells that did not exist, resorts or hotels that were never built, or new business ventures that never got off the ground.

Firms also have the responsibility to make financial information available to all potential investors. Insider trading occurs when individuals buy and sell stock on the basis of information gained through their positions or contacts with others that are not available to other investors or the general public. Such information, known only to a few insiders, gives them an unfair advantage over typical investors. Stock purchases by officers of a corporation, for instance, often precede a merger or sale that leads to temporary increases in the value of the stock. Certain laws prohibit insider trading, and the Securities and Exchange Commission prosecutes individuals found violating them.

## Advancing Social Responsibility

Many firms recognize the importance of social responsibility and take steps to see that their policies and activities make a positive impact on society. They practice social responsibility through programs of community support and social audits.

| **Community Support** | Business firms throughout the United States provide support for a wide variety of activities designed to improve their communities. Both large and small businesses contribute to the arts, build parks, donate equipment to schools, and sponsor academic scholarships. Some sponsor social programs to help the disadvantaged. Many community activities could not start up or continue without the support of business. Some firms enable employees to share their time and talent with their communities. IBM, for example, lends engineers to teach in schools. Others provide company time, materials, or facilities for employees active in community organizations. Businesspeople also participate in the Rotary, Kiwanis, Junior Achievement, and other groups that raise money for local projects or help youngsters. Firms are major contributors to charities and encourage employees to donate to organizations such as the United Way, which distributes donations among many diverse social agencies operating in an area. Through such activities, the business sector makes a significant contribution to society.

| **The Social Audit** | Some firms conduct a systematic review of their performance of social responsibility activities through a social audit. A social audit looks at the firm's short- and

KEYTERMS

**insider trading** The illegal practice of buying and selling of stock by individuals on the basis of information that they gain through their positions or contacts with others and that is not available to other investors or to the general public.

**social audit** The assessment of a firm's short- and long-term contributions to society.

long-run contributions to society. Activities reviewed might include community involvement, product safety, and the impact of business practices on the environment.

With information from a social audit, managers can evaluate how effective the current programs are and decide whether they should initiate new courses of action. Some firms spend millions of dollars each year on social responsibility activities; they need to determine whether they are spending their money wisely. Although a social audit is more informal than an accounting audit, it can be a useful tool in accessing social responsibility.

# Ethics

Social responsibility requires individuals engaging in business endeavors to behave in an ethical manner. Ethics are principles of behavior that distinguish between right and wrong.[23] Ethical conduct conforms with what a group or society as a whole considers right behavior. People working in organizations frequently face ethical questions. Management ethics is the evaluation of management activities and behavior as right or wrong. Ethical standards in business are based on commonly accepted principles of behavior established by the expectations of society, the firm, the industry, and an individual's personal values.

## Factors Influencing Ethical Behavior

To encourage ethical behavior, executives, managers, and owners of firms must understand what influences behavior in the first place. Exhibit 3.3 presents several factors that affect individuals' behavior in business: the business environment, organizational factors, and an individual's personal moral philosophy.

| The Business Environment | Almost daily, business managers face ethical dilemmas resulting from the pressures of the business environment. They are challenged to meet sales quotas, cut costs, increase efficiency, or overtake competitors. Managers and employees might sometimes think the only way to survive in the competitive world of business is by deception or cheating. Conflict of interest is another common ethical problem stemming from the business environment. Often an individual has a chance to further selfish interests rather than the interests of the organization or society. To gain favor with people who make purchasing decisions for their companies, a seller might offer special favors or gifts, ranging

**EXHIBIT  3.3**          **Factors Influencing Ethical Behavior**

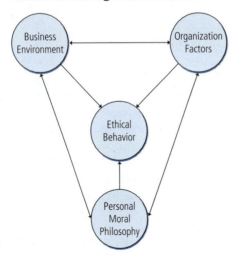

from a meal to clothing to trips. Some offer cash—a kickback—for putting through a contract or placing orders with a company. Others offer bribes. Such illegal conduct damages the organization in the long run. To limit unethical behavior, business firms must begin by expecting their employees to obey all laws and regulations.

The international business environment presents further ethical dilemmas. Businesspeople and government officials in other countries and cultures often operate according to different standards than those held in the United States. Firms sometimes have separate ethical standards for domestic and international operations.

| The Organization | The organization itself also influences behavior. Individuals often learn ethical or unethical behaviors by interacting with others in the organization. An employee who sees a superior or coworker behaving unethically might follow suit. A simply stated directive from the person at the top can set the tone in an organization. In fact, an employee's perceptions of peers and superiors in an organization are often a stronger prediction of behavior than is the employee's own system of moral and ethical values.[24]

An organization can also use rewards to influence the behavior of its members. If an individual is rewarded or is not punished for unethical behavior, the behavior will probably be repeated. Likewise, the threat of punishment and the lack of reward for unethical activities encourage ethical behavior. The severity of punishment also sends a message to other individuals who might be considering similar activities. For example, the National Collegiate Athletic Association (NCAA) has placed member institutions on probation for violating recruiting rules. Teams on probation have been barred from tournament games and from having games televised, and limits have been placed on scholarships. These penalties should discourage other university athletic programs from violating NCAA rules.

| The Individual | A person's own moral philosophy also influences his or her ethical behavior. A moral philosophy is the set of principles that dictates acceptable behavior. These principles are learned from family, friends, coworkers, and other social groups, and through formal education. The Management Highlight will help you evaluate your moral philosophy.

In developing a moral philosophy, individuals can follow two approaches: humanistic and utilitarian. The humanistic philosophy focuses on individual rights and values. Individuals and organizations adopting this philosophy would honor their moral duties to customers and workers. If a product poses harm to workers or customers, it is taken off the market. Individuals and organizations following the utilitarian philosophy seek the greatest good for the largest number of people. Pharmaceutical manufacturers who make the vaccine for pertussis, the deadly disease of whooping cough, adhere to this philosophy. Some children react to the killed bacteria in the vaccine, which is administered three times in the first two years of life. Reactions include fevers, persistent crying, and temporary unresponsiveness. The vaccine has been blamed for severe brain damage in a few children, although several studies dispute this. Despite these problems, because so many children benefit from the current vaccine, doctors continue to administer the current version while researchers work on new pertussis vaccines.

## Encouraging Ethical Behavior

Many organizations take positive steps to encourage ethical behavior. Some offer courses in ethics and include ethics in training programs. Most courses and training seminars focus on how to analyze ethical dilemmas. The emphasis is on understanding why individuals make the decisions they do rather than on teaching ethics or moral principles.

**KEY** TERMS

**moral philosophy** The set of principles that dictates acceptable behavior; learned from family, friends, coworkers, and other social groups, as well as through formal education.

**humanistic philosophy** A philosophy that focuses on individual rights and values.

**utilitarian philosophy** A philosophy that seeks the greatest good for the largest number of people.

## EVALUATING ETHICAL BEHAVIOR

Following are a number of statements that involve ethical decisions you might have to make when conducting business. Circle the number that represents your level of agreement with each statement.

| | Strongly Disagree | | | | | Strongly Agree |
|---|---|---|---|---|---|---|
| 1. It is OK take supplies such as pencils and paper home from a company office. | 1 | 2 | 3 | 4 | 5 | 6 |
| 2. I would break a company rule if my coworkers did. | 1 | 2 | 3 | 4 | 5 | 6 |
| 3. If it meant getting ahead, I would take credit for someone else's work. | 1 | 2 | 3 | 4 | 5 | 6 |
| 4. I would not turn in a fellow employee for breaking a company policy. | 1 | 2 | 3 | 4 | 5 | 6 |
| 5. If I made a mistake that could hurt the company, I would cover it up to avoid being reprimanded. | 1 | 2 | 3 | 4 | 5 | 6 |
| 6. I would not mind breaking a law to get a promotion, as long as I did not get caught. | 1 | 2 | 3 | 4 | 5 | 6 |
| 7. I would be willing to provide customers false information to make a sale. | 1 | 2 | 3 | 4 | 5 | 6 |
| 8. I see no problem with taking longer than necessary to do a job and then billing a client for the extra time. | 1 | 2 | 3 | 4 | 5 | 6 |
| 9. It is OK to take care of personal business on company time. | 1 | 2 | 3 | 4 | 5 | 6 |
| 10. I would call in sick to take a day off work. | 1 | 2 | 3 | 4 | 5 | 6 |

How are your ethical standards? Although the situations are hypothetical, they present typical business decisions. For items circled 1 or 2, you considered these behaviors unacceptable; 3 or 4 indicates you are uncertain or indifferent; and 5 or 6 suggests you believe these activities are acceptable.

Some people view the activities listed as common practices. Doesn't everyone take pens and paper home from the office? Yet many companies prohibit such actions. Some of the activities, such as misleading customers or covering up mistakes, can result in serious penalties. If you believe most of the activities are unacceptable, you have a solid ethical base from which to work. If you found most of these activities acceptable, think about them again. It might seem as though people must do such things to succeed in business. We hope that is not true.

An organization can also encourage ethical behavior through a code of ethics.[25] A code of ethics is a statement specifying exactly what the organization considers ethical behavior. Many firms, as well as trade and professional associations, have established codes of ethics. For instance, the American Medical Association (AMA) has its own code of ethics that limits the amount and types of advertising used by doctors. By enforcing codes of ethics, rewarding ethical behavior, and punishing unethical behavior, a firm limits opportunities to behave unethically.

Employees of an organization can also encourage ethical behavior by reporting unethical practices. Whistle-blowers are employees who inform their superiors, the media, or a government regulatory agency about unethical behavior within their organization. Whistle-blowers often risk great professional and personal danger by reporting the unethical behavior of others. They might be harassed by coworkers or supervisors, passed up for promotions, fired, or even threatened with damage to their property or harm to themselves or their families. Nonetheless, some organizations have developed plans that encourage employees to report unethical conduct and that provide protection for whistle-blowers.

Efforts to encourage ethical behavior will be effective only with the support of top-level management. Employees base their decisions on the guidelines and examples set by their superiors. Management must set the proper tone by never compromising ethical behavior in its dealing with customers, employees, and competitors.

**CONCLUSION**

## The Management Environment

In this chapter, we introduced the various forces in the management environment, both direct and indirect. Because these forces can have a major impact on organizations, managers must monitor the environment and take action as needed. Ignoring the management environment can lead to a host of problems and may even destroy an organization.

## Discussion Questions

1. How can internal and external environmental factors influence a manager's decisions?
2. What can a manager do to effectively monitor changes in the environment?
3. What responsibilities do managers have to behave in an ethical and socially responsible manner?

## Video Case

### Organic Valley Plants the Seeds of Social Responsibility

Many organizations treat social responsibility as if it were a separate division—the department of good deeds. They support volunteerism among employees, use environmentally friendly packaging, and sponsor special programs in the community. All these activities are to be commended. But very few commercial organizations can actually claim to be based on the principles of social responsibility. The Organic Valley Cooperative is an exception. Based in Wisconsin, Organic Valley is a cooperative of small farmers whose products are certified to be produced without pesticides, synthetic hormones, or anti-biotics, including organic milk, cheese, butter, spreads, creams, eggs, vegetables, juice, and meat.

Nearly two decades ago, a few farmers who believed strongly in the value to society of practicing organic agriculture and saving family farms got together to form a cooperative. By acting together, these farmers could better control their fate. They could control supply, negotiate with larger customers, and reach more consumers who wanted their products. And they could set their own milk prices. Instead of being forced to accept prices subject to wild fluctuations in the open marketplace, these farmers began to set their own. This practice alone might be the single most important factor in the ability of family farms to survive. In one recent year, the milk price paid to Organic Valley farmers was 60 percent higher than the price paid to conventional dairy farmers. Organic Valley has actually received criticism for this practice, particularly from its creditors. But the cooperative holds firm. "Lowering the milk price would have been as easy as falling off a log," argues Organic Valley's CEO George Siemon. "But one of our objectives is to pay our farmers a good price.... We have a pay program the farmers expect us to deliver on. These relationships are the most important thing."

Today, Organic Valley is being called the most successful organic cooperative in the world. The cooperative has 630 members farming 100,000 acres in 16 states, with a waiting list. Sales are hitting upwards of $200 million per year and growing. Member farmers are the cooperative's major stakeholders. With assistance from Organic Valley employees, the farmers govern the cooperative by serving on the board and executive committees. Organic Valley's structure is designed so that it will be able to sustain itself from one generation to the next, ensuring the survival of family farms and sustainable, organic agriculture.

Sweet Ridge Organic Dairy is one of the cooperative's farms, operated by Paul Deutsch in Westby, Wisconsin. Deutsch owns twenty-six cows that are milked twice a day and allowed to graze over pastureland the rest of the time—unlike cows in many larger, conventional dairy farms, which are kept in stalls 24 hours a day and might be given hormones or antibiotics. It costs more to run an organic dairy farm, where in addition to grass the cows are fed organic corn, alfalfa, and other grains, and the cows need more grazing land. But Deutsch isn't spending money on chemicals or vet bills. He estimates that he makes about 30 percent profit each year because consumers are happy to pay more for products they know are more healthful for themselves and their families. "Many parents have read the *Consumer Reports* studies and the National Academy of Science reports and know that organic for their kids is like seatbelts in a car," notes Theresa Marquez, Organic Valley's director of sales and marketing. "The organic category has been growing steadily at 20 percent, and organic milk, with 27 + percent annual growth, is driving the growth of the category. The implementation of the National Organic Program in the U.S.... further established the organic market as one that is here to stay. Consumers want organic."

Organic Valley has helped the economies of several rural areas. When a large federal dam project in southwestern Wisconsin was canceled after displacing more than 140 local farmers from their land, many lost their livelihoods. As Organic Valley became established, it created employment opportunities—both on the farms and in the cooperative offices—for hundreds of residents in the area. "Going organic saved our farm," says cooperative farmer Mike Gehl, whose family has operated a Wisconsin farm for 154 years and five generations. Now Gehl and others like him can look forward to the next generation of farming.

## Questions

1. In addition to the farmers, who are Organic Valley's other stakeholders?

2. Describe at least one ethical challenge that Organic Valley might face during turbulent times.

Sources: Company web site, http://www.organicvalley.coop.com, accessed August 2, 2004; Judy Ettenhofer, "Organic Valley a Big Success," *The Capital Times* (July 29, 2004): http://www.madison.com; "Organic Valley Posts Record Level Pay Price to Farmers," *OFARM* (December 30, 2003) http://www.ofarm.org; Organic Valley press kit.

## BizFlix

### Backdraft

Two brothers follow in the footsteps of their late father, a legendary Chicago firefighter, and join the department. Stephen "Bull" McCaffrey (Kurt Russell) joins first and rises to the rank of lieutenant. Younger brother Brian (William Baldwin) joins later and becomes a member of Bull's Company 17. Sibling rivalry tarnishes their work relationships, but they continue to successfully fight Chicago fires. Add a plot element about a mysterious arsonist and you have the basis of an ordinary film. The film, however, rises above its otherwise formulaic plot thanks to great acting and amazing special effects. The intense, unprecedented special effects give the viewer an unparalleled experience of what it is like to fight a fire. Chicago firefighters applauded the realism of the fire scenes.

This scene appears early in the film as part of "The First Day" sequence. Brian McCaffrey has graduated from the fire academy, and the fire department has assigned him to his brother's company. This scene shows him fighting his first real fire at a garment factory. The film continues with Company 17 fighting the fire and Brian receiving some harsh first-day lessons.

## Questions

1. What elements of the Chicago fire department culture does this scene show? Does the scene show any cultural artifacts or symbols? If it does, what are they?

2. Does the scene show any values that guide the firefighters' behavior?

3. What does Brian McCaffrey learn on his first day at work?

Source: J. Craddock Ed., *VideoHound's Golden Movie Retreiver* (Farmington Hills, MI: The Gale Group, Inc., 2000).

## Suggested Reading

Brewer, Lynn, Chandler, Robert, and O.C. Ferrell. Managing Risks for Corporate Integrity. Mason, OH: SouthWestern/Thomson Learning, 2006.

Brook, Manville, and Josiah Ober. "Beyond Empowerment: Building a Company of Citizens." *Harvard Business Review* (January 2003): 48–53.

Carroll, Archie B., "The Pyramid of Corporate Responsibility: Toward the Moral Management of Organizational Stakeholders." *Business Horizons* (July–August 1991): 39–48.

Makower, Joel. *Beyond the Bottom Line: Putting Social Responsibility to Work for Your Business and the World.* Carmichael, CA: Touchstone Books, 1995.

Pava, Moses. *The Search for Meaning in Organizations: Seven Practical Questions for Ethical Managers.* Westport, CT: Quorum Books, 1999.

Salmon, Robert, and Yolaine de Linares. *Competitive Intelligence: Scanning the Global Environment.* Oxford: Economica, 1999.

Schein, Edgar H. *Organizational Culture and Leadership.* San Francisco: Jossey-Bass, 1997.

Tichy, Noel, Andrew R. McGill, and Lynda St. Clair, (eds.), *Corporate Global Citizenship: Doing Business in the Public Eye.* Lanham, MD: Lexington Books, 1998.

Wei Choo, Chun. *The Knowing Gap: How Organizations Use Information to Construct Meaning, Create Knowledge, and Make Decisions.* New York: Oxford University Press, 1998.

## *Endnotes*

1. Edgar H. Schein, *Organizational Culture and Leadership* (San Francisco: Jossey-Bass, 1997): 58.

2. T. A. Deal and A. A. Kennedy, "Culture—A New Look through Old Lenses," *Journal of Applied Behavioral Science* (November 1983): 50.

3. Peter F. Drucker, *Post-Capitalist Society* (New York: Harper-Collins, 1993): 72.

4. Bruce Brocka and M. Suzanne Brocka, *Quality Management* (Burr Ridge, IL: Business One Irwin, 1992): 64–71.

5. Francis J. Gouillert and James N. Kelly, *Transforming the Organization* (New York: McGraw-Hill, 1995): 4–5.

6. Deal T. and Kennedy, A. (1982). *A Corporate Culture.* Addison-Wesley, Reading.

7. Schein, E. H. (1984). "Coming to a New Awareness of Corporate Culture." *Sloan Management Review,* Winter.

8. Wendy Zellner and Michael Arndt, "Holding Steady," *Business Week* (February 3, 2003): 66–68.

9. David Welch and Kathleen Kerwin, "Rick Wagoner's Game Plan," *Business Week* (February 10, 2003): 52–60.

10. Robert Levering and Milton Moskowitz, "100 Best Companies to Work For," *Fortune* (January 20, 2003): 127–52.

11. Chester Dawson, "Nissan," *Business Week* (July 22, 2002): 47–49.

12. *Statistical Abstracts of the United States* (2002): 20.

13. Rowena Rees, "Commonsense Campaign Tackles Work-Related Illness," *Works Management* (July 1995): 18–19.

14. Tatiana S. Manlova et al., "Internationalization of Small Firms: Personal Factors Revisited," *International Small Business Journal* (February 2002): 9–31.

15. Amy Borrus and Mike McNamee, "Why It's Open Season on Mutual Funds," *Business Week* (February 10, 2003): 69.

16. James D. Thompson, *Organizations in Action* (New York: McGraw Hill Book Company, 1967): chapters 2–3, p. 159.

17. Archie B. Carroll, "The Pyramid of Corporate Responsibility: Toward the Moral Management of Organizational Statekholders," *Business Horizons* (July–August 1991): 39–48.

18. Lori Bongiorno, "Big Ideas for Little Girls," *Business Week* (May 3, 1993): 38–39.

19. Charles Garfield, *Second to None* (Homewood, *IL*: Business One Irwin, 1992): 286–291.

20. Michael Wilke, "Toy Companies Take Up Diversity Banner," *Advertising Age* (February 27, 1995): 1, 8.

21. Faye Rice, "How to Make Diversity Pay," Fortune (August 8, 1994): 78–86.

22. Lee Gardenswartz and Anita Rowe, *Managing Diversity* (Homewood, *IL*: Business One Irwin 1993): 4.

23. Vern E. Henderson, "The Ethical Side of Enterprise," *Sloan Management Review* (Summer 1982): 8.

24. O.C. Ferrell and Larry Gresham, "A Contingency Framework for Ethical Decision Making in Marketing," *Journal of Marketing* (Summer 1985): 87–96.

25. O.C. Ferrell and Steven J. Skinner, "Ethical Behavior and Bureaucratic Structure in Marketing Research Organizations," *Journal of Marketing Research* (February 1988): 103–109.

# 4

# THE GLOBAL MANAGEMENT ENVIRONMENT

More than ever before, people throughout the world want the same things, whether Disney theme parks, the latest in fashion, or fast-food restaurants. The concept of "nationality" for most corporations is out of date.[1] Only a few decades ago, the world economy was the sum of the individual economies of many nations, but this is no longer the case. Thanks to joint ventures, technology, the cross-fertilization of cultures, and many other factors, a truly global economy has been created. This new global environment poses many challenges for today's managers. This chapter examines the global management environment in terms of the nature and importance of the global economy, types of organizations in the global economy, the environment for global business, regulation of international business, and multinational market groups.

## The Nature and Importance of the Global Economy

In the global economy, any product made anywhere has to compete with any product made anywhere else. Some organizations learned this the hard way. Cars made in Detroit compete with cars made in Japan; flowers grown in Florida compete with flowers grown in Colombia; wine bottled in California competes with wine bottled in France. The question facing firms in the United States and throughout the world is not whether to compete with foreign firms but how to survive in the global economy.

The answer to this question, of course, is complex. Customers are demanding better products, improved service, and lower prices, and the way to compete is through quality. Global competition means that consumers have a better choice of products for less money; management's common goal must be customer satisfaction. The inevitable conclusion is that a firm's success in the global economy will depend upon its ability to meet new competitive standards.

## The Global Boom

**International business** is the performance of business activities across national boundaries. Involvement in international business has increased steadily since World War II and is expected to continue growing into the twenty-first century. Only 60 years ago Japan was left devastated by American bombing raids during World War II. Tokyo was burned to the ground; atomic bombs leveled Hiroshima and Nagasaki. When the war ended, Japan's economy no longer existed. But Japan learned from this disaster, investing in people, and today Japan is one of the world's leading economic powers. Changes in Eastern Europe, South Korea, Vietnam, and Taiwan also suggest a global environment in which market power, not military power, will prevail. Most nations now participates in international business to some extent. Learning how to manage organizations in this new environment will be critical to American firms.

**KEY**TERMS

**international business** Business activities across national boundaries, which have increased steadily since World War II and are expected to continue growing in the twenty-first century.

MANAGEMENT HIGHLIGHT

## FOREIGN BUSINESS IN THE UNITED STATES

For each statement, circle the number that shows your level of agreement or disagreement.

| | Strongly Disagree | | | | Strongly Agree | |
|---|---|---|---|---|---|---|
| 1. Foreign individuals and firms should be restricted from purchasing assets, such as banks, farmland, and hotels, in the United States. | 1 | 2 | 3 | 4 | 5 | 6 |
| 2. Americans should purchase American-made products whenever possible. | 1 | 2 | 3 | 4 | 5 | 6 |
| 3. The United States should limit the amount of foreign goods it imports. | 1 | 2 | 3 | 4 | 5 | 6 |
| 4. Foreign companies should not be allowed to build factories in American cities. | 1 | 2 | 3 | 4 | 5 | 6 |
| 5. The United States should put a high tax on all foreign goods entering the country. | 1 | 2 | 3 | 4 | 5 | 6 |

**Feedback:**

Americans often have strong feelings about foreign companies selling products in America and competing with United States firms. If you strongly disagree with most of the statements, you favor foreign firms being able to do business in the United States. If you strongly agree with the statements, you tend to be against such business.

Some Americans fear foreign competitors because they do not fully understand them—their language, culture, or social values. Some American companies have been hurt by foreign competition; you might know people who lost jobs after firms in the Unites States closed or moved operations overseas. Conversely, some Americans have few qualms about foreign companies conducting business on United States soil. They, and you, may think that international business is exciting and that competition from all manufacturers of a product, regardless of country of origin, is fair to businesses and beneficial to consumers. Regardless of your position on this issue, you as a student of business have already realized that international business will continue to expand in the United States and throughout the world.

International management is the performance of the management process in an international business setting. The global boom has increased the importance of international management. As the desire for quality goods at lower prices increases worldwide, organizations and managers must prepare to compete in an increasingly interdependent global economy. The Management Highlight above will help you assess your thoughts about foreign firms competing in the United States.

Transportation, communication, and technology have fueled the global boom. In eighteenth-century America, all economies were local. Little emphasis was placed on regional competition, let alone national competition. With the advent of the railroad and the telegraph, nineteenth-century economies became regional or national. Firms began to compete with others in distant parts of the country. Often the firm producing the greatest quantity won out. Thus, the firms first to adopt assembly-line techniques survived. In the 1950s, fiber optics, satellites, improved transistors, and air travel made geographic distance less relevant. Firms began to compete with firms in other parts of the world. As the twentieth century progressed, firms competed even more aggressively to produce quality as well as quantity. In the twenty-first century, the firm that offers high-quality products will succeed.

## Global Opportunities

The global boom has resulted in a customer-driven economy. This means new opportunities throughout the world. For example, Russians know that their standard of living is lower than that of citizens in the West and other parts of the world. As Russia's economy changes, demand will rise for products of all types—food, clothing, appliances, leisure items, medical care, and so on. Countless new opportunities will open for firms to offer goods and services that meet these demands; firms simply need a vision for the future to act. Argentina has experienced one of the fastest and most successful processes of privatization ever. The state-owned oil company,

**KEY TERMS**

**international management** The management process in an international business setting, whose importance has increased with the boom in desire for quality goods at lower prices worldwide.

railroads, telephones, airline, utilities, and television and radio stations have been privatized.[2] Foreign investors, including many large Unites States firms, venture capitalists, and mutual fund managers, are flocking to China to invest in the world's largest emerging market.[3] China's piracy of copyrighted films, music, and software threaten its relationship with companies doing business there.[4] Western firms also are finding new opportunities in India, the world's fourth-largest economy and home to a substantial English-speaking population.[5]

Globalization also presents opportunities through global outsourcing, the strategic use of external resources by a firm to perform activities that were previously handled internally.[6] Thus, global outsourcing involves a domestic firm contracting a foreign firm to perform major functions, usually on a long-term basis. Outsourced tasks include computer programming, data management, call centers, and product engineering. The advantage of outsourcing is a reduction in costs and increased competitiveness. Firms can focus on what they do best and let other firms perform activities in which they have more expertise or an abundance of labor, or can pay lower wages. Global outsourcing has also enabled developing countries from Argentina to Vietnam to grow their economies. The leading outsourcing destinations for large companies are countries in Asia, led by China and India, as well as Russia, Brazil, and Mexico; Africa is also emerging as an outsourcing hub.[7] Tiny countries like Sri Lanka and Nicaragua are trying to attract companies interested in outsourcing. Determining the size of the global outsourcing market is difficult, but some estimates reach $1 trillion and growing.[8]

Taking advantage of global opportunities will not be easy. Firms throughout the world are poised to offer products to emerging markets. More competition means more choices, which drive the need for quality even higher. In 1980, approximately seven competitors existed in the luxury automobile market. By 1990, that number rose to fifteen, including companies in the United States, Japan, Germany, and other European countries. Competition in other industries is following the same pattern. The increased globalization of markets has led to greater competition among corporations throughout the world and an erosion in the world dominance of United States firms—a trend that is expected to continue.[9] Firms that supply high-quality products will be in the best position to survive and prosper in the global economy.

# Types of Organizations in the Global Economy

Any organization, large or small, can become involved in international business. Although international firms are perceived by the consumer as large and well-known (like Sony or IBM), numerous smaller firms also sell products in foreign markets. This section discusses multinational and global corporations and their approaches to international business.

## Multinational and Global Corporations

Firms involved in international business are commonly referred to as multinational companies. A multinational company (MNC) is an organization conducting business in two or more countries. MNCs are often based in one country, with operations, production facilities, and/or sales subsidiaries in other countries. MNCs are traditionally viewed as domestic firms that carry out activities in other parts of the world; IBM is an American firm, Grand Metropolitan is British, and Nestlé is Swiss.

Another term used to describe a type of organization emerging in the global economy is global corporation. In contrast to an MNC, a global corporation operates as if the world were a single market, and it has corporate headquarters, manufacturing facilities, and marketing operations throughout the world. A global corporation is different from an MNC because it is not anchored in a single country; national boundaries are meaningless. Global corporations pursue strategies on a worldwide basis, whereas MNCs pursue separate strategies on a country-by-country basis.[10]

**KEY** TERMS

**global outsourcing** The strategic use of external resources by a firm to perform activities that were previously handled internally in order to reduce costs, increase competitiveness, and allow firms to focus on what they do best.

**multinational company (MNC)** An organization that conducts business in two or more countries and that is typically based in one country, with operations, production facilities, and/or sales subsidiaries in other countries.

**global corporation** An organization that operates as if the world were a single market, with corporate headquarters, manufacturing facilities, and marketing operations throughout the world, and that pursues strategies on a worldwide basis.

Global corporations are not the rule yet. Many international firms are MNCs that have expanded their operations to other parts of the world. Toyota, with a large Camry plant in Georgetown, Kentucky, is considered a Japanese firm. Yet Camrys are made with predominantly American parts by American workers, have fewer defects than those made in Japan, and have actually been exported to Japan. Whereas the Big Three automakers in the United States ask consumers to "buy American," some observers argue that Camry is more American than the Ford cars made in Mexico with non-American parts. The confusion over the nationality of products is indicative of the emergence of global corporations. In the near future, global corporations will no longer be the exception. Firms that do not recognize their emerging presence face a serious threat.

## Approaches to International Business

Depending on the level of commitment an organization is willing to make, the organization can take any of several approaches to international business. Some approaches represent a low level of commitment, whereas others represent a true global commitment. These approaches include exporting, licensing, trading, countertrading, joint ventures, strategic alliances, and direct investment.

| **Exporting** | The simplest way to enter international business is exporting, or selling domestic goods to a foreign country. (*Importing* is purchasing goods made in another country.) Exporting requires the lowest level of resources and commitment. In many cases, a firm can locate an exporting agency that can provide assistance in selling products to foreign countries, thereby avoiding significant upfront investments.[11]

American imports are exceeding exports and have increased the *trade deficit,* which results when a country imports more than it exports. A *trade surplus* results when exports exceeds imports. The United States trade deficit reached a record $726 billion in 2005; the trade deficit is twice as large as it was in 1987.[12] Total imports for the United States in 2005 reached $2 trillion for the first time, whereas exports fell to $1.3 trillion.[13]

| **Licensing** | In a licensing agreement, one firm (the licensor) agrees to allow another firm (the licensee) to sell the licensor's product and use its brand name. In return, the licensee pays the licensor a commission or royalty. For example, a beverage company such as Pepsico might enter into a licensing agreement with a firm in Taiwan. The Taiwanese firm would have the right to sell Pepsi products in Taiwan and would pay Pepsico a specified percentage of the income from sales of Pepsi products. American BioScience licensed Japanese firm Taiho Pharmaceutical to develop and sell ABRAXANE, an anticancer drug.[14] Licensing offers advantages for both the licensor and the licensee. The licensor can become involved in international trade with little financial risk. The licensee gains products and technology that might otherwise be too costly to produce. But licensing does not result in a large payoff for the licensor—usually only about 5 percent of sales. Some American executives and managers believe that licensing agreements merely give away trade secrets for a meager 5 percent of sales; after the agreement expires (usually in fewer than 10 years), the licensee might continue to market the product without paying the licensor.

| **Trading Companies** | Businesses wanting to sell their products overseas might choose to sell through a trading company, which serves as a link between buyers and sellers in different countries. Trading companies are not involved in manufacturing products. They are simply intermediaries that take title to products and undertake all the activities required to move products from the domestic country to customers in a foreign country. In addition, they provide sellers with information about markets, product quality and price expectations, distribution, and foreign exchange in domestic or international markets. Trading companies assume much of the manufacturer's risk in international business.

Because they are usually favored by their governments, trading companies can facilitate entrance into foreign markets. Some countries (Brazil for one) give trading companies tax advantages. In the United States, the 1982 *Export Trading Company Act* encourages the efficient operation of trading companies, helps to finance international trade, and provides limited protection from antitrust laws when conducting export activities. After the act was passed, many major companies such as General Electric developed their own export trading companies.

| **Countertrading** | Countertrading involves complex bartering agreements between two or more countries. (Bartering refers to the exchange of merchandise between countries.) Countertrading allows a nation with limited cash to participate in international trade. The country wanting to trade requires the exporting country to purchase products from it before allowing its products to be sold there. Countertrading provides an established trading vehicle for the former Soviet bloc and other developing and Third World countries that want United States goods but lack currency to pay for them.[15] Although many companies in the United States still do not use countertrading, firms such as IBM, General Motors, Xerox, and Boeing are finding they have no choice if they wish to compete in global markets.[16]

Countertrading has several drawbacks. First, determining the true value of goods offered in a countertrade agreement is often difficult. Second, disposing of bartered goods after they are accepted is also difficult. These problems can be reduced or eliminated through market analysis and negotiation. Companies have been developed to assist firms in handling countertrade agreements. Despite these drawbacks, companies that choose not to countertrade may miss significant opportunities.

| **Joint Ventures** | Firms might also conduct international business through a joint venture, a partnership between a domestic firm and a firm in a foreign country. Because of government restrictions on foreign ownership of corporations, joint ventures are often the only way a firm can purchase facilities in another country. Glassmaker Corning, based in upstate New York, nearly collapsed a few years ago when its stock fell from $16 to $1.10 a share in a two-year period. The company survived through a joint venture with Samsung to manufacture the thin, flat glass used in making liquid crystal displays; the two companies own 60 percent of the growing market.[17]

Joint ventures are becoming more common because of cost advantages and the number of inexperienced firms entering foreign markets. Sometimes joint ventures are a political necessity because of nationalism and governmental restrictions on foreign ownership of property or industry. In environments with scarce resources, rapid technological changes, and massive capital requirements, joint ventures may be the best way for smaller firms with limited resources to attain better positions in global industries. Joint ventures might also be created to gain access to distributors, suppliers, and technology.

One major drawback to international joint ventures is that organizations can lose control of their operations. For example, because India does not allow foreign companies to own industries, Coca-Cola once entered into a joint venture with the Indian government. Despite India's huge soft drink market, Coca-Cola pulled out over a decade ago rather than risk giving up majority control and its secret formula.

## Strategic Alliance

A recent strategy for entering foreign markets is a strategic alliance. A strategic alliance occurs when two firms combine their resources in a partnership that goes beyond the limits of a joint venture. Trust is the major requirement for an effective partnership. If a firm cannot trust its prospective partners, it should not enter into a strategic alliance with them. Trust generally evolves over time,

**KEY**TERMS

**countertrading** The use of complex bartering agreements between two or more countries, in which merchandise (not cash) is exchanged between countries and by which the country wanting to trade requires the exporting country to purchase products from it before allowing its products to be sold there.

**joint venture** A partnership between a domestic and a foreign firm.

**strategic alliance** The combination of two firms' resources in a partnership that goes beyond the limits of a joint venture and for which trust is the major requirement. *See also* joint venture.

so firms must give strategic alliances adequate time to prosper. GE Money, a division of General Electric Company, formed a strategic alliance with Indian Railways Catering and Tourism Corporation (IRCTC), the world's second-largest railway, to launch its first frequent flyer program and credit card, the State Bank of India Railway Card.[18]

| **Direct Ownership** | A much more involved approach to international business is direct ownership (purchasing one or more business operations in a foreign country). Direct ownership requires a large investment in production facilities, research, personnel, and marketing activities. Many MNCs such as Ford, Polaroid, and 3M own facilities outside the United States. Through direct ownership, a firm has greater control over a foreign subsidiary.

Some well-known firms operating in the United States are actually subsidiaries owned by foreign firms. Magnavox, Pillsbury, Saks Fifth Avenue, and Baskin-Robbins are wholly owned subsidiaries of foreign multinational companies. Nonprofit organizations (such as the Red Cross) and the United States Army also own foreign subsidiaries or divisions.

Firms invest in foreign subsidiaries for a number of reasons. Direct ownership can reduce manufacturing expenses because of lower labor and operating costs. Direct ownership also enables a firm to avoid paying tariffs and other costs associated with exporting. Additionally, by paying taxes in the host country and providing employment for local residents, a foreign company can build good relations with the host government. The greatest danger of direct ownership is that a firm loses a sizable investment because of market failure or nationalization of its interests by a foreign government. When problems do arise in a foreign country, moving operations out of the country is often very difficult and expensive.

# The Environment for Global Business

The business environments of domestic and foreign markets are usually significantly different. A detailed analysis of these differences is critical in determining whether to enter a foreign market. If a manager of an MNC or global corporation is to be effective in a global environment, differences in cultural, social, economic, political, legal, and technological environments must be understood. Some questions managers should ask when analyzing global markets are listed in the Management Highlight on page 75.

## Cultural Environment

Appreciating the differences among cultures is a basic requirement for successful international management.[19] Meanings attached to body language, time, greetings, spatial patterns, and other symbols differ significantly across cultures. When products are introduced into one nation from another, acceptance is far more likely when differences between cultures are recognized and accommodated. For example, the first McDonald's in Mecca, Saudi Arabia, used meat from animals slaughtered according to Islamic rules. Conversely, Yokohama Rubber Co., based in Tokyo, had to recall auto tires with a tread pattern that resembled the Arabic word for Allah after Islamic customers protested. Yokohama apologized for its lack of knowledge of Islam, discontinued the tires, and replaced them free of charge in Islamic nations.

Managers must be willing and able to adjust to cultural differences when doing business in foreign countries. How managers communicate in different countries varies greatly. For example, managers doing business in Japan know that the Japanese value saving face and achieving harmony. Thus, to be successful, managers never put a Japanese businessperson in a position where he or she must admit failure. They approach a Japanese manager at the highest level possible in the organization. (The first person approached will be involved throughout the negotiation.) Direct communication about money is avoided if feasible. Finally, and perhaps most difficult of all, American managers must wait patiently for Japanese meetings to move forward before an agreement is reached.[20]

**direct ownership** A domestic firm's purchase of one or more business operations in a foreign country, requiring a large investment in production facilities, research, personnel, and marketing activities.

## QUESTIONS TO ASK WHEN ANALYZING GLOBAL MARKETS

**About Markets**

- How large is the market?
- How many consumers use the product?
- What is our expected market share?
- Is the market growing?

**About Competitors**

- Who are our major competitors?
- What is the market share of each competitor?
- What are the trends in market share among competitors?

**About Culture**

- What is the distribution of the population by education, occupation, and religion?
- Does our product fit the cultural values of the foreign country?
- Can our marketing program be adapted to these cultural values?

**About Consumers**

- What types of consumers buy this product?
- What are the characteristics of the consumers in terms of demographics, lifestyle, and attitudes?
- How and when do consumers use the product?
- What are their motives for buying the product?

**About Geography**

- What is the climate, elevation, and terrain of the nation?
- Is there access to the country or region by water, air, railroads, or highways?
- Can we get our products to the customer at a reasonable cost?

Business customs also play a major role in international management. In some countries, one major goal in business is to be accepted by others. Japanese workers, for instance, are more concerned with being accepted by their fellow employees than with making a profit. In the Middle Eastern oil markets, companies frequently have to do business via a "connector," who has access to the oil producers and receives a commission for this role. Differences in ethical standards influence marketing activities. Price fixing, payoffs, and bribes are acceptable behavior in some countries. In Mexico, bribes and payoffs are sometimes a way of doing business.

Many United States firms provide cross-cultural training to help managers prepare for assignments involving international business. Training covers language, culture, and history of the foreign country plus how to conduct business there. Employees are screened carefully before they are given international assignments. Firms might require that candidates for international positions speak one or more foreign languages, have lived outside the United States, and have prior international work experience.

## Economic Environment

The process of international management is also influenced by a country's economic environment. Foreign economies can be unfamiliar to managers and often fluctuate even when the domestic economy is stable. Thus the stability of the nation's economy must be determined before managers can assess the market potential for their products. Developed nations like the United States, Canada, and Japan tend to have more stable economies than less developed countries such as Ethiopia and Ecuador.

The size of the foreign market is another economic factor that must be understood before engaging in international management. A firm should verify that a market is large enough to justify the costs of introducing products there. Two factors are used to assess the size of a foreign market: population and income. A country's population must be large enough to attract a firm's interest. The acceptable size varies considerably from one company to another. Some firms market only to the largest nations such as China, India, and the United States. Other firms market products in countries with populations below one million. Managers must also investigate population trends to determine whether the country is growing.

Next, managers must examine the prospective market's income, as measured by output. Gross domestic product (GDP) is an indicator of a market's income, because it measures the market value of all goods and services produced within a country in a given year. The United States has the world's largest GDP, over $12 trillion. Gross domestic product per capita is a nation's GDP divided by the population, and it measures a nation's standard of living. United States per capita GDP is $42,101, compared to $39,658 for Sweden.[21] Sweden and the United States have a similar standard of living.

If a foreign market is large enough to capture a firm's interest, the nation's economic condition should be examined. Developed countries have high literacy rates, modern technology, and high GDP. These nations often provide the greatest marketing opportunities. In developing countries, especially in Latin America, education and technology are improving. Many less-developed countries in Africa and South Asia have lower education levels, limited technology, and very low GDP. Although current business opportunities are limited in developing and less-developed countries, long-term opportunities might be extremely favorable as these nations progress.

The nation's infrastructure (the communications, transportation, and energy facilities that mobilize the country) also indicates its economic condition.[22] The extent to which a firm can successfully promote a product in different countries partially depends on the communications media available. Similarly, the quantity and quality of transportation facilities affect a firm's ability to distribute its products. In a developed country like Italy, managers use sophisticated telecommunications systems to conduct business. In sharp contrast, many less-developed nations have neither a sizable newspaper circulation nor an adequate road or railway system. Another good measure of economic conditions is a country's energy consumption: the higher the level of consumption, the greater the market potential.

## Political-Legal Environment

Political and legal forces also shape a firm's international business activities. Managers must consider the political stability of foreign nations. Countries with intense political unrest might change their policies toward outside firms at any time. This creates an unfavorable environment for international business. In some political power struggles, production facilities have been destroyed, corporate assets seized, and the personal security of employees and their families jeopardized. Yugoslavia and Somalia are recent examples.

A government's policies toward public and private enterprise, consumers, and foreign firms influence firms' decisions to enter a foreign market and also affect the conduct of business across national boundaries. Some countries encourage and seek out foreign investors. Other countries develop barriers to prevent companies from doing business there.

A quota limits the amount of a product that can leave or enter a country. Some quotas are voluntary, such as Japan setting a target to buy 20 percent of its computer chips from United States firms. An embargo prohibits the import or export of certain goods. For instance, Muslim nations have embargoes on the importation of alcoholic beverages because alcohol consumption is a violation of Muslim values. A duty is a tax that is placed on an import or export. An exchange control limits how much profit a foreign-based firm can return to its home country.

Many countries rely on customs and entry procedures to restrict the entry of foreign products. Customs and entry procedures govern the inspection, documentation, and licensing of imports. The documents that governments require are often extensive and complex. Japan requires six volumes of standards for each car that enters the country. Without proper documentation, products do not clear Japanese customs. In France, customs documentation must be in French, which often slows product clearance. Beer cannot be imported into Mexico without a license. To obtain a license, the importer must prove that domestic demand cannot be met by Mexican brewers alone. India requires licenses for all imported goods.[23]

The highest risks for international firms are found in countries such as El Salvador, Afghanistan, and Iran, which are politically unstable and place many restrictions on business. Countries such as the United States, Australia, and South Korea are considered attractive because they are politically stable and place fewer restrictions on business.

## Technological Environment

Technology is also a major consideration when becoming involved in international business. Not all countries are at the same level of technological development. For instance, electricity is not readily available in some parts of the world so demand is not high for products requiring electricity to operate. Communications systems also differ throughout the world. Some countries lack modern broadcasting and postal services; much of the technology used for advertising cannot be used in these nations.

## Regulation of International Business

As business between nations grows, so does the number of laws and organizations involved in regulating international trade.

## Legislation

The major United States laws affecting American firms engaged in international business are summarized in Exhibit 4.1. The *Webb-Pomerene Export Trade Act* of 1918 exempts firms in the United States from certain antitrust laws if they are working together to develop export markets. The Webb-Pomerene Act does not allow companies to reduce competition in the United States or to use unfair methods of competition. The *Foreign Corrupt Practices Act*, passed in 1977, prohibits American firms from bribing foreign officials. This law spells out the penalties for companies and individuals who are in violation: companies can be fined up to $1 million, and individuals can receive a fine up to $10,000 and a prison sentence of up to five years. The *Export*

**EXHIBIT 4.1**

### U.S. Laws Affecting International Business

| Law | Purpose |
| --- | --- |
| Webb-Pomerene Export Trade Act (1918) | Exempts U.S. firms from antitrust laws if they are acting together to develop international trade |
| Foreign Corrupt Practices Act (1977) | Forbids bribing foreign officials to obtain sales for American firms |
| Export Trading Companies Act (1982) | Encourages the formation of export trading companies by eliminating antitrust barriers and allowing banks to participate in such ventures |

MANAGEMENT HIGHLIGHT

## EXPORTING E-WASTE

Have you ever heard of the term *e-waste?* Throwing an old camcorder into the trash or recycling a PC is disposing of e-waste. The EPA estimates that two million tons of high tech trash—old computers, printers, DVD players, and the like—are discarded by Americans alone each year. Electronic waste, or e-waste, is the fastest growing waste problem in the world. The quantity of waste alone is a serious problem; United States homes and businesses dispose of 133,000 PCs each day. But even more serious are the toxic ingredients in the electronic items being disposed of such as lead and mercury, which pose a severe threat to the environment.

What becomes of e-waste? It is routinely exported by developed countries to developing ones, where labor is cheap and occupational and environmental regulation is inadequate at best. The United States and other wealthy economies that dispose of most of the world's electronic products and thus generate most of the waste have relied on a convenient escape valve by exporting the crisis to developing countries in the Far East, India, Asia, and Africa. The practice is legal because the United States has not ratified the Basel Convention, which calls for a total ban on the export of hazardous waste from rich countries to poor, for any reason including recycling. To date, the United States is the only developed country in the world that has not ratified the Basel Convention.

It is estimated that 50–60 percent of the high-tech waste collected for recycling in the United States is disposed of via exporting. Trade in e-waste is causing severe harm to the countries receiving the electronic devices, because a wide range of hazardous chemicals are used in components of these obsolete products. Acid baths and toxic dumping pollute the land, air, and water, and expose residents of these poorer nations to poison. The health and economic costs of these practices are steep, and because of exporting, these costs are not paid for by western consumers. Mainland China tried to ban the practice of importing e-waste but discovered the laws are not working. The European Union, Japan, South Korea, Taiwan, and some states in the United States have introduced legislation that makes manufacturers responsible for their end-of-life products. For the present time, however, e-waste is still being exported and remains a dirty secret of the high-tech revolution.

Source: Adapted from Brad Stone, "Recycling: Tech Trash, E-Waste," *Newsweek*, (December 12, 2005): 11; "Recycling of Electronic Wastes in China & India: Workplace & Environmental Contamination," Report published by Greenpeace International (August 2005); "Exporting Harm; The High-Tech Trashing of Asia," Report published by The Basel Action Network (BAN) and Silicon Valley Toxics Coalition (SVTC), February 25, 2002.

*Trading Companies Act* of 1982 eliminates some antitrust barriers and allows banks to participate in joint ventures. (An export trading company is an organization that attempts to create exports.)

Unfortunately, many firms are able to take advantage of weak regulation in foreign countries. For example, products that are regulated in the United States, such as dangerous pesticides and drugs, might not be regulated in other countries, so firms look to these foreign markets to sell them. Third World nations are often the target of dangerous products because they have the weakest regulation. The Management Highlight above examines the growing concern over the export of dangerous electronic trash.

## International Organizations

Several international organizations exist solely to facilitate world trade. The major ones are summarized in Exhibit 4.2 and include GATT and the World Trade Organization, IMF, and the World Bank.

### GATT and the World Trade Organization

Signed in 1947, the General Agreement on Tariffs and Trade (GATT) formed an international organization of 23 nations, including the United Sates. GATT worked to reduce or eliminate tariffs and other barriers to international trade. GATT was replaced by the World Trade Organization (WTO) in 1995. Today, 128 countries agree to the guidelines established by the WTO. The *most favored nation (MFN)* principle requires that any tariff reduction negotiated between member countries be extended to all members.

Since it was organized, GATT has sponsored several "rounds" of negotiations to reduce trade barriers. President John F. Kennedy, through authority granted by the Trade Expansion Act of 1962, called for the reduction of tariffs through GATT. The Kennedy Round, which began in 1964, led to a nearly 40 percent reduction in tariffs. The Tokyo Round, held from 1973 to 1979,

**EXHIBIT 4.2**

### Organizations That Facilitate International Business

| Organization | Purpose | Members |
|---|---|---|
| General Agreement on Tariffs and Trade (GATT) and the World Trade Organization (WTO) | Formed in 1947 by 23 nations to reduce or eliminate tariffs and other barriers to international trade | 128 countries, including the United States and Japan |
| European Union (EU) | Founded in 1957 to reduce barriers among members | Austria, Belgium, Cyprus, Czech Republic, Denmark, Estonia, Finland, France, Germany, Greece, Hungary, Ireland, Italy, Latvia, Lithuania, Luxembourg, Malta, Netherlands, Poland, Portugal, Slovakia, Slovenia, Spain, Sweden, and United Kingdom |
| Latin American Free Trade Association (LAFTA) | Founded in 1960 to develop free trade among member nations | Argentina, Bolivia, Brazil, Chile, Columbia, Cuba, Ecuador, Mexico, Paraguay, Peru, Uruguay, and Venezuela |
| European Free Trade Association (EFTA) | Founded in 1960 to eliminate trade restrictions among members and develop common trade policies | Iceland, Norway, Liechtenstein, and Switzerland |
| Organization of Petroleum Exporting Countries (OPEC) | Established in 1960 to provide oil-producing nations control over prices and reduce the oversupply of oil | Algeria, Indonesia, Iran, Iraq, Kuwait, Libya, Nigeria, Qatar, Saudi Arabia, the United Arab Emirates, and Venezuela |
| International Monetary Fund (IMF) | Founded in 1944 to promote trade among member nations by eliminating trade barriers and increasing cooperation on financial issues | 184 industrial and developing countries |
| World Bank | Founded in 1946 to lend money to underdeveloped and developing countries for a variety of projects | 184 industrial and developing countries |

led to a reduction of more than 30 percent. Some nontariff restrictions, such as import quotas and unnecessary red tape in customs procedures, were also removed. In 1989, the Uruguay Round resulted in more than 100 countries agreeing to halt farm subsidies and to institute a new system of arbitration for handling disputes between countries. The recent Doha Round, also called the July 2004 package, placed an emphasis on market access designed to facilitate trade between nations.[24]

**| The IMF and World Bank |** Two international organizations have been established to help finance international trade. The International Monetary Fund (IMF) was founded in 1944 to promote cooperation among member nations by eliminating trade barriers. IMF lends money to countries that need short-term loans to conduct international trade. The World Bank was formed in 1946 to lend money to underdeveloped and developing countries for various projects such as roads, factories, and medical facilities.

## Multinational Market Groups

Companies operating in the global business environment must recognize that economic cooperation among nations is increasing. A multinational market group is created when two or more countries agree to reduce trade and tariff barriers between them. This section discusses the North American Free Trade Agreement (NAFTA), the European Union (EU), and the Pacific Rim.

## North American Free Trade Agreement

The United States, Canada, and Mexico signed the *North American Free Trade Agreement (NAFTA)*, a three-nation alliance, on August 12, 1992. The United States needed resources and a source of new labor; Canada was resource-rich but small in population; and Mexico had an abundance of oil and workers but desperately needed exports to fuel its economy. Thus, the agreement, which was approved by the respective governments in 1994, made sense to many. Trade among the three nations was $237 billion a year before NAFTA and was expected to increase dramatically.[25]

Over a decade later, NAFTA appears to be a success. The agreement has created jobs and reduced inflation without harming wages. And although some United States workers lost their jobs, the number is smaller than opponents predicted.[26] From 1993 to 2005, trade among NAFTA nations climbed 173 percent to $810 billion; Canada and Mexico are the United States' first and second largest export markets. GDP growth for the United States, Mexico, and Canada from 1993 to 2005 was 48 percent, 40 percent, and 49 percent, respectively. Over 22 million jobs were created in the United States during this period.[27]

## The European Union

The twelve-nation European Community (EC), created by the Treaty of Rome in 1957, called for eliminating most trade barriers between its members (Belgium, Denmark, France, Germany, Greece, Ireland, Italy, Luxembourg, the Netherlands, Portugal, Spain, and the United Kingdom) in 1992. Now called the European Union (EU), this multinational market group has expanded to 25 members, adding Austria, Cyprus, Czech Republic, Estonia, Finland, Hungary, Latvia, Lithuania, Malta, Poland, Slovakia, Slovenia, and Sweden. Historically, the member nations have primarily been separate markets and could not compete with the giant resources of Japan and the United States. With over 450 million consumers, the European Union is one of the largest markets in the world.[28]

The elimination of trade barriers has already meant big gains for Europe in several industries, including airlines, telecommunications, and financial services. GDP is over $11 trillion, comparable to the United States.[29] However, the broad monetary and political union of the member nations has yet to occur. Whereas single-market reform has generally been successful, the monetary unification has been less of a success. The Maastrict Treaty, an amendment to the original Treaty of Rome, mandated a single European currency. In 2002, the euro replaced the currencies of twelve member countries and became the official currency of the EU. The euro will not be a complete success until all countries of the EU adopt it. Establishing one currency would eliminate expensive currency transactions (which can cost firms billions of dollars), make selling products across borders easier for companies, and enable customers to compare prices better.

## The Pacific Rim

The Pacific Rim nations include Japan, China, Taiwan, South Korea, Singapore, Hong Kong, the Philippines, Malaysia, Indonesia, Indochina, and Australia. Firms from these nations, especially Japan, have become increasingly competitive in comparison to United States firms. Names like Toyota, Sony, and Canon are not only household words; they also represent firms that have eroded the market share of their United States counterparts General Motors, Zenith, and Kodak. Firms from Taiwan, South Korea, Hong Kong, and Singapore are expected to be even more competitive in the future.

In addition to the Asian Pacific Economic Cooperation (APEC) group (discussed in Chapter 1 "Management and Managers"), there is much speculation about future alliances. An alliance between the United States, Japan, Taiwan, China, and Hong Kong is possible. Although talk of a United States-Japanese free-trade agreement exists, any such arrangement is years away. Lack of such an agreement has led many leaders in the United States to criticize Japan's trade restrictions on products from the United States and other nations. Although the Japanese government has removed some trade barriers, foreign firms trying to do business in Japan are still confronted with barriers including the high cost of doing business and delays in receiving patents (during which time Japanese companies examine patent applications and copy new technologies), corruption (including collusion among Japanese bidders), and purchasing agents who are part of old-boy networks and refuse to buy foreign goods.

**CONCLUSION**

## The Global Management Environment

The global economy has resulted in intense competition among firms throughout the world; the way to compete is through quality. This environment presents many challenges for managers. Any product made anywhere has to compete with any product made anywhere else. By taking advantage of global opportunities and adapting to the global environment, managers can enhance an organization's likelihood of success.

## Questions

1. Describe the different approaches an organization can use to become involved in international business.

2. Why must a firm consider the environment when deciding whether to enter a foreign market?

3. What is the significance of multinational market groups to companies operating in today's global environment?

## Video Case

### Lonely Planet Travels the World

For a company such as Lonely Planet, the idea of a borderless world is nothing new. Founded in Australia by Tony and Maureen Wheeler so that they could fund their own travel dreams, the travel publisher now has offices in Australia, the United States, the United Kingdom, and France, with a total of about 450 employees. Its writers, photographers, and marketers span the globe on a regular basis in search of the best destinations for their customers to explore. However, even though the idea of globalization is built into the firm's culture, its managers face international challenges every day.

Howard Ralley, director of global marketing and promotions, is now based in Australia, after having worked at the Lonely Planet office in the United Kingdom. He is a decisive manager who says what he means and means what he ways. "You can get caught up in a lot of navel gazing, asking, 'What does global really mean?'" he quips. "Global doesn't really exist in a lot of senses. When you talk about global marketing, marketing is really all about talking with [a particular] customer, and that customer isn't global. [He or she] is concerned about the immediate environment." Thus, when Ralley and his staff get together to discuss a particular project, they consider the features of the destination, the characteristics of its culture, and the needs of the traveler as they relate to the location. The focus of a book on weekend escapes for the European traveler will be much different from the focus of a book on China.

Still, Ralley and his staff, along with the rest of the Lonely Planet employees around the world, strive to achieve consistency in the message they convey to consumers and other members of the travel industry. "There is a lot of 'globalness' that we achieve," says Ralley. "It's not about product . . . we're talking to an audience which shares many things, including a passion for travel. They believe that travel can change the world. So we work that message into individual markets." In addition, Lonely Planet employees around the world need to achieve consistency in the messages they convey to each other. The Internet has proved to be an excellent tool for handling both types of audiences. For instance, an image representing a specific book or series of books can be transmitted anywhere in the world, among Lonely Planet offices, to travel industry professionals, and to the home computers of consumers. This consistency in messages helps reinforce the Lonely Planet brand worldwide.

Ralley emphasizes the importance of conveying a unique message about Lonely Planet to distinguish the publisher from its competitors. "If a brand tries to work in all kinds of markets and you try to dumb down to the lowest common denominator," he notes, you get "blanding" instead of branding. "We all agree that travel is important," Ralley continues. "If we just did a message on that, it would make us no different from National Geographic, Fodor's, or Discovery—so that is blanding. You have to get brave in saying something new to the world. Branding is all about that distinction." Ralley does not mind that not every consumer likes Lonely Planet books. He feels that it is more important to speak with a decisive, distinctive voice.

To that end, Ralley is a decisive manager. "The world is not all happy," he said during one recent meeting when discussing with his staff the selection of representative photos for a pictorial book covering 230 countries. Ralley wanted to include a potentially controversial photo of an Ethiopian woman whose facial expression did not appear to be welcoming. His staff expressed concern that the photo would be interpreted as too political. But Ralley insisted that the photo was consistent with Lonely Planet's direct, frank approach to the world. "You face different challenges every day," he later explained when discussing his role as an international manager. "Everything you thought you knew . . . all your assumptions [about a certain culture or market] . . . you have to rethink that." And in the end, he makes the decisions. "At some point," Ralley says, "you have to call the shot."

## Questions

1. Identify at least three ways that Lonely Planet can benefit from the use of technology around the world.

2. Why is a global presence particularly important for Lonely Planet?

3. Describe at least two personal challenges that Howard Ralley faces as a manger.

Sources: Company web site, http://www.lonelyplanet.com, accessed August 5, 2004; "Lonely Planet Publications Company Profile," *Hoover's Online*, http://biz.yahoo.com, accessed July 30, 2004; Lonely Planet press packet.

# BizFlix

### *Mr. Baseball*

The New York Yankees trade aging baseball player Jack Elliot (Tom Selleck) to the Chunichi Dragons, a Japanese team. This lighthearted comedy traces Elliot's bungling entry into Japanese culture where he almost loses everything including Hiroko Uchiyama (Aya Takanashi). As Elliot slowly begins to understand Japanese culture and Japanese baseball, he finally is accepted by his teammates. This film shows many examples of Japanese culture, especially its love for baseball.

Unknown to Hiroko's father, she and Jack develop an intimate relationship. Meanwhile, Jack does not know that Hiroko's father is "The Chief" (Ken Takakura), the manager of the Chunichi Dragons. This scene takes place after "The Chief" has removed Jack from a baseball game. The scene shows Jack dining with Hiroko and her grandmother (Mineko Yorozuya), grandfather (Jun Hamamura), and father.

## Questions

1. Does Jack Elliot behave as if he had had cross-cultural training before arriving in Japan?

2. Is he culturally sensitive or insensitive?

3. What do you propose that Jack Elliot do for the rest of his time in Japan?

## Suggested Reading

Farrell, Diana. "Beyond Offshoring: Assess Your Company's Global Potential." *Harvard Business Review* (December 2004): 82–91.

Friedman, Thomas L. *The World Is Flat.* New York: Farrar, Straus and Giroux, 2005.

Ghemawat, Pankaj. "Regional Strategies for Global Leadership." *Harvard Business Review* (December 2005): 98–109.

Hampden-Turner, Charles and Trompenaars, Alfons. *The Seven Cultures of Capitalism.* New York: Doubleday, 1993.

Ohmae, Kenichi, *The Borderless World*, New York: HarperPerennial, 1991).

Porter, Michael E. *The Competitive Advantage of Nations.* New York: The Free Press, 1990.

## Endnotes

1. Kenichi Ohmae, *The Borderless World* (New York: HarperPerennial, 1991): 10.

2. "Argentina: Privatization Set to Transform the Market," *International Financial Law Review* (February 1998): 54.

3. Mark Veverka, "China Time," *Barron's* (April 17, 2006): 34.

4. "A Case for Copying," *The Economist* (November 23, 1996): 73–74.

5. Joseph Luna, "A Matter of Time: India's Emerging Economic Prowess," *Harvard International Review* (Winter 2006): 36–39.

6. Rahul Sen and M. Shahidul Islam, "Southeast Asia in the Global Wave of Outsourcing," *Regional Outlook: Southeast Asia,* 2005/2006, pp. 75–79.

7. Andy Reinhardt, "Angling to Be the Next Bangalore," *Business Week* (January 30, 2006): 62.

8. "The Global Outsourcing 100," *Fortune* (April 3, 2006): A1–A8.

9. Lawrence G. Franko, "Global Competition II: Is the Large American Firm an Endangered Species?" *Business Horizons* (November–December 1991): 14–22.

10. Jean-Pierre Jeannet and Hubert D. Hennessey, *Global Marketing Strategies* (Boston: Houghton Mifflin, 1992): 16–17.

11. Joseph V. McCabe, "Outside Managers Offer Packaged Export Expertise," *Journal of Business Strategy* (March–April 1990): 20–23.

12. "Trade Picture," *Economic Policy Institute* (February 10, 2006): 1–2.

13. Ibid, pp. 1–2.

14. Aki Tsukioka, "Taiho Pharmaceutical Licensed to Develop and Sell ABRAXANE," *JCN Newswire* (November 21, 2005): 1.

15. Matt Schaffer, "Countertrade as an Export Strategy," *Journal of Business Strategy* (May–June 1990): 33–38.

16. John P. Angelidis, Faramarz Parsa, and Nabil A. Ibrahim, "Countertrading with Latin America: A Comparative Analysis of Attitudes of United States Firms," *International Journal of Management* (December 2004): 435–444.

17. Jonathan Fahey, "Glass Menagerie," *Forbes* (April 24, 2006): 1.

18. "GE, IRCTC Form Strategic Alliance," *FinancialWire* (February 21, 2006): 1.

19. Kazuo Nukazawa, "Japan and the USA: Wrangling Toward Reciprocity," *Harvard Business Review* (May–June 1988): 42–52.

20. Philip R. Harris and Robert T. Moran, *Managing Cultural Differences* (Houston: Gulf, 1981): 189.

21. List of Countries by GDP, *Wikipedia Free Encyclopedia,* en.wikipedia.org.

22. Vern Terpstra, *International Marketing,* 4th ed. (Hinsdale, IL: Dryden, 1987): 18–19.

23. Sak Onkvisit and John S. Shaw, "Marketing Barriers in International Trade," *Business Horizons* (May–June 1988): 64–72.

24. Georg Koopmann, "Doha Development Round Perspectives," *Intereconomics* (July/August 2005): 235–240.

25. Gaylon White, "Run for the Border," *Express Magazine* (Summer 1991): 10–13.

26. Charles J. Whalen, Paul Magnusson, and Geri Smith, "NAFTA's Scorecard: So Far So Good," *Business Week* (July 9, 2001): 54.

27. "NAFTA: A Strong Record of Success," *Trade Facts,* Office of the United States Trade Representative (March 2006): 1–2.

28. "The European Union and World Trade," *EU Statistical Office—EUROSTAT,* Home page.

29. Ibid.

# Planning

# 5

# DECISION MAKING

**E**very day and in every organization, managers make decisions. Some decisions are unimportant in the larger scheme of things whereas others can affect the lives of many people for years to come. Although we generally think of decision making as an individual action, in organizations many decisions are made by groups, teams, or committees. For example, a hiring decision might be made by a personnel committee, a purchasing decision by a procurement group, and product design by a design team. Empowerment, education, democratic organizations, and advances in information technology have made group decision making quite common in organizations. This trend toward group decision making is not likely to change in the future.

## The Components of Decision Making

Regardless of its magnitude and ultimate outcome, decision making in organizations is about choosing from among several competing alternatives. A key component in the decision-making process is the amount of information that is available to the decision maker. Generally speaking, the more information the decision maker has, the better the decision will be. More information also means less risk for the decision maker and increases predictability of the outcome. Decision making is not easy. It involves a complex mixture of information, knowledge, experience, creativity, and risk taking.

An important measure of the effectiveness of an individual manager, a management team, or a worker team is the quality of decisions reached. Indeed, some have argued that the primary function of management *is* decision making and that the essence of managerial behavior is found by studying the decision-making process.

A decision is a choice among competing alternatives and the implementation of the chosen alternative. The alternatives are the means to an end or a goal. All decisions have a time horizon, or scope. *Strategic decisions* have a long-term perspective; they are related to an organization's overall strategy. *Tactical decisions* have a shorter time scope; they entail choices that must be made in the near term. However, tactical decisions must also remain consistent with the organization's strategy. Managers make many strategic and tactical decisions every day.

Decision making requires information, but the decision maker rarely has complete information. This lack of information is referred to as *uncertainty*. As author James Thompson notes, "Uncertainty appears as the fundamental problem for complex organizations, and coping with uncertainty, as the essence of the administrative process."[1]

Decision making involves one of three situations:

- *Certainty*. The decision maker has complete information about the probabilities of the outcomes of each alternative.

- *Uncertainty*. The decision maker has absolutely no knowledge of the probabilities of the outcomes of each alternative.

- *Risk*. The decision maker has some probabilistic estimate of the outcomes of each alternative.

**KEY**TERMS

**decision** A choice among competing alternatives.

Obviously, the best situation for a manager is one of certainty. Where certainty exists, the decision is clear and the outcome is known. How can you lose? The worst case for the manager is uncertainty. With little information and the inability to assign probabilities to outcomes, a manager is operating in the dark. However, most managerial decisions are made with some degree of risk. The advantage of risk is that it can be managed when alternatives are known and probability of occurrence can be assigned to outcomes.

For example, if a university knows that on the first day of the fall semester it wants to have an incoming class of three thousand students, how many students should it accept? One factor that must be taken into account is that although students apply to many schools, they attend only one. In this hypothetical case, suppose the administrators use a rational decision-making model that includes many years of past admissions data to predict a probabilistic answer. In fact, the answer might be that only 42 percent of all applicants actually attend the university. So, if the university wants three thousand students to attend the university beginning in the fall semester, its admissions office must admit 7,143 students (3000 × (1/.42)). Of course, the process is more complicated than what was just described, but the point is the same. In this example, using a rational admissions model significantly reduces uncertainty about how many students will actually attend the university for the fall semester.

As this example showed, managerial decision making entails both a process and subsequent action. A decision-making process is a series of related steps or stages leading to an action, an outcome, and an assessment. As noted earlier, as a process a decision is a choice among alternative courses of action. From a managerial perspective, a decision is also an action that someone takes, and that individual is subsequently held accountable for the outcome of the action (decision). In today's complex, information-rich organizations, the managerial decision-making process is often fragmented and rapid. In the modern work environment, a single individual is less likely to process enough information to make the best decisions for the organization. Besides dealing with the vast amount of data available for most nonroutine decisions, managers must respond to interruptions and unexpected events. As they often find, the decision-making process occurs over time rather than as a single event. Managers must learn to deal with a decision-making environment that emphasizes oral communication, brief meetings, incomplete information, and close approximations. Their decisions are often based on impressions, estimates, and personal experience. Decision making often reflects a manager's effort to make sense of the complicated environment, to attain some control over the uncontrollable, and to achieve some sense of order.

Managers are fundamentally decision makers. An organized approach to decision making—including a clear understanding of the current state of affairs, the historical basis for improving decisions, and the possible errors that can be made—enables managers to make better decisions and to reach personal and organizational goals. Management theorists have investigated decision making from many different perspectives and have developed a set of useful concepts to understand the phenomenon. To increase your awareness of the complexity of this highly social process that involves reason and emotion, risk and uncertainty, and imagination and knowledge, in this chapter we will explore the rational approach, the administrative approach, and the political approach to decision making. We will also remind the reader that many decisions are intuitive, resulting from both experience and what feels right at the moment.

## Types of Managerial Decisions

Decision making is an entirely human process; like human beings themselves, it is fraught with complexities and ambiguities. By gaining some understanding of the different concepts that researchers have used to understand decision making, the practicing manager can often avoid difficulties. For example, a manager who is used to making decisions based on intuition might notice that many of his recent decisions are less effective than they used to be. If he is aware of the distinction between *intuitive* and *rational* decision making, he might understand that his intuitions are based on personal experiences that might no longer be appropriate in a changed environment. Switching, at least temporarily, to a more rational approach could very well lead to more effective decisions.[2]

## Programmed versus Nonprogrammed Decisions

Decision making in an organization occurs during both routine operations and in unexpected situations. Herbert Simon[3] has identified two distinct categories of managerial decisions:

- *Programmed decision.* If a particular situation occurs often, a solution is designed in the form of a routine procedure. Decisions are programmed to the extent that they are repetitive and routine, and a definite procedure has been developed for handling them.

- *Nonprogrammed decision.* Decisions are nonprogrammed when they are unstructured, novel, or unique. They often represent one-time situations that require a choice among existing alternatives. There is no established procedure for handling the problem. These decisions deserve special attention and treatment because of their importance or complexity.

Managers in most organizations face making many programmed decisions in their daily operations. Such decisions should be treated without expending unnecessary organizational resources. On the other hand, the nonprogrammed decision must be properly identified as such because this type of decision can involve significant risk and uncertainty.

Despite some managers' efforts to place all organizational processes under rigorous and invariant control regimens, variation, complexity, and ambiguity in the workplace are the rule rather than the exception. Much day-to-day variation can be accommodated with routine responses, yet a creative response or nonprogrammed decision of some sort is often needed. Nonprogrammed decisions involve searching for information and alternatives that lie outside the routine decision-making process. These decisions are often time-consuming and (unlike routine decisions) demand that workers be prepared to create alternative solutions, analyze them critically, and choose a course of action.

Many organizations now use computers and software to assist with complex, nonprogrammed decisions. Boeing transformed the process of manufacturing commercial airliners when it created an online CAD/CAM system that integrated individual component designs with the final subassembly. For example, the manufacturer of a screw would design it online and submit the design, then be able to view her product used on a software model of the final assembly. The designer receives an error message for any design parameter defects (e.g., the screw was too long) immediately. The error can be corrected before the component is ever manufactured.

Programmed decisions, which do not allow for flexibility, are not always useful for workers in manufacturing jobs. Product design engineers are still often directed by management to create product assembly processes so simple that they require no input from assemblers on the factory floor. Such a simple design might be valuable to an untrained customer when assembling a product at home (e.g., a piece of home exercise equipment). But for a trained assembly worker, ordering such simple assembly processes reflects a lack of trust in the worker's ability to make nonprogrammed decisions.

One company that has succeeded in employing an innovative form of Frederick Taylor's scientific management principles on the factory floor is New United Motor Manufacturing, Inc. (NUMMI), of Fremont, California. NUMMI is a joint venture between Toyota and General Motors. NUMMI has used the principles of scientific management to create a highly programmed process flow and to increase quality, productivity, and employee motivation at the same time. How does the company manage this? It does so by allowing the workers to design the formal work standards and establish the programmed decisions. As University of Southern California Professor Paul Adler stated following a two-year study of the company, "Procedures that are designed by the workers themselves in a continuous, successful effort to improve productivity, quality, skills, and understanding can humanize even the most disciplined form of bureaucracy."[4]

Programmed and nonprogrammed decisions affect organizations daily. Sometimes managers need to react to events and make decisions. At other times they can anticipate changes and make decisions before events occur. This distinction is captured in the following discussion of two more decision types: proactive and reactive.

## Proactive versus Reactive Decisions

You might recall that earlier in this chapter, we defined the term *decision* as a choice among competing alternatives. A decision made in anticipation of an external change or other conditions is called a proactive decision. Managers who utilize a rational, proactive approach can prevent problems from developing.

A **reactive decision** is one made in response to external changes. Suppose that the ABC Router company (a manufacturer of woodworking routers) learns that their main competitor, XYZ Routing, is offering a free router accessory (a $30 value) with the purchase of their new TECH1 router. Using a reactive approach, ABC Router responds by marketing their routers in a similar fashion. In fact, ABC Router raises the stakes by offering two free router accessories and quickly working the new offer into their holiday season advertising campaign. The decision made by ABC Router is strategic, yet reactive. Their response was not based on a plan but rather in response to the plan of a competitor. Reactive decisions are not always inferior to proactive decisions, but over the long run, merely reacting to environmental stimuli is risky. Why? It suggests a lack of planning and strategy. In the next few chapters, you will see that planning and strategy formulation create a decision context. In that context, managers can make decisions that support the strategy ("we stay the course") in relation to a competitive response. This is a different situation from a reactive decision.

Noted strategy scholar Henry Mintzberg (discussed in Chapter 1, "Management and Managers") believes that top-level managers make three types of decisions: entrepreneurial, adaptive, and planning. Each of these decisions is described in Exhibit 5.1 in relation to its degree of proactivity and uncertainty.

Management history teaches that whenever possible, being proactive is better than being than reactive. Wise managers recognize that one person alone does not make things happen; whether you are the boss or the worker out on the shop floor, success depends on a team. To help focus the talents and virtues of their subordinates, managers must first provide a vision; otherwise, all decisions are reactive. Reactive decisions are not necessarily made out of context, but rather *without* a context. The ABC Router example demonstrates this point. ABC Router's decision had more to do with the decision context of another organization than its own decision context. If ABC Router's decision increases costs with no increase in customer demand, the firm might lose money on every router it sells.

Managerial vision provides the context for proactive decision making. If the vision is strong enough and communicated effectively, many employees will intuitively make decisions in support of that vision. Intuitive decisions are based on experience, and they are usually made in situations that allow little time for analysis. Rational decision making should also conform to the managerial vision for the organization, but it involves more time and prior data gathering. Intuitive and rational types of decision making next are explored next.

**KEY**TERMS

**proactive decision** A decision made in anticipation of an external change or other conditions; used by managers to prevent problems from developing.

EXHIBIT 5.1

**Mintzberg's Strategic Decision Categories**

| Decision Category | Decision Type | Nature of the Environment |
|---|---|---|
| Entrepreneurial | Proactive decisions that strategic managers make about the nature of the product and the future of the organization | These decisions are based on a higher degree of uncertainty because less information is available about customer preferences and material costs at the time of the decision. |
| Adaptive | Reactive responses to environmental conditions | Competitive actions often stimulate the organization to make a decision. A new product feature by a competitor requires a competitive product change. |
| Planning | Proactive as well as reactive decisions that develop specific reactions to reduce uncertainties related to growth, uniqueness, and efficiency | A new product launch introduces an organization's unique product, built in a "state-of-the-art manufacturing facility." The manager's goal is to increase market share in their industry segment. |

**Source:** Henry Mintzberg, "Strategy Making in Three Modes," *California Management Review,* Winter 1973, pp. 44–53.

## Intuitive Decisions

Intuitive decisions involve feelings or beliefs that one course of action is better than another. The intuitive, or "gut level," responses are said to involve more heart than head, implying that intuitive decisions have an emotional or nonrational component. Often they are the result of a unique combination of individual experience, ability, and knowledge that affords the decision maker an insight and a decision preference. Many decision makers agree that some decisions are considerably influenced by flashes of insight, or intuition. Indeed, "the intuitive insight that would save Chrysler in the 1990s came to Bob Lutz, then the company president, during a weekend drive."[5] Our emotions are what make us human, and we rely on them daily to make a variety of decisions that require little justification. We should not forget that for millennia gut feelings have often helped keep us alive, pick mates, and solve many daily problems. However, work decisions often require a sell. We need evidence and a causal pattern to convince others to support the decision. Neuroscience offers compelling evidence that we overlook our emotional response at our own peril. Intuitive decisions can be bad just as often as they can be good. An intuitive decision can lead to negative results when the following is ignored:[6]

- *Risk reward trade-off.* Risk is often minimized, and only the rewards are seen. This is the belief that a product will be a success even though no market data support that assertion.

- *Thrill of the hunt.* Winning, not the actual outcome of the win, becomes all important.

- *Fear.* Some decisions never get made because failure is subconsciously feared.

Nonetheless, decisions based purely on intuition can be premature, unnecessary, and even counterproductive. For example, one common flaw with the "merit" pay systems is that managers falsely can assume they can determine meaningful individual differences among workers' performances. If these differences are determined more by personal opinion and human biases than by facts and logical analysis, the concept of merit is lost. Such biased pay raise decisions can be destructive rather than productive in encouraging workers to perform at high levels. Although intuition is part of the decision-making process, it might be more useful for selecting among several equally viable options. Ultimately, the decision maker must be able to explain and sometimes sell the decision. Calling on the "gut" once in awhile is fine, especially when you are correct. However, making most decisions requires a more systematic approach.

**KEY TERMS**

**intuitive decision** The "gut level" feeling or belief that one course of action is better than another; not necessarily emotional or nonrational, but rather the result of a unique combination of individual experience, ability, and knowledge that affords the decision maker an insight and a decision preference.

# Systematic Decisions

Systematic decision making requires decision makers to have a goal in mind and use information to generate alternatives and make a logical choice among alternatives. The use of current and pertinent information is critical to a successful decision. It is equally important to remember that decision makers will have different preferences for one alternative. In the case of the 1986 Challenger shuttle disaster, NASA and Marshall Space Flight Center administrators had a clear preference to launch the shuttle; however, management at Morton-Thiocol, the subcontractor that built the solid rocket boosters, initially recommended "not to launch" but later reversed its decision when pressured by NASA to reevaluate the analytical data.[7] Preferences are part of being human, but ignoring the facts can be deadly. Irrefutable facts should drive the decision-making process.[8] Even though it is based on fact and data, systematic decision making has its faults. Bazerman and Chugh refer to the concept of "bounded awareness" to warn us that decision makers can be aware of information yet not be able to judge the true nature of the information before them.[9] As evidence, they point to the Vioxx ™ lawsuits. Evidence of Vioxx's potential to increase heart attacks and stroke appeared as early as 2001. Merck executives denied that they kept Vioxx on the market, knowingly exposing consumers to significant risks. The problem might have been that the evidence is not always clear and easy to understand and process. Decision making is hard work and requires more than superficial attention to detail. Bazerman and Chugh suggest the following:

- *Know what you are looking for.* Be a wise information consumer.

- *Seek expertise.* If you don't know, hire a consultant to teach you.

- *Seek information.* Examine both sides of the issues. Know your downside risk. If the decision is important, gather more information.

**KEY**TERMS

**systematic decision making** The process that requires decision makers to have a goal in mind and to use information in generating alternatives and making a logical choice among alternatives based on fact and data.

MANAGEMENTHIGHLIGHT

## DECISION MAKING: THE PMI (PLUS/MINUS/INTERESTING) APPROACH

### Scenario

A middle manager of an international firm with corporate headquarters located in New York City is faced with a decision. Should he accept a promotion that will relocate him to the London office permanently?

### Strategy

Using the PMI approach, the middle manager should approach this complex decision by listing the pluses, minuses, and interesting aspects of accepting the promotion. Positive or negative scores should be attached to each item listed based on the degree of the perceived benefit or detriment posed by each item.

### Task

For each aspect of the situation, assign a score ranging from a $+10$ to a $-10$. The following table shows how the PMI chart for his decision might look.

**Decision: Take up a new position in London?**

| Plus | Minus | Interesting |
|---|---|---|
| Better social life ($+5$) | Have to sell house ($-6$) | |
| Change of scenery ($+4$) | More pollution ($-5$) | |
| Higher salary ($+4$) | Higher cost of living ($-6$) | |
| Better promotion opportunities ($+2$) | Less disposable income ($-3$) | |
| Meet more people ($+2$) | Can afford only an apartment ($-4$) | |
| | Further away from friends and family ($-5$) | |

Total Score: $+13 - 26 = -12$

Totaling the scores, the middle manager is left with a negative score (-12), which strongly suggests that the negatives outweigh the positives, indicating that he should not accept the promotion.

Source: McGuire, R. (2002), "Decision-making," *The Pharmaceutical Journal*, 269 (November): 647-649.

| *Use information to challenge the decision.* Don't overemphasize one piece of information over another and minimize some other piece of information.

| *Share information.* Many people have part of the information. Through information sharing, all participants become more fully informed.

Before we discuss formal decision-making models, take a moment and review the previous Management Highlight on page 91. Management Highlight, which offers you an opportunity to make a decision about and the criteria you might employ to determine what to do.

# Decision Models

## Rational Decision Model

The rational decision model is a *prescriptive model*—one that advises the decision maker how decisions should be made. The rational model bases a decision on a logical, factual analysis that leads the decision maker to an optimal decision. Though this model is often criticized for its somewhat simplistic assumptions, many decisions fit its context quite well. A simple example might be a gasoline purchase, where the objective is to get as much gas as possible for your money. Suppose that while driving home from work, you see two gas stations. One station advertises regular gasoline for $2.99 per gallon; the other is selling the same grade for $2.95 per gallon. Based on the stated decision criteria, a decision maker using the rational model would choose the station with the lower price.

Rational decision models assume that, in most cases, people attempt to make logical decisions. After analyzing the facts, the decision maker chooses the alternative that offers the greatest benefits. Rational models assume little uncertainty and risk in the decision. When using a rational model, the decision maker often relies on rules and procedures to reach a decision. A virtue of the rational decision model is its general appeal to logic; arguing with the results of a rational decision is hard. However, in situations where the assumptions of the model are clearly inappropriate, the decision can suffer.

Rational decision model is most appropriate for:

| Programmed decisions

| Situations in which all the alternatives are known

| Unambiguous decisions

| Situations in which information is readily available

| Individual decision making

A key characteristic of the rational decision model is clear factual information. Rational decision making works best in a predictable, information-rich environment. Programmed decisions fit best with the rational approach. Intuitive decision making is characterized by a gut-level response to a decision context. The parameters of an intuitive decision might be less easily quantified than those of a rational decision. The decision maker relies more on instinct or a feeling, often basing the response on experience or familiarity with the situation.

## Administrative Decision Model

The administrative decision model is a *descriptive model* of decision making—it makes more realistic assumptions about the decision context and human nature. Further, it describes how people actually make decisions, not how they *should* make them. Bounded rationality[10] refers to people

EXHIBIT 5.2

**Movie Decision Model Matrix**

| Movie Preference | You | Sam |
|---|---|---|
| Movie 1 | Y* | N |
| Movie 2 | N | Y |
| Movie 3 | Y | Y |
| Movie 4 | y | n |
| Movie 5 | n | Y |
| Movie 6 | y | Y |

*Uppercase = movies evaluated; lowercase = not evaluated.

having a limited ability to process information. We can never have available all the information needed to make the very best decision, nor can we entirely understand the complexity of the information that might be brought to bear on the situation.

The administrative decision model is most appropriate for:

| A complex decision or situation with limited information

| Programmed or nonprogrammed decisions

| Preferences of individuals or a group

| Unclear alternatives

| Greater participation through group decision making

Rather than seeking an optimal decision, the administrative model assumes that the decision maker satisfices. To satisfice (a term coined by Herbert Simon) is to seek a satisfactory decision, one that is good enough but not perfect. Often the search for information reviews familiar information or areas that are understood well. The information search culminates in a limited set of alternatives. *The first alternative that proves to be a satisfactory alternative is the one chosen.*

Think for a moment about a simple entertainment decision that you might make this weekend. You and a friend, Sam, want to go to a movie. The many different types of movies, locations, and show times are some considerations that influence your preference for a particular show. You each have different viewing preferences, but you both agree on six movies you would like to see. Together, you create a combined list of movie options (see Exhibit 5.2). The first movie appeals to you, but not to Sam; the second movie appeals to Sam, but not to you; and the third movie appeals to both of you. For you and Sam, the decision is to see the third movie in your combined list. You choose the first satisfactory alternative available, and then stop your search. The sixth movie was also acceptable, but you never got that far. Remember, the two of you did not have complete knowledge of all movies available for viewing. You made a limited search and chose the first alternative that was satisfactory to both. The result of this process is a decision that both parties agree upon, though it might not be the best decision. With more time and a greater search, you and Sam might have found the best movie-going choice.

## | Political Decision Model

Unlike rational decision making, the political decision model involves nonprogrammed decisions. The decision is often ruled by political concerns rather than by a logical analysis of the situation. The important question is not what is the best decision, but rather which alternative (decision) will be accepted by the groups involved in the decision. Most organizations have multiple goals and a variety of departments. When many different groups are empowered in

EXHIBIT 5.3

**Decision-Making Models**

|  | Rational Model | Administrative Model | Political Model |
|---|---|---|---|
| Decision Type | Programmed | Nonprogrammed | Nonprogrammed |
| Decision Outcome | Optimal | Satisficed | Negotiated |
| Degree of Objectivity | High | Moderate | Moderate to low |

the decision-making process, we can expect them to have different goal preferences—which obviously increases the potential for internal conflict in an organization. Building consensus and developing agreement among diverse groups are important to arriving at a decision that is accepted by all. The alternative selected might not be optimal, or even satisfactory, but is selected through a *negotiated* agreement among the participants. The more diverse the participants in the decision-making process are, the more political the decision will be.[11]

Political decisions require the decision maker to garner the support of the groups involved in the decision to form a powerful block or coalition of support for the final decision. On the international level in 2005, President George W. Bush and Secretary of State Condoleezza Rice actively engaged in dialogue with China, Russia, and other United States allies to develop a strategy for containing the further proliferation of nuclear weapons by North Korea and Iran. The same process occurs in organizations when the CEO needs to rally employee support to accomplish goals. For example, the decision to build a new and innovative Harley-Davidson (H-D) motorcycle with a liquid-cooled V-twin Porsche engine required CEO William Davidson to build political support inside Harley. The new bike, the V-ROD, represents the future for Harley-Davidson—a way to leapfrog over the competition. Internally, Harley was firmly locked into traditional motorcycle design and manufacturing. This new product challenged employees to go beyond their comfort zone. The V-ROD required new technology, innovative design, partnerships with Porsche and other suppliers, and the creativity of H-D employees to become a success in the marketplace. Was CEO Davidson successful at coalition building inside and outside H-D? Only time will tell, but early reports from constituent groups suggest riders like the V-ROD.

Political decisions often:

| Are nonprogrammed

| Contain ambiguous information

| Entail low consensus on goals among stakeholders

| Involve groups that can influence the decision process

Exhibit 5.3 summarizes each type of decision model, indicating the decision outcome and the degree of objectivity among decision makers.

## The Process of Decision Making

The decision-making process is a manager's mechanism for seeking some desired result. The nature and structure of the process influence how effective the decision outcome is likely to be in solving or preventing the problem. But note again that decision making is a *process* rather than a single, fixed event. In most decision situations, managers go through a series of steps or stages that help them identify the problem, develop alternative strategies, analyze those strategies, choose one among the alternatives, implement the choice, and assess the results. These stages aren't always rigidly applied, and feedback is typically conceived to be a part of each step. Identifying

EXHIBIT 5.4

**Steps in a Typical Decision-Making Process**

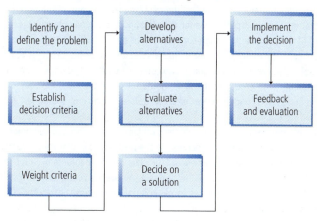

steps in the decision process is valuable; it helps the decision maker to structure the problem situation in a meaningful, rational way. A variety of models can be used. The model shown in Exhibit 5.4 depicts a typical progression of the events leading to a decision. Steps 1 through 6 of this model are the decision formulation stages; steps 7 and 8 are the decision implementation stages. The following subsections take a closer look at each step.

Understanding that *decision making is always done in the context of goals and objectives* is very important. The setting of goals and objectives is discussed in more detail in Chapter 6, "Planning," and Chapter 7, "Strategy." For now, just be aware that all behavior is goal oriented.[12] Especially in organizations, goals and objectives are needed in each area where performance influences effectiveness. If goals and objectives are adequately established, they will dictate not only what results must be achieved but also the measures indicating whether those results have been achieved. Establishing goals and objectives brings people in the organization together. And a firm's system of drawing people together is a crucial factor in its success.

**STEP 1    Identify and Define the Problem**

A **problem** is the recognition that a gap exists between a current state and a desired state. When clear goals and objectives are established, problems become apparent. To determine how critical a problem is for an organization, managers must be able to measure the gap between the level of performance specified in the firm's goals and objectives and the current level of performance. For example, a product defect rate of ten per million doesn't meet the famous "six-sigma" quality standard established by Motorola, which allows for only three defects per million.

Understanding that a problem exists is easy when there is a gap between desired results and actual results. But certain factors often lead to difficulties in precisely identifying the problem. These factors are misperception of reality, an irrational approach, and identifying only part of the problem.

**Misperception of reality.** Individual attitudes, feelings, or mental models might prevent individuals from recognizing problems. For example, prior to 1968, the Swiss dominated the world in the production of watches and clocks. They continuously improved their products and were constant innovators. Yet by 1980 their market share had collapsed, dropping from 65 percent to 10 percent. Why? Because they didn't perceive that world demand was changing from mechanical to electronic inner works. The Swiss themselves had invented the electronic quartz movement. But when Swiss researchers presented the revolutionary idea to Swiss manufacturers in 1967, it was rejected. The new movement did not fit the watch makers' mental model of watches, so they could not see its potential for the future.

**Irrational approach to the problem.** To a certain extent, this factor is seeing only one solution to the problem. The VP of engineering states "the problem is poor product design," rather than be open to the prospect that alternative explanations for the situation are equally plausible. For example, before doing any assessment of the situation, a design engineer might state, "The excessive rework we're experiencing is due to bad supplies." The engineer is suggesting a solution before the problem has been adequately identified. The supplies might indeed be low quality; but other potential explanations could also account for excessive rework, including poor employee training, outdated technology, or cumbersome process flow. Research needs to be conducted to identify the problem before suggesting solutions.

**Identifying only part of the problem.** Many problems are really manifestations of a much larger problem. For example, a retailer observes an increase in the return rate of several products. The retailer assumes that the manufacturing production process is at fault. The retailer contacts his supplier and presses for a fix. The supplier obliges but is not confident that anything was ever wrong with the product. Then, even with the supplier update, the retailer continues to experience an increase in returns. Next, sales in other products experience rapid decline, particularly in the 18–22-year-old market segment. It is not until a precipitous drop in corporate quarterly profits occurs that the CEO begins to ask hard questions. Research indicates a direct relationship between the retailer's returns and sales decline and the surge in market share growth of a new competitor. That competitor has targeted the youth market with dramatic new products, colors, and design. Additionally, the competitor's media campaign is novel, attracting customers away from the retailer. In the end, the original problem was merely a symptom of a much larger problem than increasing return rates.

## STEP 2    Establish Decision Criteria

Common criteria, or the basis on which one evaluates alternatives for a decision, might be initial cost, efficiency, and size. Analyzing cost criteria usually means that the decision maker seeks to minimize the cost associated with the initial decision. Efficiency criteria are related to the use of resources. The decision maker might specify that a decision must take into consideration the in-use cost, or what is often termed *efficiency*. Size implies space limitations need to be considered. Generally, organizations have less space as opposed to more. Criteria limitations narrow the range of decision acceptability. An acceptable decision must meet specific criteria that the decision maker sets for the decision.

Also related to setting decision criteria is the magnitude of the problem. All problems are not created equal. Deciding whether to launch a new product in response to a competitor's move is probably a more significant decision than deciding whether the employee lounge should be repainted. The process of decision making and solution implementation requires resources. Unless an organization has unlimited resources, it must prioritize its problems. This means determining the significance of each problem, which in turn involves considering three issues: urgency, impact, and growth tendency.

**Urgency.** *Urgency* is defined as the amount of time available to solve a problem. Some companies have learned that urgent problems are best dealt with at their source.[13] Ford Motor Company realized early on that the problems with the Firestone Wilderness AT tires on the Explorer sport utility vehicle (SUV) could represent a major problem.

**Impact.** *Impact* refers to the seriousness of a problem's effect. Effects might be on people, sales, equipment, or any number of other organizational variables. Whether problem effects are short term or long term, and whether the problem is likely to create other problems, are also impact-related issues. Firestone failed to recognize that the Wilderness AT problem could undermine confidence in all Firestone tires.

**Growth tendency.** *Growth tendency* refers to the future consequences of a problem. A problem could currently be of low urgency and have little impact, but if it is allowed to go unattended, its consequences could become more severe over time. The case of Ford Motor Company and Bridgestone-Firestone Tire exemplifies what can happen when a problem goes unrecognized or underestimated for too long. As the media focused daily on the rollovers caused by Firestone tires, it became clear that both Ford and Bridgestone- Firestone were at substantial financial risk from lawsuits and lack of consumer confidence in their brands—for which equity was rapidly evaporating.[14] A critical part of effective decision making is determining the problem's cause. Another critical part is determining problem significance. The more significant a problem is—as determined by its urgency, impact, and growth tendency—the more important it is that it be addressed.

**STEP 3** ## Weigh Criteria

Weighting criteria is the process of ranking the importance of decision criteria. More heavily weighted criteria are more important than those given lower weight.

**STEP 4** ## Develop Alternatives

Before reaching a decision, the decision maker needs to develop alternative solutions to the problem. This step involves examining the organization's internal and external environments for information and ideas that might lead to creative solutions to a problem. Alternatives should provide the decision maker with a range of acceptable alternatives, from which she will select only one.

**STEP 5** ## Evaluate Alternatives

Once alternatives have been developed, the decision maker must evaluate and compare them. In every decision situation, the objective is to select the alternatives that will produce the most favorable outcomes and the least unfavorable outcomes. In selecting among alternatives, the decision maker should be guided by the degree of uncertainty and/or risk associated with each alternative as well as previously established goals and objectives.

In evaluating alternative solutions, two cautions should be kept in mind. First, this phase of the decision-making process must be kept separate and distinct from the preceding step—especially in a group decision-making context. When alternatives are evaluated as they are proposed, fewer alternative solutions could be identified. If evaluations are positive, the tendency might be to end the process prematurely by settling on the first positive solution. On the other hand, negative evaluations make it less likely for someone to risk venturing what might be the best solution.

The second caution is to be wary of solutions that are evaluated as being "perfect," especially when the decision is being made under conditions of uncertainty. If a solution appears to have no drawbacks—or if, in a group setting, there is unanimous agreement on a course of action, it might be useful to assign someone to be a devil's advocate. The role of the devil's advocate is to be a thorough critic of the proposed solution. Research supports the benefits of devil's advocacy and the conflict a devil's advocate can cause, thus forcing a decision maker to reexamine assumptions and information.[15]

**STEP 6** ## Make a Decision

The purpose of selecting a particular solution is to solve a problem with the goal of achieving a predetermined objective. This means that a decision is not an end in itself, but rather only a means to an end. Although the decision maker chooses the alternative that is expected to result in achieving the objective, the selection of that alternative should not be an isolated act. If it is, the factors that led to the decision are likely to be excluded. Specifically, the steps following the decision should include implementation and follow-up.

Unfortunately for most managers, situations rarely exist in which one alternative achieves the desired objective without having some impact on another objective. If one objective is optimized, the other is suboptimized. For example, if production is optimized, employee morale might be suboptimized, or vice versa. A hospital superintendent might optimize a short-term objective such as maintenance costs at the expense of a long-term objective such as high-quality patient care. Thus the interrelatedness of organizational objectives complicates the decision maker's job.

As mentioned earlier in this chapter, the decision maker can not possibly know all the available alternatives, the consequences of each alternative, and the probability of these consequences occurring. Thus, rather than being an optimizer, the decision maker is a satisficer, selecting the alternative that meets a satisfactory standard. A satisficer is a person who accepts a reasonable alternative that is good enough but not necessarily the optimal alternative. This is not a negative comment on managerial decision making. Rather, it is a frank acknowledgment that searching for optimal solutions is usually time and cost prohibitive. Managers must be prepared to act on decisions that might have some negative implications along with the positive results they are intended to achieve.

**STEP 7** **Implement the Decision**

Any decision is little more than an abstraction if it is never implemented; further, it must be effectively implemented to achieve an objective. It is entirely possible for a good decision to be impaired by poor implementation. In this sense, implementation might be more important than the actual choice of the alternative.

In most situations, people implement decisions. Thus, the test of a decision's soundness is the behavior of the people who put it into action or are affected by it. Although a decision can be technically sound, it can easily be undermined by dissatisfied employees. A manager's job is not only to choose good solutions, but also to convert such solutions into behavior in the organization. Managers often accomplish this transformation by empowering employees to make decisions that affect work processes.

**STEP 8** **Examine Feedback and Evaluate**

Effective management involves periodic measurement of results. Actual results are compared with planned results (the objective). If deviations exist, changes must be made. If actual results do not meet planned results, changes must be made in the solution chosen, in the solution's implementation, or in the original

## NEW CAR PURCHASE DECISION

Listed below are the steps for the rational decision model and an example for a new car purchase decision. In the example, the Score and the Weighted Score yield the same decision. But, what additional information does the decision maker get by using the Weighted Score over the raw Score? Does this model makes sense to you? Identify other decisions where situations in which this type of decision-making approach would be difficult to use.

1. **State the problem.** You need to buy a new car.
2. **Establish criteria.** Determine the criteria that will serve as the basis of your evaluation.
3. **Weight criteria.** Determine the relative importance of each criterion.
4. **Develop alternatives.** Identify the comparable alternative vehicles to evaluate.
5. **Evaluate alternatives.** Perform the computation.
6. **Make a decision.** Select the vehicle with the highest score for weighted criteria.
7. **Implement the decision.** Purchase the vehicle.
8. **Evaluate feedback.** Evaluate the decision by comparing expected or advertised vehicle performance to the actual vehicle performance.

Using several structured questionnaires, one hundred and fifty students from a Midwestern university were asked to evaluate four comparable vehicles for a hypothetical purchase. Students were given manufacturers' suggested selling prices for the base models and EPA estimated MPGs for city and highway driving. Students were asked to identify criteria that were important in making their decision. Then, a list of twenty criteria was ranked by the students. The twenty were further reduced to six totally distinct criteria: price, performance, reliability, handling, safety, and styling. Next, students were asked to divide 100 points across all six criteria. This task resulted in the final weights for the criteria. Finally, a different sample of students was asked to rate each vehicle on a ten-point scale using the identified criteria. Each vehicle received a score that summated the weighted criteria. The results indicate a decision in favor of the Toyota Matrix. During class discussion, the students graded the vehicles as follows: Toyota Matrix (A), Honda Civic (A−), Chevy HHR (C+), and the Ford Focus (C−).

| | Honda Civic | Toyota Matrix | Chevy HHR | Ford Focus |
|---|---|---|---|---|
| Model Price | $14,500 | $15,200 | $12,600 | $13,900 |
| (Cty/Hwy Mileage) | (30/40) | (30/36) | (25/30) | (27/37) |
| Price (.50) | 8  8 (.50) = 4 | 9  9 (.50) = 4.5 | 10  10 (.5) = 5 | 8  9 (.50) = 4 |
| Performance (.15) | 10 10 (.15) = 1.5 | 10  10 (.15) = 1.5 | 6  6 (.15) = .9 | 8  8 (.15) = 1.2 |
| Reliability (.15) | 10 10 (.15) = 1.5 | 10  10 (.15) = 1.5 | 6  6 (.15) = .9 | 6  6 (.15) = .9 |
| Handling (.10) | 9  9 (.10) = .9 | 9  9 (.10) = .9 | 8  8 (.10) = .8 | 10  10 (.10) = 1 |
| Safety (.05) | 10 10 (.05) = .5 | 10  10 (.05) = .5 | 7  7 (.05) = .35 | 8  8 (.05) = .4 |
| Styling (.05) | 10 10 (.05) = .5 | 10  10 (.05) = .5 | 10  10 (.05) = .5 | 8  8 (.05) = .4 |
| Score | 57/60 = 95% | 58/60 = 97% | 47/60 = 78% | 48/60 = 80% |
| Weighted Score | 8.9/10 = 89% | 9.4/10 = 94% | 7.95/10 = 79% | 7/10 = 70% |

objective if it has been deemed unattainable. If the original objective must be revised, the entire decision-making process will be reactivated. The important point is that once a decision is implemented, a manager can not assume that the outcome will meet the original objective. Some system of control and evaluation is necessary to make sure the actual results are consistent with the original objectives.

Sometimes, a decision's outcome is unexpected, or it is perceived differently by different people. Dealing with this possibility is an important part of the follow-up phase in the decision process. Examining this feedback can result in different means of implementation, the selection of different alternatives, or a revised evaluation of the various alternatives.

In the Management Highlight above, examine the results of an evaluation decision to buy a new car among four different alternatives. Note how closely clumped together the final scores are. Remember, the final scores reflect the fact that these models are very similar, yet in the end one was superior to the rest.

The eight-step decision-making process is an outline of how managers in the modern workplace spend much of their time. In an increasingly technological world, even in traditional industries like agriculture and manufacturing, work has become less a matter of physical effort and more a matter of processing information. However, making effective decisions requires more than just the ability to process information and then choose among and manage alternatives. Decision making requires effective post-decision implementation, usually involving employees from various levels and functions of the organization.

Regardless of the number of steps in the decision-making process, decision making always involves people. Some decisions are made by individuals acting alone, but more often in today's organizations, as mentioned earlier in the chapter, decision making occurs in groups. The next two sections explore how decision making by individuals differs from group decision making.

# Factors That Influence Individual Decision Making

Many behavioral factors have the potential to influence decision making, and these are listed in Exhibit 5.5: individual values, personality, risk taking, and cognitive dissonance. An awareness of these factors on individual behavior enables managers to recognize their likely effect on a decision. An effective manager can then take steps to minimize the adverse impact of these forces during decision making as well as recognize when these forces are operating to influence his or her own decisions.

In a group context, many of the factors that influence individual decision making are present. Shortly we will review some of the forces that operate within a group to favor one approach rather than another.

## Individual Values

In the context of decision making, individual values are the guidelines a person uses when confronted with a choice. Most of an individual's enduring values are acquired early in life; they are a basic part of each person's personality. Other values can be acquired in adulthood and are usually associated with group membership. Examples of value orientations[16] are as follows:

- *Theoretical.* Value set based on science, order, and the discovery of truth and knowledge.
- *Economic.* Value set based on the practical, tangible, and useful.
- *Aesthetic.* Value set based on art, design, form, and harmony.
- *Social.* Value set based on human interaction and fulfillment through membership in a collective.

**KEY**TERMS

**individual values** The decision-making guidelines, mostly acquired early in life, that a person uses when confronted with a choice; a basic part of a person's personality.

**5.5**          **Influences on Decision Making**

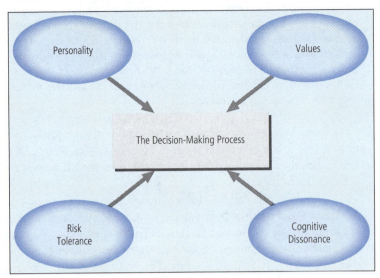

---

| *Political.* Value set based on power and dominance of others.

| *Religious.* Value set based on a higher meaning and purpose that is ethical and equitable to all.

The influence of values is evident at each step in the decision-making process. Knowing something about a person's basic value orientation tells you something about his or her decision preference. Understanding the decision maker's value orientation is particularly important when the decision is an individual decision. However, value orientation cannot be ignored in group decisions either, as people with similar value orientations often form voting blocs.

Because values play a role throughout the decision-making process, they need to be recognized by managers. As these values and beliefs are diffused and adopted throughout the organization, they become guidelines for enabling individual employees to make decisions that are in the interest of the organization.

## Personality

Making a decision is about choice and an individual's preference for one alternative over another. Personality is part of what makes us unique and is an important component of decision making. Each individual's unique personality guides preference and ultimately choices. Several studies have examined the effect of selected personality variables on the decision-making process.[17] Brim and his colleagues described how personality and situation can interact to influence the decision outcome. Brim et al. identified three sets of variables:[18] personality, the situation, and the interaction of the two. Contemporary research describes personality along several dimensions that can each have an effect on work behavior.[19] Personality variables such as introversion-extroversion, altruism, conscientiousness, ability to deal with new situations, and neuroticism can each operate in different situations to influence choice. For example, an introverted—and possibly slightly neurotic—manager decides to avoid a situation in which she is required to make a public presentation to the board of directors to make a case for an acquisition. Most of her colleagues believe that a formal presentation would be the best way to make the case for the acquisition, but she decides instead to submit a well developed position paper. In the end, the manager's personality influences the decision.

Attempting to find a decision-making profile is a risky business. According to researchers, the most important conclusions concerning the influence of these personality variables on the decision-making process are as follows:

| No one personality type is best for decision making. The Myers-Briggs type indicator is a popular personality inventory. Myers-Briggs type indicators are often used to develop insights into a persons' decision-making style. However, even Myers-Briggs cannot predict which personality type might be a better decision maker.

| Different personality factors are associated with different steps of the decision-making process.

| Gender and social status can also influence decision making. Based on these factors, the relationship of personality to the decision-making process can vary from one person to another. Thus, a person's gender and social status combine with personality to influence decision making.

## Risk Tolerance

The willingness to accept risks differs from person to person. Psychologists believe that this risk taking or risk avoiding behavior is part of an individual's personality. Risk tolerance influences decision making so strongly that researchers break it out from other personality variables and consider it separately.[20] In the same situation, a decision maker with low risk tolerance approaches the decision-making process entirely differently from a decision maker who has high risk tolerance. The person with low risk tolerance avoids risky behavior, shying away from high-risk alternatives; whereas a risk-tolerant individual views risk as an opportunity and gravitates towards high-risk alternatives. Different levels of risk tolerances in the same situation will yield different decisions. Further, many people are bolder, more innovative, and advocate greater risk taking in groups than when they are acting as individuals.

A person's risk propensity is also affected by whether potential outcomes are characterized as losses or gains. This, in turn, depends on how the decision maker frames the decision. *Framing* refers to the decision maker's perception of the decision's possible outcomes in relation to gains or losses.[21] Individuals display a greater propensity to take risks when a choice is perceived as being between losses than when it is perceived as being between gains.

## Cognitive Dissonance

The process of decision making emphasizes what occurs prior to the decision. These *pre-decision* factors, which include characteristics of the individual, characteristics of the situation, and other personal qualities, are all sources that can influence decision making. By understanding and controlling the inputs to the decision, managers can strive to be better decision makers. We also know that post-decision, a person has a tendency to revisit the basis of the choice for a decision. Marketers call this post-purchase interrogation of oneself "buyer's remorse." This *post-decision* anxiety has its roots in cognitive psychology. Recently, researchers have recognized that important individual processes are at work after a decision has been made to help the decision maker solidify the decision or take action to reverse the decision. When considerable post-decision anxiety exists, a decision maker takes action to reduce the anxiety. Such anxiety is called *cognitive dissonance.*[22] Prior to the decision, a consonance, or an agreement, existed among the attitudes, beliefs, and behavioral intentions. Cognitive dissonance is a lack of consistency among attitudes, beliefs, and behavioral intentions after a decision has been made. That is, the decision maker feels a conflict between what he believes and the consequences of his decision. As a result, the decision maker will have doubts and anxiety about his choice. Cognitive dissonance is likely to be greater when any of the following conditions exist:

- The decision is important.
- There are a number of foregone alternatives.
- The foregone alternatives have many favorable features.

Any one or all of these conditions might be present in a decision, in all types of organizations. You can expect, therefore, that cognitive dissonance will affect many decision makers across many decision opportunities.

When dissonance occurs, individuals seek to regain the consistency and harmony among attitudes and beliefs that resulted in the original decision. To do so, they might use any of the following methods to reduce their dissonance:

- Seek additional information to justify the original decision.
- Use selective perception to ignore information that does not support the decision.
- Develop an unfavorable view of alternatives not selected.
- Emphasis the positive aspects of the decision and deemphasize the negative aspects of the decision.

Not second-guessing every decision is difficult. But it is important to remember that second-guessing (or cognitive dissonance) is one of the factors that influences decision making. Also, the potential for dissonance is influenced heavily by our values, personality, and risk-taking proclivity. In addition, each factor can interact with the other. For example, there is a relationship between risk tolerance and that person's likelihood of experiencing dissonance following a decision. Both characteristics are strongly influenced by an individual's personality, perceptions, and value system, not to mention gender and social status.

## Decision-Making Style

Research indicates that people develop and use different decision styles based upon two factors: *tolerance for ambiguity* and *ways of thinking* about the decision context. Tolerance for ambiguity is a person's ability to reconcile a situation that might have multiple perspectives and interpretations. A person with a low tolerance for ambiguity has a propensity to see things in black and white. A person with a high tolerance for ambiguity is more likely to recognize a lack of clarity and not be bothered by it. Ways of thinking range from rational to intuitive. Rational decisions are factual and analytic, whereas intuitive decisions are more emotional, gut-level responses to a situation. Exhibit 5.6 shows the relationship between these key dimensions and the four common decision-making styles—analytical, directive, behavioral, conceptual—which are described in the following sections.

### Analytical Decision Maker    Analytical decision makers use a logical, analytical approach to decision making. They gather facts and other information relevant to the situation. Ambiguous situations are seen as riskier because of lack of information. Analytical decision makers assess the opportunities and risks inherent in the decision and make a rational decision based on their analysis of the situation.

EXHIBIT 5.6

**Decision-Making Styles**

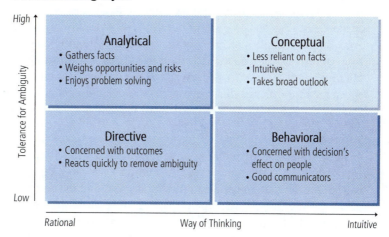

**Source:** Based on A. J. Rowe, J. D. Boulgarides, and M. R. McGrath, *Managerial Decision-making*, Modules in Management Series (Chicago: SRA, 1984), A. J. Rowe and J. D. Boulgarides, *Managerial Decision-making* (Englewood Cliffs, N.J.: Prentice Hall, 1994); G. M. Marakas, *Decision Support Systems in the Twenty-First Century*, 2nd ed. (Upper Saddle River, N.J.: Prentice Hall, 2002).

| **Directive Decision Maker** | Directive decision makers are rational and straightforward in their approach to decision making. They either avoid making decisions in highly ambiguous situations or gather more information to remove the ambiguity from the situation. The directive decision maker moves quickly to reach a final outcome.

| **Conceptual Decision Maker** | Conceptual decision makers are contemplative and tend to structure the decision situation as a mental model. They might review facts, but the focus of their thinking revolves around the cognitive assessment of the decision situation. Their assessments are often intuitive. In this process, the decision maker reviews his or her assumptions and develops alternative outcomes for different assumption sets.

| **Behavioral Decision Maker** | Behavioral decision makers are concerned with people and the affect a decision is likely to have on employees and customers. Behavioral decision makers talk to people and get their reactions to a proposed decision. They try to understand the impact of similar decisions made elsewhere. For example, a company needs to reduce employment by 500 employees. How might they best go about the employee reduction in a manner that results in the least disruption to their employee's lives?

The concept of decision styles is important; there is no single best method of making a decision. Although decision makers follow similar steps to reach a decision, their decision style often dictates the final decision. These individual differences in decision-making style mean that managers need to understand their own predominant decision-making style. Knowing your decision-making style creates an awareness of the strengths and weaknesses that our unique approach or style brings to the decision process.

## | Judgment Errors, or Bias in the Decision Process

Remember that in the administrative model, people often make decisions that are simply good enough. Sometimes that "good enough" mentality works and other times it leads people astray. To make the many decisions required at work, managers develop heuristics. A **heuristic** is a short cut that we use to simplify a decision. Often a decision heuristic works as designed and at other times acts as a bias. Several kinds of heuristics apply to judgment errors in decision making.[23]

**KEY TERMS**

**directive decision maker** A decision maker who uses a rational and straightforward approach to decision making.

**conceptual decision maker** A decision maker who is contemplative and tends to structure the decision situation as a mental model, reviewing facts, focusing on cognitive assessment (often intuitively), and developing alternative outcomes for different assumption sets.

**behavioral decision maker** A decision maker who is concerned with people and the affect a decision is likely to have on employees and customers.

| **Availability Heuristic** | Cognitive processing abilities can bias decision making in several ways. One type of bias is based on the ability to recall facts. When using the availability heuristic, an individual relies on how easily he can recall a set of facts from his memory to make a decision. For example, suppose someone asks this question: "Are there more trucks on the roads today than ten years ago?" If you regularly travel a road that is heavily congested with trucks—and you just read an article that discussed several truck accidents—you might conclude that more trucks are on the road than cars. But highway transportation data indicates that the percentage of cars and trucks on the highway has stayed about the same for the past ten years.

| **Representative Heuristic** | With the representative heuristic, one assesses a decision situation by using a stereotypical response. Imagine you are in an aircraft that is about to depart from your city. As the plane takes off, you hear a female voice announcing that the weather is clear, the destination temperature is 65 degrees, and the arrival time at the destination is 5:30 P.M. After hearing the announcement, the man in the seat behind you asks a nearby flight attendant why another flight attendant made the announcement instead of the pilot. The attendant replies that the announcement was made by the pilot; she is a woman. Obviously, the man had a stereotypic response—that all pilots are males—because he had never seen a female pilot before. He generalized from his stereotype *that all pilots are males* to reach his conclusion that the voice must be that of a flight attendant.

| **Anchoring and Adjustment** | Anchoring and adjustment is the process whereby the initial information often serves as an anchor for, or forms a lower boundary for, subsequent understanding of the situation. For example, suppose you visit three new car dealerships and the first dealership makes you an offer of $10,000 for your trade-in. That initial offer becomes that anchor point to compare the other two trade-in offers. Your expectation is set that your trade-in is worth $10,000. The second dealer offers you $11,000, and the third dealer offers you $9,500. You might describe the situation to a friend by stating that the second dealer had a high offer and the third dealer had a low offer. That $11,000 offer looks pretty good. The basis of your judgment is anchoring and adjustment from the initial offer. Now suppose that a fourth dealer in another town offers you $15,000, and you check the trade-in value on the Internet and find that $15,000 is a fair trade-in value for your area. In the end, that $10,000 set the base for what you believed the car was worth. You would have been happy with $11,000. Because of your initial anchor, it is reasonable to assume that finding out the car was worth $15,000 would be a shock. This example illustrates well that the anchoring and adjustment heuristic worked as a bias in this situation.

| **Escalation of Commitment** | Escalation of commitment is an increased commitment to a previous decision despite knowledge of contrary information.[24] Cognitive dissonance theory holds that a person's desire to reduce dissonance is also related to the desire to appear consistent to oneself. The desire to reduce cognitive dissonance becomes dysfunctional when it leads to escalation of commitment. Research has shown that individuals will escalate their commitment to a failing course of action when they view themselves as responsible for the action. According to dissonance theory, this behavior results from the individuals trying to justify that the original decision was correct by continuing support for a particular course of action.[25]

## Group Decision Making

In many organizations today, group decision making occurs in teams, task forces, and committees. Group or team decision making occurs partly because of the large volume of information needed to make effective decisions. Because group decision making involves more than one organizational member, the process builds commitment to a decision through greater member participation. Managers often have to decide whether to make an individual decision or allow the group to make the decision.[26] This is especially true for the nonprogrammed decisions that typically have the greatest outcome uncertainty and require the most creativity. Additionally, the most complex and important decisions are most often made by groups—not individuals. In many decision-making situations, problem complexity requires specialized knowledge in several different areas. Normally, the best way to get specialized knowledge in multiple areas is from an expert in each area. Further, decision acceptance is greater when a decision is made by a group.

Group decision making is not without risk. Here are several factors that contribute to increased risk and a lower-quality decision:

   | *Groupthink.* The tendency of the group to be swayed collectively can negate the benefits of group decision making.

   | *Empowerment.* Although participation generally is seen as a good thing, it allows more people in the organization access to the decision-making process. Sometimes this makes for a lower-quality decision.

   | *Corporate governance.* This dictates who can and should be part of the decision-making process. For example, corporate governance might require that a union representative be part of any decision-making committee.

   | *Politics.* Politics can occur in situations where group participants have diverse views and preferences about the decision outcome. This might lead to a decision that favors the dominant political coalition in the organization.

## | Comparing Individual and Group Decision Making

Considerable debate has centered on the relative effectiveness of individual versus group decision making. Groups usually take more time to reach a decision than individuals do. But bringing together individual specialists and experts has its benefits; the mutually reinforcing effects of their interaction often result in better decisions. In fact, a great deal of research has shown that consensus decisions with five or more participants are usually superior to individual decision making, majority vote, and leadership decisions.[27]

On the other hand, research has also found group decision making to be negatively influenced by such behavioral factors as the pressure to conform (sometimes called groupthink); the presence of a dominant personality in the group, or "status incongruity" (whereby lower-status participants are inhibited by higher-status participants and acquiesce even though they believe that their own ideas are superior); and attempts by certain participants (who are perceived to be expert in the problem area) to influence others.

Certain decisions (such as nonprogrammed decisions) appear to be better made by groups; others appear better suited to individual decision making. Exhibit 5.7 is a comparison of the group and the individual regarding specific decision-making attributes.

Groups also suffer from several common problems because of the nature of their collective interaction, including the following:

   | *Conformity.* The individual feels pressure to conform to the will of the group.

   | *Dominant personality.* One individual strongly asserts his ideas over the ideas of others in the group or takes over the group dynamics.

   | *Status differences.* Status differences between group members might give some ideas greater play.[28]

EXHIBIT 5.7

**Comparing Group versus Individual Decision Making for Five Dimensions**

| Dimension | Group | Individual |
|---|---|---|
| Knowledge | More members bring more expertise to the situation. | An individual may have greater depth and less breadth of knowledge. |
| Values | Multiple value orientation. | Single value orientation. |
| Decision quality | Research suggests that groups make better decisions than individuals. | Depends on the individual's background and experience. |
| Decision speed | Generally takes more time to process a group decision. | Generally, process time is much faster than with group decision. |
| Accountability | Locus of accountability is diffuse, making it harder to hold someone accountable. | Individual is directly accountable. |

## Group Decision-Making Methods

If groups are better suited to nonprogrammed decisions than individuals are, the manager must develop an atmosphere of group creativity. In this respect, the group decision-making process might be similar to brainstorming, in that the discussion is free-flowing and spontaneous. All group members must participate; to encourage participation, the evaluation of individual ideas must be suspended in the beginning. Still, a decision must be reached, and this is where group decision making differs from brainstorming.

When properly utilized, three techniques—brainstorming, the Delphi technique, and the nominal group technique—increase a group's creative ability to generate ideas, understand problems, and reach better decisions. Raising a group's creative capability is especially necessary when individuals from diverse sectors of the organization must pool their judgments to create a satisfactory course of action for the organization.

**Brainstorming** | Often, organizational members may not be fully aware or might not understand a situation, an idea, or how a product might be used by consumers. Brainstorming is a technique that increases knowledge about the problem and narrows the range of the problem. Brainstorming is a group technique, much like a focus group, where people with specific content knowledge are assembled to work as a group on the problem issue. The primary purpose of brainstorming is idea generation. The product of the group is a list of ideas or solutions prescribed by the problem definition. Consider this example. Suppose a company was asking itself the question, "How will people use our new product?" The organization might be concerned about product liability for unintended consumer use. The group assembled to consider this issue would brainstorm all potential product uses. Brainstorming shelters individual insecurities, such as self-consciousness, in the collective of the group. People are encouraged to speak their mind in a context where no idea is too outlandish to propose and discuss.

Here are the basic rules of brainstorming:

- Ideas are generated and evaluation or criticism is avoided. Members are encouraged to speak their mind, and no idea is considered too silly or trivial for inclusion.

- Ideas have no individual ownership; they belong to the group. This allows other members, without penalty, to make suggestions that might come in conflict with or override a previous idea.

- Ideas are prioritized, and a short list becomes the product of the group. Overlapping ideas are eliminated, or the group agrees that the list includes a specific set of ideas. Generally, the purpose of a brainstorming session is to generate ideas, not to evaluate them.

Brainstorming is commonly used in marketing, advertising, and various other fields to help generate new ideas or confirm direction. In some circumstances, however, brainstorming is less successful. Because the ideas generated are not evaluated or ranked, the groups never really conclude the problem-solving process.

**| The Delphi Technique |** The Delphi technique is a decision-making tool that relies on expert judgment in which a series of structured (directed) questionnaires are sent to the individuals (i.e., expert judges) via e-mail or by post to complete by a deadline. A staff of several people is required to solicit anonymous judgments on the topic of interest through a set of sequential questionnaires interspersed with summarized information and feedback of the opinions of participants. After a series of about three questionnaire iterations, a final report is prepared of the results of the Delphi. The structure of the Delphi requires a competent staff that can conduct a Delphi in a reasonable length of time. Delphi judges are solicited for their expertise on the topic at hand. These anonymous judges offer their expert judgment to set goals, develop priorities, or to solve a particular problem. The Delphi technique does not require the members to be in the same location. The Delphi process includes the following steps:

1. The problem or issue is defined.

2. Judges are given a series of structured questionnaires followed by summarized information of the questionnaire responses prior to the next iteration. Normally three series of questionnaire/summarized feedback documents are required.

3. A final report is compiled summarizing the conclusions and judgments of the Delphi group.

4. The final report is used as a tool by the decision maker to arrive at a decision.[29]

**| The Nominal Group Technique |** The nominal group technique (NGT) has gained increasing recognition in health, social service, education, industry, and government organizations. Researchers adopted the term nominal group technique to refer to a structured decision-making process that brings people together to make group decisions. The decision-making process is structured by rules. Thus, at first, the collection of people is a group in name only (a nominal group). The NGT begins with the facilitators assembling the group, introducing the members, providing instructions, and stating the problem. The group consists of seven to ten people who are instructed not to communicate to one another but rather to listen and follow instructions. The facilitator leads the group through the six-step process, described here:

1. A statement of the issue is presented for the group to consider. (All participants have a table, paper, and pencils readily available.) Using a PowerPoint slide that contains the issue statement is common so that everyone attending can see it.

2. Participants are allowed 15 minutes to silently generate ideas or alternatives to resolve the issue.

3. In round robin fashion, each member is asked to share one of his or her ideas with the group. The facilitator records the ideas generated by group members onto the chart or in a PowerPoint slide. Each idea on the PowerPoint slide is open for discussion, one at a time. Members can ask for clarification, but the originator of the idea is not responsible for defending it. The purpose of this step is to discuss, prioritize, and develop a list of ideas.

4. Each member is asked to prioritize items from the discussion and rank all the items from lowest to highest priority. Results are tallied and the vote is reported to the group.

5. Results are discussed for clarification, but no pressure is exerted to change the vote.

6. The final vote is taken.[30] If warranted, the list might be sent back to step four for further culling to distill the prioritize list even further.

The benefits of the nominal group technique (NGT) are that it identifies elements of the problem, encourages greater participation, and increases the likelihood of decision acceptance. However, the NGT is not perfect and has several disadvantages, including that NGT requires a trained facilitator, needs a physical environment that accommodates the seven to ten people, and works best for people with adequate writing and problem-solving skills.

Both the Delphi technique and NGT have excellent success records. There are two basic differences between them. First, in the Delphi process, all communication between participants is through written questionnaires and feedback from the monitoring staff. In NGT, communication occurs directly between participants. Second, NGT participants meet face-to-face around a table; Delphi participants are physically distant, never meet face-to-face, and are typically anonymous to one another. Practical considerations, of course, often influence which technique is used. These considerations can include the number of working hours available, costs, and the participants' physical proximity.

**CONCLUSION**

## Decision Making

Managers are decision makers. The better we understand the process of decision making, the decision context, and the factors that influence decision making, the better the decision quality will be. The trend in decision making is to encourage greater participation in decision making. Hence, we see more evidence of group decision-making opportunities that empower more stakeholders with a voice in corporate governance. Managers will always make decisions, for better or worse. But the best decisions for a situation will be made by people who not only understand the decision process, but can also apply it to achieve organizational goals.

## Discussion Questions

1. Describe an example of a typical programmed decision and a typical nonprogrammed decision in a business organization. Be sure to include an assessment explaining why your example of the decision type was appropriate to the facts of the situation.

2. Describe the differences between a rational decision, an administrative decision, and a political decision?

3. For what purpose might an organization use brainstorming in a decision-making situation?

## Video Case

### Timbuk2: CEO Sets a Course

Making decisions is a big part of any manager's job. Making the decisions that determine the direction a company will take is the job of a CEO. Mark Dwight, CEO of Timbuk2, is comfortable with this role, even though it means sometimes making unpopular decisions—or even making mistakes. Timbuk2's 45 workers tend to be young, so Dwight sees himself as the senior manager in more ways than one. "I'm the experienced executive here, and it's my charter to manage the company," he explains. "It's not a democracy. I ask the people that I think have a good perspective on [an] issue, who are affected by the issue, we discuss it, and I make a command decision based on those inputs. Hopefully, people think I make educated, informed decisions. That's my job."

Most of the decisions Dwight is referring to are nonprogrammed decisions—such as the design of a new product or the type of fabric to use. These decisions can affect sales, the brand image, and even the overall performance of the company. During one recent meeting on the new Tag Junkie bags (whose working name might be changed, requiring another decision), Dwight and his managerial staff discussed whether to invest in a costly, high-performance fabric for the bag. The cost of the fabric could potentially put the price of the bag out of reach for the average professional bike messenger. But in talking about it, the group speculated that the bag could successfully reach the motorcycle market. With night reflectors and highly durable, weatherproof fabric, the bag could be very appealing to motorcyclists—and could be offered at a higher price. Then the group discussed the working name of the product line—Tag Junkie, a term used by bike messengers and also the name of the original Timbuk2 messenger bag. Did they want to resurrect the name for the final product or try something new? The group tossed around the name Pro Series—and everyone liked the ring of it. "It sounds fast," observed marketing manager Macy Allatt. But the decision would not yet be final, because the group wanted to weigh the consequences of a name change in the bike messenger market. "Mark is the guy with the vision," says Allatt. "He will drive the decision making, but he's very open to taking input from other people. When decisions need to be made, everyone sits down and we hash it out, and when we come out of the room, we feel like we're going to make some progress."

Just about every decision facing Mark Dwight has some degree of uncertainty. He knows that he wants Timbuk2 to achieve $25 million in sales in five years; he knows he wants the firm to reach new markets such as motorcycle riders and yet rejuvenate the bike messenger market; he knows the firm needs to find new distribution channels. But there is no guarantee that a single decision is the right one. Still, Dwight believes he is ultimately responsible for deciding which way to go. "We have to make a decision and move on," he remarks. "Sometimes we make mistakes, but it's better to move to a new place than sit around and talk about it." One recent decision involved moving the production of certain bags to China to cut production costs. Despite receiving criticism for the move, particularly because so many textile factories surrounding Timbuk2's hometown of San Francisco have been closed, Dwight hung tight to his decision, insisting that transferring some production overseas would actually help the San Francisco factory stay open. So far, Dwight has been able to maintain the San Francisco plant. Increased orders for the firm's artistic Graphic Messenger Bags have actually resulted in hiring more employees at the San Francisco facility.

As a leader, Dwight doesn't mind taking the heat. "I'm a strong personality . . . It's my job to call the shots, and I can be very dictatorial about it." If he's right, future success for Timbuk2 is in the bag.

### Questions

1. What part do you think intuition plays in Mark Dwight's decision making? Why?

2. How would you categorize Dwight's leadership style? Why?

3. Using the information in this chapter, discuss Dwight's decision style and which decision model he appears most comfortable with in his daily decision making.

Sources: Company web site, http://www.timbuk2.com, accessed August 13, 2004; Brad Stone, "Homegrown," *Newsweek* (April 19, 2004): http://www.msnbc.com.

## BizFlix

### Dr. Seuss's *How the Grinch Stole Christmas*

Readers and lovers of Dr. Seuss's original tale might be put off by Ron Howard's loose adaptation of the story. Whoville, a magical, mythical land that exists inside a snowflake, features two types of life: the Whos who love Christmas and the Grinch (Jim Carrey) who hates it. Cindy Lou Who (Taylor Momsen) tries to bring the Grinch back to Yuletide celebrations, an effort that backfires on all involved. Sparkling special effects will dazzle most viewers and likely distract them from the film's departures from the original story.

This scene is an edited version of the "Second Thoughts" sequence early in the film. Just before this scene, fearless Cindy Lou entered the Grinch's lair to invite him to be the Holiday Cheermeister at the Whobilation One-Thousand Celebration. In typical Grinch fashion, he pulls the trap door on Cindy Lou who unceremoniously slides out of his lair to land on a snowy Whoville street. The Grinch now must decide whether to accept the invitation. The film continues with the Cheermeister award ceremony.

### Questions

1. What are the Grinch's decision alternatives or options?
2. What decision criteria does the Grinch use to choose from the alternatives?
3. Describe the steps in the Grinch's decision-making process.

## *Suggested Reading*

Jeffrey Pfeffer and Robert I. Sutton, "Evidence-Based Management," *Harvard Business Review* (January 2006): 4–17.

Max Bazernman and Dolly Chugh, "Decisions without Blinders," *Harvard Business Review* (January, 2006): 17–28.

Thomas Davenport, "Competing on Analytics," *Harvard Business Review* (January 2006): 29–38.

John S. Hammond, Ralph L. Keeney, and Howard Raiffa, "Hidden Traps in Decision-making," *Harvard Business Review* (January, 2006).

Jerry Useem, Julie Schlosser, Barney Gimbel, Nadira Hira, Oliver Ryan, Abrahm Lustgarten, Kate Bonomici, "How I Make Decisions," *Fortune* (June 27, 2005): V151, 106.

## *Endnotes*

1. James D. Thompson, *Organizations in Action* (New York: McGraw-Hill, 1967), 159.

2. E. Frank Harrison, *The Managerial Decision-Making Process* (Boston: Houghton-Mifflin, 1981).

3. Herbert A. Simon, *The New Science of Management Decision* (New York: Harper & Row, 1960), 5–6.

4. Paul S. Adler, "Time-and-Motion Regained," *Harvard Business Review* (January–February 1993): 97–108.

5. Alden M. Hayashi, "When to Trust your Gut," *Harvard Business Review* (February, 2001): 5.

6. Gardiner Morse, "Decisions and Desire," *Harvard Business Review* (January, 2006): 1–8.

7. Max Bazerman and Dolly Chugh, "Decisions without Blinders," *Harvard Business Review* (January 2006): 18–26.

8. Jeffrey Pfeffer and Robert I. Sutton, "Evidence-based Management," *Harvard Business Review* (January 2006): 1–12.

9. Max Bazerman and Dollu Chugh, "Decisions without Blinders," *Harvard Business Review* (January, 2006): 18–26.

10. Herbert Simon, *Administrative Behavior,* 3rd ed. (New York: Free Press, 1976).

11. Edward C. Banfield, *Political Influence* (New York: Free Press, 1961).

12. Paul Hersey and Kenneth Blanchard, *Management of Organizational Behavior* (Englewood Cliffs, NJ: Prentice Hall, 1993), 19.

13. Joann Muller, "Ford: Why It's Worse Than You Think," *Business Week* (June 25, 2001): 80–89; Muller, "Ford vs. Firestone: A Corporate Whodunit (safety crisis involving Explorer SUVs and Wilderness AT tires)," *Business Week* (June 11, 2001): 46–47.

14. Richard A. Oppel Jr., "Bridgestone Agrees to Pay $7.5 Million in Explorer Crash," *New York Times* (August 25, 2001).

15. R. A. Cozier and C. R. Schwenk, "Agreement and Thinking Alike: Ingredients for Poor Decisions," *Academy of Management Executive* (February 1990): 69–74.

16. William Guth and Renato Tagiuri, "Personal Values and Corporate Strategies," *Harvard Business Review,* 43 (1965): 123–32

17. P. A. Renwick and H. Tosi, "The Effects of Sex, Marital Status, and Educational Background on Selected Decisions," *Academy of Management Journal* (March 1978): 93–103; A. A. Abdel Halim, "Effects of Task and Personality Characteristics on Subordinates' Responses to Participative Decision-making," *Academy of Management Journal* (September 1983): 477–484.

18. Orville C. Brim, Jr., et al., *Personality and Decision Processes* (Stanford, Calif.: Stanford University Press, 1962), 46.

19. M. R. Barrick, and Michael Mount, "The Big Five Personality Dimensions and Job Performance: A Meta Analysis," *Personnel Psychology,* 44, (1991): 1–26.

20. Sim Sitkin and Laurie Weingart, "Determinants of Risky Decision-Making Behavior: A Test of the Mediating Role of Risk Perceptions and Propensity," *Academy of Management Journal,* 38, 6, (1995): 1973–92.

21. Glen Whyte, "Decision Failures: Why They Occur and How to Prevent Them," *Academy of Management Journal* (August 1991): 23–31.

22. Leon Festinger, *Theory of Cognitive Dissonance* (New York: Harper & Row, 1957), 10.

23. Bazerman, *Judgment in Managerial Decision-making,* chapter 2.

24. Barry M. Staw, "The Escalation of Commitment to a Course of Action," *Academy of Management Review,* Vol. 6, Number 4 (1981): 577–587.

25. Jerry Ross and Barry Staw, "Organizational Escalation and Exit: Lessons from the Shoreham Nuclear Power Plant," *Academy of Management Journal,* 36, 4, (1993): 701–732.

26. Victor H. Vroom and Arthur G. Jago, *The New Leadership: Managing Participation in Organizations* (Englewood Cliffs, NJ: Prentice Hall, 1988).

27. Richard A. Guzzo and James A. Waters, "The Expression of Affect and the Performance of Decision-Making Groups," *Journal of Applied Psychology* (February 1982): 67–74; D. Tjosvold and R. H. G. Field, "Effects of Social Context on Consensus and Majority Vote Decision-making," *Academy of Management Journal* (September 1983): 500–506; and Frederick C. Miner Jr., "Group versus Individual Decision-making: An Investigation of Performance Measures, Decision Strategies, and Process Losses/Gains," *Organizational Behavior and Human Decision* Processes (Winter 1984): 112–124.

28. Irving Janis, *Victums of Groupthink* (Boston: Houghton-Mifflin, 1972). Also see Graham T. Allison, *Essence of Decision: Explaining the Cuban Missile Crisis* (Boston: Little Brown and Company, 1971).

29. Andre Delbec, Andrew H. Van de ven, and David Gusstafson, *Group Techniques for Program Planning* (Glenview, IL: Scott Foresman, 1975), chapter 4.

30. Andre Delbec, Andrew H. Van de ven, and David Gusstafson, *Group Techniques for Program Planning,* (Glenview, IL: Scott Foresman, 1975), chapter 3.

# 6

# PLANNING

In the early part of the twentieth century, management theorist Henri Fayol succinctly described the functions of management as planning, organizing, leading, and controlling.[1] As a business owner, he also believed that the burdens of management could be taught to nonowners; Fayol was thus among the first to envision the role of the professional manager. So began modern management. To this day, the four core functions are rarely disputed; but not surprisingly, managers are continually challenged to change the way they plan, organize, lead, and control.

It is no accident that the first function of management is planning. Today, long after Fayol, leading management scholars continue to refer to the "primacy of planning."[2] Perhaps, because planning sets the course, common sense dictates that all other management functions must follow. Managers can then *organize* to create a structure for carrying out the plans, *lead* to motivate and engender plan participation, and *control* to ensure that plans are fulfilled as envisioned. Yes, in the final analysis, planning is seen to precede all.

This chapter examines planning as it pertains to allocating the resources of an organization as well as to using its skills, competencies, and capabilities in achieving goals. Economic success requires planning to accomplish organizational goals and objectives, but we readily acknowledge that planning often occurs without complete information. Environmental uncertainty makes planning necessary. For an organization to achieve economic success, managers somehow must cope with, and adapt to, uncertainty and change. Planning is a manager's most valuable tool for adapting to change. An organization that does not plan for the future must constantly adjust to new circumstances. For managers to have any control over the organization's direction, they must plan. Planning is proactive, allowing the organization to select the best course of action for matching its competencies with existing and future environmental opportunities. Lack of planning compels organizations to react to the actions of others. Rather than anticipating a competitive move, the organization waits for directions from the marketplace. The reactive organization is not in control; it must respond to external pressures rather than act aggressively to achieve the organization's long-term goals. Planning is the part of the management process that attempts to define an organization's future. There are different types of planning activities and different ways of putting plans together. In this chapter, you will gain an understanding of strategic, tactical, and operational plans, and then learn a six-step planning process. The chapter concludes with an overview of several planning methods, including those used in a quality-based organization.

## What Is Planning?

Planning is the process of developing action-oriented plans for achieving an organization's purpose, mission, goals, and objectives in the short term and the long term. As part of the planning process, strategic managers consider organizational, human, financial, and physical resources. They also explore opportunities and risks—including innovation, competition, and consumer demand—in the competitive marketplace. Good planning means asking tough questions about the company, customer needs, and the future. Planning guides employee behavior because it deals with future actions. In this way, planning helps organizations achieve specific results. The true test of any manager is ultimately his or her ability to achieve results (objectives and goals) consistent with the organization's values and mission. Without planning, it is impossible for organizational leaders to achieve specific outcomes.

Internally, planning is an analytical process in which organizational members chart a course of action for the organization in the years to come. Although not a flawless process, planning is necessary in order to schedule organizational actions that anticipate future needs. Even with new technological innovations, new markets, and changing consumer demographics, planning can help an organization be more competitive. Planning facilitates success by anticipating and responding to changing government demands, market conditions, and customer expectations. Effective organizational planning includes people from different areas and levels of the organization. Planning that is dominated by a few managers often lacks sufficient information and can be concerned more with the process of planning than with content or results.[3] Planning is a group activity; formal planning requires a team effort.

## Systematic Planning Occurs at Several Levels

Planning occurs at all levels of the organization. *Corporate-level* planning focuses on resource allocation issues between several divisions within the same organization. *Business-level* planning concerns how to achieve business objectives within the context of overall corporate objectives. Finally, *functional-level* planning supports specific aspects of the business level strategy, such as advertising.

To drive the planning, all three organizational levels require a rational, analytic, and systematic process that everyone understands. Like decision making, planning is most effective when it is systematic. For example, formal planning for updating the organization's personal computers requires input from many different users. These computer users must consider costs and budgets, technical specifications, and software purchases and support. Next, they will develop a plan for the timely and cost-effective acquisition of personal computers. Once the final budgets are approved, financing arrangements, delivery schedules, and operating policies can proceed. The formal planning process begins at the top of the organization but ultimately moves through the organization to include more information. In the end, the resulting plan can be evaluated to determine how successful the planning process was in achieving organizational objectives.

## Planning Involves Everyone

Effective planning requires as much information as possible to reduce uncertainty. By its very nature, planning is a complex process that must answer two questions: (1) what resources do we have, and (2) how should we use them to achieve our objectives? The first question is common across all levels; but the second question deals with allocation of resources at a much more specific level as we move down the organizational hierarchy. The time frame of the plan also varies, with the top level of the organization often looking five years into the future while the lower levels of the organization might be looking only six months ahead. Regardless of organizational level or time frame, the more that people are involved in the planning process, the more that information is available to planners. Finally, greater involvement and participation in the planning process lead to greater acceptance of the plan in the long run.

## Why Planning Is Necessary

Planning puts purpose into action. Without planning, organizations can only react to changes in the environment, technology, and customer demands. With careful planning, an organization can both anticipate and influence upcoming events.

Three characteristics of the modern organization underscore the need for planning: (1) cycle time reduction, (2) organizational complexity, and (3) global competition.

## Cycle Time Reduction

Cycle time reduction (CTR) has become a key goal for organizations. *Cycle time* refers to the length of time required to complete a process and to be ready to begin anew. For example, automobile manufacturers compete fiercely to reduce cycle time for new product development. In the 1990s, Chrysler introduced many new products. One key to the company's success was cycle time. Of the big three United States automobile manufacturers, Chrysler had the fastest new product development cycle time, bringing new offerings to market in two and one-half years. By comparison, Ford and General Motors cycle times are more than three years. Toyota leads the way with a new product development cycle time of two years. These facts indicate that time and planning often go hand in hand. The first to market has a huge competitive advantage.

High-performing, competitive organizations have realized that although economy of scale—a decrease in per-unit manufacturing cost as a result of increased size of production facilities—was formerly the key to success, today, economy of time is important. Sam Walton said that everyone thought the success of Wal-Mart was a result of placing large stores in small towns and evolving to superstores in large cities (economies of scale). In reality, he attributed Wal-Mart's success to having faster inventory turns (economy of time). Like Wal-Mart, organizations of all types are putting significant planning effort into improving functionality, reducing cycle time, and accommodating the needs of people who interact with the organization.[4]

The rise of regional air carriers JetBlue and Air Tran, among others, casts an interesting light on the concept of economy of time when you consider that their success can be attributed, in part, to attracting to their ticket windows customers who might otherwise drive to their destinations. For a closer look at how planning has helped regional carriers outperform their industry, see Management Highlight on page 115.

## Organizational Complexity

Mergers, acquisitions, restructuring, and strategic alliances all make organizations more complicated and difficult to manage. This complexity means that few organizational decisions can be made independently of other decisions. For example, design and development decisions affect production, finance, and marketing. More products and more services increase the complexity of managing daily business activities. The more markets an organization competes in, the more products it offers—and the more its competitors in the market all increase the internal complexity of their organization. For all practical purposes, before 1970 the Big Three auto organizations—GM, Ford, and Chrysler—competed among themselves. The Big Three held a commanding share of the automobile market in the United States. Now they compete among at least thirty major auto organizations worldwide. In his book *The Fifth Discipline,* Peter Senge observes that to remain competitive in the global economy, organizations must learn to be comfortable with uncertainty and complexity. Managers must develop a capacity for thinking clearly and continuously about the unknown future.[5] Planning helps organizations deal with complexity and uncertainty by providing a road map for change. With such a road map an organization can move with the forces of global competition without straying off course.

## Global Competition

Change is constant. New rivals enter the global economy each year, often dramatically affecting the existing competition. For example, because of the increasing cost of labor in the United States, many United States manufacturers have developed strategic alliances with production facilities in mainland China. Although it has increased profitability, the subsequent transfer of production to China has led to the loss of many high-paid manufacturing jobs in the

## PLANNING FOR SUCCESS: JETBLUE, AIR TRAN, AND SOUTHWEST AIRLINES

The recent problems of United Airlines and the demise of other air carriers such as Pan American and Eastern Airlines have caused financial ruin and disrupted air travel. Since the terrorist attacks of September 11, 2001, the airlines have struggled to rebuild consumer confidence while meeting strict security requirements imposed by the federal government. Airlines experiencing the most difficulty are the full-price, full-service, intercontinental air carriers. These giants have large fleets and high costs. They do business all over the world, but regularly lose money on many of the routes they serve.

Some new airlines have emerged and are capitalizing on an opportunity that major air carriers missed—the regional low-cost market. Southwest Airlines was the first to enter this market; other carriers such as JetBlue and Air Tran have since carved out different market segments.

JetBlue, which began operations on February 11, 2000, attributes its success to sound financial backing, using new planes, hiring the best people, and focusing on customer service. JetBlue offers lower fares and uses point-to-point service (i.e., no layovers), operating mainly in the eastern United States. Services include in-flight entertainment with free direct TV in each seat, security cameras, bulletproof cockpit doors, and e-ticketing.

Air Tran follows a similar low-cost strategy, with several important differences. Air Tran services a select number of United States cities from its Atlanta hub. Air Tran's feeder-service flights link Atlanta with many smaller Midwestern cities, moving travelers to and from their Atlanta hub. Their service corridor is north-to-south short runs in the East-Central region of the United States. Air Tran also services profitable regional population centers. For example, Air Tran services Central Illinois Airport in Bloomington-Normal, Illinois, linking Central Illinois to major domestic cities.

Southwest Airlines is the original innovator in low-cost regional air travel. With Dallas as its hub, Southwest pioneered low-cost, no-frills air service. At the time of this writing, it serves many cities in the continental United States. Unlike Air Tran's routes, Southwest's are limited to the continental United States.

The 1978 deregulation of the airline industry was supposed to be a boon for air travelers. Deregulation has resulted in lower airfares; but low fares also mean less service and more restrictions. The airlines industry is complex. Yet the experiences of the major air carriers over the past quarter century and the after-effects of deregulation have created new opportunities. New airlines have emerged, with new plans for meeting consumer airline needs. The modern breed of air carriers offers consumers what they want—low air fares and on-time availability. Success in the airline industry for JetBlue, Air Tran, and Southwest began with a new plan.

Source: Adapted from: Wall Street Journal, "Air Tran Swings to Third Quarter Profit." 10/24/2002; JetBlue Prospectus, 2002; A Closer Look at Airlines; available at http://airtran.com, http://jetblue.com, http://southwest.com, and ConsumerReport.org, 2003.

**EXHIBIT 6.1**

### Global Competition Requires More Planning

| Effect of Global Competition | Examples |
| --- | --- |
| New markets | Eastern European countries (such as Russia and Bulgaria); China, Korea, and Japan; India and Southeast Asia; and many Latin American countries all represent vast new markets. |
| Greater customer diversity | Customers in different countries have different needs and wants. The goal of the global organization is to compete globally, yet respond to local needs. Customers are no longer seen as one homogeneous group. |
| Increased quality and lower cost | New markets have an effect on costs. Sometimes they reduce costs with lower labor costs; at other times they increase costs with higher transportation costs. Increased information created a new awareness in customers to demand higher quality products, forcing corporations to respond. |

United States. In a global economy, new customers, new markets, and new competitors can come from across the hemisphere. They are no longer just in our own backyards, and they pose both opportunities and competitive threats for many organizations. Exhibit 6.1 summarizes the effects of global competition on the planning function. The domestic automobile industry is an excellent example of the global competitors offering superiors products while competing on a lower price structure than domestic manufacturers. The next Management Highlight describes some of the occurrences in the domestic automobile industry over the last quarter century. See if you can describe the plan that each of the three automobile manufacturers implicitly followed to better position their company in a dynamic global environment.

## ARE GM AND FORD PLANNING FOR THE FUTURE OR REACTING TO IT?

General Motors (GM) and Ford are in a quandary. Both companies are ham-strung with high production costs, the inability to produce a high-quality fuel efficient small car, and business models driven by year-end incentives. The new big three now include: GM, Toyota at #2 (overtaking Ford's long standing #2 position), and Ford at #3. The high cost of fuel and competitive pressure from international automobile manufacturers have left GM and Ford with a surplus of large gas-guzzling vehicles in a market that demands fuel efficient small cars. The result for domestic auto manufacturers is an ever-decreasing share of the domestic market. Rising costs and lower productivity coupled with a decrease in demand have resulted in losses for GM and Ford in the first half of 2006.

**GM Hourly Labor Force 1991–2004**

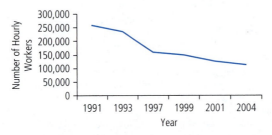

The culprits are two-fold: product and cost. GM and Ford have more production capacity than they need. Most industry analysts agree that automobile manufacturers need to operate at 90 percent capacity to make money. In addition, GM's labor cost is $72/hr, Ford's is $68/hour, and Toyota's is $45/hr in United States domestic plant production. GM estimates its healthcare costs at $1100/vehicle; at Toyota, healthcare costs are in the range of $200–$300/vehicle. Layoffs and plant closings in the United States have resulted in 50 percent fewer production workers than in 1990. To reduce labor and production costs, GM and Ford produce vehicles in Mexico and Canada. In particular, low-wage Mexico offers a substantial cost advantage with lower labor rates, healthcare costs (going forward), and technological efficiency of new plants built by GM and Ford. In fact, GM and Ford produce large high-profit SUVs and pickup trucks in Mexico for export back to the United States. Finally, pension costs are very high for GM and Ford companies. For every one worker on the assembly line, GM has three retired workers drawing a pension.

### Assignment

It is apparent from the facts presented that GM, Ford, and Toyota have each planned for the future. However, their plans were changed by the competition. For each manufacturer, describe how plans (strategy) have changed over the past 25 years. Use the facts presented in this Management Highlight and search the Internet for the latest news on the big three: GM, Ford, and Toyota.

### CHRONOLOGICAL FACTS 1980–2006: GM, FORD, AND TOYOTA

| Date | GM | Ford | Toyota |
|---|---|---|---|
| January 1980 | GM market share 44%. | Ford market share 23% | Toyota market share under 7%. |
| January 1988 | | | Toyota opens a 2000,000-unit plant in Georgetown, Kentucky. |
| January 1998–2003 | GM reduces U.S. workforce and invests in production facilities in Canada and Mexico. | | |
| June, 2005 | GM announces plans to cut 25,000 jobs, or 17% of its workforce. | | |
| November, 2005 | GM announces it plans to cut an additional 5000 hourly jobs for a total of 30,000 jobs, and close twelve plants. | | |
| January, 2006 | | Ford plans to cut 30,000 jobs over the next five years. | |

| Date | GM | Ford | Toyota |
|---|---|---|---|
| February 2006 | Improved quality but still considered average by *Consumer Reports* and J.D. Powers. | Reliability varies from product to product. High on the Lincoln Town car, low on the F-150. | Consistently ranks high in reliability. |
| June 2006 | | Announces plans to invest $9.2 billion to revamp and expand three production facilities in Mexico. | |
| July 2006 | GM market share drops to all-time low of 22%. | Ford loses #2 standing to Toyota. Ford drops to 15.3% market share. | For the first time, Toyota (16%) overtakes Ford as the #2 automobile manufacturer in the U.S. Daimler-Chrysler (10.2%) is #4. |
| August 2006 | | Ford announces the plan to idle plants cutting production by 21% in the fourth quarter of 2006. | |

Sources: Chris Isadore, "GM to Cut 25,000 Jobs by 2008," CNN (June 7, 2005); Amy Joyce, "Planned Closings Stun GM Employees" *Washington Post* (November 22, 2005); Alex Trotter, "Ford's Fight for Survival," *Fortune* (January 20, 2006); Andrew Brown, "A Surprising Ford-GM Face Off," *Fortune* (June 10, 2005); Christine Thierney, "Big 3 Market Share Dips to All-Time Low," *Detroit News* (January 5, 2005); Chris Isidore, "Ford slashes production. Automaker to have 10 plants idled for significant periods during the rest of the year as it cuts fourth-quarter output 21% from prior-year level," CNNMoney.com (August 18, 2006).

# Benefits of Planning

Planning is beneficial for all organizations; specifically, planning (1) coordinates effort, (2) identifies priorities and creates action and change, (3) defines performance standards, and (4) develops managerial skills and talent. Formal planning charts a course and communicates strategic intent to employees and other external constituents.

## Coordinates Effort

Management exists because the work of individuals and groups in organizations must be coordinated, and planning is one important technique for coordinating effort. An effective plan specifies goals and objectives for the total organization as well as each of its parts. Successful planning communicates to all levels of an organization their roles in attaining organizational goals and objectives. By working toward planned objectives, each level contributes to and is compatible with the entire organization's goals.

## Identifies Priorities and Creates Action and Change

An effective plan prioritizes activities. What is most important? What is least important? What needs to be done first? Planning answers these questions and others. Next, planning creates action and prepares an organization for change. Plans create an expectation for results. When the plans have been in place for a reasonable amount of time, results are expected. Financial results are a typical outcome of a plan, for example, increased sales or increased profits. However, the longer the time between completion of a plan and accomplishment of an objective, the greater the necessity to include contingency plans. If management considers the potential effect of a change, it can be better prepared to deal with it. Most organizations recognize that change is inevitable, but not all of them succeed in negotiating change. History provides vivid examples of the result of failing to prepare for change. Over the past decade, the collapse of many banks, savings and loans, and airlines has been largely a result of lack of preparedness.

## Defines Performance Standards

Plans create what the psychologists call behavioral expectations. In management parlance, expected behaviors are performance standards. As plans are implemented throughout an organization, the objectives and courses of action assigned to each person and group are the bases for standards that can be used to assess actual performance. In some cases, the objectives provide the standards. Managers' performance can be assessed by how close their units come to accomplishing their objectives. In other cases, the actions performed are judged against standards. A production worker can be held accountable for doing a job in the prescribed manner.

Competency-based performance is another way to ensure consistent employee response by requiring that employees performing a particular job have certain competencies, meaning a set of skills, behaviors, or other job requirements. These job-specific competencies become the basis for human resource planning, including screening, hiring, training, and compensation. Competency-based performance requires managers to complete the following activities:

- Describe the purpose of the job.
- Identify job outcomes.
- Define performance standards for each outcome.
- Identify barriers to meeting performance standards.
- Use training to enhance performance to meet standards.
- Train to achieve performance standards.[6]

Planning helps managers develop performance standards or competencies based on organizational goals and objectives. Without planning, performance standards are difficult to define, and those standards developed might be contrary to the organization's values and mission.

## Develops Managerial Skills and Talent

Planning involves managers and workers in high levels of intellectual activity. Planning is conceptual and forward-looking; it requires intelligence, experience, and a risk-taking nature. Those who plan must be able to deal with abstract ideas and voluminous information. Planning requires contingency analysis and scenario development. Using all available information, managers need to integrate what is known and develop alternative scenarios about what is unknown. One way to think about it is that planning helps managers "learn the future" before it happens.

- *Planning creates action.* Through planning, the organization's future can be improved if its managers take an active role in moving the organization toward that future. Thus, planning implies that managers should be proactive and make things happen rather than be reactive and let things happen.

- *Planning develops conceptual skills.* The act of planning sharpens managers' ability to think as they consider abstract ideas and possibilities for the future, and it reinforces the planning cycle as objectives are met through systematic actions. Thus, both the result and the act of planning benefit the organization and its managers. Through planning, managers can develop their ability to think futuristically. And, to the extent that their plans lead to effective actions, their motivation to plan is reinforced.

## Criticisms of Planning

Does planning work? Critics contend that the greatest output of formal planning is unused plans. For a variety of reasons, plans cannot always guide goal attainment. The external environment has a lot to do with the success of formal planning. Competition as well as the

**KEY** TERMS

**performance standards** In management parlance, behavioral expectations created by plans, based on the objectives and courses of action that are assigned to persons and groups and that are the bases for standards used to assess actual performance.

**competency-based performance** A way to ensure consistent employee response by requiring that the employee performing a particular job has certain competencies.

structure and dynamic nature of the industry might influence plans more than the formal planning process.

## Competition

You cannot always predict competitive actions. For instance, the introduction of a new product by a competitor might negate a year's worth of planning. In another wasteful situation, simply the lack of internal agreement among planners wastes time and resources that are better spent on other value-creating activities.

## Dynamic Environment

According to the critics, another more ominous reason that planning does not work is the dynamic nature of the industry. A company might develop plans in one direction only to find the market is moving in a different direction. As the company quickly shifts production to follow the market, their planning is now driven by short-term market trends. Although the company might be financially successful in the long term, its formal planning had nothing to do with its success.

Regardless of the criticisms of planning, it would be foolhardy to operate a business and forgo the potential benefits of planning. Lack of planning leads to a business failure more often than flawed planning does.

# Types of Planning

This section examines the different types of planning. First, we discuss the scope and timing of plans. Then we will differentiate between strategic, tactical, and operational planning. The section concludes with a comparison of single-use and standing plans.

## Scope and Timing

As we know, not all plans are created equal. Plans vary in three important ways: scope, time frame, and level of detail. For example, a fixed deadline makes the time frame a key facet. Each facet should be analyzed to determine its potential impact on the plan. The planning process takes into consideration these aspects of scope and timing:

- Scope refers to the range of activities (e.g., budgeting, human resources) covered by a plan.

- Time frame is the period considered by the plan that includes the short term, the intermediate term, and the long term.

- Level of detail concerns the specificity of the plan. All plans must be specific enough to direct actual decisions, but multiple contingencies and uncertain futures require some plans to be more general than, for example, a mattress factory's production schedule for the coming month.

## Strategic, Tactical, and Operational Planning

The type of planning process followed is determined by the goals and/or objectives to be achieved through the plan. Broad, long-term goals require strategic planning, but short-term goals with more precise objectives call for greater operational planning. Tactical planning falls somewhere between strategic and operational planning, as described in the following list:

- Strategic planning (discussed in Chapter 5, "Decision Making") is comprehensive, long-term (more than five years), and relatively general. Strategic plans focus on the broad, enduring issues for ensuring the organization's effectiveness and survival over many years. A strategic plan typically states the organization's mission and might describe a set of goals to move a company into the future. For example, it might establish a mission of market dominance in a particular product area, and set a goal to penetrate new markets based on targeted consumer research and development work.

| Tactical planning develops more specific actions or activities to implement parts of the strategic plan. It is more narrow, intermediate-term (two to five years), and specific than strategic planning. Tactics deal more specifically with a range of options available to implement a strategy. Tactical plans usually involve short-term methods of implementation such as advertising or new product introduction.

| Operational planning is focused, short-term (fewer than two years), and specific. Operational planning translates the tactical plan into clear numbers, specific steps, and measurable objectives for the short term. Operational planning requires efficient, cost-effective application of resources to solving problems and meeting objectives.

## | Single-Use versus Standing Plans

As discussed in earlier chapters, managers seek to reduce uncertainty. The planning process helps uncertainty reduction by developing a sequence for completing work. In general, work falls into two categories: it is either unique or repetitive. Work that is unique requires different planning considerations than work that is repetitive in nature. Plans are needed that consider both unique activities as well as repetitive or reoccurring activities.

The time frame for a plan typically takes the form of either single-use or standing plans. Single-use plans have a clearly specified time frame for their usefulness. For example, a task force might be established to plan the development of a new product. This single-use plan will include detailed goals and objectives, but it becomes obsolete when the product has been developed. Then the organization has no further need to consult that plan.

In contrast to the single-use plan, standing plans guide repetitive situations. A standing plan makes decision making faster, easier, and more consistent from one decision to the next because individuals armed with the same information often make quite different decisions. For ethical, strategic, and legal reasons, organizations need to limit individual decision-making discretion. To do so, organizations use standing plans to limit human behavior by using the following:

| A policy is a guideline that describes expected behavior in a specific situation or the rules that guide decision making. An example policy in a healthcare institution might be a policy for the proper retrieval and storage of medical records.

| Procedures help define rules that apply to a specific policy. In our healthcare example, the procedure used for medical records retrieval and storage might require that a digital copy of each paper document in the patient's file be maintained online for a period of five years; after five years, the patient's medical records are archived to offline storage.

| A method describes a particular sequence of activities to accomplish an objective. Generally, a manager can pick one of several methods for accomplishing an activity. If the organization prefers using one method over another, a policy manual will communicate which method to use in a specific situation.

Here is a good example of a standing plan for a hotel restaurant: For many travelers, hotels are homes away from home. Assume that a hotel's managers know their guests typically eat 50 percent of their dinners in the hotel restaurant. Based on an average occupancy rate of 65 percent,

EXHIBIT 6.2    **The Planning Process**

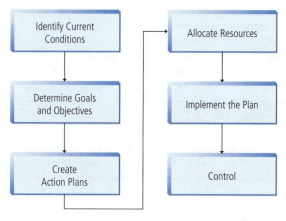

the hotel restaurant will need to prepare for a minimum of 350 meals each evening. The standing plan identifies the following allocation: 100 meals with a beef entrée, 100 with a turkey or chicken entrée, 100 low-calorie combination entrées, and 50 meals with a pork entrée. Remember that effective standing plans prove correct over the long term and can be modified if additional information becomes available.

## Steps in the Planning Process

The planning process is very much like the decision-making process presented in Chapter 5. It consists of six steps: (1) identify current conditions, (2) determine goals and objectives, (3) create action plans, (4) allocate resources, (5) implement the plan, and (6) control. This six-step process does not distinguish among the different types of plans just discussed. Instead, it is generally applicable to all types of plans, differing in the issues considered, as well as in specificity, scope, and time frame. Exhibit 6.2 above illustrates this process, and the following sections describe each step more fully.

**STEP 1**

**planning process** A six-step process: (1) identifying current conditions, (2) determining goals and objectives, (3) creating action plans, (4) allocating resources, (5) implementing the plan, and (6) control.

**competitive benchmarking** Standards for performance based on what other successful organizations have been able to achieve.

### Identify Current Conditions

Before goals and objectives can be established, the current state of the organization must be assessed. In strategic planning, for example, this assessment includes looking at the organization's resources as well as market trends, economic indicators, and competitive factors. Strategic planning takes a broad view of the organization's internal and external environments.

In operational and tactical planning, a manager's assessment of current conditions focuses less on trends and more on hard information about cash flow, market share, employee turnover ratios, and so on. In contrast to strategic planning, operational planning focuses on how to achieve specific goals and objectives.

Understanding the current conditions requires participation. That is, managers must seek out information from a broad base of organizational constituencies—for example, sales, engineering, manufacturing, and finance. Although each organizational unit may have a different perspective, managers must consider all viewpoints in order to accurately assess the organization's current situation.

Competitive benchmarking is another approach to assessing current conditions that's widely used among organizations. Benchmarking sets standards for performance based on what other successful organizations have been able to achieve. Benchmarking is one tool that provides insights into new opportunities.

**STEP 2**   **Determine Goals and Objectives**

Once current conditions are assessed, goals and objectives can be set. Managers often use these two terms interchangeably, but distinguishing between them is useful. Goals are defined as future states or conditions that contribute to the fulfillment of the organization's mission. Goals express relatively intermediate criteria of effectiveness. They can also be stated in terms of production, efficiency, and satisfaction. Customer satisfaction and productivity become workplace reality only when employees choose day-to-day behaviors that support the organization's ideals and goals. To achieve business goals, employees must understand those goals as a framework in which to perform their jobs, something that tells them which tasks are to be performed and at what level.

Objectives are short-term, specific, measurable targets that must be achieved to accomplish organizational goals. For example, an organization sets a goal of $1.2 million dollars in sales for the fiscal year. It also sets short-term objectives of $300,000 per quarter (every three months). The short-term quarterly objectives serve as benchmarks along the road to goal attainment. Failure to meet an objective signals that the goal might be unattainable. For objectives to be valuable they must be relevant, challenging, and direct employee action and behavior. Managers plan not only to determine the priority and timing of objectives but also to resolve any conflicts between objectives.

**Priority of Objectives.** It is entirely possible for an organization to have multiple goals and objectives contributing to its mission. In fact, some writers insist that the old profit-centered enterprise needs to be replaced in a postindustrial society by "multipurpose" institutions that involve employees, customers, and the public as well as investors in establishing multiple goals.

Managers always face alternative objectives. To allocate resources in a rational way, a manager must establish priorities and distinguish between objectives that are mission critical (higher priority) and those that are not. Once this distinction has been made, the manager may still be faced with the need to prioritize among the *mission-critical* objectives, because time and resources will not allow all objectives to be accomplished at once. At that point, the manager might have to seek input from others in the organization. Ultimately, however, the manager must set priorities for the organization and be prepared to carry them out.

**Conflicts among Objectives.** At any time, stakeholders—such as shareholders (owners), employees (including unions), customers, suppliers, creditors, and government agencies—are all concerned with different aspects of the organization. The process of establishing objectives and setting priorities must not overlook these interest groups, and plans must incorporate and integrate their interests. The form and weight to be given to conflicting objectives is a matter of managerial judgment. Common planning horizon trade-offs are displayed in Exhibit 6.3.

Managers must consider the expectations of the diverse groups on whom the organization's ultimate success depends. For example, present and potential customers hold power over the organization. If they are unhappy with the price and quality of the organization's products, they withdraw their support (stop buying). Suppliers can disrupt the flow of materials to express disagreement with the organization's activities. Government agencies can enforce compliance with regulations. Managers must recognize these interest groups and their power to affect the organization's objectives.

Balancing the concerns of dramatically different interest groups is difficult. However, successful organizations appear to consistently emphasize profit-seeking activities that maximize stockholder wealth. This is

**KEY**TERMS

**goal** A future state or condition that contributes to the fulfillment of the organization's mission.

**objective** Short-term, specific, measurable target that must be achieved to accomplish organizational goals.

**EXHIBIT 6.3**

**Planning Horizon and Conflicting Objectives**

| Short Term | Long Term |
| --- | --- |
| Profit | Growth |
| Efficiency | Quality |
| Daily production | Future growth |
| Market penetration | Market development |
| Stability | Growth |
| Low risk | Risk |
| Cost | Greater service |

not to say that successful organizations seek only profit-oriented objectives, but rather that they are clearly more important than other objectives.

**profitability objectives**
Objectives measured in terms of the ratios of (1) profits to sales, (2) profits to total assets, and (3) profits to capital (net worth), each measuring and therefore evaluating a different yet important aspect of profitability.

**marketing objectives**
Objectives used to measure performance relative to products, markets, distribution, and customer service, with focus on prospects for long-term profitability in terms of market share, sales volume, the number of outlets carrying the product, and the number of new products developed.

**productivity objectives**
Efficiency objectives directly measured by means of ratios of output to input; also used for comparisons across functional areas.

**physical and financial objectives** Objectives that reflect the organization's capacity to acquire resources sufficient to achieve its objectives; measured by means of numerous accounting measures, such as liquidity measures, and inventory turnover.

**quality objectives**
Objectives measured by physical characteristics of the product, or service, or that can be assessed in terms of a psychological customer perception of the product.

**planning values** The underlying decision priorities used in determining planning objectives and making decisions.

**Measuring Objectives.** Objectives must be clear, achievable, and measurable to be effective. In fact, many people believe that specific, measurable objectives increase the performance of both employees and organizations, and that difficult objectives—when employees accept them—result in better performance than easier objectives. In practice, effective managerial performance requires establishing objectives in every area that contributes to overall organizational performance.

Here are some measurements used to quantify objectives in general business areas:

- Profitability objectives include the ratios of (1) profits to sales, (2) profits to total assets, and (3) profits to capital (net worth). Managers have a tendency to emphasize the ratio of profits to sales as an important measure of profitability. Both quantities in this ratio are taken from the income statement, which organizations generally regard as a better test of performance than the balance sheet. The measures are not mutually exclusive. All three ratios are profitability objectives because each measures, and therefore evaluates, different yet important aspects of profitability.

- Marketing objectives measure performance relative to products, markets, distribution, and customer service. They focus on prospects for long-term profitability. Thus, well-managed organizations measure performance in such areas as market share, sales volume, number of outlets carrying the product, and number of new products developed.

- Productivity objectives are measured with ratios of output to input. Other factors being equal, the higher the ratio, the more efficiently inputs are used. In this way, an organization's efficiency is measured directly. This measure of productivity is also used for comparisons across functional areas.

- Physical and financial objectives reflect the organization's capacity to acquire resources sufficient to achieve its objectives. Measurement of physical and financial objectives is comparatively easy because numerous accounting measures can be used. Liquidity measures—such as the current ratio, working capital turnover, debt/equity ratio, and accounts receivable—as well as inventory turnover can be used in establishing objectives and evaluating performance in financial planning.

- Quality objectives have become increasingly important in organizations. Quality can be a measure of physical characteristics of the product or service, or it can be assessed as a psychological customer perception of the physical product. To measure service quality, A. Parasuraman, Valerie Zeithaml, and Leonard Berry offer ten dimensions that define customer satisfaction: access, communication, competence, courtesy, credibility, reliability, responsiveness, security, tangibles, and knowing the customer.[7] In the final analysis, quality is the capability to meet or exceed customer expectations.

**Planning Values.** Planning values are the underlying decision priorities used in determining planning objectives and making decisions. What is called for is a system-wide approach involving changes in a company's fundamental operations, beliefs, and values.[8] All departments act in unison to align department objectives with corporate goals. As you will see in the next chapter, an organization's mission and core values should direct action at all levels.

Harvard business professor David Garvin identified eight planning values that make up a quality-based system: performance (primary operating characteristics, e.g., speed), features (supplements to performance), reliability (no malfunctioning or need for repair), conformance (to established standards), durability (product life), serviceability (speed and ease of repair, if needed), aesthetics (appeal to taste, looks, feel), and perceived quality (customer perception).[9]

Also important to note is that planning values reflect the realities of the internal and external environments. Internal considerations are people, processes, and practices that promote quality and continuous improvement. External considerations include customer satisfaction, supplier quality and cost, and government constraints.

**STEP 3**

### Create Action Plans

To achieve its objectives, an organization needs to create action plans. Actions need to be specified prior to implementation, as part of the planning process.

Actions are specific, prescribed means that are developed to achieve objectives. Such actions determine success or failure in meeting objectives. Planned courses of action, called strategies or tactics, are usually differentiated by scope and time frame (described earlier). In any case—and whatever your organization calls it—an action plan is directed toward changing a future condition; that is, achieving an objective.

Sometimes managers can choose among alternative actions. For example, productivity increases can be achieved in various ways, including improved technology, employee training, management training, reward systems, and improved working conditions. In such cases, managers must select the most effective alternative. Often, top managers who are planning for the total organization have before them several possible courses of action. As the plan becomes more localized to a simple unit in the organization, the pool of alternatives tends to decrease, yet become more familiar.

The future is fraught with uncertainty. To reduce uncertainty, managers develop forecasts for the future. Forecasting is the process of using past and current information to predict future events. Armed with a forecast, an organization attempts to determine the likely outcomes of alternative courses of action. For example, a sales forecast would include past and current information about the organization's product, price, advertising, and cost of goods sold. External conditions to be measured include product demand, price of competing products, consumer income levels, consumer credit card interest rates, and other measures of local economic activity. Forecasts can also be useful for predicting important internal conditions, including hiring requirements, factory space needs, employee training expenditures, and healthcare costs.

**STEP 4**

### Allocate Resources

The fourth step in the planning process is allocating resources. Resources are defined as the financial, physical, human, time, or other assets of an organization. Resources are also known as *factors of production.* In creating product value, highly productive organizations use their capital, human, and material resources more effectively than do less productive organizations.

Expenditure of resources is usually controlled by use of a budget. A budget is an allocation of resources to an activity, account, or unit in the organization. For example, as part of the plan to bring a new product to market, a budget is likely to include salaries, materials, facilities, travel, and other resources. A good budget recognizes and allocates the needed resources to meet an objective.

Budgeting is both a planning technique and a control technique. As a planning technique, budgeting serves to allocate resources among competing objectives. As a control technique, budgeting compares initial allocations to actual expenditures. Often budget overruns occur that require corrective action by management.

To appreciate the complexity of the budgeting process, look at the flowchart in Exhibit 6.4. The sales budget plays a key role, as you can see by its location at the top of the chart. All other budgets are related to it either directly or indirectly. The production budget, for example, must specify the materials, labor, and other manufacturing expenses required to support the projected sales level. Similarly, the marketing budget details the costs associated with the sales level projected for each product in each sales region. Administrative expenses also must be related to the predicted sales volume. In the final step of the budgeting process, projected sales and expenses are combined to result in the financial budget, which consist of formal financial statements, inventory budgets, and the capital additions budget.

**Flexibility in Budgeting.** Forecast data are based on assumptions about the future. If these assumptions prove wrong, the budgets are inadequate. So the usefulness of financial budgets depends mainly on how flexible they are regarding changes in conditions. Organizations can achieve flexibility in two principal ways: variable budgeting and moving budgeting.

- Variable budgeting provides for the possibility that actual output deviates from planned output. It recognizes that variable costs are related to output, while fixed costs are unrelated to output. Thus, if actual output is 20 percent less than planned output, it does not follow that actual profit will be 20 percent less than that planned. Rather, the actual profit varies, depending on the complex relationship between costs and output.

EXHIBIT 6.4

**The Budgeting Process**

| Management Objectives |
| --- |

| Sales Budget | Other Income |
| --- | --- |
| • Quantity<br>• Dollar amount | • Interest<br>• Misc. income |

Less

| Production Budget | Marketing Budget | Administrative Expense Budget | Misc. Budget |
| --- | --- | --- | --- |
| • Units produced<br>• Cost of material<br>• Direct labor<br>• Factory overhead | • Promotion costs<br>• Selling expenses<br>• Advertising | • Each department | • Interest on loans |

Results in

| Financial Budget |
| --- |
| • Balance sheet |

**Source:** James H. Donnelly, Jr., James L. Gibson, and John M. Ivancevich. *Fundamentals of Management,* 8th ed. Homewood, IL: Richard D. Irwin (1992): 157. Used with permission.

- **Moving budgeting** entails the preparation of a budget for a fixed period (say, one year) with periodic updating at fixed intervals (such as one month). For example, a budget is prepared in December for the next twelve months (January through December). At the end of January, the budget is revised and projected for the next twelve months (February through January). In this manner, the most current information is included in the budgeting process. Drawing from recent experience, managers constantly revise the premises and assumptions on which the budget is based. Moving budgets have the advantage of allowing for systematic reexamination; they have the disadvantage of being costly to maintain.

Although budgets are important instruments for implementing an organization's objectives, they must be viewed in perspective as one item on a long list of demands for a manager's time.

**Criticisms of the Budgeting Process.** The major criticism of the budgeting process is its rigidity. Budgeting is often inflexible; once resource allocations are made, they are hard to change. This is largely a result of the dual nature of budgeting as both a planning technique and a control technique. On the planning side, resource allocations can be changed; but on the control side, too much change in allocation makes control impossible. Further, by strictly adhering to a planning process that relies on budgeting to allocate numbers and dollars, companies tend to overlook critical variables such as quality, customer service, and technological change. This inflexibility makes adapting to change hard for an organization, which is necessary for long-term competitive success.

Information is a useful resource in the budgeting process and needs to be allocated or distributed to members of the organization. The best decisions are made with more rather than less information. Information is perhaps the most important resource in modern, knowledge-based organizations. Without full access to the company's information—cost and market data, product developments, and so on—employees cannot be expected to help in planning.

**STEP 5**

### Implement the Plan

**Implementation** concerns the activities involved in delegating tasks, taking action, and achieving results. Without effective implementation, the four preceding steps of the planning process are pointless.

Implementation means using resources to put a plan into action. In small businesses and entrepreneurial ventures, the manager often carries out each step of the planning process, including implementation. In most large organizations, however, the manager must implement a plan through others by motivating them to carry out the plan, rewarding them for successful performance, and redirecting them when their actions lead to outcomes that differ from the objectives. Managers have three ways to implement plans through others: authority, persuasion, and policies.

**Authority.** Authority accompanies the position, not the person. In an organization, those in authority have the right to make decisions and to expect that subordinates will comply with those decisions. A manager with authority can expect employees to carry out a plan as long as it does not require illegal or unethical behavior. Authority is often sufficient to implement simple plans, but a complex plan can seldom be implemented through authority alone.

**Persuasion.** Persuasion is the process of selling a plan to those who must implement it, communicating relevant information so that those individuals understand possible implications. Persuasion requires convincing others to accept a plan based on its merits rather than on the manager's authority. Using persuasion has its drawbacks. What happens when persuasion fails? If the plan is crucial, management must then implement it by use of authority (pulling rank). Managers who have failed once in using persuasion might be well advised to limit its use in the future.

**Policies.** Policies are written statements reflecting a plan's basic values and providing guidelines for selecting actions to achieve objectives. When plans are expected to be rather permanent, policies are developed to implement them. Standard operating procedures (SOPs) are a typical example of formal guidelines used by workers and managers to make consistent decisions across consistent situations. Effective policies have these characteristics:

- *Flexibility*—A policy achieves a balance between rigidity and flexibility. In quality-based organizations, policies always leave some room for workers at all levels to exercise their discretion.

- *Comprehensiveness*—A policy must cover multiple contingencies. The degree of comprehensiveness depends on the scope of action controlled by the policy itself. Narrow issues require narrow policies.

- *Coordination*—A policy must readily coordinate among other decisions, teams, and departments. Activities must conform to the policy without building conflict across activities.

- *Clarity*—A policy must be stated clearly and logically. It must specify the aim of the action, define appropriate methods, and describe the limits of discretion provided to those applying the policy.

- *Ethics*—A policy must be ethical and responsive to cultural differences. This guideline might be most difficult to follow when an organization is doing business in a foreign country, where local standards can differ from the organization's standards as developed in another country or society. Again, judgment must often be applied.

**KEY**TERMS

**persuasion** Selling a plan to those who must implement it.

**policies** Written statements reflecting a permanent plan's basic values and providing guidelines for selecting actions to achieve objectives.

**regulation** A set of instructions for implementing a policy, also known as standard procedure.

Policies can sometimes be brief, enduring, and dramatic. Other policies, such as an organization's overall personnel policy, are longer, more detailed, and periodically updated. In any case, managers should seek to carefully define the process of policy development. For example, a key issue in personnel policy development is the question of who should be involved in developing the policy. Employee participation with management is essential in the drafting of such policies. Another issue in policy development is how and when to communicate new policies to employees. Managers must ensure that policy development processes, and the communication of policies to employees, are clear and allow for appropriate feedback.

Whereas a policy is a general guide to decision making, a regulation (or standard procedure) is a set of instructions for implementing a policy. For example, a policy of "employee empowerment" might translate into a procedure for team leaders specifying that work process changes can be instituted only after meeting with all affected employees and obtaining their approval of any changes. Team leaders might also be trained to follow specific procedures in initiating the discussion, recording employees' recommendations, and documenting the approved changes.

**STEP 6**  **Control**

Control includes all managerial activities dedicated to ensuring that actual results conform to planned results and is the final step in the planning process. Note that the controlling step and the implementation step occur virtually simultaneously. As actions are undertaken to implement the plan, measurement of the effectiveness of those actions should provide immediate feedback. Managers should be careful not to make the mistake of waiting until their actions have been completed before measuring their effectiveness. Managers receive feedback, and take corrective action, by measuring actual performance and comparing it to the standard or original plan. The process of taking corrective actions based on measurement of actual performance is known as feedback.

Managers must obtain information—feedback—that reports actual performance and permits comparison of the performance against standards. Such information is most easily acquired for activities that produce specific and concrete results; for example, production and sales activities have results that are easily identifiable and for which information is readily obtainable.

We will say more about control issues in a later chapter. For now, you should note that controlling is a necessary part of the planning function. The people responsible for taking corrective steps when actual results are not in line with planned results must know not only that they are indeed responsible, but that they have the authority to take action.

# Quality Approach to Planning

Organizations that take a quality approach to planning can choose from various specific planning methods. This section examines three of those methods: the plan, do, check, act cycle; time-based planning; and planning for continuous improvement. These approaches form the basis for quality planning. Noted consultant W. E. Deming described quality planning as the activity of (1) determining customer needs and (2) developing the products and processes required to meet those needs. Quality planning is required for every product and service within an organization, not only for goods and services sold to external customers. Total Quality Management (TQM) planning stresses employee involvement, teamwork, and a focus of the entire company on the customer. Ultimately, these quality-conscientious companies develop strategies that use new and innovative processes to produce products or services that consistently meet or exceed customer expectations.

Each of the quality approaches to planning discussed in this section emphasizes exceeding customer expectations, maintaining continuous improvement, and practicing team-based problem solving. Although all of these planning approaches are based on a similar concept of quality, each one is developed by a different thinker and has some unique aspects. At the end of this section, we will take a look at planning for continuous improvement in a quality management environment.

## The Plan, Do, Check, Act Cycle

The plan, do, check, act (PDCA) quality planning approach is conceived as a planning cycle that forms the basis for continuous improvement (see Exhibit 6.5). In the PDCA cycle, the first step is to plan the quality improvement. Second, workers perform or produce a short version or a small batch of the procedure or product. Third, workers check the results of this pilot project for compliance with standards. Fourth, workers implement the tested process. The PDCA cycle is then repeated.

Employees at Cincinnati-based Procter & Gamble (P&G) use the PDCA cycle to manage environmental quality efforts. First, they develop a *plan* to remove pollutants from each stage of production, as well as from packaging and the final product. Next (*do*) they reduce discharges to the environment and correct other potentially harmful environmental defects. Then they *check* the results, using statistics and other measurement tools. Once the results are assessed, employees (*act*) install permanent systems to maintain the quality improvement and to apply it to other aspects of the business. Using this technique, a P&G pulp mill cut landfill dumping by

6.5

**Plan, Do, Check, Act Cycle**

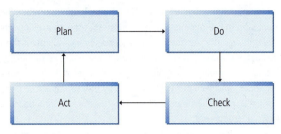

75 percent; a coffee-processing plant in Missouri added a machine to compact chaff from coffee beans, cutting solids in sewage by 75 percent. New packaging cut 3.4 million pounds of waste in deodorant product cartons. As a result of PDCA, P&G's redesigned vegetable oil bottle uses 28 percent less plastic than the earlier bottle.[10]

## Time-Based Planning

Speed can often determine the success or failure of a plan's implementation. The important period between the time a product is first considered and the time it is sold to the customer is called concept to customer. Speed in planning and delivering a product or service can be a strategic competitive advantage. All other things being equal, the prize (typically, market share) goes to the fastest organization. For example, DaimlerChrysler's new sports car, the Crossfire, completed the concept-to-customer cycle in a record-breaking twenty-four months using innovative methods for both design and production.[11] Further, paying attention to time usually forces the organization to look at other issues (e.g., design, staffing, and inspection) affecting product and service quality. For example, it is not uncommon for a product to lie untouched during 90 percent of the time allocated for its assembly. Paying attention to production speed can lead to reductions in these idle periods. Time-sensitive organizations are not only likely to deliver products to their customers faster than competitors but also likely to develop greater customer loyalty and learn more about improving the production process itself.[12]

One important initiative currently popular in many organizations is the concept of reengineering. Reengineering has been defined as "the fundamental rethinking and radical redesign of business processes to achieve dramatic improvements in critical, contemporary measures of performance, such as cost, quality, service, and speed."[13] Reengineering was largely responsible for the trend toward corporate downsizing, or "rightsizing," that swept organizations around the world during the early to mid-1990s. Many layers of management have been excised from organizations in the interest of reducing the time it takes for organizations to accomplish goals. From a reengineering perspective, this meant a reliance on a more highly educated workforce and greater use of technology to streamline the workflow, which resulted in fewer errors and higher quality products and services. On the whole, however, reengineering efforts have failed to achieve the desired objectives. Senior managers still complain that middle managers are entrenched, blocking necessary changes. And middle managers complain that senior managers have neither the vision nor the fortitude to take the enterprise through changes. To survive, managers must be willing to challenge their assumptions. An entire pattern of thought, a whole set of ideas and expectations, must be let go. According to James Champy, a founder of the reengineering approach, to speed change in the organization, managers must:

1. Abandon the quest for perfection, with its notion of the universal right way of doing things.

2. Trade in the airy abstraction of authority that comes from their title or office for the messier reality of authority based on competence and ability.

3. Broaden their age-old devotion to growth to include an equally old, but only recently rediscovered, devotion to service.[14]

Time-based planning requires new processes and structures that create the conditions for a faster cycle time. Reengineering works on the process changes needed for efficient production, but new organizational structures are also needed. A new and innovative structural change that is consistent with the principles of reengineering is known as the horizontal organization form. Unlike the more traditional vertical organizations based on a pyramidal hierarchy, the horizontal organization is flatter, more responsive, and affords better communication among participants. In the horizontal form, organization processes drive planning. Each process has fewer levels of complexity, which keeps decision making closer to the source of the decision. That is, resources and information are deployed when and where they are needed to support a core activity. In other words, unlike vertical hierarchies, horizontal organizations have resource and information needs that planning must take into consideration.[15]

Another important time-based initiative in current industry practice, as noted earlier, is called cycle time reduction (CTR). CTR is concerned with reducing the time it takes for completing organizational processes, reducing costs, and increasing customer service. A key concept in CTR is the 3 percent rule, which states that only 3 percent of the elapsed time for a process is actually needed to complete the activity. Insurance claim filing and handling is a good example: physically completing the claim might take only five minutes, but processing the claim often takes thirty days.[16]

Reengineering and CTR are two techniques used by planners in attempting to reduce completion times of key organizational processes. However, as proponents of both techniques recognize, reducing completion times is a never-ending challenge. That's why most organizations also use another form of planning that allows for the continuous improvement of the organization.

## Planning for Continuous Improvement

Effective planning and plans lead to quality outcomes as well as continuous improvements in performance. Quality pioneer Joseph M. Juran notes three main negative outcomes resulting from a lack of attention to quality in the planning process:

1. *Loss of sales due to competition in quality*—In the United States, this outcome affects almost every manufactured product, from TVs to lawn mowers to cars.

2. *Costs of poor quality, including customer complaints, product liability lawsuits, redoing defective work, and products scrapped*—Juran estimates that 20 to 40 percent of all costs of doing business are from redoing poor-quality work.

3. *Threats to society*—These run the gamut from minor annoyances like home appliance breakdowns to global disasters such as the Three Mile Island nuclear emergency; the Bhopal, India, poison gas release; and the Chernobyl, Ukraine, nuclear reactor explosion and contamination.[17]

| **Outcomes of Quality Planning** | Managers can minimize the possibility of negative outcomes by using quality-based planning methods and by establishing quality goals. Quality means knowing what your customers, clients, or patients (in the case of healthcare) want and then designing a delivery system (an organization) to provide the good or service.

Customer-driven organizations closely and continually scrutinize their system's output for quality. Ultimately, the primary outcome of quality planning is customer satisfaction and delight. Many scholars have offered advice about how best to achieve these ends. Most notably, Juran's description of quality planning includes the following main points:

| Identify customers, both external and internal.

| Determine the customer's needs.

| Develop product features that satisfy customer needs.

| Establish quality goals that meet customers' and suppliers' needs at a low combined cost.

| Develop a process to produce the needed features.

| Prove that the process can meet the quality goals under operating conditions (i.e., prove process capability).[18]

Thus, the focus of quality outcomes is on customers—both external (i.e., consumers) and internal (i.e., another department). Changes in the workplace have helped create systems for continuous improvement in many organizations. For example, American Express made a significant change when it adopted a system built on customer-based transactions. In response to its external customer requests, the company created a comprehensive delivery system that would support key customer transactions.[19]

| Quality Planning Models | Some quality planning models are revolutionary; others are evolutionary. A revolutionary planning model (e.g., traditional planning model) implements a massive, one-time change in the production process or product in order to reduce costs or improve the product in a significant way. Then no other changes or improvements are made until the next revolutionary change occurs at the end of another planning cycle. Between planning cycles, however, the original improvements tend to erode. Eventually, the improvements erode enough to initiate another plan for improvement. An evolutionary planning model makes gradual and more continuous changes based on input from inside and outside the production system. Improvements typically are not dramatic, but they are consistent and incremental.

Planning is beneficial because it allows an organization to anticipate and respond to change in a systematic manner. Planning adds value by finding ways to reduce the overall cost of doing business while also anticipating and satisfying customer needs. We recognize today the importance of quality to the consumer when considering the purchase of goods and services. But not too long ago, quality was considered a cost. Exhibit 6.6 summarizes traditional and quality-based characteristics of planning. As you can see, quality-based planning emphasizes the system rather than the employees as the source of organizational problems. Quality-based planning regards the employee as an asset.

**KEY**TERMS

**revolutionary planning model** A planning model involving a massive, one-time change in the production process or product to reduce costs or improve the product in a significant way.

**evolutionary planning model** A planning model entailing changes that are typically not dramatic, but consistent and incremental.

EXHIBIT | 6.6

### Traditional versus Quality Planning Characteristics

| Traditional | Quality |
|---|---|
| Quality is an expense. | Quality decreases costs. |
| Achieve quality through inspection. | Higher quality reduces the need for inspection. |
| Workers cause defects. | System causes defects. |
| Employ standards and quotas. | Eliminate standards and quotas. |
| Manage by fear. | Drive out fear. |
| Employees represent a cost. | Employees are an asset. |
| Focus on profit. | Focus on quality; profit will follow. |

**CONCLUSION**

## Planning

Planning is a fundamental management activity that covers any time span, from short to long term. This chapter examined various definitions of and justifications for planning, enumerated the benefits and criticisms of planning, surveyed the steps involved in planning, and looked at quality approaches to planning. These topics certainly do not cover all the important issues associated with planning. But our purpose in this chapter is to emphasize that planning is an important management function. All organizational goals and objectives flow from planning. Without a formal planning process, organizations are subject to the vagaries of environmental circumstances; they have little recourse but to react to environmental changes. Planning is a proactive activity that enables an organization to take an offensive stance, creating circumstances that are most favorable to the organization.

## Discussion Questions

1. Identify and define the three levels of planning.

2. Identify and discuss the benefits and criticisms of formal planning.

3. Provide an example of a common standing plan and a common single use plan in an organization with which you are familiar.

4. From a planning perspective, what is the difference between the terms Total Quality Management, continuous improvement, and reengineering?

5. In the discussion of time-based planning, what does the term *concept to customer* mean?

## Video Case

### Timbuk2: The Message Is in the Bag

Picture yourself on a bike, weaving in and out of city traffic, pedaling as fast as you can through a maze of streets, dodging taxicabs and pedestrians, carrying your cargo on your back. Now picture yourself making dozens of deliveries in a day, pedaling an eight- or nine-hour shift in blazing sun, pouring rain, stinging sleet, or even blowing snow. This is the life of a bicycle messenger. Timbuk2, founded in San Francisco more than fifteen years ago by former bicycle messenger Rob Honeycutt, manufactures what seems to be a specialized product: messenger bags for cyclists who make their living delivering documents door to door. Today, Timbuk2 still manufactures professional bags for bike messengers. But the firm has expanded its offerings to include fashion bags for other consumers—and its goals and plans are much broader than they were fifteen years ago.

"Our goal for the future is to remain faithful to our working-class urban roots, while expanding our unique qualities and design sensibilities to a broader range of products and a wider audience," states Timbuk2's web site. Mark Dwight, CEO of the firm, echoes this sentiment. Dwight's job as CEO is to focus on the big picture—the company's overall goals and how to achieve them. "The difference between strategy and goals is, goals are the endpoint and strategy is the way to get there. The actual steps you take would be the tactics," Dwight explains. Timbuk2's current main goal is to move from a tiny, specialized market into a broader market. "Our roots are in the bicycle messenger market . . . a subculture that is very interesting. . . . However, it isn't really a market; there's no growth there. So what we're trying to do is build from that heritage, that authenticity that gives value to our brand as a lifestyle brand," says Dwight.

Formulating the strategies to achieve the goals requires careful planning. "We are building a lifestyle brand; we are [also] trying to build brand equity because that ultimately is the value of this company," notes Dwight. "Then, when we go to sell the company or take it public, there's value there." So every effort, from the development of new products to the marketing of existing ones, focuses on strengthening the Timbuk2 brand in consumers' minds. Dwight and his staff plan to "develop a product portfolio that asserts our position in existing markets, moves into new markets, and really creates a sense of lifestyle . . . so when you think of Timbuk2 . . . you think of an emotional concept, a brand, a lifestyle."

Timbuk2 is already moving rapidly toward its goals. Sit in on a Timbuk2 planning meeting, and you willl hear lots of ideas and opinions flying back and forth—about how to design a new bag, how to market it, how to offer it over the Web. "I don't want to see any of this hardware," says Dwight, pointing to a sketch in one design meeting. "That's Coach. We're not Coach." When reminded that chrome hardware is popular among today's consumers, he does not back down. He wants Timbuk2's bags to have a look that is distinctive to Timbuk2. So far, Timbuk2 has managed to offer a variety of bags for a variety of needs—without the chrome hardware. Consumers can pick up a water-resistant yoga bag with quick-release buckles that allow yoga followers to snap out their practice mats with ease, weatherproof travel bags with destination stickers superimposed on the flaps, and colorful, messenger-style laptop computer bags for commuters who want to blend durability with style. The bags don't come cheap; with the addition of custom features, consumers can easily pay $100 or more for their Timbuk2 bags. But a good purse or travel bag from another maker can cost just as much or more.

Timbuk2 hasn't forgotten bicycle messengers, even with its new focus. The professionals can still visit the Timbuk2 web site and "build" customized professional bags—selecting from four different sizes, several fabrics, and an array of colors. In addition, as part of a celebration of the firm's heritage, Timbuk2 has planned a collaboration with Joe Urich, a San Francisco bike messenger and design student at the California College of Arts (CCA), to design two new, industrial-strength messenger bags for his colleagues. These new bags will be designed specifically to meet the requirements of working messengers. "I hope it goes well," says Urich. The project should succeed—after all, who knows better how to design a messenger bag than the messenger himself?

### Questions

1. Does Timbuk2 emphasize all three types of planning: strategic, tactical, and operational?

2. What aspects of the planning process did you observe in this review of Timbuk2?

3. Using what you know about Timbuk2, write a brief mission statement for the organization.

Sources: Company web site, http://www.timbuk2.com, August 13, 2004; "Timbuk2's Groovy Bag," *Yoga Journal*, July/ August 2004, http://www.yogajournal.com; Larry Armstrong, "Make Your PC Green with Envy," *Business Week*, http:// www.businessweek.com, June 7, 2004; "In Style Every Mile," *Organic Style*, May 2004, http://www.organicstyle.com.

## BizFlix

### The Bourne Identity

Jason Bourne (Matt Damon) cannot remember who he is, but others believe he is an international assassin. Bourne tries to learn his identity with the help of his new friend and lover Marie (Franka Potente). Meanwhile, while CIA agents pursue him across Europe trying to kill him, Bourne slowly discovers that he is an extremely well-trained and lethal agent. The story, which is loosely based on Robert Ludlum's 1981 novel, was previously filmed in 1988 as a television miniseries starring Richard Chamberlain.

This scene is an edited version of the "Bourne's Game" sequence near the end of the film. Jason Bourne kills the hired assassin who tried to kill him the day after Jason and Marie arrived at the home of Eamon (Tim Dutton). Eamon is Marie's friend but is a stranger to Jason. Jason uses the dead man's cell phone after returning to his apartment in Paris, France. He presses the redial button, which connects him to Conklin (Chris Cooper), the CIA manager who is looking for him. Listen carefully to Jason's conversation with Conklin as he walks along the right bank of the Seine River in Paris.

### Questions

1. Does Jason Bourne describe a plan to Conklin? If he does, what are the plan's elements? What is Bourne's goal?

2. Does Bourne assess the plan's execution to determine whether it conforms to his goal? If so, what does he do?

3. Was Bourne's plan successfully carried out? Why or why not? How does this scene relate to organizational strategic planning?

## Suggested Reading

Gajilan, Arlyn Tobias, "The Amazing JetBlue," *Fortune,* May 17, 2002.

Hope Jeremery and Robin Fraser, "Who Needs Budgets?" *Harvard Business Review,* Tool Kit (February 2003): Reprint Number R0302J.

Kenney, Jennifer, "Cleaning Up," *Fortune* (April 24, 2003).

Lorange, Peter and Richard F. Vancil, "How to Make Strategic Planning Work," *Harvard Business Review* (September–October, 1976).

McGrath, Rita Gunter and Ian MacMillan, "Discovery-Driven Planning," *Harvard Business Review* (July–August, 1995): Reprint Number 95406.

Mintzberg, Henry "Planning on the Left Side and Managing on the Right," *Harvard Business Review* (July–August, 1976): 49–57.

## Endnotes

1. Henri Fayol, *General and Industrial Management* (London: Sir Isaac Pitman and Sons, 1949).

2. Harold Koontz and Cyril O'Donnell, *Management: A Systems and Contingency Analysis of Management Functions,* 6th ed. (New York: McGraw-Hill, 1976).

3. Henry Mintzberg, "The Rise and Fall of Strategic Planning," *Harvard Business Review* (January–February 1994): 107.

4. James C. Wetherbe, "Principles of Cycle Time Reduction: You Can Have Your Cake and Eat It Too," *Cycle Time Research* (1995): 1–24.

5. Peter Senge, *The Fifth Discipline: The Art and Practice of the Learning Organization* (New York: Doubleday, 1990).

6. Timm J. Esque and Thomas F. Gilbert, "Making Competencies Pay Off," *Training* (January 1995): 44–50.

7. Parasuraman, Valerie A. Zeithaml, and Leonard L. Berry, "A Conceptual Model of Service Quality and Its Implications for Future Research," *Journal of Marketing* (Fall 1985), 41–50.

8. For relevant discussions of these and related management problems, see M. L. Gimpl and S. R. Daken, "Management and Magic," *California Management Review* (Fall 1984): 125–136; R. T. Pascale, "The Paradox of Corporate Culture: Reconciling Ourselves to Socialization," *California Management Review* (Winter 1985): 26–41; and Frederick D. Sturdivant, *Business and Society,* 3rd ed. (Burr Ridge, IL: Irwin, 1985).

9. David A. Garvin, "Competing on the Eight Dimensions of Quality," *Harvard Business Review* (November–December 1987): 101–109.

10. Karen Bemoski, "Carrying on the P&G Tradition," *Quality Progress* (May 1992): 24.

11. Alex Traylor, "Crossfire Just another Sexy Sports Car? Sure, but It's also a Whole New Way of Doing Business," *Fortune* (March 3, 2003).

12. George Stalk Jr. and Thomas M. Hout, *Competing against Time: How Time-Based Competition Is Reshaping Global Markets* (New York: Free Press, 1990).

13. Michael Hammer and James Champy, *Reengineering the Corporation* (New York: HarperCollins, 1993): 32.

14. James Champy, *Reengineering Management* (New York: Harper Business, 1995).

15. Frank Ostroff, *The Horizontal Organization* (New York: Oxford University Press, 1999).

16. James C. Wetherbe, "Principles of Cycle Time Reduction: You Can Have Your Cake and Eat It Too," *Cycle Time Research* (1995): 1–24.

17. J. M. Juran, *Juran on Quality Planning* (New York: Free Press, 1988), 1–2.

18. J. M. Juran, "The Quality Trilogy," *Quality Progress* (August 1986): 19–24.

19. D. Keith Denton, "Creating a System for Continuous Improvement," *Business Horizons* (January–February 1995): 16–21.

# 7

# STRATEGY

The origin of strategy, as a concept, is rooted in military planning. The word *strategy* comes from the Greek word "strategos" and means the "art of the general."[1] In a business context, a company devises a strategy that anticipates what its opponents (competitors) will do and favorably positions itself in relation to its rivals. Modern corporate strategy owes much to this traditional view, which focuses on the external environment. In the last quarter of the twentieth century, researchers began giving equal weight to a firm's internal environment. Arguably, a balanced approach views strategy as a process of matching the competencies of the organization with opportunities that are present in the larger environment.[2] Through this process, strategy helps a company perform better than the competition by creating a sustainable advantage that competitors cannot easily duplicate.[3] In this chapter, we explore how strategy creates value for organizational stakeholders through a process of analysis, decisions, and actions to achieve and maintain competitive advantage.[4] *Strategy formulation* is concerned with developing a strategic direction, environmental analysis, decisions, and plans to achieve goals and objectives; whereas *strategy implementation* represents actions taken to achieve goals and objectives.[5] In the end, strategy is the ability of the firm to use its unique resources and capabilities to exploit opportunities that are present in the external environment.

## Strategic Planning

Strategic planning is the process of developing a strategic orientation for an organization. Because it forces introspective questioning of purpose, customers, resources, and skills, strategic planning can benefit any organization. The process begins with the identification of the core competencies of the organization. Core competencies are activities, resources, skills and capabilities that the organization uses to achieve objectives. For example, a consumer goods manufacturer noted for its promotional campaigns, including a nationally recognized advertising campaign, might have a core competency based on its marketing expertise. The strategic planning process culminates in the formulation and implementation of a multilevel strategy for achieving organizational goals.

Exhibit 7.1 is an overview of the strategic planning process, and examples of each aspect of the strategic planning process are included in this chapter. As you can see in Exhibit 7.1, step 1 in the strategic planning process focuses on articulation of the organization's *purpose, philosophy, mission,* and *values.* The philosophy, mission, and values describe the organization's contribution to society, its moral and ethical beliefs, and the way it operates. Generally, the organization's CEO articulates these components, which often represent strong personal beliefs. (We'll cover the subjects of mission and goals shortly.) Step 2, *goals and objectives* describes the outcomes that the organization hopes to achieve over the short, intermediate, and long term. Objectives and goals serve many purposes including: galvanizing support among stakeholders, communicating information and holding people accountable for their actions and decisions. Step 3, *capabilities and resources,* relates to the people and assets at the disposal of the organization. Even though an organization might establish a goal, it might have neither the financial resources nor the personnel to achieve the goal. However, capabilities and resources can always be acquired or outsourced; that recognition must be an explicit part of strategic planning. *Environmental analysis,* step 4 of

EXHIBIT 7.1

**Strategic Planning Process**

| | Strategic Planning Component | Example |
|---|---|---|
| 1 | Purpose, philosophy, mission, and values | Creates a vision for the future by stating the purpose, philosophy, values, and mission of the organization. |
| 2 | Goals and objectives | Describes the short, intermediate, and long-term aspirations of the organization. Goals and objectives provide strategic direction and specific resource allocations. |
| 3 | Capabilities and resources of the organization | Identifies capabilities, employee skills, core competencies, and other resources to build competitive advantage over rivals. |
| 4 | Environmental analysis | Identifies opportunities and threats present in the external environment. |
| 5 | Strategy formulation and implementation | Develops strategic intent and thinking in managers; formulates a multilevel strategy; and implements a multilevel strategy through structure, culture, and rewards that attains organizational goals and objectives. |
| 6 | Performance | Registers the level of outcome attainment of financial performance, stakeholder satisfaction, market share, and so forth. |

strategic planning, involves exploration of all the forces affecting the organization's ability to attain its goals. Largely, these are factors present in the environment that create opportunities for the organization or threats to the organization. Favorable demographic trends, emerging markets, and new technologies, as well as government regulations, legal requirements, and rising prices for raw materials, are all understood through environmental analysis. In step 5, *strategy formulation and implementation,* the organization's managers seek to develop and execute a multilevel strategy. Strategies represent the organization's plan for navigating the competitive environment. The early phases of strategic planning focus on developing (formulating) strategy and fitting the strategy to the complexity present in the environment. In the later phases of strategic planning, strategy implementation locks in place specific organizational actions that support the strategy. Along the way, conceptual ideas are converted into action plans such as creating a TV commercial as part of an advertising campaign to support the strategy. An important part of the strategic planning process is to set target outcomes or expectations for performance. Finally, step 6, *performance,* represents the multiple outcomes of the strategic planning process. The most notable outcome of this step is profit. As you read through this chapter, the strategic planning process outlined in Exhibit 7.1 should serve as a context to help you understand the more detailed discussions of strategic management concepts and ideas that follow.

## | Developing a Mission Statement

An organization's mission is its *raison d'être* (French for "reason for being"), the fundamental purpose it's designed to serve. The organizational mission statement answers the question, "What is this organization's purpose?" for employees, customers, and other constituents. Whereas a strategy represents the path toward the attainment of a mission, goals, and objectives, the firm's mission statement describes an even more fundamental rationale for its existence.

Some organizational theorists assert that the organizational mission should be based on something even more abstract, an organizational *vision.* In other words, a mission statement should be related to vision. The vision, which usually implies the CEO's vision for the organization, is based on values, competencies of the organization, and opportunities in the future environment. The vision is important because it helps an organization to model strategic plans, and it provides a kind of touchstone for goal setting. In a constantly shifting industry environment, a vision helps avoid reactive decision making and keeps a firm focused on its long-term goals.

KEY TERMS

**mission statement** The fundamental purpose that an organization serves.

A visionary CEO in the automobile industry would be able to synthesize and integrate the impact of a new and emerging technology on vehicles of the future. As an example in the automotive industry, consider the fuel cell, which is expected to revolutionize commercial and personal transportation. A fuel cell is an electrochemical process that uses energy from a chemical reaction to create electricity. Unlike a battery, the fuel cell does not need recharging or replacing as long as it is supplied with fuel and an oxidizer. The fuel cell can be used to power electric motors that drive the wheels of the vehicle. Think of it! No oil tankers, no trucks hauling gasoline, no dependence on the Middle East, and no oil storage facilities wasting prime real estate. The question the CEO must answer is, "When will the fuel cell be commercially viable as a reliable and affordable source of power?" Hence, the CEO's vision of the future must be flexible enough to recognize that the fuel cell is coming and to prepare for integrating fuel cell technology into future products in a way that creates value for organizational stakeholders. A vision of the future probably includes the fuel cell, but the CEO has to hedge his bets on when and how it might be used in the organization.

### Characteristics of an Effective Mission Statement

To establish a mission and vision for an organization, its CEO must take the company's history into consideration. For established firms, the mission should be consistent with what is known about the firm's history. This history includes accomplishments and failures, objectives and policies, decisions, and employees. An organization must assess its history to determine its current resource base, its image, and its various capacities. Odd as it might sound, many management consultants help organizations appreciate and use organization stories—tales about experiences and events that transpired where the storyteller works. Within an organization, stories serve to legitimize power, to rationalize group behavior, and to reinforce organizational values, identity, and commitment.[6] Before the invention of writing, human cultures relied on stories to convey the history of their culture to the young and to outsiders. Similarly, organizational stories convey the history of an organization to new employees and outsiders. Managers should review organizational stories when establishing a mission statement.

Start-ups and new ventures need a mission too, but have no history upon which to base a long-term vision. Instead, such firms can look to the history of the industry they are part of, or to the history of the human needs and expectations they hope to satisfy through organized activity.

The mission statement that results from the analysis of history, distinctive competence, and the environment must be (1) customer-focused, (2) achievable, (3) motivational, and (4) specific.

Customer-Focused    Mission statements emphasize a customer focus. Many firms have faltered or failed because they continued to define themselves based on what they produced rather than on whom they served.

For enduring success, strategies must be based on the premise that customer satisfaction—and, better yet, customer delight and loyalty—is necessary. The reasons are many and fundamental. Finding new customers is far more expensive than keeping current customers. Dissatisfied customers not only fail to return and buy again, they are also likely (1) to decline to express the reasons for their dissatisfaction (which could be a source of learning and growth for the firm) and (2) to share their dissatisfaction with other potential customers. Customers, not employees, are a firm's best salespeople.

By relying too heavily on rental car and fleet markets to boost production numbers and reduce unit costs, Ford unwittingly created the perception in consumers' minds that the once-venerable Taurus had become little more than a drab vehicle suitable only for discounted bulk sales. At the same time Toyota, Ford's rival, focused on the consumer market and created a safe, reliable, and economical family car that sold without discounting and received rave reviews from automobile analysts. Ford finally admitted that it had lost sight of the real customer. Once the top-selling car in the United States, the Ford Taurus has gradually lost market share to the Toyota Camry. In speaking to reporters at the 2003 Chicago Auto Show, Jim O'Connor, who at that time headed Ford's sales and marketing division for North America, said: "Very frankly, Camry is a better product than Taurus today."[7]

**Achievable**    A mission statement should be challenging, and it must also be achievable. Unrealistic ambitions can exceed a firm's capabilities and lead to the squandering of resources. The CEO's role is to shape and set the culture and tenor of the organization. But once all stakeholders embrace that culture, ensuring that goals are implemented through strategic intent and execution is important. As noted management consultant Ram Charan advised Larry Bossidy, chairman and former CEO of Honeywell, "People think of execution as the tactical side of business, something leaders delegate while they focus on the perceived 'bigger' issues.... This idea is completely wrong. Execution has to be built into a company's strategy, its goals, and its culture. And the leader of the organization must be deeply engaged in it."[8]

**Motivational**    At all levels of an organization, the mission must serve as a source of inspiration and motivation. Effective mission statements have meaning to every employee, allowing them to translate the words of the mission into their own motivation and serving as a guide for decisions and actions.

Motivation affects the enduring effort of employees. Employee conviction and commitment to the organization's mission and goals are necessary for long-term success. With conviction, employees show dedication to the mission; with commitment, they demonstrate behavioral expression of the psychological conviction.

**Specific**    A mission statement should define in which industries the organization intends to compete—and in some cases, where it will not compete. A specific mission allows employees to focus their energy and to be more productive, making the entire firm more profitable. Broad statements of value or goodness (e.g., "the highest quality at the lowest price") do not make a good mission statement. By attempting to be all things to all people, a firm scatters its energy; doing so makes the firm less able to develop distinctive competence, which in turn makes it nearly impossible for the firm to please anyone.

Since the 1980s, mission statements have been developed by a growing number of organizations. From corporations to community groups, organizations are using these declarations to gain direction, purpose, perspective, and vision. Most mission statements are directed both inside and outside of the organization, ideally sending a strong, clear message to management, staff, clients, and prospects. While writing a mission statement, an organization needs time to reflect on what it is trying to accomplish. It needs to focus on the fundamentals: defining the business, identifying and serving stakeholders, and engendering in the employee a spirit of both loyalty and commitment.[9]

## Establishing Goals and Objectives

In an organization, the mission statement sets the tone and direction for more specific goals and objectives. The mission helps strategists develop long-term goals and short-term objectives. Strategists then convert the goals into precise actions, thus creating a context in which to develop short-term objectives. Clear goals—those leaving no doubt about the firm's intentions—inform employees where to direct their efforts. With the mission and goals as context, organizational leaders can communicate not only what needs to be done but also how it should be done (i.e., consistent with the mission). Goals facilitate management control by helping employees track their progress toward goal attainment and by serving as standards against which to compare the firm's actual performance.

## Understanding Strategic Terminology

What do strategists mean when they speak of concepts like core competence, competitive advantage, and industry environment? In this section, we define these key terms, along with several more that are commonly used in strategic management. (See the Management Highlight below for more examples.)

**Core Competence** Although an organization likely is capable of doing many things, strategic success stems from its ability to identify and capitalize on unique corporate strengths that satisfy customer needs. Core competencies are the sets of skills, resources, and capabilities that serve as a source of competitive advantage for the firm over its rivals.[10] To offer uniqueness, a core competence must be: valuable, rare, costly to imitate, and non-substitutable.[11] These unique strengths allow a company to build competitive advantage through superior efficiency, quality, innovation, or customer responsiveness.[12] This capacity is unique to the firm and valued in the market. For example, Wal-Mart's unique set of skills, resources, and capabilities—a core competence—creates unparalleled efficiency. The company purchases goods in quantity and maintains the lowest price for the product. Efficiencies gained through the purchasing and distribution processes create value that translates into the lowest price for consumers. From the Wal-Mart perspective, a superior distribution system optimizes availability and inventory cost to maintain consistent profit margins. When all is said and done, Wal-Mart uses its core competencies to compete successfully by using skills, resources, and capabilities no other firm can replicate.

MANAGEMENT HIGHLIGHT

### STRATEGIC TERMINOLOGY

| Term | Description | Focus | Examples |
|---|---|---|---|
| Planning | Analytical process that anticipates future requirements of the organization. | Affects the entire organization and takes a long-range perspective. | Indicates budgeting processes, acquisition, and merger activities. |
| Strategy | Describes how the organization will compete and create competitive advantage in the long run. | Exists at three levels: functional, competitive, and institutional. | Cost leadership is a competitive-level strategy. |
| Strategic Thinking | The ability to integrate complex information and apply that information to create greater value than competitors. | Strategic managers synthesize information about the organization's core competencies, technical advances, and competitive information. | Dell's ability to create value by selling servers rather and commodity PCs. Dell created the direct-selling market for commercial file servers. |
| Business Model | Describes the way the organization will conduct business. New business models often rely on untested and sometimes flawed assumptions. | Processes that describe the business. Contains a *narrative test* that describes what the organization hopes to accomplish and a *numbers test* that projects financial information based on assumptions. | *Successful:* Wal-Mart used mass merchandising techniques and brand-name goods to sell in rural America. *Unsuccesssful:* WebVan customers were unwilling to pay premium prices for Internet grocery shopping. |

Source: Adapted from: Joan Magretta, "Why Business Models Matter," *Harvard Business Review* (May 2002): 3–8; Richard Hammermesh, "Making Planning Strategic," *Harvard Business Review* (July–August 1986): 3–9; and Henry Mintzberg, "The Rise and Fall of Strategic Planning," *Harvard Business Review* (January–February 1994): 107–114.

| **Competitive Advantage** | Competitive advantage is built from core competencies. Competitive advantage in the marketplace allows an organization to attain greater profits than its competitors. A competitive advantage is a valuable and unique capability that a firm uses to create above average profitability. Organizations can achieve competitive advantage by performing a business activity at a lower cost than the competition or by creating uniqueness not easily duplicated by the competition. Cost savings or efficiency allows the organization to be the low-cost leader, creating a lower cost structure and achieving greater profits than the competition. A capability based on uniqueness means distinctiveness. Such an organization uses differentiation to create a product that is unlike and, in some manner, superior to those offered by the competition. That organization can then charge a premium price for the differentiated product, resulting in higher profits. Strategic management theorists Charles Hill and Gareth Jones propose that the four building blocks of competitive advantage are quality, innovativeness, efficiency, and customer responsiveness:[13]

1. *Quality*—an advantage is created by building a quality product. Lexus automobiles are known for quality as defined by fit and finish, reliability, and low level of reported defects.

2. *Innovativeness*—an advantage based on innovation creates a uniqueness that the competition does not possess. In 2003, Apple computer introduced the one-inch-thick PowerBook G4™ with a 17-inch monitor—quite big, but very thin, for a laptop. Competitors have no similar products.

3. *Efficiency*—an advantage based on efficiency reduces products costs and gives the organization more room for price reduction. In the steel industry, clearly NUCOR™ created a lower cost base than competitors. Through efficiency, they were able to increase market share by offering their products at a lower cost.

4. *Customer responsiveness*—an advantage created through customer responsiveness focuses on the needs of the product user. GM's ONSTAR™ satellite-controlled system can unlock vehicle doors if you inadvertently lock your keys in the vehicle, or inform the police of a stolen vehicle's location in real time (i.e., during a police pursuit).

| **Industry Environment** | Management strategists define the industry environment as the competition, products, customers, and any unique characteristics of a particular industry. As you can imagine, the cosmetics industry has a different structure and customer base than those of the automobile industry. By understanding the opportunities and threats presented by its industry, an organization has a head start on developing and fulfilling an effective mission.

| **Strategic Intent** | Strategic intent is the communication of an intended goal that motivates energy, allocates resources, and allows for individual discretion.[14] In the 1970s, this was exemplified by Coca Cola's ambition to be within "arm's reach" of every consumer in the world, or Honda's intent to become the number three auto maker in the United States.[15] Strategic intent includes the overall meaning or interpretation of actions, behaviors, formal communications, and decisions of an organization's stakeholders and other members of the environment. Strategic intent informs organizational stakeholders about what to expect from the organization in the future. For example, GM executives might indicate, in several different forums, that they expect to increase the company's domestic automobile market share by 5 percent over the next decade. This information alone might not indicate true strategic intent. It is information about what they would like to see happen in the future. However, the perspective changes when we know that GM plans to form strategic alliances with Suzuki to manufacture diesel engines, carry out major redesign of many models by

**KEY**TERMS

**low-cost leader** An organization that achieves a competitive advantage by performing a business activity at a lower cost than the competition.

**industry environment** The competition, products, customers, and any other characteristics of a particular industry.

2007, and eliminate the Oldsmobile division. It is the sum of all these actions, along with formal communication, that signals the true strategic intent of the organization to the external environment. By understanding the strategic intent of a competitor, a firm can better understand what its own strategic response should be.

| **Strategic Thinking** | Strategic thinking moves beyond formal planning methods and techniques. As critics have observed, formal planning is often more mechanical than truly insightful or innovative. Strategic thinking refers to the mental ability of a strategic manager to synthesize competitive implications of diverse information. To be useful, strategic thinking must produce strategies that create competitive advantage. Certainly, Michael Dell, Bill Gates, and Jack Welch are examples of people with this ability.

| **Business Model** | In many people's minds, the concept of a business model is synonymous with the Internet boom of the 1990s. Many Internet start-up companies had less than traditional approaches to business; during that period, investors often ignored business fundamentals in favor of wishful thinking. The business model describes the organizational processes an organization intends to use in conducting a viable business. Although it is no substitute for a strategy, the business model is a useful concept when applied appropriately. A reasonable business model should include two components: (1) a *narrative test* that describes what the organization hopes to accomplish; and (2) a *numbers test* that projects financial information based on assumptions about demand and costs. A good business model has a narrative that makes sense, along with the financial numbers that indicate profitability.

## Environmental Analysis Process

Strategic planning is the process of examining the organization's environment, establishing a mission, setting goals and objectives, and developing an operating plan. During the strategic planning process, strategic planners are concerned with the future of the industry and their place in it. In most organizations, strategic planning never ends. The organization is either formulating a new strategy or implementing an existing one, assessing progress, and revising current strategies.

Managers are involved in the strategic planning process in two important ways: (1) By providing information and suggestions relating to their particular areas of responsibility, they can influence the strategic planning process; and (2) by monitoring the process and responding to strategic planning documents, they help ensure not only that their department's role in the strategy is clear but also that their department has resources to support the strategy. Once the strategy has been approved, everything a department does—including the objectives established for its areas of responsibility—should be derived from the strategic plan.

Strategic planning is best conceived as a cyclical process governed by competitiveness, analysis, and innovation. Competitive organizations develop strategic scenarios of the future based on different contingencies. They attempt to anticipate the future and develop alternative responses based on a variety of competitive factors. For example, many firms have five-year strategic plans. If they are competitive, they probably revise the plan every eighteen months to two years.

## SWOT Analysis

A strategy, plan, or mission for the future begins with an assessment of the organization's current situation. A systematic, thorough analysis requires attention to four factors: *internal* strengths and weaknesses, and *external* opportunities and threats. Such an analysis is often referred to as a SWOT analysis (SWOT is an acronym for Strengths, Weaknesses, Opportunities, Threats). Historically, the SWOT analysis has provided managers with useful signals for strategic change.

EXHIBIT 7.2

**SWOT Analysis for Starbucks Corporation**

| Internal | External |
|---|---|
| **Strengths** | **Opportunities** |
| 1. Brand recognition | 1. New channels of distribution |
| 2. High-visibility outlets | 2. Product extensions (ice cream, candy) |
| 3. | 3. |
| **Weaknesses** | **Threats** |
| 1. Expensive | 1. Saturated market |
| 2. Limited drive-throughs | 2. Caffeine product substitutes |
| 3. | 3. |

Exhibit 7.2 is a partial SWOT analysis for Starbucks Corporation. What can you contribute to the breakdown of the four factors?

A company's strengths and weaknesses are usually derived from a realistic assessment of financial, human, and other internal resources. The firm's financial assets include cash, securities, receivables, and other tangible resources usually presented on its balance sheet and other accounts. Human resources are not easy to evaluate, yet they are a primary component of modern organizations. Human resources include the ideas, ingenuity, patents, and other intangible yet essential bases for competitiveness that only human beings can bring to an organization. An organization's current skills might not be useful if it makes a strategic move into a different industry requiring a different set of skills. For example, an engineering company that employs many older engineers to develop and design traditional electronics products might not be able to make the transition into the computer networking equipment industry, where electronics engineers have different skills, interests, and experience. In the end, the company might be forced to hire more engineers than originally anticipated in order to acquire the skills necessary for the industry.

Externally, the company's business environment presents both threats and opportunities. An opportunity is anything that has the potential to increase the firm's strengths. For example, a pending reduction of trade barriers may allow a firm to increase its business in another country. A threat is anything that has the potential to hurt or even destroy an organization. For instance, a change in tax laws could portend ruin for a firm that depends on the tax breaks that are to be eliminated by the change.

Even with all that we have said here about SWOT analysis, other methods of strategy planning exist. A recent approach, called the resource-based theory, suggests that organizations can build on the concept of core competencies by basing their competitive strategy on utilizing their unique resources.[16] The resources should be hard to duplicate, long-lasting, and not substitutable; further, they should create value for the organization and be valued by the customer (e.g., some people like Fords better than Chevys). Unique internal resources and capabilities are potential strengths that can help create a competitive advantage for the firm. For example, people and knowledge can be sources of a unique capability. Tacit knowledge shared by individual personalities endows a company with proprietary capabilities and creates a unique flavor or experience not available elsewhere. And if sustainable over time, it develops durability—Disney World, for example. At Disney World, company-specific resources and capabilities represent unique strengths that are difficult or impossible for competitors to replicate. Customers are willing to pay a premium price for the Disney experience. People and knowledge are two important internal resources, but others include physical resources, such as a building or location; and financial resources, such as credit or, better yet, cash reserves. The following Management Highlight describes what can happen to the value chain during times of crisis.

## FORD EXPLORER: REBUILDING THE VALUE CHAIN

What does value creation mean at Ford Motor Company? The Ford Motor Company created value in the form of quality, safety, and customer service. In fact, Ford's advertising slogan was "Quality is Job 1." In early 2000 Ford began to take heat for the increasing number of rollover accidents involving the Ford Explorer. Ford Explorers were equipped with Firestone Wilderness AT tires. While Ford and Firestone pointed the finger at one another, consumer perceptions of quality, safety, and service of each brand eroded. The long-standing relationship between Ford and Firestone, nurtured by Henry Ford and Harvey Firestone in the 1920s, began to unravel. After both companies paid out millions of dollars in litigation, Ford undertook aggressive steps to redesign the Explorer, and Bridgestone-Firestone recalled 27 million tires. It is clear that the value chain at Ford and Firestone needed attention. Where in the value chain was value created that specifically enhanced quality, or safety, or service to the customer? And more importantly where was it damaged by the Explorer/Firestone tire problem? How could the damage be repaired and consumer confidence restored? At Ford, repairing the value chain meant establishing a bold strategy to reassure the public that the Ford Explorer and the Ford Expedition SUVs were now safe and not prone to rollover accidents. The value creation centered on design (innovation) and safety (vehicle stability). The redesigned 2002 Ford Explorer was an attempt to increased quality and offer greater safety innovations than the competition. The new Ford Explorer was totally redesigned with a lower center of gravity and a more car-like responsiveness. To alleviate public concerns about safety, the Ford Expedition also received a makeover, with changes similar to those made in the Explorer. Ford CEO Jac Nassar and his successor William Clay Ford took the lead in communicating the steps Ford was taking to rebuild both product and reputation. At the heart of the message was quality, innovativeness, concern for the customer, and new technology—all aspects of the value creation. Further, this program followed up on Ford's ongoing efforts to reduce excessive car and truck production costs. It is safe to say the Explorer/Firestone tire recall was in part a result of the failure at Ford to recognize that the problem was escalating. Many Ford managers knew that the Explorer had a tire problem. They knew that it was growing larger with each passing day, but they were afraid to speak out for fear of losing their jobs. The culture at Ford didn't want to hear bad news. Ford wants that managerial culture to change. Ford's culture wasn't supporting their differentiation strategy. They know now that the culture has to support quality and safety. It is far better to catch the problem early in the cycle. Once broken, the value chain can be expensive to fix.

Source: Adapted from John Greenwald, "Inside the Ford/Firestone Fight," *Time* (May 29, 2001). Anita Kumar, "Attention Shifts to the Ford Explorer," *St Petersburg Times* (June 17, 2001).

**value chain** The stream of primary and secondary activities by which the organization acquires resources, produces the product or service, and distributes the product or service to the customer, with each value-creating activity having a cost of creation and a potential benefit, measured in terms of cost savings, quality, speed, or uniqueness.

**primary activities** The main activities of an organization: for example, inbound logistics, manufacturing the product (or creating the service), outbound logistics, marketing and sales, and service.

**support activities** Secondary activities of an organization; for example, infrastructure, human resources, research and development (R&D), and materials management.

## Value Chain Analysis

The value chain is the stream of activities the organization uses to acquire resources, produce the product or service, and distribute the product or service to the customer.[17] Each of these value creation activities has a cost of creation and a potential benefit. Value can be a measure of cost savings, quality, speed, or uniqueness. The process of creating value needs to be understood and fostered. There are activities in the product or service creation that offer the potential for cost savings or the ability to create unique value for the customer. Value chain analysis identifies organizational activities that add value to the final product or service. According to Porter, components of the value chain include primary and secondary activities that create value. Primary activities include: inbound logistics, manufacturing the product (or creating the service), outbound logistics, marketing and sales, and service. Support activities include infrastructure, human resources, R&D, and materials management. Exhibit 7.3 shows a typical value chain. Value chain analysis identifies those activities that are more efficient or different from similar activities performed by their competitors. Think about it for a moment! Burger King, Wendy's, and McDonald's perform the same value-creating activities but with quite different benefits for each firm. Similarly, Wal-Mart is noted for its superior inbound logistics system relative to its competitors. This superiority yields the company a clear cost advantage that creates the ability to lower their prices while maintaining profitability.

According to Porter, competitive advantage results from the way firms organize and perform the various activities of their value chain. To gain competitive advantage over rivals, a firm must either provide comparable buyer value and perform the value chain activities more efficiently (reducing costs) than the competition, or it must perform the activities in a unique way that differentiates the product and creates greater value and commands a premium price.

**7.3**        **Value Chain Analysis**

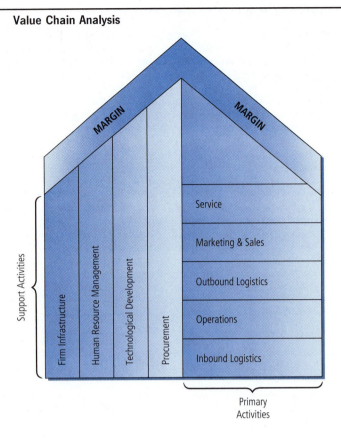

Strategy guides the way a firm organizes its functional areas. Value chain analysis helps identify sources of cost and differentiation advantage in primary and secondary activities. These hold the potential for value creation for the customer. Some companies pursue a cost leadership strategy; others follow a differentiation strategy. Regardless of the strategy, value-creating activities are critical to an organization's success. Above average profitability follows when the value created exceeds the cost of creating the product or service.[18] Successful organizations understand that the value chain helps managers view the organization as an interrelated system. By improving the components of the value chain, managers are building a better and more balanced organization that creates greater value for the customer.[19] Improvements to the system are usually made by teams of individuals representing the various value-creating functions.

## Analyzing the External Environment

Key components of an organization's environment include the socio-cultural environment, technological developments, economic conditions, political climate, and competitive environment. In the following subsections, we discuss each of these components in more detail.

**Sociocultural Environment** | Modern societies are constantly changing. Strategic planners must therefore be able to identify the changing cultural and social conditions in the environment, especially those with potential to influence the organization. Unfortunately, many organizations still fail to consider the effects such changes will have, or underestimate their impact. As noted in Chapter 3, "The Management Environment, Social Responsibility, and Ethics," many organizations use a technique known as *environmental scanning* to stay abreast of these changes. This technique, which involves acquiring and using information about events and trends in an organization's external environment, helps managers plan the organization's future courses of action. Research has shown that organizations using this technique focus primarily on the competition, customer, regulatory, and technological sectors of their environment. Information is usually received from multiple, complementary sources.[20]

Another technique used by many firms is issues management, which focuses on a single issue. A manager in the organization is often assigned leadership on the issue, and he or she is responsible for making strategic decisions regarding that issue. In the battery industry, for example, a firm might assign a manager to consider the impact of the organization's product on the physical environment. The manager engaged in issues management will consider socio-cultural factors like these: Strategically, how will the company respond to concerns of environmental groups that battery disposal should be regulated by the government? If government regulations were enacted, forecasts indicate that battery costs will double and consumer demand for batteries will decline.

| **Technological Developments** | Changes in technology can influence an organization's destiny, creating new industries or forever altering existing ones. Consider the impact of the personal computer and the Internet on business transactions over the past fifteen years. Communication and information technologies are also changing the rules of work. Telecommuting, for example, has led to "distributed work"—work activity conducted by teams of people separated from each other in time and space. Management of distributed work processes takes place using advanced communications technologies. Smart managers anticipate technological changes, adapt to their implementation in the workplace, and exploit them for competitive advantage.[21]

| **Economic Conditions** | Economic activity will be increasingly global and increasingly competitive. Every day, new players enter the worldwide economic game. New alliances form, new trading blocs come into existence, and new rules of fair competition are constantly being drafted and debated. The emerging global economy will create a more complex economic playing field than ever before. Around the world, stock markets run all night. Major investment banks can monitor and issue orders to buy and sell overnight on the international stock markets. Competitive advantage is gained by those firms with satellite and computer links to the world.

The dynamic economic environment further includes global economic considerations, downward cost pressures, and specialization based on resources, location, or knowledge. Because of these forces, managers will need to make a wide variety of strategic adjustments to remain competitive in the years ahead. New companies will emerge to satisfy new consumer needs, while other noncompetitive companies will go out of business. This era is based on fast-changing technologies and wireless instant communication making possible new products and services worldwide. It's also an era of employee empowerment and changing global relationships and structures. Traditional ways of doing business are gone forever. If companies are going to achieve success, they must stay abreast of and adapt to changing economic conditions.

| **Political Climate** | The political climate that propelled the United States to the status of a world superpower no longer exists. Nations of the world no longer need to align themselves with one of two opposing economic giants. The breakup of the former Soviet Union, the breakup of Yugoslavia, and the independence of former Soviet satellites have changed the meaning of the term *allies*. New trading partners and markets become available as politics breaks old bonds and presents opportunities to forge new ones. Business must be prepared for volatile, even revolutionary changes in geographic boundaries, contract and licensure regulations, and limitations on direct investment. As democracy rises around the world, expect much debate and even rancor as many long-oppressed nations finally get an opportunity to flex their political muscles.

**KEY**TERMS

**issues management** A technique used by many firms that is focused on a single issue.

| Competitive Environment | For any organization, the external business environment presents a mix of opportunities, constraints, and threats. Before articulating a mission, strategic planners must analyze and evaluate these conditions. The resulting mission statement should be responsive to the organization's competitive environment.

## Stakeholder Analysis

An organization's success can be controlled by people outside the organization as much as by those within. For example, a well-designed product might fail in the marketplace if it does not meet the customers' needs. If customers do not buy the product, it really does not matter how well the product was designed. Because an organization's success is thus affected by its customers, these customers are viewed as being among its stakeholders. Any group or individual having the potential to influence an organization's ability to achieve its goals and objectives is a stakeholder.[22]

Stakeholder analysis puts renewed emphasis on understanding the concerns of the numerous groups involved in achieving an organization's success or failure. All these stakeholder groups make demands on the organization. In reacting to these demands, the organization develops strategies for managing each group. Many organizations have learned the hard way that ignoring a stakeholder can have disastrous consequences. Reverend Jesse Jackson and Operation PUSH in Chicago targeted Mitsubishi Motors of America for advertising heavily to African American consumers. However, few, if any, dealerships were owned by African Americans. In the end, Mitsubishi Motors agreed to establish more African American–owned dealerships, but not before considerable damage was done to consumer confidence in the company. Organizations have also learned that customers, or stakeholders, come in a variety of forms. There are internal and external stakeholders. One important internal stakeholder who has gone through cycles of neglect in American business is the employee.

| Employees | Whereas the traditional view of strategy suggests that managers and shareholders are a company's most important assets, a customer-focused organization directs attention toward the product user and non-management employees. These stakeholders are critical in defining and adding value to the product or service. Increasingly, organizations are relying upon their own people as the source of new ideas, energy, and creativity.

The only sustainable competitive advantage for a firm in the global marketplace is its human resources. Although cash, equipment, facilities, and infrastructure can be quickly transferred, built, or acquired, human resources are not so easily or quickly developed. Strategic management of employees requires managers to dedicate time, money, and attention to employee training and development. This not only increases workers' value, but enhances their capacity for continuous improvement. In a global market, to allow a workforce to grow stagnant without ongoing training is to invite failure.

The prudent approach is to adopt a long-term strategy, and then build a sensible employee training program to develop skills that can be applied to problems throughout the organization. Employees want training that will help them make progress in their careers, but managers have to recognize that in modern organizations the meaning of *progress* has changed. Career paths in the modern organization often don't follow the traditional "corporate ladder."

Many jobs today involve collecting, organizing, and analyzing information. In short, professional work is knowledge work. To help the modern professional succeed requires not only training but also an organizational structure conducive to continuous learning. The main difference between training and learning is that training is often a group activity; learning is often more effective as an individual activity. Managers who provide both training and a learning environment for employees will create more innovation, better service, and more efficient operations than their competitors.

| Customers | Customers are the end users of the organization's products and/or services. For some companies, a variety of customers or groups might use its products and services. For example, a hotel can rent single rooms to walk-in customers, tourists in small groups,

or the business manager of a professional organization who secures rooms for thousands of convention-goers. Similarly, a household-goods moving firm might sell its full range of services to corporate clients at a discount for large volume, and at regular rates to single households that use only some of the firm's services (e.g., shipping but not packing of household goods). Careful identification of the firm's customers is essential.

Customers use the goods and services produced by a firm. Many firms are themselves customers of suppliers. Working with suppliers to ensure a steady flow of high-quality raw materials is vital to a firm's overall success.

| **Suppliers** | Suppliers provide a firm with essential raw materials for its products. Strategic aspects of supplier management include focusing on developing long-term relationships with key suppliers, focusing on building partnerships, continuously improving product quality, and driving down costs. As part of strategic planning, managers devote special attention to eliminating defective parts and to involving the supplier in the design process for the firm's product(s). This type of relationship is the basis of such process innovations as just-in-time manufacturing.

The old purchasing departments have been replaced by a new business concept called supply chain management that treats inbound raw materials strategically. A supply chain is a network of suppliers and distributors that procures materials, processes materials into finished products (sometimes this means simply materials handling), and distributes products to customers. Supply chains function in both service and product companies. The supply chain process can be simple or quite complex, depending on the product and the industry. The value-added component of each step in the chain, and the cost of the chain, both need continual monitoring.

| **Stockholders** | Stockholders are those who own a firm's stock and hence own a portion of the company. The traditional view of business in the United States placed highest priority on satisfying stockholder expectations. Because of the stockholders' exclusively financial interest, that usually meant paying close attention to the quarterly report. The upshot of this focus is a heavy emphasis on short-term profit improvements, often realized at the expense of long-term investment.

In Japan, by way of contrast, stockholders and senior management are the first to suffer in bad business times. The traditional United States approach to a downturn in the business cycle has been to lay off workers first while the firm waits for customer demand to return. A 1980 NBC News white paper, "If Japan Can, Why Can't We?" showed how Mazda of Japan, during a sales crisis induced by rising energy costs, assigned engineers to sales jobs—to learn more about the customer—without calling for layoffs.

A major responsibility of corporate management is communicating with stockholders. Perhaps the most effective communicator is the chairman of the investment firm Berkshire Hathaway, Warren Buffett, who is well known for his annual reports to shareholders. In fact, many people purchase Berkshire Hathaway stock just to have an opportunity to read Buffet's messages to stockholders. Good communication from managers to stockholders helps the latter understand a firm's long-term strategy, in turn helping to align stockholders' interests with the strategic interest of the organization.

| **Community** | The community consists of private citizens plus government and other public or regulatory agencies. Traditionally, the community is dependent on the firm; it is grateful for the salaries and taxes it pays and for its use of community suppliers and contractors. Many communities and states offer companies special inducements to bring their production to the community.

We have said that an organization must act in a legal, ethical fashion with each stakeholder; but the community also expects the firm to demonstrate a strong sense of social responsibility. Further, most communities view the firm as needing to make a positive contribution to the community—going beyond the firm's payroll, purchases, and taxes. The strategic quality-based view of the community as a stakeholder must also be considered for the long term.

**KEY**TERMS

**suppliers** Vendors that provide a firm with the essential raw materials for its products.

**supply chain** A network of suppliers and distributors that procure materials, process materials into finished products (sometimes simply handling the materials), and distribute products to customers, with each step adding value.

**stockholders** Owners of a firm's stock and hence owners of a portion of the company.

**community** The social entity consisting of private citizens, government, and other public or regulatory agencies; traditionally, dependent on the firm and grateful for the salaries and taxes it pays and for its use of community suppliers and contractors.

## Limits of Strategic Planning

Strategic planning has it limits because of unexpected events, randomness, and even the weather. Organizations develop elaborate forecasting models that produce information about future demand for a product. But then customer demographics change or a key component of the economy sours—and costs change. Forecasting the future is one method organizations use to reduce uncertainty.

Chaos theory has been applied to numerous scientific disciplines over the past decade, and it has recently been used to understand the dynamics of organizations. Essentially, chaos theory says that predictions of the future could be enormously inaccurate as a result of only slight imprecision in the measurement of existing conditions. Weather phenomena are a good example of chaotic systems. How often have you noticed your local weather forecasters being embarrassingly wrong? Usually, they are wrong because some weather conditions are just too complex to measure with great accuracy. The same is true in today's complex organizations and global economy. Managers like to be able to predict the future so that they can better prepare for it; but chaos theory suggests there might be some inherent limitations in an organization's ability to forecast the future accurately. Some theorists have even argued that the long-term future is essentially unknowable. They think managers should view as fiction the elaborate computer-modeled forecasts presented to them. The purpose of such forecasts, these theorists claim, is to allay anxiety rather than perform any genuinely predictive function. On the other hand, chaos theory provides a useful framework for understanding the dynamic evolution of industries and the complex evolution of individual companies within industries. By understanding industries and organizations as complex—perhaps chaotic—systems, managers can build better strategies.[23]

Chaos theory has its advocates, but other less controversial ideas offer others ways of making the future better for the organization. New organizational strategies and structures enable organizations to deal with complexity through constant learning and creativity. As Harvard Business School professor Rosabeth Moss Kanter states, "New organizational models offer the best of both worlds—enough structure for continuity, but not so much that creative responses to chaos are stifled."[24] Changes in the way managers understand their competitive environment are rooted in how they see the business world. Peter Senge suggests that successful organizations are learning organizations. Building a learning organization requires a manager to develop new skills, such as building shared vision, testing mental models, and engaging in systems thinking.[25] Senge's advice may help managers to better adapt to competitive pressures as well as to design an organization that fits the needs of a complex competitive environment.

## Three Levels of Strategy: Corporate, Business, and Functional

No single strategy guides all aspects of organizational activity. Strategy falls into one of three categories: corporate, business or competitive, and functional. A corporate-level strategy is described as a domain definition strategy,[26] because corporate strategy integrates complex domains (often multiple industries) in which an organization competes. For example, Altria owns both Philip Morris (PM) and Kraft Foods. Although the business was built in the tobacco industry, PM formed Altria after acquiring Kraft Foods. Clearly, the tobacco industry faces an uncertain future in the United States but is still quite profitable worldwide. The Kraft acquisition helps ameliorate the risks in the tobacco industry.

Business-level, or competitive, strategies are referred to as domain navigational strategies. Two of the most common strategies in this category are cost leadership and differentiation. Functional-level strategies describe how organizational resources are deployed in each functional area to support the business-level strategy. Common functional areas include production, marketing, accounting, and finance.

## Corporate-Level Strategy: The Big Picture

Corporate-level strategy is concerned with how best to achieve an organization's goal consistent with its mission. Organizations often compete in multiple lines of business, with some lines in different industries calling for different strategies. Common corporate strategies are concentration on a single business, diversification, and vertical integration.

**Concentration on a Single Business** | Sometimes referred to as a dominant business strategy, this strategy is focused and limited in scope. An organization using the strategy of concentration on a single business focuses, not surprisingly, on only one business. The surprise is that many organizations fall into this category. For example, Federal Express and Domino's Pizza are companies that focus on only one line of business. Federal Express is in the overnight shipping business, and Domino's is in the carry-out, freshly made pizza business. The benefits of concentration derive primarily from focusing all corporate energies in one area. But that same benefit can be a disadvantage, because all the company's "strategic eggs" are in one basket. Any economic downturn in the industry can immediately affect companies following this strategy.

**Vertical Integration** | Vertical integration affords cost advantages by owning members of the supply chain. Normally, this occurs through the outright purchase of a company that is a member of your supply chain. This process is referred to as acquisition. In an industry with few stages of production from raw material to finished goods, vertical integration makes sense. It affords greater access to limited raw materials, allows greater control over costs, and ensures a higher level of product quality. Because all stages of production are in-house, vertical integration also makes customizing the product easier. *Forward vertical integration* seeks to control the supply chain activities as the product or service moves toward the customer; for example, controlling distribution by owing trucking services or retail outlets. Members of the movie industry own distribution companies that control access and facilitate movement of film and digital media to movie venues and retail outlets. *Backward vertical integration* seeks to control the supply chain activities that precede production; for example, owning the source of the raw material used in production. The great Hollywood movie studios of the 1930s and 1940s—United Artists, Warner Brothers, MQM, Universal, and RKO—each had a stable of talented stars that were under contract to make a fixed number of movies each year. The studios already owned the production facilities. So, by contracting with the limited pool of raw material (e.g., stars like W.C. Fields, Clark Gable, and Jane Powell), they were following a strategy of backward integration. This practice is no longer feasible in the movie industry because it has proven too costly, inflexible, and inefficient. The primary consideration for a backward integration strategy is cost. If it costs less to own the member of the supply chain, you gain an advantage. However, if in-house costs are higher than market acquisition, vertical integration erodes profits.

**Diversification** | Diversification strategies are employed when a firm competes in more than one industry. Each industry has it own structure and warrants a separate strategy. Related diversification occurs when an organization diversifies into similar industries, products, and/or infrastructures. Del Monte in the preserved food industry is a good example of related diversification. Del Monte owns vegetable processing facilities, a glass jar company, and a snack food company. All these industries are related to their core products. Unrelated diversification describes the situation where the organization moves into an industry unrelated to its core business. Large global conglomerates fall into this category. Hitachi Corporation makes consumer electronics, power tools, and computers. It diversifies either by acquiring or merging with another company.

| The Portfolio Matrix Model | Portfolio analysis—evaluating an organization's current mix of products and businesses—is useful in developing corporate-level strategy. The Boston Consulting Group (BCG) developed the Portfolio Matrix to help large diversified organizations strategically manage their holdings. For example, the Coca-Cola Company manufactures, markets, and distributes more than 300 beverage brands worldwide. Some brands will succeed; others will fail. Along the way, Coke's strategic managers must decide what to do with each brand.

The dominant business on which a company has built its success, for example, Coke at Coca-Cola, might generate substantial cash surplus beyond the amount needed to sustain the product. The excess cash affords Coca-Cola Company the opportunity to expand into other profitable areas. According to the BCG, organizations use portfolio analysis to make strategic decisions across multiple lines of business.

Strategic Business Units   The first step in the BCG approach is to identify each division, product line, and so forth that can be considered a business. Each of these is called a strategic business unit (SBU). An SBU is a product or service division within a company that establishes goals and objectives in harmony with the firm's overall mission and is responsible for its own profits and losses. Each SBU has the following four characteristics:

| Has a distinct mission

| Has its own competitors

| Is a single business or collection of businesses

| Can be planned for independently of the other businesses of the total organization

Thus, depending on the organization, an SBU could be a single product, product line, division, department, or agency. Once managers identify and classify all the SBUs, they need some method of measuring their performance. This is the important contribution of the BCG approach.

An organization following the BCG approach would classify SBUs using the BCG Portfolio Matrix (see Exhibit 7.4). The matrix depends on two business indicators of strategic importance: market growth rate and relative market share. Market growth rate refers to the annual rate of growth of the market in which a product, division, or department is located. The relative market share indicates an SBU's market share. As you can see in the exhibit, this indicator ranges from a high to low relative share of the market.

**EXHIBIT 7.4**   **BCG Portfolio Matrix**

| Market Growth | | Relative Market Share | |
|---|---|---|---|
| High | | STAR — Build | QUESTION MARK — Harvest/Divest |
| Low | | CASH COW — Hold/Harvest | DOG — Harvest/Divest |
| | | High | Low |

Based on these two indicators, BCG has identified four distinct SBU classifications:

*Star.* An SBU that has a high share of a high-growth market is considered a star. Stars need a great deal of financial resources because of their rapid growth. When growth slows, they become cash cows and important generators of cash for the organization. For example, Ford's acquisition of Jaguar and revitalization of the brand ultimately recreated the cachet of the old Jaguar nameplate. Although it is a high-profit star today, it could have easily been a failure without the proper strategic guidance, resources, and customer acceptance of the final Jaguar product.

*Cash cow.* An SBU that has a high share of a low-growth market is labeled a cash cow. They produce a lot of cash for an organization, but because the market is not growing, they require less of a company's financial resources for growth and expansion. The company can thus use the money generated by its cash cows to satisfy current debt and to support SBUs in need of cash. The Coca-Cola soft drink is the cash cow of the Coca-Cola Company. The firm has been able to use the cash generated through Coke sales to buy Fruitopia, Minute Maid, Dasani, and so on.

*Question mark.* When an SBU has a low share of a high-growth market, it is identified as a question mark in the Portfolio Matrix. The organization must decide whether to spend more financial resources to build it into a star, phase it down, or just eliminate it altogether. Such SBUs frequently require high amounts of resources just to maintain their share, let alone increase it. We mentioned Ford's purchase of Jaguar in the star example. Had the market for luxury cars faltered temporarily or had Ford made decisions that affected the profitability of Jaguar, the Jaguar might easily have been reclassified as a question mark.

*Dog.* When an SBU has a low share of a low-growth market, it is classified as a dog. A dog might generate enough cash to maintain itself, or it might drain money from other SBUs. The only certainty is that dogs are not great sources of cash. In the late 1990s, for example, Time Warner made a bold strategic move to acquire America Online. It was a disaster—in 2002, AOL lost a phenomenal $100 billion. But, why did they want to buy AOL? For Time Warner, the AOL merger represented both a product and a distribution vehicle for the delivery of digital products to consumers. Following the old salesman's adage of "beating a path to the customer's door," Time Warner was buying a digital pathway to contemporary consumers. Even though their strategic intent was clear, the AOL component quickly became a cash drain, sending their combined stock price plummeting.

Depending on whether an organization's SBUs are products, product lines, or entire divisions, its portfolio matrix will include various combinations of the preceding four classifications. After completing the relevant classifications, the organization faces some strategic choices.

**Strategic SBU Choices** Any organization that operates in multiple industries or has multiple products can be analyzed using the BCG Portfolio Matrix. This technique enables managers to subject each SBU to some tough questions. If you look at Exhibit 7.4, you can see the four alternative strategies that can be selected for each category of SBU.

*Build.* If it seems that an SBU has the potential to be a star (it is probably a question mark at present), the organization would want to build that SBU. The organization might even decide to give up short-term profits to provide the necessary financial resources to achieve this objective. A firm should also build its current stars.

*Hold.* If an SBU is a successful cash cow, a key objective would certainly be to hold or preserve the market share so that the organization can take advantage of the positive cash flow.

| *Harvest.* This strategy is appropriate for all SBUs except those classified as stars. It focuses on increasing the short-term cash return without too much concern for the long-run impact. It is especially worthwhile when more cash is needed for investment in other businesses.

| *Divest.* Getting rid of SBUs with low shares of low-growth markets is often a good move.

SBUs can, and often do, change their position in the portfolio matrix. As time passes, question marks can become stars, stars can become cash cows, and cash cows can become dogs. In fact, as the market growth rate changes, an SBU can move through every category. The industry's technology and competitiveness influence how quickly these changes occur. This market fluctuation underscores (1) the importance and usefulness of viewing an organization based on its SBUs, and (2) the necessity of constantly seeking new ventures as well as managing existing ones.

There is a lot to be said for the BCG approach, but be aware that it is not perfect. Some critics have pointed out that although strategy exists at the corporate, business, and functional levels, the BCG model is most useful at the corporate level. Further, portfolio analysis often leads an organization to neglect some of its SBUs. For example, a cash cow seldom receives additional resources, because its primary purpose is to generate cash; and classifying an SBU as a dog might be a self-fulfilling prophecy when by its very definition there seems little reason to support it. Some critics are concerned that the portfolio matrix model could encourage bureaucratic aspects of planning rather than strategic thinking. Another major criticism of the model centers on its focus on market share and market growth as the primary indicators of profitability. One study found that using the BCG Portfolio Matrix actually decreased managers' ability to choose the more profitable project. Researchers Scott Armstrong and Roderick Brodie surveyed managers in six countries over a five-year period, and found that of those managers who used the BCG Portfolio Matrix in analyzing which SBUs to invest in, 87 percent selected the less profitable investment.[27]

Another criticism to consider is the simplicity of the BCG 2-by-2 matrix. This simplistic form of arraying data eliminates other important strategic variables. Yet this drawback can also be a benefit. An important reason for the popularity of this matrix seems to be that any business concept worth using has to be reducible to a fairly brief and simple form. Thus, for simplicity's sake, many complex concepts are often reduced to a 2-by-2 matrix. But the apparent simplicity of the 2-by-2 matrix is both a strength and weakness. When it is used to display concepts thoughtfully distilled from the real world, it can be very powerful. When employed to explain a situation whose considerable complexity must fit into only four boxes, it can be dangerously misleading. All these criticisms are valid; but thanks to the power of the BCG model for assessing SBU strategic positioning, the model is used extensively by managers across all industries.

For better or worse, many organizations today believe that they must be involved in e-commerce in one form or another. Firms typically achieve this objective by acquiring an Internet company. In the late 1990s, leveraged buyouts, mergers, and acquisition activity centered on Internet companies. Building an Internet presence was believed by many organizations as paramount to ensure future economic success. It turned out that many Internet companies never made a profit. Amazon.com, for example, struggles to this day to maintain profitability. One solution offered by researchers is to use portfolio analysis when assessing the viability and fit of potential acquisitions to a portfolio of investments.[28] Portfolio analysis is still a viable strategic tool for achieving a balanced investment of corporate resources.

## Business-Level Strategy: Competitive Strategy

Large organizations often compete in several industries or market segments. Each industry or market has its own competitive environment, each of which requires a unique strategy. To navigate its particular industry domain, a business needs its own competitive strategy.

EXHIBIT **7.5**

**Porter's Five Forces Model**

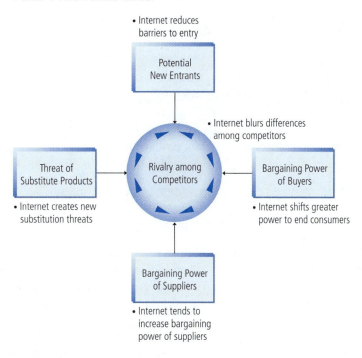

**Sources:** Based on Michael E. Porter, *Competitive Strategy: Techniques for Analyzing Industries and Competitors* (New York: Free Press, 1980); and Michael E. Porter, "Strategy and the Internet," *Harvard Business Review* (March, 2001) 63–78.

| **Porter's Five Forces** | Harvard Business School economist Michael Porter[29] has developed several useful frameworks for developing an organization's strategy. One of the most often-cited is the five competitive forces that determine industry structure (see Exhibit 7.5). Porter states that in any industry, the nature of competition is defined by five competitive forces: (1) threat of new entrants, (2) threat of substitute products or services, (3) bargaining power of suppliers, (4) bargaining power of buyers, and (5) rivalry among existing competitors.

The strength of these five forces varies from industry to industry. However, no matter the industry, these five forces determine profitability because they shape the prices firms can charge, the costs they have to bear, and the investment required to compete in the industry. For example, the threat of new entrants limits the profit potential in an industry, because new entrants seek market share by driving down prices and thus driving down profit margins. Or, powerful buyers or suppliers bargain away profits for themselves. Before making strategic decisions, managers should use the five forces model to determine the competitive structure of an industry.

| **Competitive Strategies** | According to Porter's competitive strategy model, which is illustrated in Exhibit 7.6, organizations can develop distinctive competence in three ways: cost leadership, differentiation, and focus (emphasizing either cost leadership or differentiation).

**Cost**   Cost leadership is a common strategy for creating value while maintaining a lower than average cost structure. The cost-leadership strategy means lower prices for the customer with a higher volume of business, yet lower profit margins on each item for the producer. The cost leader seeks efficiencies in manufacturing or production to maintain a low-cost position. With every gain in efficiency, the cost leader gains the ability to lower prices further while maintaining the lowest cost base in the industry. Examples of cost leaders are Wal-Mart, Aldi (a low-cost wholesale food store), and Harbor Freight Tools.

**KEY**TERMS

**five competitive forces** Defines competition in terms of five competitive forces: (1) the threat of new entrants, (2) the threat of substitute products or services, (3) the bargaining power of suppliers, (4) the bargaining power of buyers, and (5) the rivalry among existing competitors.

**cost-leadership strategy** A common strategy for creating value while maintaining a lower-than-average cost structure.

**7.6**        **Porter's Competitive Strategies**

| Cost Leadership | Differentiation |
|---|---|
| Wal-Mart | Outback Steakhouse products |

**Integrated cost leadership and differentiation strategy**

| Focus: Cost Leadership | Focus: Differentiation |
|---|---|
| Briggs & Stratton four-cycle engines | Porsche |

**differentiation strategy**
A strategy by which the firm offers a premium-priced product that is equipped with more product-enhancing features than its competitors' products.

**focus-cost leadership strategy** Serves a segment or target market for its product or service by emphasizing product consistency at the lowest possible cost.

**focus differentiation strategy** Serves a segment or target market for its product or service by creating a product that is different and superior to the competition; for example, Porsche's filling of the high-end sports car market niche with a product that differs significantly enough from its competitors to warrant a premium price.

**integrated cost leadership/ differentiation strategy**
A strategy by which an organization serves a segment or target market for its product or service by creating a product that is low cost, yet different from and superior to the competition; for example, Coca-Cola or McDonalds.

**Differentiation**    In an effort to distinguish its products, an organization using the differentiation strategy offers a higher-priced product equipped with more product-enhancing features than its competitors' products. A firm using differentiation strategy seeks to charge a premium price for its products, and it attempts to maintain high levels of customer loyalty. The firm markets and sells the product to a relatively small group of customers who are willing to pay a higher price for the premium features. This differentiation strategy leads to relatively high cost structure, lower volume production, and a higher gross profit margin per item. The differentiator firm strives for product innovation to maintain its differentiation edge. Often, advertising or marketing adds a perception of luxury that creates demand for the product because of the psychological value of buying and using it. Volvo automobiles, Starbucks coffee, and Outback Steakhouse products are marketed under a differentiation strategy.

**Focus-Cost Leadership**    A firm using the focus-cost leadership strategy serves a segment or target market for its product or service by emphasizing product consistentcy at the lowest possible cost. An example of a successful focus strategy based on *cost leadership* is Briggs & Stratton, the ultimate low-cost producer for small, high-quality, four-cycle engines. In the low-cost lawn mower market, Briggs & Stratton appears to be the engine of choice.

**Focus-Differentiation**    A firm using the focus differentiation strategy serves a segment or target market for its product or service by creating a product that is different and superior to the competition. A successful focus strategy based on *differentiation* is Porsche. Porsche fills a niche in the high-end sports car market, sticking to that market with a product that differs significantly enough from its competitors to warrant a premium price. Porche offers the ultimate driving experience in a production sports car.

**Integrated Cost Leadership/Differentiation**    A firm using an integrated cost leadership/differentiation strategy serves a segment or target market for its product or service by creating a product that is both low cost, yet different from and superior to the competition. In the global market, brands like Coca-Cola and McDonalds offer low-cost alternatives to their competitors while simultaneously offering a unique high-quality product attainable nowhere else.

# Functional-Level Strategy

Corporate-level strategy represents a broad integrative orientation to strategically manage multiple businesses in different industries. Business-level strategies are concerned with tactical

**EXHIBIT 7.7**

**Functional Strategies and Associated Activities**

| Functional Strategy | Strategic Activities |
| --- | --- |
| Marketing | Product development<br>Product positioning<br>Advertising |
| Production | Production flow<br>Continuous quality improvement<br>Production scheduling |
| Finance | Short-term borrowing<br>Capital budgeting<br>Cash flow analysis |
| Human resources | Recruitment and selection<br>Performance appraisal<br>Benefits |
| Research and development | New product development<br>Packaging innovation |

competition within a single industry. Functional strategies reflect the operational approach to implement a business-level strategy. Functional strategies are strategic actions, resources commitments, and a stream of previous decisions that follow from and support the business-level strategy. Functional level strategies are established for marketing, production, finance, human resources, and other functional areas. The functional level of strategy is the most specific level, translating more generic ideas such as differentiation into actions taken by production or marketing to create a product that is different from the competition. An example is Ford's multimillion-dollar investment in a Schuler stamping press that produces matching doors for the Ford F-150 pickup truck in one operation. This process yields better "fit and finish."[30] This piece of equipment is part of the production functional level strategy that supports Ford's business-level strategy that emphasizes increased quality. Similarly, the role of the functional marketing strategy is to create promotional and advertising programs that communicate the business-level differentiation strategy to the consumer. Functional strategies create value by supporting competitive strategies. They are successful to the degree that they actually create value—by taking action that translates into efficiency in the case of cost leadership, or by supporting aspects of product differentiation in the case of a differentiation strategy. Functional strategies create value for the consumer in production, marketing, delivery to the consumer, and post sales service support. For example, the production functional strategy might require a cost-efficient production schedule, building a minimum of 100,000 units per manufacturing run to support cost leadership strategy.

The development of successful functional strategies benefits from a thorough understanding of the source of competitive advantage for the firm. Exhibit 7.7 describes the activities included in each functional strategy that should add value to the product and support competitive advantage.

## Strategy Implementation

Strategy formulation develops a plan to achieve competitive advantage. Strategy implementation commits the organization's resources, activities, people, and structures to support the strategy. A reoccurring theme in strategy implementation is the concept of fit. Research supports the idea that successful organizations achieve a high degree of fit between their multi-level strategy and their management style, culture, systems, skill, staff, and reward system.[31] Exhibit 7.8 details the 7-S Model developed by McKinsey and Company, a group of international consultants. This model

**KEY TERMS**

**functional strategies** Strategic actions, resource commitments, and streams of previous decision that follow from and support a business strategy.

proposes that successful implementation takes the form of a *strategic fit* among the seven key organizational elements outlined. The Management Highlight on page 157 offers an opportunity to review the facts surrounding the implementation of a "Green Strategy" by several automobile manufacturers in the U.S. automobile industry and determine which one has most successfully implemented the strategy.

# Strategic Planning for the Internet

The Internet has transformed business, and no discussion of strategy should ignore this increasingly important technology. Our knowledge economy depends on information and time. Organizations need current information fast, and the Internet provides both. Organizations use the Internet in two ways. First, the Internet is *supportive* of ongoing business activities. In a sense, organizations use the Internet to do the same old things. L.L. Bean uses the Internet for an online catalog, order entry, and order fulfillment monitoring. L.L. Bean has merely automated its traditionally manual processes. Second, the Internet is *formative* to the creation of core business activities using the Internet. E* Trade Financial is an example. This firm uses information and software to make stock trades and complete other financial transactions. It has no full-service brokers; all activities are software driven, only rarely requiring human intervention. Most organizations fall into the first category mentioned, where the Internet is supportive of ongoing business activity.

Regardless of how an organization uses the Internet, three criteria drive successful e-commerce: reach, richness, and affiliation.[32] *Reach* means access—who can access your site? *Richness* is a measure of the depth of information available on the site. *Affiliation* concerns who benefits from the site. Increasingly, e-commerce is affiliating with customers rather than taking the more traditional path of affiliating with suppliers. The Internet can be a vital component of an organization's strategy if it integrates each of these three criteria into the sale of its product or service.

Michael Porter takes a more traditional view of the strategy for Internet integration.[33] He believes that the fundamentals of competition remain unchanged. In some cases, the Internet might facilitate business, and in others it might be the prime mode of business activity, but it is not likely to create a fundamental shift in competition. Organizations should begin with an e-strategy for the Internet, but ultimately, they must integrate the Internet into a multilevel strategy.

| EXHIBIT 7.8 | McKinsey's 7-S Model | |
|---|---|---|
| **Shared Values** | The beliefs, taken-for-granted assumptions, and values that guide daily group behavior. Shared values are transmitted to new members through training, mentors, stories, and rituals. | |
| **Strategy** | The organization must have a strategy or plan describing the actions that the organization will follow to achieve corporate goals. It should be clear and cause people to take specific action. | |
| **Structure** | All organizations have a structure. But is the structure supportive of the strategy? The choice of structure should be based on the strategy chosen. Structure should fit the strategy. If it does not, the structure should be changed. | |
| **Systems** | Systems are the infrastructure of the organization. These include accounting systems, information systems, and administrative systems that define the processing needs of the organization. | |
| **Staff** | These are the people who work for the organization. Does the organization have the people it needs to achieve the goals of the organization? The organization's Human Resources area is responsible for planning and development needs that are supportive of organizational goals. | |
| **Skills** | What are the organization's distinctive competencies? The organization should build on skills and competencies it already has in the market. It is less risky for an organization to build successes than to venture into uncharted waters. | |
| **Style** | Style is a euphemism for organizational culture. Remember that the culture of the organization is created by the CEO. The CEO values and philosophy are reflected in the culture that is created by the policies, decisions, and behavior of the CEO and the top management staff. | |

MANAGEMENTHIGHLIGHT

## EXERCISE

### Implementing an ECO-Friendly Strategy in the Small Car Market

The segmented nature of the automotive market forces vehicle manufacturers to follow a differentiation strategy to satisfy the needs of each segment. Increased demand for oil, higher prices, and control of supply has forced virtually all vehicle manufacturers to develop more fuel efficient vehicles. Nowhere is this more evident than in the under 2.0 liter engine small car market. Each year the American Council for an Energy-Efficient Economy gives a "green score" to vehicles manufactured around the world. Listed here are vehicles produced by General Motors, Honda, Toyota, Ford, and several different Korean manufacturers. The question is: Which manufacturer has been most successful in implementing a differentiation strategy?

### Assignment: First, for each manufacturer:

1. Compute the manufacturer's the average score for: City MPG, Highway MPG, and Green Score. Use these averages to evaluate the success of each manufacturer. Who is the leader in the industry with the highest average for City MPG, Highway MPG, and Green Score?
2. Compute the average HwyMPG/Liters for each manufacturer; which manufacturer gets the most MPGs per liter?
3. Compare HwyMPG/CYL for hybrid versus nonhybrid vehicles.
4. Rank the five manufacturers on the effectiveness of their ECO strategies.

*Note: City and Highway MPG measure the degree of goal attainment or successful strategy implementation. HwyMPG/CYL and HwyMPG/Liters are measures of the engine efficiency or resource utilization.*

| Make and Model | Manufacturer | City Mpg | Highway Mpg | Cyl | Liters | Hwympg/ Cyl | Green Score |
|---|---|---|---|---|---|---|---|
| Toyota Prius Hybrid | Toyota | 60 | 51 | 4 | 1.5 | 34 | 55 |
| Toyota Corolla | Toyota | 32 | 41 | 4 | 1.8 | 23 | 46 |
| Toyota Matrix | Toyota | 30 | 36 | 4 | 1.8 | 20 | 44 |
| Scion | Toyota | 31 | 38 | 4 | 1.5 | 25 | 42 |
| Hyundai Accent | Hyundai | 32 | 35 | 4 | 1.6 | 22 | 45 |
| Hyundai Sonata | Hyundai | 24 | 33 | 4 | 2.4 | 14 | 39 |
| Honda Insight Hybrid | Honda | 57 | 56 | 3 | 1.0 | 56 | 57 |
| Honda Civic Hybrid | Honda | 49 | 51 | 4 | 1.3 | 39 | 53 |
| Honda Civic | Honda | 30 | 40 | 4 | 1.8 | 22 | 44 |
| Honda Civic Gx | Honda | 30 | 34 | 4 | 1.7 | 20 | 57 |
| Pontiac Vibe | GM | 30 | 36 | 4 | 1.8 | 20 | 44 |
| Saturn Ion | GM | 26 | 35 | 4 | 2.2 | 16 | 43 |
| Chevrolet Cobalt | GM | 25 | 34 | 4 | 2.2 | 16 | 43 |
| Ford Escape Hybrid | FORD | 36 | 31 | 4 | 2.3 | 13 | 42 |
| Ford Focus Wagon | FORD | 26 | 32 | 4 | 2.0 | 16 | 41 |

Source: *American Council for an Energy-Efficient Economy.*

CONCLUSION

## Strategy

Strategic planning helps an organization to reduce risks and efficiently use its resources to achieve organizational goals. Strategic planning is a systematic, rational process of allocating resources in pursuit of organizational goals. The result of the strategic planning process is a *planned strategy,* though not all strategies come to fruition according to plan.[34] Critics note that strategic planning is more than a set of analytical techniques; it must be deeply ingrained in managers charged with the task of developing strategies.[35] Contrary to the very premise of strategic planning, many strategies—rather than following a formal process—actually emerge through a process of interaction between strategic planners, stakeholder negotiations, and environmental pressure from consumer, government, and special interest groups.

Strategists might plan for a specific product design; but a competitive response, changing demographics, and societal trends may alter the actual strategy implemented. This *emergent strategy* makes the strategic management process evolutionary. Keep in mind that strategy is the product of actions taken and decisions made by organizational members over time. Strategy is not an edict made by top management that all must follow obediently. Rather, top management begins with a basic plan or direction setting that is translated into action by employees at all levels of the organization. Because the strategic management process is far more complex and filled with pitfalls than most business analysts care to admit, strategic thinking is a critical skill for successful corporate leaders.

## Discussion Questions

1. A multilevel strategy consists of three levels. Identify and describe each level of a multilevel strategy.

2. Describe each component of Michael Porter's Five Forces model. Also, review the five generic strategies discussed by Porter: cost leadership, differentiation, focused cost leadership, focused differentiation, integrated cost leadership/differentiation strategy.

3. What are the three criteria that drive a successful e-commerce strategy?

## Video Case

### Timbuk2: Make the Swirl as Famous as the Swoosh

"We want to make the *Swirl* as famous as the *Swoosh*," says Timbuk2's CEO Mark Dwight with a chuckle. Although he might be joking by comparing his firm's logo to the Nike *Swoosh,* Dwight isn't kidding. When Dwight took over as head of Timbuk2 a few years ago, the company was on a downward slide, losing money because it had only one product to offer to a narrow market—a bag for bicycle messengers. Granted, the bag came in several sizes and colors—but Dwight realized that Timbuk2 couldn't survive, let alone grow, on the strength of one messenger bag. So Dwight and his managers developed corporate- and business-level strategies to achieve the goal of turning the company around and then achieving growth: increasing and broadening the product line to reach into new markets, developing the brand while remaining true to the company's heritage, finding new distribution channels, creating alliances with other firms, and outsourcing some production to maintain quality but reduce costs.

To achieve the sales goal of $25 million in five years, the Timbuk2 design, production, and marketing teams set about developing new products. Meanwhile, the sales staff renewed their efforts with Timbuk2's existing bags and customers. The expanded product line now includes yoga bags, CD cases, travel bags, duffels, graphic-arts totes, and laptop/commuter bags, among others. "We now have a [product] portfolio that you *can* shake the trees with," says Geoff Sacco. "It's not just about asking customers, can you buy some more messenger bags?" More products means more potential sales to more markets. For instance, a chic traveler might want to carry a Timbuk2 bag; a yoga student might choose a Timbuk2 bag for her yoga mat, water bottle, and other gear; a cyclist might choose the new Shortcut, a convertible waist pack that contains easy-access pockets and reflective patches for night riding.

However, Mark Dwight and his staff are determined to remain true to Timbuk2's original customers, the bicycle messengers. They are the firm's long-standing customers, and Dwight wants to be careful not to leave them behind. To that end, Timbuk2 is developing the new professional messenger bag called the Tag Junkie—referring to a term used by messengers—in collaboration with a California design student who also happens to be a bike messenger. Whenever new designs are reviewed in meetings, Dwight and his staff discuss the elements of a bag that make it stand out as a Timbuk2 brand—so that each bag is consistent with the image of the Timbuk2 brand.

Developing new distribution channels is an important strategy for Timbuk2. One is the Internet. The firm's Web site is already profitable, so building on that strength makes sense. A current popular feature of the site is "Build Your Own Bag," where customers can combine sizes, fabrics, colors, and features to create their own customized bags.

Developing products that can be used successfully with other firms' products is a creative strategy. Recently, Timbuk2 has begun manufacturing bags specifically to fit Apple laptops—much to the delight of Apple users. One reviewer who tried the Commute XL Laptop Messenger Bag for his Apple Macintosh 17" Powerbook was pleased with several features, including the strap, padded back, durable construction (a Timbuk2 hallmark), and waterproof interior (making it a good all-weather commuter bag).

Timbuk2's decision to outsource the production of some of its bags to China—most are made in a factory near the company's offices in San Francisco—drew criticism from a few customers. However, the firm defended the move by explaining that doing so actually allowed the San Francisco factory to remain open and active. The laptop bags, explains Timbuk2's Web site, "are much more complex to build and require substantially more labor and a variety of very expensive machines we don't have here in our factory." So the bags are made in China to strict Timbuk2 quality specifications—and can be sold in the United States at a more reasonable price.

To make certain that each of these strategies is being implemented effectively, Mark Dwight meets weekly with his management staff and daily with his operations staff. "We look at performance on an ongoing basis," says Dwight. "How do I know if we picked the right strategy? The results that we've seen so far indicate that we're on the right path. There are examples of other [firms] that have done the same thing and they created substantial, lasting enterprises on this strategy."

### Questions

1. How would you describe Timbuk2's corporate strategy? Business-level strategy? Why?

2. How would you define Timbuk2's core competency?

3. Identify one strength, weakness, opportunity, and threat for Timbuk2.

Sources: Company web site, http://www.timbuk2.com, accessed August 13, 2004; "Timbuk2—New Stuff," *Cross Country Skier*, January 2004, http://www.findarticles.com; product review, *mymac.com*, January 2004, http://www.mymac.com.

## BizFlix

### *Seabiscuit*

*Seabiscuit* is a 2003 American drama film based on the best-selling book *Seabiscuit: An American Legend* by Laura Hillenbrand. The film stars Tobey Maguire as Red Pollard, the jockey for Seabiscuit, an undersized and overlooked thoroughbred race horse whose unexpected successes made him a popular sensation in the United States near the end of the Great Depression. In this scene, a hospitalized Pollard is unable to ride during the final leg of the Triple Crown, so he tries to communicate to his friend and replacement jockey Charley Kurtsinger (played by Chris McCarron) what he needs to do to win the race.

### Questions

1. What aspects of strategic planning can you identify in the clip?

2. Which strategic alternative (risk seeking or risk avoiding) does Red Pollard advocate that his friend use during the race? Explain.

## *Suggested Readings*

Ghosh, Shirkir, "Making Business Sense of the Internet." *Harvard Business Review* (March–April 1998).

Kaplan Robert and David Norton, "The Office of Strategy Management." *Harvard Business Review* (October, 2005).

Mankins Michael C. and Richard Steele, "Turning Great Strategy into Great Performances." *Harvard Business Review* (July–August, 2005).

Peng, Mike W, "Institutional Transitions and Strategic Choice." *Academy of Management Review* 28(2): 2003.

Porter, Michael E, "Strategy and the Internet." *Harvard Business Review* (March 2001).

## *Endnotes*

1. Jay Galbraith and Robert Kazanjian, *Strategy Implementation* (St. Paul, MN: West Publishing, 1986): 3.

2. Charles W. Hofer and Dan Schendel, *Strategy Formulation: Analytical Concepts* (St. Paul, MN: West Publishing, 1978): chap. 1.

3. Michael E. Porter, "What Is Strategy?" *Harvard Business Review* (November–December, 1996): 62.

4. Gregg Dess and G. T. Lumpkin, *Strategic Management: Creating Competitive Advantages* (Burr Ridge, IL: McGraw-Hill-Irwin, 2003), 3.

5. Ibid.

6. Mark L. McConkie and R. Wayne Boss, "Using Stories as an Aid to Consultation," *Public Administration Quarterly* (Winter 1994).

7. "Ford Exec: Camry Better than Taurus; Ford Sales and Marketing Executive Offers Simple Reason Toyota's Sedan Outsells Ford's," Reuters wire (February 13, 2003).

8. Ram Charan, "Execution: The Discipline of Getting Things Done. How Did Honeywell Chairman Larry Bossidy Turn the Company Around? By His Maniacal Focus on Just One Thing," *Fortune* (May 28, 2002).

9. "This Month's Focus: The Mission Statement," *Manager's Magazine* (February 1995): 30–31.

10. Robert Hoskisson, Michael Hitt, and R.Duane Ireland, *Competing for Advantage* (Mason, OH: Thomson, 2004): 18.

11. Ibid. 105.

12. C. K. Prahalad and G. Hamel, "The Core Competence of the Corporation," *Harvard Business Review* (May–June 1990): 79–91.

13. Charles Hill and Gareth Jones, *Strategic Management Theory: An Integrated Approach* (Boston: Houghton-Mifflin, 1998): 113.

14. Gary Hamel and C. K. Prahalad, "Strategic Intent," *Harvard Business Review* (May–June, 1989): 63–76.

15. Ibid. Also see Michael A. Hitt, Beverly B. Tyler, Camilla Hardee, and Daewoo Park, "Understanding Strategic Intent in the Global Marketplace," *Academy of Management Executive* (May 1995): 12–19.

16. David J. Collis and Cynthia A. Montgomery, "Competing on Resources," *Harvard Business Review* (July–August, 1995).

17. Michael Porter, *Competitive Advantage* (New York: Free Press), 1985.

18. Greg Dess and Tom Lumpkin. *Strategic Management: Creating Competitive Advantages* (Boston: McGraw-Hill, 2003), 70.

19. Robert Kaplan and David P. Norton, "Using the Balanced Scorecard as a Strategic Management System," *Harvard Business Review* (January–February, 1996): 75–85.

20. Ethel Auster and Chun Wei Choo, "How Senior Managers Acquire and Use Information in Environmental Scanning," *Information Processing & Management* (September–October 1994): 607–618.

21. Samuel Fromartz, "Extreme Outsourcing: How One Business Owner Set Out to Avoid Having Employees—and Stumbled onto the Way Americans Really Want to Work," *Fortune Small Business* (May 31, 2001).

22. R. Edward Freeman, *Strategic Management: A Stakeholder Approach* (New York: Free Press, 1984), 25.

23. David Levy, "Chaos Theory and Strategy: Theory, Application, and Management Implications," *Strategic Management Journal* (Summer 1994): 167–178.

24. Rosabeth Moss Kanter, "The Best of Both Worlds," *Harvard Business Review* (November–December 1992): 9–10.

25. Peter Senge, "The Leader's New Work: Building Learning Organizations," *Sloan Management Review* (Fall 1990): 7–23.

26. L. J. Bougeois III, "Strategic Management and Determinism," *Academy of Management Review* 9 (1984): 586–596.

27. J. Scott Armstrong and Roderick J. Brodie, "Effects of Portfolio Planning Methods on Decision Making: Experimental Results," *International Journal of Research in Marketing* (January 1994): 73–84. For criticism of this research, see Robin Wensley, "Making Better Decisions," *International Journal of Research in Marketing* (January 1994): 85–90. For Armstrong and Brodie's reply to this criticism, see J. Scott Armstrong and Roderick J. Brodie, "Portfolio Planning Methods," *International Journal of Research in Marketing* (January 1994): 91–93.

28. Anthony Tjan, "Finally, a Way to Put Your Internet Portfolio in Order," *Harvard Business Review* (February 2001).

29. Michael E. Porter, *Competitive Strategy* (New York: Free Press), 1980.

30. Gary Forger, "Ford Powers Ahead," *Modern Materials Handling*, April 1, 2004

31. Raymond Miles and Charles Snow, "Fit, Fashion, and the Hall of Fame," in Glen Carroll and David Vogel, *Strategy and Organization: A West Coast View* (Marshfield, MA: Pitman Publishing, 1984), 1–19.

32. Phillip Evans and Thomas S. Wurster, "Getting Real About Virtual Commerce," *Harvard Business Review* (November–December 1999).

33. Michael E. Porter, "Strategy and the Internet," *Harvard Business Review* (March 2001).

34. Richard Hammermesh, "Making Planning Strategic," *Harvard Business Review* (July–August 1986): 3–9; and Henry Mintzberg, "The Rise and Fall of Strategic Planning," *Harvard Business Review* (January–February 1994): 107–114.

35. Henry Mintzberg, "The Rise and Fall of Strategic Planning," *Harvard Business Review* (January–February 1994): 107–114.

# Organizing

# 8

# ORGANIZATIONAL STRUCTURE AND DESIGN

Organizations are emerging with much different structures from those of yesterday. Leading the way are organizations offering quality products, adapting quickly to their customers' demands, and accommodating environmental concerns. Although management theorists do not agree on exactly what the best type of organizational structure is, a picture of a flat, lean, high-performance workplace is emerging. The average company is smaller and employs fewer people; the traditional hierarchical organization is giving way to other forms, such as the network of specialists; the model of doing business is shifting from making a product to providing customer service; and work itself is being redefined to include constant learning and critical thinking.

This chapter presents the basic elements of organizing. It begins by discussing the concept of organizing and organizational structure. Then it examines four decisions that managers make in determining organizational structure: specialization of jobs, delegation of authority, departmentalization, and span of control. Next, it explores the dimensions of organizational structure—formalization, centralization, and complexity. The final section covers organizational design, including mechanistic and organic models, the contingency approach, and other systems.

## Organizing and Organizational Structure

Organizing is the process of structuring both human and physical resources to accomplish organizational objectives. Thus, organizing involves dividing tasks into jobs, delegating authority, determining the appropriate bases for departmentalizing jobs, and deciding the optimum number of jobs in each department.[1]

Developing a responsive organizational structure is one of the most critical challenges facing managers today. Large companies like Home Depot, Southwest Airlines, and Microsoft, despite their size, have succeeded because their organizations are nimble and respond quickly to changes in the market. Many managers recognize that their organization is not responsive or flexible, that it does not act quickly. But these same managers often attribute this problem to people—departments that cannot get along, uncommitted or unmotivated employees, or the inability to develop quality products in a timely fashion. However, these are clear symptoms of problems with organizational structure.

Organizational structure is the framework of jobs, departments, and divisions that directs the behavior of individuals and groups toward achieving the organization's objectives effectively. The positive contribution of organizational structure to an organization's performance is demonstrated each time a customer is satisfied; when customers are not satisfied, chances are great that the fault is with the organizational structure. Although the organizing function refers to decisions that managers make, organizational structure reflects the outcomes of these decisions.

Organizational structure must be consistent with an organization's strategy. As explained in Chapter 7, "Strategy," strategic planning specifies *what* the organization will accomplish and *when;* organizational structure specifies *who* will accomplish what, and *how* it will be accomplished.

Many organizations, unfortunately, try to implement a new strategy with an obsolete organizational structure. The result becomes the failed initiative of the month. For instance, an organization might recognize a need to be more market driven or more quality conscious, and the result is a new program for customer satisfaction or quality improvement. But an organization does not become quality conscious simply by deciding to. Rather, it must develop an organizational structure that results in the behaviors called for by the strategy.

## Structure Supports Organizational Strategy

An effective organizational structure does not result from chance, luck, or historical accident. It is the responsibility of management to deliberately develop a structure that enhances the organization's overall strategy, taking into consideration factors such as competition and the environment. Managers, in attempting to implement a new program or directive, often encounter resistance to change. Over time, organizational structures become quite ingrained and resistant to change. This behavior is not consistent with an environment that is constantly changing, and it can place an organization in a weak position relative to competitors. To keep in step with the constantly changing environment, many organizations find themselves reorganizing on a regular basis.

Managers must also recognize that there is no single best structure for an organization. What works at IBM might be different from what works at Apple or Compaq. The challenge managers face is to design the best structure for a specific organization—the structure that facilitates getting work done well. If structure actually impedes employees from completing work and hence does not help to achieve the organization's objectives, the structure might be incompatible with the strategy. If a bank teller cannot respond to a customer's request because of a lack of authority, the problem is in the bank's structure. Likewise, if an assembly line worker does not have the knowledge or ability to perform a job effectively, the company has a problem in its structure. Often employees cannot do their best work because the organization's structure gets in their way.

## Detecting Problems in Organizational Structure

When is organizational structure a problem? Ultimately, whenever work is not getting done well, there is likely to be a problem with organizational structure. Many factors or circumstances account for such problems. Conflicts between departments or groups within an organization suggest a structure problem. These conflicts can result from personality differences, but more often they are attributable to differences in the departments' goals. For example, the marketing department is most concerned with sales and introducing new products, whereas the production department is concerned with quality control. Difficulty in coordinating work between departments, slowness in adapting to change, and ambiguous job assignments also indicate problems with organizational structure. If employees are asking which goals are most important or what work to concentrate on, organizational structure might be the underlying problem.

Structure problems can be disastrous for an organization. First, the organization becomes a collection of departments or independent groups pursuing their own goals rather than a coherent organization with a common goal. Second, the organization's structure begins to dictate its strategy rather than strategy dictating structure; in short, its structure is determining what the organization does. This situation violates an important principle of management: strategy should dictate structure. Finally, if structure is allowed to determine strategy, only strategies compatible with the existing organizational structure are acceptable. This approach severely limits the strategies that an organization can pursue effectively; it especially limits efforts toward innovation and change.

MANAGEMENT HIGHLIGHT

### GENERAL MOTORS RESTRUCTURES

On March 1, 2006, *Consumer Reports* published its top ten vehicle list, and for the first time the cars were all Japanese brands. On the same day, General Motors reported February sales fell 3 percent. In response to staggering profits and intense competition from Asian and European automakers, GM announced a plan to restructure itself into a smaller and more competitive company.

For starters, having lost over ten billion dollars in 2005, GM is cutting costs. The firm offered buyouts and early retirement packages to each of its 113,000 union employees in the United States who agreed to leave the company. Delphi, the nation's largest automobile parts maker and a unit of GM until 1999—and itself in bankruptcy—is also offering buyouts to 13,000 of its 24,000 factory workers.

Many industry experts feel this is just the beginning. On average, United Auto Workers (UAW) union members at GM and Delphi cost 67 dollars an hour including pay, pensions, and healthcare benefits. GM provides healthcare for 1.1 million employees, retirees, and dependents. This adds about 1,300 dollars to the cost of every car and truck made in the United States. Although Japanese competitors like Toyota pay healthcare benefits for their United States employees, they do not have GM's retiree health burden.

Bankruptcy is not likely to occur in the immediate future, but unless revenues are stabilized, it is a high probability down the road. One Wall Streeter familiar with GM notes that whereas other auto giants such as Chrysler and Nissan have been revived in the past, "turning GM around is a harder logistical and managerial task than the invasion of Iraq." At the least, GM will need to restructure itself at every level.

Jerry York, GM's newest board member and advisor to billionaire GM investor Kirk Kerkorian, hopes to shake things up at the auto giant. He made the following points in a speech given to auto analysts in Detroit: (1) match costs to realistic market share and revenue expectations, (2) reduce product offerings, (3) review the entire company with a clean-slate perspective, (4) sell or close noncore businesses, and (5) instill a sense of purpose. Will this save GM? As one GM employee in the dealer organization who whishes to remain anonymous said, "I can't really believe that the people who got GM into this mess are going to be the people who can get GM out."

Source: Adapted from Carol J. Loomis, "The Tragedy of General Motors," *Fortune* (February 20, 2006): 59–70; "More Flats in Detroit," *Business Week* (March 13, 2006): 31; Micheline Maynard, "GM to Offer Buyouts to All 133,000 Union Workers," Lexington *Herald-Leader* (March 23, 2006): A1, A10; Andy Serwer, "The Face of Change at GM," *Fortune* (March 6, 2006): 58.

Perhaps the greatest influence on how workers perceive their work and how they behave is organizational structure. It is management's job to design an organizational structure that enables employees to do their best work and achieve the organization's objectives. In the next section, we examine the fundamental considerations or decisions that determine organizational structure. The Management Highlight above discusses how General Motors is changing its structure to compete with rival automakers.

## Determining Organizational Structure

Most of us have worked in some type of organization, and we tend to think of structure in narrow terms: What is our own job task? To whom do we report? How much responsibility do we have? Managers responsible for designing organizational structure must think in much broader terms that describe the entire structure itself, not just the jobs that constitute it. Structure is a strategic choice. Determining the appropriate type of structure enables people to do their best work. Managers must make many decisions regarding structure; the four major decisions pertain to specialization of jobs, delegation of authority, departmentalization, and span of control.

Exhibit 8.1 summarizes the choices managers can make regarding these decisions. In general, the structure of an organization falls on the same part of each continuum. In other words, an organization structured for workers to do highly specialized jobs will also tend to group jobs according to homogeneous or common functions and assign to managers only a few workers with little authority. The following sections examine each of these decisions in greater detail.

## Specialization of Jobs

One of the manager's major decisions is determining how specialized jobs will be. Most organizations consist to some degree of specialized jobs—work is divided into specific jobs having

**EXHIBIT 8.1**

**Designing Organizational Structure**

**Specialization of Jobs**
High _____ Low

**Delegation of authority**
Centralized _____ Decentralized

**Departmentalization**
Homogeneous _____ Heterogeneous

**Span of control**
Narrow _____ Wide

specific tasks. By dividing tasks into narrow specialties, managers gain the benefits derived from division of labor: minimum training is required for jobs consisting of only a few tasks, economic gains are obtained when employees become highly efficient in those tasks, and the result is better-quality output.

| **Scientific Management versus Craftsmanship** | As you will recall from Chapter 2, "History of Management," Frederick W. Taylor, a leading proponent of specialization, did much of his work in the late 1800s and early 1900s.[2] The environment then was characterized by a smokestack economy of assembly lines and blue-collar workers—many of whom were unskilled and could not speak English. Taylor's system, the catalyst for the scientific management movement, required that tasks be broken down into their smallest elements and that problem solving be elevated to managers. Taylor, through his time and motion studies, identified basic movements that minimized effort and maximized the output of lathe operators, ironworkers, and bricklayers. This system has permeated our entire society. Specialization now applies to employees as diverse as airline pilots, nurses, and accountants. People learn a job routine and repeat the tasks over and over. If they experience problems, they must consult a supervisor or manager. Work, or execution, is clearly separate from thinking or planning.

Craftsmanship is basically the opposite of scientific management. The craftsman produces a product from start to finish by working alone or cooperatively in a small group; management provides only the means and facilities. Craftsmanship produces high-quality products but is expensive and results in low output. It is not hard to understand why scientific management replaced the craftsmanship system, which for many years was considered the only alternative. According to quality expert Joseph Juran, "Taylor's concept of separating planning from execution fitted our culture and, at the time, was very logical. You had a lot of immigrants ... some of them were completely illiterate. And they were in no position, in his [Taylor's] opinion, to make decisions on how work should be done."[3]

The strengths and weaknesses of scientific management versus craftsmanship are summarized in the Management Highlight on page 168.

As noted earlier, many people think of organizational structure in relation to their own jobs. Specialization has in some instances inspired a "that's not my job" attitude, which has seriously hurt some organizations. The system that worked so well after World War II—when America flooded the world market with affordable domestic products—is not as effective in today's complex global economy. Many organizations are searching for alternative approaches.

| **Teams and Quality Circles** | Japan was the first nation to realize that the scientific management approach to specialization would work only in an expanding market. Once

MANAGEMENTHIGHLIGHT

## SCIENTIFIC MANAGEMENT VERSUS CRAFTSMANSHIP

|  | Scientific Management | Craftsmanship |
|---|---|---|
| **Strengths** | High productivity | High skill |
|  | Lower cost | High-quality output |
|  | Higher wages | Pride in work |
|  | Unskilled workers | High job interest |
|  | Predictable scheduling | Control by worker |
| **Weaknesses** | Low morale and boredom | Low productivity |
|  | Poor quality | Higher cost |
|  | Lack of pride | Lower wages |
|  | Low job interest | Poor control |
|  | Control by managers | Scheduling problems |

markets began to shrink, Japanese firms made quality an issue and invaded markets that for years were thought to be untouchable. Basically the Japanese approach was to attack what they called *Taylorism*. It seems somewhat unfair to give Taylor sole credit for the entire system of scientific management, because others took part in its development. But the Japanese identified Taylor's concepts of time and motion with their failures: high absenteeism, low morale, and poor-quality output. While some parts of the world were experiencing the benefits of specialization, Japan was experiencing its disadvantages. Other nations are now experiencing these same disadvantages and will also have to make changes if they hope to prosper.

Many organizations are modifying and redesigning jobs so that these jobs can be performed by teams.[4] The most popular type is a problem-solving team, comprising knowledgeable workers who gather to solve a specific problem and then disband. A work team is a group of employees who work closely together to pursue common objectives.[5] Some organizations become team-based, using teams throughout the organization on a regular basis; others use teams more selectively. Some teams are directed by a manager, whereas others are self-managed. The idea behind self-managed work teams is for workers to become their own managers, which increases reliance on their creative and intellectual capabilities in addition to their physical labor. At W. L. Gore & Associates—a manufacturer of a wide range of electronic, medical, fabric, and industrial products—"associates" (the term *employee* is not used) work on self-directed teams without managers or bosses.[6] Some attempts to install self-managed work teams have failed because the team lacked skill and experience, which are prerequisites for a successful outcome.[7] Regardless which kind of team is used, teams can move swiftly, flexibly, and effectively to produce innovative products. Team members learn each others' jobs and bring their ideas together, capitalizing on workers' creativity. When truly empowered, a work team can change bored and demoralized workers into innovative and productive partners.

Quality circles are based on the belief that the people who work with the process are best able to identify, analyze, and correct the problems in any given situation. The quality circle concept originated in Japan in 1962, and Japanese firms expanded it into a highly developed system. A quality circle is a small group of people, usually fewer than ten, who do similar work and meet about once a week to discuss their work, identify problems, and present possible solutions.[8] Participation in the circle is voluntary, and the workers establish a moderator or team leader to lead discussions. The group's findings and proposals are forwarded to management.

American firms began using quality circles in the mid-1970s, and the concept grew in popularity over the next fifteen years. Unfortunately, because quality circles were merely adaptations of the scientific management system, some efforts to use them failed. The aim of managers in some cases was to increase the productivity of workers, who refused to cooperate. But these failures resulted from how the approach was used rather than from flaws in the approach itself.

KEYTERMS

**problem-solving team** A teams of knowledgeable workers who gather to solve a specific problem and then disband.

**work team** A group of employees (or "associates"), sometimes directed by a manager and sometimes self-managed, who work closely together to pursue common objectives.

**quality circle** A small voluntary group of people, usually fewer than 10, who do similar work and who meet about once a week to discuss their work and present possible solutions to management.

Quality circles cannot simply be "installed" in an organization. The concept has been most successful when used as part of an organization-wide improvement effort.

The extent to which jobs are specialized is a critical managerial decision. The important point here is that jobs vary considerably along the dimension of specialization. By changing the degree to which jobs are specialized, managers change the structure of the organization. Chapter 9, "Job Analysis, Design, and Redesign," discusses job design in further detail.

## Delegation of Authority

When designing an organizational structure, managers must also consider the extent to which authority will be distributed throughout the organization. Authority is the organizationally sanctioned right to make a decision. Managers delegate (assign) certain tasks to others, simply because one person cannot get all the work done. When delegating authority, managers must weigh the pros and cons of decentralization and centralization and strike an appropriate balance for the organization.

### Decentralization and Centralization

Authority can be distributed throughout the organization—or held in the hands of a few. Decentralization is the process of distributing authority throughout the organization. It delegates to an organization member (historically a manager) the right to make a decision without obtaining approval from a higher-level manager. The authority to identify problems or issues and recommend solutions is delegated as well. In the strictest sense, decentralization represents one end of a continuum (Exhibit 8.1) in which the authority to make decisions is shared with all members of the organization. At the other extreme, centralization is the process of retaining authority in the hands of high-level managers, who make all the decisions.

Decentralization has several advantages. Managers develop their own decision-making skills and are motivated to perform because advancement is related to performance. Managers can also exercise more autonomy, which increases job satisfaction and motivation, contributing to the organization's profitability. Hewlett-Packard attributes much of its success to decentralization, through which people and power were moved away from headquarters. Some experts think Nike's recent turnaround—for the first time in a decade, the firm experienced double-digit profit growth—began when cofounder Philip Knight delegated day-to-day control of the company.[9] Decentralization also has some disadvantages. It requires costly management training, and organizations can end up employing highly paid managers. Delegation also leads to extensive (and often stifling) planning and reporting procedures. Some managers find it difficult to make decisions, even though they have the authority, because the methods used to measure accountability are time-consuming and instill fear in the managers. The next Management Highlight on page 170 will give you some insights into your ability to delegate authority.

Instead of rushing into delegation, the manager must carefully think about the answers to these questions. The quiz points to such managerial concerns as trust, coaching, sharing of power, and building in job challenges. The quiz also highlights points that managers need to address before deciding whether delegation is a useful organizing strategy for them. Think of a time when you delegated a job or task to someone. Did you feel comfortable about delegating?

Some organizations have begun to empower workers to make decisions that typically have been made by superiors. Empowerment involves giving employees who are responsible for hands-on production or service activities the authority to make decisions or take action without prior approval.[10] For instance, a machine operator can stop production when a problem is detected, or a ticket agent can give a customer a refund without calling the supervisor. Earlier, in talking about decentralization, we referred to delegating authority to other managers. Empowerment means that production, process control, and quality assessment become part of everyone's job: all

## DELEGATION ABILITY

**Directions:** Place an X on the number that indicates how important you think the skill is for delegating job assignments or decision-making power. Circle the number that indicates how much of the skill you now possess.

| Skill Areas | Very Important/ Significant | | | Not Important/ Little | |
|---|---|---|---|---|---|
| 1. Trusting the ability of other people | 5 | 4 | 3 | 2 | 1 |
| 2. Delegating meaningful, not just routine, jobs to others | 5 | 4 | 3 | 2 | 1 |
| 3. Coaching and helping others with a new job | 5 | 4 | 3 | 2 | 1 |
| 4. Sharing power and authority | 5 | 4 | 3 | 2 | 1 |
| 5. Following up to let individuals know how they are doing | 5 | 4 | 3 | 2 | 1 |
| 6. Setting reasonable goals regarding what is to be accomplished | 5 | 4 | 3 | 2 | 1 |
| 7. Determining others' ability to make decisions | 5 | 4 | 3 | 2 | 1 |
| 8. The challenges of the delegated jobs are motivational | 5 | 4 | 3 | 2 | 1 |

**Feedback:** A person with a strong orientation toward delegation would score between 33 and 40. A score of 40 would result from placing an X on the number 5 for all eight items. Being a good delegator has several payoffs for a manager. First, delegating regular, routine tasks frees the manager's time for more important tasks. Second, employees develop and become more involved with the job because they have added responsibility. Third, having more varied tasks can break the monotony for the employee of doing the same job over and over again.

Although delegation seems simple, it requires the manager to look closely at these questions:

1. Can the employee handle delegation?
2. What will be delegated? Is it clearly stated?
3. How will the person know he or she is doing a good job, especially in terms of the delegated tasks? Are there standards of performance?
4. Is the delegator available to answer questions, coach, and provide feedback?
5. Does the employee feel good after completing the delegated task?

---

individuals are given the ability and authority to take positive actions that will lead to high quality and performance. At Federal Express, for example, "all workers are routinely expected to take whatever initiative is required to fix problems and/or extend first-rate service to a customer."[11] Chris Kearney, CEO of SPX and formerly senior counsel with General Electrics Plastics division, says that the sense of empowerment and lack of boundaries felt at GE is part of what makes it America's most advanced company.[12]

| **Chain of Command** | The delegation of authority creates a chain of command, the formal channel that defines the lines of authority from the top to the bottom of an organization (see Exhibit 8.2). As you can see, the chain of command is a series of superior-subordinate relationships, from the highest position in the organization to the lowest.

The chain of command is the communication link among all positions in the organization. It specifies a clear reporting relationship for each person in the organization and should be followed in both downward and upward communication. Generally, no individual should report to more than one supervisor.

| **Line and Staff Positions** | The chain of command includes both line and staff positions. A line position is in the direct chain of command and contributes directly to achieving the organization's goals. In Exhibit 8.3 on page 172, the president; the vice presidents of operations, marketing, and finance; the directors; and the sales managers are in line positions. A staff position facilitates or provides advice to line positions. In Exhibit 8.3, the executive assistant, the vice presidents of human resources and environmental control, and the assistant to the director of sales are considered staff positions because they provide support to others.

**KEY TERMS**

**chain of command** A series of superior-subordinate relationships, from the highest position in the organization to the lowest, that is created by the delegation of authority.

**line position** A position in the direct chain of command that contributes directly to achieving the organization's goals.

**staff position** A position that facilitates or provides advice to line positions.

8.2

**Chain of Command**

## Departmentalization

Departmentalization is the process of grouping jobs according to some logical arrangement. As organizations grow in size and as job specialization increases, determining how jobs should be grouped becomes more complex. In a very small organization like a mom-and-pop grocery store, the owner can supervise everyone. In a large grocery chain, managerial positions are created according to some plan so that the organization can run smoothly. As explained earlier, some jobs are so specialized that they are unhealthy; this issue, as you will see, is changing the way organizations group jobs. The most common bases for departmentalization are function, product, customer, and geography.

| **Functional Departmentalization** | Grouping jobs together according to organizational functions is called functional departmentalization. Generally, businesses include functions such as production, finance, marketing, research and development, and human resources (see Exhibit 8.4, page 172). The major benefit of this approach is that it establishes departments based on experts in a particular function, taking advantage of specialization. But specialization does not encourage communication across departments. Functional departmentalization works best when an organization faces a stable environment, and when tight control over processes and operations is desired.

EXHIBIT 8.3

## Differentiating Between Line and Staff Positions

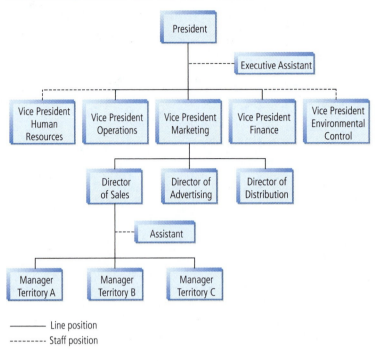

──────── Line position
-------- Staff position

EXHIBIT 8.4

## Functional Departmentalization

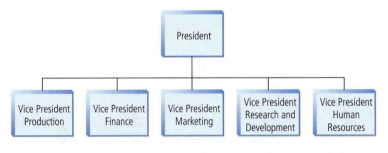

| Product Departmentalization | Product departmentalization groups jobs associated with a particular product or product line. It enables people working with a particular product to use their skills and expertise. Exhibit 8.5 illustrates how an organization groups jobs on this basis. Large organizations such as General Motors and Procter & Gamble have used this approach. The product manager might also draw on the resources of other organization members. Product departmentalization gives an organization the flexibility to develop specific strategies for different products and to grow or make acquisitions with relative structural ease. It has also been used by managers of multinational corporations with diversified product lines. But this type of grouping is expensive because it requires a manager for each product and runs the risk of duplicating effort among divisions.

EXHIBIT 8.5     **Product Departmentalization**

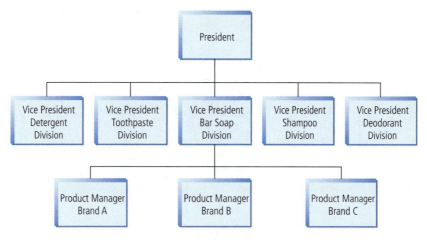

EXHIBIT 8.6     **Customer Departmentalization**

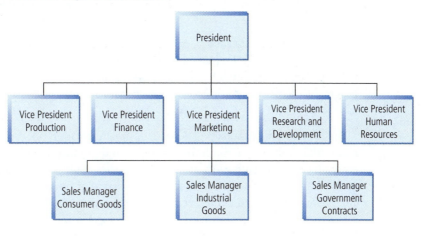

| **Customer Departmentalization** | Organizations using customer departmentalization (Exhibit 8.6) group jobs in a manner that will serve customers' needs. Organizations that have extremely large customers, or those serving diverse groups, are most likely to use this approach. For example, a firm that sells defense systems to the government might group jobs based on customers. Banks typically departmentalize on the basis of consumer and commercial accounts. Customer departmentalization can be a costly method of grouping jobs if a large staff is required to integrate the activities of several different departments.

| **Geographic Departmentalization** | Grouping jobs based on defined territories is called geographic departmentalization (Exhibit 8.7). Such a structure is useful when an organization is widely dispersed and its customers' needs and characteristics vary greatly; organizations can respond to unique customer needs in the various regions more quickly. Geographic departmentalization is the most common form used by multinational corporations (MNCs).

**8.7** **Geographic Departmentalization**

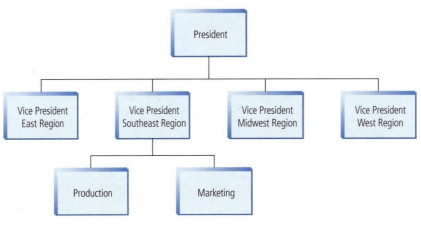

Its major drawback is that it usually necessitates a large headquarters staff to manage the dispersed locations.

**Mixed Departmentalization** | As an organization evolves over time, it might use more than one method to group jobs. Mixed departmentalization involves grouping jobs using more than one basis. Exhibit 8.8 illustrates how a bank might mix product, customer, and geographic departmentalization. In reality, most organizations group jobs using multiple bases.

**The Matrix Organization** | The matrix design attempts to capture the strengths and reduce the weaknesses of both the functional and product designs. A matrix organization is a cross-functional organization overlay that creates multiple lines of authority and places people in teams to work on tasks for a finite period of time.[13] The functional departments are the foundation, and a number of products or temporary departments are superimposed across the functional departments. The result (Exhibit 8.9) is a dual, rather than a singular, line of command. Although the matrix organization was first developed in the aerospace industry, it is now used in all types of organizations, both private and public.

As Exhibit 8.9 on page 176 shows, individuals or groups in each cell report to two managers. For instance, someone working in marketing on Product A would report to the Vice President of Marketing and Product Manager A. This arrangement is useful in speeding up innovation because each person's primary responsibility is to help produce what the organization sells. The key is to free people from bureaucratic constraints by empowering them to create winning ideas and products, while at the same time providing the structure needed to be successful.[14] Frigidaire Co., owned by Swedish-based Electrolux, uses a matrix organization that functions as a team and focuses attention on the consumer. The matrix organization has helped Frigidaire to become increasingly competitive, flexible, and market-driven.[15]

Matrix organizations have increased in popularity as organizations have decentralized and adopted project management concepts. They are most appropriate when coordination is needed in complex and uncertain environments.[16] Matrix organizations lead to efficient use of a specialized staff, offer timely response to a changing environment, enable technical specialists to interact with each other, free top-level management from day-to-day activities to spend more

**KEY**TERMS

**mixed departmentalization** The grouping of jobs using more than one criterion.

**matrix organization** A cross-functional organization overlay that creates multiple lines of authority and places people in teams to work on tasks for a finite period of time, characterized by a dual, rather than a singular, line of command.

EXHIBIT 8.8      **Mixed Departmentalization**

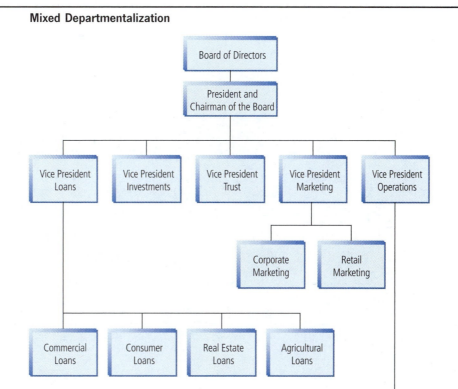

time planning, and encourage individual growth and development.[17] Because product or project groups are often employed with the matrix design, many organizations using teams and quality circles adopt this form of organization because of its flexibility and adaptability.

The matrix design has several drawbacks. The matrix can lead to confusion because individuals or groups report to more than one superior. Several bosses might place conflicting demands on subordinates or struggle with each other for power, placing workers in a compromising position. In some cases, organizations find that groups take longer to make decisions than individuals. The matrix is also costly because additional managers and staff might be needed.[18]

| **Alternative Forms of Departmentalization** | Because departmentalization reinforces specialization, some organizations are trying to involve everyone in the decision process by breaking down the barriers that often divide departments. Steelcase, Inc., a large manufacturer of office furniture, actually did away with formal departments. People work in multidisciplinary teams that encourage interaction. The physical facilities are also void of departments; they contain areas for teams to work and space for working on special projects. Executives are located in the center of the building, where everyone has equal access to them. This complex change took several years to implement but has been credited with cutting delivery cycles in half and dramatically reducing inventory.[19]

**8.9**     **The Matrix Organization**

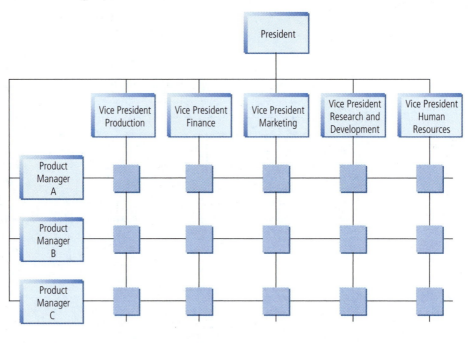

Some firms are abandoning departmentalization altogether and organizing around processes, as opposed to function, product, customer, or geography. Process organization involves basing performance objectives on meeting customer needs and identifying the processes that meet those needs. For instance, the processes that meet customer needs might be service quality or new product development. These processes, not departments, are used to organize the company. At Hallmark Cards, jobs are organized around the new product development process, according to specific holidays. There are teams for Christmas, Valentine's Day, and so on. Each holiday team includes artists, writers, lithographers, merchandisers, and accountants. Guided by project management principles, team members come from all over a 2-million-square-foot building so they can work together. Now only one team works on a Mother's Day card; previously the card had to go from one large department to the next. The time it takes to develop new cards is cut in half. Between projects or teams, workers return to their "center of excellence" for training or brief work assignments. Hallmark hopes any remaining signs of department structures eventually will disappear.[20]

## KEY TERMS

**process organization** A form of organization that bases performance objectives on identifying the processes that meet customer needs.

**span of control** The number of people who report to one manager or supervisor.

## | Span of Control

Span of control refers to the number of people who report to one manager or supervisor. This is the final decision managers must make in designing organizational structure. The objective is to determine the optimal span of control—wide or narrow. A wide span of control (or flat organization) results in a large number of workers reporting to one supervisor; a narrow span (or tall organization) results in a small number. Exhibit 8.10 compares the two structures. In the first case, two supervisors each direct eight workers; the maximum span of control is eight. There are two levels of management: a president and the two supervisors. In the second case, two department heads each direct four supervisors, and each supervisor directs four workers. The

EXHIBIT **8.10**

**Wide versus Narrow Span of Control**

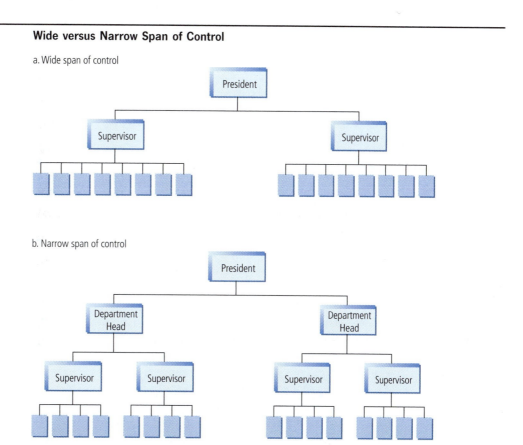

a. Wide span of control

b. Narrow span of control

maximum span of control is four, and there are three levels of management: a president, two department heads, and four supervisors.

Although there is no formula for determining the ideal span of control,[21] in the Management Highlight, we present a set of factors to consider when establishing span of control. Be aware that spans of control could be different for managers at the same level in the same organization, depending on their experience or the nature of the jobs they are supervising. Consistent with some of the trends in organizational structure already discussed (teams, quality circles, empowerment, and process organization), many firms are widening their spans of control with the objective of developing flatter, more responsive organizations in which decisions can be made without needing approval by several levels of management.

## Dimensions of Organizational Structure

The four organizational design decisions just discussed—specialization of jobs, delegation of authority, departmentalization, and span of control—determine the structure of organizations. Organizational structure provides the foundation upon which the organization functions. It also dramatically influences performance. Therefore, managers must be concerned with the entire structure and how it influences the organization. Three dimensions have been identified that enable managers to describe and understand the organizations' structure and measure differences between different organizations: formalization, centralization, and complexity.[22]

**FACTORS TO CONSIDER IN DETERMINING SPAN OF CONTROL**

1. *Competence of both the manager and the subordinates*—the more competent they are, the wider the span of control can be.
2. *Degree of interaction required among the units to be supervised*—the more extensive the required interaction, the narrower the span of control must be.
3. *Extent to which the manager must carry out nonmanagerial tasks*—the more technical and job-related work the manager has to do, the less time is available to supervise others; thus the narrower the span of control must be.
4. *Relative similarity or dissimilarity of the jobs being supervised*—the more similar the jobs, the wider the span of control can be; the less similar the jobs, the narrower it must be.
5. *Extent of standardized procedures*—The more routine the subordinates' jobs are and the more each job is performed by standardized methods, the wider the span of control can be.
6. *Degree of physical dispersion*—if all the people assigned to a manager are located in one area and are within eyesight, the manager can supervise relatively more people than when people are dispersed throughout the plant or countryside at different locations.

## Formalization

Formalization refers to the extent to which an organization's communications and procedures are written down and filed. A highly formalized organizational structure would be characterized by rules and procedures to prescribe members' behavior. Simple and routine tasks lend themselves to formalization; more complex and nonroutine tasks do not.

In general, organizations characterized by high specialization, little delegation of authority, functional departments, and narrow spans of control are more formalized. Scientific management, then, results in a high degree of formalization, whereas craftsmanship leads to less formalization. In this sense, organizations that empower workers reduce formalization.

## Centralization

Centralization, as mentioned earlier, refers to how much the authority to make decisions is dispersed throughout the organization. In a highly centralized organization, top-level managers retain decision-making authority; in contrast, a highly decentralized organization disperses decision-making authority throughout the operation. Most organizations are neither centralized nor decentralized but somewhere in between the two extremes.

In relation to the four organizational structure decisions, centralization is the result of high specialization, low delegation of authority, the use of functional departments, and narrow spans of control.

## Complexity

High specialization, product departmentalization, customer departmentalization, geographic departmentalization, high delegation of authority, and narrow spans of control result in high complexity. Complexity is defined as the number of different job titles and the number of different departments in an organization. As firms grow, divide work, and create more departments, they become more complex. Because of the dissimilarities in the jobs of both individuals and departments, a complex organization is more difficult to manage than one with few job titles and departments.

Organizations differ in how much they are formalized and centralized as well as in their degree of complexity. These differences result from managers' decisions concerning the organization's structure. No single structure is best for a particular organization. The purpose of structure is to reward and encourage behaviors that lead to accomplishing organizational objectives. Regardless of differences in how formalized, centralized, and complex organizations are, the critical issue is whether the organizational structure enables employees to do quality work. Perhaps the most important point is that managers must manage organizational structures over time and make changes in response to the changing environment.

# Organizational Design

In this chapter, we noted that organizational structure is the framework of jobs and departments that directs the behavior of individuals and groups toward achieving an organization's objectives. Structure provides the foundation within which the organization functions, and managers must design an organizational structure that enhances the organization's overall strategy. Managers have many alternatives in developing an organizational structure. Organizational design is the process by which managers develop an organizational structure. Because organizational structure is determined by specialization of jobs, delegation of authority, departmentalization, and span of control (see Exhibit 8.1), organizational design includes coordinating these dimensions of organizational structure and deciding the extent to which the organization will be specialized, centralized, and so on.

Two extreme models of organizational design—the mechanistic model and the organic model—have provided much of the framework for understanding organizational design.[23]

## The Mechanistic Model

In the early part of the twentieth century, much theory and practice in management was guided by the nature of the work and the existing organizational structure at that time. That is, many organizations, seeking a high production level, relied on unskilled workers. Factory workers were highly specialized, and little authority was delegated. Thus the term mechanistic organization describes a rigid organization that attempts to achieve production and efficiency through rules, specialized jobs, and centralized authority.

German sociologist Max Weber used the term *bureaucracy* to describe an organization based on a formal system of legitimate authority.[24] The major characteristics of Weber's bureaucracy describe the mechanistic model:

| Tasks are divided into highly specialized jobs.

| Each task is performed according to a standardized set of rules that ensures uniformity.

| Each member of the organization is accountable to a single manager.

| Business should be conducted impersonally, and managers should maintain a social distance from workers.

| Employment and advancement should be based on technical qualifications, and workers should be protected from arbitrary dismissal.

As you can see, this represents an extreme type of organization—perhaps not the kind in which you have worked or would like to work. It is important, though, to view the mechanistic model as one end of a continuum, with the organic model at the other end. Neither model is the ideal form of organizational design, and most organizations change over time. Later in this chapter you will look at other forms of more or less bureaucratic organizational design.

## The Organic Model

In sharp contrast to the mechanistic model, the organic organization seeks to maximize flexibility and adaptability. Whereas the mechanistic model is rigid and bureaucratic, the organic model encourages greater utilization of human potential. The organic model deemphasizes specialization

**KEY TERMS**

**organizational design** The process by which managers develop an organizational structure, determined by the specialization of jobs, the delegation of authority, departmentalization, and span of control.

**mechanistic organization** A rigid organization that attempts to achieve production and efficiency through rules, specialized jobs, and centralized authority.

**organic organization** An organization that seeks to maximize flexibility and adaptability, that encourages greater utilization of human potential, and that deemphasizes specialization of jobs, status, and rank.

of jobs, status, and rank. Horizontal and lateral relationships are as important as vertical relationships.[25]

The organic organization provides individuals with a supportive work environment and builds a sense of personal worth and importance.[26] Thus managers in this organization encourage and motivate employees to reach their potential. This type of organization tends to be decentralized, and communication flows throughout the organization rather than through the chain of command. Departmentalization would be based on product and customer rather than on function.

The organic model describes a more human organization. Perhaps you have already decided that this is the best type of organization, and it might look that way. Earlier in the chapter, however, you learned that the best structure is one that facilitates getting the work done well. We also said that structure sometimes interferes with quality work. But this does not mean that everything about the mechanistic model is bad in all situations, or that everything about the organic model is good in all situations. Remember, these models represent a continuum. Between these two extremes are many organizational designs—some yet to be discovered.

## Contingency Approach

In reality, there is no single best organizational design; you might remember that we identified this myth earlier. Many different circumstances influence the design decision. In some instances, the mechanistic design is more effective, whereas the organic design works best in other situations. The contingency approach suggests that different organizational designs are more effective in different situations. Managers must examine the different contingencies or circumstances surrounding the situation and select the particular approach that is most effective. The contingencies that influence this decision include technology, environment, and strategy.

**Technology and Organizational Design** | Technology refers to how tasks are accomplished using materials, equipment, and human resources to develop an organization's output. The organizational design is contingent on the type of technology that is used to convert inputs into outputs. Many studies have examined the relationship between technology and effective design. In general, the mechanistic organization is appropriate for organizations using more routine technologies. Conversely, organizations using more nonroutine technologies generally find the organic structure more appropriate.[27] For example, organizations employing simple technologies such as assembly line manufacturing can be managed through mechanistic design. Organizations that employ more complex technology to customize products for each order can be managed through organic design.

**Environment and Organizational Design** | As noted in Chapter 3, "The Management Environment, Social Responsibility, and Ethics," every organization operates in the context of a larger environment. If the environment is considered stable, little change occurs in the forces that make up the environment. Some environments are characterized by forces that are changing constantly. If these changes are unpredictable, the environment is considered turbulent. Research has shown that mechanistic organizations are most effective in stable environments, whereas organic structures are best in changing and turbulent environments.[28]

**Strategy and Organizational Design** | The strategy an organization pursues also influences the decision regarding its structure. In fact, strategy precedes structure; the organization should first develop strategy and then design a structure compatible with its strategy.[29] If the converse is true—structure determines strategy—only those strategies

**KEY**TERMS

**contingency approach**
An approach to organizational design that requires managers to examine the prevailing contingencies or circumstances and select the most effective design.

compatible with the existing structure are pursued. This can limit innovation and the organization's ability to cope with change. Finally, organizations producing a single good or service will find the organic design more compatible. As firms move away from a single product through expansion and diversification, they adopt the mechanistic design.

## Other Forms of Organizational Design

Many other forms of organizational design have been developed or are emerging in response to the rapidly changing environment. Increased global competitiveness, decentralization, buyouts and hostile takeovers, and the quality revolution are just a few of the factors causing organizations to search for new designs. This section looks at two additional forms of organizational design.

### The Multidivisional Organization

The multidivisional (M-Form) organization has emerged in western Europe and the United States during the past fifty years.[30] The multidivisional organization is a high-performance organization whose operating units or divisions are partially interdependent. Thus, each division's product is different from that of the other divisions, but all divisions share common endowments such as technology, skill, and information. Hewlett-Packard is divided into fifty semiautonomous divisions, one manufacturing hospital instruments, a second computers, a third handheld calculators, and so on. Each division sells to slightly different customers and uses different manufacturing methods, but all share a common foundation in electrical engineering, use similar manufacturing methods, and depend on a central laboratory to supplement their research.

The M-Form design attempts to strike a balance between autonomy for the divisions and control over them. Its structure represents the ambiguity common in many organizations; that is, each division is partially independent yet partially dependent on the entire organization. IBM found that as a huge, centralized organization, it simply could not react fast enough to changes in the competitive marketplace. With the M-Form, each division is expected to operate independently to maximize profits and is sufficiently autonomous to make timely decisions. But the M-Form succeeds only if divisions cooperate on things they share in common. The key is to make sure this cooperation does not stifle a division's creativity and performance. This is the delicate balance between centralization and decentralization.

### The Network Organization

A network organization is a flexible, sometimes temporary, relationship between manufacturers, buyers, suppliers, and even customers.[31] The design is dynamic in that the major components can be assembled or reassembled to meet changing competitive conditions. A major advantage of networks is that each member can concentrate on those activities it performs best. In the auto industry, everything from building factories to producing cars is getting cheaper as auto companies quit making parts and concentrate on designing cars. Members are held together by contracts and pursuit of common goals, not by the more traditional hierarchy. The term *virtual corporation* has been used to describe a temporary network of independent organizations, linked by information technology, that come together quickly to exploit fast-changing opportunities.[32] A virtual corporation has neither a central office nor an organization chart; rather, it is a series of partnerships that will more than likely terminate once an opportunity is met. Similarly, a *modular corporation* consists of a hub surrounded by a network of the best suppliers in the world. The hub is the center of activities, such as research and development; the network is made up of outside specialists that make the parts, handle deliveries, and perform accounting activities.

The network organization design is gaining popularity not only in the United States but globally. Part of its appeal, in the global context, is that network members can be added as

**KEY TERMS**

**multidivisional organization** A high-performance organization whose operating units or divisions are partially interdependent, with each division's product different from those of the other divisions, but with all divisions sharing common endowments, such as technology, skill, and information.

**network organization** A flexible, sometimes temporary, relationship between manufacturers, buyers, suppliers, and even customers, typically to meet changing competitive conditions.

needed. For example, a firm entering a foreign country for the first time might add a broker or a trading company to the network. Members that are not performing or are no longer needed can be removed. Because members pursue their distinctive competencies, quality is enhanced. Organizations can also eliminate those activities or operations that can be done better by other organizations.

**CONCLUSION**

## Organizational Structure and Design

This chapter introduced the concepts of organizational structure and design. Organizational structure is determined by specialization of jobs, delegation of authority, departmentalization, and span of control. We also discussed the three dimensions of organizational structure: formalization, centralization, and complexity. Organizational design is the process by which organizational structure is developed. The two extremes of organizational design are the mechanistic model and the organic model. The contingency approach to organizational design incorporates technology, the environment, and strategy into the design decision, suggesting that different organizational designs are more effective in different situations.

## Discussion Questions

1. Why is organizational structure critical to the success of organizations?

2. Compare the different forms of departmentalization with an emphasis on the strengths and weaknesses of each.

3. Contrast the various forms of organizational design using the mechanistic and organic models as opposite ends of a continuum.

## Video Case

### Lonely Planet: Structure That Makes Sense

When travelers Tony and Maureen Wheeler founded Lonely Planet in the early 1970s, they didn't intend to create a globe-spanning company. They didn't necessarily plan to start a publishing company. As newlyweds, they had just completed an overland trip from London through Asia, winding up in Australia. All they really wanted to do was finance their next trip—it never occurred to them to stop traveling around the world. So they wrote and published the first Lonely Planet guidebook, *Across Asia on the Cheap*; it was an instant best-seller among world wanderers.

With just two people, the Wheelers naturally did not think about organization. They traveled, wrote, and published whatever they wanted. By the mid 1970s, they had completed *Nepal and Trekking in the Himalayas* and were working on a group of guides covering Australia, Europe, Africa, and New Zealand. In 1981, *Lonely Planet India* was published and became a travel best-seller. By then, Lonely Planet had a staff of ten. It was time to get organized.

Today, Lonely Planet publishes more than 650 guidebooks, including specialized activity guides, "shoestring" or budget guides, international food guides, and phrasebooks. The firm is still owned by the Wheelers, employing 400 workers in offices in Melbourne; London; Paris; and Oakland, California. In addition, about 150 authors are traveling and writing around the world. Lonely Planet has people to create maps, take photos, design book covers, sell books, and create marketing campaigns. There are also finance people and people who work with and manage the freelancers who are roaming the world. Managing all these activities in four countries on three continents requires communication and coordination.

For example, each office is responsible for all sales and marketing efforts for its own region in order to address cultural and other environmental differences. In addition, a regional warehouse distributes all of that office's book titles to booksellers within the geographical area. Because Lonely Planet publishes books about world travel, having a presence in several key countries enhances the firm's credibility among readers. This organization gives the individual offices more flexibility in directing marketing messages to specific audiences and ensures that workers in each office know their region thoroughly. In addition, one of Lonely Planet's greatest assets is its local writers, according to David Zingarelli, managing editor for Lonely Planet USA. Being able to meet with them in person and cultivate a relationship is a great advantage. Despite their relative independence, the offices must communicate with each other. So, managers rely on the Internet for regular communication and to create consistency among marketing messages.

Although regional offices commission books for their areas—Lonely Planet USA commissions all the books for North and South America, as well as for Central America—the headquarters in Australia actually produces all the books. This centralization streamlines the production process, reduces costs by keeping cartographers and designers under one roof, and ensures that the books are designed and produced in a consistent fashion. In addition, negotiations with the printers in Hong Kong are more efficient and effective when they are conducted from a single location.

People who work at Lonely Planet love to travel, and they like the way the company is organized. "It's got all the excitement of working for a multinational . . . but without any of the . . . complexity of bureaucracy," explains one employee. "Working with other offices—Melbourne, Paris, London—as a global company and still being independently owned" is a positive experience, notes another. "It's a large company, but it's really small," he continues. Tony and Maureen Wheeler are still very much a presence in the company, visiting its worldwide offices and maintaining contact with many employees. There are some drawbacks to this far-flung method of managing; sometimes staffers grumble about the challenges of dealing with time differences, but they concede that this is a minor inconvenience. After all, if you work at a travel publisher because you love to travel, think about the possibilities. Perhaps you'll work in Australia this year and Paris next year. Maybe you've got the urge to set up shop in London. At Lonely Planet, there's almost always an opportunity to hit the road—and get paid for it.

### Questions

1. In what ways is Lonely Planet decentralized? In what ways is it centralized?

2. Does Lonely Planet have a tall structure or a flat structure? Explain briefly.

3. In what ways does Lonely Planet achieve horizontal coordination across departments or offices?

Sources: Company web site, http://www.lonelyplanet.com, accessed July 30, 2004; Lonely Planet press kit.


## BizFlix

### Reality Bites

*Reality Bites* is an American film starring Winona Ryder, Ethan Hawke, Ben Stiller, Steve Zahn, Janeane Garofalo, and David Spade. The plots follows the life of recent college graduate Lelaine Pierce (Ryder), who wants to make a documentary about her friends as a way to capture the strife and problems confronting her generation. In this scene, she is applying for a job at Wiener Schnitzel, a fast-food restaurant managed by David Spade.


### Questions

1. Using the terms from the chapter, outline the job of cashier as Spade is describing it in the clip.

2. Is the cashier position a line or staff function?

3. Describe the atmosphere at the restaurant.

## Suggested Readings

Coutu, Diane L., "Creating the Most Frightening Company on Earth." *Harvard Business Review* (September–October 2000): 143–150.

Davis, Margaret R., and David A. Weckler, *A Practical Guide to Organizational Design.* Menlo Park, CA: Crisp Publications, 1996.

Galbraith, Jay R., *Designing Organizations: An Executive Guide to Strategy, Structure, and Process.* San Francisco: Jossey-Bass, 2001.

Gibson, Cristina B., and Susan G. Cohen, eds., *Virtual Teams That Work: Creating Conditions for Virtual Team Effectiveness.* San Francisco: Jossey-Bass, 2003.

Goold, Michael, and Andrew Campbell, "Do You Have a Well-Designed Organization?" *Harvard Business Review* (March 2002): 117–124.

Hackman, J. Richard, *Leading Teams: Setting the Stage for Great Performances.* Boston: Harvard Business School Press, 2002.

Kaplan, Robert S. and David P. Norton, "How to Implement a New Strategy without Disrupting Your Organization." *Harvard Business Review* (March 2006): 100–109.

Mintzberg, Henry, *Structure in Fives: Designing Effective Organizations.* Upper Saddle River, NJ: Prentice Hall, 1992.

Walker, Carol A., "Saving Your Rookie Managers From Themselves." *Harvard Business Review* (April 2002): 97–102.

## Endnotes

1. Hugh C. Willmott, "The Structuring of Organizational Structures: A Note," *Administrative Science Quarterly* (September 1981): 470–474.

2. Frederick W. Taylor, *Principles of Scientific Management* (New York: Harper & Row, 1911).

3. Scott Madison Paton, "Joseph M. Juran—Quality Legend: Part III," *Quality Digest* (March 1992): 49–58.

4. Marshall Sashkin and Kenneth J. Kiser, *Total Quality Management* (Seabrook, MD: Ducochon, 1991): 118.

5. Charles Garfield, *Second to None* (Homewood, IL: Business One Irwin, 1992), 164.

6. Frank Shippes and Charles C. Manz, "Employee Self-Management without Formally Designated Teams: An Alternative Road to Empowerment," *Organizational Dynamics* (Winter 1992): 48–61.

7. Capozzoli, Thomas, "How to Succeed with Self-Directed Work Teams," *SuperVision* (February 2006): 25–26.

8. "The Quality Glossary," *Quality Progress* (February 1992): 20–29.

9. Stanley Holmes and Christine Tierney, "How Nike Got Its Game Back," *Business Week* (November 4, 2002): 129–131.

10. Sashkin and Kiser: 67.

11. Tom Peters, *Thriving on Chaos* (New York: Knopf, 1988), 292.

12. Morris, Betsy, "The GE Mystique," *Fortune* (March 6, 2006): 98–102.

13. Robert C. Ford and Alan W. Randolph, "Cross-Functional Structures: A Review and Integration of Matrix Organization and Project Management," *Journal of Management* (June 1992): 267–294.

14. Martin K. Starr, "Accelerating Innovation," *Business Horizons* (July–August 1992): 44–51.

15. Richard Jaccoma, "Smart Moves in Hard Times," *Dealership Merchandising* (January 1992): 164–167.

16. Paul R. Lawrence, Harvey F. Kolodny, and Stanley M. Davis, "The Human Side of Matrix Organizations," *Organizational Dynamics* (September 1977): 4.

17. Stanley M. Davis and Paul R. Lawrence, *Matrix* (Reading, MA: Addison-Wesley, 1977).

18. Stanley M. Davis and Paul R. Lawrence, "Problems of Matrix Organizations," *Harvard Business Review* (May–June 1978): 131–142.

19. Garfield, *Second to None*, 4–5.

20. Thomas A. Stewart, "The Search for the Organization of Tomorrow," *Fortune* (May 18, 1992): 92–98.

21. Robert D. Dewar and Donald P. Simet, "A Level-Specific Prediction of Spans of Control Examining the Effects of Size, Technology, and Specialization," *Academy of Management Journal* (March 1981): 5–24.

22. Richard S. Blackburn, "Dimensions of Structure: A Review and Reappraisal," *Academy of Management Review* (January 1982): 59–66.

23. Tom Burns and G. M. Stalker, *The Management of Innovation* (London: Tavistock, 1961).

24. Max Weber, *The Theory of Social and Economic Organization,* trans. A. M. Henderson and Talcott Parsons (New York: Oxford University Press, 1947).

25. C. R. Gullet, "Mechanistic vs. Organic Organizations: What Does the Future Hold?" *Personnel Administration* (1975): 17.

26. Rensis Likert, *The Human Organization* (New York: McGraw-Hill, 1967).

27. C. Chet Miller, William H. Glick, Yau-De Wang, and George P. Huber, "Understanding Technology-Structure Relationships: Theory Development and Meta-Analytical Theory Testing," *Academy of Management Journal* (June 1991): 370–399.

28. Paul R. Lawrence and Jay W. Lorsch, *Organization and Environment* (Burr Ridge, IL: Irwin, 1967).

29. Alfred D. Chandler, *Strategy and Structure* (Cambridge, MA: MIT Press, 1962); Robert E. Hoskisson, "Multidivisional Structure and Performance: The Contingency of Diversification Strategy," *Academy of Management Journal* (December 1987): 625–644.

30. Much of this discussion is based on William G. Ouchi, *The M-Form Society* (Reading, MA: Addison-Wesley, 1987), 23–25.

31. Charles C. Snow, Raymond E. Miles, and Henry J. Coleman, "Managing 21st Century Network Organizations," *Organizational Dynamics* (Winter 1992): 5–19.

32. John Byrne, Richard Brandt, and Otis Port, "The Virtual Corporation," *Business Week* (February 8, 1993): 98–102.

# 9

# JOB ANALYSIS, DESIGN, AND REDESIGN

Chapter 8, "Organizational Structure and Design," discussed how some organizations are designing structures that empower workers to make their own decisions. Workers in America have changed greatly over the past century. They are more literate and have different job objectives. People want interesting employment, recognition for good work, the chance to work with others who respect them, an opportunity to develop skills, and a voice in the design of their jobs—they want to be heard. They are no longer satisfied to simply have a job, for few of today's independent-minded workers remember what it was like to be out of work during the Great Depression of the 1930s. In those days, people had no choice but to work, and do as they were told.

Work itself is also changing. Robots do much of the work in factories, replacing many traditional blue-collar jobs. And white-collar workers, once thought to be indispensable, now lose their jobs regularly as firms decentralize. Many firms have cut jobs through restructuring and by closing plants. Organizations are being told that the front-line workers need more autonomy to make decisions. Organizations are struggling to design—or redesign—jobs more suited to today's worker and the current work environment.

This chapter examines job design. First, we discuss the steps involved in job analysis, including developing job descriptions and job specifications. Then we present three different aspects of job design: job specialization, job range, and job depth. Next, we explore approaches to job redesign, including job rotation, job enlargement, and job enrichment. Finally, we discuss the team-based approach to job design.

## Job Analysis

Before actually designing a job, an organization must determine the description of the job itself. Job analysis is the process of gathering, analyzing, and synthesizing information about jobs.[1] This time-consuming, complicated task yields vital input for job design decisions. The purpose of job analysis is to provide an objective description of the job itself.[2] This involves gathering information about all aspects of the job and pushes the organization to answer some fairly fundamental questions, as shown in Exhibit 9.1.

Job analysis is an ongoing process. As organizations evolve over time, missions and objectives change, as do conditions in the environment and the nature of the work. By analyzing and redesigning existing jobs, organizations can adapt to those changes and remain competitive. Many jobs have changed as a result of technology, global competition, and the pressure to produce quality products. Managers are learning that organizations are a collection of human beings that need to be developed and nurtured, not a collection of assets to be traded, manipulated, and motivated by fear. The following Management Highlight will help you determine whether fear is a good motivator.

Managers who use their power to create fear are most likely not accomplishing their objectives. Workers might believe they will be punished if they do not perform, which of course generates fear, but fear impedes performance rather than increases it. Managers can, of course, project an image of support and teamwork. It has been demonstrated over and over again that rewarding individuals for a job well done is more effective than the threat of punishment.

EXHIBIT 9.1

**Questions Answered by Job Analysis**

| Question | Possible Answers |
| --- | --- |
| What activities are required in a job? | Hand and body motions, use of equipment, services, communication with others |
| What skills are needed to perform the activities? | Education, previous experience, licenses, degrees, or other personal characteristics |
| What are the working conditions of the job? | Physical demands, degree of accountability and responsibility, extent of supervision, and other job environment factors |

### ARE YOU MOTIVATED BY FEAR?

Some say fear is a great motivator. This might have been true when the pyramids were built or in American "sweatshops" of the nineteenth century, but today, more and more managers are coming to the realization that individuals cannot perform unless they feel secure. Consider the following:

- Constantly being afraid of losing your job.
- Waking up each morning dreading going to work.
- Working in an environment that makes you feel insecure and inadequate.
- Having a boss who uses punishment to motivate you.

Unfortunately, many workers experience these and other fears, and the consequences can be devastating to the individual and the organization. Fear can lead to higher levels of stress and lower performance. As a result, the organization suffers. Individuals show up for work and go through the motions; this attitude can become contagious, and even more devoted workers become unmotivated and fearful.

Take a few minutes and answer the following questions. In what type of an organization would you like to work? What is most likely to motivate you to perform at your highest level? What causes you to lower your performance?

Job analysis applies to all types of jobs. Job analysis began with factory jobs, an integral part of the scientific management movement. The purpose was to use objective data to determine the single best way to design work. But eventually job analysis made its way into office and clerical jobs, and today applies to management jobs as well. Job analysis is used to help design work that enhances employee performance, not to limit workers by determining the single best way to do things. In many instances, those directly involved in doing the work are participating in the job analysis. They are closest to the task and can provide excellent information about the job.

## Steps in Job Analysis

A typical job analysis involves several steps (Exhibit 9.2). First, the job analyst must examine how each job fits into the overall organization. An overview of the organization provides a working picture of the arrangement of departments, units, and jobs. During this step, organization charts are used to examine the formal relationships among the firm's departments and units. The relationships among jobs are also examined. For example, when analyzing an assembly-line job, the analyst is interested in the flow of work to and from the assembly-line worker. Because analyzing each job would be too costly and time-consuming, the second step involves determining which jobs in the organization will be analyzed.

The third step involves collecting data about the jobs to be analyzed. Data are collected on the characteristics of the job, the behaviors and activities required by the job, and the employee skills needed to perform the job. Several methods are used to collect job analysis data. Observation is used to collect data for jobs that require manual or standardized activities, such as assembly-line work. Conducting interviews with workers, often along with observation, is

**9.2**

**Steps in a Typical Job Analysis**

probably the most widely used data collection method. Questionnaires and logs or diaries pertaining to job tasks, frequency of tasks, timing for accomplishing tasks, and so on are also used to collect information. A questionnaire called the *Job Analysis Information Format* (Exhibit 9.3) can provide basic information for use with any method employed to collect analysis data. Information collected by the job analyst is then used to prepare job descriptions and job specifications, steps four and five (see Exhibit 9.2).

## Job Descriptions and Job Specifications

The major output of job analysis is the job description. The job description is a written summary of the job: its activities, the equipment required to perform the activities, and the working conditions of the job. A job description helps the organization with a variety of activities, including planning, recruiting, and training. It also helps workers understand what a specific job entails, and what jobs fit their particular skills and interests. Exhibit 9.4 on page 190 shows a job description for a human resource manager.

Traditionally, a human resource manager was responsible for writing job descriptions. These job descriptions usually emphasize what employees should do, how they should think, and so on. In other words, they were for the most part prescriptive. Many organizations, in an effort to encourage more participation, now involve workers in developing their own job descriptions. By teaching workers how to write their own job descriptions and then having the employees and supervisors discuss and agree on a job description, workers must think about the best way to achieve desired outcomes. Rather than being prescriptive, this approach is outcome-oriented. It is used by organizations interested in empowering workers to take control of their own jobs.

The job specification is a written explanation of skills, knowledge, abilities, and other characteristics needed to perform a job effectively. The job specification evolves from the job description. The key difference is that the job description describes aspects of the job, whereas the job specification describes aspects of the person. The job specification is useful in recruiting and selecting workers.

EXHIBIT 9.3

## Job Analysis Information Format

Your Job Title_____    Code _____ Date January 1, 2007

Class Title _____    Department _____

Your Name_____    Facility_____

Supervisor's Title _____    Prepared by _____

Superior's Name_____    Hours Worked _____ AM _____ to AM
                                                                                                PM                       PM

1.  What is the general purpose of your job?

2.  What was your last job? If it was in another organization, please name it.

3.  To what job would you normally expect to be promoted?

4.  If you regularly supervise others, list them by name and job title.

5.  If you supervise others, please check those activities that are part of your supervisory duties.

| _____ Hiring | _____ Coaching | _____ Promoting |
| _____ Orienting | _____ Counseling | _____ Compensating |
| _____ Training | _____ Budgeting | _____ Disciplining |
| _____ Scheduling | _____ Directing | _____ Terminating |
| _____ Developing | _____ Measuring performance | _____ Other _____ |

6.  How would you describe the successful completion and results of your work?

7.  Please briefly describe your job duties and, if possible, how you perform them. Indicate those duties you consider to be most important and/or most difficult.

   a.  Daily duties:

   b.  Periodic duties (Please indicate whether weekly, monthly, quarterly, etc.):

   c.  Duties performed at irregular intervals:

   d.  How long have you been performing these duties?

   e.  Are you now performing unnecessary duties? If yes, please describe.

   f.  Should you be performing duties not now included in your job? If yes, please describe.

8.  Please check the blank that indicates the educational *requirements* for the job, not your *own* educational background.

   a. _____ No formal education required          d. _____ Two-year college certificate or equivalent
   b. _____ Less than high school diploma         e. _____ Four-year college degree
   c. _____ High school diploma or equivalent     f. _____ Education beyond undergraduate degree
                                                               and/or professional license

9.  Please check the amount of experience needed to perform your job.

   a. _____ None.                                 e. _____ One to three years
   b. _____ Less than one month                   f. _____ Three to five years
   c. _____ One month to less than six months     g. _____ Five to ten years
   d. _____ Six months to one year                h. _____ Over ten years

10. Please list any skills required in the performance of your job. (For example, level of accuracy, alertness, precision in working with described tools, methods, systems, etc.)
    Please list skills you possessed when you were placed on this job.

11. Does your work require the use of any equipment? Yes/No. If yes, please list the equipment and check whether you use it rarely, occasionally, or frequently.

| Equipment | Rarely | Occasionally | Frequently |
|---|---|---|---|
| a. _____ | _____ | _____ | _____ |
| b. _____ | _____ | _____ | _____ |
| c. _____ | _____ | _____ | _____ |
| d. _____ | _____ | _____ | _____ |

EXHIBIT 9.4

## Job Description of a Human Resource Manager

JOB TITLE: HUMAN RESOURCE MANAGER 

Department: HRM
Date: Jan. 1, 2007

*General Description of the Job*

Performs responsible administrative work managing personnel activities of a large state agency or institution. Work involves responsibility for the planning and administration of an HRM program that includes recruitment, examination, selection, evaluation, appointment, promotion, transfer, and recommended change of status of agency employees, and a system of communication for disseminating necessary information to workers. Employee works under general supervision, exercising initiative and independent judgment in the performance of assigned tasks.

*Job Activities*

Participates in overall planning and policymaking to provide effective and uniform personnel services.

Communicates policy through organizational level by bulletins, meetings, and personal contact.

Interviews applicants, evaluates qualifications, classifies applications.

Recruits and screens applicants to fill vacancies and reviews applications of qualified persons.

Confers with supervisors on personnel matters, including placement problems, retention or release of probationary employees, transfers, demotions, and dismissals of permanent employees.

Supervises administration of tests.

Initiates personnel training activities and coordinates these activities with work of officials and supervisors.

Establishes effective service rating system, trains unit supervisors in making employee evaluations.

Maintains employee personnel files.

Supervises a group of employees directly and through subordinates.

Performs related work as assigned.

*General Qualifications Requirements*

Experience and Training

    Should have considerable experience in area of HRM administration. Six-year minimum.

Education

    Graduation from a four-year college or university, with major work in human resources, business administration, or industrial psychology.

Knowledge, Skills, and Abilities

    Considerable knowledge of principles and practices of HRM selection and assignment of personnel; job evaluation.

Responsibility

    Supervises a department of three HRM professionals, one clerk, and one secretary.

## | Job Design

After job analyses, job descriptions, and job specifications have been prepared, an organization can use their information to design and redesign jobs. Job design is a determination of exactly what tasks must be performed to complete the work. Job design should structure job elements and duties to increase performance and satisfaction.

There is no one best way to design jobs. Managers enjoy an array of choices. The job design process involves making trade-offs regarding different characteristics of the job. Some job designs emphasize structuring jobs so that they are broken down into simple, repetitive tasks; others emphasize enjoyment of the work. There are three characteristics of job design: job specialization, job range, and job depth.

## Job Specialization

Scientific management and Frederick W. Taylor's work stimulated a great deal of interest in job specialization, which breaks down work into smaller, more discrete tasks. (See Chapter 2, "History of Management," for more information about Taylor.) The task specifies what is to be done, how it is to be done, and the exact time allowed for doing it.[3] Although specialization has been criticized because it leads to boredom and dissatisfaction, it made sense during the early twentieth century, and some of its principles are still relevant today. When Henry Ford developed the moving assembly line for manufacturing cars in 1913, job specialization led to production efficiencies. Many products made today—ranging from children's toys to this textbook to sophisticated computers—simply cannot be made by one individual; some degree of specialization is necessary.

Thus specialization is not the culprit it is often made out to be; the problem for organizations is identifying the appropriate degree of specialization. As noted in other chapters, the problems of boredom and absenteeism have plagued some companies and industries. Managerial or white-collar jobs have long been assumed to not lend themselves to specialization—managers must think, create, and communicate. Many service organizations also are finding negative consequences associated with one person performing one specialized task.[4] More and more organizations are designing jobs that enable all workers, including nonmanagerial or blue-collar staff, to be creative and enjoy their jobs. Later in this chapter, we will discuss strategies for redesigning jobs to overcome the problems associated with job specialization.

## Job Range and Depth

Two other job characteristics are range and depth. Job range refers to the number of tasks a worker performs. A greater number of tasks takes longer for one individual to complete than fewer tasks. Job depth refers to the amount of discretion a worker has in performing tasks. Jobs designed with little depth are generally at lower levels of the organization.

Job specialization is closely related to the range and depth of jobs. Generally, more specialized jobs (e.g., assembly-line workers or bookkeepers) have low range and depth. People with such jobs perform only a few tasks and have little discretion in performing them. On the other hand, less specialized jobs (e.g., teachers or scientists) have high range and depth. In service industries such as hospitality and banking, the front-line workers who actually face the customers also have jobs with high range and depth, and they can make or break the business.

Job range and depth can be used to differentiate jobs within and between organizations. Within an organization, jobs can be designed with different ranges and depths. Generally, as a person moves higher up in the organization and assumes more responsibility, job range and depth increase. But even at the same level, a machine mechanic might have higher range and depth than a machine operator. And an assembly-line job at a Ford plant might not have the same range and depth as an assembly-line job at a Toyota plant.

As is the case with specialization, the manager has the responsibility to design jobs with optimal range and depth. If an employee has too many tasks or too much discretion, the job will not be accomplished efficiently and performance will suffer. Conversely, workers performing a single task with no discretion become bored, which might also lead to poor performance.

## Job Redesign

In response to the limits of specialization, organizations began to redesign jobs to give workers more autonomy, while at the same time meeting organizational objectives for performance. Job redesign refers to an organization's attempts to improve the quality of work and give workers more autonomy. Typically, job redesign attempts to improve coordination, productivity, and product

**KEY**TERMS

**job specialization** The breakdown of work into small, discrete tasks that specify what is to be done, how it is to be done, and the exact time allowed for doing it.

**job range** The number of tasks a worker performs. *See also* job depth.

**job depth** The amount of discretion a worker has in performing tasks, with little-depth jobs generally found at the lower levels of the organization. *See also* job range.

**job redesign** An organization's evaluation of job design so as to improve the quality of work, to give workers more autonomy, and to improve coordination, productivity, and product quality, while at the same time responding to workers' needs for learning, challenge, variety, increased responsibility, and achievement.

quality, while at the same time responding to workers' needs for learning, challenge, variety, increased responsibility, and achievement.[5] Many firms are finding that workers with creativity are their greatest asset. Job specialization, associated with the scientific management movement, gives employees the least amount of autonomy and can stifle creativity. Several approaches to redesigning jobs exist (job rotation, job enlargement, job enrichment, and flextime) that give workers more autonomy. The final section of this chapter examines team-based approaches, which provide workers with the most autonomy.

## Job Rotation

The **job rotation** approach involves systematically moving employees from one job to another. Job rotation increases job range by introducing workers to more jobs and therefore more tasks. The goal is not only to reduce worker dissatisfaction caused by job specialization but also to increase worker interest and motivation.[6] For instance, workers in a tool factory might work on a machine one week, conduct stress tests the next week, pack orders the next, and so on. The strategy is to build breadth of experience, and then leadership competencies such as the ability to set direction and inspire subordinates follow.[7] Large organization like Coca-Cola are offering highly qualified business graduates the opportunity to perform a number of jobs before deciding on a position that fits them best.[8]

The major drawback of job rotation is that it does little to change the nature of the work itself. Rather than performing one task over and over again, a worker performs a variety of tasks; but in either case, the jobs are highly specialized, and workers can grow bored or dissatisfied. Inefficiencies might also result because workers must be trained for several jobs. Because of these limitations, job rotation has not been entirely successful. However, often it is used with other approaches, discussed in the following sections.

## Job Enlargement

Job enlargement was the first attempt by organizations to redesign work. In a study of mass production jobs in auto assembly plants, researchers found that workers were dissatisfied with highly specialized and repetitive tasks.[9] Based on this assumption, the job enlargement approach increases the worker's number of tasks. For example, a job could be redesigned so that a worker responsible for performing four tasks is given eight tasks to complete, thereby increasing the job range. Whereas job rotation involves moving employees from one job or task to another, job enlargement seeks to increase job satisfaction by increasing the number of tasks the worker performs, thereby reducing boredom and monotony.

Many organizations have implemented job enlargement programs, including American Telephone & Telegraph (AT&T) and Maytag. Although job enlargement requires additional training and might not remove all the boredom, many such programs have increased satisfaction. Unfortunately, job enlargement is not always successful. If workers simply end up doing four boring tasks instead of two, their job satisfaction is unlikely to rise.

## Job Enrichment

Based on Frederick Herzberg's two-factor theory of work motivation (see Chapter 12, "Motivation"), much energy has been directed at altering jobs in more meaningful ways than either job rotation or job enlargement can accomplish. Herzberg's basic theory is that workers are motivated by jobs that increase their responsibility and feeling of self-worth.[10] Job enrichment attempts to give workers more control of their activities, addressing their needs for growth, recognition, and responsibility. Job enrichment increases not only the number of tasks performed (job range) but also job depth by giving workers more opportunity to exercise discretion over their work.

EXHIBIT 9.5

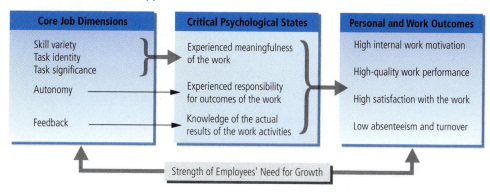

**The Job Characteristics Approach**

| Core Job Dimensions | Critical Psychological States | Personal and Work Outcomes |
|---|---|---|
| Skill variety<br>Task identity<br>Task significance | Experienced meaningfulness of the work | High internal work motivation |
| Autonomy | Experienced responsibility for outcomes of the work | High-quality work performance<br><br>High satisfaction with the work |
| Feedback | Knowledge of the actual results of the work activities | Low absenteeism and turnover |

Strength of Employees' Need for Growth

**Source:** Adapted from J. Richard Hackman and G. R. Oldham, "Motivation through the Design of Work: Test of a Theory," *Organizational Behavior and Human Performance* 16 (1976): 256.

There are several approaches to job enrichment. Some managers redesign jobs to delegate more authority to workers, whereas others remove controls and assign new tasks to make the work as interesting as possible. Job enrichment can be accomplished by redesigning jobs with some additional features, providing learning opportunities, giving workers control over resources and tasks, and letting workers schedule some of their own work.

One widely known method of job enrichment is the job characteristics approach, which looks at the job from the jobholder's perspective and not the organization's.[11] The job characteristics approach (Exhibit 9.5) suggests that jobs should be redesigned to include important core dimensions that increase motivation, performance, and satisfaction, and reduce absenteeism and turnover.[12] These core dimensions include:

- *Skill variety.* The degree to which the job requires a variety of different activities in carrying out the work, which involves a number of skills and talents.

- *Task identity.* The degree to which the job requires completion of a "whole" and identifiable piece of work—that is, doing a job from beginning to end with a visible outcome.

- *Task significance.* The degree to which the job has a substantial impact on other people's lives or work—whether in the immediate organization or in the external environment.

- *Autonomy.* The degree to which the job provides substantial freedom, independence, and discretion to the individual in scheduling work and in determining the procedures to be used in carrying it out.

- *Feedback.* The degree to which carrying out work activities required by the job results in individuals obtaining direct and clear information about the effectiveness of their performance.[13]

Presence of these core dimensions in a job is expected to create in workers three critical psychological states that are necessary for motivation and satisfaction:

- *Experienced meaningfulness.* The degree to which jobholders experience work as important, valuable, and worthwhile.

- *Experienced responsibility.* The extent to which jobholders feel personally responsible and accountable for results of their work.

**KEY**TERMS

**job characteristics approach** A job design approach suggesting that jobs should be designed to include important core dimensions and to increase motivation, performance, and satisfaction as well as reduce absenteeism and turnover.

*Knowledge of results.* Jobholders' understanding of how effectively they are performing their jobs.[14]

The more workers experience these three states, the higher their motivation, performance, and satisfaction, and the lower their absenteeism and turnover.

As Exhibit 9.5 shows, three of the core job dimensions listed earlier—skill variety, task identity, and task significance—contribute to a sense of meaningfulness. Skill variety is influenced by individual differences in the strength of growth needs.[15] Autonomy is directly related to feelings of responsibility. The more control workers feel they have over their jobs, the more they feel responsible. Feedback is related to knowledge of results. For workers to be internally motivated, they must have a sense of the quality of their performance. This sense comes from feedback.

Because people have unique capabilities and needs, managers need to be aware of the potential for individual differences to affect how the job characteristics approach works. The final part of the job-enrichment model, called *employee growth-need strength,* suggests that people with a strong need to grow and expand their potential are expected to respond more strongly to the core job dimensions than those with low growth-need strength. Thus job enrichment will probably have less effect on a person without a strong need for personal growth than on someone who values personal growth.

Managers must realize that job enrichment might change a job's skill requirements. Thus not everyone will necessarily be able to perform the enriched job, especially without additional training. And the organization might need to adjust its compensation rates for the enriched job because of the higher skill levels required.[16]

Before beginning a job-enrichment effort, managers should complete at least two actions. First, they need to thoroughly understand the job in question. Enrichment might not be feasible because of costs or other technological constraints. Second, they should consider individual preferences about enriched work. Do the employees want the work to be enriched? Obviously, accurate job descriptions and job specifications can greatly facilitate assessing these issues.

## Flextime

Another approach to redesigning jobs lets employees have input in establishing their work schedules. Flextime is a schedule that allows workers to select starting and quitting times within limits set by management.[17] Rather than working the traditional eight-hour day, workers are given greater flexibility in deciding exactly when they will work. A person might work ten hours one day and six another. Employers are increasingly permitting employees to utilize flexible work schedules.[18] Jobs designed using flextime include bank tellers, data entry clerks, lab technicians, engineers, and nurses.

Flextime programs have reportedly been successful in many instances. Over half the firms using them report such improvements as increased productivity, lower labor costs, and higher morale.[19] One study found that flextime increases performance and job satisfaction and decreases absenteeism.[20] Another study reported that satisfaction with the work schedules and with inter-actions improved significantly for both managers and nonmanagers.[21] Companies are finding that flextime builds loyalty, and that employees are committed to making flextime work.

Flextime is difficult to implement for production units with assembly lines and multiple shifts. Because work is largely machine controlled, planning flexible work schedules is a challenge. Flextime is also difficult to arrange for jobs that must be continuously covered, like those of bus drivers or retail sales clerks. A firm can also experience increased costs of heating and cooling buildings for longer workdays. It might not be possible to coordinate supervisor and subordinate work schedules, resulting in lack of supervision part of the time. Most workers might prefer similar hours—say 9 A.M. to 5 P.M.—leaving other times understaffed. Without supervision, some

**KEY**TERMS

**flextime**  A schedule that allows workers to select starting and quitting times within limits set by management; for example, working ten hours one day and six another.

MANAGEMENT HIGHLIGHT

## THE WORKPLACE OF TOMORROW

The job as a way of organizing work is slowly disappearing. Regular hours, specific duties, and standard pay no longer fit the type of work that is being done. As technology continues to change, the conditions of mass production that created jobs years age are also changing. Automated assembly lines no longer require workers to perform repetitive tasks. Knowledge entrepreneurs will replace service and factory workers in a more flexible workplace of the future. Blue-collar workers who made up 20 percent of the United States labor force in 1995 will make up 10 percent or less in the next decade.

Additionally, the automation of office work will reduce the number of nonprofessional white-collar workers to about 20 to 30 percent of the work force. The remaining 60 to 70 percent will include knowledge workers—skilled manufacturing teams, information system designers, educators, scientists, and the like.

In this type of job environment, it will be much more likely that a person will be hired for a particular project and assigned to that project's team. When the task is completed, the team disbands and workers move on to the next project; the new project might even be in a different organization. Jobs in the workplace of tomorrow will be filled with people who can work without job descriptions. Rather than performing a specific set of duties, the workers of the future will be empowered to be self-managers. Their major task will be to focus on the customer and to perform whatever activities are needed to satisfy customers rather than doing a "job." In the future, individuals will have to stay abreast of current trends and technologies so that their skills are in demand.

The workplace of the future will also be quite diverse. Three generations of employees will share the workplace: Baby Boomers, Generation X, and Generation Y. Age will no longer be an indicator of rank or privilege. Performance and achievement will be all that count in the multigenerational workplace. The fastest growing populations of the work force are the Hispanic and Asian. Managers will feel increased pressure to recognize the differences among employees in terms of age and ethnicity in designing jobs that increase creativity, innovation, and performance.

Organizations that are able to adapt to change and embrace new technologies are most likely to survive. For instance, information systems have become user-friendly and inexpensive, and offer a convenient and economical substitute for personal interactions. Rather than traditional employees working 9 to 5 in an office building, working at home has become a feasible option. Successful organizations of the future will also have to build flexibility into the job design. For example, self-managed work teams can be used to create interchangeable units that can be added quickly and efficiently to meet a specific need, such as new product development. The organization that will succeed is the one that stays current with technology, nurtures and develops its employees, and develops its entrepreneurial side.

Source: Adapted from Robert D. Ramsey, "The Workplace of Tomorrow," *The American Salesman*, January 2005, pp. 23–28; Alison Stein Wellner, "Workplace Trends," *Incentive*, September 1999, pp. 153–155; William E. Halal, "The Rise of the Knowledge Entrepreneur," *The Futurist*, November–December 1996, pp. 13–16.

employees might abuse flexible scheduling. Thus, even though flextime is appealing and some evidence suggests it has been successful, proper administration is needed to ensure success. The Management Highlight above illustrates how the job, as a way of organizing work, is changing.

## Team-Based Approach to Job Design and Redesign

Throughout most of Europe, Asia, and more recently the United States, the concept of job design is being revolutionized. The thrust of this new approach is to place greater emphasis on worker autonomy and to delegate increased decision-making responsibility. This new form of job design goes beyond traditional job-enrichment programs aimed at empowering workers, often members of teams, to make their own decisions. As noted in Chapter 6, "Planning," a team is a group of employees who work closely together to pursue common objectives. Recall also that a team cannot be effective unless it is supported by the organization's basic structure. Team-based approaches to job design and redesign provide workers with the greatest autonomy. One of the most important benefits of the team-based approach is improved communication and coordination. People learn how other jobs are done and how to coordinate efforts to work together better.[22]

The use of teams has implications not only for organizational structure but also for the design of specific jobs. Working as a member of a highly motivated, self-directed team is much different from performing several specialized tasks or performing jobs redesigned through

## APPROACHES TO JOB DESIGN AND REDESIGN

| Attribute | Job Specialization | Job Rotation | Job Enlargement | Job Enrichment | Teams |
|---|---|---|---|---|---|
| Description | Breaks work down into small, more discrete tasks. | Systematically moves workers from one job to another. | Increases the number of tasks the worker performs. | Increases the number of tasks and gives workers more control over activities. | Group works together to complete an entire task. |
| Assumptions | Production efficiencies can be achieved through division of labor. | By providing more variety, specialization reduces worker dissatisfaction. | Workers are dissatisfied with highly specialized and repetitive tasks. | Giving workers more control meets their needs for growth, recognition, and responsibility. | Teamwork reduces boredom and increases satisfaction and quality. |
| Setting | Assembly-line and mass-production jobs. | Assembly lines and settings that can entail several different jobs. | Mass-production, office, and clerical jobs. | Mass-production, office, clerical, and managerial jobs. | Mass-production, office, clerical, and managerial jobs. |
| Strengths | Workers master one job; training is minimized; useful if workers are unskilled or illiterate. | Can increase interest and motivation in the short run. | Can increase satisfaction and decrease boredom and monotony. | Provides growth and learning opportunities; redesigning jobs based on dimensions is important to workers. | Provides the most autonomy and opportunity for growth; empowers workers to make their own decisions. |
| Weaknesses | Can lead to boredom and absenteeism; little variety, responsibility, or growth. | Requires more training; doesn't change the nature of the work itself. | Requires more training; might not remove all the boredom from jobs. | Can change skill requirements, necessitating additional training; not everyone will be able to perform the enriched job. | Very difficult to implement; must overcome resistance; might be costly and time-consuming before benefits occur. |

job-enrichment programs. Although job enrichment gives workers more responsibility, these employees are still part of a large group. Work flows from one person to another, each doing a specific job. As a member of a work team, an individual participates in small-group decisions. The group decides when to perform tasks, who will perform them, and so on. The Management Highlight above provides a useful consolidation of the various approaches to job design and redesign that we have explored in this chapter.

Teams also motivate workers by moving them sideways (laterally) instead of up. With fewer promotions to give out because of decentralization, many organizations are redesigning jobs and developing teams that enable employees to transfer back and forth among teams that make different products. This approach replaces the assembly-line structure in which employees worked on one product. For instance, American Greetings Corporation redesigned 400 jobs into teams and asked workers and managers to reapply. All employees were guaranteed a job without a pay cut, and many moved laterally into a new type of work.[23] This process unleashes creativity by giving workers a change in tasks and a chance to work with different people without having to deal with the uncertainty of changing jobs or organizations.

When an organization decides to build teamwork into its structure, it must design or redesign jobs accordingly. Talking about team-based approaches is easy, but actually involving members of the organization in teamwork is difficult. Typically, developing teams involves redesigning jobs so that workers' (or teams') activities make up a whole or more complete task.[24]

Although knowledgeable workers are critical to successful teams, individual skills are substantially leveraged through teamwork. Thus managers must ensure that employees have the knowledge and skills needed to perform tasks, but more importantly, managers must create an atmosphere in which teamwork can prosper. For the most part, this attitude or philosophy flows from the top down and creates a sense of group pride, good relations with coworkers, and a spirit of teamwork that brings out the best in worker performance.[25] Training team members within this context eliminates old, counterproductive ideas and signals workers that a spirit of teamwork permeates the organization.

Perhaps the most important aspect of designing jobs for teams is empowering workers, giving them greater control over their work. This basically means that jobs must be designed so that authority equals responsibility. When individuals are made accountable for their actions, they become challenged to take responsibility for thinking, for implementing ideas, and for investing themselves in the organization.[26] Empowerment involves several conditions:

- Workers must believe their efforts can result in positive outcomes.
- Workers must have the knowledge and skills to do their jobs effectively.
- Work must be designed to form a "whole" job that is meaningful to the worker.
- Workers must have the authority to make decisions about the work on their own.[27]

Although much has been said—and many have written—about teams, organizations have been hesitant to adopt this approach for several reasons. Many executives and managers are reluctant to empower workers. Even workers themselves have been reluctant to participate in teams, fearing that teams will reduce their freedom when, in fact, teams should do just the opposite. Some workers—opting for an easier, yet more mediocre, job experience—do not want to accept accountability for their work. The large bureaucratic structures of some organizations are not conducive to designing jobs in which workers set their own schedules and production goals, have access to formerly confidential information, vote on such issues as pay raises and new hires, and make other critical decisions. Some organizations try to implement teams, but either do not go far enough in empowering workers or do not give the concept long enough to work. When truly empowered, teams can turn bored employees into productive partners. In any case, it appears that teams will continue to be an integral part of contemporary organizations.[28]

## CONCLUSION

## Job Analysis, Design, and Redesign

Job design is an important function of management. Before designing a job, managers use analysis to determine job descriptions and job specifications. This information is used to design and redesign jobs. The three characteristics of job design include job specialization, job range, and job depth. Approaches to job redesign are job rotation, job enlargement, and job enrichment. Finally, some organizations use team-based approaches to design and redesign jobs.

## Discussion Questions

1. What are the steps involved in job analysis? What are the major outputs?

2. What is the purpose of job design? What is the difference between job range and job depth?

3. What are the core dimensions of the job suggested by the job characteristics approach?

## Video Case

### Diversity at PepsiCo

Picture trying to manage and accommodate the needs of more than 140,000 people at once. Imagine a variety of voices, languages, cultures, ethnic backgrounds, families, lifestyles, ages, and geographies all vying for attention, all bearing the name PepsiCo. That's the challenge of managers throughout the PepsiCo organization. From the top of the organization on down, PepsiCo embraces diversity and inclusion in its worldwide workforce. Top executives, including CEO Steve Reinemund, believe that nurturing diversity in the organization is not only a matter of responsible ethics but also good business. Because PepsiCo offers products to such a diverse array of customers, it makes sense for the PepsiCo workforce to mirror the market. In addition, depending on where an office or facility is located, the workforce likely will reflect the local population. However, embracing a philosophy of diversity is another thing entirely from implementing it. Here is how PepsiCo takes on this global task.

Although some of the divisions might use different program models—depending on where they are located and who the population is—the Frito-Lay North American Diversity/Inclusion Model is a good example of how PepsiCo builds a measurable framework for diversity. The model was developed so that managers could implement and track diversity programs under their jurisdiction. The model addresses five key areas, ranging from "evolving the culture" to "leveraging our people systems." By following a structure, the human resource department and other managers can develop and implement specific programs to meet the needs of their employees.

One such program is the development of employee networks throughout PepsiCo's divisions. PepsiCo's employee networks are usually grassroots groups that are created on the basis of a common characteristic, such as gender or ethnic background. These networks are formed to give employees opportunities for support and mentoring as they develop their careers at PepsiCo. But the networks also perform another function: they help PepsiCo reach its diverse customer base. Ideas for new products, marketing efforts, and other projects can grow out of the employee networks. For instance, the idea for a new guacamole chip came from the Hispanic employee network, Adelante. In one recent year alone, Frito-Lay sold $100 million Lay's guacamole chips.

Regardless of the individual characteristics of a particular network, all PepsiCo employee networks have similar missions and goals:

- To become business partners that are focused on key organizational issues
- To offer resources to PepsiCo based on their unique perspectives and experiences
- To pave the way for employees to grow in their careers
- To provide opportunities for group members to network with each other and with business leaders
- To become ambassadors for PepsiCo, creating opportunities for community involvement

PepsiCo sponsors African American, Hispanic, and Asian employee networks, as well as women's networks. Each division sponsors its own networks, depending on its own population of workers. For example, Frito-Lay has the following: Black Employees Association (BEA), Adelante (Hispanic employee network), Asians in Motion (AIM), EQUAL (gay, lesbian, bisexual, and transgender employee network), and Women's Initiative Network (WIN).

In addition to the formation of employee networks, PepsiCo has established a formal, three-level inclusion training program. At level 1, division presidents and their teams participate in a course that covers issues of cultural differences and similarities; components of culture such as values and communication styles, including nonverbal cues; models for individual and organizational change; and exercises. Level 2 training is aimed at all managers throughout the United States businesses. Level 2 is designed to provide managers with the skills to lead teams of diverse workers. It focuses on enhancing self-awareness, conducting difficult conversations, recognizing people's strengths, and managing conflict.

Level 3 training is intended to reinforce the previous two levels of training for ongoing efforts to promote diversity and inclusion throughout the company.

PepsiCo believes that diversity can be harnessed as a powerful tool for growth, even during turbulent times. More than coming up with an idea for a new chip, diversity brings together groups of people who can work to meet the needs of consumers.

### Questions

1. Why is it important for upper-level managers at PepsiCo to receive diversity and inclusion training?

2. Do you think that PepsiCo's encouragement of employee networks actually works against diversity and the formation of multicultural teams? Why or why not?

Source: Company web site, http://www.pepsico.com, accessed August 16, 2004.

## BizFlix

### *U-571*

This action-packed thriller deals with a United States submarine crew's efforts to retrieve an Enigma encryption device from a disabled German submarine during World War II. After the crew gets the device, the United States submarine sinks, and they must use the German submarine to escape from enemy destroyers. The film's almost nonstop action and extraordinary special effects will look and sound best with a home theater system.

This scene is an edited composite of the "To Be a Captain" sequence early in the film. The S33, an older United States submarine, is embarking on a secret mission. Before departure, the S33's officers receive a briefing on their mission from Office of Naval Intelligence representatives on board. Executive officer Lt. Andrew Tyler (Matthew McConaughey) reports the submarine's status to Lt. Commander Mike Dahlgren (Bill Paxton). The film continues with the S33 finding the disabled German submarine.

### Questions

1. What aspects of leadership does Dahlgren say are important for a submarine commander?

2. Which leadership behaviors or traits does he emphasize?

3. Are these traits or behaviors right for this situation? Why or why not?

## Suggested Readings

Cusumano, Michael A., "How Microsoft Makes Large Teams Work Like Small Teams," *Sloan Management Review* (Fall 1997): 9–20.

Hartley, Darin E., *Job Analysis at the Speed of Reality* (Amherst, MA: Human Resource Development Press, 1999).

Herzberg, Frederick, "One More Time: How Do You Motivate Employees?" *Harvard Business Review* (January 2003): 87–96.

Purser, Ronald E., and Steven Cabana, *The Self-Managing Organization: How Leading Companies Are Transforming the Work of Teams for Real Impact* (New York: Simon & Schuster, 1998).

Senge, Peter, et al., *The Dance of Change: The Challenges to Sustaining Momentum in Learning Organizations* (New York: Doubleday, 1999).

Simons, Robert. "Designing High-Performance Organizations." *Harvard Business Review* (July–August 2005): 54–62.

## Endnotes

1. John M. Ivancevich, *Human Resource Management* (Burr Ridge, IL: Irwin, 1992), 172.

2. Frederick P. Morgeson and Michael A. Campion, "Social and Cognitive Sources of Potential Inaccuracy in Job Analysis," *Journal of Applied Psychology* (October 1997): 627–655.

3. Frederick W. Taylor, *The Principles of Scientific Management* (New York: Harper & Row, 1911), 21.

4. Greg L. Stewart and Kenneth P. Carson, "Moving Beyond the Mechanistic Model: An Alternative Approach to Staffing for Contemporary Organizations," *Human Resource Management Review* (Summer 1997): 157–184.

5. J. Barton Cunningham and Ted Eberle, "A Guide to Job Enrichment and Redesign," *Personne* (February 1990): 56–61.

6. Allan W. Farrant, "Job Rotation Is Important," *Supervision* (August 1987): 14–16.

7. Judy Orr, "Job Rotations Give Future Leaders the Depth They Need," *Canadian HR Reporter* (January 30, 2006): 17–18.

8. Erin Pooley, "Job Rotation," *Canadian Business* (October–November 2005): 109.

9. Charles R. Walker and Robert H. Guest, *The Man in the Assembly Line* (Cambridge, MA: Harvard University Press, 1952).

10. Frederick Herzberg, B. Mausner, and B. Snyderman, *The Motivation to Work* (New York: Wiley, 1959).

11. J. Richard Hackman, "Work Design," in *Improving Life at Work*, eds. J. Richard Hackman and J. L. Suttle (Santa Monica, CA: Goodyear, 1976), 96–162.

12. J. Richard Hackman and Greg R. Oldham, *Work Redesign* (Reading, MA: Addison-Wesley, 1980), 77–82.

13. Juan I. Sanchez, Alina Samora, and Chockalingam Viaweavaran, "Moderators of Agreement between Incumbent and Non-Incumbent Ratings of Job Characteristics," *Journal of Occupational and Organizational Psychology* (September 1997): 209–218.

14. Hackman and Oldham, *Work Redesign*, 72–77.

15. Robert P. Steel and Joan R. Rentach, "The Dispositional Model of Job Attitudes Revisited: Findings of a 10-Year Study," *Journal of Applied Psychology* (December 1997): 873–879.

16. Michael A. Champion and Chris J. Barger, "Conceptual Integration and Empirical Test of Job Design and Compensation Experiments," *Personnel Psychology* (Autumn 1990) 525–554.

17. Edward E. Lawler, *Pay and Organization Development* (Reading, MA: Addison-Wesley, 1981).

18. Pamela V. Rothenberg, "Alternative Work Schedules," *Journal of Property Management* (January–February 2006): 12.

19. David A. Ralston, William P. Anthony, and David J. Gustafson, "Employees Love Flextime, But What Does It Do to the Organization's Productivity?" *Journal of Applied Psychology* (May 1985): 272–279.

20. Boris B. Baltes, Thomas E. Briggs, Joseph W. Huff, Julie A. Wright, and George A. Neuman, "Flexible and Compressed Workweek Schedules: A Meta-Analysis of Their Effects on Work-Related Criteria," *Journal of Applied Psychology* (August 1999): 496–513.

21. Randall B. Dunham and John L. Pierce, "The Design and Evaluation of Alternative Work Schedules," *Personnel Administrator* (April 1983): 67–75.

22. Edward E. Lawler, *High-Involvement Management* (San Francisco: Jossey-Bass, 1991), 37.

23. Joan E. Rigdon, "Using Lateral Moves to Spur Employees," *Wall Street Journal* (May 26, 1992): B1, B5.

24. Marshall Sashkin and Kenneth J. Kiser, *Total Quality Management* (Seabrook, MD: Ducochon, 1991): 140.

25. Joseph A. Petrick and George E. Manning, "How to Manage Morale," *Personnel Journal* (October 1990): 83–88.

26. Stephen L. Perlman, "Employees Redesign Their Jobs," *Personnel Journal* (November 1990): 37–40.

27. Kenneth W. Thomas and Betty A. Velthouse, "Cognitive Elements of Empowerment: An 'Interpretive' Model of Intrinsic Task Motivation," *Academy of Management Review* (October 1990): 666–681.

28. George S. Easton and Sherry L. Jarrell, "The Effects of Total Quality Management on Corporate Performance: An Empirical Investigation," *Journal of Business* (April 1998): 253–307.

# 10

# HUMAN RESOURCE MANAGEMENT

**P**eople are the key resource in creating a successful organization. Companies that do not hire wisely will find it almost impossible to create a culture required to compete effectively. In large, formal organizations such as Toyota and Procter & Gamble, a department usually guides the human resource program. But even small organizations must take an action-oriented approach to understanding people and their needs, skills, and knowledge, and helping them meet their goals and expectations. When a strong human resource management function is in place, it facilitates the most effective use of employees to achieve an organization's goals.

For an organization to flourish, people must be the driving force; thus human resources practices, principles, and programs are the focus of this chapter. Human resource management (HRM) is discussed in relation to the activities needed to acquire, develop, retain, and utilize human resources. In doing so, eight human resource management activities are examined: equal employment opportunity, human resource planning, recruitment, selection, training and development, performance evaluation, compensation, and benefits and services. The chapter concludes with a discussion of some special issues in human resources.

## Equal Employment Opportunity

Equal employment opportunity (EEO) refers to the employment of individuals in a fair and unbiased manner. EEO has slowly become a societal priority that has needed legal and administrative guidelines to encourage action. Although EEO is usually couched in legal terminology, it is also an emotional issue.[1] Employers have been ordered to develop employment policies that incorporate laws, executive orders, court decisions, and regulations to end job discrimination.

One approach used to reach the goal of fair employment is affirmative action. The goal of affirmative action is to urge employers to make a concerted effort to promote the hiring of groups of employees who were discriminated against in the past. Employers are asked under affirmative action to use—at least in part—the race, sex, or age of a person in reaching an employment decision. Opinions regarding the impact of affirmative action are many and varied. The United States Supreme Court, in a July 2003 ruling, allowed the use of explicit racial preferences in law school admissions.[2] Research has shown that affirmative action programs have enabled a significant number of African Americans to obtain well-paying managerial positions.[3] Women, people with disabilities, and minorities other than African Americans also have benefited from affirmative action programs. Research also has shown that workers hired through affirmative action might be viewed negatively by others, regardless of their qualifications. Some white males claim they are victims of *reverse discrimination*. The jury is still out regarding the long-term impact of affirmative action.[4]

Exhibit 10.1 itemizes the major federal employment legislation whose intent is to eliminate discrimination in the American workplace. This body of laws continues to evolve through the courts. The Civil Rights Act of 1991 has long been characterized as strengthening earlier civil rights legislation and increasing the likelihood that employees will sue employers by making actionable discrimination cases subject to jury deliberation and potential damages more substantial.[5]

EXHIBIT
**10.1**

### Significant Federal Employment Laws

| Law | Provisions |
|---|---|
| Equal Pay Act of 1963 | Requires all employers covered by the Fair Labor Standards Act and others to provide equal pay for equal work regardless of sex. |
| Title VII of Civil Rights Act of 1964 (amended in 1972, 1991, and 1994) | Prohibits discrimination in employment on the basis of race, color, religion, sex, or national origin, created the Equal Employment Opportunity Commission (EEOC) to enforce the provisions of Title VII. |
| Age Discrimination in Employment Act of 1967 | Prohibits private and public employers from discriminating against persons 40 years of age or older in any area of employment because of age; exceptions are permitted where age is a bona fide occupational qualification. |
| Equal Employment Opportunity Act of 1972 | Amended Title VII of Civil Rights Act of 1964; strengthens EEOC's enforcement powers and extends coverage of Title VII to government employees, faculty in higher education, and other employers and employees. |
| Americans with Disabilities Act of 1990 | Prohibits discrimination in employment against persons with physical or mental disabilities or the chronically ill; enjoins employers to make reasonable accommodation to the employment needs of the disabled; covers employers with 15 or more employees. |
| Civil Rights Act of 1991 | Provides for compensatory and punitive damages and jury trials in cases involving intentional discrimination; requires employers to demonstrate that job practices are job related and consistent with business necessity, extends coverage to U.S. citizens working for American companies overseas. |
| Family and Medical Leave Act of 1993 | Requires all employers with fifty or more employees to provide twelve weeks of unpaid leave for family and medical emergencies. |
| Uniformed Services Employment and Reemployment Rights Act of 1994 | Protects the employment rights of individuals who enter the military for short periods of service. |

Therefore, it is in the organization's best interest for managers to develop policies and procedures that comply with the law. The best way to begin studying the relationship between HRM functions and the law is to devote time and attention to EEO. No other regulatory area has so thoroughly affected HRM as EEO; it has implications for almost every activity in HRM, including hiring, recruiting, training, terminating, compensating, evaluating, planning, disciplining, and collective bargaining.[6] Employers set up EEO programs to prevent employment discrimination in the workplace and/or to take remedial action to offset past employment discrimination.

The Americans with Disabilities Act of 1990 (ADA) requires firms to make reasonable accommodations to the needs of present and future employees with disabilities. Nearly 20 percent of the United States population is disabled.[7] The ADA was enacted to provide equal employment opportunities and reduce the high unemployment rate—nearly 70 percent—among this group of people. To date, the ADA has not fulfilled its promise.

## | Human Resource Planning

Human resource planning is a two-step process that involves forecasting future human resource needs and then planning how to adequately fulfill and manage these needs. Exhibit 10.2 points out the activities involved in needs forecasting and program planning.

As its major objective, human resource planning seeks to determine the best use of the talent and skills available to accomplish what's best for the individual and the organization. As Exhibit 10.2 shows, needs forecasting involves four specific activities. The external market conditions must be studied, as well as the firm's future human resource requirements. The firm must determine if talented and skilled human resources are available.

**human resource planning** A two-step process that involves (1) forecasting future human resource needs and then (2) planning how to adequately fulfill and manage the needs.

EXHIBIT 10.2 **The Human Resource Planning Process**

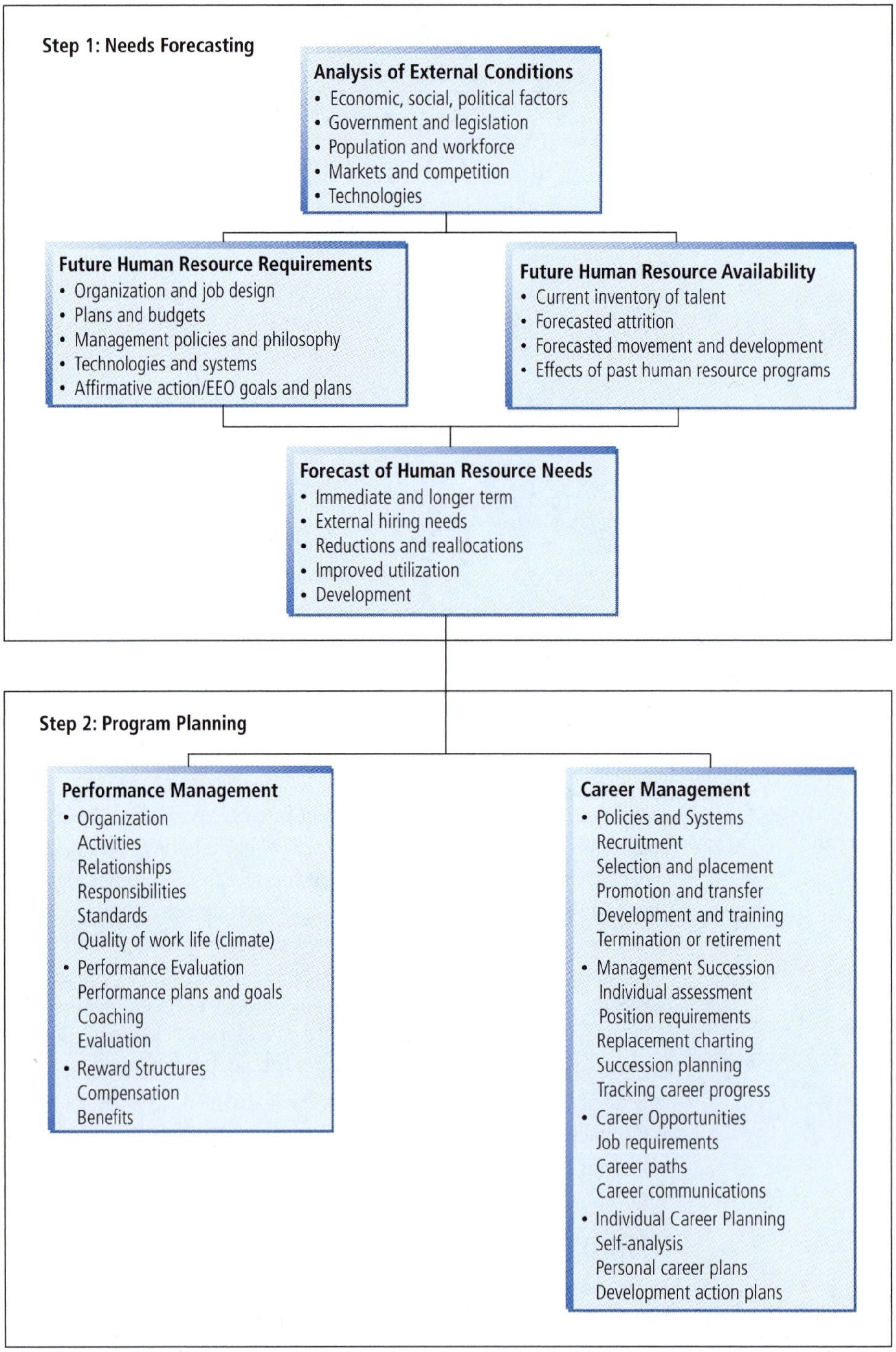

**Step 1: Needs Forecasting**

**Analysis of External Conditions**
- Economic, social, political factors
- Government and legislation
- Population and workforce
- Markets and competition
- Technologies

**Future Human Resource Requirements**
- Organization and job design
- Plans and budgets
- Management policies and philosophy
- Technologies and systems
- Affirmative action/EEO goals and plans

**Future Human Resource Availability**
- Current inventory of talent
- Forecasted attrition
- Forecasted movement and development
- Effects of past human resource programs

**Forecast of Human Resource Needs**
- Immediate and longer term
- External hiring needs
- Reductions and reallocations
- Improved utilization
- Development

**Step 2: Program Planning**

**Performance Management**
- Organization
  Activities
  Relationships
  Responsibilities
  Standards
  Quality of work life (climate)
- Performance Evaluation
  Performance plans and goals
  Coaching
  Evaluation
- Reward Structures
  Compensation
  Benefits

**Career Management**
- Policies and Systems
  Recruitment
  Selection and placement
  Promotion and transfer
  Development and training
  Termination or retirement
- Management Succession
  Individual assessment
  Position requirements
  Replacement charting
  Succession planning
  Tracking career progress
- Career Opportunities
  Job requirements
  Career paths
  Career communications
- Individual Career Planning
  Self-analysis
  Personal career plans
  Development action plans

Human resource planning also involves paying attention to the performance of the organization and the individual. Thus evaluation, developing compensation and reward programs, and coaching are important planning activities. There is also the need to select, assign, develop, and manage the careers of individuals.

Human resource planning requires the linking of external analysis and scanning with human resource management. Techniques and activities must be carefully employed to accomplish the quality and competitiveness outcomes that a firm seeks. These techniques include the use of:

- *Human resource inventories.* The skills, abilities, and knowledge that exist within the firm already.

- *Human resource forecast.* The firm's requirements based on numbers available, skill mix, and external labor supply.

- *Action plans.* The recruitment, selection, training, orientation, promotion, development, and compensation plans used.

- *Control and evaluation.* The monitoring system used to determine the degree of attainment of human resource goals.

Human resource planning involves the necessary activities that help managers reduce uncertainty about the future. For human resource plans, managers can make forecasts, plan so that change can be managed more efficiently, and display the role they play in properly managing human resources.

## | Recruitment

Whenever an organization's human resources must be expanded or replenished, a recruitment plan must be established or set in motion. Recruitment is the set of activities used to attract job candidates with the abilities and attitudes needed to help an organization achieve its objectives. Recruitment requires a sound human resource planning system that includes personnel inventories, forecasts of the supply and demand of human resources, action plans, and control and evaluation procedures. The first step in recruitment is a clear specification of needs: number of people, skills mix, knowledge, and experience level. This information is especially important so that affirmative action goals and timetables for the recruitment and hiring of minorities can be met.

If human resource needs cannot be met within a company, outside sources must be tapped. Advertisements in newspapers, trade journals, and magazines notify potential applicants of openings. Because responses to advertisements will come from both qualified and unqualified individuals, occasionally a company will list a post office box number rather than use its company name. Such advertisements, called blind ads, eliminate the need to contact every applicant, but they don't allow a company to use its name or logo as a form of promotion. Some organizations effectively use their own employees in newspaper and magazine ads.

The college campus is a major source for recruiting lower-level managers. Many colleges and universities have placement centers that work with organizational recruiters. Applicants read ads and information provided by the companies, and then they sign up for interviews. The most promising applicants are invited to visit the companies for more interviews.

To find experienced employees in the external market, organizations use private employment agencies, executive search firms, and/or state employment agencies. Some private employment agencies and executive search firms are called no-fee agencies—meaning the employers pay the search fee instead of the applicant. An organization is not obligated to hire any person referred by the no-fee agency, but the agency usually is informed when the right person is found.

**KEY**TERMS

**recruitment** The activities used to attract job candidates with the abilities and attitudes needed to help an organization achieve its objectives.

The employees responsible for recruiting are faced with legal requirements. These requirements are enforced by laws administered by the Equal Employment Opportunity Commission (EEOC). The federal government attempts to provide equal opportunities for employment without regard to race, religion, age, sex, national origin, or disability, through Title VII of the Civil Rights Act of 1964 and the Equal Employment Opportunity Act of 1972.[8] These laws have broad coverage and apply to any activity, business, or industry in which a labor dispute would hinder commerce. The laws also cover federal, state, and local government agencies.

Legal procedures regarding equal employment, opportunities, and recruitment are important to employers. Organizations must adjust to and work with these laws. Although adjustments are sometimes difficult, they seem to be a better alternative than long, costly court battles. Providing equal opportunities to all qualified job applicants makes sense both legally and morally. The vast majority of managers believe that all citizens have a right to any job they can perform reasonably well after a sufficient amount of training.

## | Selection

Selection is the process by which an organization chooses from a list of applicants the person or persons who best meet the criteria for the position available, considering current environmental and financial conditions. The selection process involves screening applicants and making decisions about which applicants to interview and which ones to hire. Firms such as Fairfield Inn and Holland American spend time and energy on their selection programs. After applicants are screened and interviewed, the firm decides whether to extend a job offer. Job candidates also enter into the decision-making process by deciding whether the job offer fits their needs and goals. Traditionally, the selection process enables the organization to attempt to accurately assess the probability that a particular candidate will succeed in the job. As noted earlier, federal mandates and legal standards affect how businesses selects employees. Exhibit 10.3 provides a list of legal versus illegal activities associated with employee screening.

The actual selection process is a series of steps. It starts with initial screening and ends with the hiring decision. Exhibit 10.4 presents each step in the process. A candidate can be rejected at any one of the nine steps. Recognizing human resource needs through the planning phase of staffing is the point at which selection begins. Preliminary interviews are used to screen out unqualified applicants. This screening often is an applicant's first personal contact with an organization. Applicants who pass the preliminary screening usually complete an application.

**KEY**TERMS

**selection** The process by which an organization chooses from a list of applicants the persons who best meet the criteria for the position available, considering current environmental and financial conditions.

---

**EXHIBIT 10.3**

### Some Legal Guidelines for Staff Selection

| Selection Screening Steps | Legal Activities | Illegal Activities |
|---|---|---|
| Test | Can be used if they have been validated | Cannot be used when there is no relationship between test results and performing the job |
| Interview information | To ask whether a person is a U.S. citizen | To require citizenship or to ask proof of citizenship |
| | To ask about convictions for crime | To ask whether a person has ever been arrested |
| Age | To require proof of age after hiring | To require a birth certificate |
| Racial identity | To keep records on racial and ethnic identity for purposes of reporting | To ask for race, creed, or national origin in application or interview |

10.4    **Typical Selection Decision Steps**

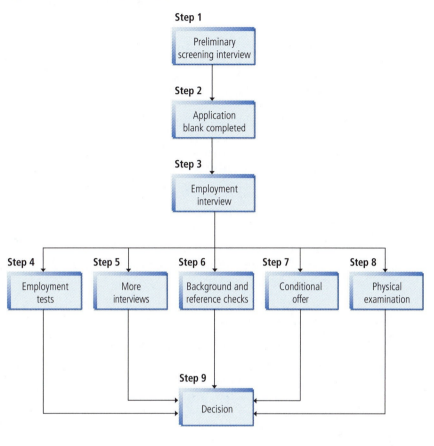

## Screening Interviews

Interviews are used throughout the selection process. Interviewers usually first acquaint themselves with the job analysis information. Second, they review the application information. Third, they typically ask questions designed to give better insight into the applicants, and they add this information to information provided on the application.

Three general types of interviews are used: structured, semistructured, and unstructured. In the structured interview, the interviewer asks specific questions of all interviewees. In the semistructured interview, only some questions are prepared in advance. This approach is less rigid than the structured interview and allows the interviewer more flexibility. The unstructured interview allows interviewers the freedom to discuss whatever they think can be important. Comparing answers across interviewees is rather difficult, however. According to a recent study, the situational interview, in which job candidates role-play in mock job scenarios, is the most accurate of any type of interview in predicting job performance (54 percent compared to 7 percent for the standard structured interview).[9]

Some firms now use online selection services to administer structured employment interviews. Although this activity does not replace the face-to-face interview, an Internet consulting service can provide a low-cost base of information about each applicant before the interviewer meets him or her. An applicant can typically complete a 100-question computer-aided interview in less than twenty minutes.[10]

## Tests

Managers often complain that they have a problem hiring and retaining successful employees. Relying solely on intuition, rather than finding objective procedures to select employees, is not adequate. Subjective procedures are not very accurate in predicting how employees actually will perform the job. One method to improve upon intuition and subjective judgments is testing. A test is a means of obtaining a standardized sample of a person's behavior.

Here are some advantages of valid selection tests (how well a test score predicts job success) and reliable selection tests (those that provide consistency of measurement):

- *Improved accuracy in selecting employees.* Individuals differ in skills, intelligence, motivation, interests, needs, and goals. If these differences can be measured, and if they are related to job success, performance can be predicted to some extent by test scores.

- *An objective means for judging.* Applicants answers the same questions under test conditions. Then their responses are scored. One applicant's score then can be compared with those of other applicants.

- *Information on current employees' needs.* Tests given to current employees provide data on their training, development, or counseling needs.

The United States Supreme Court made a landmark ruling relating to tests in the *Griggs v. Duke Power Company* case in 1971.[11] Six years earlier, Duke Power had established a policy requiring job applicants to pass a number of tests and have a high school education to qualify for placement and promotion. A group of African American employees challenged these requirements, arguing that they were denied promotions because of the company's testing policy. The Supreme Court ruled that neither the high school requirement nor the test scores showed a relationship to successful job performance.

Now, organizations using any test must carefully examine how the scores are used, and test results must be validated. The United States Court of Appeals in Chicago recently ruled that a personality test used to determine promotions was a medical exam because it asked questions that could reveal mental disabilities, and the Americans with Disabilities Act prohibits pre-employment medical exams.[12] There must be statistical proof that test scores are related to job performance. But testing still can be an important part of the selection process as well as a major tool for making decisions. The Management Highlight on page 209 discusses the importance of pre-employment testing.

## The Hiring Decision

When the human resources department has completed the preliminary screening steps—evaluation of the job application information, interviewing, and testing (if it is used)—a reference check should be conducted. Checking with previous employers can provide important information. However, fear of defamation lawsuits has caused a growing number of organizations to provide no relevant information. Courts in most states have held that former and prospective employers have a "qualified privilege" to discuss an employee's past performance. In exercising the privilege, a previous employer must follow three rules: (1) determine that the prospective employer has a job-related need to know; (2) release only truthful information about the former employer; and (3) do not release EEO-related information such as race, age, or ethnic background.[13]

**PRE-EMPLOYMENT TESTING**

All human resource managers realize that hiring the wrong employee can have negative consequences for the organization. Hiring the wrong person can lower the morale of other workers; increase the costs or training and supervision; and if the employee resigns or is let go, additional recruiting costs are incurred. Research has shown that above-average employees are worth an additional 40 percent of their salary than average workers. In terms of new hires, an above-average worker with a $40,000 salary is worth $16,000 more to the organization than an average new hire.

In spite of the obvious importance of hiring the best people, many human resource managers still rely primarily on the resume and the personal interview to make hiring decisions. Although these two screening methods are a very important part of the selection process, testing a job candidate for needed skills increases the likelihood of identifying the ideal employee. Pre-employment testing can assist the human resource manager in selecting the best qualified workers. Using pre-employment tests or software is often the most important change human resource departments can make in the hiring process. The cost of administering these tests is small in comparison to the potential cost of a bad hiring decision.

Pre-employment testing can be administered both in person and online, and can be used for a number of purposes. For example, some organizations use personality tests in interviewing to discover what a person is like and if the person is a good fit. Testing can also be used to develop a job profile and match the candidate who has specific characteristics with the appropriate job. Tests can also measure intelligence; cognitive abilities are directly related to overall job performance. Cognitive abilities tests, for instance, can be used to measure a job candidate's ability to learn. Such tests have proven to be a popular indicator of ability to learn on the job and performance. A variety of tests are available to make the selection process more successful, including:

- Job knowledge tests, which measure specific job-related knowledge

- Psychological tests, which measure personality traits

- Proficiency tests, which measure a person's ability to do the work required

- Cognitive abilities tests, which measure knowledge, learning ability, and problem-solving skills

- Interest tests, which compare a candidate's interests of successful people in a specific job

Source: Adapted from T. L. Stanley, "The Wisdom of Employment Testing," *SuperVision* (February 2004): 11–13; Adam Agard, "Pre-employmnet Skills Testing: An Important Step in the Hiring Process," *SuperVision* (June 2003): 7; Bob Hoel, "Predicting Performance," *Credit Union Management* (July 2004): 24.

# Training and Development

The training and development of human resources involves change: change in skills, knowledge, attitudes, and/or social behavior. For an organization to remain competitive, it needs to stay abreast of such changes. Maintaining technological superiority, teamwork, world-class quality performance, and social harmony among individuals with differing ethnic backgrounds and skills depends on the organization's ability to cope with change. For example, as a result of technical and software advances, computer specialists have to be continually retrained.

Training is, in short, an attempt to improve current or future employee performance. In most organizations, training is done in problem solving, problem analysis, measurement and feedback, and team building. Here are some important aspects of training:

- *Training.* The systematic process of altering employees' behavior to further organization goals.

- *Development.* The acquisition of knowledge and skills that employees can use in the present or future. Development focuses more on the long term.

- *Formal training program.* An effort by the employer to provide opportunities for the employee to acquire job-related skills, attitudes, and knowledge. At IBM, Motorola, and Xerox, all employees go through a formal training program.

*Learning.* The act by which individuals acquire skills, knowledge, and abilities that result in a relatively permanent change in their behavior.

*Skill.* Any behavior that has been learned and applied. Therefore, the goal of training is to improve skills. Motor skills, cognitive skills, and interpersonal skills are targets of training programs.

## Performance Evaluation

Performance evaluation is the systematic review of individual job-relevant strengths and weaknesses. Two processes are used in reviewing an individual's job performance: observation and judgment. Both processes are subject to bias or human error. Eliminating evaluation bias and measuring only objective indicators of performance, such as number of units produced, cost of completing a unit, or the time to finish a unit, would be ideal. But objective indicators often measure factors beyond an individual employee's control. Therefore, organizations tend to use subjective criteria, such as a manager's rating of a subordinate. And it is here that bias enters the picture, because every rater is asked to observe and then make a judgment about the observations.

Performance evaluation is a difficult process to implement, and the problems of bias are hard to overcome. The evaluation itself appears to be uncomfortable for raters as well as for those being rated. But for HRM, formal evaluations can serve the following purposes:

Make decisions easier involving promotion, transfer, pay raises, and termination

Help establish training and development programs and evaluate their success

Provide employees with feedback about strengths and weaknesses

Predict whether recruitment and selection activities lead to attracting, screening, and hiring the best-qualified human resources

Help determine what type of individual can be successful within the organization

These five purposes can be accomplished only if the evaluation system used satisfies two requirements. It must be relevant to the job or jobs being evaluated, and it must be accepted by the raters and ratees. Raters must believe in the importance of evaluation and feedback. To motivate human resources, raters must view performance evaluation as a significant part of their job. From the ratee's perspective, performance evaluation must be relevant, fair, conducted by raters familiar with ratees' job performance, and open to modification if flaws are detected. Evaluation system also must be able to discriminate between good, average, and poor performers.

Managers usually attempt to select a performance evaluation procedure that will minimize conflict, provide ratees with relevant feedback, and help to achieve organizational objectives. Basically, managers must try to develop and implement a performance evaluation program that also can benefit other managers, the work group, and the organization.

As with most managerial procedures, there are no universally accepted methods of performance evaluation to fit every purpose, person, or organization. What is effective at IBM might not work for General Mills. In fact, what is effective within one department or one group in a particular organization might not be right for another unit or group within the same company. One inherent problem with performance evaluation is that employees are generally evaluated on individual contributions, whereas the ability and willingness to work as part of a team are two of the most highly valued attributes in a worker today.[14]

**KEY**TERMS

**performance evaluation** The systematic review of individual, job-relevant strengths and weaknesses by means of observation and judgment.

EXHIBIT 10.5

**Typical Graphic Rating Scale**

Name _____ Dept._____ Date _____

| | Outstanding | Good | Satisfactory | Fair | Unsatisfactory |
|---|---|---|---|---|---|
| Quantity of work<br>Volume of acceptable work<br>under normal conditions<br>Comments | ☐ | ☐ | ☐ | ☐ | ☐ |
| Quality of work<br>Thoroughness, neatness,<br>and accuracy of work<br>Comments | ☐ | ☐ | ☐ | ☐ | ☐ |
| Knowledge of job<br>Clear understanding of the<br>factors pertinent to the job<br>Comments | ☐ | ☐ | ☐ | ☐ | ☐ |
| Personal qualities<br>Personality, appearance,<br>sociability, leadership, integrity<br>Comments | ☐ | ☐ | ☐ | ☐ | ☐ |
| Cooperation<br>Ability and willingness to work<br>with associates, supervisors, and<br>subordinates toward common goals<br>Comments | ☐ | ☐ | ☐ | ☐ | ☐ |
| Dependability<br>Conscientious, thorough, accurate,<br>reliable with respect to attendance,<br>lunch periods, reliefs, etc.<br>Comments | ☐ | ☐ | ☐ | ☐ | ☐ |
| Initiative<br>Earnest in seeking increased<br>responsibilities; self-starting,<br>unafraid to proceed alone<br>Comments | ☐ | ☐ | ☐ | ☐ | ☐ |

## Graphic Rating Scales

The oldest and most widely used performance evaluation procedure, the graphic scaling technique, has many forms: Generally, the rater is supplied with a printed form for each subordinate to be rated. The form lists various job performance qualities and characteristics to be considered. Rating scales are distinguished by: (1) how exactly the categories are defined, (2) the degree to which the person interpreting the ratings (e.g., the ratee) can tell what response was intended by the rater, and (3) how carefully the performance dimension is defined for the rater.

Each organization devises rating scales and formats that suit its needs. Exhibit 10.5 is an example of the type of rating form used in many organizations.

## Ranking Methods

Some managers use a rank-order procedure to evaluate all subordinates. Subordinates are ranked according to their relative value to the company or unit on one or more performance dimensions. This procedure usually identifies the best and worst performers, who are placed in the first and last positions on the ranking list. The next best and next poorest performers then are noted. This continues until all subordinates are on the list. The rater is forced to discriminate by the rank-order performance evaluation method.

Some problems are associated with the ranking method. First, ratees in the central portion of the list likely will not be much different from one another on the performance rankings. A second problem involves the size of the group of subordinates being evaluated. Large groups are more difficult to rank than small groups.

## Descriptive Essays

The essay method of performance evaluation requires that the rater describe each ratee's strong and weak points. Some organizations require each rater to discuss specific points, whereas others allow raters to discuss whatever they believe is appropriate. One problem with the unstructured essay evaluation is that it provides little opportunity to compare ratees on specific performance dimensions. Another limitation involves variations in raters' writing skills. Some simply are not very good at writing descriptive analyses of subordinates' strengths and weaknesses.

## Rating Errors

The numerous traditional performance evaluation methods each have problems and potential rating errors. In some situations, raters are extremely harsh or easy in their evaluations. These are called strictness or leniency rater errors. The harsh rater tends to give lower-than-average ratings to subordinates. The lenient rater tends to give higher-than-average ratings. These kinds of rating errors typically result because raters apply their own personal standards to the particular performance evaluation system being used. For example, the words *outstanding* or *average* might mean different things to various raters. Rating errors can be minimized if:

- Each dimension addresses a single job activity rather than a group of activities.

- The rater can observe the ratees' behavior on a regular basis.

- Terms such as *average* are not used on rating scales, because different raters react differently to such words.

- The rater does not have to evaluate large groups of subordinates. Fatigue and difficulty in discriminating among ratees become major problems when large groups of subordinates are evaluated.

- Raters are trained to avoid leniency, strictness, stereotyping, and other rating errors.

- The dimensions being evaluated are meaningful, clearly stated, and important.

## Compensation

Compensation is the HRM activity that deals with every type of reward that individuals receive for performing organizational tasks. It is basically an exchange relationship. Employees exchange their labor for financial and nonfinancial rewards. Financial compensation is both direct and indirect. Direct financial compensation consists of the pay an employee receives in the form of wages, salary, bonuses, and commissions. Indirect financial compensation (also called benefits) consists of all financial rewards, such as vacation and insurance, that are not included in direct financial compensation. Exhibit 10.6 presents a number of direct and indirect forms of compensation.

## Compensation Objectives

The objective of the traditional compensation function is to create a system of rewards that is equitable to employer and employee alike. The desired outcome is an employee who is attracted

**EXHIBIT 10.6**

**Types of Compensation**

| Direct | Indirect |
|---|---|
| Base pay | Education program (e.g., paying for course tuition and fees) |
| Merit pay | Protection programs (e.g., insurance) |
| Incentives<br>  Group<br>  Individual | Time away from work (e.g., vacation) |
| Cost-of-living adjustments | Perks (e.g., company car) |

to the work and motivated to do a good job for the employer. Compensation policy has seven criteria for effectiveness:

- *Adequate.* Minimum government, union, and managerial pay levels should be met.
- *Equitable.* Everyone should be paid fairly, in line with their effort, abilities, and training.
- *Balanced.* Pay, benefits, and other rewards should provide a reasonable total reward package.
- *Cost-effective.* Pay should not be excessive, considering what the organization can afford to pay.
- *Secure.* Pay should be enough to help employees feel secure and aid them in satisfying basic needs.
- *Incentive-providing.* Pay should motivate effective, productive work.
- *Acceptable to the employee.* Employees should understand the pay system and feel that it is reasonable for the enterprise and for themselves.[15]

Pay can be determined absolutely or relatively. Some people have argued that the best procedure would be a pay system set by a single criterion for the whole nation or the world (i.e., the absolute control of pay). Because absolute pay systems are not used, however, the pay for each employee is set relative to the pay of others. Pay for a particular position is set relative to three groups:

- *Group A.* Employees working on similar jobs in other organizations
- *Group B.* Employees working on different jobs within the organization
- *Group C.* Employees working on the same job within the organization

The decision to examine pay relative to Group A is called the *pay-level decision.* The objective of the pay-level decision is to keep the organization competitive in the labor market. The major tool used in this decision is the pay survey (discussed later in this chapter). The pay decision relative to Group B is called the *pay-structure decision.* The pay structure involves using job evaluation to set a value on each job within the organization relative to all other jobs. The decision involving pay relative to Group C is called *individual pay determination.*

## Compensation and Performance

Because of increasing payroll costs and competition in the global marketplace, managers throughout the world are searching for ways to increase productivity by linking compensation to employee performance.[16] High performance requires much more than employee motivation. Employee ability and health, adequate equipment, good physical working conditions, effective leadership and management, safety, and other conditions all help raise employee performance levels. But employees' motivation to work harder and better is obviously an important factor. A number of studies indicate that if pay is tied to performance, the employee produces a higher quality and quantity of work.[17] Not everyone agrees with this finding; some researchers argue that if you tie pay to performance, you destroy the intrinsic rewards a person gets from doing the job well.[18] The importance of money varies from one employee to the next. If the organization claims to have an incentive pay system but in fact pays for seniority, the motivation effects of pay will be lost. The key to making compensation systems more effective is to be sure that they are directly connected to expected behaviors. An increasing number of organizations are tying pay and bonuses to the achievement of goals and individual performance.[19]

In sum, theorists disagree over whether pay is a useful mechanism for increasing performance. Because of individual differences in employees and jobs, it seems more fruitful to redirect this research to examine (1) the range of behaviors that pay can affect positively or negatively, (2) the amount of change in worker behavior that pay can influence, (3) the kinds of employees that pay influences positively and negatively, and (4) the environmental conditions present when pay leads to positive and negative results.

## Selected Methods of Compensation

Employees can be paid for the time they work (flat rates), the output they produce (individual incentives), or a combination of these two factors.

**Flat Rates** In the unionized firm, where wages are established by collective bargaining, single flat rates rather than different rates are often paid. For example all clerk-typists might make $6.50 per hour, regardless of seniority or performance. Flat rates correspond to some midpoint on a market survey for that job. Using a flat rate doesn't mean that seniority and experience do not differ. It means that employers and the union choose not to recognize these variations when setting wage rates. Unions insist on ignoring performance differentials for many reasons. They contend that performance measures are inequitable. Jobs need cooperative effort that could be destroyed by wage differentials. Sales organizations, for example, pay a flat rate for a job and add a bonus or incentive to recognize individual differences.

Choosing to pay a flat rate versus different rates for the same job depends on the objectives established by the compensation analyst. Recognizing individual differences makes the assumption that employees are not interchangeable or equally productive. By using pay differentials to recognize these differences, mangers try to encourage an experienced, efficient, and satisfied workforce.

**Individual Incentives** Perhaps the oldest form of compensation is the individual incentive plan, in which the employee is paid for units produced. Individual incentive plans take several forms: piecework, production bonuses, and commissions. These methods seek to achieve the incentive goal of compensation.

*Straight piecework* usually works like this. An employee is guaranteed an hourly rate (often the minimum wage) for performing an expected minimum output (the standard). For production over the standard, the employer pays so much per additional piece produced. This is probably the most frequently used incentive pay plan. The standard is set through work measurement studies as modified by collective bargaining. The base rate and piece rate might emerge from data collected by pay surveys.

A variation of the straight piece rate is the *differential piece rate.* In this plan, the employer pays a smaller piece rate up to the standard and then a higher piece rate above the standard. Research indicates that the differential piece rate is more effective than the straight piece rate, although it is much less frequently used.[20]

*Production bonus systems* pay an employee an hourly rate. Then a bonus is paid when the employee exceeds the standard, typically 50 percent of labor savings. This system is not widely used.

*Commissions* are paid to sales employees. Straight commission is the equivalent of straight piecework and is typically a percentage of the item's price. A variation of the production bonus system for sales is to pay salespeople a small salary and commission or bonus when they exceed standards (the budgeted sales goal).

Individual incentives are used more frequently in some industries (clothing, steel, textiles) than others (lumber, beverage, bakery) and more often in some jobs (sales, production) than others (maintenance, clerical). Individual incentives are possible only in situations where performance can be clearly specified in terms of output (sales dollars generated, number of items completed). In addition, so that individual incentives can be applied equitably, employees must work independently of each other. Digital Equipment Company (DEC) uses an incentive system to reward whistle blowing.

| **Gainsharing Incentive Plans** | Gainsharing plans are companywide group incentive plans. Their goal is to unite diverse organizational elements behind the common pursuit of improved organizational effectiveness by allowing employees to share in the proceeds. The system has proven to be exceptionally effective in enhancing organization-wide teamwork. Gainsharing plans that use cash awards and have been in place for at least five years have shown productivity ratio improvements resulting in labor cost reductions of 29 percent.[21]

More and more companies have been implementing gainsharing plans using a formula that establishes a bonus based on improved productivity. Gainsharing rewards are normally distributed either monthly or quarterly.[22] Factors dictating a gainsharing plan's success include (1) company size, (2) age of the plan, (3) the company's financial stability, (4) unionization, (5) the company's technology, and (6) employees' and managers' attitudes. Because a gainsharing plan is expensive to administer, organizations considering it must weigh the projected benefits against costs.

Linking pay to group performance and inspiring team spirit are two reasons cited for the rising popularity of gainsharing.[23] For gainsharing to succeed, it must be supported by management. To optimize this type of group-based incentive program, management must also understand what gainsharing can and cannot accomplish.

## The Equal Pay Act

The Equal Pay Act (1963) amending the Fair Labor Standards Act is the first antidiscrimination law relating directly to women. The act applies to all employers and employees covered by the Fair Labor Standards Act, including executives, managers, and professionals. The Equal Pay Act requires equal pay for equal work for men and women. It defines *equal work* as employment requiring equal skills, effort, and responsibility under similar working conditions.[24]

Under the Equal Pay Act, an employer can establish different wage rates on the basis of (1) seniority, (2) merit, (3) performance differences (quantity and quality of work), and (4) any factor other than sex. Shift work differentials are also permissible. But all these exceptions must apply equally to men and women. Since passage of the act, the female-male earnings gap has narrowed slightly. Nonetheless, many women today continue to earn less than men who perform the same job.[25] In an effort to close the remaining earnings gap, over the past few years, there has been a growing movement to expand the widely accepted concept of equal pay for equal jobs to include equal pay for comparable jobs. Thus, for young people entering the workforce today, there is practically no difference between wages for men and women within a single job; the male-female wage discrepancy is heavily generational.

## Comparable Worth

The doctrine of comparable worth (sometimes called pay equity) does not stipulate that women and men be paid equally for performing equal work. Comparable worth is a concept that attempts

**KEY** TERMS

**gainsharing plan** A companywide group incentive plan that allows employees to share in the proceeds and whose goal is to unite diverse organizational elements behind the common pursuit of improved organizational effectiveness.

**comparable worth** A concept contending that individuals who perform jobs requiring similar skills, efforts, and responsibilities under similar work conditions should be compensated equally.

to prove and remedy the allegation that employers systematically discriminate by paying women employees less than their work is intrinsically worth, relative to what they pay men who work in comparable professions. The term *comparable worth* means different things to different people. Comparable worth relates jobs that are dissimilar in their content (for example, nurse and plumber) and contends that individuals who perform jobs that require similar skills, efforts, and responsibilities under similar work conditions should be compensated equally.

Advocates of comparable worth depend primarily upon two sets of statistics that demonstrate that women employees are discriminated against by employers. First, they point to statistics showing that women earn less than men overall.[26] Second, women have tended to be concentrated in lower-paying, predominantly female jobs. Although more women are entering the workforce, about one-fourth of all women employed in 1988 worked in three job categories: secretarial/clerical, retail sales, and preparation and service.[27]

# Benefits and Services

Indirect financial compensation, which many organizations refer to as benefits and services, consists of all financial rewards that are not included in direct financial compensation. Unlike pay-for-performance programs and incentive plans, benefits and services are made available to employees as long as they are employed by the organization. Annual surveys suggest that about 75 percent of all United States workers say that benefits are crucial to job choice. If limited to only one benefit (beyond cash), 64 percent of workers say that healthcare is most important.[28] Employee benefits and services are part of the rewards of employment that reinforce loyal service to the employer. Major benefits and services programs include pay for time not worked, insurance, pensions, and services like tuition reimbursement.

This definition of benefits and services can be applied to hundred of programs. Organizations disagree, however, about what is or is not to be included, the purposes to be served, responsibility for programs, the costs and values of the various elements, the units in which the costs and values are measured, and the criteria for decision making. Compensation decisions regarding indirect compensation are more complex than decisions concerned with wages and salaries.

## Benefits Required by Law

Benefits programs offered by organizations today are the product of efforts in this area for the past sixty years. Before World War II, employers offered a few pensions and services because they had the welfare of employees at heart or they wanted to keep out a union. But most benefit programs began in earnest during the war, when wages were strictly regulated.

The unions pushed for nonwage compensation increases, and they got them. Court cases in the late 1940s confirmed the right of unions to bargain for benefits: *Inland Steel* v. *National Labor Relations Board* (1948) over pensions, and *W W Cross* v. *National Labor Relations Board* over insurance. The growth of benefit programs indicates how much unions have used this right. In 1929, benefits cost employers 3 percent of total wages and salaries; by 1949 the cost was up to 16 percent, and in the 1970s it was nearly 30 percent. By 1990 costs of benefits and services totaled about 50 percent.[29]

## Additional Benefits and Retirement Plans

In addition to benefits required by the law (such as unemployment insurance, social security, and workers' compensation), many employers provide other kinds of benefits: compensation for time not worked, insurance protection, and retirement plans. There are many differences in employers' practices regarding these benefits. The most widely used benefits include paid vacations, holidays, and sick leave; life and medical insurance; and pension plans.

| **Childcare** | Two fairly recent additions to benefits packages are childcare and eldercare. Nearly 50 percent of today's workers are women, and as many as 70 percent of these women have children under age six at home. The Bureau of the Census reports that working mothers pay about $15.1 billion per year for childcare while they work. The United States Department of Labor states that in 1995, more than 80 percent of the women between the ages of 25 and 44 will be working outside the home at least part time. This suggests that childcare programs will become a necessity.

| **Eldercare** | People age sixty-five or older will comprise 23 percent of the United States Population by 2050.[30] Recent research shows that at least 20 percent of all employees already provide assistance to one or more elderly relatives or friends. On average, these employees spend between 6 and 35 hours per week providing this care. At least 50 percent of these employees also have children at home. The burden falls most heavily on the working woman, who traditionally cared for elderly relatives and did not work outside the home. Employees who are also caregivers to seniors experience the following problems: missed work (58 percent), loss of pay (47 percent), and less energy to do their work well (15 percent).

## Special Issues in Human Resources

The HRM activities already discussed are important and must be properly managed to ensure the efficient use of human resource abilities, skills, and experience. In addition, however, three special issues—AIDS, sexual harassment, and substance abuse—have become significant in the workplace.

### AIDS in the Workplace

For many reasons, a company should be knowledgeable about and have a plan to deal with acquired immunodeficiency syndrome (AIDS). First, morally, people are dying and organizations are likely to be involved simply by being a part of society. Second, the law of probability suggests that eventually AIDS will enter every workplace. Individuals, work groups, and departments will feel the tragedy of AIDS.

The 1992 Americans with Disabilities Act (ADA) protects individuals with AIDS from being discriminated against in the areas of hiring, advancement, compensation, training, or other conditions of employment. Under the ADA, employers can require employee physicals only if the exams are clearly job-specific and consistent with business necessity, and then only after an offer of employment has been made to a job applicant.[31]

### Sexual Harassment

According to public opinion polls, most American women believe they have experienced sexual harassment on the job. The EEOC filed more than 13,000 charges of sexual harassment in a single year.[32] As the law has evolved, two types of conduct have been found to constitute sexual harassment in violation of Title VII of the Civil Rights Act. The first type, originally identified in 1977, is the designated *tangible job benefit*, also known as *quid pro quo harassment*. This form of harassment occurs when an employee's career path is directly affected by a supervisor's unwelcome requests for sexual favors or other sexual advances.

A second type of sexual harassment is a *hostile work environment*. The elements necessary for providing a sexual harassment claim related to a hostile work environment are stated by a New York State case:

> A person would have to show that (1) he or she belongs to a protected group (i.e., female or minority group); (2) he or she was subject to unwelcome sexual harassment as defined above; (3) the harassment complained of was based upon his or her membership in the protected class; and (4) the harassment complained of affected the terms, conditions, or privileges of his or her employment.

The creation of a work environment in violation of Title VII can occur in many ways, depending on the size of the workforce, managers' sensitivity to sexual harassment, and the dynamics of the workplace. An employer can be liable for sexual harassment against an employee even when the harasser is not the actual employer; it is the organization's responsibility to protect its employee by excluding an offender from its premises.[33] Read the following Management Highlight and determine whether you think this is a case of sexual harassment.

## UNWELCOME ADVANCES

Mary is a 23-year-old gregarious nursing student working the evening shift at a large healthcare facility. Providence Health Care includes two intensive care facilities, 40 managed care practices, three out-patient surgical facilities, and ten outreach doctor's offices. The off-campus Quick Doc offices are open 8am - 10pm, but staff often arrive at 5am and stay as late as midnight. However, all doors unlock at 8am and lock at 10pm automatically. At all other times a key is required for entry. One night John, a male patient with a history of drug and psychiatric problems, showed unusual interest in Mary. In fact, he asked her out on a date. Startled by the proposition, Mary said no, but the patient was persistent. Again, Mary said no to the offer of a date and left the room. However, she felt uneasy about the situation and just wanted to forget that it ever happened to her. Yet at the same time her uneasiness made her feel that she needed to confide in someone about John. The very next day she told her supervisor that John had asked her out. Her supervisor suggested that maybe she had been too friendly with him and warned her that he was a troubled individual and to keep her distance from patients. Annoyed, Mary thought that her supervisor failed to understand that she did nothing to encourage John and that she did not want to have any interaction with him outside of work under any circumstances. In the days that followed, Mary found herself acting aloof and maintaining a distance from her patients because of her experience with John.

Several evenings later, Mary was at work and the phone rang. She answered assuming that it was one of the doctors, but it was John. He said he had been watching her every day for the past week and had followed her to work that day. He demanded that they meet after work and get to know one another. Mary was shocked and unable to respond. She instinctively hung up the phone. Shaking and on the verge of tears, she asked to speak with her supervisor. Upon hearing the situation, her supervisor told her to ignore the situation and just stay away from John. When she left work that night, she was sure she was being followed. When she arrived home, her phone was ringing but when she answered it, no one was there.

The next afternoon Mary went to work as usual. On this particular day, it was Mary's turn to close up the Quick Doc office that evening. Around 10:15 Mary was finishing up her work when the phone rang. She wasn't surprised because doctors often called in late to leave next-day patient orders or check laboratory test results. Mary answered the phone, but it wasn't a doctor—it was John! He said he was parked behind the building and wanted to talk to Mary in his car. Frightened, Mary hung up. Shaken, she tried to think about what to do next. She thought to herself, "I'm an adult and I can handle this creep." Just then there was a loud pounding noise at the back door. "Let me in, Mary!" the voice demanded. It was John. He sounded desperate. She spun around looking for help, but suddenly realized that all the other employees had gone home. She was alone in the building. Mary felt paralyzed with fear. Nothing like this had ever happened to her before. She felt unprepared and vulnerable. "What should I do?" she thought. Fear overtook judgment; she thought that she might faint as the blood seemed to drain from her arms. Mary could feel her heart pounding like a base drum. "Oh God, what do I do?" she said to herself. The pounding on the back door grew louder and it seemed that the door would give way. "Open up. I know you're in there!" he screamed.

1. Does this case have all the elements necessary for Mary to prove sexual harassment?

2. From a human resource management perspective, did Mary's supervisor do anything wrong in this situation?

3. Identify three actions that the organization might take to preclude situations like this from happening in the future.

The number of sexual harassment complains filed with the Equal Employment Opportunity Commission (EEOC) has soared by 150 percent—going from 6,127 in 1990 to 15,342 in 1996.[34] Because most victims don't file with the EEOC, these figures represent only some of the incidents. As the problem continues, managers are advised to develop a program to combat sexual harassment. Typically a company-based program involves (1) developing a sexual harassment policy and complaint resolution procedure, (2) training managers to implement the policy and procedure, (3) educating employees to recognize and confront harassment, (4) providing follow-up care after harassment incidents, and (5) monitoring the workplace for awareness of and compliance with sexual harassment policies.[35]

The seriousness of sexual harassment and why it must be dealt with through policies, increased awareness, and training are captured in this statement by the United States Merit Protection Board:

> Victims pay all the intangible emotional costs inflicted by anger, humiliation, frustration, withdrawal; dysfunctional family, and other damages that can be sexual harassment's aftermath. Victims of the most severe forms of harassment, including rape, can face not only severe emotional consequences, but also the possibility of a life-threatening disease. Some victims may leave jobs for one with a lower career path in order to escape the sexual harassment.[36]

Because of its trauma and potential impact, sexual harassment demands prompt managerial action. Employers might protect themselves from liability by taking prompt action to curb harassment when it occurs.[37] It is impossible for a worker to pay attention to the quality of production or service when harassment is occurring. Corrective action is required because of the need to protect the rights of every worker. It is also required because the law (although it is gray in some areas) indicates that employers are liable for sexual harassment. In fact, employers might also be responsible for the acts of their employees. For example, when an employer (or an employer's agent) knows—or should know—of the harassment and fails to take immediate and corrective action, the employer can be held liable. Sending a clear message that sexual harassment of any form will not be tolerated is a recommended course of action.[38]

## Substance Abuse

Substance abuse is a major problem that might affect the safety, productivity, and image of organizations.[39] Employers with substance abuse problem are less productive, have more workplace accidents, and cause higher instances of litigation.[40] An American Management Association (AMA) survey indicates that about 75 percent of major United States companies now engage in drug testing.[41] Most major corporations also conduct pre-employment substance abuse testing. Like many forms of testing, substance abuse screening has passionate opponents. Claims that it is inaccurate, an invasion of privacy, and demeaning are well articulated. But so long as substance abuse remains a problem, testing is likely to continue. It is estimated that substance abuse costs United States industry over $140 billion annually because of lost productivity.[42] Clearly, programs and policies are needed to reduce the burden of substance abuse.

Management's most powerful tool to combat substance abuse is an informed, educated workforce. Detecting substance abuse or a related problem requires careful observation and proper training. Here are some signs of possible substance abuse

- Difficulty in recalling instructions
- Frequent tardiness and absence
- Numerous restroom breaks

| Difficulty in getting along with coworkers

| Increased off- and on-the-job accidents

| Dramatic change in personality[43]

The controversy about substance detection and testing is likely to continue unabated. The need is for a policy and program that (1) explains the company's philosophy on substance abuse, (2) describes the firm's policy on testing, (3) implements a discipline and rehabilitation program, (4) communicates the program to all employees, and (5) educates managers about how to enforce a fair substance abuse policy and program.[44] The foundation of an effective approach to preventing substance abuse is a clear, coherent program.

**CONCLUSION**

## Human Resource Management

People are the most important asset of an organization. To succeed in today's competitive global markets, organizations must recruit, retain, develop, and manage human resources. Many factors—laws, compensation, and benefits—must be considered in developing an effective human resource program.

## Discussion Questions

1. What is the purpose of human resource management? Would you expect HRM to remain a top priority of management in the future? Why?

2. What are the advantages and disadvantages of the different forms of testing? Can tests help managers in the selection process? How?

3. Discuss the two forms of sexual harassment. Which of the forms is more difficult to substantiate? Why?

## Video Case

### PepsiCo Puts People First

Whether a company employs five people or five thousand people, its workers are its greatest resource. Many of today's companies view their workforce as part of their overall competitive strategy—the best people producing the best products. At large firms, which have full-time human resource (HR) departments, human resource managers such as those at PepsiCo might be viewed as strategic business partners. No longer do these managers simply sign paychecks, approve vacations, and process health benefit claims. At PepsiCo—which has HR departments across its many divisions—HR managers play an integral role in the day-to-day success of the business.

Headquartered in Purchase, New York, PepsiCo is a global organization, with more than 143,000 employees worldwide. The company produces and markets many brands that consumers know and love—PepsiCo beverages, Frito-Lay snacks, Gatorade and Tropicana drinks, and Quaker Foods. PepsiCo brand products are available to consumers in nearly 200 countries and territories. But recruiting, selecting, training, managing, and meeting the career needs of more than 100,000 workers requires planning. The company offers a variety of programs designed to help workers perform and grow to the best of their potential. To foster long-term career growth, PepsiCo has created its own PepsiCo Career Growth Model, which offers job opportunities to promote employees' knowledge, skills, and abilities in leadership capability, functional excellence, knowing the business, and critical experiences.

PepsiCo's HR managers follow their own Human Resources Competency Model, which defines four key roles played by the HR department:

| *Strategic partner.* The HR department is charged with aligning the human resource strategy with the business strategy of PepsiCo.

| *Change agent.* The department focuses on facilitating and leading organization transformation and change initiatives.

| *Technical functional expert.* The HR department emphasizes mastering and driving efficiency and effectiveness in the core information and administrative processes.

| *Employee champion.* The department drives employee satisfaction, commitment, and engagement.

Both of these models indicate a high degree of structure within PepsiCo, and the structure helps ensure that everyone's needs are met, from career opportunities to benefits. Employees have a choice of flexible benefits, ranging from healthcare to savings plans. At Quaker Oats, workers can select time off for adoption, apply for a student loan, or take a leave of absence under the QuakerFlex benefits program. At many locations, they might even enjoy free oatmeal in the morning! "The benefit package [at Quaker] is easy to understand and allows me to choose from a variety of programs that work best for me and my family," notes one facilities employee.

Regardless of job level, PepsiCo looks for the best workers to contribute to the overall performance of the company, across all of its brands. "Excellent performance ... does not happen on its own," writes chairman and CEO Steve Reinemund on the company's web site. "Our people make it happen. In order to sustain this level of success, we need to ensure that we continue to attract, retain, and develop great people in all of our businesses." At PepsiCo's online Career Center, potential job candidates will find information about what the company looks for in its employees—qualities including "a commitment to excellence" and "willingness to learn." In turn, PepsiCo offers its workers opportunities such as "exciting career challenges," "world-class training and development," and "excellent compensation." This, in essence, is PepsiCo's social contract with its employees.

Keeping all of this in mind, consider the job of Darryl Claiborne, HR manager for regional sales at PepsiCo's Frito-Lay division. Claiborne works with Frito-Lay's route sales reps, who sell and deliver their products directly to retailers. Claiborne and his reps understand the valuable contribution they make to the company—their success correlates directly with Frito-Lay's profitability. So, as an HR strategic partner, Claiborne looks for ways to help his reps manage and grow their business. Claiborne communicates regularly with his reps, checking with them on how well they are doing and where they need help. He continually reengineers their routes to make sure they can steadily increase sales. Claiborne embraces the company's "Know the Business" principles, the set of guidelines created to help managers understand the company, its mission, and the way its employees achieve success. "PepsiCo—Taste the Success!" invites the company web site. Claiborne, his route sales reps, and more than 140,000 other employees intend to do just that.

## Questions

1. In what ways could Darryl Claiborne be considered an employee champion?

2. Why is this important to PepsiCo's efforts to build human capital?

3. In essence, Darryl Claiborne engages in on-the-job training as he communicates with and accompanies his reps on their sales rounds. How is this an important part of their effectiveness as a workforce?

Sources: Company web sites, http://www.pepsico.com and http://www.pepsicojobs.com, accessed August 19, 2004; PepsiCo career and HR materials, "Knowing the Business: Resources Guide" and "Career Framework: Functional Competency Model."

## BizFlix

### Bowfinger

This film, which brought Steve Martin and Eddie Murphy together for the first time, offers a funny look at Hollywood film making. Bobby Bowfinger (Martin), perhaps the least successful director in films, wants to produce a low-budget film with top star Kit Ramsey (Murphy). Bowfinger's problem: recruit a crew and cast with almost no budget and trick Kit into appearing in his film.

Bowfinger interviews several candidates for the Kit Ramsey lookalike role. He rejects everyone until Jifferson (Jiff) Ramsey (also played by Murphy) auditions. This scene is an edited version of the "The Lookalike" sequence early in the film. It includes Jiff's audition, interview, and a brief look at his first day at work.

### Questions

1. Does Bobbie Bowfinger have a set of valid selection criteria for filling the role of a Kit Ramsey lookalike? Does Bowfinger apply the criteria uniformly to each applicant?

2. Is there a good person-job fit of Jiff Ramsey in the screen role of Kit Ramsey?

3. Do you predict that Jiff Ramsey will be successful as a Kit Ramsey substitute?

## Suggested Reading

Antilla, Susan, *Tales from the Boom-Boom Room: Women vs. Wall Street* (Princeton, NJ: Bloomberg Press, 2002).

Becker, Brian E., Mark A. Huselid, and Dave Ulrich, *The HR Scorecard: Linking People, Strategy, and Performance* (Boston: Harvard Business School Press, 2001).

Berglas, Steven, "How to Keep Players Productive," *Harvard Business Review* (September 2006): 104–112.

Cohn, Jeffrey M., "Growing Talent as if Your Business Depended on It," *Harvard Business Review* (October 2005): 62–70.

Falcone, Paul, *96 Great Interview Questions to Ask Before You Hire* (New York: AMACOM, 1997).

Gupta, Kavita, *A Practical Guide to Needs Assessment* (San Francisco: Jossey-Bass, 1999).

Kirkpatrick, Donald L., *Evaluating Training Programs: The Four Levels* (San Francisco: Berrett-Koehler, 1998).

Pfeffer, Jeffrey, "Seven Practices of Successful Organizations," *California Management Review* (Winter 1998): 96–124.

Stolovitch, Harold D., and Erica J. Keeps, *Telling Ain't Training* (Alexandria, VA: American Society for Training and Development, 2002).

## Endnotes

1. David P. Twomey, *Equal Employment Opportunity Law* (Mason, OH: Thomson/South-Western, 1994).

2. "Affirmative Action: The Flawed Remedy," *Growth Strategies* (June 2005): 2.

3. Alfred Edmond Jr., "25 Years of Affirmative Action," *Black Enterprise* (February 1995): 156–157.

4. D. Murry and James C. Wimbush, "Perceptions of Workplace Affirmative Action Plans," *Group and Organization Management* (March 1998): 27–47.

5. Ann C. Wendt and William M. Slonaker, "Discrimination Reflects on You," *HR Magazine* (May 1992): 44–47.

6. *Equal Employment Opportunity Manual for Managers and Supervisors* (Chicago: Commerce Clearing House, 1992).

7. Joel Schettler, "Equal Access to All," Training (January 2002): 44.

8. Twomey, *Equal Employment Opportunity Law,* 1–4.

9. Jennifer Merritt, "Improv at the Interview," *Business Week* (February 3, 2003): 63.

10. "HR Managers Have the Most Common Causes of Poor Candidate Selection," *Personnel Journal* (July 1995): 25.

11. Bently Baranabus, "What Did the Supreme Court Really Say? *Personnel Administrator,* (July–August 1971): 22–25.

12. Kaja Whitehouse, "Employers Face Risk with Use of a Popular Personality Test," *The Wall Street Journal* (July 13, 2005): 1.

13. M. Brown, "Reference Checking: The Law Is on Your Side," *Human Resource Measurements* (supplement to *Personnel Journal*) (December 1991): 4–5.

14. Dick Gorelick, "Evaluating Performance Evaluations," *American Printer* (November 2005): 38.

15. Thomas Patton, *Pay* (New York: The Free Press, 1977).

16. B. J. Dewey, "Changing to Skill-Based Pay," *Compensation and Benefits Review* (January–February 1994): 38–43.

17. Peter V. Leblanc, "Pay for Work: Reviving an Old Idea for the New Customer Focus," *Compensation and Benefits Review* (July–August 1994): 5–14.

18. Joel M. Stern and G. Bennett Stewart III, "Pay-For-Performance: Only the Theory Is Easy," *HR Magazine* (June 1993): 48–49.

19. Michelle Conlin, "Now It's Getting Personal," *Business Week* (December 16, 2002): 90–92.

20. Carla O'Dell, *People, Performance, and Pay: America Responds to the Competitiveness Challenge* (Scottsdale, AZ: American Compensation Association, 1986): 108.

21. Jerry McAdams, "Alternative Rewards: What's Best for Your Organization?" *Compensation and Benefits Management* (Winter 1990): 133–139.

22. Dennis Collins, Larry Hatcher, and Timothy J. Ross, "The Decision to Implement Gainsharing: The Role of Work Climate, Expected Outcomes, and Union Status," *Personnel Psychology* (Spring 1993): 79.

23. Steven E. Markham, K. Dow Scott, and Beverly L. Little "National Gainsharing Study: The Importance of Industry Differences," *Compensation & Benefits Review* (January–February 1992): 34–45.

24. A. L. Otten, "People Patterns," *Wall Street Journal* (April 15, 1994): A1.

25. Sarah E. Lockyer, "Equal Pay Still a Battle of the Sexes," *Nation's Restaurant News* (April 4, 2005): 1–4.

26. Barry Gerhart, "Gender Differences in Current and Starting Salaries: The Role of Performance, College Major, and Job Title," *Industrial and Labor Relations Review* (April 1990): 418–433.

27. "Women in Sales are Closing the Earnings Gap," *Personnel Journal* (July 1995): 28.

28. "Controlling the Costs of Employee Benefits," *The Conference Board* (1992): 8.

29. J. E. Santora, "Employee Team Designs Flexible Benefits Program," *Personnel Journal* (April 1994): 30–39.

30. "Stride Rite Halts Its Elder-Care Program," *Personnel Journal* (September 1995): 11.

31. Helen Elkiss, "Reasonable Accommodation and Unreasonable Fears: An AIDS Policy Guide for Human Resource Personnel," *Human Resource Planning* (March 1992): 183–189.

32. Terry Winkelmann, "Zero Tolerance," *T&D* (August 2005): 50–52.

33. Judy Greenwald, "Employer Held Liable for Contract Worker's Acts in Harassment Appeal," *Business Insurance* (December 5, 2005): 4.

34. Larry Reynolds, "Sexual Harassment Claims Surge," *HR Focus* (March 1997): 8.

35. Kelly Flynn, "Preventive Medicine for Sexual Harassment," *HR Focus* (March 1991): 17.

36. Jeffrey P. Englander, "Handling Sexual Harassment in the Workplace," *The CPA Journal* (February 1992): 14.

37. "Avoid Sexual Harassment Claims," *Business Owner* (November/December 2005): 8.

38. Jonathan A. Segal, "Seven Ways to Reduce Harassment Claims," *HR Magazine* (January 1992): 84–86.

39. Ncholas J. Caste, "Drug Testing and Productivity," *Journal of Business Ethics* (April 1992): 301–306.

40. Dana Michelle Baker, "Substance Abuse Prevention in the Workplace," Dissertation, Wilmington College Division of Nursing, 2003.

41. Eric Rolfe Greenberg, "Test-Positive Rates Drop as More Companies Screen Employees," *HR Focus* (June 1992): 7.

42. "Report Finds Economic Cost of Substance Abuse Exceeds $143 Billion," *Alcoholism and Drug Abuse Weekly* (January 28, 2002): 1, 4.

43. Laura A. Lynos ad Brain H. Kleiner, "Managing the Problem of Substance Abuse . . . Without Abusing Employees," *HR Focus* (April 1992): 9.

44. Martha Zetlin, "Corporate America Declares War on Drugs," *Personnel* (August 1991): 1, 8.

# 11

# INDIVIDUAL BEHAVIOR: DIFFERENCES IN PERSONALITY, PERCEPTION, AND ATTITUDES

We know that people are all different, with unique interests in academics, music, travel, cuisine, and other aspects of life. Yet for all those differences, people are remarkably similar. Medical, legal, and business organizations often classify their patients, clients, or customers based on some common trait or characteristic. Such characteristics in people are often noticeable at work. For example, "high maintenance" people require more attention; others lack compassion. Sales and marketing jobs require an outgoing person with the ability to meet and interact with people. Staff accountants might work independently on computers all day, have little interaction with other people, and need limited supervision during their work day. Managers must consider these types of personal characteristics and job characteristics to best match individuals to jobs. What is needed for success on the job in addition to technical qualifications?

## Fairness and the Psychological Contract

All people share one particular similarity—a desire for a fair and equitable workplace, but they differ in terms of the degree to which they accept departures from fairness or equity. Without a fair and equitable workplace, people will seek employment elsewhere. And nowhere is equity more apparent than in an annual salary administration process based on performance evaluation ratings. Recent research suggests that we can group people into three categories based on their reaction to deviation in fairness or equity at work. *Equity sensitive* people watch for and expect fair treatment. If they aren't treated fairly, they take action such as complaining to regain equity losses or, as a last resort, they quit. *Benevolents* are more likely to accept a little less than their fair share without complaining. *Entitleds* are people who believe that they should have more than others. They are not afraid to ask for more and are able to live with the knowledge that their salary is higher than other workers performing the same task.[1] Many situations require fair treatment by statute. But most instances of trust and fairness are the product of the attitudes and personality of mangers based on culture, custom, and the desire to avoid conflict and turnover. The implicit bargain workers make with their employers is based on trust and a sense of fair play at work.

A productive relationship between management and worker is based on fairness. Fairness is either implicit in the form of a hand shake or spelled out as in a union contract. A psychological contract is a set of expectations a worker has regarding what he or she will give and what he or she will receive from the organization.[2] Recall from Chapter 2, "History of Management," the discussion of the inducement/contribution balance. Barnard's I/C balance and Simon's "zone of acceptance" were the origins of the psychological contract. Scholars have argued that when mangers violate workers expectations of fairness, they do so at their own peril.[3] The psychological contract is based on a balanced give and take. Workers exchange their services for compensation. But often economic conditions cause management to give less and expect more from workers. Global outsourcing and the rising costs of healthcare are both contemporary examples that force

**psychological contract** A set of expectations, based on a balanced give-and-take, that workers have regarding what they will give to the organization and what they will receive from it; the exchange of workers' services for compensation.

managers to alter the long-standing agreements between management and workers. Such alterations can result in broken promises and unfulfilled commitments to workers. For example, commercial airline pilots were asked to make pay concessions for wages that they had bargained in good faith for years earlier. As a result of the prevailing competitive nature of the airline industry, pilots were faced with job loss if they refused to make pay concessions. The psychological contract, as well as the union contract, was changed to the economic disadvantage of the pilots. Harmony between management and workers (in this case, the pilots) was lost.

A fair psychological contract is one that maintains a balance that both parties can live with over time. From the individual's perspective, a fair contract means contributions consisting of effort, creativity, loyalty, and knowledge. From the organization's perspective, a fair contract means offering inducements such as wages, bonuses, benefits, challenging work, status, and security. Clearly, workers must value the inducements that sustain their level of contributions. When an imbalance occurs, workers can decrease their contributions, complain, or ultimately leave the organization. The psychological contract is an important part of the relationship between a worker and the organization.

## Individual Task Performance

At work, behavior can mean both social behaviors, such as interacting with coworkers and customers, as well as task performance, such as performing the job. People have different personalities that influence their social interaction at work as well as different abilities affecting task performance. Performance requires ability, skill, effort, and resources:

Task Performance = (Ability + Skill + Effort + Resources) + Psychological Differences

*Ability* is the capacity to perform the task, and *skill* is the proficiency in task performance. People bring varying levels of ability and skill to the workplace. Depending on ability and the task to be performed, workers must exert *effort* to complete the task. Psychological differences include personality, perception, and attitudes. For individual performance to yield results, the organization provides *resources* in the form of equipment, supplies, management support as well as worker training. Do individual psychological differences also affect task performance? Considerable research evidence supports the notion that a variety of psychological forces within each of us influences our task performance.

## Individual Differences

We have all heard that "variety is the spice of life." Variety, difference, and uniqueness present infinite opportunity. In most cases this is a good assumption, but not necessarily at the workplace. Work is often a balance between creativity and control. A manager wants predictable employee behavior that yields consistent quality work performance. Similarity makes classification possible and efficient. Successful engineers seem to have unique characteristics that are different from successful sales professionals and accountants. Career management specialists have long helped people find a career that matches their unique interests. Kurt Lewin long ago noted that behavior is a function of the person and the environment. For better or worse, behavior is a product of the interaction between the person and the situational requirements of the job.[4] For example, when a match between the person and the job requirements occurs, the result is a more satisfied and productive employee capable of superior performance. In other words, there is a fit or match between the personal characteristics and the job (environment).[5] Exhibit 11.1 describes the relationship between the person, environment, and behavior. To create the fit and manage it over time, effective managers must understand the nature of individual differences among people.[6] Managers must also recognize that many differences among people are psychological and intangible in nature rather than physiological or tangible. These affect job performance as

11.1    **Person–Environment Fit and Work Behavior**

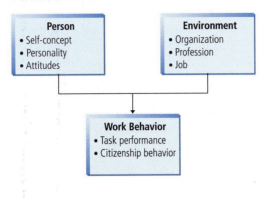

well, for example, personalities, attitudes, and perceptions. A discussion of the basis of these individual differences and why they are important to managers can begin with an examination of the notion of self.

## Self-Concept

Peter Senge tells the story of two members of the Natal tribe in a remote region of South Africa greeting one another.[7] The first man says "Sawu bona" or "I see you," and to that greeting the other man replies "Sikhona," or "I am here." Senge notes that the order of the exchange is critical. The tribe believes that you do not exist unless you are recognized by another. In essence, "a person is a person, because of other people."[8] Identity and self-concept is created and legitimized socially by acknowledgement. It is a similar situation in the workplace. A manager's identity ("authority" in Barnard's definition as described in Chapter 2) is given by the acquiescence of subordinates. What this idea suggests is that self-concept is to some extent in the hands of "others." Manager and workers give each other legitimacy that helps create identity.

The self is our source of uniqueness; it represents our values, beliefs, perceived competencies, aspirations, conscious thought, opinion, and the awareness from within that improvement is possible.[9] It registers in the mind as potential for action. One's conceptions of skills and abilities are part of this mechanism. Self-concept is our self-image, that is, the awareness of conscious thoughts that shape our personality, perceptions, attitudes, behavior, skills development, abilities, and relationships with the external world.[10] It has been said that we are what we think about. If that assumption is correct, a healthy self-concept should produce positive attitudes, actions, and behaviors that will result in successful job performance.[11] Conversely, a poor self-concept might produce negative attitudes and behaviors that will likely result in less successful job performance. If our opinion of ourselves is poor, our internal self-regulation mechanism (self-concept) limits our ability to succeed. We attempt to engage in behaviors that are consistent with our self-image.

**Self-Esteem** | An important part of self-concept is self-esteem. Researchers have found a positive relationship between self-esteem and job performance.[12] Self-esteem is a predisposition to evaluate ourselves in positive or negative terms. People with a high level of self-esteem believe that they are capable and able to perform in a variety of situations. People with high self-esteem are more likely to be self-starters, take risks, and engage in self-actualizing behavior. Failure is shrugged off by a person with high self-esteem. People with

**KEY**TERMS

**self-concept** A person's self-image, that is, the awareness of conscious thoughts that shape personality, perceptions, attitudes, behaviors, skills development, abilities, and relationships with the external world.

**self-esteem** A relatively stable predisposition to evaluate ourselves in positive or negative terms.

low self-esteem see themselves as incapable and are not likely to succeed even if they try. At work, individuals with low self-esteem avoid competition, responsibility, and challenging tasks. Failure for a person with low self-esteem reinforces their feelings of inadequacy. Research confirms that people with low self-esteem perform at a lower level than people with high self-esteem.[13] And recent research suggests that self-esteem may be relatively stable over time.[14] The role of the manager is to recognize when low self-esteem is hindering task performance and take corrective action. Through counseling and self-management, it might be possible to help people with low self-esteem increase their performance or at least minimize its impact in the workplace.

| **Self-Efficacy** | Self-efficacy is the belief in one's ability to succeed in a specific situation. It is the "can do" component within us all. Unlike self-esteem, self-efficacy needs a context or a situation, that is, situational effectiveness is evaluated at a particular time. For example, as you approach the office door of the vice president, your level of self-efficacy kicks in. High self-efficacy relaxes you and lets you plan a strategy for success. Low self-efficacy fills your head with doubts and insecurities; your situational behavior can communicate uncertainty to those around you. Self-efficacy is based on previous success, modeling by others, verbal persuasion, and psychological arousal.[15] Similar to self-esteem, self-efficacy is related to successful task performance, but unlike self-esteem, building self-efficacy requires role models and practice in a specific context or training.[16]

The relationship between self-efficacy and performance is well documented in the literature.[17] It is therefore incumbent on management to facilitate the development of self-esteem and self-efficacy in their employees in variety of ways. Two ways managers can increase low self-efficacy are through the use of role models and through training. Pairing a low self-efficacy employee with a high self-efficacy mentor can encourage the employee by enabling observation of a role model and providing a safe environment to successfully increase behavioral responses. If mentoring does not produce results, formal training to increase self-efficacy is another option. Finally, managers can offer encouragement by doing something as simple as interpreting a lack of success as an opportunity to gain more experience.

| **Self-Monitoring** | Self-monitoring is the awareness of and ability to read cues from other people in the environment and alter behavior accordingly.[18] High self-monitors are receptive to environmental cues and adjust their behavior. Low self-monitors are unaware of environmental cues and regulate behavior through internal mechanisms. Research has demonstrated that high self-monitoring managers adjust to change more readily and pick up on employee needs sooner than low self-monitors.[19] Determine whether you are a high self-monitor or a low self-monitor by completing the self-monitoring test described in the Management Highlight on page 230.

# | Personality

Kluckhohn and Murray summarized personality quite well when they noted that to some extent a person's personality is like all other people's, like some other people's, and like no other people's.[20] Individual personality varies tremendously but as mentioned earlier, we also know that many people share similar personality traits. Most personality scholars agree that the sources of personality are the interaction of heredity, environment, maturation, and learning. Heredity indicates that our personality is to a certain extent the product of genetics, that is, we are born with a predisposition to a certain level of a common set of personality traits. Environment creates the opportunity to test genetic contributions against environmental requirements, and as a result, some of the effects of heredity are minimized and other traits required for success in the environment are emphasized.

**KEY**TERMS

**self-efficacy** A person's belief in his or her ability to succeed in a specific situation; the "can-do" feeling applied to a specific context or a situation.

## SELF MONITORING
### Are You a High or Low Self-Monitor?

For the following items, circle T (true) if the statement is characteristic of your behavior. Circle F (false) if the statement does not reflect your behavior.

1. I find it hard to imitate the behavior of other people.    T    F
2. At parties or social gatherings, I do not attempt to do or say things that others will like.    T    F
3. I can only argue for ideas that I already believe.    T    F
4. I can make impromptu speeches even on topics which I have almost no information.    T    F
5. I guess I put on a show to impress or entertain others.    T    F
6. I would probably make a good actor.    T    F
7. In a group of people, I am rarely the center of attention.    T    F
8. In different situations and with different people, I often act like a very different person.    T    F
9. I am not particularly good at making other people like me.    T    F
10. I am not always the person I appear to be.    T    F
11. I would not change my opinions (or the way I do things) in order to please others or win their favor.    T    F
12. I have considered being an entertainer.    T    F
13. I have never been good at games like charades or at improvisational acting.    T    F
14. I have trouble changing my behavior to suit different people and different situations.    T    F
15. At a party, I let others keep the jokes and stories going.    T    F
16. I feel a bit awkward in company and do not show up quite as well as I should.    T    F
17. I can look anyone in the eye and tell a lie with a straight face (if it is for a good cause).    T    F
18. I may deceive people by being friendly when I really dislike them.    T    F

### Scoring

To score this questionnaire, give yourself 1 point for each of the following items that you answered T (true): 4, 5, 6, 8, 10, 12, 17, and 18. Now give yourself 1 point for each of the following items that you answered F (false): 1, 2, 3, 7, 9, 11, 13, 14, 15, and 16. Add both subtotals to find your overall score. If you scored 11 or above, you are probably a *high self-monitor*. If you scored 10 or below, you are probably a *low self-monitor*.

Source: From *Public Appearances, Private Realities: The Psychology of Self-Monitoring* by M. Snyder. Copyright © 1987 by W. H. Freeman and Company. Used with permission.

The process of maturity might also minimize the influence of one trait and increase the influence of a different trait. Finally, by learning which traits work, individuals can enhance traits that are valued or believed to be more appropriate in a particular context. Personality, then, is a stable pattern of characteristics or traits that influence behavior and describes our uniqueness.

Personality affects behavior in both positive and negative ways, and perhaps it is personality's influence on behavior that captivates our attention the most. The idea that our behavior is subject to an internal predisposition that colors behavior and perception is intriguing. Personality research includes the study of abnormal personality[21] as well as the application of personality to normal growth and development.[22] Other scholars moved in the direction of cataloging the various types of characteristics that differ among people.[23] Most scholars today support the concept of an interactive approach to personality. The interactive approach views behavior as a product of dispositional and situational factors. At work, many personality characteristics influence job performance.[24] The quest for personality traits that predict individual behavior at work recognizes that traits interact with a specific situation such as a new job (promotion), taking a different job with a more conservative organization, professional requirements (such as those for a lawyer), or just a new situation.

Today the most commonly agreed personality traits that appear to influence work behavior are referred to as the "Big Five":

| Extraversion

| Agreeableness

| Conscientiousness

EXHIBIT 11.2

**Characteristics of Big Five Personality Traits**

| Low Level | Big Five Trait | High Level |
|---|---|---|
| Irresponsible, disorganized, low self-discipline | **Conscientiousness** (low to high) | Careful, thorough, responsible, self-disciplined |
| Retiring, sober, reserved, and cautious | **Extraversion** (introvert to extrovert) | Sociable, talkative, assertive, and active |
| Irritable, ruthless, suspicious, uncooperative, and inflexible | **Agreeableness** (low to high) | Good natured, gentle, cooperative, forgiving, hopeful |
| Anxious, depressed, angry, emotional, insecure, excitable | **Emotional stability** (low to high) | Calm, enthusiastic, poised, secure |
| Down-to-earth, insensitive, narrow, crude, simple | **Openness to experience** (low to high) | Imaginative, sensitive, intellectual, polished |

**Source:** Jerald Greenberg, *Managing Organizational Behavior,* Second Edition. (Upper Saddle River: Prentice Hall 1999), 41.

EXHIBIT 11.3

**Variation in the Big Five by Job Class**

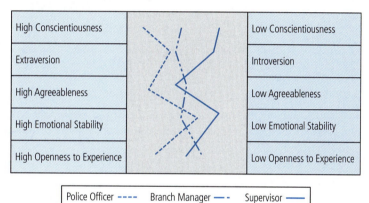

| High Conscientiousness | | Low Conscientiousness |
|---|---|---|
| Extraversion | | Introversion |
| High Agreeableness | | Low Agreeableness |
| High Emotional Stability | | Low Emotional Stability |
| High Openness to Experience | | Low Openness to Experience |

Police Officer ----    Branch Manager —-—    Supervisor ——

- Emotional stability

- Openness to new experiences

These Big Five personality traits have demonstrated a relationship to various aspects of the work environment including task characteristics, job satisfaction, commitment and task performance.[25] Exhibit 11.2 shows the ranges and characteristics associated with each of the Big Five traits.

Exhibit 11.3 shows the average scores for each of the Big Five personality traits for three occupations. The purpose of Exhibit 11.2 and Exhibit 11.3 is to illustrate how each personality dimension varies both in measurement and across occupations.

## Personality Types

Personality type classifications categorize people into personality groups that enable likely behavior to be predicted. Personality classification is common in corporate training and development. The purpose is to help people understand themselves better and to realize how their personality can influence behavior.

**Locus of Control** | Locus of control represents the extent to which individuals believe that they have control over their lives. Locus of control is divided into two types: internals and

MANAGEMENT HIGHLIGHT

## LOCUS OF CONTROL
### What's Your Locus of Control?

Below is a short scale that can give you an idea of your locus of control. For each of the four items, circle either choice a or choice b.

1. a. Becoming a success is a matter of hard work; luck has little or nothing to do with it.
   b. Getting a good job depends mainly on being in the right place at the right time.
2. a. The average citizen can have an influence in government decisions.
   b. This world is run by the few people in power, and there is not much the little guy can do about it.
3. a. As far as world affairs are concerned, most of us are the victims of forces we can neither understand nor control.
   b. By taking an active part in political and social affairs, people can control world events.
4. a. With enough effort we can wipe out political corruption.
   b. It is difficult for people to have much control over the things politicians do in office.

### Scoring Key:

The internal locus of control answers are:
1a, 2a, 3b, 4a
The external locus of control answers are:
1b, 2b, 3a, 4b

Determine which category you circled most frequently using the key to the left. This gives you an approximation of your locus of control.

Source: Debra L. Nelson and James Campbell Quick, *Organizational Behavior: Foundations, Realities, and Challenges*, (Mason, OH: South-Western/Thomson Learning), 2006.

externals.[26] People who believe that they have control over their own destiny are classified as *internals.* Internality is similar to the concept of "free will." Free will means choice, strategy, and specific outcomes. Internals make proactive choices to get the outcomes they desire. For example, internals believe that their hard work will lead to a specific reward; a student with an internal locus of control believes that spending time studying for a test will lead to high performance on the test.

Locus of control is related to many work outcomes.[27] For example, internals participate in decision making, set goals to a greater degree, and report greater job satisfaction with work than do externals. Internals take a more active role at work than do externals, and they are more likely to succeed in managerial positions, where such a predisposition is beneficial. *Externals* believe that they have little control over their lives. Externality is akin to determinism. Determinism implies that events have causes beyond the individual's control that lead to specific outcomes. Externals take a fatalistic view of life and react to it. Research indicates that internals are more independent and willing to take initiate than externals. Externals require more direction and supervision than internals. Use the Management Highlight above to determine your locus of control score.

| **Type A and Type B Personalities** | Different personalities demonstrate different generalized behaviors. Type A personalities are high-strung, active, aggressive, impatient people. Type A personalities are some times referred to as workaholics because of their tendency to accomplish as much as possible and set difficult goals for themselves. They have a strong need to dominate others and are often hostile to people who do not share their beliefs. Often these individuals experience higher levels of stress. Not surprisingly, some Type A personalities have a higher rate of coronary heart disease than their counterparts—particularly individuals that are cynical, hostile, or distrustful of others.[28] Conversely, Type B personalities have none of these tendencies. The Type B personality is more relaxed with less aggressive demeanor; time is in perspective, and they take a more long-term view of situations. The Type B personality is less likely to experience high levels of stress and coronary heart disease than the Type A personality.[29] Both types of individuals are found in the workplace, and it is important to remember the relationship of the Type A personality to stress and the potential for health consequences. Type A personalities are more likely to use tobacco and alcohol, and experience sudden death than Type B personalities.

| **Myers-Briggs Type Indicator** | Perhaps the most often discussed method of creating personality types is the Myers-Briggs Type Indicator (MBTI). It has its origin in the work of Carl Jung, who believed that although people were inherently different, they had many similarities that afforded the opportunity for classification.[30] He believed that people had different preferences for gathering (perception) and processing (judgment) information, most notably sensation-intuition and thinking-feeling. People tend to gather information by using either their senses or through intuition. Sensation is the ability to use perceptual judgment in exploring the environment. Sensation types gather information by collecting data in a systematic manner. Intuition is the connection to unconscious thought that guides safety and shapes subjective assessment processes. Intuitive types prefer to deal with more abstract ideas and show greater concern for people than facts. They gather facts and information in a holistic manner that they perceive is more likely to fit the needs of the environment.

In Jung's model, judgment is achieved through thinking-feeling. Thinking is the ability to use the mind to comprehend the surrounding complexity and to choose among alternative actions. Thinking types are more inclined to use logic and reasoning to evaluate information. Feeling refers to the emotional state that processes love, hate, pleasure, and pain. Feeling types are more likely to evaluate information using their emotions and are sensitive to the feelings of others.

According to Jung, these ways of thinking represent individual preferences to act more one way than another on the two dimensions of sensation-intuition and thinking-feeling. Jung believed that perception and judgment preferences can be combined to determine cognitive style. No single cognitive style was considered better than another. From these two dimensions Jung created four cognitive styles: Sensation-Thinking (ST), Intuition-Thinking (NT), Sensation-Feeling (SF), and Intuition-Feeling (NF). Exhibit 11.4 describes how each cognitive style operates and the fit between preferred cognitive style and the requirements of different occupations. As you might imagine, Jung's cognitive styles are helpful in matching people with careers.

Jung mentions two additional dimensions of personality: introversion-extraversion, and judging-perceiving. Jung believed that the introvert/extrovert dimension represents our preference for one source of personal energy over the other. For introverts, the source of energy is from within. For extraverts, the source of energy is the group or the social environment. Judging types are people who prefer to make decisions, evaluate, form opinions, and reach a conclusion. Perceiving types prefer to infer information from indirect sources, enjoy gathering information, and dislike the need for a quick decision.

**EXHIBIT 11.4**

### Jung's Problem-Solving Styles

| | Sensation/ Thinking (ST) | Intuition/ Thinking (NT) | Sensation/ Feeling (SF) | Intuition/ Feelings (NF) |
|---|---|---|---|---|
| **Focus of Attention** | Facts | Possibilities | Facts | Possibilities |
| **Method of Handing Things** | Impersonal analysis | Impersonal analysis | Personal warmth | Personal warmth |
| **Tendency to Become** | Practical and matter of fact | Logical and ingenious | Sympathetic and friendly | Enthusiastic and insightful |
| **Expression of Abilities** | Technical skills with facts and objects | Theoretical and technical developments | Practical help and services for people | Understanding and communicating with people |
| **Occupation** | Technician | Planner | Teacher | Artist |

**Source:** W. Taggart, and D. Robey, "Minds and Managers: On the Dual Nature of Human Information Processing and Management," *Academy of Management Review*, 6 (1981): 187-196.

The MBTI is an instrument used to measure personality and classify people into personality types. These types can then be associated with certain types of behavior and occupations. The result is a four-dimension model that results in sixteen personality types. The four dimensions are (1) extraversion-introversion (EI), sensing-intuiting (SN), thinking-feeling (TF), and judgment-perception (JP). These four categories describe different types of personalities and their expected behavioral responses. The MBTI 16-cell topology is described in the Management Highlight beginning on page 235.

The MBTI has demonstrated predictive validity, making it a practical tool for training and development of business professionals.[31] Many organizations regularly use the MBTI to help members develop a better sense of themselves and those around them. Promotion to the managerial ranks is a good example of a situation that requires a candidate have a solid understanding of the differences in employees and of how best to manage those differences. MTBI uses Jung's cognitive styles to offer a more precise match of the individual with the daily requirements of different jobs.

## Perception

Perception is the cognitive process of attention and selection, interpretation, retention, retrieval, and response to information sensed in the environment. Perception is a mental sense-making process that involves the five senses: sight, hearing, taste, touch, and smell.

An example scenario illustrates well how perception can influence interpretation. Two coworkers, Mary (a new employee) and Andy, observed their manager Hank Waters in his office talking to three people—the Vice President of Human Resources; the Chief Security Officer; and John Peters, another employee from their department. The door to the office was closed (the manager's door is rarely closed). To Mary and Andy, it looked like John Peters was in trouble. It was clear that the men were having a heated discussion about something. Mary and Andy remembered that at their department meeting earlier in the week, Hank announced that the company will fire anyone taking computer equipment home for personal use.

Mary believes that John Peters must have violated the new computer use policy and is in the process of being fired and will soon be escorted from the building by security. Mary and Andy are reminded that recently three other employees were terminated for violations of the computer use policy. However, Andy thinks no such thing! He has heard nothing negative about John's work habits or personal behavior. Thus, Andy has serious doubts that John would ever violate the computer use policy. In fact, he knew that John was a deacon in his church and the leader of the local Boy Scout troop. When the office door swung open, all four men briskly left the office without an announcement regarding the purpose of the meeting. Later that day, Andy asked Hank Waters what had occurred in his office. Hank shrugged nonchalantly and said they were merely discussing the recent NFL draft because all are avid football fans. What can you conclude about Mary and John's perceptual processes? The facts of this situation led both employees to believe that the situation appeared suspect, but Mary completely misjudged the situation and Andy had trouble making sense of it. As this example illustrates, accurate perception is important to judgment. Andy needed closure to ensure the accuracy of his perceptual process. He had to ask Hank for an explanation. Both Andy and Mary learned an important lesson that day about social perception.

An accurate perception of reality is critical for managerial success. In this example, it was obvious that Andy accurately perceived the situation. Andy's judgment process was more reflective of reality than Mary's perception. These perceptual differences among people can occur for a variety of reasons. Beliefs, values, attitudes, and expectations all filter what we see. To a large degree, we see what we expect to see. People often observe the same incident yet report remarkably dissimilar accounts of what happened. Listening to CNN, Palestinian and Israeli

## MYERS-BRIGGS TYPE INDICATOR EXERCISE

### Personality Assessment: Jung's Typology and the Myers-Briggs Type Indicator

For each item below, circle either "a" or "b." In some cases, both "a" and "b" may apply to you. You should decide which is more like you, even if it is only slightly more true.

1. I would rather
   a. Solve a new and complicated problem
   b. Work on something that I have done before

2. I like to
   a. Work alone in a quiet place
   b. Be where "the action" is

3. I want a boss who
   a. Establishes and applies criteria in decisions
   b. Considers individual needs and makes exceptions

4. When I work on a project, I
   a. Like to finish it and get some closure
   b. Often leave it open for possible change

5. When making a decision, the most important considerations are
   a. Rational thoughts, ideas, and data
   b. People's feelings and values

6. On a project, I tend to
   a. Think it over and over before deciding how to proceed
   b. Start working on it right away, thinking about it as I go along

7. When working on a project, I prefer to
   a. Maintain as much control as possible
   b. Explore various options

8. In my work, I prefer to
   a. Work on several projects at a time, and learn as much as possible about each one
   b. Have one project that is challenging and keeps me busy

9. I often
   a. Make lists and plans whenever I start something and may hate to seriously alter my plans
   b. Avoid plans and just let things progress as I work on them

10. When discussing a problem with colleagues, it is easy for me
    a. To see "the big picture"
    b. To grasp the specifics of the situation

11. When the phone rings in my office or at home, I usually
    a. Consider it an interruption
    b. Don't mind answering it

12. The word that describes me better is
    a. Analytical
    b. Empathetic

13. When I am working on an assignment, I tend to
    a. Work steadily and consistently
    b. Work in bursts of energy with "down time" in between

14. When I listen to someone talk on a subject, I usually try to
    a. Relate it to my own experience and see if it fits
    b. Assess and analyze the message

15. When I come up with new ideas, I generally
    a. "Go for it"
    b. Like to contemplate the ideas some more

16. When working on a project, I prefer to
    a. Narrow the scope so it is clearly defined
    b. Broaden the scope to include related aspects

17. When I read something, I usually
    a. Confine my thoughts to what is written there
    b. Read between the lines and relate the words to other ideas

18. When I have to make a decision in a hurry, I often
    a. Feel uncomfortable and wish I had more information
    b. Am able to do so with available data

19. In a meeting, I tend to
    a. Continue formulating my ideas as I talk about them
    b. Speak out only after I have carefully thought the issue through

20. In work, I prefer spending a great deal of time on issues of
    a. Ideas
    b. People

21. In meetings, I am most often annoyed with people who
    a. Come up with many sketchy ideas
    b. Lengthen the meeting with many practical details

22. I tend to be
    a. A morning person
    b. A night owl

23. My style in preparing for a meeting is
    a. To be willing to go in and be responsive
    b. To be fully prepared and sketch out an outline of the meeting

24. In meetings, I would prefer for people to
    a. Display a fuller range of emotions
    b. Be more task-oriented

25. I would rather work for an organization where
    a. My job was intellectually stimulating
    b. I was committed to its goals and mission

*Continued*

*Continued*

26. On weekends, I tend to
    a. Plan what I will do
    b. Just see what happens and decide as I go along

27. I am more
    a. Outgoing
    b. Contemplative

28. I would rather work for a boss who is
    a. Full of new ideas
    b. Practical

*In the following, choose the word in each pair that appeals to you more:*

29. a. Social    b. Theoretical

30. a. Ingenuity    b. Practicality

31. a. Organized    b. Adaptable

32. a. Active    b. Concentration

## Scoring

Count one point for each item listed below that you circled in the inventory.

| Score For I (Introversion) | Score For E (Extroversion) | Score For S (Sensing) | Score For N (Intuition) |
|---|---|---|---|
| 2a | 2b | 1b | 1a |
| 6a | 6b | 10b | 10a |
| 11a | 11b | 13a | 13b |
| 15b | 15a | 16a | 16b |
| 19b | 19a | 17a | 17b |
| 22a | 22b | 21a | 21b |
| 27b | 27a | 28b | 28a |
| 32b | 32a | 30b | 30a |

**Totals** _____  _____          _____  _____

| Circle the one with more points: I or E *(If tied on I/E, don't count #11)* | | Circle the one with more points: S or N *(If tied on S/N, don't count #16)* | |
|---|---|---|---|

| Score for T (Thinking) | Score for F (Feeling) | Score for J (Judging) | Score for P (Perceiving) |
|---|---|---|---|
| 3a | 3b | 4a | 4b |
| 5a | 5b | 7a | 7b |
| 12a | 12b | 8b | 8a |
| 14b | 14a | 9a | 9b |
| 20a | 20b | 18b | 18a |
| 24b | 24a | 23b | 23a |
| 25a | 25b | 26a | 26b |
| 29b | 29a | 31a | 31b |

**Totals** _____  _____          _____  _____

| Circle the one with more points: T or F *(If tied on T/F, don't count #24)* | | Circle the one with more points: J or P *(If tied on J/P, don't count #23)* | |
|---|---|---|---|

Your Score Is: I or E _____    S or N _____    T or F _____    J or P _____

Your MBTI Type Is: _____ (example: INTJ; ESFP; etc.)

## Interpretation

The Myers-Briggs Type Indicator (MBTI), based on the work of psychologist Carl Jung, is the most widely used personality assessment instrument in the world. The MBTI, which was described in the chapter text, identifies sixteen different "types," shown with their dominant characteristics in the chart on the following page. Remember that no one is a pure type; however, each individual has preferences for introversion versus extroversion, sensing versus intuition, thinking versus feeling, and judging versus perceiving. Based on your scores on the survey, read the description of your type in the chart. Do you believe the description fits your personality?

### Characteristics Frequently Associated with Each Myers-Briggs Type

| Sensing Types | | Intuitive Types | |
|---|---|---|---|
| **ISTJ** | **ISFJ** | **INFJ** | **INTJ** |
| Quiet, serious, earn success by thoroughness and dependability. Practical matter-of-fact, realistic, and responsible. Decide | Quiet, friendly, responsible and conscientious. Committed and steady in meeting their obligations. Thorough, painstaking, and accurate. | Seek meaning and connection in ideas, relationships, and material possessions. Want to understand what motivates people and are | Have original minds and great drive for implementing their ideas and achieving their goals. Quickly see patterns in external events and |

MANAGEMENT HIGHLIGHT

**Introverts**

*Continued*

| | | | |
|---|---|---|---|
| logically what should be done and work toward it steadily, regardless of distractions. Take pleasure in making everything orderly and organized—their work, their home, their life. Value traditions and loyality. | Loyal, considerate, notice and remember specifics about people who are important to them, concerned with how others feel. Strive to create an orderly and harmonious environment at work and at home. | insightful about others. Conscientious and committed to their firm values. Develop a clear vision about how best to serve the common good. Organized and decisive in implementing their vision. | develop long-range explanatory perspectives. When committed, organize a job and carry it through. Skeptical and independent, have high standards of competence and performance— for themselves and others. |

**Introverts**

| **ISTP** | **ISFP** | **INFP** | **INTP** |
|---|---|---|---|
| Tolerant and flexible, quiet observers until a problem appears, then act quickly to find workable solutions. Analyze what makes things work and readily get through large amounts of data to isolate the core of practical problems. Interested in cause and effect organize facts using logical principles, value efficiency. | Quiet, friendly, sensitive, and kind. Enjoy the present moment, what's going on around them. Like to have their own space and to work within their own time frame. Loyal and committed to their values and to people who are important to them. Dslike disagreements and conflicts, do not force their opinions or values on others. | Idealistic, loyal to their values and to people who are important to them. Want an external life that is congruent with their values. Curious, quick to see possibilities, can be catalysts for implementing ideas. Seek to understand people and to help them fulfill their potential. Adaptable, flexible, and accepting unless a value is threatened. | Seek to develop logical explanations for everything that interests them. Theoretical and abstract, interested more in ideas than in social interaction. Quiet, contained, flexible, and adaptable. Have unusual ability to focus in depth to solve problems in their area of interest. Skeptical, sometimes critical, always analytical. |

**Extraverts**

| **ESTP** | **ESFP** | **ENFP** | **ENTP** |
|---|---|---|---|
| Flexible and tolerant, they take a pragmatic approach focused on immediate results. Theories and conceptual explanations bore them—they want to act energetically to solve the problem. Focus on the here-and-now, spontaneous, enjoy each moment that they can be active with others. Enjoy material comforts and style. Learn best through doing. | Outgoing, friendly, and accepting. Exuberant lovers of life, people, and material comforts. Enjoy working with others to make things happen. Bring common sense and a realistic approach to their work, and make work fun. Flexible and spontaneous, adapt readily to new people and environments. Learn best by trying a new skill with other people. | Warmly enthusiastic and imaginative. See life as full of possibilities. Make connections between events and information very quickly, and confidently proceed based on the patterns they see. Want a lot of affirmation from others, and readily give appreciation and support. Spontaneous and flexible, often rely on their ability to improvise and their verbal fluency. | Quick, ingenious, stimulating, alert, and outspoken. Resourceful in solving new and challenging problems. Adept at generating conceptual possibilities and then analyzing them strategically. Good at reading other people. Bored by routine, will seldom do the same thing the same way, apt to turn to one new interest after another. |

**Extraverts**

| **ESTJ** | **ESFJ** | **ENFJ** | **ENTJ** |
|---|---|---|---|
| Practical, realistic, matter-of-fact. Decisive, quickly move to implement decisions. Organize projects and people to get things done, focus on getting results in the most efficient way possible. Take care of routine details. Have a clear set of logical standards, systematically follow them and want others to also. Forceful in implementing their plans. | Warmhearted, conscientious, and cooperative. Want harmony in their environment, work with determination to establish it. Like to work with others to complete tasks accurately and on time. Loyal, follow through even in small matters. Notice what others need in their day-by-day lives and try to provide it. Want to be appreciated for who they are and for what they contribute. | Warm, empathetic, responsive, and responsible. Highly attuned to the emotions, need, and motivations of others. Find potential in everyone, want to help others fulfill their potential. May act as catalysts for individual and group growth. Loyal, responsive to praise and criticism. Sociable, facilitate others in a group, and provide inspiring leadership. | Frank, decisive, assume leadership readily. Quickly see illogical and inefficient procedures and policies, develop and implement comprehensive systems to solve organizational problems. Enjoy long-term planning and goal setting. Usually well informed, well read, enjoy expanding their knowledge and passing it on to others. Forceful in presenting their ideas. |

spokesman report dramatically different accounts of the hostilities in the Middle East. Each perceives the situation from an entirely different frame of reference (using different information). Exhibit 11.5 illustrates this concept. In Figure A is a beautiful young woman. In Figure B, do you see the old woman? Most people see the beautiful woman, but what you see depends on how you perceive and process the information presented to you by the image. Perception has four components, or steps: attention and selection; interpretation; retention; and retrieving and response. (See Exhibit 11.6)[32]

**EXHIBIT 11.5**

Figure A         Figure B

**EXHIBIT 11.6**     **Four-Step Perception Process**

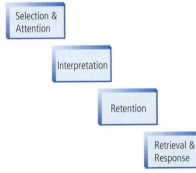

Selection & Attention

Interpretation

Retention

Retrieval & Response

**STEP 1**   **Attention and Selection**

When a person enters a new situation, that person is bombarded with information. Not all the information is necessary to make a decision or draw a conclusion. Selection is the process of seeking information that helps an individual understand a situation. Attention is the process of focusing on salient information and ignoring other information from the environment. Salient information stands out in the mind. Size, color, intensity, uniqueness, and extremes are all characteristics that make a person or an object appear salient.

**STEP 2**   **Interpretation**

Interpretation helps arrange perceptual stimuli into a specific network relationship. The process of cognitive categorization groups environmental stimuli in perceptual sets. Perceptual sets are groups of related stimuli (e.g., employee, offices, plan, deadline, and building). We then arrange several perceptual sets into a schema. A schema is a categorization or a summary of a stimulus. One schema for a meeting might be to begin on time, follow an agenda, take minutes, vote, schedule the next meeting, and adjourn on time.

**STEP 3**   **Retention**

Retention is the process of storing sensory information in long-tern memory for future retrieval. Categorized information is stored as event memory, semantic memory, and person memory. *Event memory* encodes information related to special situations or events. Birthdays, anniversaries, promotions, and conventions are all events. *Semantic memory* is our encyclopedia and dictionary. From birth, we fill it with knowledge and information we find useful or believe will be needed in the future. Procedures for running a computer or fixing a flat tire, the location on a map, and the spelling of Uzbekistan are all examples of elements stored in semantic memory. *Person memory* categorizes and stores information about all the people we know or have come in contact with. For example, the images of other people in your cash register training class for your first job might have been stored in people memory years ago. If you close your eyes, you might be able to see their face in your ''mind's eye,'' which is Step 4.

**STEP 4**   **Retrieval and Response**

The process of retrieving information is similar to running a computer program that accesses a database. Response is how that information is used; it is accessing the correct information and using it to make an informed judgment about a person, event, or object. If all goes right, the perception, memory, and decision making all work seamlessly.

## Perceptual Bias

Are perceptual processes accurate? If they are not, a situation is misperceived and or a person misjudged. Perceptual bias is the potential for error that is often inadvertently introduced into the perceptual process. The awareness that different types of errors exist makes is less likely they will be repeated in daily work situations. Several of the most common errors that bias accurate perception are selective perception, stereotyping, priming and recency, and halo effect.

**Selective Perception** | The perceptual process of filtering out information that is inconsistent with beliefs or in some other way unpleasant and not in an individual's best interest to consider is called selective perception. The title for this concept is attributed to Dearborn and Simon's classic article that describes a research study in which business executives from marketing, sales, human resources, and production were asked to determine the nature of the central problem in a short case. Marketing executives saw the problem as a marketing problem, sales executives saw the problem as a sales problem, production executives saw the problem as a production problem, and human resources executives saw the problem as a human resource problem. Clearly each executive filtered out information that didn't fit their perception of the situation. The results of the study support the concept of selective perception. Dearborn and Simon argued that the more complex the situation, the more likely it is that individuals will use existing knowledge (i.e., memory) to evaluate a situation and the less likely it is they will use information provided by the situation (i.e., new information).[33]

**KEY**TERMS

**perceptual sets** Groups of related stimuli (e.g., employee, offices, plan, deadline, and building).

**schema** A categorization or a summary of a set of stimuli.

**selective perception** The perceptual process of filtering out information that is inconsistent with beliefs or in some other way unpleasant and not in an individual's best interest to consider.

| **Stereotyping** | A perceptual shortcut for ascribing to an individual the characteristics of a group or class to which he or she belongs is called stereotyping. It is a generalization from a group to an individual. Although most instances of stereotyping are negative, stereotypes can also be positive or favorable. The common negative stereotype that men seldom use maps, seek directions, or admit they are lost can influence the recruitment process for a job that requires reading technical manuals, following directions, and asking for help as needed. It is no surprise, then, that human resource recruitment evaluators see the successful candidate for such a position as a woman. This stereotype is clearly not applicable to all males, but a widely held stereotype. Consider also the claim that Asians excel in science and mathematics.[34] This Asian stereotype is positive in nature, but still a generalization, and not true in all cases. The point is that stereotyping is a bias whether it is a positive stereotype or a negative stereotype. Why do people use stereotypes? During the attention stage, we process information. If a stereotype is resident in memory, we use it to organize the information. Stereotyping simplifies the collection and organization of information. If a stereotype is resident in memory, we stop collecting information and use the stereotype. Based on experience, the information might be modified over time. For example, the stereotype that Japanese automobile quality is superior to Korean automobile quality might be modified by higher J.D. Powers quality ratings for some Korean car models. Regardless of the situation, stereotyping results in an inaccurate perception of reality.

| **Priming and Recency** | Priming and recency are two common perceptual biases. Information primacy refers to the first information an individual encounters. Priming tends to give more weight to early information. First impressions are often used to form a judgment about a person. As part of the selection stage, priming and recency information are used at later stages of the perceptual process. Correctly or incorrectly, early information registers boldly in the mind. The first information received represents something new, unique, and special that is generalized in a unified impression of the person or object. It therefore is selectively perceived.

Another aspect of selection is recency. Representing the last information we have about a person or an object, recent information stands out as the most current and often the most important. A recent opportunity to work with a coworker that you have not worked with before is registered in the attention stage. The most recent information is then used in the remainder of the perceptual process. In many ways this makes sense. Recent information seems the most current, but it might not be the most accurate.

| **Halo Effect** | The halo effect is the tendency to select a salient positive or negative characteristic of an individual and focus on it in the attention stage. The characteristic is used to organize, interpret, and retain information about that person. In essence, the evaluator uses a single trait to filter subsequent information about the individual. A student that consistently earns high grades seems more capable and able to make better decisions than a student who earns average grades. Likewise, the student who consistently participates in class discussion and asks many questions in class is seen as more interested in school, work, and life in general—any of which might be inaccurate. It is important for managers to be aware of the halo effect during performance evaluation. Managers can inadvertently allow one characteristic to color the evaluation of a person.

## Attribution

Why does he act that way? Why did John fire Mary? Why didn't Pete say anything to the delivery driver? The answers to these questions are at the heart of attribution theory. We all seek causal explanations of events we observe, and it is no different at work. Attribution theory is a

**EXHIBIT** **11.7**    **Making Causal Attributions**

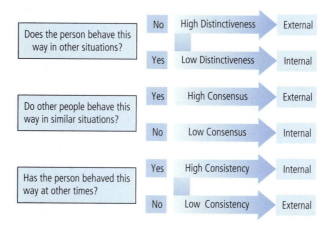

framework for determining the cause of individual behavior. The cause of behavior can be a result of either personal characteristics (internal cause) or situational characteristics (external cause).

People expect rational, logical, and predictable behavior from others. We analyze and evaluate the causes of observed behavior. Attribution is a process of sense-making, or seeking the root causes of behavior. We attribute the origin of individual behavior to either personal characteristics or environmental causes. For example, a colleague receives a promotion, and we acknowledge that she deserved the promotion because she was the most capable and talented person in the department. By this admission, we are making an *internal attribution* for the promotion. In our minds, we attribute the causes of the promotion to internal sources, to characteristics of the person. If, on the other hand, we attribute the promotion to luck, fortune, or being at the right place at the right time, we are making an *external attribution*, that is, the causes of promotion were not a result of personal characteristics but rather because of situational or environmental causes. As curious people, we want to make sense of the world around us. Researchers refer to internal causes of behavior as *dispositional* and external causes of behavior as *situational*. One popular theory of causal attribution was developed by Harold Kelly. Kelly's attribution theory uses three characteristics to evaluate the causes of a person's behavior: consensus, consistency, and distinctiveness.[35] All characteristics are relevant to understanding a specific situation. Exhibit 11.7 describes a set of questions that determines the cause of behavior as internal or external. Each characteristic is classified as low or high.

The characteristics are as follows:

- *Consensus*. The degree to which other people behave in a similar manner in this situation. High consensus means that other people behave in a similar manner. Low consensus means that others do not behave the same way in the same situation. We ask the question: Do other people behave this way in similar situations?

- *Consistency*. The degree to which the person acts the same at other times. If the person's behavior is the same at other times, consistency is high. If the person's behavior is not the same at other times, consistency is low. We ask the question: Has the person behaved this way at other times?

- *Distinctiveness*. The degree to which the person behaves in a similar manner in other situations. If the person behaves the same way in other situations, distinctiveness is low. If the person's behavior is different from situation to situation, distinctiveness is high. We ask this question: Does this person behave this way in other situations?

### 11.8  Attribution Decision Rules

|                   | Internal Attribution | External Attribution |
|-------------------|----------------------|----------------------|
| **Consensus**     | Low                  | High                 |
| **Consistency**   | High                 | Low                  |
| **Distinctiveness** | Low                | High                 |

Several examples illustrate the difference between internal and external characteristics. Consider John. He rarely studies for exams, instead relying on remembering what was said in the lecture. John, a C student, received a C grade on the second exam (high consistency). In fact, he was the only student to receive a C (low consensus). Also, John received a C on the first exam in this course (distinctiveness is low). We attribute John's performance to personal characteristics. His internal characteristics (disposition) led to his earned grade of "C."

Mary, the new marketing manager, began a PowerPoint presentation describing marketing efforts in the company's largest sales territory. She had considerable trouble accessing files, getting the video to work, and moving between one program and another. To what do we attribute her poor performance? At the end of the presentation, she apologized to the group and complained that this situation never happened to her before (high distinctiveness). Others present chimed in that the AV system in the room was unreliable and that they experienced similar results (high consensus). Further, she didn't have these problems when she made a similar presentation at corporate headquarters last week (low consistency). Mary does not complain in other situations. In this situation, we attribute her lack of success to external causes (situational). Exhibit 11.8 provides a quick reminder of the attribution theory decision rules.

Attribution theory helps determine the locus of causality of another person's behavior to either internal or external factors, but it is not without its limitations or biases. One common bias in attributing causality for another person's behavior is referred to as the fundamental attribution error. The fundamental attribution error is when an individual underestimates situational causes and overestimates personal characteristics.[36] When seeking causal attribution, an individual is likely to attribute the cause of another person's behavior to personal characteristics rather than to situational causes when the situation was the real cause of the behavior. Consider this workplace example. Ann received a low performance evaluation for her job as a customer relations specialist. We erroneously assume that Ann must be lazy or not very bright because we perceive her job as pretty easy. Often a dispositional explanation (the person) is used rather than a situational explanation (the environment) as the culprit for behavior, and we fail to assess the influence of environment. In Ann's case, high customer load or a busy service area might more likely explain her poor performance. The point is that our judgment can be clouded by an incorrect conclusion regarding the causes of behavior. We are also likely to overestimate the degree to which others share our conclusion about the causes of Ann's behavior. This is referred to as false consensus and tends to solidify judgment, often incorrectly.[37] Recent events, mood state, and whether we have a good impression of the person are all likely to bias our assessment of causal attribution.[38]

Regarding self-attribution, we attribute our successes to internal factors such as our own effort or ability. For example, we received a high grade because we studied for hours and are smart. Conversely, we often attribute the cause of our failures to situational or environmental causes. The cause of a low test grade, for example, is a result of a poor teacher or an unfair test. Attributing successes to personal characteristics and failures to situational characteristics is called the self-serving bias.

## Attitudes

An attitude is a learned predisposition about an object or a person that results in a propensity to respond in a positive or negative manner.[39] People form attitudes about many aspects of life. To a

---

**KEY TERMS**

**fundamental attribution error** In attributing causality for another person's behavior, the common tendency to underestimate situational causes and to overestimate personal characteristics.

**false consensus** The tendency to overestimate the degree to which others share our conclusion, thereby solidifying judgment, often incorrectly.

**self-serving bias** The tendency to attribute our successes to internal factors, such as our own effort or ability; for example, attributing a high grade to hard work.

**attitude** A learned predisposition about an object or a person that results in a propensity to respond one way or another; a shortcut to action; for example, the belief that it's best to be conservative or that eating pasta makes a person sleepy.

certain degree, attitudes serve as shortcuts to action. It might be that a person believes that it's best to be conservative, Fords break down more than Chevys, and eating pasta makes a person sleepy. Armed with these attitudes, no further information is needed to make a decision. In essence, attitudes shape our behavior and simplify our decision process. Further, attitudes are characterized by continuity and consistency over time. For example, people rarely change their political attitudes from one election to another. Stable political attitudes help predict voting behavior. People who publicly state that "global outsourcing is good for America" are likely to vote for the political party that shares similar attitudes. The same can be said for attitudes regarding product preference. Clearly, Coca Cola drinkers prefer Coke, and Pepsi drinkers prefer Pepsi. Although part of the cola brand preference is taste, a psychological component might be responsible as well for a preference for one product over another, and like voting, that preference is stable over time. Attitudes consist of three components: a cognitive component, an affective component, and a behavioral component:

- The *cognitive* component deals with the processing of facts, opinions, prior information, and experience, and is used to develop the concept or the idea.

- The *affective* component is an emotional attachment to the attitude or one's feelings about the attitude. Some people have a very strong attitude, and others not so strong.

- The *behavioral* component is the willingness to act in a manner that is consistent with the held attitude. If an individual's attitude toward Ford vehicles is very positive and strong, the expectation would be that the individual currently owns a Ford product and that will likely purchase another one in the future.

| **Attitude Formation** | Each component plays an important role in forming the attitude. Suppose you want to purchase a new car. The cognitive component helps you evaluate technical differences between a Ford and Chevy. The affective component provides valuable information about how you feel about the design, another person's reaction to it, and your intangible predisposition toward a particular vehicle. Finally, the behavioral component brings closure to the process. If the opportunity to purchase arises, you have formulated a predisposition and are ready to act (purchase).

## Attitudes about Work

Two important work attitudes such as those regarding job satisfaction and organizational commitment are related to task performance. Managers have the ability to influence employee behavior by understanding attitudes toward work and how these attitudes affect task performance.

| **Job Satisfaction** | Job satisfaction is the feeling of enjoyment and fulfillment a person receives from performing a particular job. Job satisfaction is measured directly by asking individual workers questions about their jobs. Job satisfaction questions can be global (e.g., "How satisfied are you with your job?") or focus on a particular facet of job satisfaction (e.g., "How satisfied are you with your supervisor?"). A high score indicates work enjoyment and a low score indicates a lack of fulfillment or lack of enjoyment from work.

Researchers have traditionally described the source of job satisfaction as related to the characteristics of the task that are more related to external sources or situational characteristics.[40] Job satisfaction has shown a positive relationship to organizational commitment and a negative relationship to absenteeism and turnover.[41] Job dissatisfaction, on the other hand, can lead to stress and other long-term health consequences if left unchecked.[42] Health professionals warn of the increased risk of heart attack and coronary disease with prolonged exposure to stressful job conditions.

**KEY** TERMS

**job satisfaction** The feeling of enjoyment and fulfillment that a person receives from performing a job.

Job satisfaction is an important predictor of many individual and organizational outcomes. Suggestions for increasing job satisfaction include:

- Pay people fairly.
- Improve the quality of supervision.
- Decentralize decision making.
- Enhance the fit between worker interest the job.[43]

| **Organizational Commitment** | Whereas job satisfaction describes the psychological relationship between the worker and work, organizational commitment describes the psychological relationship between the worker and the organization. For example, an individual might really like her job as an accountant, but she thoroughly dislikes the organization she works for and would prefer to work for another organization. Organizational commitment is the degree to which a person believes in and supports the purpose and goals of the organization and expects to continue working for the organization in the future.[44] Organizational commitment consists of three types of commitment: affective commitment, normative commitment, and continuance commitment:

- *Affective commitment* is the degree to which a person believes in the organization's purpose, philosophy, values, and goals. For example, a nurse might feel strong affective commitment to a hospital that strongly supports women's health concerns.

- *Normative commitment* is a feeling of social obligation to remain in the organization for the sake of others or to repay a debt of obligation to the other organizational members. A senior employee remains in the organization because he believes that more junior employees would be disappointed if he left or that they are dependent on him in some way.

- *Continuance commitment* is the degree to which the person believes that she will continue to work for the organization and not actively seek employment in another organization. For example, positive continuance commitment occurs when a person makes it clear to others that she have no intention of leaving the organization.

Managers need to be aware of how organizational commitment varies among employees. Not all employees are committed to the organization; many see the organization in purely economic terms. Committed employees are more likely to make sacrifices in the name of the organization, support managerial initiatives, and express greater citizenship behavior than less committed employees.

**KEY**TERMS

**organizational commitment** The degree to which a person believes in and supports the purpose and goals of the organization and expects to continue working for it in the future; three types—affective, normative, and continuance.

## CONCLUSION

## Individual Behavior: Differences in Personality, Perception, and Attitudes

The origin of individual behavior involves self-concept, the fit between an individual and the environment, perception, and personality, each of which uniquely contributes to a manager's understanding and an appreciation of why people respond to a situation in different ways. Managers are often surprised that many organizational problems can be explained by psychological theories. To what extent does personality influence behavior? Would an introvert or an extrovert be better suited for a particular job? Why does John believe that the project is doomed to failure? The answers to all these questions could be found in psychological theories that have applications in work organizations. Many personal characteristics are related to work performance. Managers who want to increase worker productivity and performance can approach the problem from an interactional view, which suggests that the manager should look at the individual (dispositional) as well as an environmental (situational) basis for a behavior. Group processes, decision making, motivation, organizational change, and leadership are all areas that can be influenced by the unique characteristics of the individual. Thus, before managers can understand group or team behavior, they should understand the implications of individual characteristics on group outcomes. Recall from Chapter 5, "Decision Making," that aspects of personality (traits) can have an effect on the decision-making process and outcome.

## Discussion Questions

1. What are the three characteristics of attribution theory that people use to determine causal attribution for another person's behavior?

2. Identify and describe the Big Five personality dimensions.

3. What is the Myers-Briggs Type Indicator used for?

4. What are the four steps in the perception process?

## Video Case

### P.F. Chang's Serves Its Workers Well

Have you ever sat down at a restaurant table and immediately thought, "This place is great?" You can tell by the atmosphere that diners are happy and staff members enjoy their jobs. Despite the hustle and bustle, people are smiling. Your server introduces himself or herself and seems genuinely glad to see you. On the flip side, you have probably been to at least one restaurant where the staff was rushed or surly, the service slow—and you do not even recall how the food tasted because the service was so poor. As a consumer, you are likely to return to the first restaurant as soon as possible and recommend it to your friends. However, you are unlikely to give the second restaurant another chance. These are the challenges that restaurant managers face every day: putting the right person in the right job, creating a team that works well together, fostering positive work attitudes, helping employees manage stress. Managers at P.F. Chang's, which owns and operates ninety-seven full-service, casual dining Asian bistros and thirty-three contemporary Chinese diners across the country, greet these challenges with gusto.

Founded in 1993, P.F. Chang's prides itself in being able to offer "fresh, contemporary, and consistently outstanding" fare at every one of its restaurants. Selections of rice, noodles, grains, dumplings, vegetables, meat, poultry, and seafood are served at each restaurant, with mixtures of traditional Chinese foods and innovative dishes from Southeast Asia. P.F. Chang's strives to create an exceptional dining experience for every customer—and that includes a friendly, knowledgeable staff. In addition to the service staff, restaurant managers must manage the chefs and other kitchen staff who operate behind the scenes. Whether guests choose the full-service casual dining experience at P.F. Chang's bistros or the quick-service, limited-menu option of the Pei Wei Asian diners, they receive the same high quality of food and service.

How does an organization this large—and spread out—foster positive attitudes and high performance among its workers? Roxanne Pronk, Regional Vice President of Operations, explains P.F. Chang's approach, which is unique among restaurants. First, she notes a particular challenge among restaurant workers: they are typically young, working for hourly wages (and tips), and struggling to establish themselves in their lives and careers. So when they arrive at work, they are not necessarily thinking about the needs of customers; instead, they are thinking about themselves. According to Pronk, most restaurants deal with these problems through the use of discipline and negative reinforcement—which results in unhappy employees and a high degree of turnover. But P.F. Chang's takes a different approach. If a worker begins to exhibit a pattern of poor behavior, such as arriving late to work, his or her manager sits down with the employee, asks whether everything is all right and how the manager might be able to help turn things around. Pronk notes that this caring and respectful treatment has a profound effect on workers' attitudes about their jobs.

By treating employees with respect, restaurant managers find that they can expect more from their staff—and get it. Unlike many hourly restaurant employees, those at P.F. Chang's have the authority to make decisions that benefit customers. For example, if a customer is dissatisfied with a meal, the server has the authority to offer a replacement or a free meal. If a customer requests butter—which is not an ingredient found in Asian cuisine—the server can ask a busboy to run to the nearest market to buy butter for the customer's meal. Giving employees the freedom to make decisions has had a huge impact on their attitude and performance, says Pronk. Of course, workers are also held accountable for their behavior and their performance, but they welcome the responsibility.

Managers at P. F. Chang's restaurant receive extensive training in how to create and nurture a positive attitude among their employees, and all workers receive an employee handbook, which clearly spells out exactly what is expected of them. In addition, every work shift at P. F. Chang's begins with a staff meeting in which the manager discusses any changes, developments, or new issues at the restaurant; this meeting acts as a sort of pep rally to motivate workers to head into their shift with an upbeat outlook.

The Chang's culture is made up of trust, respect, accountability, commitment, and passion. "We believe that every employee and member of our management team must embody our messages as well as our values," explains the web site. That's a recipe for some delicious dining.

## Questions

1. Managers at P.F. Chang's address the affective component of workers' attitudes. Why is this an important step for them to take?

2. In what ways does P.F. Chang's create organizational commitment among its workers?

3. How might a manager at P.F. Chang's use the Big Five personality factors to assess whether a candidate for a position on the wait staff would be suitable?

Sources: Company web site, http//www.pfchangs.com, accessed August 26, 2004; "Work Force Still Top Concern for CEOs," *The Phoenix Business Journal* (May 24, 2004): http://phoenix.bizjournals.com.

## BizFlix

### The Breakfast Club

John Hughes's careful look at teenage culture in a suburban high school outside Chicago focuses on a group of teenagers from the school's subcultures. They start their Saturday detention with nothing in common. Over the day they learn each others' most inner secrets. The highly memorable characters—the Jock, the Princess, the Criminal, the Kook, and the Brain—leave lasting impressions. (If you have seen the film, try to recall which actor or actress played each character.)

This scene shows the detainees at lunchtime. It is an edited version of the "Lunch time" sequence that appears in the first third of the film. Carefully study each character's behavior to answer the questions below.

## Questions

1. Which Big Five personality dimensions describe each character in this scene?

2. Which characters are externals? Which characters are internals? Explain your reasoning for classifying each character.

3. Are any of these characters Type A personalities or Type B personalities? If so, which ones?

## Suggested Reading

Jordon Kathleen, "Analyze This: Can Personality Theory Help You Lead Your Unit?" *Management Update,* Article Reprint No. U0302D (February, 2003).

MacPhail Jack and K. R. Brousseau, "Finding a Fit between Person and Position," *Harvard Management Update,* Article Reprint No. U0505D (May 2005).

Prewitt Edward, "Personality Tests in Hiring: How to Do It Right," *Harvard Management Update,* Article Reprint No. U9810C (October, 1998).

Rousseau Denise, "Changing the Deal While Keeping the People," *Academy of Management Executive,* 10 (1996): 50–59.

## *Endnotes*

1. R. C. Huseman, J. D. Hatfield, and E. A. Miles, "A New Perspective on Equity Theory: The Equity Sensitivity Construct," *Academy of Management Review* 12 (1987): 222–234.

2. Edgar Schein, *Organizational Psychology* (Englewood Cliffs, NJ: Prentice-Hall, Inc., 1965), 11–13.

3. Denise M. Rousseau, "Changing the Deal While Keeping the People," *Academy of Management Executive* 10 (1996): 50–55.

4. Kurt Lewin, "Formalization and Progress in Psychology," in Dorian Cartwright, Ed., *Field Theory in the Social Science* (New York: Harper & Row, 1951).

5. Roberts, B. W., & Robins, R. W., "A Longitudinal Study of Person-Environment Fit and Personality Development," *Journal of Personality* 72 (2004): 89–110.

6. Chatman, J., "Matching People and Organizations: Selection and Socialization in Public Accounting Firms," *Administrative Science Quarterly* 36 (1991): 459–484.

7. Peter Senge, R. Ross, B. Smith, C. Roberts, and A. Winkler, *The Fifth Discipline Fieldbook* (New York: Doubleday Dell Publishing1994), 3.

8. Ibid., 3.

9. A. P. Brief and R. Aldag, "The 'Self' in Work Organizations: A Conceptual Review," *Academy of Management Review* (1981): 75–88. Also see J. Sullivan, "Self Theories and Employee Motivation," *Journal of Management* (1989): 345–363.

10. George Mead, *On Social Psychology* (Chicago: University of Chicago Press, 1956), Chapter 7.

11. T. A. Judge, A. Erez, J. E. Bono, "The Power of Being Positive: The Relationship Between Positive Self-Concept and Job Performance," *Human Performance* 11 (1998): 167–187.

12. E. A. Locke, K. McClear, D. Knight, "Self-Esteem and Work," *International Review of Industrial/Organizational Psychology* 11 (1996): 1–32.

13. Abraham Korman, *The Psychology of Motivation* (Englewood Cliffs: Prentice Hall, 1974), 227. Also see, Mark Somers and Joel Lefkowitz, "Self-Esteem, Need Gradification, and Work Satisfaction: A Test of Competing Explanations from Consistency Theory and Self Enhancement Theory," *Journal of Vocational Behavior* 22 (1983): 303–311.

14. K. H. Trzesniewski, M. B. Donnellan, and R. W. Robbins, "Stability of Self-Esteem Across a Lifespan," *Journal of Personality and Social Psychology* 84 (2003): 205–220.

15. Albert Bandura, *Social Foundations of Thought and Action* (Englewood Cliffs: Prentice Hall, 1986).

16. Dov Eden and Arie Aviram, "Self Efficacy Training to Speed Reemployment: Helping People to Help Themselves," *Journal of Applied Psychology* (June 1993): 352–360.

17. Dana H. Lindsley, Daniel J. Brass, and James B. Thomas, "Efficacy-Performance Spirals: A Multi-Level Perspective," *Academy of Management Review* (1995): 645.

18. M. Snyder, *Public Appearances, Private Realities: The Psychology of Self-Monitoring* (New York: W. H. Freeman, 1987).

19. M. Snyder and S. Gangestad, "On the Nature of Self-Monitoring: Matters of Assessment, Matters of Validity," *Journal of Personality and Social Psychology* 51 (1986): 123–139.

20. Clyde Kluckhohn and H. A. Murray, "Personality Formation: The Determinants," in C. Kluckhohn and H. A. Murray (eds.)*Personality* (New York: Knopf, 1948), 35.

21. Sigmund Freud, *An Outline of Psychoanalysis* (New York: Norton, 1949).

22. Carl Rogers, *On Becoming a Person, 2d ed.* (New York: Houghton Mifflin, 1970).

23. Gorgon Allport, *Pattern and Growth in Personality* (New York: Holt, Rinehart, and Winston, 1961).

24. T. A. Judge, J. E. Bono, E. A. Locke, "Personality and Job Satisfaction: The Mediating Role of Job Characteristics," *Journal of Applied Psychology* 85 (2000): 237–249.

25. D. P. McAdams, "The Five-Factor Model in Personality: A Critical Appraisal," *Journal of Personality 60,* 1992, 329–361. Also see: R. R. McCrae, & P. T. Costa, Jr. (1996), "Toward a New Generation of Personality Theories: Theoretical Contexts for the Five-Factor Model." In J. S. Wiggins (Ed.) *The Five-Factor Model of Personality: Theoretical Perspectives* (New York: Guilford, 1996), 51–87. Also see: R. R. McCrae, & P. T. Costa, Jr., "Personality Trait Structure as a Human Universal," *American Psychologist* 52 (1997): 509–516.

26. J. B. Rotter, "Generalized Expectancies for Internal vs. External Control of Reinforcement," *Psychological Monographs* 80 (1966): 1–28.

27. T. R. Mitchell, C. M. Smysert, and S. E. Weed, "Locus of Control: Supervision and Work Satisfaction," *Academy of Management Journal* 18 (1975): 623–631.

28. M. Matteson and C. Preston, "Occupational Stress: Type A Behavior and Physical Well-Being," *Academy of Management Journal* 25 (1982): 373–391.

29. J. Schaubroeck, D. Ganster, and B. E., Kemmerer, "Job Complexity, Type A Cardiovascular Disorder: A Prospective Study," *Academy of Management Journal* 37 (1994): 426–439.

30. C. G. Jung, *Psychological Types,* (New York: Harcourt, 1923).

31. J. B. Murray, "Review of Research on the Myers-Briggs Type Indicator," *Perceptual and Motor Skills* (1990): 1187–1202.

32. S. T. Fiske and S. E. Taylor, *Social Cognition, 2d ed.* (Reading, MA: Addison-Wesley Publishing, 1991).

33. Herbert Simon. *Administrative Behavior, 3d ed.* (New York: Free Press, 1976) chapter 15, Selective Perception, 309–314.

34. *Valerie Strauss,* "Report Calls for Improvement in K-8 Science Education," *Washington Post,* (Friday, September 22, 2006,): A09

35. Harold H. Kelly, "The Processes of Causal Attribution," *American Psychologist* 28 (1973): 107–128.

36. L. Ross, "The Intuitive Psychologist and His Shortcomings: Distortions in the Attribution Process," L. Berkowitz, ed. *Advances in Experimental Social Psychology* (New York: Academic Press, 1977).

37. L. Ross, D. Greene, and P. House, "The False Consensus Phenomenon: An Attributional Bias in Self-Perception and Social-Perception Processes," *Journal of Experimental Psychology* 13 (1977): 279–301.

38. Erdley, C. A., and P. R. D'Agostino, "Cognitive and Affective Components of Automatic Priming Effects," *Journal of Personality and Social Psychology* 54, (1988): 741–47. Also see: J. P. Forgus, and G. H. Bowers, "Mood Effects in Person-Perception Judgments," *Journal of Personality and Social Psychology* 53 (1987): 53–60.

39. Martin Fishbein, and I. Ajzen. *Belief, Attitude, Intention and Behavior: An Introduction to Theory and Research* (Reading, MA: Addison-Wesley, 1975).

40. Frederick Herzberg, Bernard Mausner, and Barbara Bloch Snyderman, *The Motivation to Work* (New York: Wiley, 1959).

41. R. P. Tett and J. P. Meyer, "Job Satisfaction, Organizational Commitment, Turnover Intention, and Turnover: A Path Analysis Based on Meta-Analytic Findings," *Personnel Psychology* (1993): 259–293.

42. J. M. Ivancevich and M. T. Matteson, *Stress at Work* (Glenview, IL: Scott, Foresman, 1980).

43. J. Greenberg. *Managing Behavior in Organizations, 2d ed.* (Upper Saddle River, NJ: Prentice-Hall, 1999), 84–85.

44. J. P. Meyer, & N. J. Allen, *Commitment in the Workplace: Theory, Research, and Application* (Newbury Park, CA: Sage, 1997).

# 12

# MOTIVATION

**W**hy does he work so hard? Why does she go to law school at night after working all day? The actions that others take and the choices they make give us plenty to feed our curiosity. It's natural for us to want to understand the reason for human behavior. We expect people to behave rationally, we seek to understand the logic of their actions, and we judge them accordingly. The fundamental question we ask ourselves in this chapter is what motivates behavior? At work the answer to the motivation question is especially important, because presumably all work is voluntary. So we begin this chapter with the basics of motivation and then cut a path through the major theories of work motivation.

At work, managers are confronted with how best to encourage work-related behaviors, yet we know that two people in the same situation often behave quite differently. Why is that? Most motivation theorists believe that the answer is based on need. A need is a drive to achieve a specific outcome. Hedonism and Thorndike's Law of Effect[1]—the pursuit of pleasure and the avoidance of pain—inform us that people seek rewarding outcomes and avoid punishing consequences. For example, hunger is a need. When your body needs food, you act to satisfy your hunger. You break for lunch, or you hit the vending machine. Once your stomach is full, hunger no longer drives your behavior, leaving you free to attend to other things. In other words, a deficit in need causes a person to seek satisfaction of that need; but once the need is satisfied, it no longer motivates behavior. We know that eating satisfies our hunger need. From previous gastronomic experiences, we also know that some foods are enjoyable and others disagreeable to us. We seek out the enjoyable foods and avoid the disagreeable foods. In the need-satisfaction process, we make choices toward some outcomes and away from others.

Failure to understand human motivation can mean wasted time, resources, and careers. We know different people have different needs. Managers must elicit effort from workers with often vastly different levels of interest, ability, and motivation. Not all workers are motivated by the same thing (see the Management Highlight on page 251). For some workers, money is a motivator; for others, it's the opportunity to help people. Managers are constantly seeking ways to motivate people in order to increase productivity or increase the greater expression of workplace creativity. To do so, managers must motivate different types of people so that they will all contribute to the attainment of organizational goals.

In a modern society, work means economic freedom. Work allows us the benefits that money can buy, but not everyone is motivated by money. People work for many different reasons—to survive, to achieve personal goals, to feed their families, to be respected. For other reasons—taking pride in workmanship; because of ability; from a sense of obligation; for personal, peer, and social recognition; or to make a customer happy—they may excel at their jobs. Just as there are many reasons for motivation, there are also many theories to explain it. Before beginning a discussion of motivation, it is important to define what we mean by motivation. **Motivation** is the set of forces that initiate behavior and determine its form, direction, intensity, and duration. At work, these forces might be based on a need deficit (to become a lead engineer) and directed toward a goal (promotion to lead engineer). So what should a manager know about motivation? For one thing, most theories of work performance include motivation as a central concept. If managers are concerned with increasing worker commitment and productivity, they must be concerned with motivation.[2]

**KEY** TERMS

**need** A drive to achieve a specific outcome.

## WHAT MOTIVATES A WORKER?

| Intrinsic Rewards | What Organizations Can Do | Extrinsic Rewards | What Organizations Can Do |
|---|---|---|---|
| *The work itself* | Create interesting jobs that people enjoy and seek out. | *Compensation* | Explore new alternative compensation plans. For example, accumulation of paid time off rather than overtime. |
| *Work environment* | Create spaces that are natural and easily facilitate the work. | *Promotion* | Encourage promotion from within; let workers know when a move to the next level can be expected. Develop career paths within a set of jobs. |
| *Jobs with greater autonomy* | Allow workers greater control over the pace and outcome of the work. | *Corporate perks* | Provide use of company cars, golf course memberships, and other corporate facilities such as corporate parks. |
| *Social interaction among workers* | Design more group-based tasks that bring people together and encourage greater diversity. | *Stock ownership* | Create opportunities for workers to invest and share the wealth. |
| *Creative expression* | Allow workers greater freedom to change and explore new concepts and techniques. | *Funded retirement plans and 401k contributions* | Help workers build retirement assets that encourage commitment and tenure. |

---

**EXHIBIT 12.1**

## A Model of Motivation

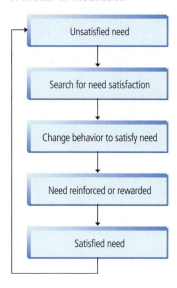

Motivation is defined in relation to a set of forces that drive behavior. Many theorists believe that motivation is driven by unsatisfied needs that people seek to satisfy. Exhibit 12.1 describes a model of motivation based on the concept of need satisfaction. For example, you have a need for greater importance in your work. With a sense of increasing tension, you become dissatisfied with your current job. This tension drives you to thoughts of returning to school and finishing your college degree. Next, you search for the best way to attend college and complete your degree program. Once you graduate and get the job you wanted, your feelings of tension are reduced. The process of motivation never ends; it is just replaced by a different need. An unsatisfied need and its associated tension cause the process to begin anew. This model helps us understand that motivation is a lifelong process driven by satisfying unmet needs.

## The Importance of Motivation

Why focus on worker motivation? The once popular view that computers and technology would make workers obsolete has been replaced by a realization that business still needs an educated workforce. Rather than seeking input and a competitive edge from a small number of key, top-level workers, companies must find ways to actively elicit the participation of all employees, and to motivate all employees to greater levels of quality performance.

To achieve organizational goals, managers must understand basic human nature. What motivates a person to work hard? What does a person want or need from work? Once this central question is answered, a reward system can be designed to satisfy these wants and needs. Although this may sound easy, it is not.

## Assumptions about Human Nature

Before beginning our discussion of motivation, let's review several important assumptions about human nature. Managers, like most of us, have very specific attitudes and beliefs about what makes people tick. As in most other aspects of life, different people have different assumptions about human nature. Assumptions are a theoretic frame of reference against which we compare our daily human interactions. To a large degree, these assumptions dictate what we expect to see and what we actually see. If we assume that most blue-collar workers are disinterested in their work, we might interpret some workers' low performance as confirmation of this lack of interest—even though the correct interpretation might be that they were poorly trained. Douglas McGregor's two contrasting explanations of human nature have been widely used to understand and shape managerial practices. His sets of assumptions (called Theory X and Theory Y) describe diametrically opposed views of managerial direction and control.[3]

Theory X states that workers are passive (if not lazy) and in need of direction and control. Thus, workers need external management through the use of force, persuasion, rewards, and punishment. McGregor described Theory X as the traditional view of direction and control.

Theory Y asserts that workers are eager to learn, be responsible, and be creative. McGregor believed that workers' capacities to learn are great and that their abilities are underutilized. If given the autonomy, workers are quite capable of self-direction and self-control. In addition, an organization's reward system must be supportive of increased employee participation.

## The Motivation Process

According to behavioral scientists, effective worker performance requires motivation, ability, and a reward system that encourages quality work.[4] In a general sense, Exhibit 12.1 describes the psychological relationship between motivation, behavior, reward, and feedback. A person's motive or motivation is characterized as a need-based state of arousal. Need deprivation increases our state of arousal or search to reduce the need deficit. At work, the term *behavior* refers to the specific work or task actions that result from a need-deficit-induced arousal. And finally, rewards are the direct consequence of our behavior. Feedback is knowledge produced about the cause-and-effect sequence that either stimulates or suppresses future states of arousal, depending on our level of need satisfaction. A reward is an attractive or desired consequence that can be either intrinsic or extrinsic. Intrinsic rewards—the intangible psychological results of work that are controlled by the worker—are inherent in the job and occur during performance of work. A task might be intrinsically motivating because it results in a feeling of accomplishment. Intrinsic rewards can have significant, yet often underestimated, impacts on job satisfaction, which as we'll see is closely linked to motivation. Extrinsic rewards are administered by another party and occur apart from the actual performance of work. An example of an extrinsic reward is a paycheck.

To be motivated, workers must also be able to do the job. Ability refers to the physical and mental characteristics that a worker requires in order to perform a task successfully. Management must do everything it can to continually develop each worker's ability through training.

Over the years, many people have developed theories describing how motivation affects work behavior. Theories of worker motivation attempt to explain people's inner workings, initiatives, and aspirations. Next, we'll examine the three basic types of motivation theories—content, process, and environmental.

## Content Theories of Motivation

Content theories (also called need theories) are based on the idea that people are driven to meet basic needs that produce satisfaction when they're met. These theories include Maslow's hierarchy of needs, Alderfer's ERG theory, Herzberg's two-factor theory, and McClelland's learned needs theory.

## Maslow's Hierarchy of Needs

Abraham Maslow's motivation theory, commonly referred to as the hierarchy of needs (Exhibit 12.2), is based on two key assumptions. First, different needs are active at different times, and only needs not yet satisfied can influence behavior. Second, needs are arranged in a fixed order of importance called a *hierarchy*.

According to Maslow's theory, behavior is triggered by a need *deficit* that drives the individual to reduce the tension it creates. Tension leads to behavior that will potentially satisfy the need. For example, a new baby in the family means a greater financial burden. As a result, the worker increases work effort to ensure a promotion and an increase in pay (raise). In Maslow's theory, the idea that the most basic unsatisfied need (in the hierarchy) influences current behavior

**EXHIBIT 12.2**      **Maslow's Needs Hierarchy**

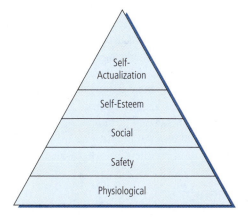

**Source:** Abraham H. Maslow, *Motivation and Personality* (New York: Harper & Row, 1954).

is called the prepotency (i.e., priority or order) of the need. This prepotency creates an urgency exerted by an unmet need that influences human behavior. In our example, the as-yet-unmet need for a promotion and raise has high prepotency. The need for greater security motivates the current behavior of the worker. Until the need is satisfied, the unmet need is said to influence behavior. Furthermore, as soon as a lower-order need is satisfied, a higher-order need emerges and demands satisfaction.

**As Exhibit 12.2 illustrates, Maslow identified five categories of needs:**

   | *Physiological needs,* such as food, sleep, and physical movement

   | *Safety needs,* such as freedom from fear or harm, stability, predictability

   | *Social needs,* such as friendship, love, camaraderie, and teamwork

   | *Self-esteem needs,* such as status and reputation

   | *Self-actualization needs,* such as the fulfillment of human potential and personal growth[5]

The hierarchy of needs gives managers a straightforward way of understanding how various work conditions satisfy employee needs. Certain basic conditions of employment (such as pay) satisfy physiological needs. Safety needs are met by safe work conditions and job security. Social needs are satisfied by interaction and communication with fellow workers. And finally, work that is fulfilling can satisfy self-esteem and self-actualization needs.

Although Maslow's ideas were a welcome relief from the emphasis on abnormal behavior that dominated the psychology of the day, they are not without some potential pitfalls. Maslow himself recognized that the hierarchy is not a stair-step approach. Humans have multiple needs that often occur simultaneously in modern society. It may make more sense to think about higher-order needs (such as esteem and self-actualization) as one set and lower-order needs (such as physiological, safety, and social needs) as another set. Using just these two categories, we can see that it is certainly possible for several needs to influence our behavior at once.

In addition, we have to consider the relative intensity of the need that we feel at a given time. Being thirsty is a relative concept. If you're in a desert and have no water, the prepotency of the need will influence 100 percent of your behavior. If you're mildly thirsty all morning but you're writing the weekly report, your behavior may be more determined by a deadline than your thirst.

Finally, Maslow's theory describes needs as internal; it says nothing about the environment's effect on behavior. How are needs determined? For example, the need for new clothes may be determined by comparing our clothes with those worn by friends, models, or prestigious people. Functionally our clothes may be fine; but in contrast to our friends' clothes, they might look old or out of style. So what might be considered a lower-order need for clothing becomes translated into a higher-order need for self-esteem. The referent for our need deficit is not internal, but external. In other words, the definition of need for new clothing is determined through other people, society, education, and religion—the external environment.

To a large degree, Maslow's ideas help us understand that everyone has basic needs that must be satisfied. One way to satisfy these needs is through work. But the complexity of the need-satisfaction process makes simple prescription problematic. Although Maslow's needs hierarchy describes a model of basic human needs, it offers little practical guidance for motivating workers.

## | Alderfer's ERG Theory

In response to several gaps in Maslow's needs hierarchy theory, Clayton Alderfer[6] developed a need-satisfaction theory of motivation that better describes human behavior. His theory is a modification of Maslow's earlier work, but it attempts to simplify Maslow's theory by including three basic needs rather than five. In addition, Alderfer introduced the concept of *frustration regression* to describe how we deal with our unmet needs. His ERG theory includes three primary needs:

| *Existence.* Basic needs for survival, food, shelter, and clothing.

| *Relatedness.* Needs that are part of building and maintaining social relationships.

| *Growth.* Intrinsic desires for knowledge, creativity, and ability to learn new and different things.

Like Maslow, Alderfer recognized a hierarchy of human needs, beginning with our most basic needs for safety and sustenance. Once our existence needs are satisfied, we progress to the next need in the hierarchy—relatedness. Once we have satisfied our relatedness needs, we become more concerned with our needs to grow and achieve whatever goals we set for ourselves—our need for personal growth.

Overall, Alderfer's theory sounds a lot like Maslow's theory, but with some unique differences. Alderfer believed that people can become frustrated in their ability to fulfill a need. Frustration regression describes the situation where we find ourselves unable to satisfy a need and, in reaction to the unsatisfied need, we regress toward a lower need. For example, in our quest to satisfy a relatedness need (i.e., becoming a member of a group), we regress toward seeking satisfaction in an existence need. Similarly, an unsatisfied growth need causes us to regress toward a desire to satisfy a relatedness need.

ERG theory offers another attempt to explain motivation in relation to need satisfaction. In his theory, Aldefer describes a hierarchy of needs and our ability to move up or down the hierarchy, depending on whether a need is satisfied. ERG theory suggests that existence and relatedness needs can be met at some point, but meeting a growth need only causes us to set higher growth goals.

## KEY TERMS

**ERG theory** A content theory, espoused by Clayton Alderfer, that is based on the concept of frustration regression to describe how we deal with our unmet needs. *See also* content theories.

**frustration regression** The situation in which we are unable to satisfy a need and, in reaction, regress to a lower need.

**hygiene factors** One of two sets of factors, that can separately explain satisfaction and dissatisfaction; also called maintenance factors, specifically the aspects of work that are peripheral to the task itself and related to the external environment.

**job context** The external environment of the job.

## | Herzberg's Two-Factor Theory

Before Frederick Herzberg's research was published, most people viewed job satisfaction and dissatisfaction as opposite ends of a single continuum. Thus many managers believed that the greater the amount of any good condition, the greater the amount of worker satisfaction. Managers further believed that eliminating undesirable working conditions would result in job satisfaction. But Herzberg believed that not being satisfied is different from being dissatisfied.

Herzberg and his colleagues were interested in identifying those factors that caused workers to be satisfied with their work. To investigate this idea, Herzberg designed a study in which data were gathered from accountants and engineers. Herzberg asked participants in the study to think of times when they felt especially good and especially bad about their jobs. Each participant was then asked to describe the conditions or events that caused those good or bad feelings. Of particular interest was the finding that participants identified different work conditions for each of the two feelings. That is, although the presence of one condition (e.g., fulfilling work) made participants feel good, the absence of that condition (fulfilling work) did not make them feel bad. Consequently, Herzberg postulated that motivators lead to satisfaction, but their absence does not necessarily lead to dissatisfaction.

Herzberg identified two factors, hygiene and motivators, that he asserts can separately explain satisfaction and dissatisfaction. Factors whose presence prevents dissatisfaction are called hygiene factors, or maintenance factors. Hygiene or maintenance factors refer to aspects of work that are peripheral to the task itself and more related to the external environment (the job context).

The term *hygiene factor* is linked to the finding that the absence of readily available rest rooms led to worker dissatisfaction. Hygiene factors include

- Company policy and administrative practices
- Technical supervision by the manager
- Interpersonal relations with the supervisor
- Worker salary, job status, and job security
- The worker's personal life
- Physical conditions of the work setting (e.g., air conditioning)

Factors whose presence leads to satisfaction are called motivators. These factors can produce high levels of motivation when they're present. Motivator factors relate directly to the job content (the specific aspects of a job). They include

- Achievement
- Recognition
- Advancement
- The task or work itself
- The worker's potential for personal learning or growth
- The worker's responsibility for results[7]

Exhibit 12.3 illustrates Herzberg's two-factor theory. The distinction between motivational and maintenance factors is often clarified by the observation that motivational factors are *intrinsic,* whereas maintenance factors are *extrinsic.*

At the time of his study, Herzberg's ideas were considered groundbreaking. He and his colleagues challenged traditionally accepted ideas about the causes and nature of job satisfaction. But when the two-factor theory was tested in other organizations, researchers found little support for the theory. Controversy over Herzberg's findings centers on three areas:

- *Method of data collection.* The information was collected via a potentially biased, structured interview format.

---

**EXHIBIT 12.3**    **Herzberg's Two-Factor Theory**

Satisfaction

Factor 1: Motivators (influence satisfaction)

- Achievement
- Recognition
- The Work Itself
- Responsibility
- Advancement and Growth

**Job Content**

Neither Satisfied Nor Dissatisfied

Factor 2: Hygiene (influences dissatisfaction)

- Supervisors
- Working Conditions
- Interpersonal Relations
- Pay and Security
- Company Policies and Administration

**Job Context**

Dissatisfaction

**Source:** Frederick I. Herzberg, "One More Time: How Do You Motivate Employees," *Harvard Business Review* (January–February 1968): 53–62.

| *Individual differences.* Individual differences were discovered to affect the two factors. For example, some workers avoid advancement.

| *Limited sample.* Conclusions were based primarily on studies of professionals (i.e., engineers and accountants), whose tasks differ significantly from other kinds of workers.[8]

Herzberg's motivational factors correspond to Maslow's higher-order needs, whereas his maintenance factors correspond to lower-order needs. Interestingly, Maslow, Alderfer, and Herzberg all provide evidence that the value of the work itself can contribute to worker motivation. Although the work of Maslow and Herzberg has its limitations, these researchers have shaped the direction of subsequent work in the field of motivation.

## McClelland's Learned Needs Theory

Another psychologist, David McClelland, paid further attention to the potential of work itself to motivate.[9] McClelland is best known for research on achievement motivation, but he also identified several other motives that have application to the work. McClelland's approach differs from Maslow, Alderfer, and Herzberg in the origin of human needs. McClelland believed that basic needs are transmitted or learned through culture and that the need for achievement was a powerful motivator. But how do you determine what these needs are and what is the mechanism that results in motivation? McClelland sought the answers to these questions. McClelland believed that a person's unconscious mind is the key to unlocking his or her particular needs. Once an individual's dominant need is identified, it then becomes a matter of understanding how best to satisfy that need.

| **Identifying the Need** | Using projective techniques, McClelland showed subjects a picture and then asked them to write a story describing what was happening in the picture and what the probable outcome would be. He believed the story would reveal the writer's needs and motives.

| **Measuring the Need** | To measure an individual's need for achievement, McClelland used the Thematic Apperception Test (TAT), which was developed by H. A. Murray, another psychologist.[10] Following Murray's work on need for achievement, McClelland and John Atkinson developed the scoring system for the Thematic Apperception Test (TAT), and McClelland used the TAT to measure need for achievement and other needs. The TAT contains pictures and asks the test taker to write a story (theme) about the picture. McClelland believed that a person's dominant needs are expressed in their description of the picture. The TAT is assessed by a trained evaluator who converts the verbal description into a numeric value suitable for analysis. McClelland contributed both a theory and a way to measure the need across people. In his later years he drew a link between the need for achievement and success at work.

| **Motivating the Individual** | Once the dominant need of the individual is identified, a strategy can be developed to satisfy the need. This may involve moving an individual to an intrinsically rewarding job rather than one that relies exclusively on pay or external recognition. It could involve recognizing the need for social contact. Or finally, it might mean a career path into management. Next we will explore the three primary needs identified by McClelland.

| **Three Dominant Needs** | Three dominant needs identified by McClelland are the need for achievement, need for affiliation, and need for power. If the dominant need identified in the individual was for achievement, then a manager should put the individual in a position

**KEY**TERMS

**Thematic Apperception Test (TAT)** A test developed by H. A. Murray to measure an individual's need for achievement, whose scoring system was later developed by David McClelland and John Atkinson; contains pictures and asks the test taker to write a story (theme) about the picture. *See also* content theories.

where he or she can fulfill that need. If the dominant need is a need for affiliation, then a situation that provides more interaction with people might allow the person to fulfill his or her dominant need.

The need for achievement is a measure of a person's desire for clear, self-set, moderately difficult goals, with feedback given based on goal achievement. High achievers are seen as self-starters, goal-oriented, or full of task initiative, all traits that firms typically value.

The need for affiliation is the desire to work with others, to interact with and support others, and to learn the lessons of life through the experiences of others. A pronounced desire for social acceptance can be a powerful motivating force in our daily lives. Work organizations are important social institutions, bringing people into regular contact with one another. The need for affiliation is Maslow's social need, applied to the individual.

The need for power is a desire to have influence and control over others. This need can be an important determinant of behavior. People dominate one another in many socially acceptable ways. People are submissive to the dominance of police, managers, tour guides, and others. It is natural and often informative to allow other people control over an aspect of our lives. Many people seek jobs that afford them the opportunity to fulfill a basic need in a socially acceptable manner, and success at many jobs actually requires people to be forceful and capable of exerting their will over others. In these positions, people with a high need for power will outperform those with a low need for power.

Like Maslow's needs theory, McClelland's theory suggests that people vary in the degree to which their motive for behavior is determined by any one or a combination of these needs. McClelland's work fits well with Herzberg's view of achievement as a motivator and with Maslow's concept of higher-order needs satisfaction as a source of motivation. In addition, McClelland's research moves beyond basic or lower-level needs as explanations for behavior. Maslow, Herzberg, and McClelland all recognize the importance of achievement and social relations as motivational factors. But it is McClelland who moves one step beyond the other theorists by adding another dimension—the need for power. As we will see, the need for power can be an important explanation for human behavior. The Management Highlight on page 259 allows you to assess your level of need for achievement, need for affiliation, and need for power. After completing the questionnaire, compute your score and compare it to the average scores of other respondents.

**KEY**TERMS

**need for achievement**
A measure of a person's desire for clear, self-set, moderately difficult goals, with feedback given based on goal achievement.

**need for affiliation** The desire to work with others, to interact with and support others, and to learn the lessons of life through the experiences of others; Maslow's social need, applied to the individual.

**need for power** A desire to have influence and control over others, which can be an important determinant of behavior.

## Managerial Application of Need Theories

The need theories reviewed in this chapter point to the conclusion that sources of individual motivation can be both internal and external. McClelland's achievement and affiliation needs, Maslow's esteem and self-actualization needs, Alderfer's growth needs, and Herzberg's intrinsic motivators—responsibility, personal growth, and the work itself—are consistent with the belief that motivation and worker commitment come from basic intrinsic needs. Reflections of these intrinsic needs are pride of workmanship and the joy of work. Maslow's physiological and safety needs, Herzberg's pay and working conditions, and McClelland's recognition that needs are acquired or learned reflect the external nature of certain needs.

With an increasingly well-educated workforce, organizations are placing more emphasis on understanding how higher-order intrinsic individual needs can be satisfied at work. However, managers often underestimate employees' need for achievement. A climate of achievement in the workplace can be cultivated in several ways. First, work that is challenging and gives the employee a sense of responsibility is motivational. Second, managers can identify and recognize contributions of individual employees rather than simply attributing a firm's success to managers. Need theories of motivation often help managers better understand the motives that drive workers to expend effort in the completion of tasks at work.

## DOES WORK MEET YOUR NEEDS?

Instructions: Using the scale provided, answer each question below in reference to a job that you have held in the past. If you have never worked, answer each question as you believe they would apply to the type of job you hope to have after graduation.

| Never | Almost Never | Seldom | Sometimes | Usually | Almost Always | Always |
|---|---|---|---|---|---|---|
| 1 | 2 | 3 | 4 | 5 | 6 | 7 |

1. I do my best work when my job assignments are fairly difficult.
2. When I have a choice, I try to work in a group instead of by myself.
3. I seek an active role in the leadership of the group.
4. I try to influence those around me to see things my way.
5. I try very hard to improve on my past performance at work.
6. I pay a good deal of attention to the feelings of others at work.
7. I find myself organizing and directing the activities of others.
8. I strive to gain more control over the events around me at work.
9. I take moderate risks and stick my neck out to get ahead at work.
10. I prefer to do my work with others.
11. I strive to be "in command" when I am working in a group.
12. I try to seek out added responsibilities on my job.
13. I do not openly express my disagreements with others.
14. I try to perform better than my co-workers.
15. I find myself talking to those around me about non-business related matters.

**Record your responses from the survey and total the three columns to arrive at your need for achievement, power, and affiliation scores.**

| Need for Achievement | Need for Affiliation | Need for Power |
|---|---|---|
| 1 | 2 | 3 |
| 5 | 6 | 4 |
| 9 | 10 | 7 |
| 12 | 13 | 8 |
| 14 | 15 | 11 |
| TOTAL | TOTAL | TOTAL |
| Divide by 5 | Divide by 5 | Divide by 5 |
| SCORE | SCORE | SCORE |

Compare Your Score to the Expected Average Score

| NACH = 4.3 | NAFF = 4.1 | NPOW = 4.1 |

Source: Adapted from Richard M. Steers, and David N. Braunstein, "A Behaviorally-based Measure of Manifest Needs in Work Settings," *Journal of Vocational Behavior*, 9 (1976): 251–261.

# Process Theories of Motivation

Process theories describe cognitive processes and decisions that help predict subsequent behavior. These theories include equity and expectancy. Whereas need theories view motivation as subconscious and instinctive, process theories view motivation in relation to workers' explicit thought processes (cognitions) and conscious decisions to select and pursue a specific alternative (choice). According to process theory, then, a worker is likely to consider a variety of methods, weighing each method based on how attractive its expected outcomes might be, before engaging in an activity. The two major process theories are expectancy theory and equity theory.

## Expectancy Theory

Need or drive theories lacked the elegance of the human condition—the ability to cognitively evaluate options, preferences, and make a choice. Expectancy theory of motivation sometimes

12.4     **Expectancy Theory**

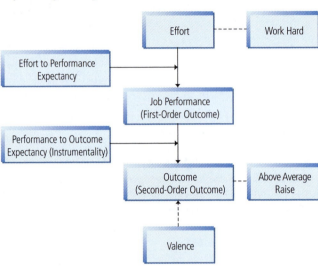

**effort-to-performance expectancy** The subjective assessment that a person can complete the job; the "can do" (perceived capability) component of an employee's approach to work.

**performance-to-outcome expectancy** The probability that hard work will be rewarded. (*See also* instrumentality).

**valence** The desirability of one outcome over another to the individual (i.e., the rewards); an outcome's desirability or preference to the individual among competing rewards.

**instrumentality** The employee's assessment of how instrumental, or likely, it is that successful task performance will be rewarded, such as with a raise; a measure of the association between performance and rewards. (*See also* performance-to-outcome expectancy).

referred to as *VIE (valence, instrumentality, expectancy) theory* described motivation as just such a process. In a nutshell, expectancy theory describes the process people use to evaluate (1) the likelihood that their effort or expenditure will yield the desired outcome, and (2) how much they want the outcome. Expectancy theory of motivation is based on three factors that determine the degree of effort to put forth (Exhibit 12.4).[11]

The first factor in VIE theory is **expectancy**—the individual's subjective assessment that an effort will lead to job performance (first-order outcome). The effort to performance expectancy is the subjective assessment that a person can complete the job. This is the "can do" (perceived capability) component of an employee's approach to work. The performance to outcome expectancy (also called instrumentality) is the probability that hard work will be rewarded. Expectancy is a probability assessment rated between 0 (certain not to produce results) and 1.0 (certain to produce results).

Valence, the second factor in VIE theory, refers to the desirability of one outcome over another outcome to the individual (i.e., the rewards). Valence represents the outcome's desirability or preference to the individual among competing rewards. Desirable rewards encourage effort; undesirable rewards discourage effort. A valence can range from negative to positive depending on whether the individual believes the outcome is personally undesirable or desirable.

The third factor is the instrumentality of successful task performance in leading to an outcome or a desired reward. If a first-order outcome is a successful completion of your job or working at an above-average level of performance, a second-order outcome might be a raise. Thus, instrumentality is a measure of the association between performance and rewards.

The valence of the potential reward, the instrumentality of the performance linked to the reward, and the expectancy of achieving the reward determine the level of effort. Then the values are multiplied to produce a force to perform for each effort. Presumably the actual level of effort will be determined by the highest VIE score.

Determining the VIE score can be complicated. For example, the levels of possible effort are often infinite rather than discrete; in other words, it's not simply a matter of effort versus no effort. An employee may not have an accurate idea of expectancy—she may not know if her efforts will produce the level of performance needed to earn a reward. The employee may also be uncertain about how performance will be rewarded. If so, the instrumentality for each level of effort cannot be determined. But for limited, discrete choices of effort (e.g., attend or not attend) and known instrumentalities (e.g., a score of 95 on an exam will guarantee the student an A grade), the calculations are simple and the research is generally supportive of expectancy theory.[12]

It's difficult to visualize expectancy theory, because it mainly involves an individual cognitive assessment of "if I do this—I will get that." Nonetheless, here are several points that can help you remember VIE theory. (You may want to look again at Exhibit 12.4.) Remember that *outcomes* are the consequences of individual behavior. What this means is that we have a choice to spend our time at work in many different ways, and some of them are more likely to lead to the outcomes we want most. *Valence* is an index of the values of competing outcomes. The outcome we choose has the highest value. Next, determine the effort-to-performance expectancy. This is the probability that an individual's effort will lead to the outcome. Finally, determine the performance-to-outcome expectancy. As the example in Exhibit 12.4 illustrates, if I perform, I will receive an above-average raise. The increased income from the raise will increase my income.

Here are some guidelines we can infer from the insights offered by expectancy theory:

- *Ask what outcomes workers desire.* Workers often prefer rewards that differ from management's assumptions. For example, for some workers in dual-career families, healthcare benefits may be irrelevant if the spouse's employer already provides them. Also, workers may prefer to get time off for child and elderly parent care rather than receive bonuses, promotions, and job transfers to new locations.

- *Break down effort-to-performance barriers.* Providing workers with tools, information, and an effective production support system will help translate effort into performance.

- *Clarify and communicate instrumentalities.* Workers who know that performance will lead to rewards are more likely to work hard. For those rewards that are controlled by management (e.g., bonuses and promotions), management must let workers know the performance level required to achieve these rewards.

- *Develop meaningful self-administered rewards.* Intrinsic rewards have a perfect instrumentality correlation (–1.0 or 1.0) and require no management action to award them. For example, developing pride of workmanship builds a self-motivated worker.

Expectancy theory provides a general guide to the factors that determine the amount of effort a worker puts forth. Expectancy theory also helps explain how a worker's goals influence his efforts. The utility of VIE theory for managers lies in its suggestion of the complex thought process that individuals use in the process of becoming motivated.

## Equity Theory

J. Stacy Adams' equity theory concerns the worker's perception of how she is being treated. In particular, equity theory is based on the *assessment process* a worker uses to evaluate the fairness or justice of organizational outcomes and the *adjustment process* used to maintain perceptions of fairness. The concepts of fairness and equilibrium (internal balance) are central to equity theory. The basic idea in equity theory is that an employee first considers his outcomes (rewards) and then his inputs (effort). Next, the employee compares his personal reward-to-effort ratio to the same ratio of

**12.5**

**Equity Theory**

**Adam's Equity Model**

$$\frac{\textbf{Outcomes}_{own}}{\textbf{Inputs}_{own}} \quad \text{EQUALS} \quad \frac{\textbf{Outcomes}_{others}}{\textbf{Inputs}_{others}}$$

where:

| | | |
|---|---|---|
| **Outcomes**$_{own}$ | = | Worker's perception of own outcomes. |
| **Inputs**$_{own}$ | = | Worker's perception of own inputs. |
| **Outcomes**$_{others}$ | = | Worker's perception of another worker's outcomes. |
| **Inputs**$_{others}$ | = | Worker's perception of another worker's inputs. |

**Restoration of Equity**

| You Feel Under-Rewarded | You Feel Over-Rewarded |
|---|---|
| 1. Ask for raise. | 1. Try to get raise for other workers. |
| 2. Lower inputs. | 2. Raise inputs. |
| 3. Rationalize why you get less than others. | 3. Rationalize why you get more than others. |
| 4. Change your comparison worker. | 4. Change your comparison worker. |

**Source:** Adapted from Ramon Aldag and T. Stearns. *Management*, 2nd ed. (Cincinnati, OH: South-Western, 1991): 422–423.

a referent. The referent is usually another employee doing basically the same work, some standard ratio based on a fair day's work, or another employee at approximately the same level in an organization.[13]

This ratio of a comparison person's outcome (rewards, recognition, pay) to inputs (time, effort, actual work performed) is called a reference ratio (Exhibit 12.5). If the employee believes that his outcomes-to-inputs ratio is lower than the reference ratio, he can (1) reduce his effort or (2) seek higher rewards to bring his outcomes-to-inputs ratio in line with the reference ratio. Conversely, if the employee's ratio is higher than the reference ratio, she can increase her effort or reduce her rewards. If Georgia feels that she's over-rewarded for her work, she might feel guilty. To reduce this tension, she could work harder or find more work to do. Her actions would reflect the need to adjust her internal state of fairness. Likewise, John, an under-rewarded worker, is off balance in the opposite direction. He too would seek an equity adjustment. If no pay increase appeared to be forthcoming, equity theory suggests that in order to create an equitable outcome, John would decrease his effort again.

Note that a worker's inputs and outcomes need not be in exact balance to one another, as long as the reference ratio imbalance matches the worker's ratio. That is, a worker may feel that she is working very hard, but may not feel unfairly treated as long as her comparison workers are also working very hard. Many workers are willing to work hard as long as the burden is shared. Equity theory helps to account for workers' feelings of mistreatment by highly paid managers.

## Environmental Theories of Motivation

Environmental theories of motivation are learning theories. Environmental theories of motivation describe how we acquire knowledge about our behavior. We learn by evaluating how our behavior is judged by other people in the environment. In this section we discuss two major environmental theories—reinforcement and social learning. Reinforcement theory states that we learn to express behavior that is rewarded and to avoid behavior that is punished. Hence, our behavior is influenced by its consequences, and we learn by the environment acting *directly* on us. Social learning theory informs us that we can also learn *indirectly* by observing the success or failures

**reference ratio** The ratio of a comparison between a person's outcome (rewards, recognition, pay) and inputs (time, effort, actual work performed).

**environmental theories** Learning theories that describe how we acquire knowledge about our behavior, specifically by evaluating how our behavior is judged by actors in the environment.

of others. When we observe the successful behavior of others, we attempt the same behavior in the hope of getting similar results. Likewise, when we observe unsuccessful behavior in another that results in a negative outcome, we avoid using the behavior that produced the negative outcome.

# Reinforcement Theory

Reinforcement theorists describe motivation largely in relation to external factors, and they suggest the conditions under which behavior is likely to be repeated. In reinforcement theory, the interpretation of motivation is different from content and process theories of motivation. Both process and content theories consider motivation a function of either internal needs or internal cognition. On the other hand, reinforcement theory (also called operant conditioning) characterizes motivation as largely determined by external factors. The consequence of our behavior determines whether the behavior will be repeated in the future. In essence, experience with past situations dictates or guides future behavior.

Noted psychologist B. F. Skinner stated that behavior is a function of its consequences.[14] Behaviors that have positive consequences are likely to be repeated, and those that have negative consequences are likely to be avoided in the future. According to reinforcement theory, workers are motivated by the consequences of their work behavior. In the process of experiencing rewards at work, workers often see a link between their own actions (i.e., their behaviors) and the reward (i.e., the consequences of their behavior). For example, a manager rewards workers at a plant that has reduced the number of accidents in the plant by holding a company-paid picnic for workers and their families.

The basis or method of distributing rewards or disincentives—and the nature of the rewards and disincentives themselves—profoundly influences behavior. Rewards may be made on a contingent or noncontingent basis. Contingent rewards are distributed based on a specific, preceding behavior. For example, a sales clerk may receive a free weekend trip for having the highest sales in her department for the preceding quarter. Noncontingent rewards are not linked to any specific behavior. For example, a paid holiday may be available to all staff regardless of their level of performance. A newly hired worker and a worker with twenty years of experience with the company receive the same reward.

Reinforcement theory deals with two types of behavior: desirable—which we want to increase, and undesirable—which we want to decrease. In the next section we will describe how reinforcement works in different situations.

**Increasing the Behavior** | Reinforcement is the process of using contingent rewards to increase future occurrences of a specific behavior. Reinforcement can take either of two forms—positive or negative. Positive reinforcement occurs when a positive consequence (reward) is applied to a desired behavior. Positive reinforcement increases the frequency of the particular behavior that it follows. *Positive* refers to the nature of the consequence; *reinforcement* refers to the strengthened likelihood of the subsequent behavior. For example, for each bag of fruit she picks, a fruit picker receives $2. Negative reinforcement occurs when an unpleasant consequence is withdrawn after the desired behavior occurs. For example, a manager stops criticizing an employee when he *achieves the daily production quota*. Both positive and negative reinforcement increase the likelihood that a desired behavior will occur.

**Decreasing the Behavior** | To decrease a current behavior, reinforcement theories suggest using either punishment or extinction. Punishment is the process of administering an undesirable consequence for an undesirable behavior. Although punishment holds many negative connotations for many people, it is a naturally occurring phenomenon in the learning process.[15] For example, a child who falls off a bicycle learns quickly to maintain

## KEY TERMS

**reinforcement theory**
Also called operant conditioning, a learning theory that characterizes motivation as largely determined by external factors, that is, the consequence of behavior (regardless of whether it is rewarded) determining whether the behavior is repeated in the future.

**operant conditioning**
*See* reinforcement theory.

**contingent rewards**
Rewards that are distributed based on a specific, preceding behavior; for example, a sales clerk receiving a free weekend trip for having the highest sales in her department for the preceding quarter.

**noncontingent rewards**
Rewards that are not linked to specific behavior; for example, a paid holiday for all staff regardless of their level of performance.

**reinforcement** Using contingent rewards to increase future occurrences of a specific behavior; can take two forms—positive or negative.

**positive reinforcement**
Reinforcement that occurs when a positive consequence (reward) is applied to a desired behavior; increases the frequency of the particular behavior that it follows.

**negative reinforcement**
Reinforcement that occurs when an unpleasant consequence is withdrawn after the desired behavior occurs.

**punishment** An undesirable consequence for an undesirable behavior, a naturally occurring phenomenon in the learning process.

balance. The famous hot stove rule suggests that being burned by a hot stove represents punishment at the most general level and in its most vivid form.[16] The hot stove rule suggests that nature is a good teacher; through it, we learn that punishment should be swift, intense, impersonal, and consistent, and it should provide an alternative.[17] Reduced to its basic components, punishment provides the recipient with useful information. As with all reinforcement, the objective is to associate the behavior with its consequence.

Although the term *punishment* is often objectionable, the concept is widely applicable to work settings. Punishment naturally occurs in all work settings. A worker drops a box on his big toe and breaks the toe. In the future, he'll either exercise greater care or risk more physical injury. Although few would disagree with the informational content in this example, it still doesn't fit our concept of punishment. We think of punishment as being yelled at or being passed over for promotion due to poor performance. But regardless of the form punishment takes, it is still the same process of applying an unpleasant consequence contingent upon the occurrence of an undesired behavior.

According to reinforcement theory, the other way of decreasing undesired behavior is through extinction (the process of nonreinforcement of a behavior). Or, more simply put, if the behavior is unrewarded, its occurrence will diminish over time. For example, an employee who tells off-color jokes at meetings could be rewarded for the behavior with laughter. By not laughing at the jokes (i.e., removing the reward), meeting attendees could eliminate the joke telling in the future.

Exhibit 12.6 illustrates the use of various reinforcement contingencies in increasing and decreasing desired and undesired behaviors.

To be effective, positive reinforcement, negative reinforcement, punishment, and extinction must be applied on a contingent basis. That is, the consequence of the behavior must be known by the worker prior to the expression of the behavior. Without this contingency, the behavior's consequence may actually reinforce a variety of behaviors, not all of them desirable. It's frequently necessary to use trial and error to determine if a consequence (i.e., possibly a reward) truly reinforces a target behavior.

The nature of the reward also helps to determine the efficacy of the reinforcement. Not all rewards produce a reinforcing effect. Some workers prefer some rewards that other workers may want to avoid. For example, one worker may want to work overtime hours to make extra income, whereas another worker may not want the additional income, given the work required. Thus,

**EXHIBIT 12.6**    **Contingencies of Reinforcement**

| | Contingencies | |
|---|---|---|
| | Applied | Withdrawn |
| Increase Desired Behavior | **Positive Reinforcement**<br><br>• Reward Applied | **Negative Reinforcement**<br><br>• Negative Consequence Withdrawn |
| Decrease Undesirable Behavior | **Punishment**<br><br>• Negative Consequence Applied | **Extinction**<br><br>• Reward Withdrawn |

"rewarding" overtime hours only to productive workers may punish rather than reinforce productivity.[18] For a reward to qualify as a reinforcer, the reward must increase the frequency of the worker's behavior. Managers use rewards in hopes of motivating employees and influencing them to perform better.

| **Managerial Applications of Reinforcement** | Several factors can influence the effectiveness of reinforcement. These principles help to ensure conditions of optimum reinforcement.

| *Immediate reinforcement.* Reinforcement should coincide as closely as is practical with the completion of the target behavior.

| *Reinforcement size.* The larger the reinforcement delivered after the occurrence of a target behavior, the greater effect the reinforcement will have on the frequency of the behavior in the future.

| *Relative reinforcement deprivation.* The more a person is deprived of the reinforcement, the greater the effect the reinforcement will have on the future occurrence of the target behavior.[19]

## | Social Learning Theory

Albert Bandura is the chief architect of social learning theory.[20] Discontent with the explanations offered by Skinner and others regarding human motivation, Bandura proposed that motivated behavior was a function of observing the success of other people and then doing what worked for them. He held that rather than being merely a function of environmental conditioning, learning was influenced by an individual's cognitive assessment of what behaviors were previously rewarded in the environment.

Exhibit 12.7 describes the social learning process. Step one is *attention,* during which another person is observed while successfully performing a behavior. Step two is *retention* of the behavioral response to memory. The observer remembers not only the specifics of the behavior but also its content. Step three is *reproduction* of the behavior exactly as it was committed to memory in the appropriate context or situation. Step four is *motivation* for the successful performance of the behavior. At this stage, the individual often administers a self-reward or is granted an external reward or recognition.

Social learning theory has many applications at work. Managers can use concepts of social learning theory to illustrate the behaviors they desire in all workers. For example, if punctuality is deemed important, managers might arrive early to work each day, signaling the importance of preparing for the day before the 8 o'clock shift begins. Similarly, the manager who pays brief visits to workers' cubicles or offices to discuss the daily schedule before a new shift starts shows through his actions that he arrives early to plan, and so should they.

We learn our work partly by watching others. In daily practice, workers observe the desired behaviors modeled by managers or successful colleagues. The modeled behaviors are those that management wants the workers to exhibit. For example, a manager always smiles and is polite and courteous to customers, or the quality work of a successful employee always seems to get noticed and rewarded by management.

In summary, then, both operant conditioning (reinforcement) and social learning theory are important explanations of human motivation. By understanding and using operant conditioning, a manager can create a work environment that automatically rewards certain behaviors (e.g., hard work) and discourages other behaviors (e.g., carelessness). Social learning theory broadens the context of learning to include the observation of other people's experiences in our own learning. In the following example, social learning theory is used to create a behavior, model the behavior, provide a

**KEY**TERMS

**social learning theory**
A learning theory proposing that motivated behavior is a function of observing the success of other people and then doing what worked for them; the influence on learning of an individual's cognitive assessment of what behaviors were previously rewarded in the environment.

EXHIBIT

**12.7**     **Bandura's Social Learning Theory**

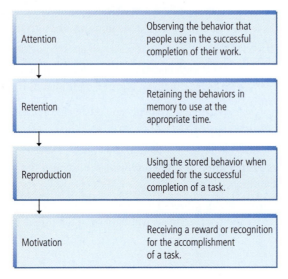

| Attention | Observing the behavior that people use in the successful completion of their work. |
| Retention | Retaining the behaviors in memory to use at the appropriate time. |
| Reproduction | Using the stored behavior when needed for the successful completion of a task. |
| Motivation | Receiving a reward or recognition for the accomplishment of a task. |

**Source:** Adapted from Albert Bandura. *Social Learning Theory* (Upper Saddle River, NJ: Prentice Hall, 1977).

context for workers to reproduce the behavior, and ultimately reward the workers for successfully reproducing the desired behavior.

At a large metropolitan hospital, the head nurse makes it clear to her department nurses that each of them should set goals for achieving daily, weekly, and monthly tasks. The head nurse follows suit; she always carries a daily planner and offers a planner to any nurse who wants one. At weekly meetings, the head nurse reviews progress from her planned activities and reports on her own degree of goal attainment. One by one, her nurses ask for planners; soon they begin exhibiting behavior similar to that of the head nurse. Over the course of a year, the head nurse finds that her nurses are 50 percent more productive, 20 percent more efficient, and report increased satisfaction with their work.

## Motivation and Reward

Although each motivation theory offers a different perspective on the nature of human motivation, one commonality across all motivation theories is the notion of reward. It's safe to say that reward is a central concept in most theories of motivation. As discussed, rewards can be intrinsic (self-administered) or extrinsic (externally-administered). Regardless of the type, managers need to know what employees value and be prepared to make those reward available contingent upon the degree of performance. Recall from Chapter 10, "Human Resource Management," that compensation comes in a variety of forms, including direct and indirect compensation. Managers also need to understand the intrinsically rewarding nature of certain jobs and the attraction in some people toward that type of work. Also, recall from Chapter 11, "Individual Behavior: Differences in Personality, Perception, and Attitudes," that some employees are highly equity sensitive, with reward seen as a central motivation for them to perform up to their potential. Managers often control the distribution of rewards large and small. Wise managers use the rewards at their disposal to create actions that result in the attainment of organizational goals.

# Goal Setting: An Applied Motivation Theory

One of the most widely researched theories of human behavior is goal-setting theory. Simply put, goal-setting theory states that people who set goals outperform those who don't set goals.[21] The organizational process of goal setting deals with (1) aligning personal and organizational goals and (2) rewarding goal attainment. Goal-setting principles are evident in such popular programs as management by objective (MBO) and self-management.

## Advantages of Goal Setting

Goals help workers to translate general intentions into a specific action. Goals, which we introduced in Chapter 5, "Decision Making," are targeted levels of performance set before doing the work. Goal-setting research emphasizes the role of conscious intentions in work.[22] That is, people with goals perform at higher levels than people without goals. Goals can help to:

- Direct attention and action
- Mobilize effort
- Create persistent behavior over time
- Lead to strategies for goal attainment.[23]

## Attributes of Effective Goals

In general, employees need to feel that working to achieve the goal is in their own best interest, not just the manager's interest. Employees also need support for their efforts, including time, tools, information, and other resources needed to do the job. Finally, employees must feel confident that their work will be rewarded.

Goal-setting theory defines goal acceptance as a psychological embracing of the goal as the worker's own aspiration; goal commitment is a behavioral follow-through, meaning persistent work effort to achieve the goal. Five goal attributes, which we discuss next, enhance the potential for goal acceptance and enduring goal commitment.[24]

| **Goal Specificity** | Specific goals are more effective than ambiguous (such as "do your best") goals. Statements of specific goals include four elements: action verb, outcome, deadline, and cost.[25] The verb (e.g., *increase, complete, reduce*) establishes the action to be followed. The outcome is expressed as a single measurable result (e.g., quarterly sales of $250,000; a completed report; increased hiring of minority job applicants). The deadline establishes the time (e.g., hour, day, or shift) when the goal should be achieved. The cost identifies the resources to be consumed in reaching the goal.

| **Goal Difficulty** | Difficult but attainable goals lead to higher performance than easy goals. A difficult but attainable goal is typically established based on relevant data, knowledge, and skills. If an employee is new and her skills are untested, she and her manager might use historical data from similar cases to assign a goal. Managers often establish an operational definition of a goal's ease or difficulty by looking at the worker's or team's prior performance record. In some cases, new tasks require employees to set a difficult goal without benefit of a historical baseline. For example, in designing the first personal digital assistant (PDA), Apple had no historical records to use as a baseline. Determining a challenging goal for completing the design required original, creative thinking.

| **Goal Feedback** | Feedback can occur at three levels: (1) in setting the goal ("What should I aim for?"), (2) in ongoing feedback after the goal is set and work commences ("How am I doing?"), and (3) in evaluating the final result ("How did I do?").

**goal-setting theory** A learning theory stating that people who set goals outperform those who do not.

**goals** Targeted levels of performance set before doing the work; can help to direct attention and action, mobilize effort, create persistent behavior over time, and lead to strategies for goal attainment.

**goal acceptance** The psychological embrace of the goal by the worker as his or her own aspiration.

**goal commitment** A worker's behavioral follow-through, a persistent work effort to achieve the goal.

In establishing an appropriate goal, the worker and manager need to exchange information on their aspirations, skills, schedules, and other work priorities. Ongoing feedback keeps the worker focused. Finally, a manager's feedback when a goal is met ("You met the goal under difficult circumstances. Great job!") mainztains the worker's faith in the goal-setting process.

| **Participating in Goal Setting** | Employees need to be involved in and have control over setting their own goals. Allowing workers to be involved in the goal-setting process encourages a higher degree of commitment to meeting those goals. Early research in goal setting emphasized assigned goals over worker participation.[26] But more recent research suggests that active employee participation in setting goals can be more effective. Employees can be involved in the goal-setting process to a greater or lesser extent, depending on their experience and skill. For inexperienced employees, management helps clarify task expectations by assigning goals based on relevant data and knowledge. These clarified task expectations are called *assigned goals*. For more experienced employees, the manager and the employee exchange information and jointly establish goals. This process produces *interactive or negotiated goals*. Finally, well-trained veteran workers can set their own goals with little or no input from the manager, resulting in *self-set goals*.

| **Competition** | Sometimes a worker's or work group's goal is defined in relation to exceeding the performance of another worker or work group. This form of competition within the firm can increase the goal's specificity and difficulty. Finding a relevant competitive standard can be the most productive way to facilitate performance initiated by goals.

However, competition also has its disadvantages. When one team's performance depends upon the performance of another team, cooperation rather than competition is necessary.

# Positive Assumptions About Employees' Work Ethic

As Douglas McGregor noted some thirty years ago, worker behavior is often a product of managerial assumptions, attitudes, and behavior toward the worker. Treat a worker with respect and dignity, and you engender trust and cooperation. If managers treat workers like dumb, replaceable machines, they should not be surprised when the workers behave according to their expectations. Conversely, if a manager treats employees as capable, ingenious, and able to develop innovative responses without guidance, these expectations may produce surprisingly positive results. This phenomenon is known as the Pygmalion effect (or self-fulfilling prophecy), whereby increasing a manager's expectations of subordinates' performance actually improves performance.[27]

Comparing the three United States auto producers (GM, Ford, and Daimler-Chrysler[28]) to the Japanese transplants, for example, Mitsubishi Motors North America (MMNA) in Illinois and NUMMI in California, on the number of work rules contained in each contract, we find some interesting facts. Work rules limit worker autonomy and discretion. Both autonomy and discretion can be important ways of involving workers in improving quality. We find the United States auto producers are far more rule-bound and oriented toward Theory X management. With fewer rules and limits on employee autonomy, the transplants from Japan follow the Theory Y approach more closely. Organizational goals can best be attained by involving all members of the organization; this is achieved only when management actively encourages greater worker participation in decision making.[29]

A participative management frames its core question about how to motivate employees something like this: How do we enable workers to feel a natural sense of pride in their work and to be self-motivated? This approach to motivation is based on the assumption that employees inherently want to do a good job. In this view, management sees employees as assets, not liabilities. Negative assumptions about employees' desire to do a good job ("if you don't watch them every minute, they're sure to slack off") are seen as counterproductive. These negative assumptions can lead to a system in which employees are motivated by fear.

## Motivation

In this chapter, we have traced the development of a theoretical basis for work motivation. Content, process, and environmental theories of motivation are useful in understanding worker behavior. To be effective in the long run, however, managers must do more than memorize theory. With an understanding of motivation theory, managers can more easily link organizational goals to individual needs. By asking the simple question, "What does this worker want from the job?" managers can use applied motivational concepts such as goal setting to meet both individual needs and organizational goals.

Motivating employees is a challenge to managers. Workers are often members of teams, empowered to make decisions that were once the domain of managers. In this environment, the manager's role is not an autocratic "enforcer," but rather a participative "coach" who gives workers the freedom to express themselves. In fact, at many companies, a new breed of manager is responding to the needs of the contemporary workforce. Knowing what motivates and when to motivate means that these managers tend to coach rather than command, prod rather than push, and empower rather than order.[30] Persuasion, influence, and altruistic appeals, not authority and power, are the tools managers use to get things done.

Worker participation in decisions made in an organization can have a positive impact on their motivation. In the workplace of tomorrow, workers will not only be given interesting tasks, but increasingly participate in decisions about how to perform them. This approach results in high intrinsic motivation; it inspires people to do high-quality work because it satisfies their need to feel good about the work for which they are responsible. In an organizational context, need satisfaction is sometimes monetary, but most often it deals with achievement. Organizations allow people to express themselves by offering the opportunity to fulfill of a wide range of human needs.

## Discussion Questions

1. Describe the process of motivation.

2. Describe the expectancy theory of motivation. Do you believe that expectancy theory accurately reflects the process of individual motivation?

3. What are the four reinforcement strategies that can be used to increase desirable behavior or to decrease undesirable behavior? Define, describe, and discuss each reinforcement strategy.

## Video Case

### P.F. Chang's Employees Taste the Fruits of Motivation

What motivates you? Do you run every morning to get fit, lose weight, or slide into that special pair of jeans? Do you study because you love what you are learning, or because you want good grades? Do you work every weekend for money to pay for college or for money to eat out with your friends? All of these motives are real and legitimate—they are what drive you to do the things you do. The same is true for workers everywhere, including P.F. Chang's bistros. It's easy to see what motivates managers and executives at P.F. Chang's: they want customers to love the food and atmosphere, they want their business to succeed and grow, and they want to earn a good living in return for their investment and hard work. "We are truly glad you are here," says P.F. Chang's motto, "and we will do everything possible to make you want to come back again." This is the biggest motivation of all—to have customers come back.

But what motivates employees at P.F. Chang's—the wait staff, bartenders, hosts, chefs and kitchen crew, bus boys and dishwashers? Historically, the restaurant industry has relied on a rigid hierarchy, with managers meting out punishments and rewards to hourly workers. The result has been a low degree of job satisfaction and a high degree of turnover. There might be some use of job rotation or job enlargement, but it is not an industry that is generally known for its embrace of a new workplace. P.F. Chang's, however, is different—and some may argue that the way its workers are treated is a major factor in the company's success.

Throughout the firm, Chairman and CEO Rick Federico introduced the concept of partnerships, rather than layers of management. Because they are empowered to hire their own team of workers, from the kitchen to the dining room, operating partners have a major stake in their restaurant's success. "Managers have a passion for the business," explains operating partner Jennifer Olson Hicks, "and we instill that in our employees." Hicks also notes that it is important for managers to be wherever they are needed in the restaurant—whether it is hosting, taking orders, or washing dishes. Setting this kind of example of commitment to the success of the organization can be a powerful motivator to employees.

All of P.F. Chang's restaurant workers are trained to understand more than just their jobs. They know the food and the way it is prepared; they know the wine list; they know what their guests want and how to provide it for them; and they know how P.F. Chang's operates as a company. In addition, the workers themselves are empowered to do just about whatever it takes to satisfy their customers. For example, wait staff are trained to guide new visitors through the Asian menu—termed the "limo ride" in company lingo—so they can select the food they will enjoy. Waiters don't just take orders, they provide a service through their knowledge of the menu, the food, and its preparation. In the kitchen, although workers may have specific jobs, ranging from line cook to sous chef, all employees understand the total picture. "Everyone knows what's going on in the kitchen," explains Paul Muller, corporate executive chef. He likens the performance of the kitchen staff to "a great baseball team."

P.F. Chang's also motivates by providing opportunity for advancement. Its continued growth "enables us to promote from within and offer members of our team the opportunity to enter management and further develop their business skills," notes CEO Federico. Finally, the firm offers a generous array of benefits, ranging from meal discounts to bonus plans to various retirement savings plans. P.F. Chang's sounds like a great place to eat—and an even better place to work.

### Questions

1. P.F. Chang's offers a menu of extrinsic rewards to its workers. What are some of the intrinsic rewards?

2. In what ways might managers at P.F. Chang's use positive reinforcement for their kitchen crew or wait staff?

3. In what ways can P.F. Chang's employees use the four elements of empowerment to achieve the highest level of performance in their jobs?

Sources: Company training materials and company web site, http://www.pfchangs.com, accessed September 8, 2004; Charles Bernstein, "Chief Execution Officer," *Chain Leader* (September 2004): 62–68; "Work Force Still Top Concern for CEOs," *The Phoenix Business Journal* (May 24, 2004): http://phoenix.bizjournals.com.

## BizFlix

### For Love of the Game

Billy Chapel (Kevin Costner), a 20-year veteran pitcher with the Detroit Tigers, learns just before the season's last game that the team's new owners want to trade him. He also learns that his partner Jane Aubrey (Kelly Preston) intends to leave him. Faced with these daunting blows, Chapel wants to pitch a perfect final game. Director Sam Raimi's love of baseball shines through in some striking visual effects.

This scene is a slightly edited version of the "Just Throw" sequence, which begins the film's exciting closing scenes in which Chapel pitches his last game. In this scene, the Tigers' catcher Gus Sinski (John C. Reilly) comes out to the pitching mound to talk to Billy.

Questions

1. What is Billy Chapel's level of esteem needs at this point in the game?

2. Do you expect Gus Sinski's talk to have any effect on Chapel? If it will, what will be the effect?

3. What rewards potentially exist for Billy Chapel? Remember, this is the last baseball game of his career.

## Suggested Reading

Conger, Jay A., "The Necessary Art of Persuasion." *Harvard Business Review* (May–June 1998).

Kerr, Steven, *Ultimate Rewards: What Really Motivates People to Achieve?* (Cambridge, MA: Harvard University Press, 1997).

Maccoby, Michael, *Why Work?—Motivating the New Workforce* (Alexandria, VA: Miles River Press, 1995).

Nicholson Nigel, "How to Motivate Your Problem People," *Harvard Business Review* (January, 2003) Reprint Number, R0301D.

## Endnotes

1. E. L. Thorndike, *Animal Intelligence* (New York: Macmillan, 1911), 244.

2. Craig Pinder, *Work Motivation in Organizational Behavior* (Upper Saddle River, NJ: Prentice-Hall, 1998), 11.

3. Douglas McGregor, *The Human Side of Enterprise* (New York: McGraw-Hill, 1960), 33–58.

4. Lyman W. Porter and Edward Lawler, *Managerial Attitudes and Performance* (Burr Ridge, IL: Irwin, 1968), 17.

5. Abraham H. Maslow, *Motivation and Personality* (New York: Harper & Row, 1954).

6. Clayton Alderfer, *Existence, Relatedness, and Growth: Human Needs in Organizational Settings* (New York: Free Press, 1972).

7. Frederick Herzberg, Bernard Mausner, and Barbara Bloch Snyderman, *The Motivation to Work* (New York: Wiley, 1959).

8. See Robert J. House and Lawrence A. Wigdor, "Herzberg's Dual-Factor Theory of Job Satisfaction and Motivation: A Review of the Empirical Evidence and a Criticism," *Personnel Psychology* 20 (Winter 1967): 369–389. Also see Joseph Schneider and Edwin A. Locke, "A Critique of Herzberg's Classification System and a Suggested Revision," *Organizational Behavior and Human Performance* 6 (1971): 441–458.

9. David C. McClelland, *The Achieving Society* (Princeton, NJ: Van Nostrand, 1963).

10. R. Murray, *Thematic Apperception Test Pictures and Manual* (Cambridge, MA: Harvard University Press, 1943).

11. Victor H. Vroom, *Work and Motivation* (New York: Wiley, 1964).

12. Hugh J. Arnold, "A Test of the Multiplicative Hypothesis of Expectancy—Valence Theories of Work Motivation," *Academy of Management Journal* (March 1981): 128–141.

13. J. Stacy Adams, "Inequity in Social Exchange," in *Advances in Experimental Social Psychology*, vol. 2, ed. L. Berkowitz (New York: Academic Press, 1965).

14. B. F. Skinner, *Contingencies of Reinforcement: A Theoretical Analysis* (New York: Appleton-Century-Crofts, 1969).

15. Albert Bandura, *Principles of Behavior Modification* (New York: Holt, Rinehart and Winston, 1969).

16. G. Strauss and L. Sayles, *Personnel: The Human Problems of Management* (Englewood Cliffs, NJ: Prentice Hall, 1967).

17. R. D. Arvey and J. M. Ivancevich, "Punishment in Organizations: A Review, Propositions, and Research Suggestions," *Academy of Management Review* 5 (1980): 123–132.

18. M. E. Schnake and M. P. Dumler, "Some Unconventional Thoughts on Punishment: Reward as Punishment and Punishment as Reward," *Journal of Social Behavior and Personality* 3 (1989): 89–107.

19. Ibid.

20. Albert Bandura, *Social Learning Theory* (Englewood Cliffs, NJ: Prentice-Hall, 1977).

21. Edwin A. Locke and Gary P. Latham, *A Theory of Goal Setting and Task Performance* (Englewood Cliffs, NJ: Prentice Hall, 1990).

22. E. A. Locke and G. P. Latham, *Goal Setting: A Motivational Technique That Works* (Englewood Cliffs, NJ: Prentice-Hall, 1984).

23. E. A. Locke, K. M. Shaw, L. M. Saari, and G. P. Latham, "Goal Setting and Task Performance: 1969–1980," *Psychological Bulletin* 90 (1981): 125–152.

24. J. R. Hollenbeck and H. J. Klein, "Goal Commitment and the Goal-Setting Process: Problems, Prospects, and Proposals for Future Research," *Journal of Applied Psychology* 72 (1987): 212–220; J. R. Hollenbeck, J. R. Williams, and H. R. Klein, "An Empirical Examination of the Antecedents of Commitment to Difficult Goals," *Journal of Applied Psychology* 74 (1989): 18–23.

25. J. M. Ivancevich and M. T. Matteson, *Organizational Behavior and Management* (Burr Ridge, IL: BPI/Irwin, 1990), 164–166.

26. G. P. Latham and G. A. Yukl, "A Review of Research on the Application of Goal Setting in Organizations," *Academy of Management Journal* 18 (1975): 824–845.

27. Helen Rheem, "Effective Leadership: The Pygmalion Effect," *Harvard Business Review* (May–June 1995): 146.

28. Daimler-Chrysler, AG is a German-owned company.

29. Sandra Rothenberg, "Knowledge Content and Worker Participation in Environmental Management at NUMMI." Journal of Management Studies, Vol. 40 (November 2003): 1783–1802.

30. Geoffrey Brewer, "The New Managers," *Incentive* (March 1995): 30–35.

# 13

# LEADERSHIP

It seems safe to say that, without someone taking charge (a leader), very little planning of purposeful action, mobilizing of resources, and motivating of organizational members would be accomplished. Make no mistake—leadership is a prime component of effective organizations; yet regrettably, leadership is often elusive. Some people believe that leadership training can enhance leadership skills in virtually anyone; still others believe that leadership is a trait or a personality dimension, that is, some people have it and others do not. What is leadership? What behaviors do leaders exhibit? What skills are necessary to become an effective leader? How does a leader differ from a manager? To better understand the concept of leadership, we address all of these questions— and possibly a few more—in this chapter. We look at related topics such as followers, the context of leaders, and power and leadership. Then we delve into the major theories of leadership, to which we devote most of our energies. An amazing array of research challenges managers to think about how they lead along a variety of insightful dimensions. We also look at possible substitutes for leadership and the role that emotional intelligence has in effecting successful leadership. Last, we analyze the concept of self-leadership, which is increasingly viewed as indispensable to organizational and personal advancement.

## What Is Leadership?

We begin by answering the question, "What is leadership?" Most scholars agree that leadership is creating a vision of the future for an organization, but leadership is also about the relationship between the *leader* and *followers,* and the *situation* in which the leadership occurs. First and foremost, leadership creates a plausible vision of the future for employees and others. The vision must be general enough to allow for change, yet specific enough to guide daily activities. Leadership further defines vision in relation to future goal attainment. For a vision to become reality, everyone in an organization must believe it and act in ways that will make the vision a reality. Just like pouring a foundation for a building signifies the beginning of a new structure, the periodic attainment of goals marks progress toward reaching a vision. Effective leadership focuses human effort and physical resources on the attainment of goals. All organizational stakeholders are influenced in one manner or another by leadership. Another aspect of leadership is the art of motivating and persuading others to follow a course of action (a plan). The leader oversees the development of strategies to achieve this end. An effective leader matches environmental opportunities with an organization's core competencies as well as with the skills of its employees. Ultimately, successful leaders build organizations that meet the needs of multiple stakeholders.

Our understanding of effective leadership has evolved and matured considerably over the years. As a historical picture of leadership, some people may think of World War II Army General George Patton barking commands from a tank turret as the troops surround him, eagerly awaiting orders. Today's generation will recall from the Hurricane Katrina evacuation the leadership of Army Lieutenant General Russel Honore, aptly nicknamed the "Rajin Cajun," barking out commands from a New Orleans street intersection, making decisions on the fly, and instilling in people a feeling of safety and control. From the business world, Microsoft's Bill Gates recently announced that he will give away much of his personal fortune to the Bill and Melinda Gates Foundation. (In 2006 the endowment was worth $27 billion.) His foundation will distribute money to educational institutions and social service organizations that assist less fortunate people around the world. During the same week, Warren Buffett agreed to donate 10 million shares of Berkshire-Hathaway stock worth $30 billion dollars to the Bill and Melinda Gates foundation. These two leaders have been successful in different industries. Their success as industry leaders has shaped their belief that they should use their extraordinary wealth for the betterment of mankind. By combining their resources, they can have a tremendous impact on the lives of the most disaffected in society. These two men have a broad vision of effective leadership that impacts people far removed from the organization.

But as society, people, and situations change, the actions of leaders must also change. Gone are the days of blind obedience to autocratic leaders; contemporary leaders rely on greater employee participation and self-leadership. Our review in this chapter describes the journey from autocratic to more participative and democratic styles of leadership. In the end, the goal of effective leadership is the efficient production of a high-quality product or service, creating value for the customer and a financial return for stockholders or owners.

Traditional models of leadership have been tested, and many doubts have been raised about their capacity to produce a competitive workforce for the twenty-first century. The trend in leadership styles is toward more participative leadership and away from the dogmatic, authoritative approaches of yesteryear. Because leaders have always been expected to be able to both manage and anticipate change, most models of leadership require the effective leader to have a vision. A vision is a clear sense of an organization's future. Without vision, leaders have nowhere to lead workers. Without an understanding of the global demands of the market, leaders are not likely to be successful. With this in mind we will begin with a brief and clear definition of leadership. Leadership is defined as the process of influencing other people to attain organizational goals.[1] Further, understanding leadership involves three components—the leader, the subordinate (follower), and the situation.[2] The interaction among the three determines the form of the leadership style as well as the relationship between the leader and each subordinate.

## Role of the Leader

Are leaders and managers different? Noted Harvard psychologist Abraham Zaleznick thinks so.[3] He believes managers focus on demands and constraints of the moment, rather than on more far-reaching matters. Unlike leaders, managers must deal with internal daily production concerns. Often managers seem more concerned with "getting things done" than with "getting the right things done." At the worst, managing is reduced to little more than people processing and product massaging. In the process, managers sometimes show little concern for the customer or the product's final use. This preoccupation with what Zaleznick calls *process* orientation leads to mediocrity. For the manager, the goal becomes preserving the status quo.

Zaleznick believes that, unlike managers, leaders are often bored with routine; or, as Tom Peters[4] puts it, they "thrive on chaos" and seek innovative and novel solutions. Rather than being preoccupied with process, the leader is concerned with substance. *Substance* is the true purpose of the work. For example, if quality is paramount, the leader must focus energy on creating quality. For a leader, substance is everything. The manager asks: "What is the best way to consistently maintain quality and meet production targets?" The leader asks an entirely different question: "For a particular product, what is quality—and how will the definition change in the future?" The difference between managers and leaders is based upon what they do. Managers deal with the pressures of the moment; they are concerned with the process surrounding the work flow. The leader is concerned with providing meaning or purpose in work for employees as well as with creating meaning in the product for customers.

Lee Iacocca's transformation of Chrysler is an example of how a leader can create vision and meaning for both workers and customers. Through Iacocca's leadership, Chrysler workers believed that they were part of the solution to problems facing the auto industry. They were creating the new Chrysler. Iacocca's leadership fostered two innovations that formed the organizational nucleus of the new Chrysler: the K-Car and the Minivan. The K-body design, or simply the K-Car as it was known at the time, was a revolutionary concept. The K-Car was a single platform design with one standard power train over which different body styles were mated, forming a standard base (low cost) with multibody fabrication that offered the consumer functionality (two doors, four doors, station wagon). The minivan is a transportation icon today, but it was not always so. The minivan was an innovative replacement for the gas-guzzling V8 station wagon. Iacocca believed that a family-sized vehicle that offered versatility and fuel efficiency was needed by consumers. He was right! Remember, at the time (early 1980s) there was no minivan—Iacocca and Chrysler created the concept and brought it to market. During this process, Iacocca had to persuade the government, stockholders, and employees that his vision for Chrysler would benefit all members of the Chrysler family and possibly even society in the long run. What followed is history—sales of the industry's first minivan went through the roof, and Iacocca brought his company back from the brink of bankruptcy. Certainly, Chrysler's customers believed that the minivan was a new alternative to the gas-guzzling station wagon. The fuel efficient minivan was a spacious people-mover the fit the needs of growing families and was gentle on the environment. Iacocca's strategic vision of new products, new markets, and new ways of creating quality and value for the consumer became a reality. Workers produced a better, higher-quality product—not just because of technology, but because they believed they could. As noted, the results were dramatically increased customer demand and profitability.

Leadership is both an individual property and a process. As an individual property, leadership is a combination of personal attributes and abilities such as vision, energy, and knowledge. As a process, leadership is the individual's ability to create a shared vision of the future and direct individual efforts at work toward the vision. Creating a shared vision requires the leader to set goals, motivate employees, and establish a supportive and productive culture in the organization. Indeed, it's often difficult to separate the individual from the process. This is because the leadership process is an extension of the leader's personality and ideas. Collectively then, individual leadership properties and the leadership process influence employee behavior.

## Followers

Leadership is the process of influencing followers. Followers are each unique with different motivations, skills, abilities, interests, experiences, and attitudes. Leaders are responsible for goal attainment. Followers are driven by their own motivations, interests, and goals. The role of the leader is to channel individual self-interest toward the attainment of organizational goals. Leaders use persuasion and other forms of influence to redirect follower's self-interest toward organizational goal attainment by exchanging organizational resources—challenging work, economic reward, status, and security—for follower compliance. Thus, effective leaders influence followers with organizational resources and their personality, often expressing personal qualities of humility, persuasion, and determination to secure compliance.[5] Leadership occurs when a follower willingly defers to a leader's influence. To gain this acquiescence, effective leaders instill trust and confidence in their followers. Effective followers support the leader by recognizing their own role in the process of being led or guided toward goal attainment. Further, organizations can develop more effective followers by creating organizational systems that encourage desirable follower behaviors. Effective followers are not passive; they do not wait to be told where to go and what to do. As author Robert Kelley notes, effective followers are not only active and technically competent, but they also understand their role in the organization. Through reflection, personal humility, and their vision of the future, effective leaders know their value to the organization and how to use their knowledge to attain organizational goals. Here are some other qualities of effective followers:[6]

| Capable of self-management

| Committed to the organization's purpose, principles, and goals

| Willing to increase their competence and skills and apply them to organizational outcomes

| Courageous, honest, and credible

What can organizations do to develop better followers? Kelly offers this advice:

| Redefine the role of the leader and the follower.

| Hone effective followership skills.

| Use the performance evaluation process and feedback to shape behavior.

| Use the organization structure to encourage effective followership.

## The Situation

The situation is the context in which leadership occurs. Often, it is the situation that determines how successful a leader can influence and persuade subordinates. When the leader is not in a good position to influence an employee, the employee might not be very responsive to influence attempts. For example, tough economic times could mean no raises or promotions. This situation limits the leader's ability to use financial rewards as a source of employee motivation. In other situations, leaders can be very effective with little or no direct intervention. Such is the case in self-leadership contexts, or in situations that encourage greater job involvement through worker autonomy. Autonomy allows the worker greater decision-making latitude. However, worker autonomy is not without limits. For example, a retail clerk might be given greater decision-making autonomy to appease a disgruntled customer. The clerk can offer the customer one of three options: an exchange, the refund purchase price, or a new product—no other options are possible. Also, the manager knows what the decision-making options are prior to granting the increase in autonomy, thus limiting the sales clerk's range of autonomy. The leadership substitute facilitates leadership without active intervention by the leader. The net result is a situation in which leadership occurs easily and naturally as a consequence of the work context.

## Power and Leadership

Influencing the behavior of others is at the core of leadership. To accomplish this, leaders use their power, which is, simply, the ability to get people to do something they otherwise would not do.[7] Managers usually have several sources of power at their disposal. The following list summarizes the various sources of power within organizations.[8] For examples of how leaders use each type of power, and why employees respond to different types of power, see Exhibit 13.1.

| Reward power is the manager's ability to allocate organizational resources in exchange for cooperation. This is probably the most widely used form of power. Rewards controlled by managers include pay raises, promotions, bonuses, and recognition.

| Coercive power, sometimes called *punishment power,* is the opposite of reward power. Coercive power is the manager's ability to apply penalties when an employee fails to

EXHIBIT

**13.1**    **Why Do Employees Respond to Different Types of Power?**

| Type of Power | Leader Action | Reason for Employee Response |
|---|---|---|
| Reward | Provides money or psychological rewards | Seeks a material reward or a feeling of job satisfaction |
| Coercive | Threatens or forces | Avoids physical force or discipline |
| Expert | Has knowledge of the situation or task | Believes that another person knows more than they know |
| Referent | Uses personal attractiveness to gain support | Has emotional attachment to the leader's beliefs |
| Personal | Uses unique combination of expert and referent power | Complies because of being influenced by leader's personal behavior |

cooperate. For example, an employee who exhibits inappropriate behavior or violates company policy might be given a below-average performance evaluation or even be passed over for promotion. But punishment power can generate fear and distrust among employees. In some situations, coercive power can be effective, but the benefits of punishment should outweigh its negative consequences before it is used to alter an employee's behavior.

| **Expert power** is based on an individual's technical or expert knowledge about a particular area. Expertise might be in the form of experience, information, or advanced education. Special knowledge allows an individual to persuade others to do as she wishes. The advertising executive who has developed many successful campaigns is sought after for advice and so has expert power.

| **Referent power** arises from an individual's personal characteristics that are esteemed by others. Referent power stimulates imitation and loyalty. Thus people we admire have referent power. When someone we admire asks us to do something, we are more inclined to do it than if someone we do not admire makes the request. We also emulate the admired person's behavior in the hope that by doing so, we will be as successful as he or she is.

| **Personal power** consists of either expert or referent power, or a combination of both. A sense of personal power comes from the belief that we can reach our goals in our own way; a sense of personal power is communicated by developing authority, accessibility, assertiveness, a positive image, and solid communications skills.[9]

**KEY** TERMS

**expert power** A type of power that is based on an individual's technical or expert knowledge about a particular area in the form of experience, information, or advanced education.

**referent power** A type of power arising from an individual's personal characteristics that are esteemed by others; stimulates imitation and loyalty.

**personal power** A type of power that consists of expert power, referent power, or a combination of both.

# | Authority

Whereas power is a personal quality, authority is granted by membership in the organization and is generally related to one's position or job. For example, by virtue of their position, managers have the decision-making authority to buy office furniture. Thus, anyone in their position can make the decision (i.e., has the authority) to buy office furniture. However, only a powerful manager can buy ugly furniture without much opposition from employees. A less powerful manager might not be able to make the same decision without meeting considerable opposition.

# | Theories of Leadership

Leadership is one of the most studied functions of management. Leadership defines that relationship between the leader and people, some of whom are inside the organization (employees), and others of whom are outside constituents. Regardless of which group is being lead, it is the leader who influences people to take actions that support organizational goal attainment.

Leadership research is voluminous, describing a variety of leadership theories, definitions, and findings. Many of these theories focus on understanding leader effectiveness. Leadership theories have evolved over time to help us understand the relationship between the leader, follower, and the situation. The evolution of leadership theory can be understood by examining three classes of theories: trait, behavioral, and contingency. Historically, trait theory and behavioral theory suggested that one leadership style was effective in virtually all situations. The characteristics of the situation or the follower were not taken into consideration. Trait and behavioral theories helped define leadership as personal characteristics and behaviors of the leader, yet they were incomplete explanations of leader effectiveness.

The trait theory of leadership, the first attempt to systematically describe effective leaders, focused on individual traits, such as a physical or personality attribute of the leader. Which traits were associated with effective leadership? The answer was debatable and depended upon on which researcher you wanted to believe, and thus the list of leader traits seemed endless. For this reason, while interesting, trait theory provided little predictive power when searching for the illusive leaders among us.

Lack of predictive power of trait theory shifted the research focus from traits to behaviors. Are particular leader behaviors associated with greater productivity, performance, or satisfaction? Early research was promising. Leader traits were an ascribed condition; all management could do is hire people with the desired trait (selection). Behaviors were different; people often changed their behavior from one situation to the next. Leader behavior theory created an opportunity for greater precision in leading and training future leaders. The behavioral theory of leadership focused on two types of leader behaviors: (1) those that emphasized the task accomplishment, and (2) those that showed concern for worker feelings. Effective leaders were thought to exhibit both behaviors, suggesting that these behaviors would be effective in all situations. In essence, behavioral theories failed to take into consideration how the unique issues of a situation affect leadership style.

Contingency theories of leadership were the first class of leadership theories to take into consideration contingencies of the situation or the follower. Contingency leadership models state that the effective leader's behavioral style is contingent on the situation. Contingency theorists make different assumptions about people's behavior. Some believe that people have a favored behavioral predisposition that they express in all situations. Other contingency theorists believe that leader's change their behavior to fit the characteristics of the situation. For example, a manager who is also a parent switches his behavioral response depending on whether he is talking to a subordinate or his child.

Subsequent leadership theorists have sought alternative explanations for effective leadership, including visionary leadership and substitutes for leadership.

## Trait Theory of Leadership

Today we tend to notice effective leaders—Bill Gates at Microsoft, Peg Whitman at eBay, Larry Ellison of Oracle, and Anita Roddick at The Body Shop—and ask what personal characteristics make them effective. This question is at the root of the trait theory of leadership, which as described earlier identifies effective leaders based on certain physical and psychological attributes (e.g., intelligence, height, articulateness). Trait-based leadership focuses on the traits of those who have emerged or assumed power as the leader and on the traits of those leaders believed to be effective. For example, Edwin Ghiselli found that among other traits, leader initiative, self-assurance, decisiveness, and maturity are important for leader success.[10] Exhibit 13.2 is a summary of some other common leadership traits.

Trait theory was an early attempt to find those elusive qualities of the individual that are necessary for effective leadership. Researchers identified individual traits such as personality, skills, and physical characteristics. These early studies focused on the idea that effective

EXHIBIT 13.2

**Some Common Leadership Traits**

| Capacity | Intelligence, alertness, originality, and judgment |
|---|---|
| Achievement | Knowledge, accomplishments, and scholarship |
| Responsibility | Dependability, initiative, persistence, and aggressiveness |
| Participation | Activity, sociability, cooperation, and adaptability |
| Status | Popularity, and social status |

**Source:** Adapted from Bernard Bass, *Stogdill's Handbook of Leadership*, revised and expanded ed. (New York: Free Press, 1981), 66.

leadership was a naturally occurring phenomenon among people. The question was, if certain traits could be identified in individuals, then could organizations more efficiently select people with high leadership potential? In response to the often conflicting research results and a lack of clear support for trait theory, psychologist Ralph Stogdill[11] reviewed the findings of trait theory research from 1904 to 1947. He concluded that something other than traits worked to determine leader effectiveness. Traits did not appear to transfer well from one situation to another. In other words, a leader might be successful in one situation but not in another; finding traits did not seem to be the answer. As a result of the work of Stogdill and other leadership researchers, the focus of leadership effectiveness shifted from a quest for universal traits toward understanding situational requirements. However, it is still a widely held belief that effective leaders share certain common traits but that these traits alone do not explain why these leaders are effective.

Trait theory constitutes an important yet incomplete approach to leadership. Although supporters of trait theory were unsuccessful in explaining leader effectiveness, it is important to recognize that individual qualities are still important. The lesson from trait theory is that such qualities are not the exclusive source of leader effectiveness; rather, individual characteristics, the situation, and leader behaviors are all contributors. Clearly, not all effective leaders are tall—nor are they all exceptionally smart. Further, serious cultural differences exist; attributes seen as positive in some cultures are seen as negative in others. For example, American leadership practices have tended to endorse direct, forceful leaders. But not all successful leaders are dominating, extroverted, or self-confident. The trait approach is a simple—perhaps too simple—method of trying to identify or predict effective leadership. Yet, at the same time, it presents an appealing potential explanation for the effectiveness of people like Sam Walton and Lee Iacocca.

A disadvantage of trait theory is that it generally ignores the workers. Lists of traits also fail to give weight to the relative importance of the many possible traits. For example, is decisiveness more important than intelligence? In addition, due to their focus on small groups of leaders, many trait studies had limited ability to generalize, especially across cultures and countries. Most of all, trait theory studies were inconsistent in their findings and in their value to management. Trait theory does suggest that some value can be found in giving attention to both the task and the workers. The deficiency of trait theory in explaining significant variance in leadership effectiveness has led to the behavioral models of leadership. The following Management Highlight presents a contemporary perspective on gender differences of leaders.

## Behavioral Theory of Leadership

As research shifted away from the idea that leaders are endowed with certain characteristics, it moved toward the notion that different leaders have or could develop distinct leadership styles. As explained earlier, this approach, known as the behavioral style, defines leader effectiveness based on *leader behaviors*—what the leader does rather than which traits the leader has. Researchers have identified specific behavioral styles, which we examine next.

## DO MEN AND WOMEN HAVE DIFFERENT LEADERSHIP TRAITS?

Though the subject of men's and women's leadership traits has been debated a great deal, and with mixed opinions, author Judy Rosener has identified certain leadership style differences. She has found that through socialization, men and women are taught differently. Thus, although both men and women both make good—and bad—leaders, understanding the different leadership styles they use is important. One caveat is in order: the following characteristics should be considered suggestive rather than definitive, because they apply in some cases and not in others. The most effective leader will combine the positive traits of both men and women and use them appropriately.

**Characteristics Attributed to Men.**

- *Lead by command and control*—This works best in the military but has drawbacks when managing across gender lines.

- *Encourage rewards for services rendered*—This is the traditional reward system, much like the old barter system. Creating more flexibility in what an organization rewards is very important in helping a diverse group of workers to find success.

- *Rely on positional power*—Because males have held many of the power positions, it is not surprising that they derive power from their position.

- *Follow a hierarchical structure*—Historically, leaders have relied on lines of authority in getting the job done. As TQM has gained popularity, the end result is a flatter organization, and following a hierarchical structure might become more difficult.

- *Take action*—Aggressive, take-charge managers have succeeded in the past, and they will succeed in the future, though an overly aggressive stance turns workers off.

- *Think analytically*—Leaders with this trait have a great track record, especially when combined with intuitive thinking.

**Characteristics Attributed to Women.**

- *Share power and information*—Power, to some extent, stems from position and information and can be used to influence others. Women are skilled at maintaining power through relationships and are more willing to share power than men.

- *Enhance self-worth of others*—Female leaders tend to build their coworkers' esteem. This trait builds employee commitment and is essential in managing a diverse group.

- *Encourage participation*—This is a powerful and important characteristic of a leader. Employees feel motivated when they know they are part of the organization and that their opinions count.

- *Get others excited about their work*—Female leaders place great emphasis on process as well as product; they want to enjoy the journey. This trait is useful because it helps employees find intrinsic value in their work.

Source: Adapted from Judy B. Rosener, "The Valued Ways Men and Women Lead," *Human Resources* (June 1991):149; Judy B. Rosener, "Ways Women Lead," *Harvard Business Review* (November–December 1990): 119–125; and Lee Gardenswartz and Anita Rowe, *Managing Diversity* (Burr Ridge, IL: Business One Irwin, 1993), 356–361.

| **Origin of Leader Behavior Model** | In the leader behavioral model, effective leaders focus not only on the work, but also on workers' attitudes and expectations. A task-oriented behavioral style consists of behaviors such as setting goals, giving directions, supervising worker performance, and applauding good work. Beginning with scientific management, regular attention has been given to the leader's role and responsibility for task accomplishment. But as we learned from the human relations movement, focusing attention on task completion alone was insufficient. Workers not only required specific direction, but they also had personal and social needs that managers should consider if they hoped to

attain optimal performance from the worker. A relationship-oriented behavioral style emphasizes individual needs, showing empathy for worker needs and feelings, being supportive of group needs, establishing trusting relationships with workers, and allowing workers to participate in work-related decisions. It allows compassion, and recognizes that each individual employee is a human being, not a production machine. Thus, the leader behavior model recognized that both behaviors were important, but the quest for the effective leader must somehow reconcile these disparate behaviors. Two famous research programs, one at the University of Michigan and the other at the Ohio State University, began the study of the relationship between leader behaviors and work group performance.

| **Michigan Leadership Studies** | Studies conducted by the Social Science Research Center at the University of Michigan focused on identifying and measuring behaviors of effective leaders. This early work by Rensis Likert and his colleagues identified two important leader behaviors: job-centered and employee-centered leader behaviors. These two categories of leader behaviors represent a behavioral predisposition toward task or task-related activities, such as planning and scheduling, or toward behaviors that focus on the needs of the employees, such as concern for individual needs and compassion. At first they found that an employee-centered leader was more effective than a job-centered leader, but the original study did not separate cause and effect. Did an employee-centered leader produce good work, or did good work produce an employee-centered leader? More careful subsequent research found that whereas employee-centered leaders did create more positive worker attitudes, job-centered leaders achieved higher worker productivity.[12] The Michigan studies identified dimensions of leader behavior and created a survey methodology to measure leader behaviors. Ultimately, the Michigan studies contribution was to show that leader behaviors were related to group performance. In their series of studies, Michigan researchers found that effective leaders used different behaviors from ineffective leaders.

| **Ohio State Leadership Studies** | At about the same time as the Michigan studies were conducted, the Ohio State studies followed a similar stream of research to identify and measure leader behaviors. The major contributions of the Ohio State Leadership Studies researchers were the identification of leader behaviors and the development and validation of a questionnaire to measure leader behaviors. As originally designed, the LBDQ (Leader Behavior Description Questionnaire) measured two dimensions of leader behavior: initiating structure and consideration, similar to task- and relationship-oriented behavioral styles, respectively.[13] Leaders emphasizing *initiating structure* usually follow a behavioral pattern that insists workers follow rigid work methods, requires that the leader be informed of worker behavior, emphasizes work productivity over workplace harmony, encourages greater effort, and controls the planning and scheduling of work rather than encouraging employee participation. Leaders emphasizing *consideration* appreciate a job well done, stress high morale, treat workers as their equals, encourage greater employee control over work, allow employee greater discretion and autonomy over workflow, and are friendly and approachable. Subsequent studies generally found that leaders who score high on both behaviors are more effective than leaders scoring low on these behavioral styles.

The Ohio State Leadership Studies revealed that the quest for the effective leader was neither simple nor easy. For even when a leader exhibited a consistent, well-trained, and focused set of initiating structure or consideration behaviors, no one leader behavior consistently emerged as most effective in all situations. Some workers did not respond well to initiating structure leaders. At times, consideration behavior yielded higher task performance; at other times, it detracted from task performance. Dissatisfaction with the ability of behavioral style theories to explain effective leadership led researchers to examine the role that characteristics of the situation or characteristics of the follower play in determining leadership effectiveness.

**13.3** | **The Leadership Grid**

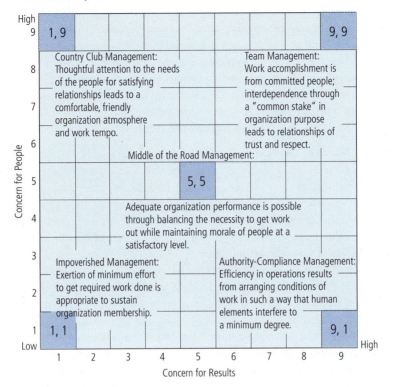

**Source:** The Leadership Grid® (formerly the Managerial Grid by Robert R. Blake and Jane S. Mouton) from R. R. Blake and A. A. McCanse, *Leadership Dilemmas–Grid Solutions* (Houston: Gulf Publishing, 1991), 29. Copyright © 1991 by Scientific Methods, Inc. Reproduced by permission of the owners.

In the end, the genesis of leader behavior research is found in the works of Frederick Taylor (scientific management), with his concern for the task; and Elton Mayo's (human relations movement), with his focus on the social needs of the individual. Both contribute to worker productivity. Perhaps it is only logical for leader behaviors to express the conscious management need for control of production, and the recognition that employees want to be treated with respect, dignity, and fairness.

| **Leadership Grid**® | Basing their early work on the leadership research conducted at the University of Michigan and Ohio State University, Robert R. Blake and Jane S. Mouton developed what was originally called the Managerial Grid® and in later editions the title was changed to the Leadership Grid® as a vehicle for leader behavior assessment and development.[14] In a series of questionnaires and structured seminars, Blake and Mouton used the grid to assess leadership orientation. The Leadership Grid incorporates both task orientation (concern for results) and people orientation (concern for people) into a two-dimensional matrix grid (Exhibit 13.3). *Concern for people* and *concern for results* are each arrayed along a nine-point continuum. A leadership style with a high concern for people and low concern for results would be represented by cell (1, 9)—Country Club—suggesting an emphasis on relationship building and the needs of people.

In the reverse situation, a leadership style with high degree of concern for results and low concern for people would be located at cell (9, 1)—Authority-Compliance—suggesting a strong concern for task completion and very little concern for the worker. In the midrange position is the leader who is moderate on both dimensions, represented by the cell (5, 5)—Middle of the Road or Balanced—suggesting a balance between task accomplishment and demonstrating concern for the worker. A leader rated at the top on both dimensions would be in cell (9, 9)—Team Management—suggesting a leader with common stakes, commitment, mutual trust, and respect. This technique demonstrates that rather than indicating distinct or different leader behaviors, the results and people orientations are usually more or less present in all managers. Leaders must be able to demonstrate concern for both people and results.

Further, Blake and Mouton believe that Team Management—cell (9, 9)—representing high people orientation and high task orientation, is the preferred leadership style. The rationale for their belief is that a leader must not only support the worker, but structure the work setting toward task achievement. At the opposite end of the matrix is Impoverished Management—cell (1, 1). This cell represents the leader with low task orientation and low people orientation; clearly, an undesirable situation and untenable in the long run.

Finally, through a series of seminars, leaders are guided more toward the (9, 9) orientation. A positive feature of the Leadership Grid is its recognition that both types of leader behaviors are important, and that people bring different orientations or predispositions to the management process. Two negative features of the Leadership Grid are (1) effective leadership is defined the same way in all situations, and (2) leader behavior can be changed through seminar participation. In contrast, contingency theory states that successful leaders match their behavior to particular situations.

## Situational Leadership Theories

In response to the lack of success in trait theory and behavioral theory, researchers turned to the situation as a determinant of effective leadership. We will review the following situational leadership theories in this chapter: Fiedler's Contingency Theory of Leadership, Hersey-Blanchard Situational Leadership Theory, Path-Goal Leadership Theory, Leader-Member Exchange Theory, and Substitutes for Leadership Theory. Situational leadership theories describe effective leadership as a process of adjusting leader behavior to the characteristics of the situation. Accordingly, situational leadership theories prescribe the appropriate leader behavior as one that best fits the constraints of a specific situation. Further, leader effectiveness is contingent on displaying behavior appropriate to the situation's demands. In this context, situational leadership theories (1) identify important leadership situations, and (2) suggest various leadership behaviors that increase worker satisfaction and productivity.

Three contrasting approaches to leadership situational effectiveness have emerged. One fits the leader to the situation (i.e., assign a manager to the situation that matches his fixed leadership style); the second fits the leader's behavior to the situation (i.e., expect a manager to change her behavior in response to the situation); and the third considers how characteristics of the situation replace or nullify leader behaviors. The first approach assumes a leader's behavioral style is relatively fixed or not easily changed; thus, the best course is to find the situations in which particular leaders are most effective and avoid those in which they are least effective. Is this always possible? Probably not, but the idea has merit. If we can find the situations in which a manager's dominant leadership style is most effective, both leader and follower are best served. An example of this approach to situational leadership is Fiedler's Contingency Theory of Leadership (discussed in the next section).

In the second approach to leadership situational effectiveness, it is assumed that both the leader's decisions and the work situation are relatively fluid and subject to change. This perspective removes the assumption of a rigid leadership style that nothing can change. It views managers as adaptive and able to respond effectively to different people and situations. Examples of this approach are the Hersey-Blanchard Situational Leadership Theory and Path Goal Theory of Leadership, which are explained later in this section.

A third situational theory is the Substitutes for Leadership, which identifies *substitutes* or aspects of a situation that make leader behavior redundant; and *neutralizers,* which are characteristics of the task or organization that make leader behaviors ineffective.

These approaches to situational leadership hold merit and have research support, but the second approach—fitting the decision to the situation—appears to offer a more realistic view of human nature. Leaders face people with different personalities, abilities, and motivations. To assume that a leader would treat them all alike is simplistic at best. Finally, the situational impact of substitutes for leadership is often overlooked by leaders. Each of these approaches represents different perspectives on leadership effectiveness.

| **Fiedler's Contingency Theory of Leadership** |   In the mid-1970s, Fred Fiedler developed one of the first situational theories of leadership.[15] Contingency theory, sometimes called least preferred coworker (LPC) theory, describes effective leadership as a behavioral predisposition of the leader matched with a favorable situation. This theory asserts that the leader's behavioral style must first be measured and determined. Next, says Fiedler, a situation has to be found or created that is conducive to the leader's fixed style. Thus, Fiedler's Contingency Theory of Leadership matches the characteristics of the individual to the requirements of the situation.

**Determining Leadership Style**    Fiedler believes that the leader's personality determines how they are likely to respond to their workers. Based on previous behavioral research, Fiedler states that people have a primary orientation (or leadership style) that emphasizes task completion or concern for people. He also notes that a person's primary orientation is fixed and thus not likely to change over time. A task-oriented leader is consistently more concerned with getting the work done. A relationship-oriented leader is consistently more concerned with workers' feelings and understanding the impact of personal problems on work performance.

**Measuring Leadership Style**    Fiedler measures leadership style in reference to how the leader treats her least preferred coworker. Fiedler developed a series of questions that form the LPC (Least Preferred Coworker) scale to measure the leader's attitude about her least preferred coworker. The LPC scale measures the leader's behavioral style relative to task orientation and people orientation. One way to think about the LPC score is that it represents an enduring, or consistent, personality characteristic of the leader. With this measure, a leader who identifies her LPC in terms that are critical of the worker's *task* initiative and accomplishment is described as task oriented. In contrast, if the leader identifies her LPC in relatively positive terms (that is, prefers not to work with this person but finds little to criticize), she is described as people oriented.

**Situational Characteristics**    In his work, Fiedler identified the following three situational characteristics:

| *Leader-member relations* represent the follower's trust and confidence in the leader. To be effective, a leader must be able to influence the follower and elicit cooperation. High trust and confidence makes for high leader-member relations. Conversely, low trust and a lack of confidence create a situation described as low leader-member relations.

| *Task structure* is the degree to which a task is well defined and clearly understood. A high degree of task structure represents a situation with a well-defined, easily understood job.

EXHIBIT 13.4

## Fiedler's LPC Theory of Leadership

| | High Leader Control | | | Moderate Leader Control | | | Low Leader Control | |
|---|---|---|---|---|---|---|---|---|
| | I | II | III | IV | V | VI | VII | VIII |
| Leader-Member Relations | Good | Good | Good | Good | Poor | Poor | Poor | Poor |
| Task Structure | High | High | Low | Low | High | High | Low | Low |
| Position Power | Strong | Weak | Strong | Weak | Strong | Weak | Strong | Weak |
| Recommended Leadership Style | Task-Oriented | | | Relationship-oriented | | | | Task-Oriented |
| Very Favorable to Leaders | | | | → | | | | Very Unfavorable to Leaders |

**Source:** Adapted from Fred E. Fiedler, "The Effects of Leadership Training and Experince: A Contingency Model Interpretation," *Administrative Science Quarterly*, 17 (1972): 455; Fred E. Fiedler, "How to Engineer the Job to Fit the Manager," *Harvard Business Review* (September–October, 1965).

In a situation with low task structure, the job is ill-defined and the specific steps for task completion are unclear.

 *Position power* is the power available to the leader to reward or punish the follower. Leaders with high position power can and do reward their followers for successes, and they discipline inappropriate behavior. Leaders with low position power lack the power to gain compliance through reward and punishment; such leaders find it difficult to gain compliance from their followers.

Fiedler combines these three characteristics into eight cells, describing various situations that leaders are likely to confront in an organization (Exhibit 13.4). The situations range from being relatively favorable to the leader to unfavorable. For each situation, Fiedler also identifies recommended leadership styles. In Exhibit 13.4, we can see that the manager experiences a high degree of control in cells I–III, a moderate degree of control in cells IV–VII, and a low degree of control in cell VIII.

In the following situations, Fiedler recommends the task-oriented leadership style:

 Difficult work situations, in which the leader has poor relationships with workers, little power over workers, and an unstructured task (Exhibit 13.4, cell VIII).

 Relatively undemanding work situations, in which the leader has good relationships with workers, high power over workers, and a clearly structured task (Exhibit 13.4, cells I–III).

In contrast, Fiedler says the relationship-oriented leadership style works best in moderately difficult situations (neither easy nor difficult) (Exhibit 13.4, cells IV–VII).

**Criticisms of Fiedler's Contingency Theory**   LPC theory has its critics. Despite being developed more than thirty years ago, the theory has limited research support. In fact, some studies have been quite critical of contingency theory—especially regarding Fiedler's strong belief that leaders have a fixed style that does not change in going from one situation or person to another.[16] In many organizations today, Fiedler's fixed leadership style seems at odds with the requirements for success. Successful leadership requires flexibility and adaptability—not inflexible, autocratic responses. In addition, some note, the measurement of leadership style using the concept of a least preferred coworker as a referent is an indirect and sometimes unreliable approach.

MANAGEMENT HIGHLIGHT

## LEADERSHIP IN STRESSFUL SITUATIONS

| High-Stress Situation | Low-Stress Situation |
|---|---|
| High stress limits the effectiveness of your cognitive ability. Previous experience replays a successful strategy. **Rule:** In high-stress situations, use experience to guide decision making. **Action:** Select a manager who has experience with the nature of the stress encountered in the situation. Clearly avoid inexperienced managers. Also, an intelligent leader may not have the time of composure to use native intelligence. | Low stress allows time to bring cognitive resources to forefront. Cognitive resources provide a broad array of alternatives. **Rule:** Use your intelligence to guide decision making. **Action:** Preferably, select an intelligent manager. The low dynamics of the situation allow the manager time and composure to rely on cognitive resources. Experience may be useful but intelligence will increase range of options and decision-making capacity. |

*Fiedler's Cognitive Resources Theory.* Fiedler's recent work has focused on stress and leadership effectiveness. Stressful situations present another contingency for the leader. Leaders rely on their cognitive resources, which are developed through education, experience, and personality, to make decisions. Therefore, Fiedler says, intelligent leaders are more likely to be effective than less intelligent leaders. Fiedler and Garcia pondered the question, "Is an effective leader an intelligent leader or an experienced leader?" In other words, what resources do effective leaders rely on to make decisions? What Fiedler and Garcia found was that the degree of stress (i.e., a situational constraint) confronting the manager influences leader effectiveness. In stressful situations, the leader tended to focus on the source of the stress instead of the situation, thereby leading to ineffective performance. Fiedler found that in high-stress situations, effective leaders tended to rely on their previous experience with a similar situation. In low-stress situations, effective leaders relied more on their intelligence to resolve the issue.

Fielder and Garcia have heightened our awareness about the consequences of stress on leader effectiveness. The general message these authors send is that in high-stress situations, leaders should rely on their experience; in low-stress situations, they should rely on their intelligence. Fiedler and Garcia believe that in stressful leadership situations, rather than trying to invent a new program, leaders perform better when they use a program that worked well in a similar situation. However, in less stressful situations, leaders have time to evaluate the situation, and they perform better by using intelligence to resolve the situation.

**Source:** Fred E. Fiedler and Martin M. Chemers, *Leadership and Effective Management* (Glenview, IL: Scott Foresman, 1974).

F. E. Fiedler and J. E. Garcia, *New Approaches to Leadership, Cognitive Resources and Organizational Performance* (New York: Wiley, 1987).

Fiedler, F.E., "The Contribution of Cognitive Resources to Leadership Performance," In L. Berkowitz(ed.), *Advances in Experimental Social Psychology* (NY: Academic Press, 1986).

Although this relatively unique method of assessing a leader's style has been questioned, Fiedler's own research shows an improvement over noncontingent approaches to leadership. He describes different situations in which the leader will have the most power and influence with subordinates, thus giving the leader greater control over the outcome of the work. Fiedler's contingency-based LPC theory is still considered an important explanation of situational constraints on leader behavior. More recently Fiedler's contingency theory has focused his research on the relationship between stress and leadership effectiveness. Stress is another important situational factor that can impact the degree of leader effectiveness. The Management Highlight above describes how resources used by the leader in a situation depend upon the level of stress present in a situation.

**Hersey-Blanchard Situational Leadership® Theory** Ken Blanchard and Paul Hersey believe that leaders can and should adjust their behavior to suit the decision-making situations they confront in the workplace. For leaders, the most important of these situations is dealing with people in their formal leadership capacity. The Hersey-Blanchard Situational Leadership® theory uses the traditional dimensions of concern for production (task behavior) and concern for the worker (relationship behavior).

Exhibit 13.5 presents the theory in graphic form. In the topmost chart, task behavior (guidance) is the amount of task-specific direction a worker needs; relationship behavior (supportive behavior) is the amount of emotional support needed to complete a task. The leader's allocation

EXHIBIT 13.5

**Hersey-Blanchard Situational Leadership® Theory**

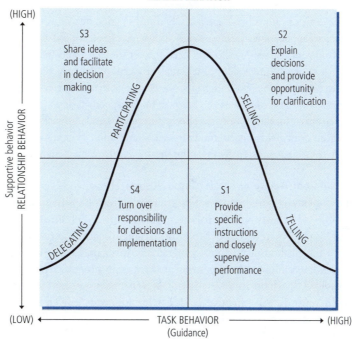

**LEADER BEHAVIOR**

(HIGH)

Supportive behavior — RELATIONSHIP BEHAVIOR

S3
Share ideas and facilitate in decision making

PARTICIPATING

S2
Explain decisions and provide opportunity for clarification

SELLING

S4
Turn over responsibility for decisions and implementation

DELEGATING

S1
Provide specific instructions and closely supervise performance

TELLING

(LOW) ← TASK BEHAVIOR → (HIGH)
(Guidance)

**FOLLOWER READINESS**

| HIGH | MODERATE | | LOW |
|---|---|---|---|
| R4 | R3 | R2 | R1 |
| Able and Willing or Confident | Able but Unwilling or Insecure | Unable but Willing or Confident | Unable and Unwilling or Insecure |

FOLLOWER DIRECTED · LEADER DIRECTED

of guidance to supportive behavior depends on the level of follower readiness (willingness, confidence, ability), as shown in the bottom chart.

In making a situational assessment, the leader also considers group performance in relation to decision making and dispute resolution. Based on follower readiness and group interaction, four leadership styles are recommended—telling, selling, participating, and delegating. Each style affects the degree of leader directedness. As we can see in Exhibit 13.5, follower readiness levels R1 and R2 require greater leader direction than do R3 and R4, which allow greater follower participation in decision making and less leader direction. Follower readiness also determines the

**KEY**TERMS

**follower readiness** The degree of willingness, confidence, and ability of followers. *See also* Hersey-Blanchard Situational Leadership® theory.

degree to which the leader shares decision-making authority. The higher the readiness, the more willing the leader is to allow greater follower autonomy in decision making. This makes sense because the leader wants predictable outcomes. A good leader is not likely to let a follower make decisions until he or she is ready to make good decisions. The theory describes a mutually beneficial model of leadership. Ready followers, capable of independent action, require less leader intervention; less ready followers need greater guidance and more leader intervention.

On the positive side, Situational Leadership® theory suggests there is no one preferred leadership style. The best leadership style is the one that best matches the situation. Leadership style depends on the readiness of the follower for independent action. Although the Hersey-Blanchard theory builds on early work and offers additional considerations, it too has its critics.[17] The theory has been criticized for its methods as well as substance. In other words, the model may not depict reality or be as consistent with earlier work (i.e., the Managerial Grid®) as the authors suggest.

| **Path-Goal Theory of Leadership** | Robert House and Terrence Mitchell's path-goal leadership theory is based on the expectancy theory of motivation. The role of the leader is twofold: (1) clarify for the follower the path by which an individual can achieve personal goals (salary increases and promotions) and organizational outcomes (increased productivity and profitability); and (2) increase rewards that are valued by the follower. In a sense, the leader facilitates the organizational learning process. To do this, the leader engages in behaviors that help followers better understand how their actions are linked to organizational rewards. An effective leader helps followers engage in behaviors that lead to the rewards followers' value. In essence, the leader motivates followers toward outcomes valued by the individual and the organization.

Path-goal theory identifies four types of leader behaviors:

| *Directive behavior.* The leader makes clear task expectations by setting goals, structuring work flow, and providing advice and comments through regular performance feedback. This leader behavior is similar to the traditional leader behavior known as initiating structure.

| *Supportive behavior.* The leader demonstrates concern for the follower and, when problems occur, is ready and willing to offer advice or just listen. Supportive behavior is the same as the traditional leader behavior known as consideration.

| *Participative behavior.* The participative leader actively seeks ideas and information from workers. Participative behavior implies that followers actually participate in making decisions that affect them. For participative style to be effective, workers must perceive that their participation is meaningful and will be used by management.

| *Achievement behavior.* Achievement leadership translates into setting expectations and task goals at a high level. This involves making the job challenging but not impossible to accomplish.

These four behaviors form a repertoire of meaningful actions that a leader might exhibit under different work situations. The theory also suggests that leaders have the ability to increase rewards that are valued by the follower. Leaders are effective to the extent that they can motivate their followers, influence their ability to perform, and increase their job satisfaction. The model specifies that a follower's attitudes and behaviors are influenced by two factors: leader behaviors and situational factors. Followers' attitudes and behaviors include their level of job satisfaction and their ability to perform their task. Situational factors (sometimes referred to as environmental factors) include task requirements, the work group, and the formal authority structure. Personal characteristics of the follower include locus of control and perceived ability.

Path-goal theory prescribes which leader behaviors are likely to be effective with different situational constraints. Leaders are expected to change their behavior toward the follower when situational changes occur. From the workers' perspective, the leader behaviors must be seen as facilitating or enabling workers to accomplish both immediate task goals and their own personal goals.

The theory suggests, for example, that the following matches between leader behaviors and situations result in effective leadership:

- Directive behavior is suggested for situations that require more task structuring, monitoring, and feedback. Directive behavior may be particularly appropriate for a new employee with limited job experience.

- Supportive behavior might be suitable in a situation where workers know the job well, are experiencing delays or "client conflict," and just need to know that they are doing the right thing.

- Participative behavior is appropriate for workers who know their jobs well enough to make meaningful contributions to decisions that affect themselves and their department.

- Achievement behavior is suitable in situations where high performance is in the best interest of both the employee and the organization. A sales department that compensates employees on a commission basis would provide an opportunity for achievement-oriented leader behavior. Here achievement-oriented leader behavior sets high sales expectations that, when met, yield the sales department greater financial rewards. Achievement-oriented leadership works best when the followers have a high need for achievement.

In summary, path-goal leadership theory views the leader as the vital link between the organization and the individual. Leaders need to motivate workers to understand how their work efforts are tied to valued salary increases, promotions, praise, recognition, and respect. Exhibit 13.6 presents the path-goal theory.

---

**EXHIBIT 13.6**  **Path-Goal Theory**

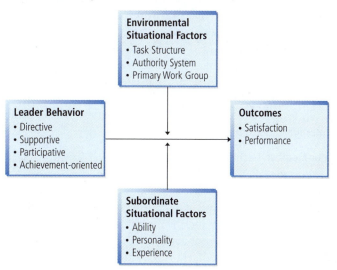

**Source:** Adapted from R. J. House and T. R. Mitchell, "Path-Goal Theory of Leadership," *Journal of Contemporary Business* (Autumn 1974): 81–97; R. J. House, "A Path-Goal Theory of Leader Effectiveness," *Administrative Science Quarterly* (September 1971): 321–338.

EXHIBIT | 13.7          Substitutes for Leadership

| Substitutes for Leadership | In many work situations, traditional approaches to leadership are ineffective or sometimes just not possible. Authors Steven Kerr and John Jermier believe that situational characteristics can reduce the need for traditional leadership.[18] They identify three situational attributes that include characteristics of the subordinate, the task, and the organization. These characteristics can act as either neutralizers or substitutes for leadership.

In certain situations, leader behavior can be neutralized by an organizational characteristic. A neutralizer is any situation that prevents the leader from acting in a specified way. For example, a union contract may require that all union members in the organization receive the same raise, regardless of job performance. This situation neutralizes the leader's ability not only to reward or reinforce positive behavior but also to sanction negative behavior. In this illustration, the union contract prohibits the leader from rewarding top performers at a higher rate than low performers. The leader loses the ability to influence worker behavior.

In other situations, substitutes for leadership replace the need for traditional leadership. As a characteristic of the subordinate, a new hire needs more task supervision. New employees often require more direct, task-oriented leader behaviors. But training and education can reduce the need for task-oriented leader behaviors; so in effect, training and education serve as substitutes for leadership. Finally, a characteristic of the task can also be a substitute for leadership. An intrinsically rewarding job replaces the need for direct supervision. Exhibit 13.7 gives examples of substitutes for leadership.

| Leader-Member Exchange Theory | Unlike other situational leadership theories, leader-member exchange theory (LMX) is based on the concepts of social exchange and attribution that occur between the leader and followers.[19] Leader-member exchanges are often described in terms of the power and influence of the leader and the role making and resource exchange between the leader and the member. Although many leadership theories describe leadership behavior as universal across people, the facts speak otherwise—few leaders are really that egalitarian. More likely is the situation where the leader shares demographics, attitudes, hobbies, interests in sports, and other social interests with some followers (or subordinates) and not others. It is not unusual for a leader and a follower to become friends. Most of us have found ourselves associating with leaders outside work. While we may be friends with our boss today, in the future we might have a different boss with whom we do

not care to associate outside of work. Likewise, leaders form strong bonds with some followers and not with others. Leader-member exchange theory is an attempt to understand leadership from the perspective of the relationships existing between the leader and each follower.

Leader-member exchange theory, sometimes called the vertical dyad linkage model,[20] explains effective leadership in relation to the role-making process that occurs between the leader and followers. Leaders develop different relationships with each subordinate. These relationships are based on a variety of factors including compatibility, attitudes, and interests. In the process of negotiating a relationship with each subordinate, the leader enters into exchanges with each subordinate. A low-exchange relationship is based on rules and procedures. As long as the subordinate complies with the rules, the subordinate receives benefits from the leader. A high-exchange relationship involves the allocation by the leader of more discretionary rewards such as support, travel, a new computer, and so on in exchange for compliance from the subordinate. The leader's intent is to build commitment and encourage task accomplishment. However, codependence between the leader and the follower can develop. This results in greater resource allocations by the leader in exchange for compliance and task performance by the follower.

From a practical standpoint, leaders often find themselves working with a small number of people—not their whole department. In many cases, group formation is often at the discretion of the leader. LMX theory suggests that *in-group* members are more likely to be included in important decision-making groups than are *out-group* members. Over time, in-group and out-group membership becomes entrenched. When this situation occurs, the result is that in-group members are more informed and better respected in the unit, department, or organization than are out-group members. Too often out-group members, holding the same job with the same leader, are in the unenviable position of not being highly regarded by the leader, and may be denied information and interesting group assignments.

Leader-member exchange theory describes both of the preceding situations as common. Over time, the leader forms a so-called in-group based on friendship, respect, and admiration for some of the followers. Other followers who hold less respected relationships with the leader are relegated to the out-group. The in-group shares a special relationship with the leader that provides security, information, and privilege. The out-group includes people the leader believes are unmotivated and lacking in commitment and loyalty. Leader-member exchange is an attribution theory that helps us better understand leader behavior and the differential treatment of followers.

## Transformational and Transactional Leadership

Early in the chapter, we considered the differences between leaders and managers. We also discussed trait theory—an early theory suggesting that leaders have certain characteristics that can be identified or may be developed in those who are deficient in the trait. For many years, trait theory took a back seat to behavioral and situational explanations of leadership; today most management scholars use the terms *managing* and *leading* to refer to two different processes.

Several theorists use the term transformational leadership to describe an inspirational form of leader behavior based on modifying followers' beliefs, values, and ultimately their behavior. Bernard Bass refers to this process as leadership that creates "performance beyond expectations."[21] For example, Lee Iacocca transformed Chrysler not just by changing products alone, but also by changing worker and customer attitudes. To succeed in the short term, workers had to make better products and accept pay concessions; customers needed to believe his "Buy American" sales pitch. Similarly, Larry Quadracci's inspirational leadership transformed a small Midwestern printer, Quad Graphics, into a highly profitable national corporation. Home Depot

**KEY TERMS**

**leader-member exchange theory** A leadership theory that explains effective leadership in terms of the role-making process between the leader and followers.

**low-exchange relationship** A leader-follower relationship based on rules and procedures. *See also* high-exchange relationship.

**high-exchange relationship** The allocation by the leader of more discretionary rewards, with the intent to build commitment and encourage task accomplishment. *See also* low-exchange relationship.

**transformational leadership** An inspirational form of leader behavior that is based on modifying followers' beliefs, values, and ultimately their behavior.

struggled for several years of sagging stock prices in the 1990s before hiring back one of its founders, Pat Farrah; the self-proclaimed "radical," Farrah was given much of the credit for the retailer's initial success. Although the stock price slipped in the late 1980s and early 1990s, since Pat Farrah's return in 1995, the stock price has soared; Home Depot stock shot up 28,000 percent from its IPO in 1981.[22] Pat Farrah is a tough boss and relentless worker, but people are energized by his charismatic leadership style.

In contrast, transactional leadership is more closely related to both behavioral and situational leader behaviors. Transactional leaders appeal to their followers' rational exchange motive. Workers exchange labor for wages. Leaders help clarify the path from effort to reward. For the worker, it is a form of self-interested exchange—do this and you get a reward. For the leader, it is a process of keeping workers riveted to organizational goals.

Both transactional and transformational leadership are valid approaches to leadership. Transformational leadership helps us to realize that leaders who transform organizations are unique. As you will recall, early trait theorists were unsuccessful in identifying physical attributes and personality types needed for effective leadership. But transformational leadership research holds the promise that individual qualities are a critical element in transforming an organization. Successful companies often have bold, dominant leaders who guide, inspire, and create a vision of the future. Larry Ellison of Oracle, Steve Jobs in the early years of Apple Computer, and Jack Welch of GE are examples of leaders who made a difference in the performance of their organizations.

Do leadership traits exist? Sure they do. But can we teach people these traits and expect them to go out and transform organizations? Certainly not! It is foolish, however, to assume that some people are genetically endowed with leadership traits whereas other people lack them. Finding that elusive leader within requires more than having a requisite set of traits. Nor should we assume that leaders just magically appear as the circumstances require. On the contrary, leadership is personal and situational, requiring an investment in education, skill building, experience, and—undoubtedly—some luck.

## Emotional Intelligence

Recent work by Daniel Goleman[23] suggests that emotional intelligence plays a key role in leader success. According to Goleman, emotional intelligence allows people to more effectively manage themselves and their relationships with others. Contemporary organizations are more complex and diverse, and they employ a highly educated workforce that enjoys instant access to a variety of information. Leaders have to deal not only with a new workforce, but also with a more complicated business environment. The Enron and Arthur Andersen debacles exemplify the complexity of the business environment and the problems leaders face in seeking financial success. Leadership is a balance, tempering the leader's vision for the future with the expectations of corporate constituents. To do so, leaders need to understand themselves and how other people react to them.

Effective leadership requires more than intelligence and experience; it also requires emotional intelligence. Emotional intelligence consists of self-awareness, self-regulation, motivation, empathy, and social skill.[24] Exhibit 13.8 defines the components of emotional intelligence and provides some example behaviors.

## Self-Leadership

Two societal trends will greatly affect future leadership approaches. First, a highly educated workforce in a democratic society will seek greater decision-making participation and other forms of power sharing. Second, a highly competitive world economy has led to the necessity for

EXHIBIT 13.8

### Emotional Intelligence

| Components | Definition | Behaviors |
|---|---|---|
| **Self-Awareness** | The ability to recognize and understand your moods, emotions, and drives, as well as their effects on others | Self-confidence<br>Realistic self-assessment<br>Self-deprecating sense of humor |
| **Self-Regulation** | The ability to control or redirect disruptive impulses or moods | Trustworthiness<br>Integrity |
| | The propensity to suspend judgment to think before acting | Comfort with ambiguity<br>Openness to change |
| **Motivation** | A passion to work for reasons that go beyond money or status | Strong drive to achieve<br>Optimism |
| | A propensity to pursue goals with energy and persistence | Organizational commitment |
| **Empathy** | Ability to understand the emotional makeup of other people | Expertise in building and retaining talent |
| | Skill in treating people according to their emotional reactions | Service to clients and customers |
| **Social Skill** | Proficiency in managing relationships and building networks | Effectiveness in leading change<br>Persuasiveness |
| | Ability to find common ground and build rapport | Expertise in building and leading teams |

**Source:** Adapted from P. Salovey and J. Mayer, "Emotional Intelligence," *Imagination, Cognition, and Personality no.* 3 (1990): 185–211; D. Goleman, *Emotional Intelligence* (New York: Bantam:1995); D. Goleman, "Leadership That Gets Results," *Harvard Business Review* (March–April 2000): 79–90.

increased cost-cutting measures. For instance, United States firms have historically used more middle managers than their foreign competitors. To be more competitive, United States firms have permanently reduced their white collar workforce. Both trends make a shift toward greater worker control more likely in the future.

Shifting societal trends call for new leadership strategies. For effective leadership in the future, two things must occur. First, leaders must engage in behaviors that actively encourage workers to gain control over their work destiny. Empowering workers means sharing power, which takes a confident, secure leader as well as willing, able workers. Second, workers need to develop the requisite self-control strategies such as self-management and self-leadership. New leadership approaches to managing increasingly competitive markets will, of necessity, increase worker participation in the decision-making process. As noted earlier, this means more democratic rather than authoritarian leaders.

A pioneer in leadership, Lincoln Electric in Cleveland, Ohio, has earned a reputation for product quality. Lincoln's leadership system assumes workers are self-motivated and capable of self-management. Workers can rearrange tasks, and any improvement in quality of output earns the worker more money, so both the employee and the company benefit. Teamwork and reliability are rewarded; some employees are doubling their base pay with incentive compensation. Each manager is responsible for about 100 employees, who are graded on their ability to work without a supervisor. Likewise, Johnsonville Sausage has encouraged greater participation and self-leadership for some time. As the CEO at Johnsonville put it, "I went from authoritarian control to authoritarian abdication." But he was glad he did for in the result was increased performance and greater worker satisfaction.[25]

Self-leadership is a management philosophy that encompasses a systematic set of behavioral and cognitive strategies leading to improved performance and effectiveness.[26] This philosophy

**KEY**TERMS

**self-leadership** A management philosophy that encourages individual employees to develop their own work priorities that are consistent with organizational goals.

encourages individual employees to develop their own work priorities that are consistent with organizational goals. What happens to the manager in the self-leadership process? Interestingly, rather than abdicating control, the manager must actively encourage the development of self-leadership capabilities in subordinates.

Developing self-leadership might not be as easy as it sounds. Many people believe that workers would jump at the chance for more control, but some actually resent it. Why would this be? Mainly, this resistance is from fear of the unknown. For decades, workers have been encouraged to complete their work according to procedures and standards designed by their managers or specialists. With the self-leadership approach, workers are asked to assume new responsibilities. Often, workers believe they are untrained or unable to accomplish this new role successfully. One way to increase worker self-control is to use empowerment to overcome worker resistance or fear. Empowerment is the process of providing workers with skills, tools, information, and—above all—authority and responsibility for their work. Worker empowerment gives workers direct control over many aspects of their work. Self-leadership transfers control of directing individual work behavior from the manager to the worker. Leadership becomes an internal process. Real empowerment involves the worker's commitment to self-management, which is the use of work strategies that help to control daily activities in order to achieve organizational goals.

The manager's role in the self-leadership organization is to encourage workers to develop self-control skills. By self-control, we mean the workers' ability to control their own work destiny in both the short and long term. Self-leadership deemphasizes external forms of control. The primary vehicle leaders use to encourage self-leadership is role modeling, a process by which leaders exhibit behaviors that they expect other employees to follow. For example, leaders need to set goals for themselves in ways that their employees can observe. Although the idea of role modeling seems simple, in reality it seldom happens. For role modeling to be successful, it must be apparent to the worker that the manager is demonstrating a work behavior she would like the employee to emulate. Further, the worker needs to see some connection between adopting the behavior and achieving positive outcomes. Research also suggests that workers are most likely to emulate the behavior of successful managers.[27] You may want to determine your own level of self-leadership skills. Complete the following Management Highlight and compute your score.

## Behavioral Self-Management

Behavioral self-management refers to a set of strategies that help people gain greater control over their lives; common strategies include self-set goals, self-observation, self-rewards, self-cueing, and self-designed jobs.

- With self-set goals, the initiative for setting the goal and the level of the goal itself comes from the worker, not the manager. Self-set goals are consistent with the firm's overall goals and are based on the worker's commitment to the firm's goals. Self-set goals free the manager from traditional supervisory duty and empower workers with a greater sense of personal control. This autonomous approach to goal setting is recommended as a matter of ethics, not just effectiveness.[28]

- Self-observation is a process in which a worker monitors his own behavior and notes actions, events, or outcomes. The self-leadership philosophy assumes that workers can monitor their own behavior. Self-observation includes keeping performance records. For example, a package delivery worker might keep a notebook recording the time of each delivery. Self-observation increases worker empowerment and autonomy.

## SELF-LEADERSHIP ASSESSMENT
### Directions

Self-leadership consists of six dimensions: self-observation, self-goal-setting, self-cueing, self-reward, self-punishment, and practice. Answer the questions in the table honestly, and then compute a score for each dimension and interpret your score using the information that follows the table. Finally, calculate your overall score, and then calculate your overall score excluding the self-punishment score (X) and including the self-punishment score (XX). Was your self-leadership score high, moderate, or low? What did you find surprising about self-leadership score?

| | | Describes Me Very Well | Describes Me Well | Describes Me Some-what | Does Not Describe Me Very Well | Does Not Describe Me At All |
|---|---|---|---|---|---|---|
| 1. | I try to keep track of how well I'm doing while I work | 5 | 4 | 3 | 2 | 1 |
| 2. | I often use reminders to help me remember things I need to do. | 5 | 4 | 3 | 2 | 1 |
| 3. | I like to work toward specific goals I set for myself. | 5 | 4 | 3 | 2 | 1 |
| 4. | After I perform well on an activity, I feel good about myself. | 5 | 4 | 3 | 2 | 1 |
| 5. | I tend to get down on myself when I perform poorly. | 5 | 4 | 3 | 2 | 1 |
| 6. | I often practice important tasks before I actually do them. | 5 | 4 | 3 | 2 | 1 |
| 7. | I usually am aware of how I am performing on an activity. | 5 | 4 | 3 | 2 | 1 |
| 8. | I try to arrange my work area in a way that helps me positively focus my attention on my work. | 5 | 4 | 3 | 2 | 1 |
| 9. | I establish personal goals for myself. | 5 | 4 | 3 | 2 | 1 |
| 10. | When I have successfully completed a task, I often reward myself with something I like. | 5 | 4 | 3 | 2 | 1 |
| 11. | I tend to be tough on myself when I have not done well on a task. | 5 | 4 | 3 | 2 | 1 |
| 12. | I like to go over an important activity before I actually perform it. | 5 | 4 | 3 | 2 | 1 |
| 13. | I keep track of my progress on projects I am working on. | 5 | 4 | 3 | 2 | 1 |
| 14. | I try to surround myself with objects and people that bring out my desirable behaviors. | 5 | 4 | 3 | 2 | 1 |
| 15. | I like to set task goals for my performance. | 5 | 4 | 3 | 2 | 1 |
| 16. | When I do an assignment especially well, I like to treat myself to something or engage in an activity that I enjoy. | 5 | 4 | 3 | 2 | 1 |
| 17. | I am often critical of myself concerning my failures. | 5 | 4 | 3 | 2 | 1 |
| 18. | I often rehearse my plan for dealing with a challenge before I actually face the challenge. | 5 | 4 | 3 | 2 | 1 |

*Continued*

*Continued*

### Directions for Scoring

Total your responses for F, X, and XX by adding the numbers you circled for each of the statements indicated in the parentheses.

| | Self-Leadership Category | Score |
|---|---|---|
| **A.** | Self-observation (add numbers circled for statements 1, 7, and 13) | |
| **B.** | Cueing strategies (add numbers circled for statements 2, 8, and 14) | |
| **C.** | Self-goal setting (add numbers circled for statements 3, 9, and 15) | |
| **D.** | Self-reward (add numbers circled for statements 4, 10, and 16) | |
| **E.** | Self-punishment (add numbers circled for statements 5, 11, and 17) | |
| **F.** | Practice (add numbers circled for statements 6, 12, and 18) | |
| **X.** | Total Score, including self-punishment | |
| **XX.** | Total Score, not including self-punishment | |

### Interpreting your score

Your score for A–F suggests your current self-leadership tendencies concerning six self-leadership strategies. Your score on A can be interpreted as follows:

1. A score of 3 or 4 indicates a very low level of the strategy.
2. A score of 5 to 7 indicates a low level of the strategy.
3. A score of 8 to 10 indicates a moderate level of the strategy.
4. A score of 11 to 13 indicates a high level of the strategy.
5. A score of 14 or 15 indicates a very high level of the strategy.

Research suggests that the higher the score on A–D and F, the higher the performance. A high score on E may detract from your overall performance. With that in mind, use the XX total score for further analysis.

1. A score of 15 to 22 indicates a very low overall level of the strategies.
2. A score of 23 to 37 indicates a low overall level of the strategies.
3. A score of 38 to 52 indicates a moderate overall level of the strategies.
4. A score of 53 to 67 indicates a high overall level of the strategies.
5. A score of 68 to 75 indicates a very high overall level of the strategies.

Source: Adapted from Charles C. Manz, *Mastering Self-Leadership: Empowering Yourself for Personal Excellence, Self-leadership* (Englewood Cliffs, NJ: Prentice Hall, 1992); Charles C. Manz and Henry Sims, *Leading Workers to Lead Themselves: The External Leadership of Self-Managing Work Teams*, and Charles C. Manz and Henry Sims, *Super-Leadership: Leading Others to Lead Themselves* (Englewood Cliffs, NJ: Prentice Hall, 1989).

**KEY**TERMS

**self-rewards** Also called self-administered rewards, rewards that workers give themselves, based on their accomplishments.

**Self-rewards** (also called *self-administered rewards*) recognize our own accomplishments. A worker monitors, evaluates, and applies a reward for the successful completion of a task. Self-rewards enable the individual to personally recognize that a performance milestone has been surpassed. An example of self-reward is giving yourself break time only after completing a major portion of the assigned task. Another type of self-reward is recognizing the naturally rewarding aspect of the work itself—for example, reminding yourself that it feels good to do your best or that it is intrinsically rewarding to clear your desk of pending cases each day. Although these ideas have a simplistic edge, they get back to basics and are powerful motivators. The worker decides the measure and worth of an activity rather than adhering to a universal definition. Self-administered rewards add meaning and purpose to work. In essence, the worker knows what she is supposed to do, she does it, and then pats herself on the back or rewards herself with a break.

When a mechanic lays out the necessary tools before commencing work, he is practicing self-cueing—the process of planning or making arrangements for an activity prior to its performance. This practice helps to prevent defects from occurring during the execution stage. One type of self-cueing, *behavioral rehearsal,* involves practicing an activity under simulated or controlled conditions. For example, the night before a meeting with a customer, a sales team might conduct a role play in which some members of the sales team play the role of the customers and ask appropriate questions, giving the sales team a chance to rehearse their answers.

Self-designed jobs allow workers to propose and design work-process changes rather than having superiors simply impose external constraints on them. This can result in a personal sense of competence, self-control, and purpose. At the Federal Express facility in Memphis, Tennessee, in response to the problem of late-arriving and mislabeled packages, management implemented a system called *minisort.* But the minisort process was inefficient and unpopular among workers. One worker observed, "If you got on someone's nerves, they sent you to minisort." So a team of 12 workers was appointed to solve the problem. The team cut minisort staff from 150 to 80 workers (saving $30,000), clarified minisort tasks, and implemented prevention measures that cut the number of packages sent to minisort in the first place from 10,000 down to 4,000 per night. In four months the number of late packages dropped from 4,300 to 432. The team's work actually caused a decrease in its members' own wages, yet as one worker said, "For management to listen to me, that's important."[29]

## Cognitive Self-Management

Not all self-management strategies are observable and measurable. Using cognitive self-management principles, the individual worker creates mental images and thought patterns that are consistent with the firm's goals. Two basic cognitive self-management strategies are opportunity building and positive self-talk.

The process of seeking out and/or developing new possibilities for success is referred to as opportunity building. An oft-told marketing story involves two shoe salespeople who are sent to sell shoes in a foreign country. The negative thinker reports to the firm's headquarters, "Opportunities nonexistent. Nobody here wears shoes." The positive thinker says, "Opportunities unlimited. Nobody here wears shoes." Thus, depending on how we perceive and define a problem, an obstacle may be converted to an opportunity.

Positive self-talk is the process of creating mental imagery that reinforces a worker's sense of self-esteem and enhances effectiveness. For example, a customer service agent, upon dealing with an angry customer, reminds herself that she has been successful in calming and satisfying angry customers in the past by listening for important words or phrases used by the customer. By maintaining her self-confidence, the agent is using positive self-talk to help her manage a difficult situation.

## Developing a Self-Leadership Culture

The process of developing an effective self-leadership culture begins with a commitment from the top levels of management. Three keys to establishing a self-leadership culture are sharing information, training, and reinforcement.

*Sharing information.* Self-managed workers need a great deal of information. Many traditional management secrets must become part of their information base. Workers need information concerning costs and profits if they are to set goals and commit to certain actions. When they are informed, workers become more willing to accept responsibility for their actions. In addition, open communication sends a message to employees that they are respected and trusted.[30]

|   *Training.* Training in the use of self-management strategies might focus on improving communication skills, team building, or developing the various self-management strategies discussed in this chapter. Training helps to reinforce managerial policy statements at all levels of an organization. Managers may feel threatened by the idea of a self-managed workforce, so in addition to training, they also need assurance that they will continue to have an important role in organizational success.

|   *Reinforcement.* In addition to sharing information and conducting training programs, the administration of performance rewards can help to reinforce the use of self-management behaviors. For instance, a "team player" or "star performer" award might be issued to an employee who demonstrates outstanding self-leadership ability.

## Leadership Challenges

Critical global issues confront the economy and firms as we face the twenty-first century.[31] The most effective managers will be those who understand leadership as a broad, empowering tool, and who have a special capability to develop self-managed leadership in others.

Effective leadership in the future will most likely mean leading others to lead themselves. Workers will have to develop self-management skills; those who do so are better able to control the pace and flow of their work. To facilitate this process, effective leadership in the future must also encourage employees to develop self-leadership skills. Here is a summary of some challenges future leaders will face:

|   Increasing global competition

|   Emphasis on speed, service, and information

|   Lean and flexible work demands for more value-added labor and reduced indirect labor costs

|   Need to employ untrained, unskilled, and disenfranchised employees

|   Fewer low-skilled jobs available as more low-skilled workers enter the market

|   Increasing gaps, particularly (1) between elite, skilled employees with lifetime employment and a working underclass with limited skills and few employment options; and (2) between knowledge-intensive, highly educated employees and labor-intensive, unskilled employees

|   Employee demands for greater participation; shift to teams, skill-based pay, and cooperation with the firm

|   Further expansion of information technologies; flatter, decentralized organizations with greater employee need for self-management

Empowering workers through self-leadership is a good start, but it may not be enough when an organization's competitive position has eroded. Visionary transformational leadership may be required to resuscitate a poorly performing organization. Take the reign of IBM CEO Louis Gertsner Jr., who faced tremendous challenges from the beginning. The once mighty IBM had lost market share and was unable to change the organization to match the needs of the future. For IBM to regain competitive ground in the computer industry, Gertsner had to communicate a new vision of IBM to employees, customers, and competitors. Gertsner transformed the firm's image, changing not only how IBM thought about itself but also how consumers viewed IBM. In the 1950s, the transformational leadership of Thomas Watson Jr. was the cornerstone of IBM's success for the next three decades. Gertsner called on the creativity of the IBM spirit and reconstituted the Big Blue of yesteryear. Through his leadership, he rebuilt the ailing giant and crafted a new vision for IBM in the future.

**CONCLUSION**

## Leadership

Effective leadership requires an employee-oriented viewpoint—putting people first. By placing the interests of employees above their own, leaders gain loyalty, respect, and motivated workers. Effective leaders listen to subordinates, acquiring the necessary information to make sound decisions. As we noted early in the chapter, leaders and managers are different. Effective leaders encourage employees to develop supportive work relationships with others; communicate their personal values and organizational commitment; and articulate a vision of what the organization can be in the future. Moreover, effective leaders move the organization in new directions, by rejecting the status quo, communicating and explaining decisions, favoring risk and change, and generating a feeling of value and importance in work.[32] In the workplace of the future, effective leaders will be employee centered, customer focused, and respected for their ability to develop employees to their full potential.

The mix of skills needed to be an effective leader is changing. Effective leaders need *technical skills*—including specialized knowledge, analytical ability, and the ability to use tools and techniques of the discipline. They also need *conceptual skills*—the ability to see the enterprise as a whole and recognize how the various parts of the organization interact. Finally, leaders need *human skills*—the ability to work effectively as a group member to build cooperative effort.[33] But additionally, management scholars suggest that future leaders need three new skills. They will need the personal skill to *manage ambiguous situations,* the organizational skills to *manage and understand complex systems,* and the leadership skill to *direct the work of groups* as well as individuals.[34] Leaders will continue to make use of these skills, with greater emphasis on human skills such as communication and team building. Effective leaders will be those who can successfully navigate their way through the conflicting organizational goals and changes demanded in the marketplace.

## Discussion Questions

1. Describe the differences between trait theory of leadership, behavioral leadership theory, and contingency theory of leadership.

2. What is the difference between a transformational leader and a transactional leader?

3. What are some of the ways that people can use self-management principles to gain more control over their lives?

## Video Case

### Leadership at P.F. Chang's

How do you manage 97 bistros and 33 diners at once? This isn't a riddle, but is actually the daily challenge of Rick Federico, chairman and CEO of P.F. Chang's, which owns and operates a chain of Asian restaurants across the country. During the time he has been head of the company, Federico has assumed the huge tasks of taking the company public and launching Pei Wei, the firm's chain of diners. In addition, he has developed management teams and laid out clear expectations for his employees. He has earned the respect of his managers, his workers, his customers, and even his competitors. He has won accolades and leadership awards. "Rick has done a great job of building a strong team culture and has built an organization that is based upon quality of execution," notes one colleague. "He has built P.F. Chang's into a concept that is craved and loved by its customers and team members." These characteristics are the attributes of a leader.

Rick Federico knows the restaurant industry. He began his career as a dishwasher for a steak house and worked his way up the management chain. So he understands everyone's job, from busboy to chef to manager. Perhaps that is why he feels comfortable fostering a team atmosphere at P.F. Chang's, giving employees the authority to make decisions to please customers and ultimately benefit the restaurant. And because he has so many contacts throughout the industry, he is able attract the best staff, from hourly employees to restaurant managers. At the same time, he maintains a clear vision for the company as a whole. He believes that restaurants based on an Asian menu will continue to grow in popularity—and that developing a recognizable Asian brand is a huge opportunity. Everything at P.F. Chang's two types of restaurants—bistros and diners—is designed with this vision of growth in mind. From tableside cooking to replicas of twelfth-century Chinese murals, the entire P.F. Chang's dining experience is intended to leave a strong impression on customers, which is exactly what Federico wants.

Although the restaurant industry in general has suffered during the past few years, P.F. Chang's has managed to grow. Federico is both philosophical and practical about the obstacles that every restaurant faces during uncertain times. "While so many of the challenges that face our industry are out of our control, our greatest challenge is also our greatest opportunity: our people," he says. "We are in the hospitality service industry, and our business is to provide our customers with an outstanding dining experience each and every time they walk through our doors." One way he accomplishes this goal is by empowering employees to make decisions, such as fulfilling special requests from customers. And because of its success, P.F. Chang's has been able to create hundreds of jobs across the country while other restaurant chains are laying off workers.

Federico expects results from every team, manager, and worker. But he expects no less from himself. "I'm a reflection of our employees," he muses. "I surround myself with people better than I am in certain areas." He believes his greatest tasks as a leader involve remaining focused on his customers, his workers, and the food they serve. As P.F. Chang's grows, he wants to be sure that the quality of service, atmosphere, and food are always at their highest. He's not afraid to look in the mirror for the solution to a problem. "I suppose the day I'm not an effective leader, I'll be out of here," he admits. More likely, he'll be busy coming up with ways to make P.F. Chang's bigger, better, and eventually, a household name.

## Questions

1. Describe some of Rick Federico's personal leadership traits.

2. Would you characterize Rick Federico as a charismatic or transformational leader? Why?

3. Which of the five sources of power does Rick Federico use?

Sources: Company web site, http://www.pfchangs.com, accessed August 26, 2004, Charles Bernstein, "Chief Execution Officer," *Chain Leader* (September 2004): 62–68; "Work Force Still Top Concern for CEOs," *The Phoenix Business Journal* (May 24, 2004) http://phoenix.bizjournals.com.

## BizFlix

### Apollo 13

This film dramatically portrays the Apollo 13 mission to the moon that almost ended in disaster. Only innovative problem solving and decision making amid massive ambiguity saved the crew. Almost any scene dramatically makes this point. Flight Director Gene Kranz wrote a book describing the mission and the actions that prevented disaster.

A zero gravity simulator, a KC-135 four-engine jet aircraft (NASA's "Vomit Comet"), helped create the film's realistic weightless scenes. These scenes required 600 parabolic loops over 10 days of filming. This scene is a composite built from portions of the "Carbon Dioxide Problem" sequence, which occurs a little after the midway point of the film, and parts of the "With Every Breath . . ." sequence, which appears about seven minutes later. The scene's first part follows the nearly complete shutdown of the Apollo 13 module to save battery power. Mission Control has detected rising carbon dioxide levels in the module, which could kill the astronauts if NASA engineers on the ground cannot solve the problem. The film continues with the Apollo 13 crew building a carbon dioxide filter designed by the engineers.

**Source:** J. Craddock Ed. *VideoHound's Golden Movie Retreiver* (Farmington Hills, MI: The Gale Group, Inc.), 2000. [0][0].

Questions

1. What is the problem in this scene?

2. What are the engineers' options for solving the problem?

3. Does this scene show innovation and innovative behavior? If so, in what form?

## Suggested Reading

Collins, Jim, "Level 5 Leadership," *Harvard Business Review* (July–August, 2005) Reprint Number R0507M.

Goleman, David, Richard Boyatzis, and Annie McKee, "Primal Leadership: The Hidden Driver of Great Performance," *Harvard Business Review* (December 2001): 42–51.

Manz, Charles, and Christopher Neck. *Mastering Self-Leadership: Empowering Yourself for Personal Excellence*, Third Edition. Upper Saddle River, NJ: Prentice Hall, 2004.

McGill, Michael, and John Slocum, "A Little Leadership Please," *Organizational Dynamics* 26 (Winter 1998) 26: 39–49.

Pagonis William G., "Leadership in a combat Zone," *Harvard Business Review - Best of HBR* (December, 2001) Reprint Number, R0111H.

Teerlink, Rich, "Harley's Leadership U-Turn," *Harvard Business Review* (July–August 2000): 3–7.

## Endnotes

1. R. Tannenbaum, I. R. Weschler, and F. Massarik, *Leadership and Organization* (New York: McGraw-Hill, 1961): 24.

2. R. Tannenbaum and Warren H. Schmidt, "How to Choose a Leadership Pattern," *Harvard Business Review* (May–June 1973) (Classic reprint originally published in *HBR* in 1958).

3. Abraham Zaleznick, "Leaders and Managers: Are They Different?" *Harvard Business Review* (1977): 31–42; "Real Work," *Harvard Business Review* (1989): 52–64; Abraham Zaleznick, "The Leadership Gap" *Academy of Management Executive* (February 1990): 7–22; and Abraham Zaleznick. *The Managerial Mystique* (New York: Harper & Row, 1989): 1–42.

4. Tom Peters, *Thriving on Chaos* (New York: Knopf, 1987), 561.

5. Jim Collins, "Level 5 Leadership," *Harvard Business Review* (July–August 2005) Reprint Number, R0507M.

6. Robert E. Kelley, "In Praise of Followers," *Harvard Business Review* (November–December 1988): 3–8.

7. Robert Dahl, "The Concept of Power," *Behavioral Science* 2 (1957): 201–215.

8. John R. P. French Jr. and Bertram Raven, "The Bases of Social Power," in *Studies in Social Power*, ed. Dorwin Cartright (Ann Arbor: University of Michigan Press, 1959): 150–167.

9. Patricia Haddock, "Communicating Personal Power," *Supervision* (July 1995): 20.

10. Edwin E. Ghiselli, "Managerial Talent," *American Psychologist* 71 (October 1963): 631–641.

11. Ralph M. Stogdill, "Personal Factors Associated with Leadership," *Journal of Applied Psychology* (January 1948): 35–71.

12. Rensis Likert, *New Patterns of Management* (New York: McGraw-Hill, 1961).

13. Edwin A. Fleishman and James G. Hunt, eds., *Current Developments in the Study of Leadership* (Carbondale, IL: Southern Illinois Press, 1973), 1–37.

14. R. R. Blake and Jane S. Mouton, *The Managerial Grid* (Houston: Gulf Publishing, 1964); R. R. Blake and A. A. McCanse, "The Leadership Grid®," in *Leadership Dilemmas—Grid Solutions* (Houston: Gulf Publishing Company, 1991).

15. Fred E. Fiedler and Martin M. Chemers, *Leadership and Effective Management* (Glenview, IL: Scott Foresman, 1974).

16. Victor Vroom, "Leadership," in *Handbook of Organizational Psychology,* ed. Marvin Dunnette (Chicago: Rand McNally College Publishing, 1976), 1316.

17. R. K. Hambleton and R. Gumpert, "The Validity of Hersey-Blanchard's Theory of Leader Effectiveness," *Group and Organization Studies* 7, no. 2 (1982): 225–242. Also see C. L. Graeff, "The Situational Leadership Theory: A Critical Review," *Academy of Management Review* 8 (1983): 285–296.

18. Steven Kerr and John M. Jermier, "Substitutes for Leadership: Their Meaning and Measurement," *Organizational Behavior and Human Performance* (December 1978): 375–403.

19. George Graen, "Role-Making Processes in Organizations," in *Handbook of Organizational Psychology,* ed. Marvin Dunnette (Chicago: Rand McNally College Publishing, 1976).

20. Chester Schriesheim, C. A. Castro, and C. C. Coliser, "Leader-Member Exchange Research: A Comprehensive Review of Theory, Measurement, and Analytic Procedures," *Leadership Quarterly* 10 (1999): 63–113. Also see George Graen and Mary Uhl-Bien, "Relationship-Based Approach to Leadership: Development of Leader-Member Exchange (LMX) Theory over the Past 25 Years: Applying a Multilevel Multi-Domain Approach," *Leadership Quarterly* 6 (1995): 219–247.

21. Bernard M. Bass, *Leadership: Performance Beyond Expectations* (New York: Free Press, 1985), 43; and Bernard M. Bass, "Leadership: Good, Better, Best," *Organizational Dynamics* (1985) Winter, vol. 13: 26–40.

22. *Nancy Meyer.* "Farrah Back at Home Depot," *HFN The Weekly Newspaper for the Home Furnishing Network* (Oct 2, 1995) v69 n40, 1–2.

23. Daniel Goleman, "Leadership That Gets Results," *Harvard Business Review* (March–April 2000): 80–90.

24. Daniel Goleman, "What Makes a Leader?" *Harvard Business Review* (November–December 1998): 93–102.

25. W. Baldwin, "This Is the Answer," *Forbes* (July 5, 1982): 52. Also see Ralph Stayer, "How I Learned to Let My Workers Lead," Harvard Business Review (November–December, 1990).

26. Charles C. Manz and Henry P. Sims Jr., *Superleadership* (New York: Berkeley, 1990), xviii.

27. Howard Weiss, "Subordinate Imitation of Supervisor Behavior: The Role of Modeling in Organizational Socialization," *Organizational Behavior and Human Performance* 19 (1977): 89–105.

28. M. Sashkin, "Participative Management Is an Ethical Imperative," *Organizational Dynamics* 12 (1984): 5–22.

29. Martha T. Moore, "Sorting Out a Mess," *USA Today* (April 10, 1992): 5B.

30. Rich Teerlink, "Harley's Leadership U-Turn," *Harvard Business Review* (July–August 2000): 4–7.

31. See M. Porter, "Why Nations Triumph," *Fortune* (March 12, 1990): 94–98. Also see J. Dreyfuss, "Get Ready for the New Work Force," *Fortune* (April 23, 1990): 165, 168, 172, 176, 180–181.

32. F. A. Manske Jr., *Secrets of Effective Leadership* (Memphis, TN: Leadership Education and Development, Inc., 1987).

33. Robert L. Katz, "Skills of an Effective Administration," *Harvard Business Review* (September–October, 1974): 23–35.

34. Management Update, "Three Skills for Today's Leaders," *Harvard Business Review* (1999): 3–4.

# 14

# INTERPERSONAL AND ORGANIZATIONAL COMMUNICATION

The view that communication is critical to organizational excellence dates back at least to 1938, when Chester Barnard wrote his famous book, *The Functions of the Executive.*[1] In it, Barnard described one of the major responsibilities of executives as developing and maintaining a system of communication. It is a fact of workaday life that managers and employees alike must solve increasingly complex problems. And, increasingly, researchers and practitioners are examining the role that effective communication has in propelling individuals to overcome barriers, work through problems, and achieve goals. Do you believe that employee retention and productivity can be improved simply by communicating more forthrightly and more frequently to workers about how their pay and salary increases are determined?[2] In fact, research does support the proposition that constructive conversations of this type drive up performance.

As you'll see in this chapter, communication is an important part of the leadership function; and leading, as we have stressed earlier, is a core function of management. Managers cannot be effective as leaders if they cannot communicate well. Successful leaders have vision; they set direction and mobilize resources.[3] Whereas leaders don't necessarily create budgets, they do have a clear picture of what they want the organization to be and communicate that vision just as clearly to other members of the organization. This chapter's topic is interpersonal and organizational communication. First, we discuss the nature and scope of communication. Then, we examine various types of interpersonal and organizational communication. Next, we look at barriers to organizational communication and strategies for facilitating communication. Finally, we discuss how information and communication technology are impacting communication in the workplace.

## Communication

The term *communication* is a common one. Most of us have used it in one way or another to describe our interactions with others. Historical figures are often compared by their ability to communicate. TV, radio, and newspapers are referred to as communication media (the plural of *medium*); the telephone and computer are called communication devices. Unfortunately, communication is often taken for granted, though it is a complex activity. Failure to understand this complexity often leads to problems with communication.

Communication is defined as the exchange of information between a sender (source) and a receiver (audience). If meaning is not shared, communication has not taken place. A production worker stopped her machine to fix it because it was making defective products. The foreman came by and ordered: "Run it," so she turned the machine back on. When asked to explain her behavior, the worker replied, "He ordered me to make defectives."[4] The foreman surely didn't mean to order the worker to make defective products, but that's the message that was communicated.

KEY TERMS

**communication** The exchange of information and the sharing of meaning between a sender (source) and a receiver (audience).

EXHIBIT **14.1**        **The Communication Process**

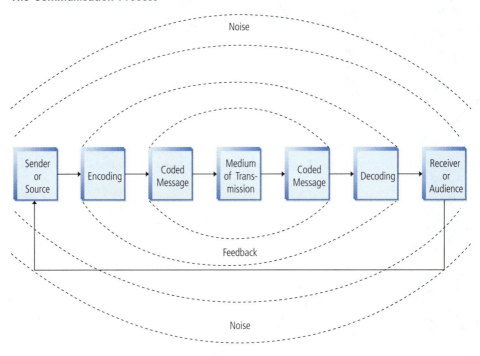

## The Communication Process

Communication can be described as a process in which a message is encoded and transmitted through some medium to a receiver who decodes the message and then transmits some sort of response back to the sender. It is through the communication process that the sharing of a common meaning takes place. As Exhibit 14.1 shows, communication begins with a sender—a person, a group, or an organization that has a message to share with another person or group of persons.

In organizations, executives, managers, workers, departments, and even the organization itself can be the source of a message. Executives must communicate not only with the board of directors and top-level managers, but also with groups and individuals outside the organization such as stockholders, regulators, and customers. Managers must communicate with managers in other departments, superiors, subordinates, customers, and suppliers. Workers must communicate with superiors, customers, and each other. Clearly, we could go on and on. The point is that every organization member is a source with a message to communicate to internal and external parties.

A message is an idea or experience that a sender wants to communicate. Messages can be communicated both verbally and nonverbally. For instance, a manager may want to communicate a process to a worker. This can be done in many ways: by explaining the process, illustrating it, or providing a written explanation. The critical issue is that the message is presented in such a way that the manager conveys the intended meaning.

To convey meaning, the sender must encode the message by converting it into groups of symbols that represent ideas or concepts. Encoding translates ideas or concepts into the coded message that will be communicated. We use symbols (languages, words, or gestures) to encode ideas into messages that others can understand. When encoding a message, the sender must use symbols that are familiar to the intended receiver. A person with a message to communicate should know the audience and present the message in language that the audience can grasp. A computer company developing a sales presentation targeted at a nontechnical audience should ensure that its presentation is written and delivered using words and graphics familiar to that audience. In referring to concepts, the sender should use the same symbols that the receiver uses to refer to those concepts, and should avoid using symbols that can have more than one meaning.

To relay the message, the sender must select and use a medium of transmission (a means of carrying an encoded message from the source to the receiver). Ink on paper, vibrations of air produced by vocal cords, and electronically produced airwaves such as radio and TV signals are examples of transmission media. If a sender relays a message through an inappropriate medium of transmission, the message may not reach the right receivers. Organizations use memos, meetings, reward systems, policy statements, production schedules, and many other mediums to communicate with members. Some may not always be appropriate.

Decoding is the process by which the receiver interprets the symbols (coded message) sent by the source by converting them into concepts and ideas. Seldom does the receiver decode exactly the same meaning that a sender encoded. When the receiver interprets the message differently from what the sender intended, the cause may be noise (interference that affects any or all stages of the communication process). Noise has many sources, such as competing messages, misinterpretation, radio static, faulty printing, or use of ambiguous or unfamiliar symbols. Yelling at a subordinate may result in noise, even though the manager uses familiar words to convey the message. Noise may be present at any point in the communication process.

Feedback is the receiver's response to the sender's message. During feedback, the receiver becomes the source of a message that is directed back to the original sender, who then becomes a receiver. Thus, communication can be viewed as a circular process, as Exhibit 14.1 shows. But feedback may not take place immediately. For instance, a consumer products manufacturer may advertise the benefits of a product (the message), but the consumer may not actually purchase the product (feedback) until some time after receiving the source's message. In organizations, effective feedback must be two-way, engaging, responsive, and directed toward a desired outcome.[5] Goals can best be achieved when people in organizations communicate with each other and work cooperatively. It is often nonmanagers who are closest to production problems, suppliers, and customers. If they do not have the capacity to provide feedback, managers will miss out on valuable information.

The communication process has a channel capacity, a limit on the volume of information that it can handle effectively. Channel capacity is determined by the least efficient component of the communication process. With verbal communications, there is a limit to how fast a source can speak and how much a receiver can decode. If a manager transmits more than one message, the communication process may not be totally effective. The audience (receivers) may not be able to decode all the messages at the same time, especially if these messages are inconsistent. For instance, suppose a manager at a branch bank says to all the new tellers that customers are important; but he also tells them to close their windows early so that they can balance their windows and get out of the bank on time. The result is longer lines at closing times, and the new tellers do not get the message that customers are important.

## Selecting a Communication Medium

Media selection is a critical aspect of effective communication. A communication medium is a conduit or channel through which data and meaning are conveyed.[6] Communication media include oral, written, and nonverbal delivery systems. Exhibit 14.2 provides examples of

**KEY**TERMS

**medium of transmission** A means of carrying an encoded message from the source to the receiver; for example, ink on paper, air vibrations produced by vocal cords, and radio and TV signals.

**decoding** The interpretation of a message's symbols by the receiver, who converts them into concepts and ideas.

**noise** Interference that affects any or all stages of the communication process and that may be present at any point in the communication process.

**feedback** The receiver's response to the sender's message, during which the receiver becomes the source of a message that is directed back to the original sender, who then becomes a receiver.

**channel capacity** A limit on the volume of information that can be transmitted effectively, as determined by the least efficient component of the communication process.

**communication medium** A conduit or channel through which data and meaning are conveyed; includes oral, written, and nonverbal delivery systems.

**14.2**

**Alternative Communication Media**

| Oral | Written | Nonverbal |
|---|---|---|
| Face-to-face contact | Computer printout | Touch |
| Telephone | Letter | Eye contact |
| Speech | Electronic mail | Body language |
| Video conference | Memo | Time |
| Intercom | Bulletin board | Space |

communication media. Managers must determine which media to use when sending and receiving information. Suppose, for instance, a sales manager wants to communicate a new compensation plan to the selling force. How should the new plan be communicated? What media should be used? Would letters, memos, oral presentations, telephone calls, or some other medium work best? The answers to these questions will likely affect the success of the new compensation program.

One factor that has been stressed in choosing media is the media richness (media's capacity to convey data).[7] One medium may be richer than another; that is, one medium may have a greater capacity to carry data than another. Data-carrying capacity refers to the degree to which a medium can effectively and efficiently convey data. Thus, the best medium can be determined by its richness or effectiveness. Research has shown that managers rely most on media richness when making media selection choices.[8]

Several criteria are used to evaluate a medium's richness: the medium's capacity for timely feedback; its capacity for multiple uses, such as audio and visual; the extent to which the message can be personalized; and the variety of language, such as natural and body language, that can be used.[9] Face-to-face contact is the richest medium because feedback is the fastest, both audio and visual cues can be used, the message is personal, and a variety of languages can be used. Conversely, formal numeric media such as computer printouts are the least rich because feedback is very slow and data-carrying capacity is limited to visual information.

Suppose a firm's sales manager decides that the most effective way to inform the selling force about the new compensation plan is through face-to-face communication. The meaning of the spoken word; the rate, pitch, and force of the verbal message; and facial expressions can all combine to give a single, powerful message. Each salesperson will have the opportunity to see the manager, hear the message, interpret it, and give and receive feedback. This seems to be the best way to ensure the new plan's success. Unfortunately, the firm has thousands of salespeople in several countries throughout the world. Face-to-face communication is simply not possible.

In addition to richness, several other factors must be considered in selecting a communication medium. First, cost must be weighed against the medium's speed of transmission and its overall effectiveness. A telephone call, for instance, may be the fastest and most effective medium when speed is critical in communication, even though a letter would be much less expensive. Some messages have a greater impact when delivered in person. Communicating a promotion personally, or both in person and by letter, may convey the maximum impact. Second, the purpose of the communication influences the media choice. To communicate technical or quantitative information, a written report may be most effective. Third, the extent to which interaction is necessary should be considered when selecting a medium. A performance review could be in writing, but a face-to-face meeting would allow for questions, feedback, and understanding. Finally, the receiver's capabilities also influence which medium is selected. A receiver who tends to forget oral communication may need written reminders, providing documentation for the future.

**KEY**TERMS

**media richness** A medium's capacity to convey data.

**data-carrying capacity** The degree to which a medium can effectively and efficiently convey data.

In summary, media choice depends on the situation's requirements. Some situations may call for oral communication, some for written, and others for a combination. Always select a communication medium that most effectively conveys the intended message to the target audience.

## The Role of Communication in Organizations

Throughout this book, we have discussed several functions of management, including planning, organizing, and leading. Controlling will be discussed in the next part of the book. Management is largely a profession that functions through the vehicle of communicating with people—most good managers are good communicators. Indeed, managers need technical, analytical, and conceptual skills to perform their functions and develop a culture that is conducive to quality. But communication is an essential part of all other management functions and processes. Put another way, "The job of the manager is, ultimately, communication, regardless of how varied or specialized the activity of the moment might be."[10]

Many managers stress open communication as a means of improving organizational effectiveness and quality. The goal of constantly improving quality can be achieved only if it supersedes differences, jealousies, competition between individuals and departments, and turf battles. Silence has been attributed to failed products, broken processes, and poor career decisions; indeed, breaking the silence can lead to a flow of ideas from all levels of the organization.[11] But open communication requires more than simply maintaining open offices. It also involves managers' accessibility to workers, day-to-day interaction with employees, and breaking down barriers and resistance to change. If an organization decides to implement teams, communication is essential. Resistance to the change should be expected. Here communication helps people deal with change, work through it, and adapt to the new way of doing things, whether it be working in teams or some other change. In short, communication pervades every aspect of the organization — every individual, team, or department, and each external relationship with customers, suppliers, and competitors. The organization cannot achieve its goals without open, two-way communication.

## Interpersonal Communication

Individuals spend a great deal of time in organizations interacting with each other. Interpersonal communication is communication between two people, usually face-to-face.[12] Other communication media such as the telephone or e-mail also can be used to communicate interpersonally; e-mail is preferred to the telephone by 80 percent of business professionals responding to a survey.[13] Through interpersonal communication we develop and maintain human relationships—the basic social units of any organization. Thus interpersonal communication is the fundamental building block of organizational communication.

## Oral Communication

Oral communication takes place when the spoken word is used to transmit a message. Conversations can take place in person, via telephone, or through some other mechanism that allows individuals to speak to one another. Oral communication enables prompt, two-way interaction between parties. Many meetings and conferences that involve people from different locations, even different parts of the world, are conducted using TV hookups so that participants can interact personally. Perhaps the major benefit of this type of communication is that ideas can be interchanged and prompt feedback can be provided. Questions can be addressed, positions and issues debated, and a plan for action or resolution established. Oral communication that takes place in person also allows the use of gestures, facial expressions, and other emotions such as tone of voice.

Oral communication, because of its immediacy, can result in poor communication. If, for instance, a person becomes angry, noise enters the communication process. Messages that are not clearly encoded may also fail to communicate the intended idea. A hurried manager may give an oral instruction or initiative without thinking about the outcome. (Recall what happened when the foreman instructed the factory worker to turn the machine on.) Even though feedback is immediate, it might be without thought, reducing the quality of the communication. Individuals often feel the need to respond immediately in a face-to-face meeting, when in fact they should take some time to prepare a well-thought-out response.

## Written Communication

Transmitting a message through the written word is called written communication. This type of communication can help eliminate the problem we just discussed. Written messages allow a manager to think about the message, reread it several times, and perhaps get others to review the message before it is transmitted. The receiver can take time to read the message carefully and accurately. Written messages are also more permanent than oral, providing a record of the communication. Whether it is a long report or a short memo, written communication can be referred to in the future as needed. Managers often find it necessary to document their decisions for legal reasons.

Despite the advantages of written communication, managers generally prefer to communicate orally. Written communication takes more time to prepare and does not allow interaction or immediate feedback. Managers rely on two-way communication to resolve problems quickly. It takes much longer to get ideas on paper, to distribute them to others, and to receive written responses; a telephone call or meeting is quicker. Written communication, by its formal nature, can also discourage open communication. E-mail, a form of written communication, is timelier and enables a quick response, perhaps explaining its popularity.

## Nonverbal Communication

All intentional or unintentional messages that are neither written nor spoken are referred to as nonverbal communication. Examples include vocal cues, body movements, facial expressions, personal appearance, and distance or space. A certain look or glance, seating arrangements at a meeting, or a sudden change in voice tone can communicate a strong message. Nonverbal messages can be powerful, depending on the situation. For instance, a salesperson's ability to actively listen and detect the other party's nonverbal communication cues often determines whether the relationship is successful.[14]

The difficulty with nonverbal communication is that in order to accurately decode a message, the receiver must know the specific background or frame of reference of its source. Suppose that on her first day of work, a new employee witnesses her boss screaming at a coworker. She's shocked, and asks the coworker if this happens often. He explains that the boss is a great guy and a great manager, will do anything for you, but happens to yell all the time. Now she has a different perspective. On the other hand, imagine the effect when a manager who is known to be cool and calm—and rarely changes expressions—suddenly glares at someone in a meeting.

Managers must recognize that nonverbal communication can occur unintentionally. After being on the job for about three months, a computer programmer comes to the conclusion that his supervisor does not like him. He is so concerned that he decides to look for another job; but he decides to talk to his supervisor before quitting. He tells the supervisor, "Obviously I did

## IMPROVING NONVERBAL COMMUNICATION SKILLS

Here are some tips for improving your nonverbal communication skills.

**Maintain eye contact.**

Establish eye contact with the person or group you are communicating with, and remember that it signals interest and credibility. Eye contact has been identified as perhaps the most powerful aspect of effective communication.

**Use posture to project a positive image.**

Lean toward your communication partner, showing an interest in what the other person is saying. Sit or stand erect and at eye-level with the person to whom you are speaking. Avoid the extremes of being too stiff or too loose.

**Use gestures appropriately.**

Natural, relaxed movements or gestures communicate self-confidence and can be used to support a point. Conversely, some gestures such as repeatedly touching your nose or removing your glasses can be distracting. Some gestures should be avoided—for instance, crossing the arms signals defiance and even anger.

**Think about how you look.**

People form impressions of others immediately, often based on dress and appearance. The way a person dresses and looks can command respect; good grooming also shows respect for others. Wear serious clothing when you want to be taken seriously—dark suits and conservative grooming, for example.

**Learn to read others.**

Don't forget to *listen* to what others are saying and experiencing through nonverbal communication. It is critical to pay attention to others and present your message accordingly.

Sources: Adapted from Dan Danbom, "Goes Without Saying," *Business Finance* (April 2006): 56; Lillian Chaney, "Presenter Behaviors," *SuperVision* (June 2006): 8–9; Sarah Hanson, "How Body Language Can Win Business," *Director*: 32.

something to upset you." The manager looks at him without emotion, tells the programmer he is doing a great job and can expect a nice raise at his six-month review, and offers no other explanation. The point? Managers have to understand the potential of nonverbal communication and realize that they might be unintentionally sending the wrong message. The preceding Management Highlight suggests several ways to improve nonverbal communication skills.

Nonverbal communication is important to multinational corporations (MNCs) operating in a foreign country. People in different countries and cultures have different sets of nonverbal symbols and meanings. Nonverbal cues such as touch, body language, and personal distance are used differently across cultures. Managers encounter difficulty in interpreting nonverbal communication while working in foreign countries. Likewise, they are uncertain what nonverbal messages they may be transmitting. A business deal could be adversely affected if someone from a foreign country misinterprets a nonverbal message. Representatives working in a foreign country should receive adequate training in that country's nonverbal customs.

## Empathic Listening

For some time now, you have been reading this book that we have written. Reading and writing are both forms of interpersonal communication, but they are not the only ones. Speaking and listening are other forms. We all have a lot of experience speaking, but perhaps listening is the one form of communication that we have the least experience with. In his best-selling book *The 7 Habits of Highly Effective People,* Stephen Covey suggests that the key to effective listening is to seek first to understand, and then to be understood.[15] Covey describes empathic listening as listening with the intent to understand. This is not easy—it requires looking at an issue from another person's point of view. It requires listening not only with your ears, but with your eyes and your heart as well. Successful management starts with empathic listening.[16]

Distractions such as interruptions, telephone calls, and unfinished work are a major barrier to effective listening. Creating an environment free of such distractions will improve listening.

**KEY**TERMS

**empathic listening**
Listening in which the listener attempts first to understand and then to be understood; requires looking at an issue from another person's point of view.

Many listeners also take detours during a communication. For instance, if someone mentions a word that brings out certain emotions, we become distracted and tune out the message. Many receivers also begin to mentally debate a point, thinking ahead and planning a response. When you do this, you're likely to miss the message.

It is not easy to listen, but we can all start by taking time to listen. Relax, try to close out other distractions, and give both your mental and physical attention to the other person. Help the other person relax by assuming a nonthreatening listening posture, maintaining eye contact, and assuming a warm facial expression. This demonstrates that you, the listener, are interested in what is being said.

Communication can also be improved by giving and requesting constructive feedback. If people say what they think others want to hear, feedback is of limited value. Honest feedback can be used to determine whether the listener understood the intended message. Effective listeners focus on the message's meaning, postpone judgments until the communication is complete, actively respond to the speaker, and avoid focusing on emotionally charged words.

Effective, empathic listening takes time and practice. Listening with empathy puts you on the same level with another person. Listening is difficult when you do not understand the other person. Effective listening is not a passive exercise; it is an active skill that requires full participation. Good listeners take notes, ask questions, and are totally attentive to what is being said. Although listening may not come naturally to all of us, with practice, we can become better listeners and reap the benefits of effective communication. This next Management Highlight will help you evaluate your listening skills.

Students need to practice good listening skills in all their classes. Without listening ability, learning is difficult. Are you a good listener? How can you determine your listening skill weaknesses?

# Organizational Communication

We noted earlier that individuals and groups must communicate effectively for organizations to be successful. In this section, we examine formal and informal channels of organizational communication and their impact on the communication process. It is the manager's job to ensure that effective, efficient channels are available to facilitate communication. Exhibit 14.3 illustrates the forms of organizational communication, both formal and informal. Managers must understand these forms; they must also be aware of the barriers to organizational communication and know how to remove them.

## Formal Channels of Communication

Formal channels of communication are the official paths prescribed by management. These formal channels generally follow the organization's chain of command. Information can be communicated downward, upward, or horizontally; and it can be oral, written, or nonverbal.

| Downward Communication | Information flows down the organizational hierarchy from managers and supervisors to subordinates through downward communication. As Exhibit 14.3 shows, this communication follows the formal lines of authority prescribed by the chain of command. Downward communication generally involves job instructions, manuals, policy statements, memos, motivational appeals, and other forms of formal instruction or feedback. Downward communication has been associated with job performance and job satisfaction.[17] Downward communication is not always adequate, because workers need more information than just job instructions. They also need to know, for instance, what other members of the organization are doing. Nevertheless, downward communication is important because lack of communication from superiors can leave workers misinformed, feeling disconnected, and less satisfied with their jobs.

MANAGEMENTHIGHLIGHT

## LISTENING SKILLS

### Directions

Place an X on the number that indicates how important you think the specific skill is for good listening. Then place a circle around the number that indicates your estimation of your present skill level in listening to people.

| Skill Areas | High/ Excellent | | | Low/ Poor | |
|---|---|---|---|---|---|
| 1. Regarding what the other person says as important—at least to the speaker | 5 | 4 | 3 | 2 | 1 |
| 2. Listening without interrupting | 5 | 4 | 3 | 2 | 1 |
| 3. Not rushing the other person | 5 | 4 | 3 | 2 | 1 |
| 4. Giving full attention to the other person | 5 | 4 | 3 | 2 | 1 |
| 5. Not responding judgmentally | 5 | 4 | 3 | 2 | 1 |
| 6. Adjusting to the other person's pace of speaking | 5 | 4 | 3 | 2 | 1 |
| 7. Listening objectively | 5 | 4 | 3 | 2 | 1 |
| 8. Responding both to what is said and to what is left unsaid | 5 | 4 | 3 | 2 | 1 |
| 9. Checking to be sure that the other person heard correctly | 5 | 4 | 3 | 2 | 1 |
| 10. Maintaining confidentiality | 5 | 4 | 3 | 2 | 1 |

Give your overall rating of the quality of your listening skills, with 10 being the highest rating and 1 being lowest: 10 9 8 7 6 5 4 3 2 1.

### Feedback

Both students and managers have completed the Listening Skills quiz. Based on many responses, the two skill areas in which respondents seem to be the weakest are (2) listening without interrupting and (4) giving full attention to the other person. People seem to have a knack for interrupting others and for not listening to what is being said. Any item that has an X on the 1 or 2 rating may require attention on your part. Also, a gap between an X and a circle equal to two or more numbers indicates a discrepancy between perceived importance and skill level. Each of these ten areas is extremely important.

Listening skills can be improved by:

- Talking less

- Avoiding hasty judgments

- Taking notes

- Letting the person finish talking

- Asking questions

- Paying attention

**upward communication** Information that flows up the organizational hierarchy, from subordinates to supervisors and managers; necessary for managers to evaluate the effectiveness of downward communication and for workers to feel they are a meaningful part of the organization.

One problem managers face is deciding which, and how much, information to communicate to subordinates. Too much information, especially if it is irrelevant, is eventually ignored. Every Friday some salespeople find dozens of reports and summaries in their mailboxes—many of them useless—and begin to ignore the material. Unfortunately, some of it may be valuable. Managers who wish to empower workers must provide quality information that can enable workers to improve. This may also require communicating information that was once considered only for managers, such as financial and performance data.

**| Upward Communication |** Information that flows up the organization from subordinates to supervisors and managers is called upward communication. This type of communication is necessary for managers to evaluate the effectiveness of downward communication. It also enables workers to feel they are a meaningful part of the organization. Many types of messages are communicated upward, including suggestions for improvements, feelings about the job or the organization, problems or grievances, requests, and responses to

14.3 **Formal and Informal Channels of Communication**

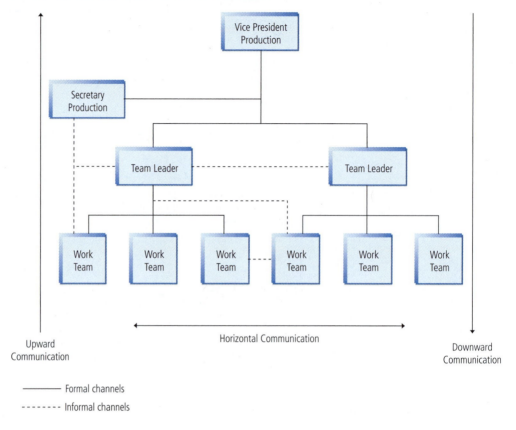

downward communication. Many workers face a dilemma concerning what they should communicate to superiors. In any event, upward communication should be encouraged, because it helps to drive fear out of the organization. A factory worker must not be afraid to tell the supervisor that the machine is making defective products.

Obviously, information is not effective unless it is accurate. Upward communication is often distorted in one way or another to make it more acceptable to managers. Workers may be reluctant to report problems if they think managers will blame them. Managers should create an environment in which workers feel comfortable reporting good news and bad. Empowered workers are more likely to report accurate information than less powerful or fearful employees. Managers can demonstrate that upward communication is valued by replying or acting promptly and positively.

| **Horizontal Communication** | Messages flow between persons at the same level of the organization through horizontal communication. This includes staff meetings, face-to-face interactions, and sharing of information through memos and reports. Horizontal communication is needed to coordinate the activities of diverse but independent units or departments. For instance, the manager of marketing and sales needs to communicate with the manager of production to avoid under- or overstocking a product.

Traditionally, horizontal communication took place more among managers than nonmanagers. But as organizations have begun to utilize work teams and quality circles, workers from different units or departments are often called together to work on a project or problem. Many organizations are placing increasing emphasis on horizontal communication. In their book *Re-inventing the Corporation,* John Naisbitt and Patricia Aburdene observe, "The top-down authoritarian management style is yielding to a networking style of management, where people learn from one another horizontally, where everyone is a resource for everyone else, and where each person gets support and assistance from many different directions."[18] Horizontal communication between subsidiaries of the same multinational corporation can be a problem, especially when subsidiaries are located in countries where different languages are spoken. Research suggests that corporate training should focus on the broad spectrum of international communication rather than on increasing the knowledge of any one language.[19]

## Informal Channels of Communication

Informal channels of communication are outside of the official chain of command established by management (see Exhibit 14.3). One informal channel of communication is the grapevine. The grapevine cuts across formal channels of communication and carries a variety of facts, opinions, rumors, and other information. All organizations, large or small, have grapevines; it is futile for managers to try to eliminate this informal channel. Conversely, communications must be managed effectively so that the grapevine is not the main source of information. When properly nurtured, the grapevine can help managers get a feel for the morale of organizations, understand the anxieties of the workforce, and evaluate the effectiveness of formal communication efforts.[20]

Although grapevines do not always have negative consequences, they are frequently troublesome to managers. A middle manager once learned she was being considered for an impending transfer when she received a telephone call from a real estate agent in another part of the country. She eventually discovered that the real estate agent's contact at corporate headquarters had learned about the transfer and passed it on to the realtor. Unfortunately, the woman's supervisor had not yet told her about the transfer. The grapevine can also be the source of harmful rumors and gossip; it is especially dangerous when managers manipulate it to communicate with employees instead of using normal, open communication channels. Managers can control the grapevine to some extent by communicating accurate, timely information, by maintaining and cultivating open channels of communication in all directions, and by moving quickly to dispel rumors and correct inaccurate information.

Despite its limitations, the grapevine offers an abundance of operating data, generates corporate memory, and can communicate important insights with speed and economy. As organizations move toward the new paradigm of flat, borderless, and globally dispersed network organizations, informal communication—more than ever before—provides an important source of needed information.

## Barriers to Organizational Communication

Communication is not always effective. Breakdowns occur for many reasons. Some can simply be attributed to poor habits—lack of preparation or vague directions. Barriers such as these can be overcome without too much difficulty if the communicator is willing to work at it. Other barriers can be much more difficult to overcome. In this section, we examine common barriers to organizational communication.

**KEY**TERMS

**grapevine** An informal channel of communication that cuts across formal channels of communication and that carries a variety of facts, opinions, rumors, and other information.

## Personal Characteristics

One major barrier to organizational communication is the personal makeup of the parties involved. People have attitudes about work-related matters, conditions in the world, their personal lives, and communication in general. Some individuals have defensive attitudes and interpret messages as an order or threat. Some people simply have incompatible personalities. Others feel inferior or threatened, become defensive in an attempt to cover up their feelings, and respond aggressively. Constantly being on the offensive is an obstacle to communication.

Another problem involves the parties' credibility. Source credibility refers to the receiver's confidence and trust in the source of a message. If the receiver has little or no faith in the source, it will be difficult for the two parties to communicate. For example, a recent study reported that when auditors thought a client's reputation was not squeaky clean, they were less likely to believe the client, and in turn collected more audit evidence than usual.[21] Individuals lose credibility when they pass along inaccurate information or fail to follow through with directives or initiatives. New leaders are often greeted with a sense of excitement and hope by other members of the organization. But if they make promises they don't keep—pay raises, new offices, lower taxes, and so on—they lose their credibility and their ability to communicate effectively.

Several other personal characteristics can inhibit communication. Some individuals tend to be disorganized, which carries over to their communication efforts. Poor listening habits on the part of the receiver are also a communication barrier. As mentioned earlier in the chapter, some people, rather than listening, are thinking ahead to how they will respond and thus do not receive the message. Receivers might also have certain predispositions and tune out the communicator because the message is not consistent with their beliefs. Finally, individuals might be biased because of age, gender, looks, or some other factor, and these biases inhibit the communication process. Such biases are especially alarming as the workforce becomes more diverse.

## Frame of Reference

As individuals, we all have different backgrounds and have had many different experiences that shape the meanings we assign to words. There is a great deal of difference between you or me saying, "I'm starved," as we head to a restaurant, and a child who hasn't eaten in ten days uttering the same words. We have a different *frame of reference,* so we may have difficulty achieving common understanding. When a parent tells a child, "I never had so many toys when I was a kid," the child may find it difficult to understand because the parent and the child have different frames of reference. Likewise, if a supervisor and a subordinate or two coworkers have different backgrounds and experiences, organizational communication may suffer.

A related problem in communication concerns people blocking out information they are not comfortable with. Selective perception occurs when people screen out information that is not consistent with their beliefs or background. When people receive information that conflicts with what they believe, they tend to ignore it or distort it to make it conform to their beliefs. Managers, for instance, generally analyze problems based on their frame of reference. In other words, a sales manager analyzes a problem from the sales point of view, whereas an environmentalist analyzes problems based on a different set of beliefs.

Conflicting frames of reference and selective perception can hamper organizational communication in various ways. As individuals move up the organizational hierarchy, for instance, they may develop different frames of reference. A salesperson who is concerned with closing the deal and a sales manager who must be concerned with cost control and other management issues might each attach different meanings to words. Likewise, an individual in the production department might have a different frame of reference from a marketing staffer. This can reduce the effectiveness of upward, downward, or horizontal communication.

One challenge faced by organizations implementing teams is breaking down barriers between individuals and departments. Because traditional organizations are structured to encourage competition among individuals, units, departments, or divisions, these entities develop their own frames of reference. This makes it difficult for people to communicate and work together toward the same goal. In the worst scenario, individuals care only about their own job and their own department's performance. A worker is rewarded for reaching a production quota; quality control and customer satisfaction are somebody else's problem. Under these circumstances, effective communication is difficult, and the organization's overall performance is likely to suffer.

## Resistance to Change

All organizations go through change, whether it be a new sales program, new leadership, or new owners. Change is a constant in today's organizations. Yet no matter how innocuous or even beneficial change may be, we all have a human tendency to resist it. Change triggers rational and irrational emotional reactions because it involves uncertainty. People resist change for several reasons: they fear the loss of something they value; they mistrust management; they view the change differently from those initiating it; or they have low tolerance for change.[22] Whatever the reason, resistance to change is a significant barrier to communication. When firms change the way employees do their jobs—by reengineering business processes or implementing new systems—they must be prepared to deal with resistance to change.[23]

The CEO at a major bank felt that change was needed due to the branch managers' lack of interest in doing anything other than making loans and performing administrative duties; the managers had little interest in other management issues confronting the bank. The CEO decided to schedule monthly meetings with all bank officers, including branch managers, to discuss broad issues like the bank's overall goals, personnel policy, productivity, strategies, and compensation programs. At the meetings, the managers expressed few ideas on how they could assume more managerial responsibility. The CEO increased the number of meetings, then asked for individual reports to obtain each manager's input on how to deal with management problems and issues. The results of this approach were even more disappointing. The reports demonstrated a clear lack of communication between the CEO and the branch managers. In this case, the branch managers' resistance to change proved to be a significant barrier to the CEO's objective of prompting managers to take on more responsibility.

## Facilitating Organizational Communication

Although some barriers to communication cannot be completely removed, organizational communication can be facilitated in several ways. By understanding the barriers and striving to be better communicators, individuals can improve the communication process. In some cases this may be relatively simple, perhaps accomplished just by breaking a few bad habits. In other cases, improving communication can be a lengthy, ongoing, demanding process. The Management Highlight on page 316 examines how storytelling can be used to facilitate organizational communication.

### Developing Communication Skills

Perhaps the best way to facilitate communication is to develop the skills needed to be a better communicator. Both managers and nonmanagers need to develop communication skills. Managers must improve their ability to understand workers and to be understood. With more individual responsibility, workers must also be able to communicate effectively. Individuals can acquire these skills through managerial training programs in communication.

We have already discussed the importance of *listening* in effective communication. A good communicator listens with *empathy*. By understanding the feelings of others, the communicator

**FACILITATING ORGANIZATIONAL COMMUNICATION THROUGH STORYTELLING**

Many organizations are discovering that storytelling is a powerful way to improve communication. Stories are fundamental to communication, learning, and thinking; they are the most effective way of storing, retrieving, and disseminating information. Hearing a story requires active participation on the part of the listener. Sharing personal ideas and experiences in the form of stories makes information more tangible and memorable. In short, stories provide a valuable set of tools for organizations. Below are some of the benefits storytelling provides:

- Develops and nurtures partnerships and teamwork

- Empowers individuals to explore controversial subjects

- Motivates, inspires, and builds credibility

- Provides the impetus for change

- Builds commitment and momentum through the sharing of success stories

- Helps shape the culture of the organization

- Helps individuals and units negotiate their differences

- Inspires others to tell their stories, and then learn from them

Sources: Adapted from Terrence L. Gargiulo, "Power of Stories," *The Journal of Quality and Participation* (Spring 2006): 4–9; Christine van Winkelen, "Connecting Individual and Organizational Knowledge," *Knowledge Management Review* (May/June 2006): 3; Hilary McLellan, "Corporate Storytelling Perspectives," *The Journal of Quality and Participation* (Spring 2006): 17–21.

can anticipate how a message will be decoded. And by encouraging *feedback,* the communicator can determine whether the message was properly decoded. The use of *simple language* can also facilitate communication. Complex language and the use of confusing or misleading terms introduces noise into the communication process. Good communicators also *question* others, asking for ideas and suggestions, thus encouraging participation. They *initiate* new ideas and calls for action, and *evaluate* the ideas of others, offering insightful summaries.

## Minimizing Resistance to Change

As we said, many workers resist change, which is a major barrier to communication. By minimizing resistance to change, managers can help facilitate the communication process. Otherwise change will be poorly implemented, resulting in no change at all or a very short-term, superficial change. In some instances, because of the resulting miscommunication and lack of trust, organizations are worse off after the change effort fails. To implement change successfully, the communication strategy must explain why the change is necessary; create a clear and compelling plot line; be developed with an understanding of those involved in the process; and support engagement.[24]

Managers have several methods to minimize resistance to change.[25] One way is to deal with change before it occurs, through education and communication. Preparing people for change helps cut down on resistance. Also, by having those who are affected by the change participate in it, managers can increase these people's commitment to the change. Being supportive when change is being implemented is critical. Managers can show their support by being understanding, being a good listener, and going to bat for subordinates on important issues. Reducing resistance to change can also be accomplished through negotiation and agreement. Regardless of which method is used, managers responsible for implementing change must overcome resistance to change in order to facilitate effective communication and a successful change effort. An organization is more likely to adapt to change if it has many means of two-way communication that reach all levels and that all employees can understand.

## Communicating with a Diverse Workforce

Managers increasingly face the prospect of communicating with a diverse workforce, which makes communicating more difficult. To facilitate communication in such an environment, managers must be aware of diversity and understand its value. Differences in gender, race, culture, and the like can influence how people interpret (decode) messages. A good communicator should not only be aware of an individual's background and experiences, but also anticipate the meaning that person will attach to different messages.

The globalization of the world's economy has placed increased emphasis on cross-cultural communication. Whenever two parties have different cultural backgrounds, communication breakdowns can result. People often tend to communicate based on their own background or culture. Thus, when communicating with someone from another culture, they are more likely to send a message that is not intended or to misinterpret a message they are receiving. Effective listening skills are especially important for individuals involved in cross-cultural communication.

Communicating with an increasingly diverse workforce is critical to an organization's viability. This is not a question of civil rights or affirmative action, which are something different. It concerns the demands a diverse workforce places on the communication skills of managers and coworkers. It requires not only the skills in listening, empathy, feedback, and language already discussed, but also skills in understanding other cultures, as well as the ability to overcome hidden biases and stereotypes about other people.

## Conducting Communication Audits

The communication audit is a useful tool for managers to use in understanding and improving organizational communication. A communication audit is a systematic method of collecting and evaluating information about an organization's communication efforts. The purposes of a communication audit are to:

- Provide information about communication behavior in the organization

- Provide a means for diagnosing discontent or revealing problems in communication

- Provide a clear picture of current communication patterns and determine those aspects that could be most affected by change

- Provide a before-and-after picture of organizational communication in relation to change

Benefits of communication audits are described in the next Management Highlight.

There are no black-and-white guidelines for conducting a communication audit. Information can be collected from managers and workers via surveys, interviews, observing operations, and reviews of formal and informal reports and procedures used in communicating. Organizations use many different formats when conducting a communication audit.

As firms in the next decade struggle with such issues as global competition, downsizing, and reorganization, communication in organizations is taking on increased significance. Effective communication characterizes successful organizations, whereas poor communication leads to such problems as lower quality and productivity, anger, and mistrust. Through effective communication, individuals can solve complex problems and achieve organizational goals.

## Information and Communication Technology

In today's workplace, using information and communication technologies (ICTs) as a communication tool is commonplace. Blogs, group-messaging, and computer networks, to name a few, are changing the way we communicate in modern organizations. In this section, we examine

---

**KEY TERMS**

**communication audit**
A systematic method of collecting and evaluating information about an organization's communication efforts with the purposes of providing (1) information about communication behavior in the organization, (2) a means for diagnosing discontent or revealing problems in communication, (3) a clear picture of current communication patterns and how they might be affected by change, and (4) a before-and-after picture of organizational communication in relation to change.

MANAGEMENT HIGHLIGHT

## BENEFITS OF COMMUNICATION AUDITS

| Improved productivity

| Positive impact on programs

| Reduced communication costs

| More efficient use of time

| Verification of facts

| Better use of information and communication technology

| Improved morale

| A more vibrant organizational culture

| Discovery of hidden information resources

| Communication changes

Sources: C. W. Downs, *Communication Audits* (Glenview, IL: Scott, Foresman, 1988); G. M. Goldhaber and D. P. Rogers, *Auditing Organizational Communication Systems. The ICA Communication Audit* (Dubuque, IA: Kendall/Hunt, 1979); and S. Hamilton, *A Communication Audit Handbook: Helping Organizations Communicate* (New York: Longman, 1987).

some of these communication technologies, as well as collaboration technologies that assist employees working together—sometimes down the hall and sometimes across the world—in exchanging ideas and solving problems.

## Communication Technologies

A variety of information technology tools are allowing coworkers to share information more efficiently. Nearly everyone working in an organizational environment uses voice answering systems and e-mail. Many businesses are switching from traditional telephone service to *Voice over Internet Protocol (VoIP)*, which allows callers to use a broadband internet connection and eliminate telephone charges. *Wireless networks* use radio waves to connect to the Internet; these networks have increased the use of laptop computers and other portable devices such as the BlackBerry. Wireless networks and free public wireless connections (Public Wi-Fi) allow business communication to occur anywhere at anytime without interrupting access to company files, software programs, and e-mail. For instance, as part of its first major design overhaul in thirty years, McDonald's added Wi-Fi access.[26] As a result of wireless networks and Wi-Fi, more people are working from their homes or other remote sites, a practice called *telecommuting*.

Some companies provide their own protected Web site to share internal information, called an *intranet*. A typical intranet handles: company announcements; e-mail; information about policies, procedures, and frequently asked questions; employee directories; personnel forms and information; and a variety of other documents, discussion forums, and employee information. For instance, at the Japanese firm Sharp Corporation, factory workers are trained over the company intranet.[27] One of the major benefits of developing an intranet is that it uses Internet technology but is available only to people within the company.

Another advancement in communication technology that is especially helpful to disabled workers is *voice recognition* software. Computers equipped with this software allow users to dictate up to 160 words a minute with accurate transcription. Professionals with heavy dictation loads also find this a useful means of creating documents, entering data, writing e-mails, even surfing the web—all by voice. Voice recognition software is becoming much more common in cars, where hands-free operation can improve safety. With the Acura TL system, the driver can control navigation, climate, and audio systems by speaking. As voice recognition software is becoming more efficient, expect to see it used in a wide variety of applications, for example, a Chinese-speaking business person talking to an English-speaking associate.[28]

## Collaboration Technologies

Information technologies are not only reshaping the way individuals communicate; they are changing the way groups interact and make decisions. Today's rapid pace of business and increasing global competition are driving the development of innovative collaboration technologies. *Voice conferencing* enables two or more callers from different locations to share a call. Individuals from different sites can collaborate or conduct a conference via telephone. Organizations also rely on *videoconferencing* to hold meetings or present information by using computer networks as audio and video equipment. Different groups can see each other and interact in real time even though they might be thousands of miles apart. With the increasing costs of travel, voice conferencing and videoconferencing is gaining popularity in many firms. Videoconferencing has boosted the efficiency of speech and language interpreters at the Alameda County Medical Center in Oakland and at San Francisco General Hospital, where patients speak thirty-five different languages. The Video Medical Interpretation project, as it is known, cuts the average time an interpreter spends with a patient from 37 minutes to 17 minutes by reducing the drive time of interpreters. It is estimated that the system will save the two hospitals at least $420,000 annually.[29]

By taking advantage of PCs and the Internet, a growing number of organizations are using *web conferencing* to conduct meetings. Although this technology continues to evolve, it typically uses screen sharing, voice communication, text messaging, and shared applications, such as software that would allow individuals to work on a proposal together. For example, WebEx and Microsoft Live Meeting are making this technology more accessible. IBM estimates that web conferencing cuts its expenses by $20 million annually.[30]

*Weblogs,* or *blogs,* let people author interactive running diaries on opinions, ideas—anything. Blogs can be used by companies to share information with employees, introduce new products, and communicate with customers. Blogs also allow for responsive communication so that employees and customers can respond quickly and efficiently. For instance, customers visiting a blog can leave public comments that can be shared with future visitors. Likewise, organizations use blogs internally to create a journal of employee responses over time. Blogs are a simple mechanism for people to communicate and share ideas. Aerospace giant Boeing has joined other large firms such as Walt Disney, General Motors, and McDonald's in using blogs. The company's two public blogs give Boeing a direct link to the general public, whereas internal blogs allow employees to raise issues and concerns anonymously.[31]

## CONCLUSION

## Interpersonal and Organizational Communication

Communication is critical to the success of organizations. Successful communication requires shared meaning between the sender of a message and the receiver. Managers function by communicating with others through both formal and informal channels. Barriers to communication include personal characteristics of the parties involved, conflicting frames of reference and selective perception, and reactions triggered by change. Communication can be facilitated by understanding the barriers and striving to be better communicators. Information and communcation technologies are also improving organizational communication.

## Discussion Questions

1. What is the meaning of the term *communication?* What are the advantages and disadvantages of oral, written, and nonverbal communication?

2. Describe the communication process and provide an example of each component.

3. How is information and communication technology changing the way we communicate in organizations?

## Video Case

### NEADS Creates Partnerships between People and Dogs

Suppose you woke up one day and couldn't see. Or perhaps you couldn't hear, couldn't speak, or couldn't walk. How would you communicate and interact with the world around you? Today's technology provides solutions to some of these challenges, but there is a live solution as well: assistance dogs. The National Education for Assistance Dog Services (NEADS) acquires, trains, and matches dogs with people who need assistance. Founded in 1976 as a nonprofit organization, NEADS is based in the rural community of Princeton, Massachusetts, where it adopts and trains dogs to serve their new owners.

Communication is central to success at NEADS. Communication between trainer and dog, between interviewer and client, between trainer and interviewer, and among the trio of client, trainer, and dog is a well-established process. Executive director Sheila O'Brien describes the importance of the process this way. "The match of client and dog is the most important thing that we do, because if we make a bad match, we can't salvage it in any way, shape, or form." Thus, while a trainer begins to work with a dog, developing the skills it will need in its new role—such as responding to a doorbell, ringing telephone, or activated smoke alarm—an interviewer reviews a client's application and conducts an in-person interview to learn as much about the client as possible. If the person has a hearing loss, the interviewer will ask how the loss occurred, how severe it is, and what the prognosis might be. Clients answer questions about lifestyle: Do they live in the city or the country? Do they work outside the home? How many people live in the home? Do they travel a lot? and so forth. They also have a chance to describe their expectations and preferences—whether they want a large or small dog, an energetic or quiet dog, a male or female dog. "The interviewer does have to listen on many levels," notes Sheila O'Brien. "[The interviewer must] ask questions and listen to the answers." Once the interview is complete, the interviewer and trainers meet to try to match dogs with clients.

The match meeting is lively. By now, the trainers know the characteristics of the dogs, and the interviewers know the personalities of their clients. "Match meetings have a lot of give and take," says O'Brien. "The lines of communication have got to be open." Sometimes, a match may seem close—but needs some tweaking. So a trainer will work further with the dog, and ultimately the client-dog pair, to create a smooth relationship.

Because NEADS staffers deal with different types of individuals, ranging from hearing-impaired clients to dogs in need of training, they are open to all kinds of communication. They don't view communication barriers as an obstacle. "I think my staff is of the opinion that the sky is the limit when it comes to communication," says O'Brien. If hearing or speaking is an issue, she explains, "We don't necessarily rely on voice...we rely on body language." Hand signals are often the best means of communication between a dog and a hearing-impaired client, so both are trained for their new language. Clients who will be receiving dogs live at the NEADS facility for two weeks while they learn how to communicate with their new partners. "We have to be open to a wide variety of communication skills," says O'Brien. "We'll do what works. We'll use any kind of communication we can."

In its three decades of existence, NEADS has trained more than 650 client-dog teams. Because the program has been so successful, there is currently a two-year waiting period for clients who have been accepted into NEADS to receive their dogs. But when the match is made, it lasts a lifetime.

### Questions

1. How would you describe the capacity and richness of the NEADS match meeting as a communication channel?

2. According to one study, the impact of facial expressions on message interpretation is 55 percent. How might this finding be used at NEADS?

3. Why are listening skills so important at NEADS?

Source: Organization web site, http://www.neads.org, accessed September 2, 2004.

## BizFlix

### *Patch Adams*

Hunter "Patch" Adams (Robin Williams), a maverick medical student, believes that laughter is the best medicine. The rest of the medical community believes that medicine is the best medicine. Unlike traditional doctors who remain aloof, Patch Adams wants to be close to his patients. Williams's wackiness comes through clearly in this film, which is based on a true story.

This scene comes from the film's early sequence "The Experiment," which takes place after the students' medical school orientation. Patch Adams and fellow medical student Truman Schiff (Daniel London) leave the University Diner. They begin Patch's experiment for changing the programmed responses of people they meet on the street. Along the way, they stumble upon a meat packers convention where this scene occurs.

### Questions

1. What parts of the communication process appear in this scene? Note each part of the process that you see in the scene.

2. Do you think Patch Adams is an effective communicator? Why or why not?

## *Suggested Reading*

Clarke, Boyd, and Ron Crossland, *The Leader's Voice: How Communication Can Inspire Action and Get Results* (New York: SelectBooks, 2002).

Dunning, Stephen, *The Springboard: How Storytelling Ignites Actions in Knowledge-Era Organizations* (Woburn, MA: Butterworth-Heinemann, 2000).

Jones, Elizabeth, Bernadette Watson, John Gardner and Cindy Gallois, "Organizational Communication: Challenges for the New Century." *Journal of Communication* (December 2004): 722–750.

Keller Johnson, Lauren, "Does E-Mail Escalate Conflict?" *Sloan Management Review* (Fall 2002): 14–15.

Lepsinger, Richard, and Anntoinette D. Lucia, *The Art and Science of 360 Degree Feedback* (San Francisco: Jossey-Bass, 1997).

McAfee, Andrew P., "Enterprise 2.0: The Dawn of Emergent Collaboration." *Sloan Management Review* (Spring 2006): 21–28.

Munzoni, Jean-Francis, "A Better Way to Deliver Bad News." *Harvard Business Review* (September 2002): 21–28.

Perlow, Leslie, and Stephanie Williams, "Is Silence Killing Your Company?" *Harvard Business Review* (May 2003): 52–58.

Wenger, Etienne, Richard McDermott, and William M. Snyder, *Cultivating Communities of Practice* (Boston: Harvard Business School Press, 2002).

## *Endnotes*

1. Chester Barnard, *The Functions of the Executive* (Cambridge, MA: Harvard University Press, 1938).

2. Lin Grensing-Pophal, "Communication Pays Off," *HR Magazine* (May 2003): 76–82.

3. Frank M. Corrado, *Getting the Word Out* (Burr Ridge, IL: Business One Irwin, 1993), 10.

4. W. Edwards Deming, *Out of the Crisis* (Cambridge, MA: Center for Advanced Engineering Study, Massachusetts Institute of Technology, 1986), 78.

5. Lawrence R. Birkner and Ruth K. Birkner, "Communication Feedback: Putting It All Together," *Occupational Hazards* (August 2001): 9–10.

6. Stephen R. Axley, "Managerial and Organizational Communication in Terms of the Conduit Metaphor," *Academy of Management Review* (July 1984): 428–437.

7. Sim B. Sitkin, Kathleen M. Sutcliffe, and John R. Barrios-Choplin, "A Dual-Capacity Model of Communication Choice in Organizations," *Human Communications Research* (June 1993): 563–598.

8. Patricia J. Carlson and Gordon B. Davis, "An Investigation of Media Selection among Directors and Managers: From 'Self' to 'Other' Orientation," *MIS Quarterly* (September 1998): 335–362.

9. Richard Daft, Robert H. Lengel, and Linda Klebe Trevino, "Message Equivocality, Media Selection, and Manager Performance: Implications for Information Systems," *MIS Quarterly* 1 (1987): 353–364.

10. Richard K. Allen, *Organizational Management through Communication* (New York: Harper & Row, 1977), 2.

11. Leslie Perlow and Stephanie Williams, "Is Silence Killing Your Company?" *Harvard Business Review* (May 2003): 52–58.

12. Gary L. Kreps, *Organizational Communication* (New York: Longman, 1986), 53–54.

13. Charles Whaley, "Phone Calls Are Futile," *Computing Canada* (May 23, 2003), 13.

14. Al Auger, "Speak Not . . . Sell a Lot," *Advisor Today* (March 2003): 76.

15. Stephen R. Covey, *The 7 Habits of Highly Effective People* (New York: Fireside, 1990), 237.

16. Wayne K. Tandy, "Non-Tech Talk: Leadership and Management," *ITE Journal* (May 2000): 20–21.

17. Jose R. Goris, Bobby C. Vaught, and John D. Pettit Jr., "Effects of Communication Direction on Job Performance and Satisfaction: A Moderated Regression Analysis," *Journal of Business Communication* (October 2000): 348–368.

18. John Naisbitt and Patricia Aburdene, *Re-inventing the Corporation* (New York: Warner Books, 1985), 62.

19. Mirjaliisa Charles and Rebecca Marschan-Piekkari, "Language Training for Enhanced Horizontal Communication: A Challenge for MNCs," *Business Communication Quarterly* (June 2002): 9–29.

20. Lorenzo Sierra, "Tell It to the Grapevine," *Communication World* (June–July 2002): 28–48.

21. Philip R. Beaulieu, "Reputation Does Matter," *Journal of Accountancy* (January 2002): 87.

22. John P. Kotter and Leonard A. Schlessinger, "Choosing Strategies for Change," *Harvard Business Review* (March–April 1979): 106–116.

23. Marianne Kolbasuk McGee, "Political Skills Required," *Information Week* (April 23, 2003): 62–64.

24. Roger D'Aprix, "Four Essential Ingredients for Transforming Culture," *Strategic Communication Management* (April/May 2006): 22–225.

25. Kotter and Schlessinger, "Choosing Strategies for Change," p. 112.

26. Pallavi Gogoi, Michael Arndt, and Abed Moiduddin, "Mickey D's McMakeover," *BusinessWeek* (May 15, 2006): 42.

27. Kenji Hall and Hiroko Tashiro, "Better than Robots," *BusinessWeek* (December 26, 2005): 46.

28. Stephen H. Wildstrom, "Hello Again, Speech Recognition," *BusinessWeek* (May 22, 2006): 20.

29. Matt Hambler, "Hospitals Expand Videoconferencing," *BusinessWeek* (June 5, 2006): 21.

30. Spencer E. Ante, "IBM," *BusinessWeek* (November 24, 2006): 84.

31. Stanley Holmes, "Into the Wide Blog Yonder," *BusinessWeek* (May 22, 2006): 84.

# 15

# GROUPS AND TEAMS IN ORGANIZATIONS

**C**ollective action is an integral part of all organizations. Without groups, organizations would have to rely solely on individuals to complete both daily tasks and longer-term assignments. As you can imagine, many activities would be impossible without the collective efforts of two or more people. An action as simple as lifting a box might be near impossible if someone wasn't around to help you. Be thankful, then, that collective action is a natural extension of individual effort. Our prehistory suggests that hunting in groups for food and communal living increased chances of survival for all. Armies, sporting teams, bridge clubs, and church choirs are everyday examples of collective behavior known as groups. As we all recognize, group behavior has a power unmatched by individual action. Any organization may ignore an individual's demand for a salary increase; but the same demand, when made by a union, could cripple the organization's productive capacity if ignored. For these reasons and others, it is natural and important for future managers to learn the dynamics of group behavior.

In this chapter, we describe types of groups, how they function, and what factors are likely to turn any group into a highly effective component of the organization. The chapter ends with a discussion of team-driven enterprises, whose notions of work and how work is managed continually challenge the status quo. But first we need to draw the distinction between a group and a team, and this chapter begins with a few key definitions.

*Groups* and *teams* are terms often used interchangeably to represent the same idea. However, there is a clear distinction: *group* is a general concept, whereas *team* is more specific. A group is defined as two or more people, who are aware of each other, interact to collectively accomplish a goal, and perceive themselves to be a group.[1] Groups often occur naturally, to accomplish a goal such as moving a log or pushing a car from a ditch. In an organization, a naturally forming group might be people who were all hired in the same department at about the same time and attend the same training session. A team consists of several people who work as a collective, have complementary skills, share a common purpose, and are mutually accountable for an outcome. Teams compensate for member variability; exhibit more autonomy and interactivity; and exhibit more self-direction than a group. A team is also a group that holds membership in the organization, but its purpose is more specialized and directed toward a specific organizational goal of that organization (e.g., a State Farm Insurance Company disaster response team). Whereas a group might be part of an organized activity, a team has a task, resources, leadership, and a goal. Further, a team is a self-managing collective that experiences synergy through shared information, interaction, interdependence, and the bond of a common goal. Teams often have resources at their disposal and have greater decision-making autonomy than a conventional group. The integrated work of several teams makes larger goals attainable.

In this chapter, we consider the roles of both groups and teams, with an eye on the performance or outcomes of the group or team. As you read, bear in mind that most of the ideas that apply to groups also apply to teams.

## Groups

Groups are a common fixture of organizational life. Much of the daily work of organizations is performed by groups. But not all groups work to achieve the goals of the organization. From an organizational perspective, there are two categories of groups: the informal group and the formal group. All other types of groups or teams are variants of these two basic forms of collective behavior.

## Informal Groups

An informal group arises when two or more people engage in voluntary collective activity for a common purpose. Friendship groups and interest groups are two types of informal groups commonly found in organizations.

> **Friendship Group.** A friendship group is a collection of people with similar values or beliefs who get together for a common purpose—possibly just to have fun.

> **Interest Group.** An interest group is a collection of people addressing a specific subject. An example would be five people from different walks of life who meet regularly to discuss art and attend plays.

Informal group actions generally are not recognized by the organization. However, work associations are often springboards into friendship groups and interest groups such as quilting, woodworking, Habitat for Humanity, or shopping excursions. Membership in an informal group provides the individual with new ways of understanding daily life experiences. These new worldviews often translate into action at work. For example, working in a quilting circle at church on Sunday might lead to the idea that the best way to accomplish a work task is by using a group rather than assigning a single person to complete the task. Though not directly related to work organizations, informal groups are found in all organizations. Our ability to join one or more informal groups is greatly enhanced when we regularly interact with diverse groups of people. Most large organizations fit this description quite well. Membership in large organizations increases our exposure to different informal groups that we might join. With an informal group, the "joining" part is often rather casual. People join informal groups for a variety of reasons. One of the most common reasons for group membership is that it satisfies an individual need. Possibly it is a need for greater social interaction; maybe a need for increased self-worth encourages membership in a high-status group; or the possibility that the member joins a group with similar values to her own.

## Formal Groups

Groups are formal to the extent that membership is based on the employee's position in an organization. A formal group consists of two or more people who engage in organizationally required actions for a common purpose. Such a group is a permanent part of the organization. A marketing department is an example of a formal group. The role definition and membership requirements for a formal group are quite explicit. Thus, to maintain membership in the marketing department, a marketing manager might have to reach targeted sales goals for assigned products.

## Command Group

A command group is composed a leader and the subordinates reporting to the leader. The earlier example of the marketing department is a command group, as is a president and her staff of vice-presidents. Command groups represent jobs formally responsible for different departments, processes, or tasks within the organization. Although information flows both up and down, the term *command* signifies direction for action comes from the level above it.

## Work Groups

Within a formal group, such as a customer relations department, are many work groups. A work group is defined as two or more people in a work organization who share a common purpose. This common purpose is usually the completion of a task. The work group is the smallest formal organizational personnel arrangement. As such, a work group represents the most basic level of collective work activity. To govern the relationship between the group and the organization, the group has assigned reporting relationships, a formal leader, and, often, specific instructions to guide task completion. For many years, the formal work group with external supervision was the mainstay of productive effort in organizations.

## Characteristics of Effective Groups

An effective group is one that fully utilizes the abilities of its members in the attainment of group goals. A group continues to be effective as long as it can elicit contributions from members. Another way of thinking about the relationship between a member and the group is as a type of exchange. The group member gives time, energy, knowledge, and ability; in exchange, the group gives the member need satisfaction. Group membership holds the potential to satisfy several basic human needs. Individual member needs that are met through group involvement include need for achievement, need for affiliation, and need for power.[2] When a group has successfully attained a specific goal, its members are often encouraged to know that goal attainment would have been impossible without their efforts. Likewise, successful group members interact. For many individuals, group membership at work is their primary attachment to other people. Group interaction is an important part of human interaction as well as a necessary component of work.

An effective group doesn't just happen by accident; it is created, managed, and developed over time by managers and group members. Yet, not all groups will be effective. Managers are responsible for periodic group evaluation (even self-managing groups have a manager who is responsible for that group). Managers can use the qualities or characteristics of effective groups (Exhibit 15.1) as a basis for diagnosing problems in poorly performing groups.

**KEY TERMS**

**work group** The smallest formal organizational personnel arrangement, two or more people in a work organization who share a common purpose, usually the completion of a task.

EXHIBIT 15.1

**Characteristics of Effective Groups**

**Source:** Adapted from R. Likert, *New Patterns of Management* (New York: McGraw-Hill, 1961), 166.

Like the need for affiliation, the need for power can be fulfilled in a socially acceptable way at work. Work-group hierarchy allows some group members a degree of control over other group members' activities. People are accepted into the group, their behavior is scrutinized, and they are encouraged or discouraged based on group members' evaluation of them. The group leader or a designated leader might derive a real sense of personal power from these types of value-adding activities. But beyond these issues of group functioning are other, more enduring issues. For example, how does an effective group continue to function at high levels over time? What mechanisms sustain the group when high-performing members leave?

## Role Making in Groups

All work groups are defined not only by the roles that their members perform, but also by the hierarchy or status of these roles. As discussed in Chapter 1, "Management and Managers," a *role* is a set of shared expectations regarding a member's attitude and task behavior within the group. At the most basic level, a group will have available two roles: leader and member.

The greater the group's task complexity, the more roles will emerge. Group member agreement about the role to be performed is referred to as the sent role. Essentially, the sent role embodies the formal requirements of the role within the group. The received role is the role recipient's individual translation of what the sent role means to him or her. In other words, the sent role may be received differently by different people. The enacted role is the manner in which the received role is expressed or redefined by the individual assuming the role.[3] This role is defined by how formal group expectations are transmitted, filtered, and processed for action by the role occupant. We all have different backgrounds, values, education, and beliefs about how the job should be done. All these factors are brought to the forefront during the role creation and enactment processes.

## Problems in Role Making

Role creation within groups is not without its share of problems. Common problems include role conflict, role ambiguity, and role overload.[4]

**| Role Conflict |** Role conflict represents the incompatibility between the role's requirements and the individual's own beliefs or expectations. Remember, we all assume multiple roles in many different aspects of our lives. For example, a worker could simultaneously hold the roles of mother, wife, devoted church leader, manager, and engineer. It is easy to see that many of these different roles have required behaviors that can conflict with one another.

**Such internal conflict can come from a variety of sources.**

| Interrole conflict occurs when two different types of roles collide. A manager may have to fire an employee who is also a friend and the coach of his son's Little League team. The friend part of him does not want to fire the man, but his job requires him to do so.

| Intrarole conflict occurs when two similar roles come in conflict, for example, when your boss tells you to increase productivity and your workers are pushing for better working conditions. In this example, you are simultaneously a subordinate and a superior. Further, you believe not only that the organization needs greater productivity, but also that the work rules make for dissatisfied and unmotivated workers.

| Intersender conflict occurs when contradictory messages come from the same source. Your boss preaches that quality is the most important aspect of your work. However, he insists on hiring low-skilled workers who cannot fully utilize the robotics that are a major determinant of quality in the company.

Person-role conflict occurs when an individual's beliefs are in direct conflict with the requirements of his or her role. For example, suppose you know that a product batch is defective and that shipping the products could possibly cause consumer injury and increase liability for the firm. You've also received a memo from your boss, who insists your job is to help build sales volume by expediting the shipment of as many products as possible. You know shipping the product is wrong, but you feel compelled to make your volume quota.

| **Role Ambiguity** | In role ambiguity, the requirements of a role are not clear. In general, role ambiguity results when the role occupant is not sure how to fulfill role requirements. Simple, routine roles rarely generate ambiguity. In a routine role, for instance, an assembly-line job, role requirements are specific or decision criteria are simple. Professional roles present a greater chance of role ambiguity. Managers often face technical situations that they are not trained to fully understand. In such situations, managers may experience ambiguity in choosing between two courses: Should they consult a staff specialist (which might waste time), or go with the subordinate's judgment? Whether the outcome is positive or negative, managers know full well that they will be held responsible.

| **Role Overload** | Role overload is a condition in which a task's demands overwhelm the role occupant's ability to perform the task. Too much, too little, or conflicting information can surpass the role occupant's ability to perform the task at a satisfactory level. With the emphasis on "lean organizations" and the corresponding reduction of America's white-collar workforce, it is very likely that role overload will be a common contributory symptom of role stress reported by those who remain employed.

Role conflict, role ambiguity, and role overload are all potential problems that can decrease a group's effectiveness. Managers must recognize these problems, which can undermine a group's overall performance.

## Group Norms

Group norms define the borders of acceptable member behavior. Usually, intergroup behavior is thought of as a positive force in group productivity. But norms can actually have a negative effect on group output. Take, for example, the restriction of output. A work group might easily produce twenty-five units in an hour. Yet if the group's strategy is to suppress output, the norm enforces lower effort and lower output. Norms represent a form of control over intermittent or random behaviors by group members—be they positive or negative behaviors. However, norms are not developed for all situations or circumstances that the group might encounter, only for those that hold some importance for the group. The group uses rewards and sanctions to encourage acceptance of the norm. Group members who adhere to the norm may receive praise or recognition for their devotion to group norms. Completing a project ahead of schedule may be rewarded with a Friday afternoon off.

Member acceptance of a norm is referred to as conformity. Because it creates a system of shared values among veteran group members as well as newcomers to the group, conformity is important. On the one hand, newcomers may be amazed by group performance or behavioral expectation.[5] But new members quickly learn to meet group expectations if they want to maintain a good standing in the group. On the other hand, veteran members of the group help create and enforce group norms. Without group norms, the group's expectations would be vague at best. For this reason, groups with clear normative expectations are more effective at attaining group goals—and in the process, creating greater member satisfaction—than are groups with comparatively limited normative guidance. Exhibit 15.2 presents some common group norms and their purposes, with example situations in which the norms are enforced.

**15.2**

**Typical Group Norms**

| Group Norm | Purpose | Example Situation |
|---|---|---|
| Rotate leadership | Avoid dominance of one person. | Mary is an accountant and has a low tolerance for ambiguity. |
| Timeliness | Make deadlines. | The product launch will be a week later than expected; the product testing group missed their deadline. |
| Loyalty | Maintain confidential information. | When asked by the head of another department to divulge a new employee's salary, John referred the question to his boss, thus maintaining confidentiality. |
| Fairness | Share rewards equally among the group. | In the department, vacation requests are based on rotation. The last person to request last year gets first pick this year. |

**Group norms are communicated in one of four ways:**

- Explicit statements by the group leader
- Explicit statements by group members
- Critical events in the group's history
- Past group experiences[6]

Most often, group norms develop through efforts of the group leader. The leader communicates the group's wishes and values to new members and reinforces them with existing members. But the leader may not always be present in a norm-signaling situation. In this instance, coworkers may communicate the conformity to the group norm. For example, suppose a member of the counter crew at a fast-food restaurant observes a coworker's negative attitude toward customers. He might quickly take the worker aside and remind her that if the customer complained, the entire crew could be reprimanded for her poor attitude. If the rude worker fails to alter her inappropriate customer behavior, she might be shunned by other crew members until her behavior improves.

Another impetus for the development of group norms might be a critical event in the group's history. Say, for instance, that a group representative has been outmaneuvered in a staff meeting to the group's disadvantage. This could force a group norm to develop regarding how ideas are presented to other groups to ensure a successful outcome for the group.

## Cohesiveness

A group has cohesiveness to the extent that (1) the group can do its work effectively, attract new members when necessary, and maintain the group over time; and (2) group members are able to influence one another.[7] Cohesiveness is a way of describing how well the group functions. Highly cohesive groups are good problem solvers. Further, in both work and social situations, members of cohesive groups interact more than people in less cohesive groups do.

By developing interaction skills, cohesive groups set the stage for greater success in their attempts to gain social influence. Social influence regulates deviation from accepted norms.[8] Group members can gang up on an individual member who is acting in ways the group believes are in conflict with group norms. For example, over a period of weeks, task group members on an auto assembly line might notice that one group member's "quality emphasis" is slipping. Each group member may pick a different time or approach to encourage the deviant worker to rethink how he does his job. This type of positive social influence may well make the deviant worker aware of his actions and bring him closer to the group norm. But if the worker's behavior is intolerable to the group, the social influence may be shifted toward the group leader—perhaps even forcing the leader to fire the worker for nonconformity to the quality norm.

## Groupthink

Group decision making is not without some degree of risk. Group norms and conformity tendencies may actually suppress opposing or contrary perspectives. Irving Janis calls this concept groupthink. Groupthink is "a mode of thinking that people engage in when they are deeply involved in a cohesive in-group, when members' strivings for unanimity override their motivation to realistically appraise alternative courses of action."[9] Groupthink has been given as an explanation for the decision-making process that led to the Kennedy administration's disastrous 1961 Bay of Pigs invasion of Cuba. In essence, groupthink means suppressing or ignoring countervailing ideas that represent a threat to group consensus or unanimity. Unfortunately, when the group is wrong, group consensus doesn't mean very much in the long run. It is important to note, however, that within the same group, groupthink can occur during one decision-making situation and not another.[10]

## Cultural Diversity

Groups are increasingly characterized by cultural diversity. Whether at work, at school, or during leisure time, cultural diversity exists in groups whose members differ by gender, age, ethnic background, disability status, religious affiliation, and lifestyle. Changing demographics and greater immigration bring greater diversity to the labor pool and ultimately to work. Over time, this means greater cultural diversity in work groups. Growing globalization and the addition of more women and minorities to the workforce mean that by 2020, a culturally diverse workforce will be the norm in most organizations.

Managing diverse groups has become a critical challenge in corporate America; firms that do not include diversity as part of their business plan will be at a competitive disadvantage.[11] For instance, one study found that firms receiving Department of Labor recognition for exemplary affirmative action programs are better able to recruit, develop, and maintain human resources, providing a competitive advantage.[12] Several approaches have been used to enhance cooperation and communication among culturally diverse groups, including multicultural workshops; female and minority support groups and networks; managerial reward systems based on managers' ability to train and promote women and minorities; fast-track programs targeted at women and minorities who demonstrate exceptional potential; and mentoring programs pairing women and minorities with senior managers.[13] At Ameritech, for example, a black advocacy panel was formed to review corporate policy on affirmative action and works to improve diversity at top levels.[14]

## The Group Development Process

Now that we have reviewed the different kinds of groups, we can examine how groups develop in a four-stage process of forming, storming, norming, and performing.[15] Group development describes the progression from a collection of people literally tossed together for a common purpose to a well-functioning whole whose effectiveness stands the test of time.

**STEP 1** ### Forming

Forming refers to the actual beginning of the group, when members get to know one another and start to understand each other's abilities and deficits. In the formation stage, the collection of people quickly comes together as a functioning unit. Members temporarily accept formation rules and orders in an effort to initiate the group. With the process under way, formal group functions are defined, and the beginnings of a hierarchy emerge. Sometimes, formal organizational task requirements dictate group purpose. A formal leader is often appointed to facilitate group development.

**KEY**TERMS

**groupthink** A mode of thinking that people engage in when they are deeply involved in a cohesive in-group, when members' strivings for unanimity override their motivation to realistically appraise alternative courses of action.

**group development** The progression from a collection of people literally tossed together for a common purpose to a well-functioning whole whose effectiveness stands the test of time.

**forming** The beginning of the group, when members get to know one another, start to understand each other's abilities and deficits, come together as a functioning unit, appoint a formal leader, define formal group functions, and start to develop a hierarchy emerge.

STEP 2

### Storming

As the name suggests, this is the most tumultuous stage in the group development process. Storming refers to the group's coming to grips with inherent conflicts and developing solutions that keep the group focused on its work. During this stage, members learn to accept one another's individual differences. With this acceptance comes the beginning of a collective "group personality" that reflects their similarities and minimizes their differences. This collective viewpoint is the result of sharing common work, values, and purpose. Along with personality emergence comes informal vying for power or control of the group. Specialization through subgroups also begins to develop. Group members negotiate roles that are needed for effective group functioning, and members adopt those roles.

STEP 3

### Norming

During the norming stage, the group charts its long-term vision of group purpose and how it will function over time. The process of achieving all members' agreement on the group's long-term vision is referred to as developing shared values. The group's norms are the unwritten guides to behavior. Conformity to norms is enforced through rewards and sanctions. Members who adhere to norms reap the benefits the group has to offer—such as status, affiliation, and personal growth. Deviance from group norms may subject the member to punishment, humiliation, or ostracism.

STEP 4

### Performing

The group is now at the performing stage, in which the group functions as a highly effective unit. During this stage, a group that has remained together for a long time is fine-tuning group functioning. Group members carefully redefine group roles as needed. They decide how best to balance needs of the group and the organization. At this stage the group is most able to develop the skills of current members, recruit new members, and perform the group's work at a high level. By the time the group reaches the performing stage, all individuals have learned their roles in the group. The faster the group reaches the performing stage of development, the more effective the group.

Often, short-term groups have to disband and merge their membership into other task groups. Some authors consider this "ungrouping" process a separate stage.

At each new stage in the group development process, the group is confronted with increasingly difficult decisions. One of the greatest challenges is how best to reward individual contribution and still maintain the group's integrity. In fully mature groups, individual efforts have been well integrated into specific group functions. Over time, the group's success or failure becomes evident. This is largely determined by how well the group performs its assigned functions and contributes to the organization's overall effectiveness.

## Teams

As we discussed in the beginning of the chapter, teams and groups are different. Exhibit 15.3 reviews some of the practical distinctions between a group and a team. Regardless of the distinction, teams have become a widespread business phenomenon in recent years. Success stories of the team concept include Chrysler's initial product development of the Viper sports car as well as the use of cross-functional and cross-national work teams at Ford and Mazda.[16] These examples highlight the advantages of using self-managing, cross-functional teams to decrease product development time and/or increase overall product quality. Because effective work teams can be valuable assets to a firm, people who can successfully facilitate team interactions play an increasingly important role in organizations throughout the world.[17]

Although historically the use of teams has tended to be most prevalent in Japanese firms, the team approach seems to be gaining momentum in the United States as well.[18] More than twenty years ago, management expert and college professor Edward Lawler estimated that about 150 manufacturing plants (fewer than 1 percent of all organizations) in the United States used some sort of self-managing team approach. In 1990, he estimated about 7 percent of the manufacturing firms in the United States used a team approach.[19] Today, the consensus is that 15 percent of all manufacturing involves the use of teams. In fact, corporate leaders are

EXHIBIT 15.3

**Distinctions Between a Group and a Team**

**What Is the Difference Between a Group and a Team?**

| Working Group | Team |
|---|---|
| Strong, focused leader | Shared leadership roles |
| Individual accountability | Individual and mutual accountability |
| Group's purpose is the same as the organization's mission | Specific team purpose defined by the team |
| Individual work products | Collective work products |
| Efficient meetings | Open-ended problem-solving meetings |
| Measures its effectiveness by its influence on others (financial performance) | Measures performance directly by assessing collective work products |
| Discusses, decides, and delegates | Discusses, decides, and does real work together |

**Source:** Adapted from Jon R. Katzenbach and D. K. Smith, "The Discipline of Teams," *Harvard Business Review* (March–April, 1993): 111–120.

increasingly relying on self-managed teams in all aspects of their businesses.[20] New hires are evaluated on their ability not only to work effectively within a team, but to direct the work of multiple teams. Project management skills have become essential to the upwardly mobile manager in dealing with time and cost, which are critical aspects of project management. All projects of any consequence have a deadline and limited resources.

This section begins by examining the characteristics of teams and the advantages of teamwork. Other topics include team effectiveness, implementing work teams, and developing team-driven companies. We conclude by looking at how organizations can overcome employees' resistance to teamwork.

## Characteristics of Teams

An effective team has many hands, all helping to shoulder an otherwise individual burden. Teams are often responsible for all aspects of their work; they are given a goal or goals, a budget, and a deadline. The team is expected to perform the task and produce the output in accordance with the workflow of the organization. The result is efficiency, increased reliability, and innovation. For example, during recruitment, product design teams, creative advertising teams, and human resource management teams might each be charged with the responsibility of interviewing and recommending a prospective employee.

**Generally, three characteristics can be used in describing the work of a team:**

- Teams have a specific task.
- Teams are self-managing.
- Teams have decision-making autonomy.

As mentioned earlier, two other factors are common to the team—resources and time. Resources mean a budget, and time takes the form of a deadline for task completion. Additionally, an effective team reward recognizes the collective effort, not individual performance.

**However, not all teams are the same; a few distinctions are in order.**

- Work team. Describes a special type of organizational work group that is self-managed and has considerably more decision-making autonomy than some work groups. The primary difference between a work team and a work group is the way in which a team is governed and the special bond among team members.
- Task team. Is less permanent than a work team. A task team is a formal group of people working on a temporary job. When its work is completed, a task team disbands.

**KEY** TERMS

**task team** A formal group of people working on a temporary job, disbanding when its work is completed.

**EXHIBIT** 15.4

### Skills of Effective Team Members

| Problem Solving | Interpersonal | Technical |
|---|---|---|
| • Thinking | • Facilitating | • Discovery |
| • Creativity | • Influencing | • Organization |
| • Discussion | • Listening | • Analysis |
| • Decisiveness | • Supporting | • Synthesis |
| • Implementation | • Visioning | • Clarification |

**Source:** Adapted from Eileen K. Aranda, Luis Aranda with Kristi Conlon, *Teams: Structure, Process, Culture, and Politics* (Upper Saddle River, NJ: Prentice Hall, 1999), 18; and Jon R. Katzenbach and Douglas Smith, ''The Discipline of Teams,'' *Harvard Business Review* (March–April 1992): 112–120.

| Management team, composed of several people from different functional or operating areas, brought together to plan, implement, and manage ongoing organizational activities.

Effective teams need members with the requisite skills to help the team achieve their goals. Regardless of the type of team, all team members need problem solving skills, interpersonal skills, and technical skills. Exhibit 15.4 lists the qualities of each skill team members need to possess or acquire to be effective team members. Think about your last team experience and complete the next Management Highlight on page 333 to determine how ready your team was to perform.

## Virtual Teams

The term virtual team refers to the collaborative activities of several people, working together on computer networks, who use common software and share common data. Expensive office space and the environmental impact of increased automobile usage and automobile parking make virtual teams practical. As a cost-saving measure, Allstate Insurance in Northbrook, Illinois, encourages employees to telecommute to minimize parking problems and the cost of office space. Many industries outsource work that may still need internal coordination and control. The result is a virtual team with internal members, domestic outsourced member, and other international outsourced members. All members form the virtual team. It is not unusual for members to never meet face to face during the duration of team interaction. Virtual teams of this nature are commonly used in the banking, insurance, and publishing industries for performing tasks that can be digitized and decomposed into technical components.[21]

The advent of personal computers and groupware (group-based software) made possible the collaborative work by geographically dispersed users. Using groupware, virtual team members can interact in real time, modifying and updating designs or other elements in a database. Virtual teams are common in the publishing industry, in new product design, and in many other applications. Boeing Aircraft developed the 777 aircraft on a computer network that linked in-house services and all external subcontractors. Many participants in the development process were members of virtual teams. Design team members shared information and used virtual-space renderings of design elements to ensure that parts from different vendors fit together. The result is a high-quality, high-reliability product that airlines and air travelers can count on for safe, reliable, and economical service.

## DETERMINING TEAM READINESS

**Instructions:**

Using the scale provided, answer each question below in reference to a job that you have held in the past. If you have never worked, answer each question as you believe it would apply to the type of job you hope to have after graduation.

| Never | Almost Never | Seldom | Sometimes | Usually | Almost Always | Always |
|-------|-------------|--------|-----------|---------|---------------|--------|
| 1 | 2 | 3 | 4 | 5 | 6 | 7 |

1. If you want to be a good team member you need to fit in.
2. I change my behavior to match the expected member's behavior.
3. Most team members believe that supporting the team is very important.
4. Team members work well together.
5. Our team is like a well-oiled machine.
6. When a team member is sick, another team member picks up the slack.
7. Our team is made up of a diverse group of people.
8. Team members bring different perspectives to the team.
9. Team members come from different social, racial, or ethnic groups.
10. Out team works well together.
11. Our team works better now than it did in the past.
12. Team members know each other well enough to anticipate how other team members will perform.
13. Team leadership is achieved by having a common sense of direction.
14. Team leadership is leadership by consensus.
15. Our team is self-directed.

Record your responses from the survey and total the three columns to arrive at your need for each dimension.

| | Conformity | | Cohesiveness | | Diversity | | Development | | Leadership |
|---|-----------|---|--------------|---|-----------|---|-------------|---|------------|
| 1 | Conform1 | 4 | Cohes1 | 7 | DIV1 | 10 | DEV1 | 13 | LEAD1 |
| 2 | Conform1 | 5 | Cohes2 | 8 | DIV2 | 11 | DEV2 | 14 | LEAD2 |
| 3 | Conform1 | 6 | Cohes3 | 9 | DIV3 | 12 | DEV3 | 15 | LEAD3 |

| TOTAL | TOTAL | TOTAL | TOTAL | TOTAL |
|-------|-------|-------|-------|-------|
| Divide by 3 | Divide by 3 | Divide by 3 | Divide by 3 | Divide by 3 |
| SCORE | SCORE | SCORE | SCORE | SCORE |

Compare your score to the expected maximum average score of seven (7) for each scale.

Here are some benefits of the virtual team:

| Geographically dispersed people can work together online.

| Reduces employee cost per transaction.

| Decreases time to complete a project.

| Reduces transmittal and paper costs.

| Increases work quality.

| Allows greater work integration from several people.

## | Advantages of Teamwork

Though teamwork is not a panacea, it does allow for more input from a variety of perspectives. A major advantage of teamwork is quick response time. Although in the past group decision making has been criticized for slow response, teams are more likely charged with a sense of urgency. In the same sense, teams usually are given "hard target" deadlines that they must meet as a condition of effective performance. Another advantage of a team is higher quality output at every step of the production process. Whether the product is an advertisement, software, or an automobile, teamwork enhances the outcome. Generally, when more people are involved in a task, they make better decisions. Employee participation through team membership means greater commitment, motivation, and ultimately satisfaction with the final outcome of team effort. Finally, self-directed teams typically handle job assignments, plan and schedule work, make decisions that affect the team, and take action on problems—all with minimal direct supervision.

The self-regulating nature of the team allows for greater error detection and correction on the spot rather than at projection completion. Even in today's highly automated assembly facilities, almost every workstation has a switch within easy reach that the worker can use to stop the assembly line when something is wrong. Stopping the assembly line was far more difficult twenty years ago; it required managerial intervention. Because it was more trouble then to correct errors on the spot, most errors just slipped through. Immediate error correction means that fewer defects make it through final assembly, which yields higher-quality products. Thus procedures, methods, and practices of both the organization and its work groups must be physically and psychologically attuned to production requirements. In doing so, teams have become a focal component in, for example, delivering quality medical services, solving sales problems, and making factories more productive.

Teamwork affords many benefits, such as allowing one employee to compensate with his or her strength for another employee's weakness. Everyone on a team has a chance to contribute ideas, plans, and figures; but anyone on a team may expect to find some of his or her best ideas vetoed by team member consensus. However, a good team also has a social memory. As a collective, the team should be able to "remember" the contributions of individuals for the good of the group. Over time, contributing members play a major role in shaping the group's activities. In summary, teams:

- Provide a quick response time and focused energy
- Offer better-quality decisions
- Engender greater member commitment and acceptance of ideas
- Allow greater employee participation
- Afford workers greater autonomy and self-governance

But teams are not without their problems; the team-building process is often flawed from the start. Employees need time to get accustomed to working in teams. Team members need to know not just why teams are being used, but where each team fits into the larger picture. If employees feel teams are being used to reduce the size of the workplace or to make them do more work, they will sabotage the process. The team approach is certain to fail when managers do not create a supportive environment for the team. And all too often, organizations find that team leaders eventually resort to human nature and refuse to share authority with the rest of the team.[22] To overcome the pitfalls of teamwork, external leadership of the team-building process is needed to create an infrastructure that allows teams to thrive. If teamwork is successful, the rewards are lower costs and higher-quality products or services.[23] In the Management Highlight on page 335, you can try your hand at deciding when a team is a bad idea.

## Team Effectiveness and Team Interaction

In the same way that organizational effectiveness is a measure of organizational success, team effectiveness is a measure of team success. It follows, then, that moving from understanding the social psychology of groups to building successful teams is not such a large leap. In this section, we'll examine the topics of implementing work teams and overcoming resistance to teamwork.

## WHEN IS A TEAM A BAD IDEA?

MANAGEMENTHIGHLIGHT

Are teams always the right way to organize people to attain organizational goals? After reading these three scenarios, you make the call—which team is a bad idea?

**Team Scenario 1.** Physician Management Services Inc. manages five healthcare offices. Each office has five physicians and a staff of fifteen nurses, technicians, and clerical workers. Each office receives a budget based on a per capita (known as capitation) dollar amount for each patient under its care. In other words, each office has only so much money to spend on each patient. All physicians meet monthly to decide how best to treat each patient and allocate their budget on patient care. Even though an expensive new treatment might be available, if it cannot be provided in-house, it is against corporate policy to prescribe the treatment. Further, any physician can propose a less expensive treatment than that called for in the attending physician's plan. *A binding vote by all physicians is taken based on cost and other factors.*

**Team Scenario 2.** Provident Health Care, a struggling HMO, has been ordered by the board of directors to cut costs in order to increase profits. The organization's two-pronged strategy for success is to sign new patients and keep service costs low on existing patients. Dr. Henry wants to schedule a surgical procedure for a patient covered by Provident Health Care. Although the procedure is not common, it is well accepted and offered at most hospitals. Provident's care manager discusses the request with a team of administrators, area clerical specialists, and their in-house physician, but finally authorizes only a less expensive procedure. *Dr. Henry believes that his patient is being afforded inferior service.*

**Team Scenario 3.** PanJen Corporation has a team of employees that reviews all new-hire applicants who seek posted jobs. The team's role is advisory to the HR department, but its wishes are rarely disregarded. Each member of the team represents a different group in the company, and each member has a different agenda. In team decision making, politics often rule the day. Sometimes the techies rule; sometimes those calling for diversity are heard; sometimes the team bases its decision solely on an applicant's qualifications. *The trouble is, managers never know if (or when) they will get the best person for the job.*

---

A team is a work group with a common goal. Team effectiveness represents the outcomes, or results, of the team's efforts such as efficiency, satisfaction, and goal attainment. Assuring team success requires that the team has a common purpose, that specific goals flow from that purpose, that team members have complementary skills, that the team has a shared agreement about how the work will be done, and that there is mutual accountability for team action.[24] Research from cardiac response teams suggests that the team leader plays an important role in a team's success. Successful teams have a team leader who is willing to be accessible; does not try to "go it alone," but rather asks for input from other team members when necessary; and is not afraid to be "human," admitting mistakes and then moving forward.[25] Further, team effectiveness can be enhanced by building teams with greater emotional intelligence.[26] Team-based emotional intelligence is rooted in the group processes described earlier in this chapter.

Research on group dynamics suggests that team effectiveness is best understood using a systems model that describes the inputs (or context), processes, and outputs (or outcomes) of group interaction (Exhibit 15.5).[27] Context consists of structure, strategies, leadership, and rewards. Structure includes the members' personalities and abilities as well as the overall size of the group. Structure dictates what the team can accomplish. Strategy clarifies, among several action plans, the one that the team intends to use in achieving its goals. For example, a team wanting to increase quality may use a strategy that intentionally slows down the production process, thus allowing workers more time to complete their tasks. The final inputs to context are leadership and rewards. Team leadership must facilitate the team's overall strategy and goals, provide resources, communicate vertically, and reward performance.

Team rewards are one motivation for a team member to work in unison. Although extrinsic rewards such as money and promotions are important on an individual level, team rewards serve as a powerful motivating force. Team recognition may be equally important to an individual. We have all seen sporting events where a player on the winning team reports an

**System's Model of Team Effectiveness**

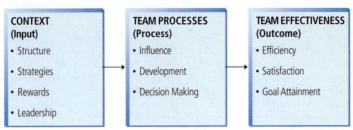

incredible feeling of accomplishment, even though her individual contribution to winning the final game was minor. And at NASA mission control, the images of a successful spacecraft landing tell a similar story of taking pride in team membership and achieving a difficult goal. Similarly, on an everyday level, work teams revel in their daily successes, knowing that their contributions made a difference. A supportive team environment that is fair to all engenders trust. Research indicates that employees view a process as fair if they are involved in the process early on, have the process clearly explained to them, and hold realistic expectations for the outcomes to follow from the process.[28]

By looking again at Exhibit 15.5, you can see that the inputs define how the team processes of the work group will unfold. Three separate processes occur in all work teams: influence, development, and decision making. The process of influence is a necessary and important part of the overall well-being of the team. Particularly in autonomous work teams or self-managing work teams, mutual influence allows all members access to change other members' minds or challenge unrealistic assumptions. But not all influence is productive. "Social loafing" and "free riding" occur when one group member does less work than others, knowing full well that his or her contribution will be hidden in the group effort.[29] Mutual influence should be viewed as inevitable and healthy. Team development involves the process of activities, interactions, and sentiments that occur as time passes. A major part of team development involves its members' attachment to and identification with the team. For example, wearing union jackets or company clothing outside the work environment indicates pride and group identity. Further, members quickly learn that not all groups are equal. Those groups that provide an opportunity for enjoyable and productive work are valued by members and nonmembers alike.

Goal attainment, efficiency, and member satisfaction are all team outcomes (see Exhibit 15.5). From a managerial perspective, thinking about the human component of the team is important. In an environment in which teams are the primary productive unit, managers need to understand how well the team interacts on a continuous basis. Similarly, a team that has successfully attained an important goal is also likely to experience a high level of job satisfaction and feel a unique sense of inter-team loyalty. For all practical purposes, the highly effective team is one that experiences high levels of expected work outcomes such as quality, productivity, or reliability.

## Implementing Work Teams

Management theorists have continually emphasized the importance of teamwork to the overall success of an organization. If we recall from Chapter 1 the open systems input, output, and processing (IPO) model, which characterizes the organization as consisting of three subsystems, we can see that teams are essential in the operation of each subsystem. One strong theme that runs

MANAGEMENT HIGHLIGHT

## RULES FOR CREATING EFFECTIVE SELF-MANAGED TEAMS

| Team Development | Description |
|---|---|
| *Organize around processes rather than tasks.* | Organize around core processes, identify the critical processes, and assign teams responsibility related to process, not to their functional area. |
| *Create horizontal structures by grouping subprocesses.* | Create cross-functional, project-based teams with clear objectives, diverse membership, and limited external management. |
| *Reengineer the process.* | Develop processes that are responsive to customers and teams to support them. Patient healthcare requires clerical support, nurses, physicians, technicians, and administrative team members. |
| *Give self-managed teams greater control over processes and process performance.* | Self-managed teams are responsible for multiple tasks and have discretion over the methods of work, task schedules, assignment of members to different tasks, compensation, and feedback about performance for the group as a whole. |
| *Link team performance to customer satisfaction.* | Everything should be driven by the customer; successful performance also means customers have been satisfied. |
| *Assign performance objectives to teams, not individuals.* | Successful attainment of objectives must be a group effort and not the result of one or two individuals. Multiple member involvement is critical to developing a sense of the collective. |
| *Assign managerial tasks to the team where feasible.* | Self-managed means just that—limited external leadership. Teams should be responsible for activities such as hiring, evaluating, and scheduling. |
| *Train team members to develop cross-functional skills and competencies.* | Team members need multiple skills that support the work of the team or replace team members lost to illness, turnover, or reassignment. |
| *Empower team members with information.* | Information should go directly to those who can use it in their jobs. Trained and empowered workers know how to use information. |
| *Put team members in touch with customers.* | Know your customers, both internal and external. Visit them and understand their problems. Problem-solving teams can bring team members closer to customers. Knowledge of customer needs is then reflected in team work. |
| *Reward skill development and team performance.* | Performance evaluation should focus on team achievements rather than on individual achievements. Talking about teamwork while evaluating and rewarding individuals is counterproductive. |

Source: Adapted from Frank Ostroff, *The Horizontal Organization* (Oxford University Press, 1999); Daniel Goleman, "Leadership that Gets Results," *Harvard Business Review* (March–April, 2000): 80–90; Charles C. Manz and Henry P. Sims, Jr., *The New Superleadership: Leading Others to Lead Themselves* (Berrett-KoehlerSan Francisco, 2001); Richard Hackman as cited in Charles C. Manz and Henry P. Sims, Jr., "Leading Workers to Lead Themselves: The External Leadership of Self-Managing Teams," *Administrative Science Quarterly* (March 1987): 106.

throughout the management literature is the need for teams and teamwork. At every level, companies need teamwork. The aim of a team is to improve the input and the output at any stage of operations.

Three main features of effective self-managed teams are (1) extensive worker control over operating decisions, especially those traditionally made by supervisors, foremen, and quality inspectors; (2) high levels of feedback from the work itself (e.g., self-charting, online computerized reports); and (3) cross-training so that each worker can perform many functions (i.e., job de-specialization).

As described in the above Management Highlight, in a team-driven organization, work is designed around customers, not tasks. Senior managers are responsible for processes that are critical to satisfying customers. Self-directed work teams make decisions regarding hiring, scheduling, and so on. Fewer people are needed between senior managers and work teams, and their job is to facilitate, not control. This, in part, explains why so many mid-level management positions are being phased out in companies today.

## | Overcoming Resistance to Teamwork

The transition to teams isn't always easy. Following are some of the many problems encountered when building teams: confusing team building with teamwork, haphazard team planning, starting teams before assessing team needs, training team members individually, and not making teams accountable. Team members also have a tendency to become so intent on some of the group's issues that they forget to use effective team processes. Team members have to be trained not only to get along but also to work together as a team. Organizations must develop a system for planning teamwork. First, team needs must be defined; then team members should be trained as a team. Teams must also be accountable for what they have learned in training and what they do at work. Teams flourish when managers make room for spontaneity, value speaking out, encourage intellectual exchange, and select self-motivated people.[30]

Teams are not without their opponents. Often, teams mean fewer managers. Middle management is often the primary target for staff reduction when the team approach is implemented. A shift to teams and flatter organizations may reduce managers' opportunities for advancement. Unions are also opponents of work teams, whose self-regulating nature threatens the unions' traditional power and roles. Teams, they claim, threaten a union's very existence by posing a long-term threat to workers' job security and other union benefits. Through self-governance, teams resolve grievances, discipline workers, and award pay raises. Traditionally, these functions were part of the union's contractual relationship with the organization.

Teamwork is an important part of today's work environment. But team success comes only if workers are empowered to solve problems and make decisions, cultivate a natural sense of pride in their work, are self-managed, and receive group-based rewards and recognition for their accomplishments. If these elements are all present, teams can make important contributions to providing their customers with high-quality products or services.

## CONCLUSION

## Groups and Teams in Organizations

Organizations will increasingly utilize teams as they continue to reduce costs and downsize. After years of reorganizing and outsourcing, organizations are left with a lean core of knowledgeable employees. By necessity, many of these organizations are forced to rely on greater worker participation in the decision-making process through empowerment. With job security increasingly tenuous, and new compensation plans encouraging less reliance on salary (as in the past) and greater compensation in the form of stock options, employees need to adapt to the changing work world. Upgrading skills in their teamwork, technology, and management education will all be essential for career success.

In the years ahead, workers will also be evaluated more and more as a group. Performance will be based on group productivity, and group members will be expected to improve their skills and help others perform better. Rewards will be based on group rather than individual performance, and the entire group will be held accountable for its actions. Teams will establish their own identity by devising their own name and by promoting personal relationships. In short, the emphasis in groups will be on promoting cooperative teamwork.

The workplace of tomorrow will be even more diverse than today's. This will make the management of teamwork an even greater challenge for organizations than it is today. As corporate leaders begin to understand the impact of diverse groups on their organizations, their commitment to diversity will become much stronger. This means increased resources allocated for diversity training—for recruiting, training, and retaining qualified workers with diverse backgrounds. Managers will learn that a diversified workforce is a major asset in the twenty-first century.

## Discussion Questions

1. What is the difference between a formal and an informal group? Also, provide examples of informal groups and formal groups that you have observed.

2. Think about your experience as a group member. Describe how each stage of group development occurred in your group.

3. According to the text, what are the characteristics of an effective team?

## Video Case

### The NEADS Team: People and Dogs

All the teams you have encountered in this chapter have been teams of people. NEADS, the National Education for Assistance Dog Services, functions with teams of people as well. But another type of teamwork is central to the mission of NEADS: the team of human and dog. NEADS acquires, raises, trains, and matches service dogs to meet the needs of people with limited physical mobility or deafness. A typical service dog may be trained to respond to a blaring smoke alarm or ringing telephone, nudge a light switch on or off with its nose, or retrieve items for an owner. Because this partnership is intended to last a lifetime, it is important for the match to be perfect.

It takes about two years to train a service dog—and that requires a lot of teamwork. Since NEADS is a nonprofit organization, it must be creative in the way it recruits and uses volunteers. These volunteers include high school students, families, and prisoners. High school students may help NEADS puppy trainers begin to expose the youngest dogs to experiences they will encounter in their lives as service dogs, such as sitting by a wheelchair or walking next to a cane. Families become part of the team when, at four months of age, the puppies are placed in foster care for the next part of their education. Volunteer families agree to feed, love, and raise the puppies so that they become accustomed to the distractions and energy of the real world. Professional dog trainers from NEADS visit regularly to work with the families and dogs to ensure that the dogs receive the proper training in preparation for their later work. Since 1998, prison inmates in Massachusetts and Connecticut have participated in a foster care program as well. While a puppy lives at the prison, a small team from NEADS visits regularly to monitor the puppy's development. Another set of volunteers participates in a program called Pups on Parole, during which the volunteers take the puppies outside the prison for field trips to shopping malls, supermarkets, business districts, parks, and the like. In addition, a professional trainer works with the prisoners and puppies. The partnership with prisons has required another level of teamwork—with state agencies. NEADS executive director Sheila O'Brien says this relationship has been highly successful. "The commissioner felt very strongly that inmates should give back to the society that they violated, in a safe way." Working with the dogs has proved to be a safe and effective program for inmates. In fact, the dogs who live with prisoners return to NEADS more advanced in their readiness for formal training than those who live with families.

The puppies live in their foster homes until they are about a year and a half old—then they return to the NEADS farm to continue their education. Here, they receive advanced training from professional dog trainers. When a dog's training is complete, its new owner arrives on campus for a two-week stay, during which the person and dog become a team. The dog and person have been matched through an extensive process that involves a team of people interviewers and dog trainers. During this intensive get-acquainted and training period, "they learn to love each other, respect each other, and work together," explains O'Brien.

O'Brien emphasizes that, "Even though the concentration at this point is on the team, meaning two—the dog and the person—there are still many team members working behind the stage to facilitate this coming together." She refers to volunteers who raise funds to cover the cost of receiving a dog, as well as those who greet new clients and help them become familiar and comfortable with the NEADS campus. "What makes these teams work so cohesively is that everyone knows what the outcome should be," says O'Brien. "Everyone is working toward getting a dog and person together and making sure this dog provides the independence that this disabled or deaf person needs. Everyone has that in sight. Everyone just works toward that end."

## Questions

1. Describe the characteristics of a typical NEADS team, using the criteria discussed in the chapter.

2. What factors determine the cohesiveness of NEADS teams?

3. Describe a situation in which conflict might arise in a NEADS team.

Source: Organization web site, http://www.neads.org.

## BizFlix

### Apollo 13

This film recreates the heroic efforts of astronaut Jim Lovell (Tom Hanks), his crew, NASA, and Mission Control to return the damaged Apollo spacecraft to earth. Examples of both problem solving and decision making occur in almost every scene. This scene takes place during day five of the mission about two-thirds of the way through the film. Early in Apollo 13's mission, Jack Swigert (Kevin Bacon) stirred the oxygen tanks at the request of Mission Control. After this procedure, an explosion occurred, causing unknown damage to the command module. Before the scene takes place, the damage has forced the crew to move into the LEM (Lunar Exploration Module), which becomes their lifeboat for return to earth.

## Questions

1. Describe how Jim Lovell attempts to encourage teamwork to help resolve the situation.

2. There are three people in this situation. Are they a group or a team? Justify your answer.

3. Use Exhibit 15.4 to evaluate the skills of mission commander Jim Lovell and his crew.

## Suggested Readings

Druskat Vanessa Urch and Steven B. Wolff, "Building the Emotional Intelligence of Groups," *Harvard Business Review* (March 2001): 80–90.

Katzenbach, Jon R., and Douglas Smith, "The Discipline of Teams," *Harvard Business Review* (March–April 1992): 112–120.

Polzer Jeffrey, "Identity Issues in Teams," *Harvard Business School,* Reprint 90403-095 (February 06, 2003): 1–10.

Thompson, Leigh, "Improving the Creativity of Organizational Work Groups," *Academy of Management Executive* 17, no. 1 (2003): 96–109.

Wageman, Ruth, "Critical Success Factors for Creating Superb Self-Managing Teams," *Organizational Dynamics* (Summer 1997): 49–61.

## Endnotes

1. Edgar Schein, *Organizational Psychology* (Englewood Cliffs: Prentice Hall, NJ): 67, 1965.

2. David McClelland, *The Achieving Society* (Princeton, NJ: Van Nostrand, 1961). Also see David McClelland and David H. Burnham, "Power Is a Great Motivator," *Harvard Business Review* (March–April 1976): 100–110.

3. George Homans, *The Human Group* (New York: Harcourt, Brace, 1950).

4. Robert L. Kahn, D. M. Wolfe, Robert P. Quinn, J. D. Snock, and R. A. Rosenthal, *Organizational Stress: Studies in Role Conflict and Role Ambiguity* (New York: Wiley, 1964).

5. Meryl Reis Louis, "Surprise and Sense-Making: What Newcomers Experience in Entering Unfamiliar Organizational Settings," *Administrative Science Quarterly* (June 1980): 226–251.

6. Daniel Feldman, "The Development and Enforcement of Norms," *Academy of Management Review* 9, no. 1 (1984): 47–53.

7. Dennis Organ and Thomas Bateman, *Organizational Behavior* (Plano, TX: Business Publications, 1986), 473.

8. Marvin Shaw, *Group Dynamics: The Psychology of Small Group Behavior* (New York: McGraw-Hill, 1971), 192–204.

9. Irvin Janis, *Groupthink,* 2nd ed. (Boston: Houghton Mifflin, 1982), 9.

10. Christopher P. Neck and Gregory Moorhead, "Groupthink Remodeled: The Importance of Leadership, Time Pressure, and Methodical Decision-Making Procedures," *Human Relations* (May 1995): 537–557.

11. James B. Strenski, "Stress Diversity in Employee Communications," *Public Relations Journal* (August–September 1994): 32–35.

12. Peter Wright, Stephen P. Ferris, Janine S. Hiller, and Mark Kroll, "Competitiveness through Management of Diversity: Effects on Stock Price Valuation," *Academy of Management Journal* (January 1995): 272–287.

13. Catherine Ellis and Jeffrey A. Sonnenfeld, "Diverse Approaches to Managing Diversity," *Human Resource Management* (Spring, 1994): 79–109.

14. Michele Galen and Ann Theresa Palmer, "Diversity: Beyond the Numbers Game," *BusinessWeek* (August 14, 1995): 60–61.

15. Tuckman, Bruce, "Developmental Sequence in Small Groups," *Psychological Bulletin,* 63 (1965): 384–399.

16. David Woodruff, "The Racy Viper Is Already Winning for Chrysler," *BusinessWeek* (November 4, 1991): 36–38; and James B. Treece, "How Ford and Mazda Share the Driver's Seat," *BusinessWeek* (February 10, 1992): 94–95.

17. Greg Burns, "The Secrets of Team Facilitation," *Training & Development* (June 1995): 46–52.

18. James P. Womack, Daniel T. Jones, and Daniel Roos, *The Machine That Changed the World* (New York: Harper Collins, 1991), 92.

19. Edward E. Lawler, "The New Plant Revolution Revisited," *Organizational Dynamics* (Autumn 1990): 5–14. Lawler estimated the number of plants as "somewhere between 300 and 500" (p. 9).

20. C. C. Manz, "Self-Leadership: Toward an Expanded Theory of Self-Influence Processes in Organizations," *Academy of Management Review* 11 (1986): 585–600.

21. Thomas Friedman. *The World Is Flat* (Farrar, Straus, and Giroux. New York: Free Press, 2005).

22. Kenneth Labich, "Elite Teams," *Fortune* (February 19, 1996): 90–99.

23. C. C. Manz and H. P. Sims Jr., *The New SuperLeadership: Leading Others to Lead Themselves* (San Francisco: Berrett-Koehler, 2001).

24. John Katzenbach and Douglas Smith, "The Discipline of Teams," *Harvard Business Review* (March–April 1993).

25. Amy Edmondson, Richard Bohmer, and Gary Pisano, "Speeding Up Team Learning," *Harvard Business Review* (October 2001): 1–12.

26. Vanessa Urch Druskat and Stephen B. Wolff, "Building the Emotional Intelligence of Groups," *Harvard Business Review* (March 2001): 80–90.

27. Marilyn Gist, Edwin A. Locke, and M. Susan Taylor, "Organizational Behavior: Group Structure, Process, and Effectiveness," *Journal of Management* 13, no. 2 (1987): 237–257.

28. W. Chan Kin and Renee Maurborgne, "Fair Process: Managing the Knowledge Economy," *Harvard Business Review* (July–August 1997): 66–74.

29. S. G. Harkins, B. Latane, and K. Williams, "Social Loafing: Allocating Effort or Taking It Easy?" *Journal of Experimental Social Psychology* 16 (1985): 457–465.

30. Michael Pacanowsky, "Team Tools for Wicked Problems," *Organizational Dynamics* (Winter 1995): 36–51; and see Harold J. Leavitt and Jean Lipman-Blumen, "Hot Groups," *Harvard Business Review* (July–August 1995): 109–116.

# Controlling

# 16

# CONTROL SYSTEMS

**C**ontrol is a fundamental management responsibility, closely linked with the planning and organizing processes. It also has an important impact on motivation and team behavior. Control is both a process (e.g., working to keep things on schedule and according to plan) and an outcome (e.g., the product has met standards). In traditional terms, the controlling function includes all activities that a manager undertakes in attempting to ensure that actual results conform to planned results. For instance, control systems implemented at El Paso Field Services Company's Thompsonville, Texas, gas plant enabled the plant operator to reduce unexpected upsets caused by tower flooding using a flooding prevention strategy, which included online estimation of liquid rates and automatic exchanges balancing to limit liquid production and feed rates.[1] In some contexts, the controlling function of management is a very technical thing indeed.

But like many management terms, control has different meanings to different people and manifests in different ways, depending on a host of variables. Not surprisingly, an individual's concept of control often reflects a personal perspective. Statisticians may think of control in relation to numbers (variances, means, errors, control limits); engineers, in relation to specifications, monitoring, and feedback; and managers, in relation to directing the activities, attitudes, and performance of subordinates.

To achieve results, some characteristics of all organizations must be controlled: key among them are production and operations, financial resources, human resources, and organizational change and development. In this chapter, we examine the various elements of the control process, the types of control, and quality control systems.

## Elements of the Control Process

Control is a process used (1) to evaluate actual performance, (2) to compare actual performance to goals, and then (3) to take corrective action to reduce discrepancies between performance and goals.[2] Quality statistician Walter Shewhart elaborated these three elements within the control process under the concepts of specification, production, and inspection[3] (see Exhibit 16.1).

> *Specification.* Specification is the statement of the intended outcome. Control requires the specification of a standard. A standard is an operationally defined measure used as a basis for comparison. Specification fully describes the preferred condition, which may take the form of a goal, standard, or other carefully determined quantitative statement of conditions.

> *Production.* Production means making the product or delivering the service. Shewhart defines this element as the work required to achieve objectives. It's important to note that this element of the control process applies as much to service as to manufacturing.

> *Inspection.* Inspection is a judgment concerning whether the production meets the specifications. Inspection determines whether corrective actions need to be taken.

EXHIBIT 16.1

**Steps in the Control Process**

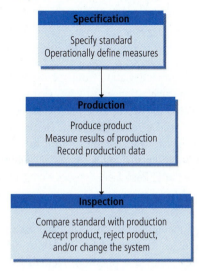

**Specification**
Specify standard
Operationally define measures

**Production**
Produce product
Measure results of production
Record production data

**Inspection**
Compare standard with production
Accept product, reject product,
and/or change the system

Clear specification of a performance standard requires an operational definition. An operational definition converts a concept into measurable, objective units.[4] For example, the concept of *weight* can be operationally defined in terms of grams, pounds, or another standard measure. These measures are not subject to personal interpretation. In contrast, the concept of *heavy* can be interpreted differently by different people. For some, six ounces is heavy; for others, six pounds is heavy. An operational definition should bring uniform agreement to the meaning of a concept.

The process of setting performance standards must begin with a strategy, conveyed in terms of operationally defined measures. Operational measures underlie the control process. Not only do they control operations through finished-product or after-service inspections; they also enable workers to evaluate processes as they are occurring.

Production and operations are controlled by performance standards. Standards determine the activity or outcome to be measured. Control of production and operations requires measurement to identify deviation from standards. Through measurement and assessment, workers can find possible improvements within the product or process and indicate where to initiate change. The act of measuring errors or defects often has an immediate, direct effect on reducing them.

It is important to point out that control applies to all types of organizations, not just manufacturing. Businesses that provide a service must also be concerned with controlling their operations and the quality of their work. Service organizations control performance principally through employee training. Small and large firms alike have recognized the importance of giving employees the knowledge and information they need to serve customers. Home Depot, the hardware and home repair discounter, has made an art of empowering employees to exceed each customer's expectations. Home Depot does not conduct extensive marketing surveys but rather relies on its associates, who are trained to ask customers what they want and expect.

Inspection in traditionally managed companies typically occurs at the end of production or upon the provision of a service. Quality management discourages this type of inspection. In fact, of quality pioneer W. Edwards Deming's fourteen points, the third states, "Cease dependence on mass inspection." As Deming put it, "Routine 100 percent inspection to improve quality is equivalent to planning for defects, acknowledgment that the process has not the capability required for the specifications."[5] Quality-based firms use statistical sampling techniques concurrent with the production process to ensure that most products or service encounters exceed performance specifications.

When statistical sampling indicates a deviation from specifications, corrective action may be necessary. People undertaking corrective actions must know that they're responsible, and they must have the authority to effect change. Job descriptions that have specific, operationally defined performance objectives are necessary to control performance. Responsibilities that fall between the jobs of two individuals should be avoided. For the control function to be most effective, operationally defined objectives, clear authority, and accurate information are requisite.

# Types of Control

Management has numerous control methods at its disposal. Each has strengths and limitations. Managers must decide what type of control system to employ in different situations. Some control techniques have very specific, limited application. Nonetheless, all control techniques must be economical, accurate, and understandable.

The techniques managers use to control production and operations can be classified under three main types: preliminary control, concurrent control, and feedback control.

## Preliminary Control

Preliminary control focuses on preventing deviations in the quality and quantity of resources used in an organization. For example, human resources must meet the job requirements as defined by the organization; employees must have the physical and intellectual capabilities to perform assigned tasks. Materials used in production must meet acceptable levels of quality and must be available at the proper time and place. Capital must be on hand to ensure an adequate supply of plants and equipment. Financial resources must be available in the right amounts and at the right times.

Preliminary control procedures include all managerial efforts to increase the probability that actual results compare favorably with planned results. From this perspective, policies are an important means of implementing preliminary control, because policies are guidelines for future actions. It's important to distinguish between *setting* policies and *implementing* them.[6] Setting policy is included in the planning function, whereas implementing policy is part of the control function.[7] Similarly, job descriptions are aspects of the control function because they predetermine the activity of the jobholder.[8] At the same time, however, we must distinguish between defining and staffing the task structure. Defining jobs is part of the organizing function; staffing them is part of the controlling function.

Management needs to be concerned with preliminary control of processes in four areas: human resources, materials, capital, and financial resources.

| **Human Resources** | The organizing function defines the job requirements and predetermines the skill requirements of jobholders. These requirements vary in degree of specificity, depending on the nature of the task. Preliminary control of human resources is achieved through the selection and placement of managerial and nonmanagerial personnel. Exhibit 16.2 shows the steps involved before a person actually begins to work at a firm. Each step along the way, including placement, is a preliminary control step during which the potential worker's skills, abilities, and attitudes are assessed for his or her qualifications for a given position.

**KEY**TERMS

**preliminary control** Control that focuses on preventing deviations in the quality and quantity of resources used in an organization.

**16.2**    **Preliminary Control of Human Resources**

Candidates for positions must be recruited from inside or outside the firm, and the most promising applicants must be selected based on matching skills and personal characteristics to the job requirements. The successful candidate must be trained in methods and procedures appropriate for the job. Most organizations have elaborate procedures for providing training on a continual basis.

Appropriate attention to preliminary control of human resources ensures that the organization will have a match between its needs and individual skills, abilities, and attitudes. With increasing emphasis on information and knowledge as the primary focus of global business, the search, selection, and placement of people is an increasingly vital function. Where human resource professionals had been relegated to staff support in the past (typically, under the rubric *personnel*), many firms today have line positions for human resources. This significant shift reflects the growing awareness that competitive advantage can be gained through proper screening and development of people. In their human resource planning, managers should distinguish between procedures designed to obtain qualified subordinate managers (staffing) and those designed to obtain qualified nonmanagers and operatives (selection and placement). Although basic procedures and objectives are essentially the same, the distinction is important because managerial competence is a fundamental determinant of the organization's success. The Management Highlight on page 348 asks you to evaluate human resource controls you have experienced in your life.

| **Materials** | The raw materials that are converted into a finished product must conform to quality standards *before* they are used in the production process. At the same time, a sufficient inventory or delivery system must be maintained to ensure a continuous inflow of raw materials so that the manufacturer can meet customer demand.

MANAGEMENTHIGHLIGHT

### CONTROLLING HUMAN RESOURCES

Think of some *ineffective* human resource controls you have experienced in school, at work, or in other aspects of your life. Describe them and answer the following questions for each:

- Why was the control ineffective?

- How could the control be changed to make it effective?

Numerous methods that use statistical sampling to control the quality of materials have been devised. These methods typically involve inspection of samples rather than an entire lot. Thus, statistical methods are less costly; but there is a risk of accepting defective material if the sample is nonrandom or, by chance, contains none of the defective items.

We do not provide a complete discussion of statistical sampling procedures in this text. However, the essence of the procedures can be described. As an example, suppose management establishes a standard that it will accept no more than a 3 percent defect rate from a supplier. The incoming material would be inspected by selecting random samples and calculating the percentage of defective items in the sample. Based on this sample, managers must make a decision to accept or reject the entire order, or to take another sample. This method is not perfect. Based on the sampling technique, managers could reject an entire lot even though the overall defect rate is less than 3 percent, or they may accept a lot even though the defect rate is greater than 3 percent. The control system used is based on balancing the relative costs of these two types of potential errors.[9] We'll say more about the role of statistics in control later in this chapter.

| Capital | The acquisition of capital reflects the need to replace existing equipment or to expand the firm's productive capacity. Managers of this process are often faced with complicating factors such as financial risk and uncertainty about potential outcomes.[10] Capital acquisitions are controlled by establishing criteria of potential profitability that must be met before the proposal is authorized. Such acquisitions ordinarily are included in the capital budget, an intermediate and long-run planning document that details the alternative sources and uses of funds. When connected with strategic planning, capital budgeting has been found to improve financial performance.[11] Several major imperatives are driving managers to wager money on capital budgets: customer service, quality, productivity, and capacity expansion. Managerial decisions that involve the commitment of present funds in exchange for future funds are termed investment decisions. The methods that serve to screen investment proposals are based on economic analysis. The following are several widely used capital control methods. Each involves formulating a standard that must be met to accept the prospective capital acquisition.

Payback Method    Payback is the simplest method of capital control, and it is widely used. One study of Swedish corporations found the payback method was the most used method of capital control in all industries.[12] The payback method calculates the number of years needed for the proposed capital acquisition to repay its original cost out of future cash earnings. For example, a manager is considering implementing new information technology that would reduce labor costs by $20,000 per year for each of the four years of the new technology's expected life. The cost of the technology is $40,000. If we use the 36 percent marginal tax rate on corporations with taxable income over $10 million, the

**KEY**TERMS

**capital budget** An intermediate and long-run planning document that details the alternative sources and uses of funds.

**investment decisions** Managerial decisions that involve the commitment of present funds in exchange for future funds, based on economic analysis.

**payback method** A measurement of profitability involving the calculation of the number of years needed for the proposed capital acquisition to repay its original cost out of future cash earnings.

additional after-tax cash inflow from which the machine's cost must be paid is calculated as follows:

| | | |
|---|---|---|
| Additional cash inflow before taxes (labor cost savings) | | $20,000 |
| Less: Additional taxes | | |
| Additional income | $20,000 | |
| Depreciation ($40,000/4) | $10,000 | |
| Additional taxable income | $10,000 | |
| Tax rate | 0.36 | |
| Additional tax payment | | $3,600 |
| Additional cash inflow after taxes | | $16,400 |

The payback period can be calculated as follows:

$40,000/$16,400 = 2.44$ years

The proposed new information technology would repay its original cost in about two and one-half years; if the predetermined standard requires a payback of three years or fewer, the information technology would be an appropriate investment.

The payback method suffers many limitations as a standard for evaluating capital resources. It does not produce a measurement of profitability. More important, it does not take into account the time value of money; that is, it does not recognize that a dollar today is worth more than a dollar at a future date. Other capital control methods do include these important considerations. The primary reason for using the payback method is that in situations where the technology changes rapidly and new products become obsolete quickly, corporations should look for investment opportunities that pay back within a short period of time.

**Rate of Return on Investment**   One alternative measure of profitability, consistent with methods ordinarily employed in accounting, is the simple rate of return on investment. Using the preceding example, the calculation would be as follows:

| | |
|---|---|
| Additional gross income | $20,000 |
| Less: Depreciation ($40,000/4) | $10,000 |
| Taxes | $3,600 |
| Total additional expenses | $13,600 |
| Additional net income after taxes | $6,400 |

The rate of return is the ratio of additional net income to the original cost:

$6,400/$40,000 = 16\%$

The calculated rate of return would then be compared to some standard of minimum acceptability, and the decision to accept or reject would depend on that comparison. In this case, if the standard rate of return were 10 percent, the purchase of the information technology would be a good investment. The measurement of the simple rate of return has the advantage of being easily understood. It has the disadvantage of not including the time value of money. The discounted rate of return method overcomes this deficiency.

**Discounted Rate of Return**   The discounted rate of return is a measurement of profitability that takes into account the time value of money. It is similar to the payback method, except that cash inflows and outflows are considered. The method is widely used because it is considered the correct method for calculating the rate of return. Based on the preceding example,

$$\$400,000 = \frac{\$16,400}{(1+r)} + \frac{\$16,400}{(1+r)^2} + \frac{\$16,400}{(1+r)^3} + \frac{\$16,400}{(1+r)^4}$$

where $r = 23\%$

The discounted rate of return ($r$) is 23 percent, which is interpreted to mean that a $40,000 investment repaying $16,400 in cash at the end of each of four years has a return of 23 percent.

The rationale of the method can be understood by thinking of the $16,400 inflows as cash payments received by the firm. In exchange for each of these four payments of $16,400, the firm must pay $40,000. The rate of return—23 percent—is the factor equating cash inflows and present cash outflow. This rate of return can be compared to a company minimum standard to determine its acceptability.

| **Financial Resources** | Adequate financial resources must be available to ensure payment of obligations arising from current operations. Materials must be purchased, wages paid, and interest charges and due dates met. The principal means of controlling the availability and cost of financial resources is budgeting—particularly cash flows and working capital budgets.

These budgets anticipate the ebb and flow of business activity when materials are purchased, finished goods are produced and inventoried, goods are sold, and cash is received.[13] This operating cycle results in a problem of timing the availability of cash to meet obligations. When inventories of finished goods increase, the supply of cash decreases as materials, labor, and other expenses are incurred and paid. As inventory is depleted through sales, cash increases. Preliminary control of cash requires that cash be available during the period of inventory buildup and be used wisely during periods of abundance. This requires the careful consideration of alternative sources of short-term financing during inventory buildup, and alternative short-run investment opportunities during periods of inventory depletion.

Managers use certain ratios to control financial resources. For example, the control standard may be stated in the current ratio (the ratio of current assets to current liabilities), and a minimum and a maximum set. The minimum ratio could be set at 2:1 and the maximum at 3:1, which would recognize the cost of both too little and too much investment in liquid assets. The control would involve corrective action taken when the actual current ratio deviates from the standard. Other financial ratios contributing to control of financial resources include the acid-test ratio, inventory turnover, and average collection period. These ratios are discussed in greater detail in the section on feedback control methods.

## | Concurrent Control

Concurrent control involves monitoring ongoing operations to ensure that objectives are pursued. The standards guiding ongoing activity are derived from job descriptions and from policies resulting from the planning function. Concurrent control is implemented primarily by the supervisory activities of managers. Through personal, on-the-spot observation, managers determine whether the work of others is proceeding in the manner defined by policies and procedures. Delegation of authority provides managers with the power to use financial and nonfinancial incentives to effect concurrent control.

Concurrent control consists primarily of actions of supervisors who direct the work of their subordinates. Direction refers to the acts of managers when they (1) instruct subordinates in proper methods and procedures and (2) oversee subordinates' work to ensure that it is done properly.

Direction follows the formal chain of command, because the responsibility of each superior is to interpret for subordinates the orders received from higher levels. The relative importance of direction depends almost entirely on the nature of the tasks performed by subordinates. The supervisor of an assembly line that produces a component part requiring relatively simple manual operations may seldom engage in direction. On the other hand, the manager of a new product research unit must devote considerable time to direction. Because research work is inherently more complex and varied than manual work, it requires more interpretation and instruction.

Directing is the primary function of the first-line supervisor, but at some point every manager in an organization engages in directing employees. The direction given should be within the stated organizational mission, goals, and objectives. As a manager's responsibilities grow, the relative time spent directing subordinates diminishes as other functions become more important.

The scope and content of directing vary according to the nature of the work being supervised. In addition, several other factors determine differences in the form of direction. For example, because direction is basically a process of personal communications, the amount and clarity of information are important factors. Subordinates must receive sufficient information to carry out the task, and they must understand the information they receive. On the other hand, too much information and detail can be distracting.

The tests of effective direction are similar to the tests of effective communication. To be effective, a directive must be reasonable, understandable, appropriately worded, and consistent with the organization's overall goals. Whether these criteria are met is not the manager's decision. Rather, the subordinate decides. Many managers have assumed that their directives were straightforward and to the point, only to discover that their subordinates failed to understand or to accept them as legitimate.

## Feedback Control

Feedback control methods focus on end results. Corrective action is directed at improving either the resource acquisition process or the actual operation. This type of control derives its name from its use of results to guide future actions. A simple illustration of feedback control is a thermostat, which automatically regulates the temperature of a room. Because the thermostat maintains the preset temperature by constantly monitoring the actual temperature, future results (activation of heating or cooling units at time $x$) are directly and continually determined by feedback (room temperature at time $x - 1$). Room temperature at time $x$ then feeds back to control the heating and cooling units at time $x + 1$, and so on.

In the following two subsections, we outline feedback control methods widely used in business: financial statement analysis and standard cost analysis.

**| Financial Statement Analysis |** A firm's accounting system is a principal source of information that managers can use to evaluate historical results. Periodically, the manager receives a set of financial statements that usually includes a balance sheet and income statement. These financial statements summarize and classify the effects of transactions in assets, liabilities, equity, revenues, and expenses—the principal components of a firm's financial structure. The balance sheet describes an organization's financial condition at a specified point in time. The income statement is a summary of an organization's financial performance over a given time period.

A detailed analysis of the financial statement's information enables management to determine the adequacy of the firm's earning power and its ability to meet current and long-term obligations. Managers must have measures of and standards for profitability, liquidity, and solvency. Whether a manager prefers the rate of return on sales, on owner's equity, on total assets, or a combination of all three, it is important to establish a meaningful norm—one that is appropriate to the particular firm, given its industry and stage of growth. An inadequate rate of return negatively affects the firm's ability to attract funds for expansion, particularly if a downward trend over time is evident.

The measures of liquidity reflect the firm's ability to meet current obligations as they become due. The widest known and most often used measure is the current ratio (the ratio of current assets to current liabilities). The standard of acceptability depends on the particular firm's operating characteristics. Bases for comparison are available from trade associations that publish industry averages. A tougher test of liquidity is the acid-test ratio, which relates only cash and near-cash items (current assets excluding inventories and prepaid expenses) to current liabilities.

The relationship between current assets and current liabilities is an important one. Equally important is the composition of current assets. Two measures that indicate composition and rely on information found in both the balance sheet and income statement are the accounts receivable turnover and the inventory turnover. The accounts receivable turnover is the ratio of credit sales to average accounts receivable. The higher the turnover, the more rapid the conversion of accounts receivable to cash. A low turnover would indicate a time lag in the collection of receivables, which in turn could strain the firm's ability to meet its own obligations. Appropriate corrective action might be tightening of credit standards or a more vigorous effort to collect outstanding accounts. The inventory turnover also facilitates the analysis of appropriate balances in current assets. It is calculated as the ratio of cost of goods sold to average inventory. A high ratio could indicate a dangerously low inventory balance in relation to sales, with the possibility of missed sales or a production slowdown. Conversely, a low ratio might indicate an overinvestment in inventory to the exclusion of other, more profitable assets. Whatever the case, the appropriate ratio must be established by the manager, based on the firm's experience within its industry and market.

Another financial measure is solvency, the ability of the firm to meet its long-term obligations, that is, its fixed commitments. The solvency measure reflects the claims of creditors and owners on the firm's assets. An appropriate balance must be maintained—a balance that protects the interest of the owner yet does not ignore the advantages of long-term debt as a source of funds. A commonly used measure of solvency is the ratio of net income before interest and taxes to interest expense. This indicates the margin of safety; ordinarily, a high ratio is preferred. However, a very high ratio combined with a low debt-to-equity ratio could indicate that management has not taken advantage of debt as a source of funds. The appropriate balance between debt and equity depends on many factors. But as a general rule, the proportion of debt should vary directly with the stability of the firm's earnings.

Firms also use *debt ratios* to assess the amount of financing being provided by creditors. Two popular debt ratios are the debt/equity ratio and the debt/asset ratio. The debt/equity ratio is a measure of the amount of assets financed by debt compared to that amount financed by profits retained by the firm and investments (stocks and other securities). The debt/asset ratio is an expression of the relationship of the firm's total debts to its total assets.

| **Standard Cost Analysis** | Standard cost accounting systems are considered a major contribution of the scientific management era. A standard cost system provides information that enables management to compare actual costs with predetermined (standard) costs. Management can then take appropriate corrective action or assign to others the authority to take action. The first use of standard costing was to control manufacturing costs. In recent

**KEY**TERMS

**liquidity** The firm's ability to meet current obligations as they become due.

**current ratio** The widest known and most often used measure of liquidity, expressed as the ratio of current assets to current liabilities.

**acid-test ratio** A measure of liquidity that relates only cash and near-cash items (current assets excluding inventories and prepaid expenses) to current liabilities.

**accounts receivable turnover** A measure of liquidity expressed as the ratio of credit sales to average accounts receivable.

**inventory turnover** A measure of liquidity that is calculated as the ratio of cost of goods sold to average inventory; facilitates the analysis of appropriate balances in current assets.

**solvency** The ability of the firm to meet its long-term obligations, that is, its fixed commitments, its measure reflecting the claims of creditors and owners on the firm's assets.

**debt/equity ratio** A measure of the amount of assets financed by debt compared to the amount financed by profits retained by the firm and investments (stocks and other securities).

**debt/asset ratio** An expression of the relationship of the firm's total debts to its total assets.

**standard cost system** A cost system that compares actual costs with predetermined (standard) costs, enabling management to take appropriate corrective action or assign to others the authority to take action.

years, standard costing has also been applied to selling, general, and administrative expenses. Here we discuss standard manufacturing costs.

The three elements of manufacturing costs are direct labor, direct materials, and overhead. For each of these, an estimate must be made of cost per unit of output. For example, the direct labor cost per unit of output consists of the standard usage of labor and the standard price of labor. The standard usage derives from time studies that fix the expected output per labor hour; the standard price of labor is fixed by the salary schedule appropriate for the kind of work necessary to produce the output. A similar determination is made for direct materials. Thus, the standard labor and standard materials costs might be as follows:

| | |
|---|---|
| Standard labor usage per unit: | 2 hours |
| Standard wage rate per hour: | $5.00 |
| Standard labor cost (2 × $5.00): | $10.00 |
| Standard material usage per hour: | 6 pounds |
| Standard material price per pound: | $.30 |
| Standard material cost (6 × $.30): | $1.80 |

The accounting system enables the manager to compare incurred costs and standard costs. Today, cost accounting practices are undergoing significant changes to keep pace with the rapidly evolving manufacturing environment. Activity-based accounting, a new system of cost accounting based on activity, has been advocated by many academicians and practitioners. Its underlying principle is that activities consume resources and products consume activities. The labor costs of supporting departments can be traced to activities by assessing the portion of each person's time spent on each activity, which can then allow for restatement of departmental cost in activities and their associated costs. Activity costs then are traced to the product based on the amount of activity volume each product consumes. The overall impact is more accurate product cost information.

## Quality Control Techniques

The total quality movement has brought with it a set of tools and techniques for controlling organizational processes. Three approaches in particular—statistical process control, total quality control, and total quality management—are in wide use in a broad spectrum of industries. These approaches are all similar in their focus on exceeding customer expectations as a central value. Another central value is a focus on the system (in contrast to the traditional focus on the worker) as the source of most production or service errors or defects.

## Statistical Process Control

The approach of statistical process control has long played an important role in business and industry. Statistical process control (SPC) is based on two assumptions: (1) nature is imperfect, and (2) variability exists everywhere in systems. Therefore, probability and statistics play a major role in understanding and controlling complex systems. Charts, diagrams, and graphs are conceptual tools managers can use to summarize statistical data, measure and understand variation, assess risk, and make decisions. The Management Highlight on page 354 summarizes the seven tools of quality control. Statistics is defined as "that branch of applied mathematics which describes and analyzes empirical observations for the purpose of predicting certain events as a basis for decision making in the face of uncertainty."[14]

Statistics come in two varieties: descriptive and inferential. Descriptive statistics are a computed measure of some property of a set of data, making possible a statement about the data's

## SEVEN TOOLS OF QUALITY CONTROL

1. **Flow charts** provide a visual description of the steps in a process or work activity. The sequence of events that makes up the process is shown. Generally, flowcharts begin with inputs, show what takes place to transform these inputs, and end with outputs. Flowcharts are especially helpful in visualizing and understanding how things are currently being done, and how they can be done differently to improve the process.

2. **Run charts** are used to plot measurements taken over specific time intervals such as a day, week, or month. Usually the quantity measure is plotted on the vertical axis, and time is on the horizontal axis. The run charts can be used to determine how something is changing over time, and whether problems are taking place at certain periods of time.

3. **Control charts** show the result of statistical process control measures for a sample, batch, or some other unit. Such charts can be used to study variation in a process and to analyze the variation over time. A specified level of variation may be acceptable, but deviation beyond this level is unacceptable.

4. **Fishbone diagrams**, also called cause-and-effect diagrams, look like a fishbone. The problem, such as a defect, is defined as the effect. Events that contribute to the problem are called causes. The effect is the "head" of the fishbone, and the causes are the "bones" growing out of the spine. The fishbone chart can be used to see how different causes occur and lead to a problem. Once the causes are identified, corrective measures can be implemented.

5. **Pareto charts** are used to display the number of problems or defects in a product over time. Fairly simple to construct, Pareto charts display the results as bars of varying lengths. The basic premise of the Pareto chart is that only a few causes account for most problems.

6. **Histograms** also called **bar charts**, show the frequency of each particular measurement in a group of measurements. This information is useful in analyzing the variability in a process.

7. **Scatter diagrams** show the relationship between two characteristics or events, such as the relationship between diameter and strength for samples of wires. By measuring these two variables and plotting the results, quality control managers can observe how one variable changes as the other changes.

meaning. An example of a descriptive statistic is the average (mean) time the customer service department takes to answer the telephone. Other descriptive statistics include the mode (the most common data point) and the median (the point at which 50 percent of the other points lie above, and 50 percent below). Mean, median, and mode are also often referred to as measures of central tendency.

Inferential statistics are computations done on a set of data, or among several sets of data, that are designed to facilitate prediction of future events or to guide decisions and actions. An example of an inferential statistic might be the correlation of (a) the average time the customer service department takes to answer the telephone with (b) customer attitudes about the organization. It might be found that faster average response time is correlated with increased customer satisfaction. In that case, this statistic would be a catalyst to action centered on reducing telephone response time.

Because variation exists in any process, no two products or service encounters are exactly alike. The control of quality is largely the control of variation. The job of statistical process control is to limit this variation within an acceptable range. For example, statistical process control is used to control the variation in the weight of packages of biscuits; underweight packages result in customer dissatisfaction, whereas overweight packages reduce profits.[15] So how do we determine what is acceptable variation?

There are two types of variation in any system—random and nonrandom. Random variation is often referred to as the "normal" variation of a system. Random variation potentially affects all components of a process. Nonrandom variation is not considered to be part of the normal cause processes of a system. This type of variation leads to unpredictable outcomes, something management wants to eliminate.

Random and nonrandom variation are explained in turn by two different types of causes: common and special. Common cause variation is just the random variation in a system, and typically, it cannot be completely eliminated. Managers should work to minimize the range of common cause variation as part of their continuous improvement process. Range refers to the extreme upper and lower measures of a variable. But, given the assumption that the perfect system is not likely to be achieved, managers need to be aware that some common cause variation is likely to remain.

Special cause variation, on the other hand, is a result of some *external* influence upon a system. This could be anything from drug abuse by workers to earthquakes. Managers want to eliminate special cause variations to the extent possible. In our examples, this would be done by screening workers and offering drug abuse counseling, or by locating in areas not prone to earthquakes. A stable system is one that has eliminated special cause variation and is subject only to the unavoidable (yet reducible) common cause variation.

For example, consider a firm that wants to establish quality control over one of its key suppliers. One critical measure may be the percentage of orders that are delayed each week. To develop a baseline, the company may randomly sample 100 orders each week from this supplier for, say, 20 weeks to develop a mean percentage of orders that are delayed. With these data, it is possible, using well-tested statistical methods, to establish upper and lower control limits. The range of values within these limits would be the range of expected variation due to common causes. If the mean percentage of delays during the 20-week baseline period is .06, and the upper and lower control limits are .11 and .01, respectively, any subsequent weeks where the percentage of delays is between these values is probably a result of common cause variation (e.g., traffic conditions, worker absences, misplaced orders).

However, if for several weeks the manager notices that the percentage of delays is above .11 (or below .01), a special cause may be operating and action might need to be taken. Some possible special causes are (1) the supplier was bought out and is under new management, and (2) a trucker strike is delaying deliveries. Managers use statistical measures to know when key processes are affected by special cause variation and need immediate attention.

The practice of quality management in any type of organization—whether it's service, manufacturing, retail, nonprofit, or something else—can benefit from applying statistical methods to organizational processes or customer expectations. Although statistical techniques are common to most quality management environments, each manager must decide how best to apply these techniques to his or her own organization. What is common across organization types is the fundamental purpose of quality control—to minimize variation.

## Total Quality Control

In traditional production management, quality control consisted of assigning the last person on the assembly line the responsibility of ensuring that the product worked. Today, quality control begins at the beginning; that is, quality control is maintained from the design process through manufacturing, sale, and use of the product. The sum of all these efforts is called total quality control. The principles of total quality control can be applied equally well to either products or services. Customers will always seek products and services of consistently high quality. To understand how total quality control can transform an organization, consider that each worker within a company can be viewed as providing a product or service for some other individual, and that the product or service can be evaluated using the tools of total quality control (see Management Highlight on page 354).[16]

Armand Feigenbaum is often credited with coining the term total quality control (TQC).[17] TQC represents a more comprehensive form of quality control than SPC, although it recommends using statistics to improve quality. According to Feigenbaum,

> Total quality control is an effective system for integrating the quality-development, quality-maintenance, and quality-improvement efforts of the various groups in an organization so as to enable marketing, engineering, production, and service to perform at the most economical levels which allow for full customer satisfaction.[18]

The fundamental purpose of TQC is to manufacture products or deliver services that meet the level of quality demanded by customers. TQC's emphasis is on customer satisfaction. Feigenbaum identifies several TQC benchmarks: quality is what the customer says it is; quality is a way of managing; quality and innovation are mutually dependent; quality requires continuous improvement; and quality is implemented with a total system connected with customers and suppliers.[19]

According to Feigenbaum, there is no such thing as a permanent quality level. Demands and expectations for quality are constantly changing. A distinction of good management is personal leadership in mobilizing the knowledge, skill, and positive attitudes of everyone in the organization to recognize that what they do to make quality better helps to make everything in the organization better. Quality is also essential for successful innovation for two reasons. The first reason is the rapid speed of new product development. The second is that when a product design is likely to be manufactured globally, where international suppliers must be involved in every stage of development and production, the entire process must be clearly structured.[20]

In a quality-based system, control is a conscious, positive, preventive stance created in the system. TQC begins with planning—planning that is aimed at preventing quality problems. Here are some concerns addressed by quality planning:

- Establishing quality guidelines.
- Building quality into the design.
- Procurement quality.
- In-process and finished product quality.
- Inspection and test planning.
- Control of nonconforming material.
- Handling and following up on customer complaints.
- Education and training for quality.[21]

## | Total Quality Management

Total quality management (TQM), the generic name given to the Deming approach to quality-based management, is heavily oriented toward treating the *system* as the primary source of error or defects in manufacturing or service work. Although quality management uses myriad statistical techniques to control processes, it also provides some fundamental lessons for control from a human psychology perspective. Deming stresses in his fourteen points such goals as "pride of workmanship," "self-improvement," and "drive out fear" (see the Management Highlight on page 357). These are all elements of the "softer" side of management (the nonquantitative side), but they are equally important to master. Managers who use only SPC are likely to ignore the need for pride in workmanship that most workers share. Thus, the *total* in TQM requires

## DEMING'S 14 POINTS OF TOTAL QUALITY MANAGEMENT

1. *Create constancy of purpose for improvement of product and service.* Deming suggests a radical new definition of a company's role. Rather than to make money, the company's role is to stay in business and provide jobs through innovation, research, constant improvement, and maintenance.

2. *Adopt the new philosophy.* Americans are too tolerant of poor workmanship and sullen service. We need a new religion in which mistakes and negativism are unacceptable.

3. *Cease dependence on mass inspection.* American firms typically inspect a product as it comes off the assembly line or at major stages along the way; defective products are either thrown out or reworked. Both practices are unnecessarily expensive. In effect, a company is paying workers to make defects and then to correct them. Quality comes not from inspection, but from improvement of the process. With instruction, workers can be enlisted in this improvement.

4. *End the practice of awarding business on price tag alone.* Purchasing departments customarily award business to the lowest-priced vendor. Frequently, this leads to low-quality supplies. Instead, buyers should seek the best quality in a long-term relationship with a single supplier for any one item.

5. *Improve constantly the system of production and service.* Improvement isn't a one-time effort. Management is obligated to continually look for ways to reduce waste and improve quality.

6. *Institute training.* Too often, workers have learned their job from another worker who was never trained properly. They're forced to follow unintelligible instructions. They can't do their jobs well because no one tells them how to do so.

7. *Institute leadership.* The supervisor's job isn't to tell people what to do or to punish them, but to lead. Leading consists of (1) helping people do a better job, and (2) learning by objective methods which workers need individual help.

8. *Drive out fear.* Many employees are afraid to ask questions or to take a position, even when they don't understand what their job is or what's right or wrong. They will continue to do things the wrong way or not do them at all. Economic losses from fear are appalling. To ensure better quality and productivity, people must feel secure.

9. *Break down barriers between staff areas.* Often a company's departments or units are competing with each other or have goals that conflict. They don't work as a team so that they can solve or foresee problems. Worse, one department's goals may cause trouble for another.

10. *Eliminate slogans, exhortations, and targets for the workforce.* These never helped anybody do a good job. Let workers formulate their own slogans.

11. *Eliminate numerical quotas.* Quotas take into account only numbers, not quality of methods. They're usually a guarantee of inefficiency and high cost. To hold their jobs, people meet quotas at any cost, without regard for damage to their company.

12. *Remove barriers to pride of workmanship.* People are eager to do a good job and are distressed when they can't. Too often, misguided supervisors, faulty equipment, and defective materials stand in way of good performance. These barriers must be removed.

13. *Institute a vigorous program of education and retraining.* Both management and the workforce must be educated in new methods, including teamwork and statistical techniques.

14. *Take action to accomplish the transformation.* A special top management team with a plan of action is needed to carry out the quality mission. Workers can't do it on their own, nor can managers. A critical mass of people in the company must understand the 14 points.

**Sources:** W. Edwards Deming, *Out of the Crisis*, 2nd ed. (Cambridge, MA: MIT Center for Advanced Engineering Study, 1986); Lloyd Dobyns and Clare Crawford-Mason, *Quality or Else* (Boston: Houghton Mifflin, 1991); and Marshall Sashkin and Kenneth J. Kiser, *Total Quality Management* (Seabrook, MD: Ducochon Press, 1991).

managers to be familiar with a wide range of facts about the workplace, both those that can be described mathematically and those that cannot.

Let's examine just a few of the important elements of TQM, including the worker's role and the manager's role in a TQM environment.

| **The Worker's Role in TQM** | Workers play an important role in implementing TQM programs. Deming provides an example of successful worker quality control in the

production of stockings. Managers with the stocking company first recognized a problem in production costs when they faced a situation in which costs were soon to exceed revenues. Management hired a statistician to help them diagnose their problem. The statistician recommended that the company send 20 supervisors to a 10-week training course to learn techniques for charting the number of defective stockings. When the supervisors returned, they were asked to apply some of the principles they had learned.

In all but two cases, defects fell within statistically established control limits with a mean defect rate of 4.8 percent per production worker (called "loopers" in the stocking business). Next, individual loopers were charted. Management found (1) an excellent looper whose skills were passed on to others by training them, (2) a looper who improved markedly with eyeglasses, and (3) a looper whose performance changed dramatically after charting. One of the loopers remarked, "This is the first time that anybody ever told me that care mattered." Within seven months, the mean number of defects dropped to 0.8 percent. Instead of 11,500 stockings rejected each week, only 2,000 were rejected.[22]

A quality-based system of control must be built on worker trust and pride of workmanship, which provides a basis for worker self-control.[23] In this quality-based view, control must be seen as an internal, individual process before it can result in an external process. Control becomes an internal quality guide practiced by all employees rather than an external set of rules applied by managers. Juran defines self-control as "A means of knowing what the goals are ... a means of knowing what the actual performance is ... a means for changing the performance in the event that performance does not conform to goals and standards."[24]

Although workers play an important role in implementing a TQM approach, management has the responsibility of leadership. In most organizations, workers below the managerial level are unlikely to lead a revolution in organizational philosophy. It's up to management to steer the ship. Managers must create the vision for the organization. This is no different in a TQM environment or a scientific management environment. What is different is the behavior of managers.

| **Management's Role in TQM** | Quality-based management believes control of work processes is effected first by the workforce, then by automation, then by managers, and finally by upper managers. Upper management is responsible for creating the system; workers are trained to maintain control. Thus, a quality-based approach locates control at the lowest levels of the firm—the workers on the line who provide the service.[25]

The traditional managerial control function has focused on supervision during the production process. Supervision has been widely practiced as a traditional method of keeping an eye on workers—that is, looking for mistakes. Some managers have even resorted to using information technologies to eavesdrop on employees. This type of practice has debilitating effects on performance and is ethically questionable. In some cases, the corporate trend toward downsizing and rightsizing has led workers lower down in the corporate hierarchy to tell bosses only what they think they want to hear, even resorting to lying. Extreme pressure to perform can lead to improper behavior.

The responsibility for quality control ultimately rests with management; however, managers must also promote worker self-management. To further employee self-management, managers must develop worker participation programs and policies. With knowledge of the company's costs and goals, workers can practice control with minimal supervision. Management's job is to ensure that workers have the knowledge, the tools, and the power to prevent problems from arising. Managers must also encourage employee suggestions and cost consciousness by recognizing and implementing worker quality improvement decisions. And, if there are problems, management should give workers the first opportunity to solve them.

Managers need patience to transform their organizations using the principles and tools of TQM. Workers are not always readily willing to embrace new practices. Managers are responsible for creating an atmosphere filled with enthusiasm for change and improvement.[26] Most workers want responsibility and control over their work. Most will understand and accept a new approach to their work if management demonstrates commitment to improving the system. That means workers need to be trained in the tools and techniques of TQM, SPC, and TQC. They need to be empowered to control their work processes. And they need to be encouraged constantly to develop pride in their work and their organization. These elements of quality are the least quantifiable, but no less important.

**CONCLUSION**

## Control Systems

Control is an important responsibility of managers. The three elements of the control process are specification, production, and inspection. The techniques managers use to control production and operations include preliminary control, concurrent control, and feedback control. The total quality movement has given rise to three additional approaches for controlling organizational processes: statistical process control, total quality control, and total quality management.

## Discussion Questions

1. Describe the difference between preliminary, concurrent, and feedback control.

2. Explain the role of statistics in quality control.

3. What is total quality management (TQM)? Discuss the worker's role and the manager's role in TQM.

## Video Case

### Control Is Key to Peapod's Online Grocery Service

Imagine a big food fight—tomatoes, peanut butter, eggs, bread flying across the room. The grocery industry is a like a food fight without the mess. It is so competitive that only the strongest survive. Now imagine trying to survive in the *online* grocery industry, where customers can't see, smell, or touch the goods, and they expect their orders to be accurate and arrive on time. Finally, picture being one of the few companies to ride out the original dot.com storm. Those are daunting challenges for any firm. But Peapod, the online grocery service founded in 1989 by brothers Andrew and Thomas Parkinson, is succeeding on all three fronts.

Peapod introduced a new concept 15 years ago: the convenience of shopping for groceries online. Plenty of skeptics said the idea wouldn't fly, but some consumers and businesses were intrigued and began to order their groceries online. When many dot.coms of the era began to fail, Peapod hung on. Mike Brennan, vice president of marketing for Peapod, explains that the firm was able to survive because its founders focused on controlling the quality of their goods and services, as well as their costs. Meanwhile, competitors that entered the market with far more investor funding fell by the wayside. A company called Webvan actually raised $1 billion in capital—and is nowhere to be seen today. HomeRuns.com and Streamline.com are also gone.

Quality and service have been Peapod's highest priorities since the beginning. "The biggest hurdle was convincing consumers they could shop online and still maintain control over the quality of their picks," notes CEO Marc van Gelder. "That's been Peapod's cornerstone all along. Today, customers see us for what we are: a lifestyle solution for their busy lives." Whether an order is fulfilled through one of Peapod's own freestanding warehouses or in any of its eight smaller "warerooms," which are adjacent to Peapod's supermarket partners Stop & Shop and Giant Food, it must be accurate; contain the highest quality meats, seafood, and produce; and be completed quickly. Peapod works closely with its suppliers to select the best fresh foods and store them in controlled climates to ensure the longest freshness with minimal waste.

Customer service is controlled on a daily basis. When a call comes in from a customer, it is immediately routed to the department best equipped to deal with it. If there is a problem, it is corrected within 24 hours, which reduces the number of subsequent calls. Fewer customer service calls means more satisfied customers, better service, and less money spent on staffing the customer service department.

Transportation is one of Peapod's largest costs. Mike Brennan explains that when a delivery truck goes out on a route, the costs are fixed no matter how many deliveries the truck actually makes. That's because the truck requires maintenance and fuel, and the driver needs to be paid. So, it is more cost effective to send out a truck with 10 customer orders than it is to send out the same truck with 4 orders. To control some of these fixed transportation costs, Peapod developed the Smart Mile program, which sets a minimum number of deliveries each truck must make. Under the program, each truck must have on board between 14 and 25 deliveries before it can leave the distribution center. However, Peapod must still coordinate delivery times with its customers, or its service will begin to falter. That's why Peapod offers customers a discount in delivery fees if they agree to choose certain time slots. Mike Brennan believes that the Smart Mile program is vital to Peapod's profitability and ultimate success.

Finally, Peapod's growth must be controlled. Although the firm is still based in Chicago, it has expanded into markets where its grocery partners are located. Peapod began serving the Washington, DC, area several years ago, in conjunction with Giant Food. Recently, delivery was expanded to the Baltimore area, making the service available to nearly 250,000 new households. With industry research revealing that online grocery shopping is a growing trend, Peapod plans to grow, too. By keeping its costs, quality, and service in control, this dot.com survivor could win the ultimate food fight.

## Questions

1. What types of feedforward controls might Peapod use in the next few years?
2. Using the feedback control model, identify at least two standards that Peapod might establish.

3. Do you think decentralized control would be effective at Peapod? Why or why not?

Sources: Company web site, http://www.peapod.com, accessed September 8, 2004; "Peapod Grocery Delivery Service Coming to Baltimore," *Baltimore Business Journal*, August 11, 2004, http://baltimore.bizjournals.com; "Online Groceries Keep Expanding, Quietly," *MSNBC News*, May 16, 2004, http://www.msnbc.com; "Online Grocery Shopping Finally Becoming Profitable," *Food & Drink Weekly*, April 28, 2003, http://www.findarticles.com.

## BizFlix

### Brazil

*Brazil* take place in a retro-futuristic world in which automation prevades every facet of life, but paperwork, inefficiency, and mechanical failures are the rule. *Brazil* stars Jonathan Pryce in the role of Sam, a low-level bureaucrat. In this scene, Sam inadvertently gets wrapped up in an intrigue surrounding the so-called terrorist Harry Tuttle (played by Robert DeNiro), who is actually a renegade heating technician for whom the Ministry of Central Services has issued an arrest order. The clip moves quickly, so you may need to review it several times to really grasp the nuances in the coversation.

### Questions

1. What kind of control is being used by Central Services?

2. Tuttle describes a paradox of control. What is it?

3. What kind of control does Tuttle seem to prefer? Explain.

## Suggested Readings

Anderson, Erin, "How Right Should the Customer Be?" *Harvard Business Review* (July/August 2006): 59–67.

"Can Benchmarking Provide Evidence?" *Harvard Business Review* (January 2006): 69.

Cokins, Gary, *Activity-Based Cost Management: An Executive's Guide* (New York: Wiley, 2001).

Cole, Robert E., "Learning from the Quality Movement: What Did and Didn't Happen and Why?" *California Management Review* (Fall 1998): 43–73.

Crosby, Philip B., *Quality Is Free: The Art of Making Quality Certain* (Mentor Books, 1992).

Deming, W. Edwards, *Out of the Crisis* (Cambridge, MA: MIT Press, 2000).

George, Michael L., *Lean Six Sigma: Combining Six-Sigma Quality with Lean Production* (New York: McGraw-Hill, 2002).

## Endnotes

1. "Low-Maintenance Control Systems Improve NGL Recovery at Texas Gas Plant," *Oil and Gas Journal* (May 19, 2003): 56–63.

2. Joseph M. Juran, *Juran on Leadership for Quality: An Executive Handbook* (New York: Free Press, 1989), 145.

3. Walter A. Shewhart, *Statistical Method from the Viewpoint of Quality Control* (Washington, D: Graduate School, U.S. Dept. of Agriculture, 1939), 1.

4. W. Edwards Deming, *Out of the Crisis* (Cambridge, MA: Center for Advanced Engineering Study, Massachusetts Institute of Technology, 1986), chapter 9, esp. pp. 276–277.

5. Deming, *Out of the Crisis,* p. 28.

6. Peter Lorange and Declan Murphy, "Considerations in Implementing Strategic Control," *Journal of Business Strategy* (Spring 1984): 27–35.

7. George Schreyogg and Horst Stenman, "Strategic Control: A New Perspective," *Academy of Management Review* (January 1987): 91–103.

8. Luis R. Gomez Mejia, Henry Tosi, and Timothy Hinkin, "Managerial Control, Performance, and Executive Compensation," *Academy of Management Journal* (March 1987): 51–70.

9. Joel G. Siegel and Matthew S. Rubin, "Corporate Planning and Control through Variance Analysis," *Managerial Planning* (September–October, 1984): 33–36.

10. Michael R. Walls, "Integration Business Strategy and Capital Allocation: An Application of Multi-Objective Decision Making," *Engineering Economist* (Spring 1995): 247–266.

11. Jane Beckett-Camarata, "An Examination of the Relationship between the Municipal Strategic Plan and the Capital Budget and Its Effect on Financial Performance," *Journal of Public Budgeting, Accounting, and Financial Management* (Spring 2003): 23–40.

12. "Capital Budgeting Methods among Sweden's Largest Groups of Companies," *International Journal of Production Economics* (April 11, 2003): 51–69.

13. Frank Collins, Paul Munter, and Don W. Finn, "The Budgeting Games People Play," *Accounting Review* (January 1987): 29–49.

14. Gabriel A. Pall, *Quality Process Management* (Englewood Cliffs, NJ: Prentice-Hall, 1987), 94.

15. Susanta Kumar Gauri, "Statistical Process Control Procedures for Controlling the Weight of Packets of Biscuits," *Total Quality Management and Business Excellence* (July 2003), 525–535.

16. Thomas Pyzdek, *What Every Manager Should Know about Quality* (New York: Marcel Dekker, 1991), 3.

17. A. V. Feigenbaum, *Total Quality Control* (New York: McGraw-Hill, 1991); Mary Walton, *The Deming Management Method* (New York: Perigree, 1986), 122–130 and Kaoru Ishikawa, *What Is Total Quality Control?* (Englewood Cliffs, NJ: Prentice Hall, 1985), 90–94.

18. Feigenbaum, *Total Quality Control,* p. 5.

19. Feigenbaum, p. 828.

20. Feigenbaum, pp. 828–833.

21. Pyzdek, *What Every Manager Should Know about Quality,* pp. 3–4.

22. Deming, *Out of the Crisis,* pp. 380–387.

23. Juran, *Juran on Leadership for Quality,* chapter 5.

24. Juran, pp. 147–148.

25. Juran, pp. 148–150.

26. Richard A. Roberts, "You Want to Improve? First You Must Change," *SuperVision* (May 2003): 8–10.

# 17

# MANAGING ORGANIZATIONAL CHANGE AND DEVELOPMENT

**C**hange is inevitable, but it can be evolutionary or revolutionary. *Evolutionary change* occurs gradually, sometimes almost without notice. Behavioral change, such as an increased tolerance for differences, is an outgrowth of evolutionary societal changes. *Revolutionary change* is abrupt—it happens, and the change is forever. Technological advances, such as the introduction of a new chemical compound or the release of a new microprocessing device, make existing products quickly obsolete. Managers must navigate this changing domain, determining whether they face evolution or revolution. They have a twofold obligation to meet daily operational demands as well as adapt to changing future circumstances.

To some managers, change appears to be occurring at an unprecedented and accelerating rate. Perhaps these managers believe this era is uniquely challenging because much of modern organizational change is driven by external forces, such as market competition or technology. In the 1950s and 1960s, large American firms had few competitors and there was little pressure for organizational change. Social, demographic, and economic changes of the past few decades have altered the competitive landscape. Today the economic picture is far different from that of even a few years ago. Global competition, which gives consumers more choices, is a major driver of organizational change, and it is a phenomenon that has become reality slowly over about the past 20 years. This global nature of competition requires that managers think of ways to change their organization continuously to gain competitive advantage. Managers must consider their company as well as speculate about the future of the industry and its economic circumstances.

This chapter examines four targets of change and how to overcome resistance to change. It presents a model for managing change in organizations, the role of change agents, and the strategy of change.

**During the past decade, managers have led the following organizational changes:**

- *Internet access and local computer networks*—increasing worker productivity and connecting the company to suppliers.

- *E-commerce*—using the Internet to market products or services.

- *Flexible work systems*—offering job sharing, telecommuting, and other innovative approaches.

- *Empowerment*—sharing power with more organizational stakeholders. Management has given the worker more power in the workplace, including involvement in decision making, planning, and customer satisfaction.

- *Restructuring and downsizing*—restructuring to decrease costs mainly by reducing the number of workers required to run the organization. Many organizations have downsized to become leaner, with less middle management and fewer layers in the corporate hierarchy.

- *Quality*—implementing strategies to increase product quality. Such tangible outcomes as high reliability, fewer defects, and better fit and finish are today's management mantras.

# Change Targets

At the most general level of distinction, change has four targets. *Organization-wide* change targets, such as restructuring or Total Quality Management TQM, have an impact on the entire organization. *Group* change targets focus on several people working collectively toward a common goal. For example, using new group decision-making software to enhance group performance requires a change in how the group functions and group members interact. *Intergroup* change targets address the nature of the interaction between groups. Introducing groupware software into the organization requires different groups to change their behavior and attitudes. *Individual* change targets focus on the person, or in this case, the employee. Safety training required by the Occupational Safety and Health Administration (OSHA) is an example of change targeted at the individual and possibly attempting to change both attitudes and behavior.

These changes, which take place in American business and industry, can be summarized as follows: (1) global competition; (2) restructuring; (3) technological advances; and (4) digital technology, including the Internet and e-commerce. These changes will pressure managers to make a wide variety of adjustments if they want their companies to remain competitive in the twenty-first century. New companies will come into being, and old ones that do not change their strategies will die. This is an era of instant communication and fast-changing technologies. It is an era in which customers demand quality and value; it is also an era of employee empowerment and changing global relationships and structures. Traditional ways of doing business are gone, along with comfortable relationships. Letting go of systems and habits that have developed over a lifetime is hard, but for companies to achieve and maintain success, they must continuously reinvent themselves.[1]

Over the past decade, many companies have tried to remake themselves into better competitors. Their efforts are carried on under many banners: total quality management, reengineering, rightsizing, restructuring, and cultural change. In almost every case, the goal has been the same—to cope with a new, more challenging market by changing the way business is conducted. A few of these change programs have been very successful. A few have been utter failures. Most fall somewhere in between, though with a distinct tilt toward the failure end of the scale. The lessons learned from these failures will be relevant to more and more organizations as the business environment becomes increasingly competitive. One lesson companies have taken away is that change involves numerous phases that, together, usually take a long time to complete. A second lesson is that critical mistakes in the management of any of the phases can have a devastating impact on the success of the change effort.[2]

The following sections discuss some forces of change. Frameworks and models are presented that can serve not only as blueprints for ordering managerial thinking about change but also as guidelines for first diagnosing and then managing change. In a later section, we will discuss various intervention methods in relation to change.

# Change Forces

Today's organizational domain includes unpredictable and uncontrollable domestic and international forces. New developments in mergers and acquisitions, regulation, privatization, downsizing, union-management collaboration, high-involvement participation, plant closings, reengineering, management of culturally diverse workers, and environmental protection occupy managers' time. These and many other forces from outside and inside the organization demand attention.

As mentioned in the introduction to this chapter, organizations around the world have been experiencing increasingly rapid change for much of the second half of the twentieth century.

With the globalization of markets, worldwide telecommunications, and increasingly rapid and efficient travel over the past decade, the need for organizations to continuously reinvent themselves is greater than ever. The average United States business lasts only about forty years. Complex and rapid changes in the world's economic and social climates heighten the threat of survival. Organizations that learn to respond creatively to an uncertain future develop the ability to transform themselves when they confront the chaos of a constantly changing competitive environment.[3]

## Strategies for Change

All change strategies have one common purpose—adaptation. The success of a change strategy rests on its ability to be adapted to changing circumstances in a timely manner; otherwise, an organization risks becoming noncompetitive and ultimately going out of business. Change strategies help the organization adapt to changing circumstances while creating greater value for organizational stakeholders. Exhibit 17.1 shows three contemporary change strategies.

The three strategies listed in Exhibit 17.1 can be described as follows:

| Restructuring is a revolutionary change that focuses on the redesign of the organization's structure. In most cases, it means "de-layering," or eliminating units or departments. It can also mean the consolidation of functions. The purpose of restructuring is to create value by both increasing performance and reducing costs.

| Reengineering is a revolutionary change that focuses on an organization's processes. As part of a larger system, a process is a series of activities or tasks that require external inputs in the creation of outputs. For example, purchasing, manufacturing, and sales represent three common organizational processes. The purpose of reengineering is to create value by redesigning efficient organizational processes that meet customer needs.[4]

| Continuous improvement is the evolutionary process of reexamining organizational practices. Continuous improvement processes first identify key organizational performance indicators at all levels of the organization. Next, they periodically compare an actual organization transaction against standards. The goal is to compare actual performance against a standard and make needed adjustments to better serve the customer.[5]

These three organizational change strategies are common, but they do not guarantee success. Their success depends largely on top management support, employee commitment, and the organization's ability to make tough decisions. Change strategies can be effective only to the degree that their leader has a good understanding of the industry and its future direction.

## Internal Forces

Internal change forces are pressures that come from within the organization. Internal sources for change can be a need for cost reduction, negative morale or poor employee attitudes, and the overall organization design (structure).

**KEY**TERMS

**restructuring** A revolutionary change that focuses on the redesign of the organization's structure, eliminating units or departments, but possibly meaning the consolidation of functions.

**process** A series of activities or tasks that require external inputs to create value by redesigning efficient organizational processes to meet customer needs.

**continuous improvement** The evolutionary process of reexamining organizational practices, first identifying key organizational performance indicators at all levels of the organization and then periodically comparing an actual organization transaction against standards.

**internal change forces** Pressures that come from within the organization.

---

EXHIBIT 17.1

**Contemporary Organizational Change Strategies**

| Strategy | Purpose |
|---|---|
| **Restructuring** | Efficiency—Eliminate organizational layers and people to reduce costs. |
| **Reengineering** | Efficiency—Provide better service through the redesign of organizational processes. |
| **Continuous Improvement** | Increase quality or service—Conduct ongoing assessment of product or service, including customer satisfaction. |

| Cost Reduction | Sometimes the internal pressure is the cost of producing a microchip or car. For example, unit cost increases; therefore, pricing the product at a reasonable amount to make a sale is a force that might signal a need for change. If the product costs too much to produce, it cannot be priced competitively.

| Employee Attitude | Poor worker morale over some inequity in the reward system could be an internal pressure point that a manager becomes aware of and must address. Although attitudes can be difficult to observe directly, increased grievance rates, absenteeism, or turnover might suggest poor or decreasing morale. Identifying internally driven forces for change is sometimes difficult. Is poor morale caused by the culture, the structure, or the manager; or does the worker bring this attitude to work? This is a difficult question to answer.

| Organization Design | A common problem that calls for an assessment of the current organization design is a mismatch between a new strategy and an old structure. For example, suppose that as part of a new strategy, a CEO mandates a 20 percent cost reduction, including staff, for all departments. The resulting plan called for some departments being absorbed into other departments, and still others eliminated. Such a change is likely to be a mismatch between a new strategy and the old structure. Remember, the old structure was in support of the old strategy—not the new strategy. For optimal performance, the new strategy needs a new structure.

Regardless of changes or development efforts in an organization's environment, mission, or structure, employee satisfaction and quality of work life remain significant concerns. Although morale and motivation are not often the impetus for such change programs, they are almost always tied inextricably to problems. One of a manager's most effective tools for understanding and diagnosing issues is the organizational survey. Surveys can be conducted by using questionnaires or through interviews. They help managers stay in touch with the forces of change that are at work among employees. By staying in touch with these forces, managers can anticipate changes and turn them to positive outcomes.[6]

## | External Forces

External change forces are pressures that originate outside the organization; they can be a signal that change is needed. External sources for change can be governmental actions, competitive forces, and social forces.

| Governmental Forces | In 1991, an executive order of the governor created the California Environmental Protection Agency (EPA). The agency's mission was to restore, protect, and enhance the environment to ensure public health, environmental quality, and economic vitality. In the process of fulfilling its mission, the California EPA created laws that required organizations to alter their way of conducting business. For example, automobile emissions laws mandated lower amounts of emissions. Automobile manufacturers failing to meet the environmental requirements would be unable to sell any vehicles in the state of California—and California accounts for 30 percent of all domestic vehicle sales. Manufacturers had to comply or risk substantial losses.

Sometimes a government mandate has mixed blessings. Take the example of the use of oxygenators to meet environmental requirements. Typically, gasoline refiners use MTBE (a hydrocarbon oxygenator) to meet emission standards. However, MTBE is toxic and has a negative impact on the environment. Ethanol, a form of alcohol, is an environmentally friendly substitute for MTBE. California and other states have given ethanol producers an economic boost by eliminating MTBE use in their states. As a result, MTBE sales have dropped but ethanol sales have increased. This is an unintended benefit for ethanol producers and good news for the environment. Ethanol can be used as an additive to increase octane ratings in gasoline and also results in lower emissions at the same time. However, it is more expensive than MTBE. The change in California law will ultimately create more demand for ethanol, resulting in production efficiencies and lowering the price in the long run.

| **Competitive Forces** | Competitors force change by introducing new products, new supplier relationships (business-to-business software connections), new uses of technology, or new legal strategies. The success of General Motors in the diesel engine market is one example of competitive change. GM's successful Duramax™ diesel engine is quiet, produces no smoke and less odor, and has greater fuel efficiency than similar diesel engines produced by Ford and DaimlerChrysler. In response, Ford and DaimlerChrysler had to develop similar attributes in their diesel engines or risk a significant loss of market share in the diesel truck market.

| **Social Forces** | Concern with equity and fairness is a hallmark of American life. Our emphasis on cultural diversity today is a powerful external force that often causes organizations to change their practices. Sometimes cost prohibitions make organizations less than enthusiastic about change, but the law encourages and often mandates a timeline for change. Integrating and utilizing the talents of a more diverse workforce, and effectively rewarding this culturally diverse workforce, will require changes in attitude, interpersonal interaction, and perception. Changes in managers' cultural awareness are also needed.

# Resistance to Change

Any change, no matter how clearly beneficial to employees and the organization as a whole, will meet with and can be sabotaged by resistance. Management scholar Paul Lawrence noted many years ago that resistance to change is more often a social or human problem than a technical one.[7] The failure of many recent large-scale efforts at corporate change can be traced directly to employee resistance. Total quality management (TQM) is an example. Evidence shows that many firms that have attempted to apply TQM in their organizations have gained little competitive advantage. Similarly, many reengineering efforts have also fallen short of expectations.[8] A major reason for these disappointing results is employee resistance to change. The following are reasons that people resist change:

- *Self-interest.* Some employees resist change because they have a personal interest in the way things are currently done. They know how to successfully complete the work as it is defined today; they are comfortable with their boss and peers and threatened by change. For most people, interactions at work are based on technical knowledge and expertise. Think about how threatening the introduction of desktop computing and e-mail was to people whose expertise was based on old methods, ideas, and technology, such as microfiche and fax machines. Many employees felt unable to learn new technology and resisted efforts to be taught. When such changes take place, people often fear a loss of social position that can accompany decreasing expertise. They know that fewer people will seek them out as a source of knowledge and expertise in the future.

- *Habit.* For many employees, the routine of working the same way day after day has a certain appeal. Life is a pattern of getting up, going to work, coming home, and going to bed. People become accustomed to sameness; they get in the habit of doing tasks a certain way. Changes in personnel, work flow, structure, or technology threaten the continuation of a pattern or set of habits.

*Fear.* Change introduces uncertainty and a degree of fear. People fear possible failure when having to learn a new way or trying to become accustomed to a new leader. Employees are sometimes given an opportunity to relocate and take a different, better-paying job in the firm, but such changes are considered risky, and they introduce the possibility of failing.

*Peer pressure.* Peers often apply pressure to resist change. For example, peers might resist the introduction of automation because they assume, sometimes correctly, that fewer workers will be needed to perform the job. These peers can create pressure on their colleagues, who might otherwise emotionally and personally support automation and its potential to improve productivity.

*Bureaucratic inertia.* Large government institutions, educational institutions, and business organizations have a built-in resistance to change because of the traditional rules, policies, and procedures. The refrain is: "This is how we've done things for years." Why change? The Big Three auto manufacturers had a degree of built-in resistance to the smaller Japanese cars that arrived in the 1970s. These smaller, more gas-efficient cars caught the attention of American consumers—especially after the gas shortages of 1973. But the Big Three simply did not respond in a timely or aggressive fashion. All three were steeped in traditional thinking about small cars—especially Japanese autos.

Inflexible rules, policies, and procedures preclude the use of adaptive changes in any organization. Bureaucracy, red tape, and traditional ways of conducting business are difficult to overcome. Often managers know they are in a bureaucratic maze but have difficulty wrestling free of barriers, delays, and stonewalling.

## Reducing Resistance to Change

Before an organization can implement changes, its leaders must not only overcome or reduce resistance but also encourage and build support for those changes. There are no simple, foolproof prescriptions for reducing resistance, but the following six options might prove useful.

**Education and Communication** | When lack of information is the problem, managers will find it especially helpful to explain in meetings, memos, or reports why change is needed. Open communication helps people prepare for change. Paving the way, showing the logic, and keeping everyone informed lowers resistance. This option is usually time-consuming. The emphasis of a communications plan should be proactive rather than reactive. All messages should be consistent and repeated through various channels such as videos, memos, newsletters, e-mail, and regular meetings.

**Participation and Involvement** | Bringing together those who will be affected to help design and implement the change likely will increase employee commitment. Empowering employees, paying attention to customers, and customizing the change program to company culture all contribute to successful implementation. Behavioral change is essential to long-term success. Change means new attitudes, behaviors, and often a new way of thinking about the familiar. It might mean embracing new technology.

**Facilitation and Support** | When implementing change, managers must be supportive. They must provide training opportunities and help facilitate the change by showing concern for subordinates, being good listeners, and going to bat for their employees on important issues. Behaviors exhibited by leaders and managers can influence employees' attitudes and perceptions about their work and their organization. Research conducted during a change effort in the marketing and sales division of an international pharmaceutical firm showed that different types of behaviors for managers and senior managers were significantly related to employee attitudes and perceptions.[9] Managers need to behave in ways that show commitment to the change as well as support employees while they are learning to deal with the change.

| **Negotiation and Agreement** | Resistance can be reduced through negotiation. Discussion and analysis can help managers identify points of negotiation and agreement. Negotiated agreement involves giving something to another party to reduce resistance. For example, convincing a person to move to a less desirable work location might require paying that individual a bonus or increasing the monthly salary. Once this negotiation agreement is reached, others might expect the manager to grant similar concessions in the future.

| **Manipulation and Co-optation** | Manipulation involves the use of deception to convince others that a change is in their best interests. Holding back information, playing one person against another, and providing one-sided information are examples of manipulation. Co-opting an individual involves giving the person critical of the change a major role in the design or implementation of the change. For example, during the federal government bailout of Chrysler Motors, Chrysler appointed then president of the UAW Douglas Fraser to Chrysler's board of directors. The union had demanded a wage increase, or a strike would follow. However, once Fraser was a member of the board, he had a new understanding of the situation. Chrysler turned an adversary into a member of a decision-making body, thus co-opting Fraser. In the end, the strike was averted by using the strategy of co-optation.[10]

| **Coercion** | In using coercion, managers engage in threatening behavior. They threaten employees with job loss, reduced promotion opportunities, poor job assignments, and loss of privileges. The coercion is intended to reduce a person's resistance to the management-initiated change. Coercive behavior can be risky because it can generate bad feelings and hostility.[11]

Regardless of the methods employed, the goal of the change agent is to reduce resistance to the change. Companies that are successful in implementing change report much greater employee commitment to change initiatives, smaller productivity fluctuations during implementation, and significantly shorter implementation timelines. At the end of the day, managers who overcome resistance to change; collect data that identifies each factor causing the resistance; develop strategies to reduce the resistance; and apply these strategies to the affected groups.[12]

## A Model for Managing Change in Organizations

Change is, obviously, a process that occurs over time. Managers first recognize that change is needed and then initiate the process. For example, suppose a firm's CEO recognizes that the competition has reduced the price of its product, resulting in increased sales and market share for price cutters. To ensure that her organization has the ability to better control future pricing, the CEO wants to reduce overall costs to gain pricing flexibility. Her solution is to begin an organization-wide restructuring. Although the impetus for restructuring was external, the organization will have many internal changes in the form of new processes, altered structures, and different people to ultimately reach the CEO's goal of reducing system-wide costs.

EXHIBIT 17.2

**A Model for Managing Change in Organizations**

| Assessment | → | Intervention | → | Evaluation |
| Unfreeze | | Change | | Refreeze |

EXHIBIT 17.3

**Process Model for Managing Change**

① Identify Forces for Change
 • Internal
 • External

② Recognize a Need for Change

③ Diagnose Problem

④ Assess Alternative Intervention Strategies

⑤ Select Intervention Strategy

⑥ Perform Evaluation

**KEY**TERMS

**unfreezing** The first stage in the process of change, readying people for the change.

**intervention** In the process of change, the second stage, the change itself.

**refreezing** The final stage in the process of change, implementing the change.

Noted psychologist Kurt Lewin developed an elegant and concise model of change. He believed that change occurs in three stages. The first stage in the process of change is unfreezing, or readying people for the change. The second stage involves the intervention, or actual change. The final stage is refreezing, or implementing the change. The model illustrated in Exhibit 17.2 is based on Kurt Lewin's general concept of change as well as other factors that influence change. Exhibit 17.3 illustrates a more detailed process model for managing change, which emphasizes six distinct stages that managers must consider when making decisions.

These stages are described in detail here.

**STEP 1**  **Identify Forces for Change**

The forces that drive a change can be internal or external. For example, an internal force (employees) generates concerns about compensation, but an external force (the market) might actually stimulate the change in compensation practices because of the organization's inability to hire sufficient employees to conduct business. As this example illustrates, the impetus for change can come either from an internal force, an external force, or a combination of the two forces.

**STEP 2**  **Recognize a Need for Change**

Managers must recognize that change is needed or that the present state is inadequate. Recognition is easy when the magnitude of the problems (such as market-share losses, equal employment opportunity discrimination suits, rising turnover, or declining profit margins) is significant. Unfortunately, the indicators that change is needed are not always dramatic. A loss here and there, a complaining group of customers, a disgruntled technician, or a lost contract can also be small signs that change is necessary.

Some companies have adopted a new technique for helping managers recognize the need for change. The technique is known as the sense-and-respond (SR) model. The SR model involves sensing change earlier and responding to it faster. According to Steve Haeckel of the IBM Advanced Business Institute, the SR model requires managers to be very good at conceptual thinking.[13] That means managers must be able to think broadly and to entertain simultaneously two or more (possibly contradictory) ideas about issues. The SR model requires managers to build an organizational context that delegates operational decision making and the design of adaptive systems to the people or teams accountable for producing results (beginning of the unfreezing stage). The model encourages all employees to be alert to changes in the environment and to act on those changes to improve the company's competitive position.[14]

**STEP 3**

### Diagnose the Problem

Diagnosis is an analytical process that generates valuable information to determine the exact nature of a problem or the need for change. Although direct observation is quite common, diagnosis can be conducted using a variety of techniques.

**Force Field Analysis.** Force Field Analysis is a popular diagnosis strategy developed by Kurt Lewin. This technique is a means of diagnosing situations and analyzing the various change strategies that can be used in a particular situation.

**Gap Analysis.** Gap analysis identifies the difference between the current state of the organization and the desired state of the organization. Once the gap is identified, Force Field Analysis becomes a useful tool. Before undertaking any change strategy, managers will find it useful to determine what they have working in their favor (driving forces) and what forces are working against them (restraining forces).

- Driving forces are those forces affecting a situation that are pushing in a particular direction; they tend to initiate a change and keep it going. In relation to improving productivity in an organization, examples of driving forces are words of praise from a manager, effective reward systems, and a high level of employee involvement in decision making.

- Restraining forces are those forces that act to restrain or decrease driving forces. Low morale, anger, or inadequate work tools are examples of restraining forces. Equilibrium is the point at which the sum of the driving forces equals the sum of the restraining forces.

To understand these concepts, imagine that you manage a fast-food restaurant. If you decide to initiate a significant change in the restaurant, some driving forces might be customer demand, competition, cost pressures, government regulations, and franchise policies. Restraining forces might include lack of resources, low employee morale, low employee skill level, employee resistance to change, or lack of knowledge.

In utilizing Force Field Analysis for developing a change strategy, managers can use these guidelines:

- *When driving forces far outweigh the restraining forces* in power and frequency in a change situation, managers interested in driving for change can often push on and overpower the restraining forces.

- *When restraining forces are much stronger than the driving forces*, managers interested in driving for change have several choices: (1) They can give up the change effort, realizing that it will be too difficult to implement; or (2) they can pursue the change effort, but concentrate on maintaining the driving forces in the situation while attempting, one by one, to change each of the restraining forces into driving forces—or somehow to immobilize each of the restraining forces so that they are no longer factors in the situation. The second choice is possible, but very time-consuming.

- *When driving forces and restraining forces are fairly equal* in a change situation, managers probably will have to begin pushing the driving forces, while at the same time attempting to convert or immobilize some or all of the restraining forces. The Management Highlight on page 371 describes an exercise that helps you better understand the complexities of Force Field Analysis using a contemporary problem.

**STEP 4**

### Assess Alternative Intervention Strategies

Managers must assess several different intervention methods and choose one of them. Intervention methods are discussed later in the chapter, including survey feedback, team building, empowerment, and foresight-led change.

MANAGEMENT HIGHLIGHT

## FORCE FIELD ANALYSIS: UNDERSTANDING THE PRESSURES FOR AND AGAINST CHANGE

The Force Field Analysis is a beneficial tool for analyzing all the forces for and against change. By carrying out the analysis, a manager can strategically strengthen the forces supporting a decision that will induce change, and subsequently, reduce the impact of opposition to it.

To conduct a Force Field Analysis, follow these steps

1. List all forces for change in one column, and all forces against change in another column.
2. Assign a score to each force, from 1 (weak) through 5 (strong).
3. Draw a diagram showing the forces for and against change. Show the size of each force as a number next to it.

Now apply what you have learned to the scenario below.

### Scenario

The United States is faced with an energy crisis resulting from the rising costs of oil, which inevitably contributes to the rising costs of gasoline. In order to help alleviate some of the pressures, domestic automobile manufacturers have introduced alternative fuel vehicles. However, a majority of the United States population have not adopted such cars. What are the forces for and against change toward the diffusion of alternative fuel vehicles in the United States domestic market?

A simple example of a Force Field Analysis for the above scenario might look like this.

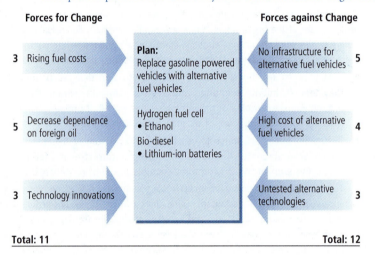

To implement the plan, the analysis might suggest a number of changes to the initial plan:

- By creating an infrastructure for alternative fuel vehicles, you could eliminate one force against change.

- By increasing government tax breaks to owners, you could reduce alternative-vehicle costs to consumers (reduce vehicle cost by 2).

It appears that the domestic automobile market has not, to date, embraced the benefits of alternative fuel technology. In fact, the forces against change have kept the market at or near status quo. Suggested changes could swing the balance from 12:13 (against change), to 12:6 (in favor of change).

---

STEP 5

### Select Intervention Strategy and Implementation

After evaluating the pros and cons of various change techniques, the manager should select one or some combination of alternatives and then implement it. This is the intervention, or change, phase of the model described in Exhibit 17.3. Implementation often is not given enough consideration when attempting to bring about lasting change. At this point refreezing begins.

STEP 6

### Perform Evaluation and Begin the Process Again

Managers want to learn whether changes have occurred, and if so, what has been accomplished. Is the profit margin improved? Has morale improved? Have customers returned to the brand? Measuring change over time is difficult because many uncontrollable influences often affect the original change effort. For example, in the middle of a structural change, suppose a new government regulation is passed that directly affects employees in the units undergoing change. Suppose the regulation demands that employees file additional government paperwork, even though employees have continually complained about too much paperwork. Low morale prevails. Did the structural change cause the lower morale, or did the new regulation? It would be hard to say what is behind the lower morale.

## Measurement

Measuring skills, attitudes, and values before, during, and after change is often difficult. But measurement is necessary for evaluating the effectiveness of a change. When a complete measurement is not possible or cost effective, general reactions to change can be assessed. Example reactions to a change might include (1) global reaction—Did you like the change program? (2) learning—What was learned? and (3) outcomes—Is quality of output higher, lower, or about the same?

Based on years of research and attempts to measure changes in reaction, learning, behavior, and outcomes, some general guidelines are useful:

  *Measurements should be conducted over a period of time.* Soon after change has occurred, participants might be generally excited and interested because they are being asked for responses. Conducting measurement over a period of time will identify lag effects, extinction effects, and long-term results.

  *Compare groups that have undergone change with those that have not undergone change.* Comparisons are a form of internal benchmarking—how does a unit that was changed compare regarding outcomes or behavior with a unit that was not changed?

  *Avoid exclusive reliance on quantitative measures.* Quantitative measures include cost, profit, units produced, and defective units. Managers must also consider qualitative questions. What do participants say? How do participants look? What do participants do without being asked? These types of qualitative measures provide insight into the effects of change.

Guidelines like these can be applied to both small and major changes. Unfortunately, too many organizations bypass evaluation because it is difficult. However, change is a continual process, and starting over requires feedback. If done properly, the evaluation step can provide feedback for the next cycle of change; that is, the model output becomes an internally based force for change.

## Types of Change Agents

A change agent is an individual or a team of individuals whose responsibility it is to practice the stages suggested in Exhibit 17.3. Typically, a professional outside consultant leads the change effort but needs considerable help from inside the organization during the diagnosis stage, most preferably from the top level of the organization. Four types of change agents have been identified: outside pressure (OP), people-change-technology (PCT), analysis for the top (AFT), and organizational development (OD).[15]

## Outside Pressure

The outside pressure (OP) change agent is an individual or a group that is not regularly employed by the firm but still applies pressure on the firm to change. For example, many parts of the world have witnessed a shift from a manufacturing-based economy toward a predominantly service-based economy driven by digital technology, knowledge or intellectual capital, and information. In the mass production era, people made their career choices at about the time they graduated from high school and then stuck with them. Today, organizations know that to survive into the next century, they must obtain high performance from their workers. As a result, organizations are continually eliminating nonproductive functions and constantly reassessing, reshuffling, and retraining staff. Intelligent career and life planning in the knowledge-service era necessitates ongoing assessment, decision making, problem solving, and the creation of opportunities. Because of societal changes, organizations must change the career paths they create for people.

## People-Change-Technology

The people-change-technology (PCT) change agent attempts to bring about change via various behaviorally oriented techniques. It focuses on the individual. Normally these change agents are professionals using standardized assessment techniques. To be successful in the long term, most change programs must involve more than superficial, isolated behavioral changes. A system-wide approach involving changes in a company's fundamental operations, beliefs, and values is called for. Resistance to change can also be reduced if employees understand how the changes will increase organizational effectiveness and ultimately lead to greater job security and more meaningful work.[16]

## Analysis for the Top

Analysis for the top (AFT) agents offer advice about how best to change technology and structure to increase overall organizational effectiveness. Reengineering, restructuring, and technology change are methods used by AFT agents. AFT consultants focus their efforts on improving the organization's relationship with the external environment as well as overall system efficiency and effectiveness.

## Organizational Development

Organizational development (OD) change agents use behavioral science techniques to facilitate systemic change that is neither a quick fix nor superficial. Normally, organizational development is seen as a long-term approach to improve organizational effectiveness and targets the entire organization. The role of the OD change agent is to follow the steps outlined in Exhibits 17.2 and 17.3, which include diagnosis, intervention, and evaluation. Qualities of a successful OD change agent include: *technical competence* in the intervention strategies used in the planned change, *leadership skills* to champion the change process, and strong *interpersonal skills* to persuade and influence participants.[17]

Which change agent(s) should be used to introduce a total quality management program or a program about quality of work life? Four factors to consider are the nature of the force for change, that is, internal or external; the target of the change; the degree of problem severity; and the time frame for improvement. In general, the greater the outside pressure for change, the easier it is to persuade participants of the need for change. In fact, some managers have even successfully invented the pretext of outside pressure to encourage change within their organization.

## How Does a Leader Change an Organization?

How does organizational change occur? Change occurs because a leader takes action. But what specific action? Meaningful organizational change can occur in a surprisingly limited number of ways. Five common ways organizations can fundamentally change what they do and how they do it are structural, technological, cultural, task, and behavioral (people) change.[18] Organizational change is classified as planned change and reactive change. *Planned change* is proactive and driven by a vision for a specific outcome. A planned change is the product of a strategic choice by the organization's leadership to change the structure, technology, culture, task, or behavior of people in the organization. *Reactive change* is a change that is unanticipated by the organization and made in response to an external force. Pushing diversity training in response to a competitor's effort to do the same is an example of reactive (external) force for change. But for the competitor, the training might have been an integrated planned change.

Organizational change means reconfiguring work. Culture, structure, technology, the task, and behavior of people can all be reconfigured in a variety of ways that meet the requirements of internal or external forces for changes. As Exhibit 17.4 shows, a change in one element of the model is likely to affect other elements of the model. Also, the depth of the change can influence the durability and sustainability of the change over time.

## Changing the Culture

Organizational culture creates the character and uniqueness of the organization. The leader or founder develops and encourages a particular type of culture. Organizations vary considerably in cultural expression, as Deal and Kennedy note.[19] For example, a healthcare system with a religious affiliation has different values and beliefs from a county-run hospital. For an organization to change, the basic values, beliefs, and assumptions that drive employee behavior on a daily basis must change. Employee identification with the culture and organizational goals shape behavior. When an organization wants to make a major change that affects all employees, it must expect to change its culture in the process.

An organization's culture is an enduring system of values, beliefs, attitudes, and assumptions widely held and shared by groups and individuals inside the organization that create a unique organization. Educational institutions, businesses, and law firms are examples of organizations with different cultures. Cultural uniqueness comes from the way in which the leader creates a culture that is specific to that one organization. Culture socializes members and increases predictable behavior, thereby increasing social control of organization members.

The organizational culture is referred to as the *dominant culture*. Within the dominant culture can be many subservient subcultures. For example, the dominant culture at GM under Jack Smith was informal, reflective of his personal leadership style. However, the design subculture at GM was more characteristic of the culture of artists and design professionals than the dominant culture. Subcultures coexist within the dominant culture to reflect different approaches to work from one organization to another. Information systems, art and design, or advertising are all unique subcultures that meld into the dominant culture without conflict—they know their limits.

Three ways to change an organizational culture are as follows:

- *Hiring and retention.* Carefully staffing people who will enhance the culture and contribute to its development over time
- *Socialization.* Training and socializing new employees to inculcate the values of the culture
- *Role modeling.* Identifying successful role models and pairing role models with new employees to develop cultural continuity over time

Once created or changed, a culture can be institutionalized in the following ways:

- *Creating stories that dramatize the culture.* State Farm Insurance Company traces its origins to the "Farmer from Merna, IL." Most State Farm employees have heard the story of the "Framer from Merna" and understand the significance of the story: anything is possible if you work hard.[20]

| *Using rites and rituals to define uniqueness.* Retirement, promotion, dismissal, and leadership succession can all help define and showcase the culture.

| *Using language that is shared by members of the culture.* Using language that is unique to a organization, industry, or profession enables employees to feel like "insiders," further building cultural bonds.

| *Create symbols that portray the culture.* Trademarks, logos and other symbols create corporate identity. Corporate cars, appointments to prestigious committees, and travels by corporate jet can also have symbolic significance by creating meaning within the organization.[21]

Leaders create change as much by their inaction as by their action; failure to act can be interpreted negatively by employees looking for a cue from the leader, so the leader must attend to shaping the culture on an ongoing basis. To modify or fundamentally change the culture, a leader can use the preceding ideas in the following sequence:

1. *Benchmark the current culture*—Determine what kind of culture (if any) currently defines the organization. How does it compare to other similar organizations in the industry?

2. *Communicate the new culture*—Inform employees about the values and beliefs that define the new and developing culture.

3. *Appoint new leaders*—Sever ties with the old culture and showcase the leaders of the new culture.

4. *Create a system of shared meaning*—Build the culture with stories, rituals, symbols, and language that uniquely defines the new culture.

5. *Socialize new members and reward old members*—Create opportunities and activities that inform new members what is expected for success. Reward members of the culture who are meeting or exceeding those expectations in a visible and public manner.

Where cultural features support past ineffective or failed strategies, they can constrain change. Generating change involves (1) understanding the powerful force of culture; (2) aligning culture with positive ethical and equitable values; and (3) devising sound reward, educational, and socialization systems. In a growing number of firms, leaders realize that changing culture can also require changing organizational structures.

## | Changing the Structure

Organizational performance is superior when structure supports strategy. A mismatch between the strategy and the structure results in lower levels of performance.[22] As an example, in the 1930's GM invented the multidivisional structure to support a growth through acquisition strategy. GM acquired Oldsmobile, Chevrolet, Cadillac, and Pontiac from their original owners. Alfred Sloan used the divisional structure to achieve a higher degree of control and financial performance from each division. The lesson from the GM experience is that a company should first develop a plan (i.e., a strategy) and then create a structure than supports the strategy. Research supports this idea that as strategy changes, structural change is generally required for optimal performance.[23]

In the early 1980s, General Motors decided to change their organizational structure in response to changing competitive circumstances. During this period, GM was facing increased competitive pressures from other domestic automakers and the Japanese automobile industry. Their strategy was to pool resources and become more like their successful Japanese competitors. GM needed to decrease time to market and dramatically decrease costs to remain competitive. Their hope was to consolidate design, fabrication, and assembly within their new structure. GM's long-standing and successful divisional structure, which included Chevrolet, Pontiac, Oldsmobile Cadillac, and Buick, had been in place since the 1930s. In 1984, they replaced it with two new divisions. One division included Chevrolet, Pontiac, and Chevrolet-Canada (CPC); and the other included the luxury brands of Buick, Oldsmobile, and Cadillac (BOC). The restructuring was a disaster for a number of reasons. The new strategy was ill-defined and poorly implemented because it diluted divisional identity and loyalty for both employees and customers. The structural change was massive and driven by cost-cutting, not vision; it was a management edict with little employee participation or commitment. Finally, GM failed to understand the culture at GM. When the company suggested naming a new combined division for Buick, Oldsmobile, and Pontiac to BOC, many current and retired employees objected—a clear indicator of their threatened identity and strong loyalty to a particular product division, not to all divisions, which they viewed as friendly competition.[24]

As the GM example illustrates, as changes become more intense and rapid, and as competition becomes more innovative, managers must be more responsive and astute at modifying their structures. But at the same time the work of the organization must continue. Organization structure has two requirements: (1) meet short term needs for control and consistency, and (2) meet long term needs for adaptation to future circumstances. A structure should get the work of the day completed and be adaptive to the needs of tomorrow. Greater use of decentralized structures, network structures, or virtual organizational structures, and team structures will push decision making closer to the point of the decision, increasing responsiveness and flexibility.

## Changing Technology

Technological change is the shift from one method of converting inputs to outputs to another method. In a very real sense, technological change represents progress. New technology should make the tasks individuals perform in organizations easier, better, and more efficient. For example, rather than use a security guard in the lobby, a corporate headquarters changes to a swipe card (similar to a credit card) to identify persons entering the building, authorize building access, and record time of entry and exit. The swipe card technology offers greater control at a lower cost.

Behavioral change is also critical. People must embrace the new technology and use it. In the early days of personal computing, the PC was viewed as a curiosity and not as a substitute for the mainframe. It took a fundamental change in technology to create integrated networks connected via broadband to the Internet. However, not all employees jumped on the digital bandwagon. It took both technological breakthroughs and behavioral change to increase overall organizational effectiveness.

Typically, the push for technological innovation comes from outside the organization. Organizations adopt new technology to remain current and competitive. For instance, new Computer Numerical Control (CNC) devices that afford greater precision and less waste in leather cutting operations replaced handcrafted methods because they were more efficient and used by the competition. Successful technological innovations drive efficiency and quickly diffuse new technology throughout the industry. However, the rate at which the new technology can be adopted by users of the new technology is influenced by the following five areas:

- *Relative advantage.* The degree to which the new technology is better than the old technology it replaces. The better the technology performs, the faster the rate of adoption.

- *Compatibility.* The degree of consistency with the values and experiences of the employees. For example, computer keyboards have a similar layout to the typewriters they replaced. Knowledge of typing was transferable to the new technology.

- *Complexity.* The degree of difficulty in understanding and adopting the new technology. Users will resist technology that is difficult to use.

| *Divisibility.* The degree to which the new technology can be phased in a little at a time to ease the transition. The ability to preview a new technology in limited operation eases adoption fears.

| *Communicability.* Ease of technology adoption across the organization. The easier it is to transfer the technology to employees, the quicker that technology will be used. A server that rolls out the latest version of new software is a good example of rapid communication of the technology across the organization.[25]

## Changing the Task

Task organization is an element of structure. Task structure is a form of control that limits the variability of human behavior. The goal of changing the task is to increase individual effectiveness. Job enrichment researchers found that increasing the variety of tasks performed and the ability to have greater control over work increased employee motivation and led to increased job performance.[26] More recently, Hackman and Oldham's Task Characteristics Theory offered a more integrated approach to task design.[27] Task Characteristics Theory describes five dimensions of a task that vary independently: variety, autonomy, identity, feedback, and significance (see Chapter 9, Exhibit 9.5). Each dimension can be varied to enrich the task, allowing employees more or less control over their work. Increased autonomy allows workers greater decision-making discretion. Variety increases the range of work performed. Greater feedback from a supervisor informs employees where improvement can be made.

Changing the task might occur in response to a change in structure, technology, culture, or behavior. For instance, a new computer network that allowed a bank teller access to account history might also require a change in task structure to a require the teller to use the additional information in certain situations. In the end, the decision to change task structure was caused by a change in technology, and that change may affect behavior (our next topic).

## Changing Behavior

People must change their behavior in a specific way for meaningful organizational change to occur. In general, people change their behavior to match their beliefs and attitudes. Organizations work hard to change employee attitudes in anticipation of behavioral change. Persuasion, influence, and training programs are all methods used daily in organizations to create a deep-rooted behavioral change.

If organizational change is going to occur, then in almost all instances individuals must change their behavior. For example, sexual harassment exposes the organization to considerable liability. Once a diagnosis is made that current behavioral norms fail to address sexual harassment, some type of intervention is needed to create behavioral change. In order to conform to the law, an organization hires an OD consultant to further diagnose the severity of the problem, develop an intervention that will increase awareness of the topic, clarify the organizations response to allegations of sexual harassment, implement the intervention, and evaluate the intervention. The goal of the intervention is to change employees' current behavior to a more socially and legally acceptable form of behavior regarding interaction with the opposite sex at work. Exhibit 17.4 describes the relationships between these four types of organizational change on their effect on the task. These changes do not occur in isolation; each one affects the other as well as affects the task performed by the individual.

## Organizational Development Interventions

Organizational development (OD) interventions are tools, methods, and techniques used to transition the organization from current practices to desired future practices. OD change agents have to balance their involvement inside the organization with the need for employee buy-in,

**17.4**

**Types of Organizational Change**

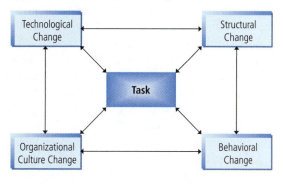

**17.5**

**Transition Model of Change**

participation, and commitment that will sustain the change over the transition period. An organization-wide change such as restructuring might take six months to a year to complete. Successful planned change is controlled by top management with the goal of increasing organizational effectiveness. Successful OD is characterized by changing people's attitudes, perceptions, and behaviors regarding a specific aspect of the work environment.

## Lewin's Model of Change

Intervention describes a method, technique, or means of change that improves individual effectiveness, group effectiveness, organizational effectiveness, or all of these entities. An intervention can respond to forces for change, or it can create forces that give employees the impetus to accept change more readily. Beckhard and Harris have taken Lewin's model and broadened it. Exhibit 17.5 describes a similar approach to Lewin's that considers change as a transition from (1) the current state, to (2) the transition state, to (3) the future state. The *current state* describes the existing organization form, including strategy, structure, culture, and processes. The *transition state* describes the movement away from one type of organizational form toward another. The final state is the *future state*, characterized by a new organizational form.[28]

Types of interventions include individual, group, intergroup, and organization-wide. The type of intervention selected depends on the problem diagnosis, its cost, the time available, the organization's culture, management's confidence in the anticipated results, and the depth of change. Depth of intervention is defined as the degree of change that an intervention is intended to bring about.[29] A *shallow intervention* seeks mainly to provide information that is helpful to make improvements. A manager coaching a subordinate is an example of shallow intervention. *Moderate-depth interventions* such as team building are intended to alter attitudes and perceptions. Different perspectives are presented and analyzed with the result being better understanding, greater tolerance of other viewpoints, and modification of negative stereotypes.

**depth of intervention**
The degree of change that an intervention is intended to bring about, such as shallow, moderate, or deep.

A *deep intervention* is intended to bring about psychological and behavioral changes that are reflected in improved job performance. Sensitivity training is an example of deep intervention.

Today, many organizations attempt organizational change through training with little thought about the depth of the intervention. However, with any type of deep intervention, caution should be exercised and the use of qualified experts should be a top requirement. For example, sexual harassment training and diversity training discuss situations that might be uncomfortable or disturbing to some participants and should, therefore, be facilitated only by trained personnel. The idea is to facilitate change in the organization in a positive direction and not to unintentionally hurt people. Sometimes, though, legal requirements mandate employees have a clear and detailed understanding of the ethical, moral, legal, and liability implications of their actions or the actions of their subordinates.

The following sections discuss only a few of the many intervention methods available to stimulate changes in people, culture, structure and task, and technology. As is often the case, no single method is effective in every case.

## Survey Feedback

Survey feedback is the process of collecting attitudinal data from individuals about the organization. Data is usually analyzed at the division, department, and unit levels. It is a shallow intervention method because it does not attempt to directly effect psychological or behavioral changes of each individual. This method is typically conducted in four stages.[30] First is the planning stage, during which a change agent works with top management to design the questions to be used in a survey. Next, data are collected from a sample or an entire unit population (department, division, organization). Data might be collected using a survey questionnaire, interviews, historical records, or some combination of data collection techniques. In the third stage, the change agent categorizes, summarizes, and interprets information collected during the survey and prepares reports. Finally, in the fourth stage, employees are given feedback, meetings are held to discuss the findings, and action plans for overcoming identified problems are developed and implemented.

Survey feedback is a popular intervention method. It is efficient, seeks member participation, and provides much job-relevant information. The hope is that greater information-sharing yields a better understanding of the challenges people face. For success, survey feedback needs top management's endorsement and involvement. Survey feedback is a two-way street. Managers receive information from employees, and employees expect that managers will act on their feedback.

KEYTERMS

**survey feedback** The collection of attitudinal data from individuals about the organization and its analysis at the division, department, and unit levels; typically conducted to overcome identified problems.

**team building** A moderate-depth intervention that attempts to improve diagnosis, communication, cooperation, and the performance of members and the overall team; helps work groups perform at a higher level.

## Team Building

Teamwork is quickly becoming an essential component of most organizations today. An effective team communicates well, cooperates, stimulates its members, and provides recognition and rewards. Team building is a moderate-depth intervention that attempts to improve diagnosis, communication, cooperation, and the performance of members and the overall team. Be careful not to confuse team building with the widespread use of teams in most organizations. *Team building* is the term used to refer to helping work groups perform at a higher level. It is not focused on solving workplace problems through teams, but rather in making a team out of a work group.

Team-building interventions often work toward establishing specific goals and priorities, analyzing a group's work methods, examining the group's communication and decision-making processes, and examining interpersonal relationships within the group. With these group functions in place, the group can more easily explicitly recognize each group member's contributions (both positive and negative).[31]

The process by which these aims are achieved begins with *diagnostic* meetings. Often lasting an entire day, the meetings enable all team members to share with other members their perceptions of problems. If the team is large enough, subgroups engage in discussion and report their ideas to the total group. These sessions are designed to allow expression of all members' views and to make these views public. In this context, diagnosis emphasizes the value of open confrontation of issues and problems that previously were discussed in secrecy.

Identifying problems and concurring on their priority are two important initial steps in team building. But a *plan of action* must also be agreed on. The plan should call on each group member, individually or as part of a subgroup, to act specifically to alleviate one or more problems. If, for example, an executive committee agrees that one problem is a lack of understanding of and commitment to goals, a subgroup can be appointed to recommend goals to the total group at a subsequent meeting. Other team members can work on different problems. For example, if problems are found in the relationships between members, a subgroup can initiate a process for examining each member's role.

Team building is also effective when new organizational units, project teams, or task forces are being created. Typically such groups have certain characteristics that need to be altered if the groups are to perform effectively—for example:

- Ambiguity about roles and relationships
- Members having a fairly clear understanding of short-term goals
- Group members having technical competence that puts them on the team
- Members often paying more attention to the team's tasks than to the relationships among team members

In the last case, the new group will focus initially on task problems but ignore the interpersonal relationship issues. By the time relationship problems begin to surface, the group cannot deal with them, and performance begins to deteriorate.

To combat these characteristic tendencies, a new group should schedule team-building meetings during the first weeks of its life. Meetings should be held away from the work site; one- or two-day sessions often suffice. The format of such meetings varies, but essentially their purpose is to enable the group to work through its timetable as well as each member's role in reaching group objectives. An important outcome of such meetings is to establish an understanding of each member's contribution to the team and of the reward for that contribution. Although reports on team building indicate mixed results, the evidence suggests that group processes improve through team-building efforts.[32]

## Leadership Grid®

**Leadership Grid** | Robert R. Blake and McCanse created the Leadership Grid® as a vehicle for leader behavior assessment and organizational development.[33] In a series of questionnaires and structured seminars, Blake and McCanse used the grid to assess leadership orientation. The Leadership Grid is described in detail in Chapter 13, "Leadership" (refer to Exhibit 13.3 on page 282.) In brief, the Leadership Grid is an OD technique that helps people understand the primary dimension of their leadership style: task orientation (concern for results) or people orientation (concern for people). The Leadership Grid technique is based on a two-dimensional matrix grid with *concern for people* on the Y axis and *concern for results* on the X axis. Each axis is incremented on a nine-point continuum. A leadership style with a high concern for people and low concern for results would be represented by cell (1, 9)—Country Club—suggesting an emphasis on relationship building and the needs of people.

In the reverse situation, a leadership style with high degree of concern for results and low concern for people would be located at cell (9, 1)—Authority-Compliance—suggesting a strong concern for task completion and very little concern for the worker. In the midrange position is the leader who is moderate on both dimensions, represented by the cell (5, 5)—Middle of the Road or Balanced—suggesting a balance between task accomplishment and demonstrating concern for the worker. A leader rated at the top on both dimensions would be in cell (9, 9)—Team Management—suggesting a leader with common stakes, commitment, mutual trust, and respect. This technique demonstrates that the results and people orientations are usually more or less present in all managers. Leaders must be able to demonstrate concern for both people and results.

The OD consultant uses a series of seminars to shape a participant's leadership style. First, the OD consultant uses the Leadership Grid to assess the participant's current leadership style. If the leadership style is one-dimensional—that is, focused on only one of the two dimensions—the OD consultant attempts to help the participant develop a leadership style that is high on both consideration and production. Blake and Mouton believe that Team Management—cell (9, 9)—representing high people orientation and high task orientation, is the preferred leadership style. The rationale for their belief is that a leader must not only support the worker but also structure the work setting toward task achievement. At the opposite end of the matrix is Impoverished Management—cell (1, 1). This cell represents the leader with low task orientation and low people orientation; clearly, an undesirable situation and untenable in the long run.

Finally, a positive feature of the Leadership Grid is its recognition that both types of leader behaviors are important, and that people bring different orientations or predispositions to the management process. A negative feature of this approach, and many other OD techniques, is the assumption that leader behaviors can be readily changed through seminar participation.

## Process Consultation

Process consultation is performed by an OD consultant who specializes in this particular OD technique. Process consultants observe the various organizational processes and determine the effectiveness of each process. Typical organizational processes include decision making, performance evaluation, leadership, team interaction, conflict resolution, and communication. When a particular process is deficient in some way, the OD consultant makes recommendations for corrective actions to management. Next, programs are developed to resolve the problems. For example, an organization with an ineffective decision-making process would be exposed to a multistep program that develops skills in different aspects of decision making. The goal of the process consultation is to pinpoint problems and develop solutions that lead to a more effective organization in the future.

## Empowerment

Empowerment is an important part of changing an organization; it is achieved through encouraging greater participation by managers and workers. As noted earlier, empowerment is a process that increases people's involvement in their work (design, flow, interactions, decision making). Empowerment is not limited to individual actions; in fact, the growth of teamwork in organizations often leads to the opportunity for greater group decision-making autonomy or group empowerment. To the degree that the preceding occurs, empowerment can be a high-depth intervention.

Empowerment involves far more than giving employees greater decision-making ability. It can also involve altering the organizational structure from centralized to decentralized. At its most practical level, empowerment requires behavioral change, structural change, and cultural change together. Successful empowerment of employees requires the following:

| The freedom to accept decision-making responsibility

**KEY**TERMS

**empowerment** An important part of change in an organization, the increase of people's involvement in their work (design, flow, interactions, decision making), often leading to the opportunity for greater group decision-making autonomy.

| A decentralized structure that presents the opportunity to make a decision at lower levels in the organization

| A culture that values sharing power

| Management who actively encourages even greater employee involvement strategies such as self-management and the use of teams

| Use of technological solutions (e.g., Internet, cell phones, and digital imaging) to distribute greater information to individuals at lower level of the organizational hierarchy[34]

The business world today is captivated by the idea that team structure yields superior results to those produced by individual performance. However, not all companies are rushing ahead to manage their businesses through the use of employee teams. Three commonly agreed upon reasons that teams have not gained more traction are (1) teams are not easy to manage, (2) team performance is not easily measurable, and (3) equitable team compensation is often difficult.

But the issue is really more about hiring the right people. Ultimately, managers achieve competitive success by working with people, not by replacing them or limiting the scope of their activities. It entails seeing the workforce as a source of strategic advantage, not just as a cost to be minimized or avoided. Firms that take this different perspective are often able to successfully outmaneuver and outperform their rivals.[35]

Over the long term, empowerment is only one intervention among several possible. Indeed, workers are motivated by a sense of achievement, recognition, enjoyment of the job, promotion opportunities, responsibility, and the chance for personal growth. Worker motivation and performance are tied directly to the style of management and to the principles of positive or negative reinforcement.

## The Strategy of Change: Foresight-Led Change

In their book, *Competing for the Future,* Gary Hamel and C. K. Prahalad argue that most organizations do not spend enough time thinking about the future of their industry and their business. In fact, these authors state that organizations typically fall under the "40/30/20 rule." This rule reflects their finding that about 40 percent of senior executive time is spent looking outward (i.e., outside the business). Of the time spent looking outward, only 30 percent is spent peering three or more years into the future. And of that time spent looking into the future, only about 20 percent is spent attempting to build a collective view of the future. Thus, on average, senior management spends less than 3 percent of its energy ($40\% \times 30\% \times 20\% = 2.4\%$) building an organizational perspective of the future.[36]

To compete effectively for the future, organizations must develop what Hamel and Prahalad call industry foresight-led. According to them, "industry foresight-led is based on deep insights into the trends in technology, demographics, regulation, and lifestyles that can be harnessed to rewrite industry rules and create new competitive space."[37] The authors distinguish this term from the more commonly used *vision,* which they dislike because it connotes unreality and intangibility.

Foresight-led change involves looking into the future, determining what the future is projected to be, and then using that insight to change an organization in the present. Stretch target is another term for describing this "pull" approach to change (as in pulling an organization into the future).

Stretch targets reflect a major shift in the thinking of top management. Executives are recognizing that incremental goals, however worthy, invite managers and workers to perform the same comfortable processes a little better every year. Unfortunately, the all too frequent result is

**KEY**TERMS

**industry foresight-led** A strategy of change that involves looking into the future, determining what the future is projected to be, and then using the insight to change the present organization.

**stretch target** Another term for describing the "pull" approach to change (as in pulling an organization into the future).

EXHIBIT

17.6

**Guidelines for Stretch Targets**

**Stretch targets should:**

| Be measurable

| Give teams autonomy and power

| Modify work structures to support change

| Develop a culture of support and encouragement

**Source:** Adapted from Kenneth R. Thompson, W. Hochwarter, and Nicholas J. Mathys. "Stretch Targets: What Makes Them Effective?" *Academy of Management Executive* 11, 3 (1997): 54.

average performance. Stretch targets require big leaps of progress on such measures as inventory turns, product development time, and manufacturing cycles. Imposing such imperatives can force companies to reinvent the way they conceive, make, and distribute products. Exhibit 17.6 provides guidelines on setting stretch targets.

For CEO John Snow of CSX, the $9.5-billion-a-year railroad and shipping company, stretch targets were a natural extension of his business approach. In 1991, CSX's return on capital hovered well below its capital charge—in the 10 percent range. Snow's bold goal was to make sure CSX would earn the full cost of capital by 1993 and thereafter. As Snow predicted, the stretch target he established forced managers to look hard at the railroad's core problem—that the company's fleet of locomotives and railcars sat loafing much of the time at loading docks and seaport terminals. Raising the company's return on capital would mean working the massive fleet far harder than had ever been attempted.

Having set the target, Snow then got out of the way. The strategy proved to be a winner. Since 1991, while handling a surge in business, CSX has eliminated from its rolling stock 20,000 of its 125,000 cars—enough to form a train stretching from Chicago to Detroit. That caused capital expenditures for supporting the fleet to shrink from $825 million a year to $625 million. CSX is now earning its full cost of capital.[38]

For most of the twentieth century, organizations orchestrated change management based on what has been called the strategy-structure-systems doctrine. The doctrine took hold as organizations increased in size and complexity, leading senior managers to delegate most of the operating decisions to division-level managers. Senior managers then recast their own jobs as defining strategy, developing structure, and managing the systems required to link and control the company's parts.

This approach to management has been successful for more than fifty years. It has enabled central managers to maintain contact with increasingly far-flung operations. But, while senior managers saw these increasingly sophisticated systems as necessary links to operations, those at the operational level felt them to be burdens that too often called them to heel.

Today, top-level managers at some of the most successful organizations are creating organizational change through people, information, and technology. Management's challenge is to use technology to create useful information that engages the unique knowledge, skills, and abilities of every individual in the organization. Managers are developing a management philosophy based on a more personalized approach that encourages diverse viewpoints and empowers employees to contribute their own ideas.

As managers pay more attention to organizational culture, they need to have some insight into how it can be shaped and managed. As a closing thought on implementing organizational change, review the Management Highlight on page 384 for several problems common to all large-scale organizational changes.

**KEY**TERMS

**strategy-structure-systems doctrine** A change management strategy, utilized mainly in large, complex organizations, in which leading senior managers delegate most operating decisions to division-level managers and then recast their own jobs as defining strategy, developing structure, and managing the systems required to link and control the company's parts.

MANAGEMENT HIGHLIGHT

**PROBLEMS IMPLEMENTING ORGANIZATIONAL CHANGE**

Implementing organizational change is not easy. Asking people to stop doing what they know works and then to learn a new method is often a traumatic experience for them. Some soul-searching and thoughtful action by management, however, can alleviate the root causes of their concerns:

- *Power*—Every organization has a pattern of political relationships that can make or break the change efforts. Management needs to build support for the change among powerful actors.

- *Anxiety*—The thought of something new can be frightening. What will happen to me? How long do we have to wait to find out our new assignment? These questions are common and reveal the anxiety surrounding change. Managers need to understand the source of anxiety and help minimize it during the transition phase.

- *Control*—Often, rapid change feels like a loss of control. Who is in charge now? If I ask John to complete the assignment, what guarantees do I have that he will complete the task?

Source: Adapted from David Nadler and Michael Tushman, *Competing by Design: The Power of Organizational Architecture* (New York: Oxford University Press, 1997).

## Change and the Influence of the Founder

The power to make change happen is often largely vested in management and most notably in the founder of the company. It is the founder's vision and values that create mental images of the future in the minds of employees. The founder's energy and enthusiasm often engage employees to produce greater effort and higher levels of task performance.[39] Everyone recognizes the role played by the late Dave Thomas, founder of Wendy's International, in creating and shaping the future of Wendy's. But not everyone knows that above all, Thomas believed in clear, clean communication to all organizational stakeholders.[40] Improved communications, initiated by the leader, must be a top priority. Merely informing workers that change is coming is not enough to guarantee success. Communication must be a two-way process. Participation creates more information about the impact of a change. However, along with empowering employees, managers must maintain some controls to keep the change process on target.

The chief executive officer (CEO) communicates a commitment to support a total change in the way everything is done in the organization. The CEO must commit to establishing a companywide communication program that involves managers and workers. The communication must include the following:

- Specific actions required to implement the change
- Distinction between what is important from what is merely desirable
- Action plans for achieving concrete timely results
- CEO involvement that symbolizes the importance of a change
- Benefits of the implemented change to the organization

Management must be prepared for resistance to change that affects any normal pattern or set of procedures. Because change often affects culture, to become effective and ingrained, the change might take several years. Although managers can initiate change, change must be adopted by everyone in the organization. This next Management Highlight on page 385 offers some guidelines for managing organizational change.

Institutionalizing a change and achieving consistency between goals and performance measures is one of the most important tasks of upper management. Once a goal has been achieved, the company can shift its focus to the next priority. This building-block approach has produced concrete results for some companies, and many others are now adopting it. For example, when former CEO

## MANAGING ORGANIZATIONAL CHANGE

At one time or another, all organizations are confronted with the reality that a major change in the way business is conducted is necessary. To successfully achieve needed change, having a plan is helpful. Here, we offer a general set of guidelines for the process of change, ideas about how to reduce resistance to change, and an example based on a change toward greater quality.

| Step | Process for Creating the Change | Process for Reducing Resistance to Change | Example: Creating a Change Toward Greater Quality |
| --- | --- | --- | --- |
| Step 1 | Establish a sense of immediacy. | Facilitate and support. | Create performance standards. |
| Step 2 | Create a leadership team. | Manipulate and co-opt. | Develop visible quality for product or service. |
| Step 3 | Create and communicate a vision. | Educate and communicate. | Build in reliability and consistency. |
| Step 4 | Encourage involvement. | Participate and involve. | Create durability. |
| Step 5 | Set short-term goals as guides to behavior. | Negotiate and foster agreement. | Emphasize the value or uniqueness of the product or service. |
| Step 6 | Change the institution's strategies, structures, and processes. | Engage in explicit and implicit coercion. | Build a reputation for quality. |

Source: Adapted from John P. Kotter and Leonard A. Schlesinger, "Choosing Strategies for Change," *Harvard Business Review* (March–April 1979); John P. Kotter, "Leading Change: Why Transformation Efforts Fail," *Harvard Business Review* (March–April 1995): 59–67; David A. Garvin, "Competing on the Eight Dimensions of Quality," *Harvard Business Review* (November–December 1987): 101–109; and Ronald F. Ricardo, "Overcoming Resistance to Change," *National Productivity Review* (Spring 1995): 5–12.

Carly Fiorina created a mega-giant with the Hewlett-Packard/Compaq merger, she also needed to create a cultural change that emphasized efficiency. At the time of the merger, the new HP had a substantial share of the consumer PC market, however, that was not enough to guarantee financial success even with economy-of-scale efficiencies to create a durable competitive advantage in a global market. Carly Fiorina carried on the vision and values that Bill Hewlett and Dave Packard infused in the company so many years before. Change is necessary, but change should be consistent with the vision and values that form the guiding principles of the company going forward.

Achieving significant change in the workplace is a long-term challenge for managers of any type of organization. One of the most difficult obstacles to overcome is giving up too early in the implementation process. For those companies that persevere, it has been worth the struggle.

## Change and Conflict Management

Although an organization's managers and employees might recognize that change is inevitable, new ideas and old ways are often on a collision course. Change means greater uncertainty; it generates conflict among organizational members, who often have different strategies for managing change. As we discussed earlier in the book, uncertainty decreases our ability to understand and effectively manage the future. The uncertainty inherent in change is no different. Whether conflict occurs inside or outside of an organization, the people, groups, and organizations it affects will seek strategies that maximize their outcomes in the aftermath of the change.

Conflict is a struggle between competing ideas and/or values. Author L. R. Pondy developed a five-stage model of conflict.[41] *Latent conflict* represents the underlying source of the conflict. For example, the sales department is rewarded for volume or the amount of units its employees sell. As a source of latent conflict, the production department might be more concerned with a steady flow of product that is easy to produce. *Perceived conflict* describes the situation where both

EXHIBIT **17.7** | **Managing Conflict Resolution**

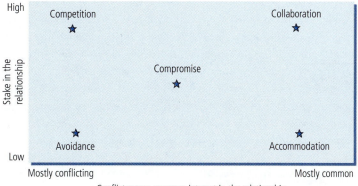

**Source:** Adapted from Thomas Ruble and Kenneth Thomas, "Support for a Two-Dimensional Model of Conflict Behavior," *Organizational Behavior and Human Performance* 16 (1976): 145.

departments become aware of the basic differences between their departments. *Felt conflict* occurs when one of the parties to the conflict takes some action that disadvantages the other party. For example, an e-mail is circulated in which the writer makes it clear that production and sales are at odds with one another. *Manifest conflict* is the actual or open conflict between the parties. It could take the form of verbal attacks or more subtle political actions to further a position. Finally, the *conflict aftermath* describes the long-term consequences of the conflict to the parties as well as other members of the organization. It often takes years to smooth over bitter disagreements and organizational actions.

How do organizations go about managing conflict? Exhibit 17.7 offers a rational yet strategic approach to understanding a conflict participant's level of involvement in the conflict; it also offers strategies to maximize the participant's outcomes in the aftermath of the conflict.

As Exhibit 17.7 shows, these five strategies depend on two factors: (1) your stake in the relationship, and (2) whether your interest in the relationship is common or conflicting. The strategies and situations in which they are appropriate are described in the following list:

- *Avoidance.* Low stake in the relationship and conflicting interests. You have little to gain by becoming involved in the conflict.

- *Collaboration.* High stake in the relationship and mostly common interests. It is in your interest to develop an ally and work together for your collective good.

- *Compromise.* Middle-ground position with no strong position on either dimension, yet a willingness to see the conflict resolved to the mutual benefit.

- *Accommodation.* Low stake in the relationship and mostly common interests. A low stake means that you can afford to yield to the needs of the other party to preserve the common interests that bind you together.

- *Competition.* High stake in the relationship and mostly conflicting interests. Direct conflict requires a defensive strategy to protect your interests.

Conflict is never as clear or concise as examples make it out to be. However, managers who are armed with a model to help understand the nature of the conflict, as well as a set of strategies to choose from, have much going in their favor.

# Managing Organizational Change and Development

We began this chapter by saying that "change is inevitable." We can now update that statement by adding that organizational change is inevitable. It is important for a manager to be willing and open to change—and, in fact, to seek it out. By reading the environment correctly and embracing change, a manager will maintain currency in her discipline and be an asset to her employer. However, no manager is an island. The organization must encourage and reward risk taking in the form of successful organizational change. A wise admonition is that it is foolish to change for the sake of change. More to the point, pursuing change because other organizations are changing will be ineffective. Strategic change or change that is driven by plans, values, and vision will endure and be rewarded in the marketplace.

## Discussion Questions

1. According to the chapter discussion, origins of change are either internal or external. With that discussion in mind, provide an example of a change that has an external origin.

2. Identify and describe each of the four modes of change.

3. Describe Pondy's five-stage model of conflict. What post-conflict problems are likely to endure even after the conflict has been resolved.

## Video Case

### Original Penguin Spreads Its Wings

Change is hard for companies—especially for large companies, which have large numbers of people and systems to manage. But in many cases, change can be positive, especially when it is in response to an opportunity for growth. Chris Kolbe is a master of change. Now vice president of Original Penguin, Chris essentially runs the division for its parent company, Perry Ellis International. He got there by finding himself in the unique position of rediscovering a languishing bird—and bringing it back to life.

Original Penguin was a 1950s icon—the penguin logo appeared on Munsingwear Penguin knit sport shirts for men, mostly golfers. Eventually, its popularity faded, and Perry Ellis International later acquired the brand. Chris Kolbe was working in merchandising at retailer Urban Outfitters when he conceived the idea of rejuvenating the penguin—but with a new twist and for a new market. Starting with a few new shirts, which sold out almost immediately, the "new" Original Penguin began to grow, and Perry Ellis tapped Kolbe to complete the transformation as head of a new venture team.

Despite the fact that the Original Penguin flagship store in New York boasts an oversized vintage photo of Kolbe's family, including his father wearing one of the "original" Munsingwear Penguin golf shirts, Kolbe recognizes that the fashion industry is a hotbed of change—and any clothing company that wants to survive must embrace innovation. "The fashion business is a young business," observes Kolbe. "It's about having fresh ideas. . . . What can happen is, if you stop having those brands in your pipeline, things start to dry up. . . . We realized Penguin could be one of those brands." So Kolbe and his team have focused on designs and clothing items that appeal to a younger market, both men and women, between the ages of 17 and 30.

Although Kolbe could certainly be called the idea champion for this project, he does not work alone. He has a team of highly creative fashion-industry professionals, including David Bedwell, Creative Director. "We changed the brand a bit to really reach out to a different market today than maybe the market it was reaching in the past . . . yet keeping a classic twist on it," says Bedwell.

Consumers who wander into the new Original Penguin store will find an entire line of trendy, yet classic clothing and accessories. "We try to create an environment that our clothes will live in," explains Bedwell. Store displays show quirky, unconventional clothing combinations—such as a striped top with plaid pants. And visitors may wander through the "garden" or the "bedroom" to look at different outfits. Yes, shoppers can still buy knit sport shirts—in new colors and designs—but they can also pick up belts, shoes, and even bikinis.

If it sounds as though Kolbe and his team have free rein from Perry Ellis, they don't. Instead, they have a loose rein. They have a great deal of freedom to take risks, be creative, and make decisions. But Perry Ellis is taking the ultimate risk, and Kolbe knows that. The company does require regular updates on key financial and sales numbers. "The best thing about being young is you don't know the odds you're up against.... The risk for Perry Ellis was equally significant because they finance everything," says Kolbe.

Kolbe envisions the current fashion lines as the beginning of more innovation for Original Penguin and Perry Ellis. He also understands that change takes time and patience. "It takes a couple of years to see results, so it takes a certain amount of perseverance," he acknowledges. But he is excited about the future. "We've been able to bring a lot of influence and fresh ideas to a company that was searching. You can start to be a catalyst for a larger business."

### Questions

1. In what ways might creativity be designed into the Original Penguin division of Perry Ellis International?

2. Why has it been important for Perry Ellis to give freedom to a new venture team in order to relaunch Original Penguin?

3. In what respects does Original Penguin represent a cultural change for Perry Ellis?

Source: Company web site, http://www.originalpenguin.com, accessed July 30, 2004.

## BizFlix

### October Sky

The movie *October Sky* is based on the autobiographical book *Rocket Boys* by Homer Hickam. An all-star cast is led by Jake Gyllenhaal, who plays Homer Hickam. As a teenager, Homer is facing a dreary future as a coal miner until he sees the Soviet satellite *Sputnik* pass over his small mining town of Coalwood, West Virginia. A new interest in rockets infects Homer, who begins to experiment with model rockets in the summer of 1957. Soon, Homer has convinced several of his friends to join him in designing a rocket to enter in the National Science Fair, where they hope to win college scholarships as a result.

### Questions

1. Are Homer and his friends working toward evolutionary change or revolutionary change? Explain.

2. Were the boys using a planned change or a reactive change in their efforts to achieve success? Identify the elements of their approach that are evident in the clip.

## *Suggested Reading*

Abrahamson, Eric, "Change without Pain," *Harvard Business Review* (July–August 2000): 75–79.

Charan Ram, "Home Depot's Blueprint for Culture Change," *Harvard Business Review* (April 2006) Reprint R0604C.

Hammer Michael, "Deep Change: How Operational Innovation Can Transform Your Company," *Harvard Business Review* (April 2004) Reprint R0404E.

Hirschhorn, Larry, "Campaign for Change," *Harvard Business Review* (July–August 2002): 2–7.

Pascale Richard Tanner and Jerry Sterin, "Your Company's Secret Change Agents," *Harvard Business Review* (May 2005) Reprint R0505D,

Sugarman, Barry, "A Learning-Based Approach to Organizational Change: Some Results and Guidelines," *Organizational Dynamics* 30 (2002): 62–76.

## Endnotes

1. Howard Isenberg, "The Second Industrial Revolution: The Impact of the Information Explosion," *Industrial Engineering* (March 1995): 15.

2. John P. Kotter, "Leading Change: Why Transformation Efforts Fail," *Harvard Business Review* (March/April 1995): 59–67.

3. Tom Broersma, "In Search of the Future," *Training & Development* (January 1995): 38–43.

4. Michael Hammer and James Champy. *Reengineering the Corporation* (New York: Harper Collins, 1993), 31, and Frank Ostroff. *The Horizontal Organization* (NewYork: Oxford University Press, 1999).

5. D. Keith Denton, "Creating a System for Continuous Improvement," *Business Horizons* (January/February 1995): 16–21.

6. Allan H. Church, Anne Margiloff, and Celeste Coruzi, "Using Surveys for Change: An Applied Example in a Pharmaceuticals Organization," *Leadership & Organizational Development Journal,* 1995, 16(4): 3–11.

7. Paul Lawrence, "How to Overcome Resistance to Change," *Harvard Business Review* (May–June), 1954, reprinted in *HBR* (January–February 1969): 110.

8. Barry K. Spiker and Eric Lesser, "We Have Met the Enemy . . . ," *Journal of Business Strategy* (March/April 1995): 17–21.

9. Allan H. Church, "Managerial Behavior and Work Group Climate as Predictors of Employee Outcomes," *Human Resource Development Quarterly* (Summer 1995): 173–205.

10. Biography of Douglas Fraser, http://www.frasercenter.wayne.edu/about/fraser.asp, accessed April 10, 2003.

11. Perry Pascarella, "Resistance to Change: It Can Be a Plus," *Industry Week* (July 27, 1987): 45ff.

12. Ronald F. Recardo, "Overcoming Resistance to Change," *National Productivity Review* (Spring 1995): 5–12.

13. Robert M. Randall, "The Sense-and-Respond Model," *Planning Review* (May/June 1995): 43–44.

14. Stephan H. Haeckel, "Adaptive Enterprise Design: The Sense-and-Respond Model," *Planning Review* (May/June 1995): 6–13.

15. Noel Tichy, "How Different Types of Change Agents Diagnose Organizations," *Human Relations* (December 1975): 771–779.

16. Judith A. Neal, et al., "From Incremental Change to Retrofit: Creating High-Performance Work Systems," *Academy of Management Executive* (February 1995): 42–54.

17. Gerald Zaltman and Robert Dunchan, *Strategies for Planned Change* (New York: John Wiley and Sons, 1977).

18. Harold Leavitt, "Applied Organizational Change in Industry: Structural, Technological, and Humanistic Approaches," in James March, Ed., *Handbook of Organizations* (Chicago, IL: Rand McNally and Company, 1965).

19. T.E. Deal and A. Kennedy, *Corporate Cultures* (Reading, MA: Addison-Wesley, 1982); also see Edgar Schein, *Organizational Culture and Leadership* (San Francisco, CA: Sage Publishing, 2d ed., 1992).

20. Karl Schriftgeisser, *Farmer from Merna* (New York: Random House, 1996).

21. H. M. Trice, and J. M. Beyer, "Studying Organizational Culture through Rites and Ceremonials," *Academy of Management Review* (1984): 9, 653–669.

22. Alfred Chandler, *Strategy and Structure: Chapters in the History of the American Industrial Enterprise* (Cambridge, MA: MIT Press, 1962); also see Oliver E. Williamson, *Markets and Hierarchies: Analysis and Antitrust Implications* (New York: Free Press, 1975).

23. Richard Rumelt, *Strategy, Structure, and Economic Performance*. Cambridge, MA: Harvard University Press, 1974.

24. Maryann Keller, *A Rude Awakening: The Rise, Fall, and Struggle of the American Automobile Industry* (New York: Harper Collins, 1989); Also see David Nadler and Michael Tushman, *Competing by Design: The Power of Organizational Architecture* (New York: Oxford University Press, 1997).

25. Everett Rogers, *Diffusion of Innovations* (New York: Free Press, 1965), chapter 5.

26. Frederick Herzberg, B. Mauser, and B. Snyderman. *The Motivation to Work*. New York: John Wiley and Sons, Inc., 1959.

27. J. Richard Hackman and Greg Oldham, *Work Redesign* (Addison-Wesley Publishing, 1980); also see Ricky W. Griffin, *Task Design: An Integrated Approach* (Glenview: Scott, Foresman and Company, 1982).

28. Richard Beckhard and R. Harris, *Organization Transitions* (Reading, MA: Addison-Wesley, 1977).

29. Roger Harrison, "Choosing the Depth of Organizational Intervention," *Journal of Applied Behavioral Science*, (1970): 181–202.

30. Wendell L. French and Cecil H. Bell, Jr., *Organizational Development: Behavioral Science Interventions for Organizational Improvement* (Englewood Cliffs, NJ: Prentice-Hall, 1990), 170.

31. Cynthia Reedy Johnson in "An Outline for Team Building," *Training* (January 1986): 48; Richard L. Hughes, William E. Rosebach, and William H. Glover, "Team Development in an Intact, Ongoing Work Group," *Group and Organizational Studies* (June 1983): 161–181.

32. Kenneth P. deMeuse and S. Jay Liebowitz, "An Empirical Analysis of Team-Building Research," *Group and Organizational Studies* (September 1981): 357–78.

33. R. R. Blake and Jane S. Mouton, *The Managerial Grid* (Houston: Gulf Publishing, 1964); R. R. Blake and A. A. McCanse, "The Leadership Grid®," in *Leadership Dilemmas—Grid Solutions* (Houston: Gulf Publishing Company): 29, Copyright © 1991 by Scientific Methods, Inc.

34. W. Alan Randolph, "Navigating the Journey to Empowerment," *Organizational Dynamics* (Spring 1995): 19–32.

35. Jeffrey Pfeffer, Toru Hatano, and Timo Santalainen, "Producing Sustainable Competitive Advantage Through the Effective Management of People," *Academy of Management Executive* (February 1995): 55–72.

36. Gary Hamel and C.K. Prahalad, *Competing for the Future* (Boston, MA: Harvard Business School Press, 1994), 4.

37. Ibid, p. 76.

38. Shawn Tully, "Why to Go for Stretch Targets," *Fortune* (November 14, 1994): 145–155.

39. Edgar Schein, "The Role of the Founder in Creating Organizational Culture," *Organizational Dynamics* (1983): 13–28.

40. "Wendy's to Cite Thomas in the New Dave's Way Ads," *Nation's Restaurant News* (June 3, 2002): 3.

41. L.R. Pondy, "Organizational Conflict: Concepts and Models," *Administrative Science Quarterly*, Vol. 2 (1967): 296–320.

# GLOSSARY

**3 percent rule** A key concept in cycle time reduction (CTR), a rule stating that only 3 percent of the elapsed time for a process is actually needed to complete the activity.

## A

**Ability** The physical and mental characteristics that a worker requires to perform a task successfully; can be increased through training.

**Accounts receivable turnover** A measure of liquidity expressed as the ratio of credit sales to average accounts receivable.

**Acid-test ratio** A measure of liquidity that relates only cash and near-cash items (current assets excluding inventories and prepaid expenses) to current liabilities.

**Actions** Specific, prescribed means that are developed to achieve objectives and that determine success or failure in meeting objectives.

**Activity-based accounting** A system of cost accounting, based on activity and advocated by many academicians and practitioners, asserting that activities consume resources and products consume activities.

**Adaptive learning** According to Peter Senge, an early stage that a firm goes through in becoming a learning organization; characterized by learning through adapting to its successes.

**Administrative decision model** A model of decision making that makes realistic assumptions about the decision context and human nature; describes how people actually make decisions, not how they *should* make them.

**Affirmative action** An approach used to reach the goal of fair employment by which employers are encouraged to make a concerted effort to promote the hiring of groups of employees who were discriminated against in the past.

**Agrarian economies** Economies prevalent largely before 1830 that were based on small, family-owned farms and small shop production.

**Analytical decision maker** A decision maker who gathers facts and other information relevant to the situation, who uses a logical, analytical approach to decision making.

**Analytical skill** The skill that enables someone to analyze or logically diagnose even complex problems.

**Anchoring and adjustment** is the process whereby the initial information often serves as an anchor for, or forms a lower boundary for, subsequent understanding of the situation.

**Attitude** A learned predisposition about an object or a person that results in a propensity to respond one way or another; a shortcut to action; for example, the belief that it's best to be conservative or that eating pasta makes a person sleepy.

**Authority** The organizationally sanctioned right to make a decision.

**Availability heuristic** A type of bias based on the individual's ability to recall facts accurately.

## B

**Balance sheet** A financial statement that summarizes a firm's assets, liabilities, and equity; describes an organization's financial condition at a specified point in time.

**Behavioral decision maker** A decision maker who is concerned with people and the affect a decision is likely to have on employees and customers.

**Behavioral science** A behavioral management theory that views workers as much more complex than the "economic man" described in the classical approach or the "social man" described in the human relations approach.

**Behavioral self-management** A set of strategies that help people gain greater control over their lives, commonly including self-set goals, self-observation, self-rewards, self-cueing, and self-designed jobs.

**Behavioral theory of leadership** A theory of leadership that is focused on two types of leader behaviors: (1) those emphasizing the task accomplishment and (2) those showing concern for worker. *See also* trait theory of leadership.

**Benefits and services** Indirect financial compensation consisting of all financial rewards that are not included in direct financial compensation and made available to employees as long as they are employed by the organization. *See also* indirect financial compensation.

**Bounded rationality** The limited ability of people to process information.

**Brainstorming** A group technique, much like a focus group, in which people with specific content knowledge work as a group to generate ideas or solutions prescribed by the problem definition.

**Budget** An allocation of resources to an activity, account, or unit in the organization.

**Bureaucracy** A management approach based on formal organizational structure with set rules and regulations that rely on the specialization of labor, an authority hierarchy, and rigid promotion and selection criteria.

## C

**Capital budget** An intermediate and long-run planning document that details the alternative sources and uses of funds.

**Centralization** The retention of authority in the hands of high-level managers, who make all the decisions.

**Chain of command** A series of superior-subordinate relationships, from the highest position in the organization to the lowest, that is created by the delegation of authority.

**Change agent** An individual or a team of individuals, typically an outside professional consultant, whose responsibility is to practice the stages of change.

**Channel capacity** A limit on the volume of information that can be transmitted effectively, as determined by the least efficient component of the communication process.

**Chaos theory** The theory that predictions of the future can be enormously inaccurate as a result of only slight imprecision in the measurement of existing conditions.

**Classical management** A management theory that emphasized greater workforce productivity.

**Classical organization theory** A theory that concentrates on top-level managers and problems of managing the entire organization.

**Code of ethics** A statement specifying what the organization considers ethical behavior.

**Coercive power** Sometimes called punishment power, the manager's ability to apply penalties when an employee fails to cooperate.

**Cognitive dissonance** A lack of consistency among attitudes, beliefs, and behavioral intentions after a decision has been made; the conflict a decision maker feels between what he or she believes and the consequences of a decision.

**Cognitive self-management** A form of self-management in which the individual worker creates mental images and thought patterns that are consistent with the firm's goals. *See also* opportunity building; positive self-talk.

**Cohesiveness** A group characteristic that describes how well the group functions; reflects how well (1) the group can do its work effectively, attract new members when necessary, and maintain itself over time and (2) group members are able to influence one another.

**Command group** A group that is composed of a leader and subordinates reporting to the leader.

**Common cause variation** The random variation in a system that typically cannot be completely eliminated.

**Communication** The exchange of information and the sharing of meaning between a sender (source) and a receiver (audience).

**Communication audit** A systematic method of collecting and evaluating information about an organization's communication efforts with the purposes of providing (1) information about communication behavior in the organization, (2) a means for diagnosing discontent or revealing problems in communication, (3) a clear picture of current communication patterns and how they might be affected by change, and (4) a before-and-after picture of organizational communication in relation to change.

**Communication medium** A conduit or channel through which data and meaning are conveyed; includes oral, written, and nonverbal delivery systems.

**Communication skill** The ability to communicate so that other people understand and to seek and use feedback from employees to ensure understanding.

**Community** The social entity consisting of private citizens, government, and other public or regulatory agencies; traditionally, dependent on the firm and grateful for the salaries and taxes it pays and for its use of community suppliers and contractors.

**Comparable worth** A concept contending that individuals who perform jobs requiring similar skills, efforts, and responsibilities under similar work conditions should be compensated equally.

**Compensation** The human resources management activity dealing with every type of reward that individuals receive for performing organizational tasks—financial and nonfinancial, direct and indirect.

**Competency-based performance** A way to ensure consistent employee response by requiring that the employee performing a particular job has certain competencies.

**Competitive advantage** The advantage that can be gained through lower cost or differentiation.

**Competitive benchmarking** Standards for performance based on what other successful organizations have been able to achieve.

**Competitive scope** The breadth of a firm's target within its industry.

**Competitors** In the business world, organizations that produce similar goods or services; usually rival firms competing for the same group of customers.

**Complexity** The number of job titles and the number of departments in an organization.

**Computer skill** The ability to use business software and related technology.

**Concept to customer** The important period between when a product is first considered and when it is sold to the customer.

**Conceptual decision maker** A decision maker who is contemplative and tends to structure the decision situation as a mental model,

reviewing facts, focusing on cognitive assessment (often intuitively), and developing alternative outcomes for different assumption sets.

**Conceptual skill** The ability to see the big picture—how each part of the organization fits and interacts with other parts to accomplish goals.

**Concurrent control** A measurement of profitability involving the monitoring of ongoing operations to ensure that objectives are pursued; implemented primarily by the supervisory activities of managers through personal, on-the-spot observation, but also by their delegation of authority.

**Conflict** A struggle between competing ideas and/or values.

**Conformity** The acceptance by an organization's members of a norm, important because it creates a system of shared values among veteran group members as well as newcomers to the group.

**Consideration** A dimension of leader behavior, by which leaders emphasize concern for the worker, that is, appreciating a job well done, stressing high morale, treating workers as their equals, and encouraging greater employee control over work. *See also* initiating structure.

**Consumerism** The activities of individuals, groups, and organizations aimed at protecting consumer rights.

**Content theories** Also called need theories, job design theories based on the idea that meeting people's basic needs produces satisfaction.

**Context** The environment in which a team operates, including organizational structure, strategies, leadership, and rewards, as well as the members' personalities and abilities and the overall size of the group; dictates what the team can accomplish.

**Contingency approach** An approach to organizational design that requires managers to examine the prevailing contingencies or circumstances and select the most effective design.

**Contingency leadership model** A leadership model stating that the effective leader's behavioral style is contingent on the situation or followers.

**Contingency theory** A management theory describing the unique aspects of the situation that effect performance such as technology and the environment.

**Contingent Rewards** Rewards that are distributed based on a specific, preceding behavior; for example, a sales clerk receiving a free weekend trip for having the highest sales in her department for the preceding quarter.

**Continuous improvement** The evolutionary process of reexamining organizational practices, first identifying key organizational performance indicators at all levels of the organization and then periodically comparing an actual organization transaction against standards.

**Control** The final step in the planning process consisting of all the managerial activities to ensure that actual results conform to planned results; simultaneous with implementation.

**Control charts** Charts that show the result of statistical process control measures for a sample, batch, or some other unit; used to study variation in a process and to analyze the variation over time.

**Controlling** Requires three elements: (1) established standards of performance, (2) identify deviations between actual performance and the established standards, and (3) action to correct performance that fails to meet the standards.

**Co-opting** Giving a person who is critical of change a major role in the design or implementation of it.

**Core competencies** The activities, resources, skills, and capabilities that the organization uses to achieve objectives.

**Cost focus** A competitive strategy that emphasizes gaining advantage through cost control in a narrow market area.

**Cost leadership** A strategy that involves keeping costs and prices lower than those of competitors.

**Cost-leadership strategy** A common strategy for creating value while maintaining a lower-than-average cost structure.

**Countertrading** The use of complex bartering agreements between two or more countries, in which merchandise (not cash) is exchanged between countries and by which the country wanting to trade requires the exporting country to purchase products from it before allowing its products to be sold there.

**Cultural diversity** The differences among and within cultures.

**Culture** The system of behaviors, rituals, and shared meanings that distinguish a group or an organization from other similar units.

**Current ratio** The widest known and most often used measure of liquidity, expressed as the ratio of current assets to current liabilities.

**Customer departmentalization** The grouping of jobs, usually in organizations with extremely large customers or those serving diverse groups, in a manner that serves customers' needs.

**Customers** The end users of the organization's products and/or services.

**Customs and entry procedures** Procedures that govern the inspection, documentation, and licensing of imports.

**Cycle time reduction (CTR)** The reduction of cycle time (the length of time required to complete a process and to be ready to begin anew).

## D

**Data-carrying capacity** The degree to which a medium can effectively and efficiently convey data.

**Debt/asset ratio** An expression of the relationship of the firm's total debts to its total assets.

**Debt/equity ratio** A measure of the amount of assets financed by debt compared to the amount financed by profits retained by the firm and investments (stocks and other securities).

**Decentralization** The distribution, or delegation, of authority throughout the organization; the sharing of decision-making authority with all members of the organization.

**Decision** A choice among competing alternatives.

**Decision sciences** Modern management theories decision making, information systems, mathematics, and statistics to aid in making choices.

**Decisional role** The role of the manager, acting as entrepreneur, disturbance handler, resource allocator, and negotiator.

**Decision-making skill** The skill that enables a manager to make the appropriate decisions for achieving the organization's goals.

**Decoding** The interpretation of a message's symbols by the receiver, who converts them into concepts and ideas.

**Delphi technique** A decision-making tool in which several expert judges solicit anonymous responses through a series of sequential questionnaires, interspersed with summarized information and feedback of the opinions of participants, after which a final results report is prepared.

**Departmentalization** The grouping of jobs according to a logical criterion.

**Depth of intervention** The degree of change that an intervention is intended to bring about, such as shallow, moderate, or deep.

**Descriptive statistics** Statistics computed as a measure of some property of a set of data, making possible a statement about the data's meaning.

**Diagnosis** The analytical process that generates valuable information to determine the exact nature of a problem or the specific need for change.

**Differentiation** A strategy that attempts to improve a firm's competitive position by developing unique products.

**Differentiation strategy** A strategy by which the firm offers a premium-priced product that is equipped with more product-enhancing features than its competitors' products.

**Direct financial compensation** Compensation that consists of the pay an employee receives in the form of wages, salary, bonuses, and commissions.

**Direct ownership** A domestic firm's purchase of one or more business operations in a foreign country, requiring a large investment in production facilities, research, personnel, and marketing activities.

**Direction** The acts of managers when they (1) instruct subordinates in the proper methods and procedures and (2) oversee their work to ensure that it is done properly.

**Directive decision maker** A decision maker who uses a rational and straightforward approach to decision making.

**Discounted rate of return** A measurement of profitability that takes into account the time value of money; similar to the payback method, except that cash inflows and outflows are considered.

**Diversification** A strategy employed when a firm competes in more than one industry, with each industry having it own structure and warranting a separate strategy.

**Domain definition** A class of corporate-level strategies that integrates the complex domains (often multiple industries) in which an organization competes.

**Domain navigational strategy** A class of business-level, or competitive, strategies.

**Dominant culture** The core values shared by most of the employees in an organization; for example, Disney's emphasis on quality goods and services.

**Downward communication** Information that flows down the organizational hierarchy from managers and supervisors to subordinates, following the formal lines of authority prescribed by the chain of command.

**Driving forces** Forces tending to initiate a change and to keep it going.

**Duty** A tax placed on an import or export.

## E

**Economy of scale** A decrease in per-unit manufacturing cost as a result of increased size of production facilities.

**Economy of time** Enhancing profitability by increasing functionality, shortening cycle time, and meeting the needs of people who interact with the organization; for example, Wal-Mart's success with fast inventory turnovers.

**Effectiveness** The ability of the organization to achieve its goals.

**Efficiency** Amount of resources to produce a product or service.

**Effort-to-performance expectancy** The subjective assessment that a person can complete the job; the "can do" (perceived capability) component of an employee's approach to work.

**Embargo** Prohibition of the import or export of certain goods; for example, the Muslim nations' embargo on the importation of alcoholic beverages.

**Emotional intelligence** A characteristic of individuals that allows them to effectively manage themselves and their relationships with others.

**Empathic listening** Listening in which the listener attempts first to understand and then to be understood; requires looking at an issue from another person's point of view.

**Empowerment** An important part of change in an organization, the increase of people's involvement in their work (design, flow, interactions, decision making), often leading to the opportunity for greater group decision-making autonomy.

**Enacted role** How the received role is expressed or redefined by the individual assuming the role, as transmitted, filtered, and processed for action by the role occupant. *See also* received role; sent role.

**Encoding** Converting the message into groups of symbols that represent ideas or concepts; translates ideas or concepts into the coded message that will be communicated.

**Environmental analysis** The assessing of the information gathered through environmental scanning to reconcile inconsistencies and interpret findings.

**Environmental complexity** The number of forces in the environment that influence the organization.

**Environmental scanning** The collection of information about forces in the management environment through observation, reviewing publications, and research.

**Environmental theories** Learning theories that describe how we acquire knowledge about our behavior, specifically by evaluating how our behavior is judged by actors in the environment.

**Environmental uncertainty** The degree to which managers can predict how environmental factors will change and the impact of the changes on the organization.

**Equal employment opportunity (EEO).** The employment of individuals in a fair and unbiased manner; a societal priority that has needed legal and administrative guidelines to encourage action.

**Equilibrium** The point at which the sum of the driving forces equals the sum of the restraining forces.

**Equity theory** A job design theory that concerns the worker's perception of how he or she is being treated, based on the assessment process a worker uses to evaluate the fairness or justice of organizational outcomes and the adjustment process used to maintain perceptions of fairness.

**ERG theory** A content theory, espoused by Clayton Alderfer, that is based on the concept of frustration regression to describe how we deal with our unmet needs. *See also* content theories.

**Escalation of commitment** An increased commitment to a decision, despite information indicating its failure, due to a person's desire to reduce dissonance and to appear consistent to oneself.

**Ethics** Principles of behavior that distinguish between what a group or society as a whole considers right and wrong.

**Euro** The official unit of currency of the European Union.

**Evolutionary activity** Activity that occurs gradually over long periods of time.

**Evolutionary planning model** A planning model entailing changes that are typically not dramatic, but consistent and incremental.

**Exchange control** A limit on how much profit a foreign-based firm can return to its home country.

**Expectancy theory** The theory based on an individual's subjective assessment that an effort will lead to job performance and that job performance will lead to a first-order outcome.

**Expert power** A type of power that is based on an individual's technical or expert knowledge about a particular area in the form of experience, information, or advanced education.

**Exporting** Selling domestic goods to a foreign country.

**External change forces** Pressures that originate outside the organization, sometimes signaling that change is needed.

**External environment** The set of forces outside the organization that have a direct or indirect impact on the firm's activities, some of which are controllable and others not.

**External strategies** Organizational attempts to change environmental circumstances, thereby reducing environmental uncertainty.

**Extinction** In reinforcement theory, a way of decreasing undesired behavior through nonreinforcement, that is, the diminishing over time of an unrewarded behavior.

**Extrinsic rewards** Rewards that are administered by another party and that occur apart from the actual performance of work; for example, a paycheck.

# F

**False consensus** The tendency to overestimate the degree to which others share our conclusion, thereby solidifying judgment, often incorrectly.

**Feedback** The receiver's response to the sender's message, during which the receiver becomes the source of a message that is directed back to the original sender, who then becomes a receiver.

**Feedback control** A type of control that uses results to guide future actions, like a thermostat, which automatically regulates the temperature of a room.

**First-line management** Managers who are responsible for the organization's basic work; often called supervisors, managers, or foremen.

**Fishbone diagrams** Diagrams that look like a fishbone, in which the problem is defined as the effect (the "head" of the fishbone) and the events that contribute to the problem are called causes (the "bones" growing out of the spine); also called cause-and-effect diagrams.

**Five competitive forces** Defines competition in terms of five competitive forces: (1) the threat of new entrants, (2) the threat of substitute products or services, (3) the bargaining power of suppliers, (4) the bargaining power of buyers, and (5) the rivalry among existing competitors.

**Flat rate** A rate of pay, established by collective bargaining, for all workers in a job category, regardless of seniority or performance.

**Flextime** A schedule that allows workers to select starting and quitting times within limits set by management; for example, working ten hours one day and six another.

**Flowcharts** Charts that shows the sequence of steps in a process or work activity, generally beginning with inputs, showing what takes place to transform these inputs, and ending with outputs.

**Focus differentiation strategy** Serves a segment or target market for its product or service by creating a product that is different and superior to the competition; for example, Porsche's filling of the high-end sports car market niche with a product that differs significantly enough from its competitors to warrant a premium price.

**Focus-cost leadership strategy** Serves a segment or target market for its product or service by emphasizing product consistency at the lowest possible cost.

**Focused differentiation** A competitive strategy that involves providing a competitive and unique product and/or service to a narrow market area.

**Follower readiness** The degree of willingness, confidence, and ability of followers. *See also* Hersey-Blanchard Situational Leadership® theory.

**Force Field Analysis** A means of diagnosing situations and analyzing the various change strategies that can be used in a particular situation.

**Forecasting** The process of using past and current information to predict future events.

**Formal group** Two or more people who engage in organizationally required actions for a common purpose.

**Formalization** The extent to which an organization's communications and procedures are written down and filed.

**Forming** The beginning of the group, when members get to know one another, start to understand each other's abilities and deficits, come together as a functioning unit, appoint a formal leader, define formal group functions, and start to develop a hierarchy emerge.

**Friendship group** A collection of people with similar values or beliefs who get together for a common purpose— possibly just to have fun.

**Frustration regression** The situation in which we are unable to satisfy a need and, in reaction, regress to a lower need.

**Functional departmentalization** The grouping of jobs according to organizational functions, which works best in a stable environment and when tight control over processes and operations is desired.

**Functional strategies** Strategic actions, resource commitments, and streams of previous decision that follow from and support a business strategy.

**Fundamental attribution error** In attributing causality for another person's behavior, the common tendency to underestimate situational causes and to overestimate personal characteristics.

## G

**Gainsharing plan** A companywide group incentive plan that allows employees to share in the proceeds and whose goal is to unite diverse organizational elements behind the common pursuit of improved organizational effectiveness.

**Gantt chart** A tool developed by Henry Gantt, that visually depicts the steps in a process, the time and the sequence of steps required to complete the entire project.

**Gap analysis** Analysis that identifies the difference between the current state of the organization and its desired state.

**General environment** The overall environment containing the elements that affect all organizations.

**Generative learning** According to Peter Senge, a stage that a firm goes through in becoming a learning organization and that requires "seeing the systems that control events."

**Geographic departmentalization** Grouping jobs based on defined territories; enables organizations to respond to unique customer needs in various regions quickly.

**Global corporation** An organization that operates as if the world were a single market, with corporate headquarters, manufacturing facilities, and marketing operations throughout the world, and that pursues strategies on a worldwide basis.

**Global outsourcing** The strategic use of external resources by a firm to perform activities that were previously handled internally in order to reduce costs, increase competitiveness, and allow firms to focus on what they do best.

**Goal** A future state or condition that contributes to the fulfillment of the organization's mission.

**Goal acceptance** The psychological embrace of the goal by the worker as his or her own aspiration.

**Goal commitment** A worker's behavioral follow-through, a persistent work effort to achieve the goal.

**Goals** Targeted levels of performance set before doing the work; can help to direct attention and action, mobilize effort, create persistent behavior over time, and lead to strategies for goal attainment.

**Goal-setting theory** A learning theory stating that people who set goals outperform those who do not.

**Grapevine** An informal channel of communication that cuts across formal channels of communication and that carries a variety of facts, opinions, rumors, and other information.

**Gross domestic product (GDP)** The total value of goods and services produced by a nation.

**Group** Two or more people who are aware of each other, who interact to collectively accomplish a goal, and who perceive themselves to be a group.

**Group development** The progression from a collection of people literally tossed together for a common purpose to a well-functioning whole whose effectiveness stands the test of time.

**Group norms** The borders of acceptable member behavior, usually thought of as a positive force in group productivity but sometimes having a negative effect on group output.

**Groupthink** A mode of thinking that people engage in when they are deeply involved in a cohesive in-group, when members' strivings for unanimity override their motivation to realistically appraise alternative courses of action.

**Groupware (group-based software)** Software that enables geographically dispersed virtual team members to interact in real time, modifying and updating designs or other elements in a database.

## H

**Halo effect** The tendency to select one salient (positive or negative) characteristic of an individual, focus on it, and use it to organize, interpret, and retain information about the person.

**Hawthorne effect** The unexpected results of the Hawthorne Studies indicated that productivity increased in relation to the presence and attention of the researchers. *See also* Hawthorne Studies.

**Hawthorne Studies**  Famous studies conducted by Elton Mayo at Hawthorne Works of Western Electric in Cicero, Illinois; initially aimed to determine the relationship between the intensity of illumination and the efficiency of two groups of workers. *See also* Hawthorne effect.

**Hersey-Blanchard Situational Leadership® theory**  The situational leadership theory, developed by Ken Blanchard and Paul Hersey, asserting that leaders can and should adjust their behavior to suit situations in the workplace. *See also* situational leadership theories.

**Hierarchy**  An organizational with specialized skills necessary to the purpose of the firm.

**Hierarchy of needs**  Abraham Maslow's motivation theory that is based on needs and includes two key assumptions: (1) different needs are active at different times and only unsatisfied needs can influence behavior, and (2) needs are arranged in a fixed order of importance, called a hierarchy. *See also* content theories.

**High-exchange relationship**  The allocation by the leader of more discretionary rewards, with the intent to build commitment and encourage task accomplishment. *See also* low-exchange relationship.

**Histograms**  Charts that show the frequency of each measurement in a group of measurements; useful in analyzing the variability in a process; also called bar charts.

**Horizontal communication**  Messages that flow between persons at the same level of the organization; needed to coordinate the activities of diverse but independent units or departments.

**Horizontal organization form**  Compared to the more traditional vertical organizations based on a pyramidal hierarchy, a flatter and more responsive organizational form.

**Hot stove rule**  A metaphor suggesting that being burned by a hot stove represents punishment at the most general level and in its most vivid form and that punishment should be swift, intense, impersonal, and consistent, while providing an alternative.

**Humanistic philosophy**  A philosophy that focuses on individual rights and values.

**Human relations approach**  A behavioral management theory that focuses on individuals working in group settings and in which managers and workers are studied in relation to what occurs in the group.

**Human resource management (HRM)**  The activities needed to acquire, develop, retain, and utilize human resources, specifically: (1) equal employment opportunity, (2) human resource planning, (3) recruitment, (4) selection, (5) training and development, (6) performance evaluation, (7) compensation, and (8) benefits and services.

**Human resource planning**  A two-step process that involves (1) forecasting future human resource needs and then (2) planning how to adequately fulfill and manage the needs.

**Hygiene factors**  One of two sets of factors, that can separately explain satisfaction and dissatisfaction; also called maintenance factors, specifically the aspects of work that are peripheral to the task itself and related to the external environment.

**Implementation**  A step in the planning process that consists of delegating tasks, taking action, and achieving results; using resources to put a plan into action.

**Income statement**  A financial statement that summarizes a firm's revenues and expenses; a summary of an organization's financial performance over a given time period.

**Indirect financial compensation**  Also called benefits, compensation that consists of all financial rewards that are not included in direct financial compensation; for example, vacation and insurance. *See also* benefits and services.

**Indirect forces**  Forces in the external environment that influence an organization, but not directly in its daily operations; categorized as social-cultural, economic, global, technological, and political-legal.

**Individual incentive plan**  A compensation plan in which the employee is paid for units produced, whether in the form of piecework, a production bonus, or a commission.

**Individual values**  The decision-making guidelines, mostly acquired early in life, that a person uses when confronted with a choice; a basic part of a person's personality.

**Industrial economy**  An industry-based economy, prevalent between 1830 and 1950, that was ushered in by technological revolutions, beginning with the invention of steam power, which created the energy necessary for mass production.

**Industry environment**  The competition, products, customers, and any other characteristics of a particular industry.

**Industry foresight-led**  A strategy of change that involves looking into the future, determining what the future is projected to be, and then using the insight to change the present organization.

**Inferential statistics**  (*See* page 354) Computations done on a set of data, or on several sets of data, that are designed to facilitate the prediction of future events or to guide decisions and actions.

**Informal group**  Two or more people who engage in a voluntary collective activity for a common purpose.

**Information system**  A computerized system that helps managers make better decisions by permitting them to gather and accurately process large volumes of data.

**Informational role**  The role that establishes the manager as the central point for receiving and sending information.

**Infrastructure**  The communications, transportation, and energy facilities that mobilize a country; an indicator of its economic condition.

**Initiating structure**  A dimension of leader behavior emphasizing work productivity over workplace harmony. *See also* consideration.

**Input, processing, and output (IPO)**  The three subsystems of a system.

**Insider trading**  The illegal practice of buying and selling of stock by individuals on the basis of information that they gain through their positions or contacts with others and that is not available to other investors or to the general public.

**Inspection**  A judgment concerning whether the production meets the specifications and whether corrective actions need to be taken.

**Instrumentality**  The employee's assessment of how instrumental, or likely, it is that successful task performance will be rewarded, such as with a raise; a measure of the association between performance and rewards. (*See also* performance-to-outcome expectancy).

**Integrated cost leadership/differentiation strategy**  A strategy by which an organization serves a segment or target market for its product or service by creating a product that is low cost, yet different from and superior to the competition; for example, Coca-Cola or McDonalds.

**Interest group** A collection of people addressing a specific subject of mutual interest.

**Internal change forces** Pressures that come from within the organization.

**Internal environment** The set of factors within an enterprise that influence how work is done and how goals are accomplished and that, taken together, create a culture within the organization.

**Internal strategies** Tactical actions that organizations can choose when adapting the organization, thereby reducing or at least managing environmental uncertainty. *See also* adaptive learning (Chapter 2).

**International business** Business activities across national boundaries, which have increased steadily since World War II and are expected to continue growing in the twenty-first century.

**International management** The management process in an international business setting, whose importance has increased with the boom in desire for quality goods at lower prices worldwide.

**International Monetary Fund (IMF)** Founded in 1944 to promote cooperation among member nations by eliminating trade barriers; lends money to countries that need short-term loans to conduct international trade.

**Interpersonal communication** Communication between two people, usually face-to-face, but possibly by telephone or e-mail; the fundamental building block of organizational communication.

**Interpersonal role** The figurehead, leader, and liaison roles.

**Interrole conflict** Conflict resulting from the collision of two different roles.

**Intersender conflict** A conflict resulting from contradictory messages coming from the same source.

**Intervention** In the process of change, the second stage, the change itself.

**Intrarole conflict** Conflict between two similar roles.

**Intrinsic rewards** The intangible psychological results of work that are controlled by the worker, that are inherent in the job, and that occur during performance of work.

**Intuitive decision** The "gut level" feeling or belief that one course of action is better than another; not necessarily emotional or nonrational, but rather the result of a unique combination of individual experience, ability, and knowledge that affords the decision maker an insight and a decision preference.

**Inventory turnover** A measure of liquidity that is calculated as the ratio of cost of goods sold to average inventory; facilitates the analysis of appropriate balances in current assets.

**Investment decisions** Managerial decisions that involve the commitment of present funds in exchange for future funds, based on economic analysis.

**Issues management** A technique used by many firms that is focused on a single issue.

## J

**Job analysis** The process of gathering, analyzing, and synthesizing information about jobs, with the purpose of providing an objective description of the job itself.

**Job characteristics approach** A job design approach suggesting that jobs should be designed to include important core dimensions and to increase motivation, performance, and satisfaction as well as reduce absenteeism and turnover.

**Job content** The specific aspects of a job, including achievement, recognition, advancement, the task or work itself, the worker's potential for personal learning or growth, and the worker's responsibility for results.

**Job context** The external environment of the job.

**Job depth** The amount of discretion a worker has in performing tasks, with little-depth jobs generally found at the lower levels of the organization. *See also* job range.

**Job description** The output of job analysis, the written summary of the job: its activities, the equipment required to perform the activities, and the working conditions of the job.

**Job design** The determination of the tasks to be performed to complete the work and the structuring of job elements and duties to increase performance and satisfaction.

**Job enlargement** A job design approach that increases the number of tasks a worker is responsible for, with the purpose of increasing job satisfaction by reducing boredom and monotony.

**Job enrichment** A form of job design that increases not only the number of tasks performed (job range) but also job depth by giving workers more opportunity to exercise discretion over their work, thereby giving workers more control of their activities and addressing their needs for growth, recognition, and responsibility.

**Job range** The number of tasks a worker performs. *See also* job depth.

**Job redesign** An organization's evaluation of job design so as to improve the quality of work, to give workers more autonomy, and to improve coordination, productivity, and product quality, while at the same time responding to workers' needs for learning, challenge, variety, increased responsibility, and achievement.

**Job satisfaction** The feeling of enjoyment and fulfillment that a person receives from performing a job.

**Job specialization** The breakdown of work into small, discrete tasks that specify what is to be done, how it is to be done, and the exact time allowed for doing it.

**Job specification** The written explanation of skills, knowledge, abilities, and other characteristics needed to perform a job effectively; describes aspects of the job holder, whereas the job description describes aspects of the job.

**Joint venture** A partnership between a domestic and a foreign firm.

## K

**Kaizen** The Japanese word for the continuing improvement of everything an organization does.

**Knowledge economies** Economies that are based on information and intangibles, such as computer software and financial services, and that resulted from the development of computer technology during World War II.

## L

**Leader-member exchange theory** A leadership theory that explains effective leadership in terms of the role-making process between the leader and followers.

**Leadership** The process of influencing other people to attain organizational goals.

**Leading** The process of influencing and persuading people to attain organizational goals.

**Level of detail** The specificity of the plan.

**Licensing** An agreement in which one firm (the licensor) allows another (the licensee) to sell the licensor's product and use its brand name, and requires the licensee to pay the licensor a commission or royalty.

**Line position** A position in the direct chain of command that contributes directly to achieving the organization's goals.

**Liquidity** The firm's ability to meet current obligations as they become due.

**Low-cost leader** An organization that achieves a competitive advantage by performing a business activity at a lower cost than the competition.

**Low-exchange relationship** A leader-follower relationship based on rules and procedures. *See also* high-exchange relationship.

## M

**Management** A process of achieving organizational goals and objectives through the efforts and contributions of other people.

**Management ethics** The principles by which management activities and behaviors are evaluated as right or wrong.

**Management level** Vertical specialization of the management process, authority to act and to use organizational resources within specified limits.

**Management team** Several people from different functional or operating areas, brought together to plan, implement, and manage ongoing organizational activities.

**Managers** Individuals who use the principles of management to guide, direct, or oversee the work and performance of others.

**Manipulation** The use of deception to convince others that a change is in their best interests.

**Market growth rate** The annual rate of growth of the market in which a product, division, or department is located.

**Marketing objectives** Objectives used to measure performance relative to products, markets, distribution, and customer service, with focus on prospects for long-term profitability in terms of market share, sales volume, the number of outlets carrying the product, and the number of new products developed.

**Matrix organization** A cross-functional organization overlay that creates multiple lines of authority and places people in teams to work on tasks for a finite period of time, characterized by a dual, rather than a singular, line of command.

**Mechanistic organization** A rigid organization that attempts to achieve production and efficiency through rules, specialized jobs, and centralized authority.

**Media richness** A medium's capacity to convey data.

**Medium of transmission** A means of carrying an encoded message from the source to the receiver; for example, ink on paper, air vibrations produced by vocal cords, and radio and TV signals.

**Message** An idea or experience that a sender wants to communicate, verbally or nonverbally; for example, a manager communicating a process to a worker by explaining it, illustrating it, or providing a written explanation.

**Method** A sequence of activities to accomplish an objective; usually communicated in a policy manual. *See also* standing plan.

**Middle management** Managers who plan, organize, control, and lead the activities of other managers and who are subject to the management of a superior.

**Mission statement** The fundamental purpose that an organization serves.

**Mixed departmentalization** The grouping of jobs using more than one criterion.

**Moral philosophy** The set of principles that dictates acceptable behavior; learned from family, friends, coworkers, and other social groups, as well as through formal education.

**Moving budgeting** Budgeting for a fixed period (say, one year) with periodic updating at fixed intervals (such as one month).

**Multidivisional organization** A high-performance organization whose operating units or divisions are partially interdependent, with each division's product different from those of the other divisions, but with all divisions sharing common endowments, such as technology, skill, and information.

**Multinational company (MNC)** An organization that conducts business in two or more countries and that is typically based in one country, with operations, production facilities, and/or sales subsidiaries in other countries.

**Multinational market group** A group of two or more countries that agree to reduce trade and tariff barriers among them.

## N

**Need** A drive to achieve a specific outcome.

**Need deprivation** A condition leading to a state of arousal or the search to reduce the need deficit.

**Need for achievement** A measure of a person's desire for clear, self-set, moderately difficult goals, with feedback given based on goal achievement.

**Need for affiliation** The desire to work with others, to interact with and support others, and to learn the lessons of life through the experiences of others; Maslow's social need, applied to the individual.

**Need for power** A desire to have influence and control over others, which can be an important determinant of behavior.

**Negative reinforcement** Reinforcement that occurs when an unpleasant consequence is withdrawn after the desired behavior occurs.

**Network organization** A flexible, sometimes temporary, relationship between manufacturers, buyers, suppliers, and even customers, typically to meet changing competitive conditions.

**Neutralizer** Any situation that prevents the leader from acting in a specified way.

**Noise** Interference that affects any or all stages of the communication process and that may be present at any point in the communication process.

**Nominal group technique** A structured, six-step decision-making process that brings seven to ten people together to make group decisions that are structured by rules, the initial group being a group in name only (a "nominal" group).

**Noncontingent rewards** Rewards that are not linked to specific behavior; for example, a paid holiday for all staff regardless of their level of performance.

**Nonverbal communication** All intentional or unintentional messages that are neither written nor spoken.

**Norming** The stage in group development when the group charts its long-term vision of group purpose and how it will function over time.

# O

**Objective** Short-term, specific, measurable target that must be achieved to accomplish organizational goals.

**Occupational Safety and Health Administration (OSHA)** Passed in 1970, federal legislation whose primary purpose is to ensure safe working conditions by establishing standards with which employers must comply.

**OD** *See* organizational development (OD).

**OP** *See* outside pressure (OP) change agent.

**Open system** A system that is open to influences from the environment.

**Operant conditioning** *See* reinforcement theory.

**Operational definition** A definition that converts a concept into measurable, objective units; for example, the concept of *weight* can be operationally defined in terms of grams, pounds, or another standard measure.

**Operational planning** Planning that is focused, short-term, and translates the tactical plan into clear numbers, specific steps, and measurable objectives.

**Operations management** A sphere of management science that includes the areas of purchasing, materials management, production, inventory and quality control, maintenance, and plant management.

**Opportunity building** Seeking out and/or developing new possibilities for success.

**Oral communication** The communication that takes place when the spoken word is used to transmit a message, either in person, on the telephone, or through another mechanism that allows individuals to speak to one another; enables prompt, two-way interaction between parties.

**Organic organization** An organization that seeks to maximize flexibility and adaptability, that encourages greater utilization of human potential, and that deemphasizes specialization of jobs, status, and rank.

**Organization stories** Tales about experiences and events that transpired in the storyteller's workplace and that legitimize power, rationalize group behavior, and reinforce organizational values, identity, and commitment.

**Organizational commitment** The degree to which a person believes in and supports the purpose and goals of the organization and expects to continue working for it in the future; three types—affective, normative, and continuance.

**Organizational design** The process by which managers develop an organizational structure, determined by the specialization of jobs, the delegation of authority, departmentalization, and span of control.

**Organizational development (OD)** A long-term approach to improve organizational effectiveness that targets the entire organization.

**Organizational performance** An outcome that assesses the degree to which an organization is both efficient in using resources and effective in attaining its stated goals.

**Organizational socialization** The process by which managers and coworkers offer consistent help to newcomers in developing skills and

evolving into accepted team members who understand and are committed to the firm's culture.

**Organizational structure** The framework of jobs, departments, and divisions that directs the behavior of individuals and groups toward achieving the organization's objectives effectively.

**Organizations** Structural arrangements of people brought to accomplish a goal or goals.

**Organizing** The structuring of both human and physical resources to accomplish organizational objectives; involves dividing tasks into jobs, delegating authority, determining the appropriate bases for departmentalizing jobs, and deciding the optimum number of jobs in each department.

**Outcomes** The team outcomes of goal attainment, efficiency, and member satisfaction.

**Outside pressure (OP) change agent** An individual or group that is not regularly employed by the firm but that applies pressure on the firm to change.

# P

**Pareto charts** Charts used to display the number of problems or defects in a product over time, displaying the results as bars of varying lengths.

**Path-goal leadership theory** A leadership theory, in which the leader's role is twofold: (1) clarify the path by which followers can achieve personal goals and organizational outcomes and (2) increase the rewards valued by followers; four types of leader behaviors: directive, supportive, participative, and achievement.

**Payback method** A measurement of profitability involving the calculation of the number of years needed for the proposed capital acquisition to repay its original cost out of future cash earnings.

**PCT** *See* people-change-technology (PCT) change agent.

**People-change-technology (PCT) change agent** A change agent that attempts to bring about change by means of various behaviorally oriented techniques and that focuses on the individual; normally professionals using standardized assessment techniques.

**People skill** The skill that enables someone to work with others.

**Perception** The cognitive process of attention and selection, interpretation, retention, retrieval, and response to information sensed in the environment.

**Perceptual sets** Groups of related stimuli (e.g., employee, offices, plan, deadline, and building).

**Performance evaluation** The systematic review of individual, job-relevant strengths and weaknesses by means of observation and judgment.

**Performance standards** In management parlance, behavioral expectations created by plans, based on the objectives and courses of action that are assigned to persons and groups and that are the bases for standards used to assess actual performance.

**Performance-to-outcome expectancy** The probability that hard work will be rewarded. (*See also* instrumentality).

**Performing** The stage in group development in which the group functions as a highly effective and perform the group's work at a high level.

**Personal power** A type of power that consists of expert power, referent power, or a combination of both.

**Personality** A stable pattern of characteristics or traits that influences behavior (positive or negative) and that describes a person's uniqueness.

**Person-role conflict** A conflict that occurs when an individual's beliefs are in direct conflict with the requirements of his or her role.

**Persuasion** Selling a plan to those who must implement it.

**Physical and financial objectives** Objectives that reflect the organization's capacity to acquire resources sufficient to achieve its objectives; measured by means of numerous accounting measures, such as liquidity measures, and inventory turnover.

**Plan, do, check, act (PDCA)** A quality planning approach that is conceived as a planning cycle for continuous improvement; a repetitive cycle of (1) planning the quality improvement, (2) workers performing a pilot, (3) workers checking the results of the pilot, and (4) workers implementing the tested process.

**Planning** The development of action-oriented plans for achieving an organization's purpose, mission, goals, and objectives in the short and long term.

**Planning process** A six-step process: (1) identifying current conditions, (2) determining goals and objectives, (3) creating action plans, (4) allocating resources, (5) implementing the plan, and (6) control.

**Planning values** The underlying decision priorities used in determining planning objectives and making decisions.

**Policies** Written statements reflecting a permanent plan's basic values and providing guidelines for selecting actions to achieve objectives.

**Policy** A guideline that describes expected behavior in a specific situation.

**Political decision model** A decision-making model whose aim is not to make the best decision, but rather to make the decision that will be accepted by the groups involved in making it.

**Pollution** The contamination of water, air, and land.

**Positive reinforcement** Reinforcement that occurs when a positive consequence (reward) is applied to a desired behavior; increases the frequency of the particular behavior that it follows.

**Positive self-talk** Creating mental imagery that reinforces a worker's sense of self-esteem and enhances effectiveness.

**Power** The ability to get people to do something they otherwise would not do. *See also* Coercive power; expert power; personal power; referent power; reward power.

**Preliminary control** Control that focuses on preventing deviations in the quality and quantity of resources used in an organization.

**Prepotency** In Maslow's theory, the idea that the most basic unsatisfied need (in the hierarchy) influences current behavior; for example, an unmet need for a promotion and a raise. *See also* hierarchy of needs.

**Primary activities** The main activities of an organization: for example, inbound logistics, manufacturing the product (or creating the service), outbound logistics, marketing and sales, and service.

**Priming** The tendency to give more weight to early information; using first impressions to form a judgment about a person. *See also* recency.

**Proactive decision** A decision made in anticipation of an external change or other conditions; used by managers to prevent problems from developing.

**Problem-solving team** A teams of knowledgeable workers who gather to solve a specific problem and then disband.

**Procedure** A rule that applies to a policy.

**Process** A series of activities or tasks that require external inputs to create value by redesigning efficient organizational processes to meet customer needs.

**Process organization** A form of organization that bases performance objectives on identifying the processes that meet customer needs.

**Process theories** Theories describing cognitive processes and decisions that help predict subsequent behavior; view motivation in relation to workers' explicit thought processes (cognitions) and conscious decisions to select and pursue a specific alternative (choice). *See also* equity theory; expectancy theory.

**Processes** Processes that occur in all work teams: influence, development, and decision making.

**Product departmentalization** The grouping of jobs according to a particular product or product line, thereby enabling people working with a particular product to use their skills and expertise.

**Production** Making the product or delivering the service; defined by Shewhart as the work required to achieve objectives.

**Production management** A sphere of management science that focuses on manufacturing technology and the flow of material in manufacturing.

**Productivity objectives** Efficiency objectives directly measured by means of ratios of output to input; also used for comparisons across functional areas.

**Profitability objectives** Objectives measured in terms of the ratios of (1) profits to sales, (2) profits to total assets, and (3) profits to capital (net worth), each measuring and therefore evaluating a different yet important aspect of profitability.

**Psychological contract** A set of expectations, based on a balanced give-and-take, that workers have regarding what they will give to the organization and what they will receive from it; the exchange of workers' services for compensation.

**Punishment** An undesirable consequence for an undesirable behavior, a naturally occurring phenomenon in the learning process.

**Pygmalion effect** Also known as the self-fulfilling prophecy, a theory that an increase in a manager's expectations of subordinates' performance actually improves performance.

## Q

**Quality circle** A small voluntary group of people, usually fewer than 10, who do similar work and who meet about once a week to discuss their work and present possible solutions to management.

**Quality objectives** Objectives measured by physical characteristics of the product, or service, or that can be assessed in terms of a psychological customer perception of the product.

**Quality planning** As described by W. E. Deming, (1) determining customer needs and (2) developing the products and processes required to meet those needs

**Quota** A limit on the amount of a product that can leave or enter a country; sometimes voluntary.

## R

**Range** The extreme upper and lower measures of a variable.

**Rate of return on investment** A measure of profitability in terms of the percentage of the return on an investment.

**Rational model**  A decision making model that assumes the decision maker uses a logical approach to select the best alternative to reach a decision.

**Received role**  The role recipient's individual translation of what the sent role means to him or her. *See also* enacted role; sent role.

**Recency**  The tendency to regard the last information obtained about a person or an object as the most current and often the most important; might not be the most accurate. *See also* Priming.

**Recruitment**  The activities used to attract job candidates with the abilities and attitudes needed to help an organization achieve its objectives.

**Reengineering**  Rethinking and radically redesigning processes to dramatically improve cost, quality, service, and speed.

**Reference ratio**  The ratio of a comparison between a person's outcome (rewards, recognition, pay) and inputs (time, effort, actual work performed).

**Referent power**  A type of power arising from an individual's personal characteristics that are esteemed by others; stimulates imitation and loyalty.

**Refreezing**  The final stage in the process of change, implementing the change.

**Regulation**  A set of instructions for implementing a policy, also known as standard procedure.

**Reinforcement**  Using contingent rewards to increase future occurrences of a specific behavior; can take two forms—positive or negative.

**Reinforcement theory**  Also called operant conditioning, a learning theory that characterizes motivation as largely determined by external factors, that is, the consequence of behavior (regardless of whether it is rewarded) determining whether the behavior is repeated in the future.

**Related diversification**  A strategy employed when an organization diversifies into similar industries, products, and/or infrastructures.

**Relationship behavior (supportive behavior)**  The amount of emotional support needed to complete a task. *See also* Hersey-Blanchard Situational Leadership® theory.

**Relationship-oriented behavioral style**  A style of behavior that emphasizes individual needs, showing empathy for worker needs and feelings, being supportive of group needs, establishing trusting relationships with workers.

**Relative market share**  The market share of an SBU.

**Representative heuristic**  A type of bias based on a stereotypical response.

**Resources**  The financial, physical, human, time, or other assets of an organization; also known as factors of production.

**Restraining forces**  Forces that act to restrain or decrease driving forces.

**Restructuring**  A revolutionary change that focuses on the redesign of the organization's structure, eliminating units or departments, but possibly meaning the consolidation of functions.

**Revolutionary activity**  Activity that occurs periodically to forever alter the nature of business transactions.

**Revolutionary planning model**  A planning model involving a massive, one-time change in the production process or product to reduce costs or improve the product in a significant way.

**Reward**  An attractive or desired consequence that can be either intrinsic or extrinsic.

**Reward power**  The manager's ability to allocate organizational resources in exchange for cooperation.

**Role**  A pattern of expected behavior often associated with a job or profession.

**Role ambiguity**  Unclear role requirements, usually resulting when the role occupant is not sure how to meet requirements.

**Role conflict**  The incompatibility between the role's requirements and the individual's own beliefs or expectations.

**Role modeling**  A technique by which leaders exhibit behaviors that they expect of other employees.

**Role overload**  A condition in which a task's demands overwhelm the role occupant's ability to perform the task.

**Run charts**  Charts used to plot measurements taken over specific time intervals, such as a day, week, or month, usually with the quantity measure plotted on the vertical axis and time on the horizontal axis.

## S

**Satisfice**  A term, coined by Herbert Simon, that means to seek a satisfactory decision, one that is good enough but not perfect; the first alternative that proves to be a satisfactory alternative.

**Scatter diagrams**  (*See* page 354) Diagrams that show the relationship between two characteristics or events.

**Schema**  A categorization or a summary of a set of stimuli.

**Scientific management**  A management theory that concentrates on increasing workforce productivity.

**Scope**  The range of activities (e.g., budgeting, human resources) covered by a plan.

**Selection**  The process by which an organization chooses from a list of applicants the persons who best meet the criteria for the position available, considering current environmental and financial conditions.

**Selective perception**  The perceptual process of filtering out information that is inconsistent with beliefs or in some other way unpleasant and not in an individual's best interest to consider.

**Self-concept**  A person's self-image, that is, the awareness of conscious thoughts that shape personality, perceptions, attitudes, behaviors, skills development, abilities, and relationships with the external world.

**Self-cueing**  Planning or making arrangements for an activity prior to influence event performance.

**Self-designed jobs**  Jobs that allow workers to propose and design work-process changes rather than having superiors impose constraints and that can result in a personal sense of competence, self-control, and purpose.

**Self-efficacy**  A person's belief in his or her ability to succeed in a specific situation; the "can-do" feeling applied to a specific context or a situation.

**Self-esteem**  A relatively stable predisposition to evaluate ourselves in positive or negative terms.

**Self-leadership**  A management philosophy that encourages individual employees to develop their own work priorities that are consistent with organizational goals.

**Self-management**  The use of self-imposed work strategies helping to control the daily activities that achieve organizational goals.

**Self-observation** Workers' monitoring of their own behavior, noting their actions, events, or outcomes and keeping performance records.

**Self-rewards** Also called self-administered rewards, rewards that workers give themselves, based on their accomplishments.

**Self-serving bias** The tendency to attribute our successes to internal factors, such as our own effort or ability; for example, attributing a high grade to hard work.

**Self-set goals** Goals that are set at the initiative of the worker, not the manager, and empower workers with a greater sense of personal control.

**Semistructured interview** An interview in which only some questions are prepared in advance, allowing the interviewer more flexibility; less rigid than the structured interview.

**Sender** A person, a group, or an organization that has a message to share with another person or group of persons.

**Sent role** The formally required role of the group. *See also* enacted role; received role.

**Shared values** The group's values on its long-term vision, which have all members' agreement.

**Single-use plan** A plan that is used only one time and for a specific purpose.

**Situation** The context in which leadership occurs; often determines how successfully a leader can influence and persuade subordinates.

**Situational characteristics** In contingency theory, the three characteristics of situations which Fiedler identified (leader-member relations, task structure, and position power) and combined into eight cells, describing various situations that leaders are likely to confront in an organization. *See also* contingency theory.

**Situational leadership theories** Theories on leadership prescribing that the appropriate leader behavior is the one that best fits the constraints of a specific situation and that leader effectiveness is contingent on displaying behavior appropriate to the situation's demands.

**Skill** An ability or proficiency in performing a particular task.

**Social audit** The assessment of a firm's short- and long-term contributions to society.

**Social learning theory** A learning theory proposing that motivated behavior is a function of observing the success of other people and then doing what worked for them; the influence on learning of an individual's cognitive assessment of what behaviors were previously rewarded in the environment.

**Social responsibility** The awareness that business activities have an impact on society and the consideration of the impact in decision making.

**Solvency** The ability of the firm to meet its long-term obligations, that is, its fixed commitments, its measure reflecting the claims of creditors and owners on the firm's assets.

**Source credibility** The degree of confidence and trust that receiver places in the source of a message, without which communication between two parties is difficult.

**Span of control** The number of people who report to one manager or supervisor.

**SPC** *See* statistical process control (SPC).

**Special cause variation** The variation in a system that is a result of an external influence on a system; for example, drug abuse by workers or earthquakes.

**Specification** The statement of the intended outcome, fully describing the preferred condition, which may take the form of a goal, standard, or other carefully determined quantitative statement of conditions.

**Stable system** A system in which special cause variation has been eliminated and that is subject only to common cause variation.

**Staff position** A position that facilitates or provides advice to line positions.

**Stakeholder** Any group or individual, within the organization or outside it, having the potential to influence an organization's ability to achieve its goals and objectives.

**Standard cost system** A cost system that compares actual costs with predetermined (standard) costs, enabling management to take appropriate corrective action or assign to others the authority to take action.

**Standard of living** A nation's standard measured in terms of gross domestic product (GDP) per capita, that is, GDP divided by the population.

**Standing plan** A plan that guides repetitive situations; makes decision making faster, easier, and more consistent from one decision to the next.

**Statistical process control (SPC)** A type of process control based on the two assumptions that (1) nature is imperfect and (2) variability exists everywhere in systems and therefore probability and statistics play a major role in understanding and controlling complex systems. *See also* total quality control (TQC).

**Statistics** The branch of applied mathematics that describes and analyzes empirical observations for the purpose of predicting certain events as a basis for decision making in the face of uncertainty.

**Stereotyping** A perceptual shortcut for ascribing to an individual the characteristics of group or class to which he or she belongs.

**Stockholders** Owners of a firm's stock and hence owners of a portion of the company.

**Storming** The stage in group formation when it comes to grips with inherent conflicts and develops solutions that keep the group focused on its work and members learn to accept one another's individual differences.

**Strategic alliance** The combination of two firms' resources in a partnership that goes beyond the limits of a joint venture and for which trust is the major requirement. *See also* joint venture.

**Strategic business unit (SBU)** Within a company, a product or service division that establishes goals and objectives in harmony with the firm's overall mission and is responsible for its own profits and losses.

**Strategic planning** Decision making that is comprehensive, long-term focuses on the broad, enduring issues for ensuring the organization's effectiveness.

**Strategy-structure-systems doctrine** A change management strategy, utilized mainly in large, complex organizations, in which leading senior managers delegate most operating decisions to division-level managers and then recast their own jobs as defining strategy, developing structure, and managing the systems required to link and control the company's parts.

**Stretch target** Another term for describing the "pull" approach to change (as in pulling an organization into the future).

**Structured interview**  An interview in which the interviewer asks the same set of questions of all interviewees.

**Substitutes for leadership**  Any replacement for traditional leadership; for example, replacement of the task supervision that a new hire needs with job training and education.

**Suppliers**  Vendors that provide a firm with the essential raw materials for its products.

**Supply chain**  A network of suppliers and distributors that procure materials, process materials into finished products (sometimes simply handling the materials), and distribute products to customers, with each step adding value.

**Support activities**  Secondary activities of an organization; for example, infrastructure, human resources, research and development (R&D), and materials management.

**Survey feedback**  The collection of attitudinal data from individuals about the organization and its analysis at the division, department, and unit levels; typically conducted to overcome identified problems.

**SWOT analysis**  A systematic and thorough analysis of the organization's current situation, with attention to (1) internal strengths, (2) internal weaknesses, (3) external opportunities, and (4) external threats.

**Synergistic effect**  The sum total effect of all systems components, as in an organization in which each of its parts performs a specific function.

**Synergy**  The assumption that a system is greater than the sum of its parts.

**System**  A collection of interrelated entities (subsystems) that operate interdependently to achieve common goals.

**Systematic decision making**  The process that requires decision makers to have a goal in mind and to use information in generating alternatives and making a logical choice among alternatives based on fact and data.

**Systems theory**  A way of thinking about organizations and management problems from a systems point of view. *See also* system.

## T

**Tactical planning**  Planning that develops specific actions or activities to implement the strategic plan. more narrowly focused and specific than the strategic plan.

**Task behavior (guidance)**  The amount of task-specific direction a worker needs. *See also* Hersey-Blanchard Situational Leadership® theory.

**Task environment**  The environment containing elements that can have an immediate impact on organizational success.

**Task-oriented behavioral style**  A style of behavior that focuses on tasks, such as setting goals, giving directions, supervising worker performance, and applauding good work.

**Task team**  A formal group of people working on a temporary job, disbanding when its work is completed.

**Team**  Several self-managing people who work as a collective, have complementary skills, share a common purpose, and are mutually accountable for an outcome, having a task, resources, leadership, some decision-making authority, and a goal.

**Team building**  A moderate-depth intervention that attempts to improve diagnosis, communication, cooperation, and the performance of members and the overall team; helps work groups perform at a higher level.

**Team effectiveness**  A measure of the outcomes, or results, of the team's efforts, such as efficiency, satisfaction, and goal attainment.

**Technical skill**  The skill that enables someone to use specific knowledge, techniques, and resources in performing work.

**Technological imperative**  An organization theory asserting that, as technological complexity increases, different organizational structures are needed for optimal results.

**Technological innovation**  The process consisting of all the activities that people carry out to translate technical knowledge into a physical reality, that is, into a usable or useful product or service; progresses from the most basic research to wide-scale marketing.

**Technology**  The conversion process used in organizations to transform raw materials into a complete product.

**Test**  A means of obtaining a standardized sample of a person's behavior.

**Thematic Apperception Test (TAT)**  A test developed by H. A. Murray to measure an individual's need for achievement, whose scoring system was later developed by David McClelland and John Atkinson; contains pictures and asks the test taker to write a story (theme) about the picture. *See also* content theories.

**Theory X**  According to McGregor, Theory X assumes that workers are passive and need direction to keep them focused. A Theory X manager will have a control orientation.

**Theory Y**  A management theory asserting that workers are eager to learn, responsible, and creative, and that their capacities to learn are great and their abilities underutilized.

**Theory Z**  A management approach, developed by William Ouchi in 1981, that combines American and Japanese management practices.

**Time frame**  The period covered by a plan, including short-term, intermediate-term, and long-term components.

**Top management**  A small group of senior executives (usually including a chief executive officer, president, or vice president) who are responsible for the performance of the entire organization.

**Total quality control (TQC)**  A more comprehensive form of quality control than SPC, quality control that uses statistics to integrate the quality-development, quality-maintenance, and quality-improvement efforts of the various groups in an organization, allowing for full customer satisfaction; name coined by Armand Feigenbaum. *See also* statistical process control (SPC).

**Total quality management (TQM)**  The generic name given to the Deming approach to quality-based management, which treats the system as the primary source of error or defects in manufacturing or service work.

**TQC**  *See* total quality control (TQC).

**TQM**  *See* total quality management (TQM).

**Trading company**  An intermediary that takes title to products and undertakes to move them from the domestic country to customers in a foreign country, assuming much of the manufacturer's risk.

**Trait theory of leadership**  The attempt to systematically describe effective leaders by focusing on individual traits, such as a physical or personality attribute. *See also* behavioral theory of leadership.

**Transactional leadership**  A leadership theory in which leaders appeal to their followers' rational exchange motive (labor for wages).

**Transformational leadership**  An inspirational form of leader behavior that is based on modifying followers' beliefs, values, and ultimately their behavior.

## U

**Unfreezing** The first stage in the process of change, readying people for the change.

**Unrelated diversification** A strategy employed when an organization moves into an industry unrelated to its core business, usually by either acquiring or merging with another company.

**Unstructured interview** A type of interview that allows interviewers the freedom to discuss whatever they think is important but that makes comparing answers across interviewees difficult.

**Upward communication** Information that flows up the organizational hierarchy, from subordinates to supervisors and managers; necessary for managers to evaluate the effectiveness of downward communication and for workers to feel they are a meaningful part of the organization.

**Utilitarian philosophy** A philosophy that seeks the greatest good for the largest number of people.

## V

**Valence** The desirability of one outcome over another to the individual (i.e., the rewards); an outcome's desirability or preference to the individual among competing rewards.

**Value chain** The stream of primary and secondary activities by which the organization acquires resources, produces the product or service, and distributes the product or service to the customer, with each value-creating activity having a cost of creation and a potential benefit, measured in terms of cost savings, quality, speed, or uniqueness.

**Values** The set of convictions that specific modes of conduct are personally or socially preferable to other modes of conduct.

**Variable budgeting** Budgeting recognizing the possibility that actual output deviates from planned output and that variable costs are related to output, while fixed costs are unrelated.

**Virtual team** The collaborative activities of several people, working together on computer networks, who use common software and share common data.

**Vision** A clear sense of an organization's future.

**Viziers** Ancient managers who used the managerial functions of planning, organizing, leading, and controlling.

## W

**Whistle-blowers** Employees who inform their superiors, the media, or a government regulatory agency about unethical behavior in their organization, thereby often risking great professional and personal danger.

**Work group** The smallest formal organizational personnel arrangement, two or more people in a work organization who share a common purpose, usually the completion of a task.

**Work team** A group of employees (or "associates"), sometimes directed by a manager and sometimes self-managed, who work closely together to pursue common objectives.

**World Bank** Formed in 1946 to lend money to underdeveloped and developing countries for various projects such as roads, factories, and medical facilities.

**Written communication** Transmitting a message through the written word, allowing the receiver to think about the message, reread it several times, and perhaps get others to review the message before it is transmitted, and providing a record of the communication.

# INDEX

Note: Page numbers in bold type indicate that the term is defined on that page. Page numbers followed by "f" indicate figures.